James Anthony Froud

History of England from the Fall of Wolsey to the Defeat of the Spanish Armada

James Anthony Froud

History of England from the Fall of Wolsey to the Defeat of the Spanish Armada

ISBN/EAN: 9783741182464

Manufactured in Europe, USA, Canada, Australia, Japa

Cover: Foto ©Andreas Hilbeck / pixelio.de

Manufactured and distributed by brebook publishing software (www.brebook.com)

James Anthony Froud

History of England from the Fall of Wolsey to the Defeat of the Spanish Armada

HISTORY OF ENGLAND

FROM

THE FALL OF WOLSEY TO THE DEFEAT OF THE SPANISH ARMADA.

REIGN OF ELIZABETH.

VOLUME V.

LONDON: PRINTED BY
SPOTTISWOODE AND CO., NEW-STREET SQUARE
AND PARLIAMENT STREET

HISTORY OF ENGLAND

FROM

THE FALL OF WOLSEY

TO

THE DEFEAT OF THE SPANISH ARMADA.

BY

JAMES ANTHONY FROUDE, M.A.

LATE FELLOW OF EXETER COLLEGE, OXFORD.

VOLUME XI.

LONDON:
LONGMANS, GREEN, AND CO.
1870.

CONTENTS OF VOLUME XI.

CHAPTER XXV.

	PAGE
Development of the character of Elizabeth	1
Her favourites	2
The Bishop of Ely and Hatton Garden	5
State of France	12
Proposed Latitudinarian League	13
Haarlem taken	14
Exploits of Drake	15
Alva in favour of an English Alliance	15
Treachery of English officers in the Low Countries	16
Recall of Alva	17
Spanish offers of peace	18
Battle of Mook Heath	19
Melancholy letter from the Prince of Orange	20
State of parties in England	22
Philip II. refuses an asylum to English Catholic refugees	23
Elizabeth promises to reconsider her secession from the Church	25
Burning of Anabaptists in England	27
Story of Edward Woodshawe	27
Siege of Leyden	31
Sir Henry Cobham's mission to Spain	31
Debate in the Spanish Cabinet	33
Philip's answer to Cobham	35
Position of the States	38
Perplexity of the English Council	40
Champagny's mission	41

	PAGE
Wentworth's speech in Parliament	42
Death of Requescens	43
Treatment of St. Aldegonde by Elizabeth	44
Her anger with the Prince of Orange	45
She meditates a change of policy	46
Castelnau de Mauvissière sent to England	48
Duke of Alençon a suitor to Elizabeth	49
He joins La Noue and the Huguenots	50
Unsatisfactory peace signed at Paris with the Protestants	54
The Catholics disregard it	55
Ravages of Spanish mutineers in the States	58
The Seventeen Provinces unite against Spain in the Treaty of Ghent	59
Arrival of Don John of Austria	59
Mission of M. Schwegenhem to Elizabeth	59
She refuses to assist the Protestants	60
Effects of her work	63
Sir John Smith sent to Madrid	64
His interview with Archbishop Quiroga	66
Liberty enjoyed by Mary Queen of Scots	70
Margaret, Countess of Lennox	71
Plots with Lady Shrewsbury	72
Her grandchild, Lady Arabella Stuart	73
Elizabeth will not see treason	74
Her letter to Lord Shrewsbury	75
Her correspondence with Regent Morton	78
Her treatment of Bishops	82
Archbishops Parker and Grindal	83
The Spanish troops evacuate Holland	84
Don John intends to break the treaty	86
Fluctuations in Elizabeth's policy	87
Severities to recusants	88
League with the States	91
Story of Oxenham, the rover	91
Francis Drake sails from Plymouth	94
Don John defeats the States' army at Gemblours	95
Their indignation at Elizabeth's want of faith	96

CHAPTER XXVI

	PAGE
Assassination of Escobedo	98
Don Bernardino Mendoza sent to England	99
First interview with Elizabeth	102
She receives Count de Retz	104
Alençon offers to assist the States	106
Sir James Crofts bribed by Philip	108
Elizabeth repudiates the bonds which she had given to the States	109
Distress of her Ministers	110
The Regent Morton	114
Resigns Regency	118
Duke of Guise proposes to invade Scotland	119
Mission of the Abbot of Dunfermline to Elizabeth	121
She rejects the Scotch proposals	123
Will give no money	124
Philip Sidney declines to carry her message to the States	125
The States lose patience	126
The battle of Rymenant gained for them by the English	127
Elizabeth changes policy again	129
She receives the Burgundian crown jewels	130
Closes her direct dealings with the Netherlands	130
Her last matrimonial adventure	133
She invites Alençon to visit her	138
Death of Don John, Alexander of Parma becomes Regent	139
Battle of Alcazar, and death of Sebastian of Portugal	141
Prosperity of England	142
Audacity of the pirates	142
Alençon leaves the States	144
M. Simier brings Elizabeth his letter	147
Opinions in England on the marriage	149
Demands of Alençon	151
Leicester's marriage to Lettice Knollys	153
Alençon's personal appearance	154
Pamphlet by John Stubbs	156
General dislike in England of the Alençon marriage	160
Stubbs loses his hand	162
The marriage treaty suspended for two months	163

viii   Contents.

	PAGE
And then allowed to drop	164
Cecil's advice to the Queen	165
Catholic plot against England	167
The Refugees at Rheims	169
Meditated Jesuit invasion	171
The missionaries of disaffection	172

CHAPTER XXVII.

Relations between England and Ireland	173
Cruel effects of the Queen's economy	174
The Earl of Essex appointed governor of Ulster ...	175
Submission of Tirlogh Lenogh and Sir Phelim O'Neil	177
Submission and pardon of the Earl of Desmond ...	178
Massacre of the O'Neils at Belfast	180
Campaign of Essex in the north	183
Murder of the wives and children of the Scotch chiefs	185
Sir Henry Sidney again made Deputy	186
Progress of Sidney in Munster	187
Granny O'Malley	188
Ovations and executions	189
State of religion in Ireland	190
Catholic revival	191
Report of Sidney on the Established Church	192
Execution of justice in the South	195
Sir Nicholas Malby at Athlone	196
Revolt and punishment of the Burkes	197
Death of Essex	199
Anarchy, temporal and spiritual	200
Sir William Drury President of Munster	201
Symptoms of approaching rebellion	202
Dr. Nicholas Sanders	203
Overtures to Spain for interference in Ireland	205
Coldness of Philip	206
Sanders and James Fitzmaurice sail for Ireland with a commission from the Pope	207
They land at Dingle	208

Contents.

	PAGE
They call on the Earl of Desmond to join them	209
Murder of English officers at Tralee	211
The rising of the Geraldines	212
Death of James Fitzmaurice	213
Energy of Sanders	214
Malby destroys Ashketyn	215
Desmond declares for the insurrection	216
The Earl of Ormond commissioned to suppress it	217
Supplies sent from England	218
Ormond and Pelham take the field	219
Massacre of the people, and capture of Carrigafoyle	220
Invasion of Kerry, and narrow escape of Sanders	222
Killarney in the 16th century	225
Death of Sir James of Desmond	226
Rising in the Pale	227
Lord Grey de Wilton Deputy	228
Defeat of the English in Glenmalure	229
An Italian and Spanish force lands in Kerry	230
The fort at Smerwick	231
Divisions among the Irish	232
The English fleet ordered to Smerwick	233
Lord Grey goes thither with the army	234
Bombardment and capture of the fort	235
Execution of the garrison	237
Death of Sanders	239
Collapse of the rebellion	240
English intended clemency	241
Executions on all sides	242
Despondency of Lord Grey	243
General despair and cruelty	245
Dress and habits of an Irish nobleman	246
Executions in Dublin	248
The Geraldines in the forest	249
Burghley's censure on the English barbarities	250
Elizabeth desires to try milder methods	251
Preparations for the last campaign	254
Desmond refuses to submit	255
Ormond marches into Kerry	256
Catholic ferocity	257
Desmond a wanderer in the mountains	258

Betrayed and killed ... 259
Ulick and Shan Burke ... 261
Arrest of Archbishop Hurley ... 263
Who is tortured and hanged without trial ... 264
Grey succeeded by Sir John Perrot ... 265

CHAPTER XXVIII.

Esme Stuart, Count d'Aubigny, sent by the Jesuits to Scotland ... 266
Reorganisation of the French faction at the Scotch Court 267
Philip invited to assist the Catholics there ... 270
Alarm of Elizabeth ... 271
Danger of the Earl of Morton ... 272
Elizabeth tempts Morton to commit treason ... 276
Changes her mind too late ... 277
And when he fails, deserts him ... 278
Arrest of Morton, and confinement in Dumbarton Castle 281
Charged with the murder of Darnley ... 282
Obligation of Elizabeth to protect him ... 284
She remonstrates, threatens, and does nothing ... 287
Dexterity and treachery of d'Aubigny ... 290
Fresh efforts to save Morton ... 292
Final resolution of the Queen not to interfere ... 294
Trial and sentence ... 297
The last morning ... 297
Death of Morton, and victory of the Catholic faction ... 301
The Jesuit invasion of England ... 302
The Pope sanctions the murder of Elizabeth ... 304
Elizabeth's tolerant policy towards the Catholics ... 306
Parsons and Campian ... 308
Their early history ... 309
The Seminary at Rheims ... 311
The English mission resolved upon ... 313
Difficulty in the position of the English Catholics ... 315
New construction of the Bull of Pope Pius ... 315
Agitation in the Court ... 316
The Queen appeals to the country ... 318

Parsons and Campian land in England	320
Reception in London	321
Letter of Campian to the General of the Jesuits	322
He challenges the Protestant divines	325
Arrests of Jesuits	326
Use of torture	327
Sufferings of the Catholics	329
Priests in the pay of Walsingham	330
Exultation of Campian	331
Meeting of Parliament	333
Dispute between the Queen and the House of Commons	334
Bill for the repression of treasonable practices	336
Complaint against the Anglican bishops	337
Lukewarmness of the Catholic laity	339
Campian publishes his 'ten reasons'	341
Lyford Grange	342
Campian's last sermon	344
His capture	345
Execution of Everard Harts	347
Campian is tortured	348
Six Catholic noblemen promise Mendoza to take arms	350
Disputation in the Tower chapel	352
Trial of Campian and his companions	353
Execution of Campian, Sherwin, and Bryant	356
Reflections on the treatment of the Jesuits	360
Failure and success of persecution	363
Burghley's Execution of Justice, with Allen's reply	365

CHAPTER XXIX.

The Alençon marriage revived	368
Early life of Sir Francis Drake	371
Portrait of Drake	372
Preparations for the great voyage	373
The Pelican sails from Plymouth	374
Mr. Thomas Doughty	375
Magellan's Straits	377
Return of Captain Winter to England	378

	PAGE
Valparaiso and Tarapaca	379
Lima	380
Pursuit and capture of the Cacafuego	381
Description of Drake and his ship	383
Two Spanish cruisers fear to attack him	385
He sails for California	386
Agitation in Spain and England	387
Anxiety of Philip to avoid a war	388
Feeling in the City of London	390
Convention between Mendoza and Elizabeth	392
Drake searches for a North-eastern passage	393
Failing to find it, he returns by the Cape of Good Hope	394
The Pelican on a coral reef	395
Safe arrival in England	396
Mendoza demands the restoration of the plunder	397
He is supported by Burghley and Sussex	399
False returns of the bullion	400
Favour of Drake with the Queen	402
She determines to restore nothing	403
Alençon	405
Spanish conquest of Portugal	406
Uneasiness of France and England	407
Advice of Burghley	408
The crown of the Low Countries offered to Alençon	410
Elizabeth promises to marry him	412
Arrival of Alençon's secretary	414
Incredulity of Mendoza	416
A French embassy	418
Conditional marriage treaty	419
Manœuvres to escape	421
Irritation in Paris	422
Likelihood of a rupture with Spain	422
Don Antonio, the Portuguese pretender	424
Proposed expedition to Terceira	426
Walsingham is sent to Paris	430
Elizabeth's dilemma	430
Misgivings of Walsingham	433
She sends Alençon money	435
Hard treatment of Don Antonio	436
Remonstrances of Mendoza	439

	PAGE
Final refusal to restore Drake's plunder	441
Mendoza advises Philip to reconcile himself with Elizabeth	443
Alençon again in England	445
The kiss at Greenwich	446
Fresh hesitation	448
The Queen decides that she will not marry	450
Alençon goes to Holland	453
Installed Duke of Brabant	454
The Queen determines on a league with Spain	455
Resentment of the French court	456
She inclines to the marriage once more	458
Alternative prospects	460

CHAPTER XXX.

D'Aubigny created Duke of Lennox	463
Disposition of James	464
Relations between Scotland and France	465
Proposed association of James and Mary Stuart in the crown	466
Mission of Captain Errington	469
Negotiations with the Queen of Scots	470
Elizabeth attempts to play her off against her son	472
Letter of Mary Stuart to Mendoza	474
The Jesuits in Scotland	475
The Scotch Catholics make advances to Spain	476
Correspondence with the Catholics in England	478
Proposed treaty between Elizabeth and the Queen of Scots	479
Intended invasion of England by the Duke of Lennox	480
Irresolution of Philip	482
Jesuit plot for invasion and insurrection	484
The Duke of Guise	486
Episcopacy in Scotland	487
The Earl of Arran	488
Sir Robert Montgomery	489
Action of the General Assembly	490
Tumult in Edinburgh	492
Alarms of Lennox	493

	PAGE
Eagerness of the Queen of Scots	494
Defeat of the French at Terceira	497
The raid of Ruthven	500
Captivity of James	502
Scene in Edinburgh	503
Discovery of the Jesuit plot	504
The Earls of Angus and Ruthven apply for help to Elizabeth	507
Elizabeth refuses	509
French intrigues	512
Appeal of Mary Stuart	513
La Mothe Fenelon comes to London	516
Proposed alliance between France, England, and Mary Stuart	517
The Lady Arabella	519
Lennox retires from Scotland	521
Danger of James	522
Elizabeth receives Lennox in London	524
Lennox and Mendoza	526
Fresh plans for insurrection	528
Hesitation of the English Catholic nobles	529
Treachery of Lennox	530
His sudden death in Paris	532
Parties in Scotland	535
Renewed negotiations for an arrangement with the Queen of Scots	537
Secretary Beale at Sheffield	538
Mary Stuart consults Mendoza	541
Mendoza advises her to temporise	543
Commissioners from Angus and Ruthven sent to Elizabeth	544
Conditions on which Scotland will be her ally	546
Elizabeth demands the extradition of the Jesuit Gaspar Holt	549
She declines the Scotch proposals	551
And will not part with money	552
Continuation of the treaty with Mary Stuart	554
Which also she declines to conclude	556

CHAPTER XXXI.

	PAGE
Large sums advanced to Alençon	559
Plots to assassinate the Prince of Orange	561
Orange wounded by Jaureguy	563
Enthusiastic delight of the Catholics	565
The Prince recovers	566
The French conspiracy	569
Catastrophe at Antwerp, and flight of Alençon	570
Ineffectual attempt at reconciliation	573
Elizabeth again purposes to assist Spain in the reconquest of the United Provinces	576
The Paris plot	579
Guise prepares to invade England	580
Negotiations with Spain	582
Letter from Mendoza to Philip	583
James escapes from the Protestant nobles in Scotland	587
Revolution at the Scotch Court	589
James places himself at Guise's disposition	592
Guise ready to sail, waits only for support from Spain	594
Charles Paget sent over to arrange the landing	595
Walsingham is sent to Scotland	598
Complaints of James	599
The King of Navarre applies to Elizabeth for support	603
Her sharp practice	605
Impatience of the Duke of Guise	606
Divisions among the Catholics	607
Attempt to assassinate Elizabeth	609
Death of Somerville and Arden	611
Arrest of Francis Throgmorton	612
His confession on the rack	613
Arrest of the Earls of Arundel and Northumberland	616
Difference of opinion in the English Council	617
Fresh executions of Seminary priests	619
Expulsion of the Spanish Ambassador	620
Violent scene with the Council	624
Parry's plot	627
Parry and Morgan	629

xvi   *Contents.*

	PAGE
The Low Countries	632
Difficulties of James	636
He again writes to Guise	637
And to the Pope	638
Parties among the English Catholics	641
Protestant plot to seize the King of Scots	643
The Lords are betrayed, and fly	647
Capture and execution of Ruthven	648
Mary Stuart's instructions to her son	649
Elizabeth makes fresh efforts for a compromise	652
Reopening of the treaty with the Queen of Scots	655
She stands on 'proud terms'	660
The treaty is dropped	661
Letters of M. Fontenay from Scotland	663
Curious account of the character of James	664
Scotch politicians	669
Mary Stuart's hold over her son	671

CHAPTER XXV.

IN the fall of Edinburgh Castle and the provisionary arrangement with Spain, the first great Catholic conspiracy against Elizabeth was finally extinguished. The recusants, disheartened at their desertion by Philip, flung their cause upon Providence, and the whole island settled down in a sullen but unresisting acquiescence. While the danger lasted, the Queen had not shown to advantage. Sir Francis Walsingham, not once only, but at every trying crisis of her life, had to describe her conduct as 'dishonourable and dangerous;'—dishonourable, because she never hesitated to break a promise when to keep it was inconvenient, and dangerous from the universal distrust which she had inspired in those who had once relied upon her. But her disposition to compromise, her extreme objection to severity or coercion, were better suited to conciliate defeated enemies. Whether it was policy, or that, like Hamlet, she 'lacked 'gall,' she never remembered an injury. She fought with treason by being blind to it, and made men loyal in spite of themselves by persistently trusting them.

Her manners were eminently popular. She was hard of feature and harsh of voice: 'her humours,' as Sir T. Heneage expressed it, 'had not grown weak with 'age:' but she was free of access to her presence, quick-witted, and familiar of speech with men of all degrees.

She rode, shot, jested, and drank beer; spat, and swore upon occasions; swore not like 'a comfit-maker's wife,' but round, mouth-filling oaths which would have satisfied Hotspur,—the human character shewing always through the royal robes, yet with the queenly dignity never so impaired that liberties could be ventured in return.

The public policy of the realm was in the main directed by Burghley, but his measures were at all times liable to be suspended or reversed. She had a second ear always open to Catholic advisers—pensioners, some of them, of Spain—in the household and the cabinet. Her ladies of the bedchamber were for the most part the friends and correspondents of Mary Stuart. Her favourite courtiers, men like Lord Oxford and Lord Henry Howard, were the most poisonous instruments of Spanish intrigue. Her 'new minion,' as he was spitefully called abroad, Leicester's rival, Sir Christopher Hatton, was a Catholic in all but the name. The relations of Elizabeth with these persons, however insolently remarked upon by the refugees and malignants, were never generally misunderstood, and if regretted, were regretted only for public reasons by her wiser statesmen.

Leicester, no doubt, she would have liked well to marry. Leicester had been an object at one time of grave suspicion, and even Cecil's mind once misgave him, on the ambiguous position in which this nobleman stood towards his sovereign. But the Spanish Ambassador de Silva enquired curiously into the scandals which were flying, and satisfied himself that they were without foundation. And the absolute silence afterwards of Mendoza, on a subject on which hatred would have made him eloquent, is a further and conclusive answer to the charges of Allen and Sanders.[1] Leicester con-

---

[1] In the enormous mass of Mendoza's correspondence at Simancas, there is not a single imputation upon the personal character of Elizabeth.

tinued till his death an object of exceptional regard. Hatton, a handsome, innocent, rather absurd person, was attached to her on the footing of a human lapdog, and he repaid her caresses with a genuine devotion, ridiculous only in the language in which it was expressed.[1] Elizabeth had nicknames for every one who was about her person: Burghley was her 'spirit'; Leicester, her 'sweet Robin'; Oxford, her 'boar'; Hatton, her '*Lidds*,' her 'sheep'; her mouton, Anglicised into 'Mutton.' The letters addressed to her by statesmen are remarkable for the absence of formality, for language, often of severe and startling plainness, unseasoned with a compliment. She kept her intelligence for Burghley and Walsingham, and gave her folly to the favourites. The hard politician of the cabinet exacted in the palace the most profound adulation; she chose to be adored for her beauty, and complimented as a paragon of perfection.

Her portraits are usually without shadow, as if her

A youth calling himself Arthur Dudley, and professing to be the son of Elizabeth and Leicester, was presented to Philip in 1585, by Sir Francis Englefield. His story was inquired into, and he was treated as an impostor.

[1] Sir Harris Nicolas, very strangely as it appears to me, construes Hatton's letters to Elizabeth as an evidence of a discreditable connection between them. And yet one of the strongest love passages is followed by an urgent entreaty to her to marry, and it is not to be supposed he ever thought she could marry him. 'This is the twelfth day since I saw the brightness of that sun that giveth light unto my sense and soul. I wax an amazed creature. Give me leave, madam, to remove myself out of this irksome shadow, so far as my imagination with these good means, may lead me towards you: and let me thus salute you: Live for ever most excellent creature, and love some man to show yourself thankful for God's high labour in you. I am too far off to hear your answer to this salutation. I know it would be full of virtue and great wisdom; but I fear for some part thereof I would have but small thanks.'—*Hatton to the Queen*, June 17, 1573. *Life of Hatton*, by Sir H. Nicolas, p. 27.

features radiated light. Sometimes she was represented in more than mortal character; as an Artemis with bow and crescent; as the Heathen Queen of love and beauty, as the Christian Regina Cœli, whose nativity[1] fell close to her own birthday, and whose functions as the virgin of Protestantism she was supposed to supersede. When she appeared as a mere woman, she was painted in robes, which it is to be presumed that she actually wore, broidered with eyes and ears as emblematic of omnipresence—or with lizards, crocodiles, serpents, and other monsters, emblematic, whatever they meant besides, of her own extraordinary taste.

Hatton tells her when he is writing to her, that 'to see her was heaven, and the lack of her was hell's torment.' 'Passion overcomes him,' as he thinks upon her sweetness. Leicester 'is but half alive' when he is absent from 'her most blessed presence.' Even in business of state she was not proof against flattery. Mendoza could divert her at any time from disagreeable subjects by turning the conversation upon her personal excellencies.[2] Sir John Smith, when sent on a visit to the Court of France, found it prudent to dispraise the Queen and ladies there to her Majesty's advantage.[3]

And there were no attentions which more certainly brought substantial wages. The public service was conducted most thriftily—ministers of state had

---

[1] Sept. 1. Eliz. born Sept. 7.
[2] 'Divertiendola dellas platicas con otras a que yo estaba cierto habia de dar oydos, como decirle quan buena estaba.'—*Mendoza al Rey*, 31 Marzo, 1578. *MS. Simancas.*
[3] 'I assure your Majesty of my faith there is more beauty in your Majesty's finger than in any one lady among them all. I had heard the French Queen before I saw her commended to be very fair and of good presence. Clear skinned she is, but very pale and without colour; her face reasonably well formed, but for majesty of a princess, God knows she has none,' &c.—*Sir John Smith to Elizabeth*, April, 1576. *MSS. Spain. Rolls House.*

their reward in doing the business of the country. Walsingham spent his private fortune in his office, and ruined himself. Sir Henry Sidney declined a peerage, his viceroyalty in Ireland having left him crippled with debt. Sir James Crofts excused his accepting a pension from Spain, on the ground that the Queen allowed him nothing as controller of her household. Lord Burghley has left on record in his own handwriting, that the grants which he had received from his mistress had not covered his expenses in attending upon her: that he had sold lands of his own to maintain his state at court, and that the fees of his Treasurership did not equal the cost of his stable.[1] But the largesses withheld from statesmen were given lavishly to the favourites and flatterers. Their office perhaps being ignominious, required a higher salary. Leicester, who inherited nothing, his father's estate having been confiscated, became the wealthiest nobleman in England. Sinecures, grants of land, and high places about the court, rewarded the affection of Hatton. Monopolies which made their fortune 'to the utter undoing of thousands of her Majesty's subjects,'[2] were heaped on them and others of their kind—cheap presents which cost the Queen nothing. To Hatton was given also the Naboth's vineyard of his neighbour the Bishop of Ely; the present Hatton Garden, so named in memory of the transaction.[3]

---

[1] 'In my whole time I have not for these 16 years been benefited from her Majesty so much as I was within four years of King Edward. I have sold as much land of value as ever I had of gifts from her Majesty. I am at charge by attendance upon court, and by keeping of my household specially in term time by resort of suitors, more than any councillor in England. My fee for the Treasurership is more than hath been for these 300 years. It doth not answer to my charge of my stall, I mean not my table.'—*Burghley to Wm. Herle*, Aug. 14, 1585. *Autograph MSS. Domestic, Rolls House.*

[2] D'Ewes' Journals, p. 241.

[3] The reluctance of the Bishop to part with his property called out the

Without family ties, with no near relations, and without friends save such as were loyal to her, for their celebrated letter in which 'the Proud Prelate' was told that if he did not instantly comply with the Queen's wishes, 'by God she would unfrock him.' The Bishop still inclining to resist, was brought to reason by means so instructive on Elizabeth's mode of conducting business, when she had not Burghley or Walsingham to keep her in order, that Lord North, the person whom she employed, may tell the story in his own words. 'This last denial,' Lord North wrote to the Bishop, 'being added, my Lord, to her former demands, hath moved her Highness to so great a misliking as she purposes presently to send for you and hear what account you can render for this strange dealing towards your gracious sovereign. Moreover she determines to redress the infinite injuries which of long time you have offered her subjects. For which purpose, to be plain with your lordship, she has given me order to hearken to my neighbours' griefs, and likewise to prefer those complaints before her Majesty's Privy Council, for that you may be called to answer, and the parties satisfied. She has given orders for your coming up, which I suppose you have already received, and withal, you shall have a taste to judge how well she liketh your loving usage.

'Now to advise you, my Lord, I wish you from the bottom of my heart to shake off the yoke of your stubbornness against her Majesty's desires, to lay aside your stiffnecked determination and yield yourself to her known clemency. She is our God on earth. If there be perfection in flesh and blood, undoubtedly it is in her Majesty; for she is slow to revenge and ready to forgive. And yet my Lord she is right King Henry, her father, for if any strive with her, all the princes in Europe cannot make her yield. You will say to me, you are determined to leave your bishoprick in her Majesty's hands, to dispose thereof at her good pleasure, and I know that you have so reported among your friends. Your wife has also counselled you to be a Latimer, glorying, as it were, to stand against your natural prince. My lord let not your wife's shallow experience carry you too far. You see that to court you must come. The Prince's good favour and grace will be altered from you; your friends will be strange. It will be no ease for your age to travel in winter, and I know well how you are horsed and manned for that purpose. It will be no pleasure for you to have her Majesty and the Council know how wretchedly you live, how extremely covetous, how great a grazier, how marvellous a dairyman, how rich a farmer, how great an owner. It will not like you that the world know of your decayed houses, of the lead and brick that you sell from them, of the leases that you pull violently from many; of the copyholds you lawlessly enter into, of the free lands which you wrongfully possess, of the tolls and imposts which you raise, of God's good ministers which you causelessly displace.

'All this I am to prove against you, and shall be most heartily sorry to put it in execution. Wherefore, if

country's sake rather than her own, Elizabeth concealed the dreariness of her life from herself, in the society of these human playthings, who flattered her faults and humoured her caprices. She was the more thrown upon them because in her views of government she stood equally alone, and among abler men scarcely found one to sympathise with her. She appears in history the Champion of the Reformation, the first Protestant Sovereign in Europe, but it was a position into which she was driven forward in spite of herself, and when she found herself there, it brought her neither pride nor pleasure.

In her birth she was the symbol of the revolt from the Papacy. She could not reconcile herself with Rome without condemning the marriage from which she sprung; but her interest in Protestantism was limited to political independence. She mocked at Cecil and 'his brothers in Christ.' She affected an interest in the new doctrines, only when the Scots or the Dutch were necessary to her, or when religion could serve as an excuse to escape an unwelcome marriage. When the Spanish Ambassador complained of the persecution of the Catholics, she answered that no Catholic had suffered anything who acknowledged her as his lawful sovereign, and that in spiritual matters, she believed as they did.[1]

---

you love place, the preservation of your credit, and the continuance of her Majesty's favour, conform yourself and satisfy her request, which, if you list to do, no doubt the Queen is so inclined to good as I trust she will not only forget what is past and spare your journey, but also thankfully accept your doing herein. Thus all things may be pacified, which I will gladly bring to pass. Her Majesty shall receive pleasure, her servants preferment and some profit, and yourself honour and long comfort.—Your loving friend, R. NORTH.

'November 20, 1576.'

Comment would be thrown away upon this letter. It is among the MSS. at Hatfield, and endorsed by Burghley, to whom the bishop probably sent it.

[1] 'Me replicó que no castigaba á los Catholicos sino por no confesarla por reyna: que en lo demas creya lo que ellos.'—*Don Bernardino de Mendoza al Rey*, xvii. de Junio, 1578. *MSS. Simancas.*

Fanatics, Puritan or Papist, she despised with Erasmian heartiness. Under her brother and sister she had witnessed the alternate fruits of the supremacy of the two theological factions. She was determined to hold them both under the law, which to her had more true religion in it than cartloads of creeds and articles. Puritanism drew its strength from the people. The Popish priests were a regiment of the Bishop of Rome. She would permit no authority in England which did not centre in herself. The Church should be a department of the State, organised by Parliament and ruled by the national tribunals. The moderates of both parties could meet and worship under its ambiguous formulas. There should be no conventicles and no chapels, to be nurseries of sedition. Zealots who could not be satisfied might pay a fine for their precision, and have their sermons or their sacraments at home.

She never ceased to hope that foreign princes would see things as she saw them. To the intelligent latitudinarian his principles appear so obviously reasonable that he cannot understand why they are not universally accepted. Elizabeth desired only a general peace, outward order and uniformity, with liberty to every one to think in private as he pleased. What could any man in his senses wish for more? So long as there was no Inquisition, she could not see why the Calvinists should refuse to hear mass. So long as their subjects would conform to the established ritual, kings might well be satisfied to leave opinion alone. It was to this consummation that her foreign policy was always directed. It was for this reason that she always resisted the advice of Burghley and Walsingham to put herself at the head of a Protestant League. Unwillingly and at long intervals she had sent secret help to the Prince of Orange and the Prince of Condé—not, however, to emancipate the Low Countries, or change the dynasty of France, but only to prevent the triumph of the spirit of the Council of Trent, and to bring Philip and the House of Valois to extend over Europe a government analogous to her own.

Events were too strong for her. Her theory was two centuries before its time; and nations can only be governed on principles with which they sympathise themselves. Yet Elizabeth may be fairly credited with a general rectitude of purpose; and for the immediate purpose of keeping England quiet and preventing civil war, she was acting prudently and successfully. She could not forget that she was a sovereign of a divided people, and that all her subjects, as long as they were loyal, were entitled to have their prejudices respected. The Anglo-Catholics and Catholics were still three-quarters of the population; united in sympathy, united in the hope of seeing the old creed restored in its fulness, and as yet only differing in a point of order. All alike were thriving under the peace and prospering in their worldly comforts, while France and Flanders were torn in pieces by civil war. If she had struck openly into the quarrel, Germany would probably have followed, and Romanism might perhaps have been driven back behind the Alps and Pyrenees; but as, in doing so, she would have created the deepest resentment in England, the attempt might also have cost her her own throne, and she might have been herself more successful in provoking rebellion than Mary Stuart or the emissaries of the Pope. Her first duty was to her own people, and both for herself and England there were protecting conditions which war would forfeit, but which would hardly fail her as long as she remained at peace. The massacre of St. Bartholomew had brought France no nearer to Spain. Spain was reluctant as ever to permit the Guises to interfere by force for Mary Stuart. French politicians could not allow Philip to invade and conquer England. Philip had made an effort to cut the knot. Chapin Vitelli's dagger was to have disposed of Elizabeth, and Mary Stuart and the Duke of Norfolk were to have taken the crown with Alva at their backs; but Norfolk's head had fallen and Mary's last friends at Edinburgh had been hanged, and Philip had retraced his steps, had washed his hands of his English friends, and was once more on good terms with his sister-in-law. The Bull declaring her deposed was ostentatiously and universally ignored; Charles IX. made a league with her in the face of it; the Spanish Council of State had denied its validity; and Elizabeth was entitled to believe that she was still regarded by her brother sovereigns as one of themselves. Mary Stuart remained her heir presumptive; the Catholics, both at home and abroad, were allowed to look forward to her accession; and the Queen judged rightly, that after so disastrous a failure, both they and Philip would prefer to wait for a peaceful alteration by the order of inheritance, rather than risk the chances of a fresh insurrection or an internecine war. For the foreign Protestants she considered that she did enough by maintaining her own position. While she remained upon the throne, England was an asylum for the persecuted of all nations, a neutral territory from which they could maintain the struggle with their oppressors. If she refused to help them herself they found allies among her subjects. English congregations contributed money. English volunteers flocked to the standard of Condé and Orange. English privateers threatened Spanish commerce, and threw supplies into

Rochelle. The mere existence of a powerful kingdom out of communion with Rome was a continual obstruction to an ultramontane policy. In refusing to permit the succession to be settled positively either for Mary Stuart or against her, Elizabeth was accused of neglecting the interests of the nation, and caring only for her own quiet. Sometimes in mockery, she would tell the Council that she would come back after her death and see the Queen of Scots making their heads fly. She advised Hatton to buy no land and build no houses. When she was gone, she said, there would be no living for him in England.[1] A policy, however, could not have been only selfish, which was attended with unceasing risk to her own life. Every year that could be saved to peace was so much gain to England; and she persisted in hoping that through weariness and necessity the Catholic Powers would throw over the Council of Trent, and allow Europe to be settled on some quiet and moderate terms. How she worked in detail, how uncertain, how vacillating, how false and unscrupulous she could be, when occasion tempted, has appeared already and will appear more and more; but her object in itself was excellent, and those who pursue high purposes through crooked ways, deserve better of mankind, on the whole, than those who pick their way in blameless inanity, and if innocent of ill, are equally innocent of good.

Five years now passed, to England precious years of breathing-time. The storm continued to rage on the Continent. The annals of England are almost a blank; and the leading incidents may be passed over rapidly.

Charles IX., in consenting to the massacre of St. Bartholomew, had said that if tried at all it should be

---
[1] The Queen of Scots to the Archbishop of Glasgow, August 4, 1574. LABANOFF, vol. iv.

universal. From fifty to sixty thousand human creatures had been murdered; but indignation created heretics faster than the sword could destroy them. The whole country beyond the Loire revolted, and the civil war broke out fiercer than ever. Anjou was driven from Rochelle after a fruitless four months' siege, in which he lost twenty thousand men; and the throne of Poland falling vacant, and the queen-mother coveting it for her second son, the Court swung round. Peace was patched up, leaving Catholics and Huguenots as they stood before the massacre. Catherine made advances again to the Prince of Orange and Count Louis, and by their help she secured the election. Anjou left France for his new kingdom, only to be recalled to it a few months after by his brother's death. The sickly princes of the House of Valois followed each other fast to the tomb. But the Queen-mother continued to rule, and in her hatred of Spain stretched out her hand to Orange who, desperate of other help, seemed inclined to let the past be past and accept it, bloodstained as it was. He had offered the sovereignty of the States to Elizabeth. In possession of Holland and Zealand, he had told her that she would be 'head of the religion' and mistress of the seas. The rest of the States would revolt from Spain and come to her devotion, and no enemy would dare to quarrel with her. If she refused, they would not submit to the Spaniards. They were prepared to die first if necessary; but he warned her fully that before they were destroyed 'they would entangle the country 'with such a devil as should root out thence the name of 'Spaniards for ever.' 'The French King was ready to 'help them, and to the French King they would go.'[1]

The Prince was evidently desperate: the danger to

---
[1] Mr. Herle and the Prince of Orange, June 11, 1573.—*MSS. Flanders.*

England of the annexation of the Provinces to France was only one degree less than of their reconquest by Alva; and to prevent the States from taking any wild step, which could not be retraced, she sent Orange money for his immediate necessities, and an attempt was made among the more moderate of the European powers to compel Philip to grant the Provinces reasonable terms. After a communication between Walsingham and Maximilian, deputies met informally at Speyr in the autumn of 1573 from England, Switzerland, and the German States, to draw up the conditions of a league—a league which was to be neither Catholic nor Protestant, but composed of men of all creeds, who would combine to resist oppression. The contracting parties were to disclaim all intention of meddling with religion. They quarrelled with no faith. Doctrines and forms of worship were left indifferent. The object of the confederation was to enforce justice, order, liberty of conscience, and the common rights of humanity.[1]

The project never passed beyond an outline. Dogmatism was more sacred than humanity. Lutherans and Calvinists could not act together, far less could Protestants and Catholics. But it breathes the very spirit of Elizabeth. And that such a thing should have been tried at all shows that even in the sixteenth century there were minds which theology had failed to calcine.

Orange meanwhile was left to struggle on with such help as volunteers could give him. On the 12th of July, 1573, the town of Haarlem surrendered to Alva. The siege had cost him twelve thousand of his troops,

---

[1] Confederacion entre los Reyes, Duques, Principes, Villas libres, Republicas y Señorias de Alemannia, Inglaterra, Escocia, Suyça y Flandes, assi de una como de otra Religion, para opponerse a la tyrannia de algunos enemigos de piedad y virtud. Hecha en Espira, a xv. de Octubre, 1573.—TYTLER, vol. v.

but as he had found severity hitherto useless, he determined to make Haarlem an example of what he called clemency. The garrison, consisting chiefly of English, French, and Scots, was put to the sword. A few of the principal citizens were selected for execution, but the town was not, like Mechlin, given over to pillage, and private property was generally spared. The Duke then moved on Alkmaar, hoping that it would open its gates. But Alkmaar was obstinate as Haarlem had been. He tried one desperate assault, but failed, and it appeared clear to him that he would have to conquer the two Provinces inch by inch. One town had already cost him an army recruited with enormous difficulty from Italy and Spain. Holland and Zealand formed a great intrenched camp, intersected by dykes, canals, and rivers. The sea was open behind, and as long as Protestant Europe, as long especially as England, continued to throw in men and powder, the problem appeared a hopeless one.

The natural remedy would have been to hold Elizabeth responsible for the acts of her subjects, and to threaten her with war unless she checked them. She had herself given further provocation. In the spring of 1571, when the Spanish ambassador had been discovered to be a party to the Norfolk conspiracy, a hint was given to the western privateers, and a young adventurer sailed out of Plymouth harbour more enterprising and more audacious than the dreaded Hawkins himself. In the last disastrous expedition many English sailors were left prisoners in the hands of the Spaniards. Most of them had been released by Hawkins' ingenuity, but some had been left in Mexico, to be burnt by the Inquisition. Francis Drake set out to revenge his comrades. He spent the summer in the West Indies burning, killing, and taking prizes.[1] Then putting himself in communication with escaped negro slaves in the woods at Panama, he landed and intercepted the mules which were bringing the gold and silver over the isthmus. He secured an enormous booty, sufficient to tempt half the pirates in the world to the Spanish main, and returned safe with it to England, fortune so standing his friend that he caught another gold ship on his way home, which was also of immense value.[2] Elizabeth was personally compromised: and this time she showed no desire to evade her responsibility. She was known to have had shares in the adventure. Drake presented her with a negro slave whom he had taken in a house at Carthagena. She showed him publicly at court as a curiosity. A priest, implicated in some recent treason, was executed about the same time in London with the usual cruelties;[3] while she continued to harass Philip with demands for the expulsion of the English refugees from Flanders, which had been promised in the provisional treaty. Out of such a condition of things it appeared as if only war could follow; but Alva, who unlike the Catholics generally, had formed a high estimate of Elizabeth's power, preferred any humiliation to driving her into an alliance with Orange. He considered Drake's performance a fair equivalent for the Ridolfi conspiracy. So far from advising Philip to demand reparation of his sister-in-law, he saw in it only a further motive for seeking a close alliance with her.

---

[1] At Nombre de Dios he killed eighteen Spaniards, and cut out and carried off a loaded galloon which was lying in the harbour.—*Memoria que ha dado el Consejo de las Indias de los robos hechos en ellas por Ingleses.* 1572. *MSS. Simancas.*

[2] Protest of Antonio y Guaras to Elizabeth, 1573.—*MSS. Simancas.*

[3] *Martyrio hecho en persona de un Catholico en Inglaterra,* Junio 19, 1573. In the hand of de Guaras.—*MSS. Simancas.*

'If your Majesty had listened to me,' he said, 'if you had not trusted Chapin Vitelli, and had attended to the considerations which I placed before you, these present difficulties would not have arisen. It is now of the highest importance to show Europe that there will be no war between England and Spain.'[1]

Even the question of the volunteers the Duke was not inclined to press upon Elizabeth. She had recalled Sir Humfrey Gilbert, the only officer who held a commission from herself. With the rest he discovered for himself a more successful method of dealing. England was swarming with adventurers of no particular creed, careless whom they served so they served their own interests. Some hundreds of these made advances to Alva through Antonio de Guaras, the Spanish factor in London. Alva directed them to offer their swords to the Prince of Orange, obtain employment with the garrison at Flushing, and either betray the town or burn the Dutch fleet.[2] The plot was revealed to Cecil and defeated: but others followed. Spanish gold was used and promised freely. Colonel Chester, an English officer in Walcheren, undertook, for 30,000 crowns, to introduce the Spaniards into the island.[3] Two others, Captain Poole and Captain Ralph Hasleby, proposed to kill or carry off Orange:[4] and Hasleby actually tried it. Another scoundrel, a Captain Wingham, sought a situation in the Prince's

---

[1] Alva to Philip, July 7. Compare Philip to Alva, July 8. Alva to Secretary Cayas, July 8. Cayas to Alva, July 17.—*Correspondence of Philip II.* GACHARD.

[2] The story of the negotiation is at Simancas, in the hand, I think, of Don Gueran de Espes, the late ambassador, who was then at Paris.— Compare Ralph Lane to Cecil, May, 1573. *MSS. Flanders.*

[3] Antonio de Guaras to Philip, 1573.—*MSS. Simancas.*

[4] 'El Capitan Poole y Ralph Haselby, en tiempo del Duque de Alva habian offrecido de entregar vivo el de Orange o matarle.'—*Puntos de cartas de Antonio de Guaras*, 1574. *MSS. Simancas.*

household with the same purpose. Then two more, a Captain Ellice and a Colonel Balfour, were found engaged in the same trade.[1] And at length the Prince, shocked and frightened at the treachery which surrounded him, and unable to distinguish friend from foe, was obliged to dismiss all the English companies and send them home. The irritation caused by a measure so necessary, yet so painful, was followed by fresh differences tending further to alienate England from the Prince's cause.

Alva, at his own request, was now recalled. He returned to Spain leaving behind him an eternal memory of infamy because he had not succeeded. Those who attempt to extinguish a revolution in blood play for a high stake. If they win, their cruelties pass in history as the necessary severities of a wise and courageous rule. If they fail, they are ministers of Satan to be for ever execrated and abhorred. Yet the difference after all may be only in the intellectual appreciation of the circumstances; and if the honour is deserved in the one case, the shame may be unmerited in the other. Alva was conscious of nothing but that he had tried to do his duty to his master. It had proved too hard for him, and he gladly relinquished it to another.

There was now to be an attempt at milder treatment.

---

[1] In August, 1574, De Guaras writes: 'Hasleby and Chester have returned to England. It is arranged that Captain Ellice and Colonel Balfour shall follow the Prince to Delft or Rotterdam, and there take or kill him. They hope they may get possession of one or other of these towns. If they kill the Prince, and also obtain a town for us, they expect 10,000 crowns for the colonels, as much more for each of the captains, and a further sum for the men. If they take the town, but miss the Prince, they will be content with 15,000 crowns among them all. If they secure the Prince without the town, they expect 10,000, the colonels to have in addition a pension of a thousand crowns, and the captains one of three hundred. The agreement is to be drawn up in writing. Ellice says he has been long in the Prince's service and hates him.'

His successor Don Louis de Requescens, Grand Commander of Castile, brought with him an offer of peace: peace upon terms short of the absolute submission demanded by Alva, with a saving to the Provinces of their old rights of self-government, on condition of reunion with the Church. This point conceded, and the mass restored in the churches, the Spanish army would be withdrawn, and the States would be governed as before the revolt under their own laws, administered by their own countrymen. To the common sense of Europe it seemed a fair proposal—a concession to the temper which had been shewn in the meeting at Speyr. The re-establishment of the Catholic religion did not imply persecution. Unsupported by foreign troops the Bishops would have been powerless for anything save the maintenance of external order. The chapels of the Calvinists would have been closed, but private opinion would have remained unenquired into, and the Protestants of Holland and Flanders would have been in the same position as the Catholics in England.

English practical understanding decided at once that these offers ought to have been thankfully received. The Queen, who allowed no 'liberty of worship' herself, could not consistently demand it for others, even if she had thought that it could be prudently granted: and when the Prince and the States sternly refused they were considered to be offering gratuitous obstacles to the settlement of Europe. The English Catholics came forward in numbers making contributions for Requescens or taking service in the Spanish army.[1] Trade had reopened under Alva's

[1] 'Muchos gentilhombres, soldados y marineros, y otros de nuestro pays, ha pocos dias que viniéron á esta tierra para ofrecer su servicio al Rey contra sus rebeldes; y viendo que cada dia llegan aqui tanto numero de Catholicos de nuestra nacion para servir al Rey, he hecho quanto ha podido que su Excellencia formase un regimiento de Ingleses Catholicos.'—

treaty, between London and Antwerp; the Flushingers insisted on a right of search lest munitions of war should be carried to the enemy; and ugly quarrels rose in consequence. The channel privateers, not being particular about creeds, plundered Dutch merchantmen.[1] Vessels from Holland were robbed even at the quay at Sandwich, and no redress could be had. The interference of England on behalf of the States was made more impossible than ever.

Nor was this the worst. In the spring of 1574 the Prince of Orange and his two brothers, Count Louis and Count Henry, collected an army of Huguenots in France, with the connivance of Catherine de Medici, crossed the Meuse, and were making their way towards Zealand, when they were intercepted at Mook Heath and forced into an engagement by Don Sancho d'Avila. The sea was the friend of the Hollanders, the land was their enemies'. Their entire force was destroyed, and Louis and Henry were killed.[2]

Requescens, snatching the opportunity, published an amnesty, from which fourteen names only were excepted. He invited the provinces to reflect upon the favourable disposition of his sovereign, and to take ad-

---

Relacion de M. de Copley. 1574. *MSS. Simancas.*

[1] Here for instance is one case out of eleven reported September 7, 1573:—'Cornelius Williamson, of Dort, sailing out of Yarmouth, was boarded and utterly spoiled. The mariners of the said ship were most cruelly handled; and being tied with ropes were cast into the sea and greatly tormented for to know whether they had money. They hanged up the said Cornelius with a rope about his neck until he was almost dead, and when he was come to his wits, they stripped him all naked and cast him eight times tied with a rope and with stones at his legs 18 or 20 feet deep in the sea till they knew where his money was, and so took his money and of his mariners with all their gear, and the anchors, cables, and victuals of the said ship, and left the master wholly naked.'—*MSS. Flanders.*

[2] Battle of Mook Heath, April 14, 1574.

vantage of offers which might not be within their reach again. Out of the seventeen states only two were prolonging the revolt. For the sake of Holland and Zealand, the great commercial cities of Flanders and Brabant had to submit to a prolonged military occupation, to see their laws suspended, their trade ruined, and their industry paralysed by taxation. Broken-hearted by his last misfortune, and utterly dispirited, the Prince now felt that the end was probably near, and that nothing would be soon left to him but to follow Count Louis to the grave. 'Our people,' he wrote to his one remaining brother, Count John, 'have now lost all heart, and if the 'enemy invade us he will find slight resistance. Our 'destruction will be the destruction of the religion 'throughout the world. The turn of the Germans will 'come, and the turn of the English also, who, in imagined 'prudence, have temporised and waited upon events.'[1] If 'you can think of anything, do it. I am myself so over-'whelmed with business, and so stupefied with sorrow, 'that I am equal to little more. I undertook to hold 'these States for two years, single-handed, against all the 'force which Spain could bring against us. Those years 'are expired, and if we are to stand longer we must 'have assistance. If it cannot be, and if we must needs 'perish, in the name of God be it so. They cannot take 'from us the honour of having done what so small a 'handful of men never did before. We have held this 'little spot of ground unfriended, and we have kept our 'consciences undefiled. God is all powerful, and I trust 'we may yet be preserved. At worst, it shall cost the 'Catholic King half Spain and half his subjects, ere he

---

[1] 'Les Allemans se pourront avec le temps bien appercevoir le domage, comme aussy feront les Angloys, qui s'attendans aux évènements et leurs de nos affaires ont, comme ils estimoient par grande prudence humaine, toussjours voulu temporiser.'

'make a final end of us.'¹ This letter fell into the hands of Requescens, and was sent by him to England as an evidence of the condition to which the Prince was reduced. The two years' treaty being at the same time almost expired, he intimated that if Elizabeth would interfere no further, his master was willing to do what till now he had always refused, and renew the old league which Charles V. had made with her father. What was she to do? If the Prince would but have accepted the terms which Philip offered, all would have been well. With the nobler aspect of Protestantism, with its deep, passionate loathing of falsehood—loathing intense as that with which the first Christians shook themselves free of the heathen idolatry,—with this she had no kind of sympathy. She did not understand what it meant. But the States, however desperate their situation, intended to fight to the death, and when crushed they would require to be held down by force. A Spanish army would continue to be a dangerous neighbour; Spanish fleets would lie in the Scheldt; and the Dutch, having lost all they valued, might have no objection to assist in an enterprise against England. Spain might consent, at present, to the league, but while the difference of religion continued, wise men were of opinion that the alliance could not be permanent. England's turn, as the Prince said, must and would come at last. Meanwhile the sea towns were untaken; the two provinces were at Elizabeth's disposition if she would have them; with the certainty, at the same time, of a sharp and severe war, and the possibility of an insurrection at home. The parties into which England was divided were both represented in the Council. Walsingham and Leicester were for joining the Prince, but Burghley and Bacon, who had

---

¹ The Prince of Orange to Count John. May 7.—*MSS. Flanders.*

hitherto acted with them, threw their powerful weight into the other scale. Don Pedro de Valdez was coming with an armada from Cadiz to assist Requescens. Walsingham would have had him set upon and destroyed in the Channel. Burghley thought that with division at home, and with Ireland so vulnerable behind them, the risk was too great to be ventured. If the Prince threw himself as he threatened upon France, even Burghley considered that it would be even better to join Philip actively, and assist in the reduction of the Provinces. England would thus earn a right to a voice in the conclusion, and secure the Hollanders some kind of terms.[1] The Spanish trade was of great importance: and a fresh interruption of it would lead to serious discontent in London. For Spain to consent, in defiance of the Pope, to a closer alliance with an excommunicated sovereign would be a significant fact which would have its weight with the English Catholics; and the nation generally had not yet come to look on Spaniards as enemies. The old connection was still far more popular than the new friendship with France; and even with the Protestants the horrors of St. Bartholomew had eclipsed the doings of the Blood Council. Philip, it was said in London, never made an unjust war. Philip was true in word and deed, and in his severities respected the usages of humanity.[2] The Spanish party

---

[1] 'El gran Tesorero y el gran Chanciller respondiéron á sus compañeros del Consejo que si la Reyna se pusiese en ello, que con buena causa el Rey de España les podria cisma y fuego en su reyno por Irlanda, y que no eran de parecer de tal acceptacion; y que en caso que á Francesas se entregase el de Orange que lo estorbaria por lo que tocaba á Inglaterra en favor del Rey de España.' Antonio de Guaras á Çayas; 25 de Agosto, 1574. MSS. Simancas.

[2] La Mothe-Fénelon says it was argued in the English Council, 'Qu'il ne s'estoit veu ni ne se voyoit rien au Roy d'Espaigne pour quoy la Royne leur Meistresse deubt rejetter son amitié, ny luy denier la sienne, puisqu'il la venoit rechercher. Car il s'estoit tousjours monstré prince veritable et certain, plein de grande

carried the day. De Valdez passed up the Channel unmolested to give Orange what every one expected must be his final blow; while Don Bernardino de Mendoza, Philip's master of the horse, came across from Brussels with a complimentary letter to Elizabeth, bringing with him also, in evidence of his master's sincerity, several hundred Englishmen who had been taken prisoners in Holland.

Nor was this all. The King had consented, at Alva's entreaty, that the Catholic refugees should be forbidden to remain in his dominions. The condition, so long evaded, was now actually enforced. The Earl of Westmoreland, the Countess of Northumberland, the Nortons, and the other waifs and strays from the rebellion of 1569, were informed that they must seek an asylum elsewhere. A seminary of English Priests which had been established at Douay, was broken up by Requescens, to be received in France by the Duke of Guise, and provided with a new home at Rheims. Weary of ineffectual intrigues which had ended only in increased severities to the Catholics whom they had wished to befriend, the Spanish Council had resolved, at least for the present, to turn their backs upon English conspirators, and relinquish the hope of recovering England to the Church by revolution.[1] 'Amazed,' 'incredulous,' the refugees

---

moderation et d'integrité; qui n'avoit point men de guerres injustes ni qui ne feussent necessaires et n'avoit usé en icelles ni fraude ni mauvaise foy ni exercé aulcuns actes cruels qui feussent hors du debvoir de la guerre ni contre les termes de la justice.'—*Dépêches*, vol. vi. p. 217, &c.

[1] Spanish lay statesmen looked on these clerical incendiaries as coldly as Charles V. had looked on Pole. Secretary Aguilon writing from Paris to Cayas, says:—

'Yo no se porque no cierran allá las puertas á todos los Ingleses, Escoceses y Irlandeses que van con invenciones. Pues es cosa llana que el dia que su Mag⁴ pensase emprender contra alguna de aquellas provincias, le romperian abiertamente Franceses la guerra, juntandose con los otros; porque ni á ellos les está bien que su Mag⁴ tenga pid en ellas ni su Mag⁴ que ellos, y entretanto no sirven las idas y venidas de los susodichos sino hacer mas

struggled against their fate. They petitioned the Pope to publish a construction of the Bull of Deposition, which would implicate any Catholic Prince who made a treaty with Elizabeth, and would make rebellion an obligation of faith to the Catholics remaining in England.[1]

Gregory, however, was too well advised. He could not afford, for the sake of a handful of passionate fanatics, to embroil himself both with France and Spain; and Sanders and Allen, and Parsons and the Archbishop of Cashel, and the noble lords and ladies of the North, whose fault was fidelity to the cause of which Philip was the European champion, were dismissed over the frontiers at the request of the heretic Elizabeth, and requested to return no more. It was a hard measure, yet at once a political triumph to the English Government of immense moment, and in itself not undeserved. The object which these people had set before themselves, had been to kindle a war of religion, and to carry fire

---

daño á la pobre Reyna de Escocia y á los Catholicos. Por mala que sea la Reyna de Inglaterra, estando las cosas de Flandes como estan, conviene temporizar con ella, y aun diré mas adelante que despues de estar pacificos aquellos estados les estará siempre bien el amistad y correspondencia de Inglaterra. Pues se ha visto el daño que habrria perdido les ha resultado.—*Aguilon á Cayas*, 5 de Maio, 1575. TEULET, vol. v.

Whatever may be thought of the chivalry of Elizabeth's conduct to Orange, language of this kind shows that she was no dupe to false pretences, and that in her unwillingness to precipitate a war she had real ground to go upon. The Spaniards were sincerely anxious to remain at peace with her, if the Pope and the priests would let them alone.

[1] 'Sententia excommunicationis sive interdicti: Vis ea est. Primum quod nulli Christiano cum iis populis neque conversari neque commercia habere licet contra quos ea lata est. Deinde quod subditi principum eorum contra quos ea lata est liberantur in posterum ab omni obedientiâ fide officio jurisjurandi religione quâ antea tenebantur, neque deinceps possunt solum, sed etiam debent, contra eosdem ferro arma ut contumaces tanquam hereticos schismaticos rebelles Deo ipsi invisos trucidare vastare diripere ferro flammâ furcâ coercere omni daniquo ratione de irâ deflexos in viam reducere. Fiat. Fiat. Amen. —*Copia de la sentencia de excommunion que pidiéron los Catholicos de Inglaterra.* 1574. *MSS. Simancas.*

and sword through the country which claimed their
allegiance. They had flooded Europe with libels, 'in
'which Medea was made a saint,' and the spotted garments of the Queen of Scots had been hung upon Elizabeth. The English Reformation was represented as a
monstrous product of lust and tyranny and spoliation,
and Cromwell, Cranmer, Burghley, every statesman and
thinker whom Protestant England had produced, were
held up as pandars to the wickedness of Henry
VIII., and his bastard daughter. Elizabeth insisted
that Philip should set a mark of disapproval on them,
and Philip yielded.

As a set off Mendoza invited Elizabeth to reconsider
her secession from the Church, and her answer was not
positively unfavourable. Present change she said was
impossible, but she gave him hopes that she would
consider about it at a more favourable moment. The
commercial differences were settled. The ships and
cargoes seized on both sides had been long sold, but the
accounts were produced and balanced, and the Spanish
treasure, the original ground of quarrel, was allowed for
in the general estimate. One question only was left
open, which Philip reserved for his own special consideration, on what terms English factors and merchant
ships were to be allowed to make use of Spanish port
towns and harbours. The Holy Office claimed absolute
authority in Spanish waters, and forbade 'the accursed
thing' within gunshot of their shores. English seamen
who had had Prayer-books on board with them, had been
imprisoned in the Inquisition dungeons, and their vessels
and cargoes confiscated. The Queen insisted that the
deck of an English ship was English soil. 'I assure
'you,' she said to De Guaras, 'it is a thing my father
'would not have borne, nor will I bear it, and unless

'your King takes better order with these men, I must
imprison subjects of his in return.' 'Understand me,'
she continued, 'you know the proverb—old wine, old
bread, and an old friend. The French say, our reconciliation cannot stand. Let the King and me prove
their word false.'[1] A special minister was sent to
Madrid, to insist on concession, and Sir Henry Cobham,
who had been dismissed from the Spanish court four
years before with scanty courtesy, was pointedly selected
for the purpose.

Elizabeth too, on her part, was ready to do what she
could to gratify Philip, and she took the opportunity of
showing him that the English for whom she demanded
toleration, were not the heretics with whom they were
confounded. Among the fugitives from the Provinces,
who had taken refuge in England, was a congregation
of Anabaptists—wretches abhorred in the eyes of all orthodox Anglicans. Twenty-seven of them were arrested
in Aldgate, and brought to trial for blasphemous opinions
on the nature of Christ's body. Four of them carried
faggots at Paul's Cross, recanted, and were pardoned.
Eleven who were obstinate were condemned in the
Bishop of London's court, and delivered over to the
secular arm. The incongruous element of Elizabeth's
Council would have perhaps been split in pieces by an
execution on so large a scale. 'Great pains were taken'
to move them. One more woman at last yielded. The
rest were banished, but enough had not been done to
vindicate Anglican orthodoxy. One of the first four,
Hendrick Tenwort, had relapsed, and with another of
the remainder, John Wielmacher, was selected for a sacrifice to the Spanish alliance. The sentence was not
carried out without protest. John Foxe the martyro-

[1] De Guaras to Cayas, Jan. 1575.—*MSS. Simancas.*

logist, who was occupied at the time on the history of
the Marian persecution, wrote to Elizabeth to remonstrate.[1] He obtained a month's reprieve to give the
unfortunate creatures time to abjure, but they persevered
in impenitence, and they were burnt on the 22nd of
July, 'in great horrour, crying and roaring.'[2] The propositions for which they suffered, with the counter
propositions of the orthodox, have passed away and become meaningless. The theology of the Anabaptists
may have been ridiculous, their theories of civil government mischievous; but they were not punished in the
service even of imagined truth; the friends of Spain about
the Queen wished only to show Philip that England
was not the paradise of heresy which the world believed.

A high-born offender of the opposite kind had a near
escape at the same time, from the second edge of Elizabeth's sword of justice. The story is curious as illustrating the character of many of the English adventurers, who were wandering on the Continent. Among
the refugees who were ordered to leave Flanders, was a
person named Edward Woodshawe, who took the opportunity of writing to Lord Burghley to ask for pardon
and employment. Woodshawe was singularly open in his
account of himself. He had been 25 years in the Low
Countries; at first in the household of Count Egmont,
'with whom he had lived in all luxury.' On Egmont's
arrest, he went back to England, 'but neither his uncle
'Leveson, of Wolverhampton, his cousin Arden, of Park
'Hall, in Warwickshire, nor any of his other relations
'would help him with two angels.' 'He had been
'brought up like a gentleman, seldom knowing what it

---

[1] 'Id unum valde deprecor, ne pirae ac flammae Smithfieldianae, jam diu faustissimis tuis auspiciis huc usque sopitae, sinas nunc recandescere.'— *Fox to Elizabeth.* SOAMES, p. 116.

[2] Stowe.

'was to lack or want.' 'And therefore,' he said, 'with other companions who were in straits as well as myself, I was forced to give the onset, and break up a house in Warwickshire, not far from Wakefield.'

With the 20l. which came to his share from this transaction, he went again to Flanders, and was employed by Alva, 'Whom he took God to witness he loved as the devil in hell.' He prayed Burghley to overlook his offences, and to give him an opportunity of retrieving his character. 'Having long followed the wars,' he said, 'and experimented this wavering world, what he took in hand he would do, so that no man in the world should know of his affairs. Her Majesty, Lord Burghley, and himself, could understand each other. Their secrets need go no further,' and he 'protested before God, and swore by his holy name on the damnation of his soul,' that he would be true. He was intimate with Requescens, intimate with Lord Westmoreland, Lord Morley, the Archbishop of Cashel, the Nortons, and the priests who had been at Douay. If he could be of use in Spain, Chapin Vitelli would introduce him to the King, and he could obtain an appointment in the Palace.

'There,' he went on, 'if you like to employ me, I will obtain intelligence of all that goes forward, and of any plot against England. I will deal as circumspectly, as wisely, as faithfully as I would crave at God's hands to receive my soul into his mercy. And therefore, though your honour has no acquaintance with me, yet mistrust me not. For, by the living God, if your honour will cause to be made there in England, a certain lingering poison, and send it hither by a trusty messenger to me, not letting him know what it is, but forge some other matter, and let me have command-

'ment from your honour to whom I shall give it, and
'therewith you shall try me what I am, for the service
'of the Queen's majesty and my country. And doubt
'not, but I will handle it secretly as reason requires for
'my own safety; what letters your honour writes to me,
'I will tear them in pieces for fear of afterclaps, and I
'trust your honour will do so by my letters.'[1]

The open cruelties of Philip II. have not stained his reputation so deeply as his employment of assassins; the blackest spot in Alva's scutcheon is his recommendation of the murder of Elizabeth: but public men rarely sink below the average of the morality of their age. An English gentleman, honourably connected, who had been in the service of the Viceroy of the Netherlands, could write to the first minister of his country, confessing to a burglary, offering to poison his friends who had given him shelter and wages, and expecting to be admitted to the confidence of the Queen herself.

Nor is this the strangest part of the story. Lord Burghley condescended to make use of this man. He did not send the poison, but he intimated that there were other ways in which his correspondent might deserve his pardon for the affair at Wakefield; and with this encouragement, Woodshawe wrote that he had a dear friend in De la Motte, the Governor of Gravelines, whom he described as a greedy ruffian, 'that two hundred 'pounds would give courage to attempt anything:' with De la Motte's help he proposed to surprise Calais, which he had ascertained to be 'carelessly guarded.' Or failing this, he could betray his English comrades.

'For my other pretence,' he wrote, when the Calais plan was abandoned, 'if it please your honour to send

---
[1] Edward Woodshawe to Burghley, Sept. 3, 1574.—MSS. Flanders.

'me your whole mind, whatever your honour command
'me to do, if I do it not secretly and effectually, never
'trust man for my sake. What I have been, God for-
'give me my folly: but what I am, I pray God give me
'grace that I may do that service to the Queen's
'Majesty and my country which my faithful heart is
'willing to do.'[1]

The English Government had more than once shewn the refugees that to escape from England was not necessarily to escape altogether. Story had been kidnapped and hanged, the Earl of Northumberland had been bought from the Scots and beheaded. The lesson had produced some effect, but it needed to be repeated. Lord Westmoreland had applied for pardon, and had almost obtained it, when he fell back under the influence of the Countess of Northumberland, and was again 'prac- 'tising' against the Queen. He had been attainted, and his life was forfeited. Cecil employed Woodshawe to entrap him, take him prisoner, and bring him to London. The ingenious scoundrel wound himself into the Earl's favour, sending report of his progress as he went along. When the Earl, with the other exiles, were ordered finally out of Flanders, Woodshawe advised him to go to Liége, and laid an ambuscade for him on the way, intending, ' by God's grace to carry him dead or alive to England.'[2]

Fortunately for Burghley's reputation, the plot failed. Woodshawe disappears from history, and the Lord Treasurer had to submit to the humiliation of receiving advice from Leicester to have no further transactions with persons of abandoned character.[3] He could have defended himself on the ground that

---

[1] Woodshawe to Burghley, Nov. 30 —MSS. Flanders.
[2] Woodshawe to Burghley, Feb.
27 and March 13, 1575.—MSS. Ibid.
[3] Leicester to Burghley, March, 1575.—MSS. Hatfield.

Westmoreland, being an attainted traitor, had no rights left him, in law or honour; but Philip, on the same plea, might have defended the assassination of Orange.

To return to Sir Henry Cobham. The instructions which he carried with him were not limited to English interests. His first business was with the Inquisition. If the Holy Office persisted in interfering with the merchants, he was directed to say that 'the amity could not 'continue.' The English were not heretics. They merely 'professed a difference' in the observation of the rites and forms of the Church. The Queen recommended her brother-in-law 'to be guided rather,' in these questions, 'by such as were of noble birth and 'temporal vocation, than by such as had their oaths to 'the Church of Rome, and preferred the particular 'affairs of the Pope before the service of the King.'

But beyond this which concerned herself, Elizabeth went a step further. A gleam of success had lighted the fortunes of the gallant Orange on the arrival of De Valdez. Requescens had attacked Leyden, and the ever memorable defence of the city had ended in the flight and ruin of the besieging army. Negociations for peace followed, but had been broken off on the old point of toleration. The Queen, in her capacity of mutual friend, now proposed to mediate. She made the most of the offers which the States had pressed upon herself. The King, she said, ought to be aware that 'in Christendom he had no such friend as she had been.' The States were ready to return to their allegiance if they would have toleration on the terms of the Peace of Passau, and Philip need not hesitate to allow what had been allowed by his father. This one concession would be sufficient; or if the Prince made difficulties afterwards, 'she promised to join with the King by force to 'compel the disobedient that should impeach it.' On the other hand, if the war was to continue, she said plainly that she would be driven into some other course. She did not wish to injure the King, but she could not, in the interests of England, let the Netherlands be annexed to France, and in default of help from her it was to France that they would certainly turn.[1]

The weight of the message lay in the last paragraph. A war of religion would not be tolerated in England, but a war to prevent the aggrandisement of France would be warmly popular. It was thought that Philip knew enough of English politics to comprehend the distinction.

To the Spanish people generally the mission was most unwelcome. The reception of a heretic minister was in itself a scandal which had been overcome only by a dispensation from the Pope.[2] Cobham could hardly find so much as a lodging at Madrid. The King, in his first interview, was cold and ambiguous: and the Nuncio, notwithstanding the Pope's permission, recommended between advice and command, that the ambassador should be dismissed without a second audience.[3] Elizabeth might be negociated with at Brussels, or an emissary might be sent to London, but Madrid was the second city of the Catholic world. Shocked at the dreadful presence of the accursed thing among them, the Council even reopened the whole question of the alliance. Hopper, President of the Council for the Netherlands, admitted that Elizabeth had grounds of

---

[1] Heads of a message to the King of Spain, July 1, 1575. Instructions to Sir H. Cobham. Drawn by Walsingham and signed by the Queen, July.—*MSS. Spain.*

[2] 'Como el Santo Oficio ha hecho muy complidamente, procurando para ello y para mayor seguridad de la conscienca disimuladamente el consentimiento de la Santa Sede Apostolica.'—*Parecer de Hopperus*, Oct. 1575. *MSS. Simancas.*

[3] A su Mag^d del Nuncio, 24 de Nov^{br} 1575. Sobre echar de aqui á Cobham.—*MSS. Ibid.*

complaint. Her life had been attempted, and she knew it,[1] but she was a schismatic, and no fit ally for Spain. 'The 'honour of God,' he argued, 'forbade ambiguous friend-'ships. She had been at the bottom of all the confusion 'in Europe. The rebels were now at their last gasp, and 'his Majesty should trust in God and finish the work.'

Quiroga, Archbishop of Toledo and Inquisitor-General, took the same view. 'The Queen of England,' he said, 'neither was nor ever could be an honest friend 'of Spain. She was a tyrant, and had murdered Ca-'tholics. She had revolutionised Scotland, and would 'never cease to trouble the world. Her present overtures 'were deceit. She knew Chapin's intentions against her, 'and women and princes never forgave."[2]

Then Alva rose. Alva, with his experience of Haarlem and Leyden, knew better the resources yet remaining to the rebellion, and understood better also the personal disposition of Elizabeth. 'Diplomacy was not 'action,' he urged; 'and the alliance which he recom-'mended need stand only as long as it was useful. Con-'venience was the measure of obligation even between 'Christian States, far more, therefore, between a Christian 'and a heretic.[3] An English ambassador could do no 'harm at Madrid, a Spanish ambassador in London would 'have mass in his house, would protect the Catholics, and 'prevent persecution. The Queen was well disposed to 'Spain. It was supremely important to humour her incli-'nations, and prevent her from drawing closer to France. 'In affairs of State, as in philosophy, imagination was a

---

[1] 'Tanto mas habiendose ella offendido una vez por haber entendido que se machinaba algo contra su persona y Reyno.'—*Parecer de Hopperus. Ibid.*

[2] 'Y que en fin Doñas y Coronas nunca perdona.'—*Parecer de Quiroga.*

MSS. *Ibid.*

[3] 'Siendo su intencion que dure mientras durara la necessidad como lo hacen los Principes Christianos uno con otro, quanto mas con la Reyna herege.'—*Parecer de Alva. Ibid.*

'powerful element. It was no question of conscience, 'and the King could throw her over when he pleased.'[1]

So construed the alliance was less alarming. Quiroga himself was willing to make allowances. 'The thing 'desired was not so bad but that it might be made good 'by circumstances.' The English trade would no doubt be useful, and implied diplomatic intercourse. The difficulty lay in the details. Was an English ambassador at Madrid to be allowed to use a heretic service? Was the Holy Office to see its authority impaired in the port towns?

Beaten on the main argument, President Hopper stood out against concession in details. 'There were 'men about the King,' he said, hitting at Alva, 'who 'pretended that scruples were out of place in politics,' 'that princes should look to interest, and leave theory 'to philosophers and divines. This was a doctrine 'of atheists and enemies of mankind. Politics should 'have no foundation but the will of God, and what 'was not of God was of the devil.'[2]

The King, inclining always to what he called piety, was deeply perplexed. He was willing to carry out what had been undertaken by Mendoza in England, but he hesitated at the further step, and Alva was in despair. Unless the Inquisition could be controlled, he saw that the alliance would fall in pieces. The Queen would take up the cause of the States, and Drake would be let loose upon the gold fleets. 'Cobham,' he wrote to Secretary Cayas, 'has just rushed into my room to kill 'me. I have Cobham at one ear and Hopper at the 'other, and between them both I am at my wits' end.

---

[1] 'Que los negocios de Estado se fundan en Imaginacion como los filosofos, y que pues es cosa temporal que la puede soltar quando quisiera.' —*Pervew de Alva. Ibid.*

[2] Recuerdo de Hopperus.—*MSS. Ibid.*

'Hopper will ruin all. The Queen of England will
'throw herself on France: the objection will be the same
'as long as she lives, and Hopper is such an obstinate
'ass that I can drive no conviction into his head. The
'King knows what I think, and I shall say no more.
'The Englishman is ready to tear me in pieces because
'he and his mistress are called heretics.'[1]

In still more passionate tones he complained of
Quiroga. 'The Inquisitor-General,' he said, 'has no
'right to notice offences not committed on Spanish
'soil, nor if the English do wrong while on shore
'should he touch the property of any but the offenders
'themselves. I have argued with him, but he is
'as hard as a stone,'[2] and unless we yield in this we
'lose England, and all will be over with Flanders. His
'Majesty, no doubt, should respect the Holy Office, but
'it cannot be right to play into the hands of God's
'rebels and his own. I beseech his Majesty with tears
'to listen to me. Without this concession all else will
'be nothing. I will not give up hope. I will snatch
'at every twig that offers.'[3]

Between his various advisers, Philip was as uncertain
as Elizabeth. Alva recommended him to renew his
father's old League, or make another special treaty, to
stand till the Low Countries were conquered. Philip
was afraid, on one side, of committing misprision of
heresy; on the other, of adding England to his other
enemies. At length he gave Cobham in writing the
following answer. 'He would send an ambassador to
'London, and he would receive an Englishman at
'Madrid, but only on these conditions. His own minister
'must have the sacraments of the Church, as a matter of

---

[1] Alva to Cayas, Nov. 1575.
[2] 'Esta como una peña dura.'
[3] Alva to Cayas, Nov. 25.— *MSS. Simancas.*

'course. As positively, no unauthorised service could be
'permitted in Spain. The utmost indulgence which
'would be extended to a foreign resident would be that
'he should not be compelled to hear mass. It would be
'more agreeable to all parties, therefore, if the person
'selected could be a Catholic, otherwise the Queen must
'send some reasonable person well inclined to the alliance.
'The offer of mediation he was obliged to decline. If his
'insurgent subjects would submit unconditionally, he
'would receive them to mercy at her Highness's hands,
'but he would adventure all his estate, rather than
'license any exercise of religion other than the Catholic
'Roman. As to the merchants and seamen, strangers
'must observe the laws established by the Inquisition,
'and if they offended must be punished by the law. The
'religious administration was independent of himself, and
'he was bound by his oath to respect the privileges of
'the Inquisition.'[1]

The principal matter was thus really left in the Archbishop's hands, and the lives and properties of Englishmen were insecure as ever. Alva, however, made a private arrangement with Cobham, for the fulfilment of which, he said, he would be himself responsible. Out of special regard for the Queen, the law against heresy should be so far relaxed that no English subject should be liable to arbitrary arrest and examination.[2] The English, in return, if they chose

---

[1] Answer to Sir H. Cobham, Nov. 1575.—*MSS. Simancas.*

[2] A marginal note shows that Quiroga had given a sort of consent but had refused to commit the Inquisition by a positive engagement. 'Esto fué conforme a lo que habia dicho el Inquisidor General que aunque todos los estrangeros que han hereticado fuera del Reyno son castigados por ello se disimularia con los Ingleses. Pero que no se les habia de decir que procedia de la Inquisition porque no lo tomasen por ley o permission, y asi se pusó en papel a parte y se lo dió al Duque de Alva.'—*Dies eras del Duque de Alva*, 2 de Deciembre. *MSS. Simancas.*

to enter Spanish churches, must behave as others did. If they encountered the Holy Sacrament in the streets they must kneel, nor must they proselytise or introduce heretical books.

With this reply Cobham took his leave. It is needless to say that Alva's engagement was not observed by the Inquisitors, and the natural good-will between the English and the Spaniards was changed to hatred by the cruelties to which Elizabeth's subjects were still systematically exposed. But the utmost had been done on both sides to prevent the disintegration of the old alliance.

The King of Spain himself was really acting in good faith. The exiles had fitted out a Catholic English pirate fleet. Don John of Austria, their favourite candidate for the hand of the Queen of Scots, had given them encouragement; but Philip had been coldly unfavourable.[1] Requescens's army had received its chief supplies from England, and when Orange threatened to stop the trade between the Thames and Antwerp, Elizabeth sent to tell him 'that she would not bear it at 'his hands, and would sooner join her forces to those of 'Spain' to compel him to submit.[2] The French court, encouraged by the success at Leyden, was willing to risk a war for the incorporation of the Provinces; Orange desperate of help from England was inclining to agree; while the States of Holland, dreading France

---

[1] Sir Francis Englefield writes in cipher to Cotton, the pirate admiral: 'I am sorry and angry to see your service and diligence so ill requited by them that are to receive the chief profit. I have written in all fidelity both to Spain and Rome. From the first I have no answer; which shews their little favour in whatever should cost them any penny. From the second I have answer, that the importance of your service is imparted to Don John and the chief cardinals, and shall be followed to the uttermost of their small credit.'—*MSS. Domestic.* Oct. 1575.

[2] Instructions to Daniel Rogers, June 8, 1575.—*MSS. Flanders.*

only one degree less than they dreaded Spain, hoped that Elizabeth would take up their cause. They threw themselves at her feet, imploring to be accepted as her subjects, and professed to desire nothing so much as to be annexed to the English crown.[1]

Cobham had not at that time returned; it was uncertain what answer he would receive; and decision was so difficult, that Burghley hesitated, and was disposed to change his opinion for Walsingham's.[2] He drew out in his usual manner the alternatives of the situation.

Three possibilities only lay before the States. They must either be conquered by Spain, or be assisted either by England or by France. If they were conquered, they would be governed thenceforth by Spaniards, and England 'would be neighboured by a 'nation, which for religious and other quarrels, would 'take advantage to subvert the Estate.' If they were supported by France, 'they would be at the command-'ment of that crown,' 'and with their havens and ships, 'France would control both England and Scotland, and 'all the narrow seas.' The conclusion seemed irresistible that England, whether she liked it or not, must interfere, and either help the Prince of Orange with money till the King of Spain would agree to toleration, or 'receive the States on their own offers as subjects to 'the crown.'[3]

Time was pressing. The Prince sent the Queen

---

[1] Daniel Rogers, Oct. 9.—*MSS. Flanders.*

[2] 'If my ability were I would gladly help the plough with you in the ridge or furrow, till the yoke was pulled off my neck.'—*Burghley to Walsingham, MSS. Domestic.*

[3] Consideration of the difficulties that may or are likely to ensue upon the not aiding and maintaining the Prince of Orange and Estates in Holland. In Lord Burghley's hand, Oct. 17, 1575.—*MSS. Flanders.*

word that 'she had offers made her that, if she would
'embrace them, her posterity would thank God for her;'
submit to Spain, however, they never would, 'for they
'feared a massacre of Paris;' and if she refused they
would 'seek other aid.' It was the dilemma which
Elizabeth had foreseen when she told Philip that if he
would not make peace, she must act on her own judgment; she could not let the provinces become French.
Had she been so disposed, she could not move with
decency till Cobham came; she sent again to Requescens, however, urging peace, and bidding the messenger
use his eyes and ascertain the dimensions of the Spanish
forces.[1] She wrote more gently to Orange. She
called herself the best real friend that he possessed
in Christendom. She wished to help him, but a war
with such a power as Spain was a serious consideration.
She had sent a minister to Philip, she said, and she
had still hopes that he would consent to a compromise.
Meanwhile she asked for an account of his resources,
and implied and all but promised that if the King was
obstinate she would help him.[2]

Requescens, frightened at her attitude, dispatched
M. de Champagny[3] to protest, while St. Aldegonde, the
Prince's most faithful friend, and two councillors, Paul
Buys and Francis Maldesen, came as commissioners
from the States.

Their arrival in England was simultaneous with the
return of Cobham, whose report did not tend to clear
the situation. It was conciliatory on the whole, but the
offered mediation was refused. Towards the States there

---

[1] Instructions to Mr. Corbet, Oct. 11. Burghley's hand.—*MSS. Flanders.*

[2] Instructions to John Hastings sent to the Prince of Orange, Oct. 29.—*MSS. Ibid.*

[3] Brother of Cardinal Granville, and Governor of Antwerp.

was no concession, and the lives and properties of English traders were still only secured by a verbal promise of Alva. The Council sat day after day unable to resolve. The heads of the guilds, with the leading merchants and manufacturers, were called in to assist in the consultation. Leicester, Walsingham, Bedford, Knollys, Mildmay, and privately Burghley, were for accepting the offers of the States. The men of the city, with the Spanish party among the peers, were for peace and alliance with Philip. The controller of the household, Sir James Crofts, insisted that the Queen's revenue sufficed barely for the ordinary expenditure, and that taxation in a doubtful cause would be resented by the country.[1] Elizabeth herself, furious that the quiet of Europe should be sacrificed to Protestant preciseness, was so vehement, that one day, according to De Guaras, after a stormy discussion, she flung out of the council chamber, and locked herself into her room, crying out that the Council would destroy her.[2]

The objections of the city were silenced by the opportune arrival of news from Cadiz illustrating the value of Alva's engagements. A ship belonging to Sir Edward Osborne, one of the first merchants in London, had been seized and condemned by the Inquisition. The crew

---

[1] Speech on the question of giving aid to the Prince of Orange, in French. *MSS. Flanders,* 1575. The translator attributes it to the Chancellor. But there was no Chancellor in England at this time, the Great Seal being held by Sir Nicholas Bacon, as Lord Keeper. The person meant must be the Controller Crofts who is specified by De Guaras as having advocated the Spanish side. —*Cartas de Antonio de Guaras,* Dec. 31. *MSS. Simancas.*

[2] 'Ha tenido aviso cierto de que hizó la Reyna demostraciones con mucho descontento y con muchas voces sobre que no era de parecer de enviar fuerças declaradamente a Zelanda y Holanda, y se entró en su aposento sola cerrandole, dando voces que por ello la ponian en perdicion. Y los que alli estaban y sus damas las daban mayores diciendo que sino abria que quebrarian la puerta, no pudiendo sufrir que estuviese sola con aquella pena.'—*Ibid.*

were in a dungeon at Seville, no offence being charged
against them beyond the fact that they were heretics.
If this was to be the order of things peace was indeed impossible. Champagny was dismissed with a cold answer.
St. Aldegonde was told that one more remonstrance
would be tried with Spain, and unless the Queen could
obtain a formal promise that her people should be no
more molested she would 'receive the States into her
'protection.' She could not declare war immediately.
She must consult Parliament, and allow time to the
merchants to call in their ships. But she could send the
Prince some money, and would insist meanwhile on a
suspension of arms. If the Spanish Government refused
redress 'she would have a more probable occasion in the
'sight of the world to proceed to the open aiding of them.'[1]

Champagny before he retired demanded the arrest
or expulsion of St. Aldegonde in return for the banishment of the refugees. Elizabeth declined on the
ground that St. Aldegonde being commissioned to
her by the States, was protected by his position. Cobham, fresh from Madrid, was ordered to Brussels to tell
Requescens that peace must be made 'or her Majesty
'would be forced for her own safety to put in execution
'some remedy for her relief that she would not willingly
'yield unto,'[2] while Parliament was summoned immediately to provide the necessary means.

Parliament made no difficulty. The States were not
spoken of by name, but a large subsidy was voted for
'the defence of the realm.' The session promised to
pass off for once without unpleasantness, when a question burst out which produced an ill-timed exasperation,

---

[1] Two answers to the Hollanders. In Walsingham's hand and Burghley's, Jan. 15, 1576.—*MSS. Flanders.*

[2] Instructions to Sir H. Cobham, sent to the Commendator, March, 1576.—*Flanders.*

and flung the Queen into the worst of humours with the Protestants and all belonging to them. She ruled the pulpits of the Churches: she imagined that she could do the same with the House of Commons; and more than once she had intimated that she would allow nothing to be discussed there affecting religion where the initiative had not been taken by the Bishops. On the same principle on which she prohibited Puritan conventicles and forbade Catholics to preach in public or say mass, she checked the tongues of the Reformers in Parliament. While secular questions were best resolved by debate, religious animosities she always attempted to suffocate.

The Protestant members resented the interference with their inherited liberty of debate, and the Queen gave them an advantage by including subjects in her prohibition immediately within the province of the House. Wentworth, member for Tregony, rose to complain 'that not only were they forbidden to speak of 'religion, but now they were to be silent on matters 'touching the interests of every tradesman in the realm.' 'The customs duties were suspended in favour of noble-'men and courtiers; honest men were robbed in thou-'sands that three or four persons connected with the 'palace might be enriched: and yet Parliament was 'expected to be silent. Either a rumour was spread 'about the House that her Majesty was offended, or a 'message would come down desiring that this or that 'complaint should not be mentioned. He wished such 'rumours and messages were buried with the father of 'them in hell.'[1]

---

[1] Speech of Mr. Wentworth, 18th of Elizabeth, D'Ewes' Journals. Another passage in the speech curiously illustrates the growing bitterness against the Bishops. 'Her Majesty,' he said, 'forbade us in the last ses-

The times were too dangerous for loyal subjects to quarrel with the Queen. The question raised was, to say the least of it, unreasonable. If she granted monopolies, she had governed with singular economy, had rarely troubled her subjects for money, had restored the currency, and punctually paid her father's, brother's, and sister's debts. Her credit stood so high that she could borrow money at Antwerp at five per cent., when Philip could not borrow on any terms at all.[1] Wentworth was stopped by the Speaker before he could conclude his speech. He was Star-chambered, and sent to meditate for a month in the Tower. He then made his submission on his knees on the floor of the House, and was pardoned ' to the great contentment of all present.'[2]

In the conduct of the House the Queen had little to complain of; but this small accident, combined with other causes, occasioned one of those periodical fits of ill humour, to which she was always liable, against the Protestants. She had been dragged into encouraging the States against her inclination: the sudden death of Requescens before Cobham could reach him gave her

---

sion to deal with any matter of religion, but only what was laid before us from the Bishops, and nothing was done, for God would not that His holy Spirit should descend all that session on the Bishops. I have heard from of old that the banishment of Pope and Popery, and the restoring of true religion had their beginnings from this House and not from the Bishops. I have heard that few laws for religion had their foundation from them. I was one of others sent last Parliament to the Archbishop of Canterbury, for the Articles of Religion then passed this House. He asked why we put out of the book the Articles for the Homilies, consecrating Bishops, and such like. "Sir," said I, "we were so occupied with other matters we had no time to examine them, how they agreed with the word of God." "You mistake," said he, "you will refer yourselves wholly to us therein." "No, by the faith I bear to God," said I, "we will pass nothing before we understand what it is—that were but to make you Popes. Make you Popes who list," said I. "We will have none."'

[1] Edward Castelyn to Walsingham, March 4.—MSS. Flanders.
[2] D'Ewes' Journals.

an excuse for altering her mind, and having determined not to send the help which her Parliament had given her the means of sending, she tried to gain credit with Spain by making her refusal as offensive as possible. After all her gracious promises, St. Aldegonde and his companions were sent away with an answer in writing that she would neither assist the States herself nor permit them to seek help from France. Her own agents had been entertained always at the public cost in Holland. The emissaries of the Prince of Orange were made to pay their own expenses, and were hustled out of the country with threats and insults.

As much surprised as mortified, they returned to the Hague. Long as they had experienced the vacillations of the strange woman whose friendship they had sought so humbly, the suddenness of the last change bewildered them.[1]

Burghley sent them word that their rejection was no act of his, that their cause should never want such support as he could command. It was hinted 'that her 'Majesty's answer was but a manner of connivance, 'which was necessary for the season;' but they went away in profound indignation; and the despair of the States was only less than their exasperation.

It was the darkest moment in the Prince's fortunes.

---

[1] 'The poor men were in a marvellous passion for the answer they had received, which they had the less expected at her Majesty's hands, whom they had always accounted gracious and no tyrant. They had deserved well, and were, therefore, unworthy of this uncourteous dealing and rejection, and thought it very hard if they being free men should be forbidden to seek aid to preserve their lives. It would bring them by despair to fear no evil, that they could not hope for any good. It would have sufficed, they said, without this aggravation, that they had spent here so much time, and consumed great sums of money, that might have been better employed. They had come over at her Majesty's invitation, and were sent away, not only without thanks, but threatened also if they did not yield their own throats to be cut.'— *Wm. Herle to Burghley*, March 23, 1576. *MSS. Flanders*.

The Spaniards, whose progress had not been checked by the Viceroy's death, had cut Holland in two. They had taken the islands of Tholen, Duiveland, and Schowen. Boisot, the hero of Leyden, was killed in an attempt to save Zierichsee, and with the fall of that town, Philip's troops were again established upon the sea. For want of the money, which Elizabeth had first promised and then refused, the Dutch fleet was dissolving.[1] The Anglo-Catholic buccaneers seized ship after ship of the Dutch, and flung the crews into the sea. The fierce Hollanders in savage despair, repaid cruelty with cruelty. The next step was a general arrest of all Dutch vessels in English harbours, and the Prince in retaliation seized the London merchant fleet in the Scheldt, worth, it was said, 200,000*l.*

Elizabeth, it is quite clear, again believed that the States were about to be overwhelmed, and that her most prudent course was now to assist in their overthrow. She wrote a letter to the Prince, 'the like of which,' he said, 'he had never received from any in the world.' She sent Sir William Winter to extricate the fleet by force or practice. She bade him tell Orange not to think that she needed his friendship; the King of Spain was on cordial terms with her; and whether he was foe or friend, she could defend her own shores; if the ships were not released, she would make open war upon the States.[2]

They were surrendered instantly, with an apology to Winter, but the Queen was not satisfied. She said she had been insulted. Her honour was compromised. She

---

[1] 'The Prince has engaged to pay his mariners in confidence of the sum promised. If he is frustrate his force is lost. He begs her Majesty to consider it is but a bare loan, and all Holland and Zealand are bound for it. His extremity is such that he must be succoured or he is undone.'—*M. de G. to Walsingham, from Flushing,* Aug. 30. *MSS. Flanders.*

[2] *Flanders MSS.* May and June, 1576.

thought of seizing Flushing, to hold as a pawn, in the coming settlement with Spain.

It was at this time, and probably under the weight of this last blow, that the Prince meditated embarking with as many of the inhabitants of the States as their ships would carry, and migrating to a new home beyond the Atlantic. 'He was greatly amazed when he under-
'stood assuredly that her Majesty would be avenged
'of him by way of arms. Although necessity might have
'induced him to forget some part of his duty towards
'her Majesty, yet his state and condition was rather to
'be pitied and tendered with compassion, than perse-
'cuted with hatred, especially on a Christian Prince's
'part.'¹ Never, however, was Prince, either Christian or heathen, less open than Elizabeth to sentimental considerations. She was meditating a complete reversal of policy, which if begun could hardly stop short of reunion with Rome. Warnings were not wanting, but the tone in which they were made showed how real was the danger. 'Her Majesty,' wrote some one, who was most likely Walsingham, 'considers herself forced, in
'respect of her honour, to enter into action against the
'Prince of Orange. The Prince has been a bridle to
'Spain hitherto, and kept war out of our own gate.
'If Spain assail him now by land, and the Queen of
'England by sea, he must fall, and what can her
'Majesty look for but such mischief as Spanish malice
'can yield? Spain will then assist France to put down
'the religion. The number of malcontents at home is
'increased, and if the King of Spain attack England he
'will find so great a party within the realm as is
'grievous to a good subject to think of. There are but
'three possible courses—to maintain the Prince of Orange

---

¹ M. de G. to Walsingham, Aug. 10.—*MSS. Flanders.*

'and the Huguenots, to seek reconciliation with Spain,
' and for her Majesty to settle her estate at home. To
' the first, men are now unwilling to move her, for that
' her Majesty has with very bitter speeches repaid those
' that first advised her to assist the Protestants, and
' thinks it against her conscience to maintain rebels.
' In reality that advice deserved rather praise than
' blame. The Prince of Orange is her soundest friend.
' The King of Spain daily consumes her Majesty's sub-
' jects by fire, and confiscates their goods. Such of her
' subjects as are loyal, would all have her support the
' Prince. Those who make a conscience of maintaining
' rebels are themselves rebels in heart, and will become
' disaffected when time shall serve. Reconciliation with
' Spain it is unlikely can ever be. *If religion were
' the only impediment, then, perhaps, it was likely recon-
' ciliation might follow by changing religion,* but though
' in outward show religion shall be the pretext, the
' crown shall be the mark which no change of religion
' can save. The repose which her Majesty has hitherto
' enjoyed has wholly depended on the Princes her
' neighbours' troubles at home. These troubles will
' not long continue. She must look to the peril out of
' hand, which can neither abide long delay of consulta-
' tion, nor stay in execution of that which may tend to
' the prevention thereof.'[1]

To understand the meaning of Elizabeth's present attitude, we must turn to her relations with another country. Charles IX. and his brother, who had just succeeded him as Henry III., had been successively suitors for her hand. The negociation which fell to the ground with the massacre of St. Bartholomew, was

---

[1] A brief discourse laying forth the uncertainty of her Majesty's pre- sent peace and quietness. Abridged. Aug. 1576. *MSS. Domestic.*

revived afterwards in behalf of the third brother, Francis of Alençon, a pock-marked, unhealthy dwarf. Catherine de Medici, it will be recollected, when the religious objections were raised by Anjou, hinted that she had another son, from whom no such difficulty need be anticipated. Alençon, in the terrors which followed the massacre, had thought of flying for refuge to England. He had friends about the court; and when the danger passed off, the Queen-mother, who believed that sooner or later Elizabeth would be compelled to marry, held his pretensions continually before her eyes. La Mothe Fénelon was recalled. His place at the English Court was taken by Castelnau de Mauvissière, a politician of the middle and moderate party, who had no love for the Pope, hated the Guyses and Spain, regarded the English alliance as a guarantee for the quiet of France, and looked on a marriage between Alençon and the Queen as the sure means of making the alliance permanent.

The position of heirs presumptive was always uneasy, and Alençon's, when his brother came to the throne, was no exception. 'Monsieur,' as he was now called, was detained at court with Henry of Navarre, both of them essentially prisoners. The King was jealous of him, and the Guises, who aspired to supersede the house of Valois, inflamed the ill feeling. But for his mother, it was thought that means would have been found to rid Alençon out of the world.[1] The peace had after

---

[1] 'There have been many practices against Monsieur by the Guises, whereby the King has been in many passions against his brother, and has been sometimes advised to use all severity against him; and if it had not been for the help of the Queen-mother it hath been thought it had been hard with Monsieur before this time, for the Queen-mother has always been a stay to him, as a mother and also as a stay for herself against the Guises.'—*Valentine Dale to Sir T. Smith, from Paris,* Sept. 3, 1575. *MSS. France.*

all given little respite to the Huguenots, the Catholic nobles, in their different governments, respecting the promises made to them no further than suited their own pleasure. Alençon was suspected of intending to take up their cause, and the King concluded, after much hesitation, that it would be well, both for himself and France, if Elizabeth would take him for a husband. The princes and princesses of the sixteenth century hung suspended between a prison and a throne. The matrimonial crown of England might make Monsieur dangerously powerful; but there were objections to murder, and the closest prison could not be made conclusively secure. The marriage, on the whole, appeared to be the safest alternative.[1] Mauvissière told Walsingham, 'that he 'could not sleep at night, for his desire to bring about 'a matter so much for the repose of Christendom;'[2] while Elizabeth herself, as usual, played with the suggestion, gave a favourable though indecisive answer, but insisted on her old condition, that she must see her bridegroom before she could make up her mind.

Alençon himself was all eagerness. To him it had long appeared that, with so poor an outlook in France, a marriage with Elizabeth, though she was twice his age, 'would make him the happiest man alive:' and as his hopes, if he remained longer in captivity, might be cut short by a Guisian poniard, he became anxious to place himself where his life would be safe, and where he could fly to England when he pleased.

---

[1] 'The king demanded with very great affection, et ne se peult il faire encore? The Queen-mother cast out words sometimes alone, sometimes the King being present, to feel what she could understand of the Queen's Majesty's disposition, and certain it is both the King and Queen-mother would with all their hearts the matter was ended, if they thought it might be compassed, and might trust Monsieur at liberty.'— *Valentine Dale to Sir T. Smith,* Sept. 3, 1575. *MSS. France.*

[2] Manvissière to Walsingham, Sept. 4.—*Ibid.*

The Guises, dreading the effects of such an alliance on the prospects of Mary Stuart, pressed the King to commit his brother to the Bastile. On the 15th of September, when the Cardinal of Guise was in the royal closet on this particular errand, Monsieur borrowed a carriage from a friend, slipped out of the Louvre in disguise, and made his way to St. Cloud. Several hundred mounted gentlemen were waiting to receive him, and in a few days he was with La Noue on the Loire, at the head of a Huguenot army. All had been prepared for a rising. He wrote to his brother, to say that he had fled only to save his life. He put out a Proclamation, in which he styled himself Protector of the liberties of France.[1] Condé was at Strasburgh, ready to march on Paris; while Casimir, brother of the Elector Palatine, entered Lorraine with 10,000 Reiters, meaning to cross France and join La Noue.

The King, in real or affected dismay, remained idle in the palace. He shut himself into his room, saw no one, and 'lay tormented on his bed,' with his mother at his side. Hating and fearing equally both Guises and Huguenots, he could form no plan and trust none of his Council.[2] The Duke of Guise flew to Lorraine, and partially checked Casimir, but was wounded and disabled in a skirmish. The treasury was empty; the Catholics were without leaders and disorganised. The Queen-mother, as usual, undertook to mediate, and went off to La Noue's camp to see Monsieur. The Huguenots having been deceived so often, demanded substantial guarantees that the promises made them should be observed. They required the free exercise of their

---

[1] Gouverneur-général pour le Roy et Protecteur de la liberté et bien publique de France.—*Dale to Burghley*, Sept. 21. *MSS. France.*

[2] 'Ipse sibi timet et metuit omnes, desideratur in eo animus et consilium.'—*Dale to Burghley*, Sept. 21. *MSS. Ibid.*

religion in every part of France, with eight large towns to be selected by themselves out of those already in their possession, to be garrisoned by their own men. Condé asked besides for Boulogne, and Casimir for the payment of his expenses with Metz, Verdun, and Toul as securities.

The Queen-mother promised everything—but the Huguenot leaders refused to dissolve their forces till their terms were actually complied with. Alençon sent to Elizabeth, to tell her that she was his chief hope on earth, that he longed to see her; that his chief motive in escaping was, that he might be sure of access to her most precious person; and that meanwhile, he relied on her support. If she would join in a formal league with himself and Casimir, they might dictate terms to Europe; if that could not be, he begged her to lend him, at all events, some money; and undertook to make no peace in which she was herself not comprehended.[1]

Elizabeth's position towards France was briefly this. She could not yet trust the King, who had been the chief instrument in the massacre of St. Bartholomew. If the Guises became dominant they were likely to join Spain, and interfere in England for Mary Stuart. If the Huguenots got the better of them without help from her, they would join the Prince of Orange, and earn the gratitude of France by the annexation of the Netherlands. A hold upon Alençon was therefore extremely desirable. She sent money—she replied with gracious vagueness, that she would think about the League; that she approved of what he was doing, understanding that it was not directed against the King, but against his 'ill advisers,' 'whose passions would not suffer him to

---

[1] Instructions to La Porte sent to the Queen of England by the Duc d'Alençon. Nov. 27, 1575. *MSS. France.*

'enjoy quietness at home, nor friendship with his best
'affected confederates."¹ La Noue meanwhile was in
correspondence with Walsingham, and keeping a watch
on Monsieur, of whom he felt uncertain so long as his
mother was at hand to play upon him.²

It was at the same moment that St. Aldegonde and
his companions arrived in London with the offer of the
States; and the Queen had two cards in her hand, to play
either or both as suited her convenience. The Huguenots used their momentary superiority — Condé set
himself in motion at Strasburgh, and advanced slowly
on the Paris road. Casimir pushed on towards the Loire,
Guise, who had recovered from his wound, following
him and pressing for help from Philip.

The French King, only anxious for peace, became more
than ever desirous to dispose of his brother in England.
He told the English minister, that 'if he might see the
'Duke so matched, he would sing Nunc dimittis; and
'that if he died without children he would settle his
'crown on her Majesty's offspring.'³ He wrote to Elizabeth descanting on her divine perfections, and promising
that if she would accept Alençon, she should find more
than a brother in himself.⁴

'Her Majesty,' said Walsingham once, impatiently,
'trusts much in fortune. I would she would trust more
'in Almighty God.' Yet Elizabeth might be pardoned
for relying on a power which so steadily befriended her,
and in nothing more than in the character of the two
great sovereigns which divided Catholic Europe. The
weakness of Henry and the bigotry of Philip were alike
defences to English independence. She had assisted

---

¹ Her Majesty's secret letter to the Duc d'Alençon. Walsingham's hand.—MSS. France.
² Walsingham to Burghley, Nov. 22.—MSS. Ibid.
³ Dale to Elizabeth, Dec. 19.
⁴ The King of France to Elizabeth, Dec. 1575.—MSS. France.

Alençon; she had not offended the King. But the issue was still uncertain. Should Monsieur's victory be complete he was morally certain to offer help to the Low Countries, and in that case she could only prevent the States from throwing themselves into his arms by becoming herself their protectress. Should he be defeated, she might require the help of the States herself, in the coalition which might then be formed against her. So long as the uncertainty lasted, therefore, she amused St. Aldegonde with fair words and promises. In February, the King of Navarre slipped from the Court as Alençon had done. Rumours prophetic of the future said that he was playing at dice with Guise, in the King's cabinet, when suddenly 'great round drops 'of blood appeared upon the board between them;' and Navarre believing it to be an omen of his fate, if he waited longer, fled to his friends.[1]

The Protestants had now their natural leader among them, and never before or after had so fair a chance of complete success. Money only was wanting. Alençon applied again to Elizabeth. He asked only but for means to keep Casimir's Reiters two months longer in the field, and the whole government of France would then, he trusted, be in his hands.

But Elizabeth had done as much as she cared to do. A little more and Alençon would be too strong. The Court confirmed the concessions which the Protestants demanded. The old edicts of toleration were renewed; they were declared equal with Catholics in the eye of the law, and La Noue was allowed to keep his eight towns. These terms were considered by Elizabeth sufficiently liberal. The two factions would balance each

---

[1] This curious story was current in Paris a week after.—*Dale to Walsingham*, Feb. 14. *MSS. France.*

other, and England would be in no danger from either. She stipulated for, and exacted, the repayment of the sum which she had advanced to Monsieur. But Condé did not obtain Boulogne, no securities were given to Casimir, and peace on these conditions was signed at Paris, on the 24th of April.

The danger was now held to be passed. St. Aldegonde therefore was dismissed with cold comfort. Thomas Randolph was sent to Paris to tell Henry and Alençon, that she would rather assist the King of Spain than allow them to meddle in the Low Countries. The marriage overtures fell through, being no longer needed till the reappearance of danger should revive them.[1]

Randolph, who was not admitted to his mistress's secrets, could not understand what she was about. He saw the Protestants left imperfectly secured. A little more money, and Casimir, and La Noue, and Condé, and Henry of Navarre, would have occupied Paris and have dictated their own conditions. 'Better it would have 'been,' thought Randolph, 'had the Queen dealt substan- 'tially with them whom she thought to profit by, and ' either not have gone so far or not have left the cause ' for a little.' 'Never was such an opportunity thrown ' away,' he wrote to Walsingham. 'Do not think it ' choler or perverse humour in me, but rather duty to ' my dear mistress, that I see daily so many ways tend- ' ing to her greatness, and yet either impoliticly over- ' thrown or negligently omitted, even for nought or ' little when it was put into her hands. I can say no ' more, but as the mad knave in Terence did—

'Doleo bolum tantum ereptum nobis è faucibus.

' I know not by what means I may retrahere illud ar-

---

[1] Instructions to Thomas Randolph, sent to the French King. April 2, 1576. *MSS. France.*

'gentum [*sic*], which if I had in my hands the King
'should full dear buy his peace.'[1] But what the cause
had lost Elizabeth supposed that she had herself gained.
When she encouraged revolting subjects with one hand,
she played with their sovereign with the other. She
conceived that she had placed France in such a position
that it could neither coalesce with Spain against her,
nor be dangerous by ambitious projects elsewhere. She
could now afford to throw off the Hollanders, or to
follow out her scheme of reconciliation with Philip, by
assisting in their suppression.

It was not a noble, not a long-sighted policy. Walsingham had more than once to characterise his mistress's proceedings by the words 'dishonourable and 'dangerous,' and Walsingham was not a man who used such expressions lightly. But it suited her temper. She prided herself on the skill with which she handled delicate manœuvres. It was economical. It gained time. She lived, as the phrase is, 'from hand to mouth,' and trusted to her good luck to stand her friend.

A few months proved Randolph's simplicity to have been wiser than the Queen's cunning. The Catholic nobles in France laughed the Edicts to scorn. Complaints were useless, for there was no central authority to attend to them. Alençon and the King were reconciled, and Alençon was won away from his late friends. Guise, supplied with dollars from Madrid, threatened the Huguenot towns. The States General met at Blois in November. The Protestants stayed away. A resolution was passed with Alençon's consent that the Edicts were impracticable, and that only one religion could be tolerated; that the Protestant ministers must either submit or go into exile; and that Condé and Navarre

---

[1] Randolph to Walsingham, April 25 and April 17.—*MSS. France.*

should lose their rank as princes of the blood, unless they were reconciled with the Church.[1]

The Catholics were now entirely in the ascendant; the Court was governed by the Duke of Guise; Elizabeth had overreached herself by her refinements, the danger which she most dreaded was at her door; when an extraordinary accident reversed the whole position of affairs.

Alva had expected that the Netherlands could be made to pay the cost of their conquest. He had ruined the Netherlands, but he had not relieved the Spanish exchequer. In the eight years which followed his appointment as governor, Philip had spent upon the war thirty-two millions of English money. His resources were now severely tried. Requescens could not wring another stiver from the Provinces; the bankers would not lend; and when Requescens died, the King of Spain was unable to resolve upon his successor, and left his army for many months unpaid and uncommanded, to mutiny. Zierichsee was taken on the 21st of June, 1576. The soldiers who had performed so brilliant a service clamoured in return for their wages, and as there were no wages to be had, they pillaged Schowen, and then marched through Brabant, plundering as they went to Alost. A shout of indignation rose throughout Belgium. The nobles, orthodox believers as they were, assembled at Brussels to concert measures for self-protection. If rapine and murder were to be the rewards of their loyalty, they began to doubt whether

---

[1] It is noticeable that when the breach of faith with the Huguenots was first proposed, alone of all the nobles present, one 'Mirabeau of Poitou' protested that he would leave the court and the estates and withdraw to his home if such impolitic and dishonourable speeches were permitted to be made.—*Advertissements par Blois*. Nov. 1576. *MSS. France.*

after all they would not consult their safety by making common cause with the Prince of Orange. Don Sancho d'Avila, who commanded at Antwerp, with the captains of the garrisons in Ghent, Maestrecht, and Valenciennes, threatened destruction to the cities under their charge if the country revolted. In the absence of a governor there was no one to restrain the license of the army; and the hungry Spaniards, soldiers and officers alike, were ready to take advantage of the first excuse for indiscriminate pillage. After long hesitation, Philip had selected his illegitimate brother Don John to succeed Requescens; but Don John had not yet arrived, and the delay was fraught with ruin. The scheme for his marriage with Mary Stuart had been the difficulty. Guise wished it, and the English Catholics wished it. But Philip, to whom Don John was as much an object of suspicion as Alençon or the King of France, was utterly discouraging. Philip meant to remain on good terms with Elizabeth, nor had he the slightest intention of promoting his brother to an independent sovereignty. Ardent Catholics throughout Europe had their hearts fastened on the enterprise of England. Don John's appointment had been postponed, from a fear that he might abuse his opportunity and act upon their instigation. He was sent to his government with a prohibition to meddle in English politics at all; and Philip's secretary, the unlucky Escobedo, was sent with him as a check on his ambition, and a spy upon his actions.

Don John notwithstanding still allowed his thoughts to wander in the forbidden direction. Information, true or false, reached Elizabeth that on his passage through France, he had held an interview with Guise, where it had been arranged that as soon as the Huguenot towns were reduced, they were to make a joint demand upon her for the release of the Queen of Scots.[1] Escobedo betrayed Philip's trust, and encouraged what he had been commissioned to prevent. To conquer England, conquer the Netherlands through England, and win a throne for himself, appears to have been Don John's fixed idea as he hastened to his government. The condition in which he found the Provinces dispelled rapidly these visionary schemes.

M. Champigny, hitherto the most loyal of the Belgian nobles, was at the head of the new movement. Orange seizing the opportunity, had sent circulars through the seventeen states, urging the people to rise and defend their liberties. Champigny had responded cordially, and the Spanish officers, to read a lesson, as they pretended, to the incipient mutiny, had dropped the reins on the neck of the army, and given over the threatened towns for the soldiers to work their will upon. Mastrecht was sacked on the 20th of October, and several hundreds of the citizens were murdered. A fortnight later Antwerp itself found a yet more dreadful fate. The palaces of its merchant princes, the magnificent Bourse, the warehouses which lined its quays for miles, a thousand houses and public buildings, were given to the flames. The banks were pillaged. The wealth of the richest city in the world became the prey of men who were no better now than the banditti of their own forests, and eight thousand men, women, and children, were either killed or flung into the river.

Touched to the quick at last, the slow-moving Flemings sprung to arms. Ghent feared the same fate as

---

[1] Sir Amyas Paulet, who had succeeded Dale as ambassador at Paris, heard of the interview from Guise's secretary. He made further enquiries and assured himself that it had really taken place. *Paulet to Burghley*, April, 1577. *Paulet to Walsingham*, May 9, 1577.—*MSS. France.*

Antwerp. Thousands of patriots poured in, and enclosed the Spanish garrison in the citadel. The States General assembled there with representatives from the entire Netherlands. The Prince of Orange came in person out of Holland, and on the 8th of November, the seventeen provinces were once more united in the Treaty of Ghent for common defence against the Spaniards. They pledged their faith to each other to expel all foreign troops, and never again under any pretence to admit them. They resolved to insist for the future on being governed under their own laws. In the heartiness of the first reunion they suspended everywhere the laws against heresy, the ultimate settlement of religion being referred to a special convocation which was to meet when the liberation should be complete.

Two days before the conclusion of this momentous treaty, Don John arrived at Luxemburg, and there he thought it prudent to remain. The Protestant and Catholic elements, hitherto in most deadly enmity, were for the present united against him. It was uncertain whether the union would continue, or whether the difference of creed would not prove too powerful a disintegrant. One large influence Don John could count upon with confidence. To priests and monks sacked cities were of less moment than the maintenance of orthodoxy. The confessional would be in his favour from the first, and the pulpit when the first passion had cooled down.

The States, after subscribing the treaty of Ghent, dispatched M. Schwegenhem, who had been Alva's commissioner for the reopening of the trade, to Elizabeth to ask for advice, encouragement, and as usual, for an immediate loan. It was no longer Holland and Zealand struggling half conquered on the edge of destruction: all the Provinces were standing erect, shoulder to shoulder, in strength sufficient, if their union held, to defy Spain to do its worst. Don John had been told that if he would accept the treaty of Ghent, and dismiss the Spaniards, he would be received quietly as governor; on this condition, however, the States General peremptorily insisted. But below the outward unanimity a thousand countercurrents were already seething and eddying. What France would do under existing influences could hardly be guessed. Guise, who was thoroughly Spanish, desired to join Don John. The King and the politicians had their eyes upon the Catholic Provinces, and tried to persuade them to accept a French protectorate.

Some weeks passed before Elizabeth could see her way. While the horror of the Antwerp fury was fresh, while patriotism was stronger than religious hatred, and the Prince of Orange was the idol for the moment of all the States which had signed the treaty, it might have been thought that she would have seen, and would for her own sake have used, so splendid an opportunity. It would be safer for the Queen, said Orange, to ally herself with peoples and with a great cause, than with Princes who sought their own convenience and were not to be relied upon.[1] But Elizabeth despised 'peoples,' and cared nothing for the 'great 'cause.' She feared Don John. She meant to take advantage of his difficulties to obtain securities for herself and England. But then, and always, she wished the Provinces to remain Spanish. The Prince of Orange and the Protestants were her good friends; but she

---

[1] Daniel Rogers to Walsingham, July 20, 1577. *MSS. Flanders.*

dreaded the spread of their principles as complicating
the problem of pacification. If she did too much she
might find herself at war with Spain; if too little France
was ready to step in, and take the place which had been
first offered to herself.

The situation was exactly suited to the character of
her diplomacy. She decided to lend, not give, a certain
sum of money—forty thousand pounds. Twenty thousand were sent in bullion on the spot, the rest followed
soon after. She stipulated that she was to be repaid in
full, in eight months. She had an excuse ready for
Philip, that she was merely enabling the States to pay the
arrears of the Spanish army, to prevent further violence.
She sent Dr. Wilson to the States, to caution them
against listening to the promises which would be made
them by Don John. She sent Sir Edward Horsey to
Don John, to tell him that she had forbidden the States
to renounce their allegiance to Spain. She said generally, that she would help the Provinces to maintain
their liberties. She intimated privately to Schwegenhem, who was a Catholic, that she had no liking for
the Prince of Orange, that peace must not be imperilled
by difficulties about liberty of conscience, and that as a
condition of her support the States must accept whatever religion the King of Spain might be pleased to
impose on them.[1]

On this point she was limpidly clear. She was determined that there should be no mistake about it. The
creed in which the Hollanders had been brought up

---

[1] 'Sa Ma^{tè} leur a presté de l'argent a condition de se maintenir en l'obeisance du Roy et de recevoir telle religion que leur Roy vouldra et non aultre. C'est ce que M. de Schwegenhem leur a dict de la part de sa Ma^{tè}.'—*Villiers (chaplain to the Prince of Orange) to Walsingham.* Feb. 4, 1577. *MSS. Flanders.*

would do as well for them as it had done for their fathers.[1]

The differences of opinion already existing were not likely to be diminished by this message. To the Hollanders, religion was the soul and centre of the revolt. If they would have yielded on that one point, they might have been quit of the Spaniards, and have had their country to themselves when they pleased, without seeking assistance from Elizabeth. After five weeks' confusion and correspondence, the States proposed, and Don John agreed, that the Spanish army should be paid the arrears of its wages and should go; and that the government should be carried on as before the rebellion by the States themselves. So far, the pacification of Ghent was accepted. The further clauses stipulating for the suspension of the laws against heresy, were to be referred to Philip's pleasure, and were to stand in force till that pleasure was known. Orange was no party to this arrangement. Advantage had been taken of his absence from Brussels to hurry it to a conclusion.

---

[1] Not through Schwegenhem only, but by other means she had expressed her resolution on the matter. The Prince of Orange found soon after—

'Que sa Ma^tè avoit deliberé de conseiller Messieurs des Estats de maintenir la religion Romaine en laquelle ils ont esté nes et esleves, chose qui nous seroit tant prejudiciable que rien ne nous sçauroit venir plus mal à propos en ce temps-cy.'

And again later—

'Depuis les miennes du jour d'hier j'ay reçeu ung extraict de l'article touchant la volunte de sa Ma^tè en ce qui touche la religion Romaine, lequel a esté tiré du rapport de M. de Havrech. Aussi que tant s'en fault qu'elle vouloist ingerer d'y Introduire aucune nouvellete que mesmes au contraire desiroit bien sa Ma^tè qui accuseries qu'elle ne permettroit en façon quelconque que nouveaute y fust introduite et moins qu'on intentast chose prejudiciable à l'obeïssance de nostre souverain Prince et Seigneur naturel ou à la religion Catholique en laquelle estions nes et nourries et nostre Prince vouloit que nous fussions maintenes.'—*The Prince of Orange to Davison*. Jan. 4 and 5, 1578. *MSS. Flanders.*

Orange, to whom truth and falsehood in these matters were not only of principal but of exclusive importance, who had taken up arms for no other cause whatever except liberty of conscience, was unable to comprehend so sublime a development of indifferentism.

There was no representative present from the Northern States, not only not from Holland and Zealand, but neither from Utrecht, Gelderland, Friesland, Gröningen, nor Overyssel. Efforts had been made to prevent a resolution till the opinions of these provinces could be heard, but the reasons urged for delay were to the Catholic Walloons an additional motive for haste. The Prince suspended his assent. The seven Provinces supported him in demanding acceptance pure and simple of the Ghent Treaty. But intrigue and Elizabeth's influence had done their work, and Don John by the vote of the majority was admitted as Governor.

It was Elizabeth's work, distinctly hers, and wherever her hand can be traced, the same purpose can be invariably discovered. As her father held the balance between France and Spain, and could choose for his motto the proud 'Cui adhereo præest,' so Elizabeth aspired to hold the same relation between peoples and sovereigns, between Protestants and Catholics; certain that the Protestants would stand by her when she might need their assistance, because they were the weaker side, but not choosing to take their part, choosing rather to appear indifferent or hostile to them, lest if she demanded toleration for others, the Catholic powers and her own Catholic subjects would make an answering demand upon herself. In distinct opposition to Walsingham, she felt assured that Philip desired to be on good terms with her, and that the dreams of Don John would find no support or countenance from his master if the provocation did not come from herself. She was told that the Catholic powers understood each other, that Alençon was now to marry the Infanta, that Guise and Alençon, and Don John, with Spain and the Papacy behind them, intended to invade England, tear from her hands the imprisoned Queen of Scots, and lift her to the throne. She did not believe it. She waived aside the leadership of Protestant Europe so often thrust into her hands. Her sympathies were with established sovereigns, and order, and law, and she sought her friends among her own equals.

Further and immediate communication was now necessary with her brother-in-law. Among the Catholics or Anglo-Catholics at her court (the words meant the same thing in all but dependence upon Rome), there was a certain Sir John Smith, a courtier, a believer in kings, an accomplished Spanish scholar, with an English orthodoxy of creed, and an equally English contempt for the priests who were its ministers. Him Elizabeth chose for a second mission to Madrid, either to reside as ambassador there or to return, as might seem most expedient; at all events to explain her conduct in the Netherlands, to renew her offer of mediation, and to require a more distinct protection for the English traders. Other ships had been seized besides Sir Edward Osborne's, the seamen thrown into dungeons, and the cargoes confiscated. With the Netherlands problem returned upon his hands, the King, she thought, would see the necessity of now keeping the Inquisition under control.

On Smith's arrival, the Spanish Council assembled as before. The bigots tried their strength. The Bishop of Cuença, like Hopper and Quiroga, insisted again that the Queen of England was a heretic; that God forbade dealings with such people, that an interference with the Inquisition in their behalf was a thing that was not to be endured. But Alva had this time a distinct majority on his side. He persuaded the most influential of Philip's advisers that they had to thank Elizabeth that the entire Provinces were not in arms against them, that on the score of religion they had nothing to fear from her, that she had thrown her weight upon the orthodox side, and that she was an invaluable ally to the Catholic Powers, in resisting the demand for toleration.[1] For her own sake she would not ask for others what she did not allow in England; all else that she might desire the King could reasonably concede; and if the Spanish troops were really forced to leave the Netherlands, her friendship would be indispensable.[2] The reasoning was entirely convincing. Philip wrote an affectionate letter to Elizabeth thanking her for her proposal of mediation. He said that he would gladly avail himself of it if Don John failed to come to an understanding with the States without her. For himself, meanwhile, he assured her that he was, and ever would remain, her constant friend.[3]

The Inquisition difficulty still remained. The Inquisition, as Secretary Cayas explained, was an ecclesiastical tribunal, over which the King himself had no regular authority. It was surrounded with the terrors which superstition and practical fear combined to inspire, and Cayas spoke of it as a mysterious force which it was dangerous even to attempt to meddle with. An Englishman, brought up in the traditions of Henry VIII., felt none of these timidities. The creed might be sacred, but Inquisitors were mere priests, who meddled with the persons and properties of the Queen's subjects.

Quiroga, Archbishop of Toledo, was the first subject in the Peninsula. Next to the King in his place in Council, superior to the King in wielding the irresponsible

---

[1] 'No osara pedir lo de la Religion, pues demas que sabe quan mal lo tomaria V. Mag⁴, ella haria contra su misma, que quiere que sus vassallos la obedezcan en la religion que tiene, y no podria pedir otra cosa á su Mag⁴.'—*Parecer de Alva*, 1577. *MSS. Simancas.*

[2] 'Saliendo los Españoles ea fuerça que V. Mag⁴ tenga por amiga á aquella Reyna y obligada como lo quedaria contra los Estados quando no cumplieren lo que hubieren prometido.'—*Ibid.*

[3] Carta de su Mag⁴ á la Inglesa con Juan Smith.

powers of the Holy Office, he was a person before whom princes stood with bated breath, while meaner citizens knelt as he passed along the streets. Smith had more than once applied for an interview with this august personage. Quiroga, who five years before had refused to deliver the message of the Council to Cobham lest he should defile himself by speaking to an excommunicated Englishman, sent cold answers that he could not see him. Sir John, who had encountered Archbishops in London and had not found them formidable, did not choose to be put off in this way. He went one evening to the palace, brushed past the porter, ascended the stairs, and forced himself into the sacred presence.

It was after supper. The Archbishop was in his private room with the Condé de Andrada and two priests. He stared haughtily at the intruder, who proceeded to tell him, with entire coolness, that he considered he had been treated with scanty courtesy. He was the minister of a great Queen, he said, and as such, was entitled to be received and heard when he had anything to communicate. The promises made to Cobham had been broken. The Holy Office had continued to ill-use English seamen who had committed no offence, to rob, imprison, and otherwise injure them. He must request the immediate release of those who were at present in the Inquisitors' hands, with compensation for the injuries which they had sustained.

The Archbishop had remained while the Ambassador was speaking, dumb with anger and amazement. At last, finding his voice, and starting from his seat in fury, he exclaimed:—'Sirrah!'[1] I tell you, that, but

---

[1] 'Yo os digo.' Sirrah is too mild a word; but we have no full equivalent. 'Os' is used by a king to subjects, by a father to children, more rarely by a master to a servant. It is a mark of infinite distance between a superior and inferior. 'Dog' would, perhaps, come nearest to the Archbishop's meaning in the present connexion.

'for certain respects, I would so chastise you for these words that you have spoken, that I would make you an example to all your kind. I would chastise you I say, I would make you know to whom you speak in such shameless fashion.'

'Sirrah!' replied Smith in a fury too, and proud of his command of the language which enabled him to retort the insult, 'Sirrah! I tell you that I care neither for you nor your threats.'

'Quitad os!' 'Be off with you!' shouted Quiroga, foaming with rage, 'leave the room! away! I say.'

'If you call me Sirrah,' said Smith, 'I will call you Sirrah. I will complain to his Majesty of this.'

'Complain to whom you will,' said the Archbishop. 'Be off with you! Go!'

'Be off yourself,' retorted the Englishman, moving however to the door; the graceful interchange of insolence continuing till the Ambassador was out of hearing, and the Archbishop following and railing at him from the head of the stairs.[1]

Philip was greatly distressed, but his desire to gratify Elizabeth overcame his awe of the Inquisitor-General. He apologised to Smith. He entreated, he argued, and at last insisted, that the Holy Office should make concessions. The prisoners at Seville were released and their property restored. The promises made to Cobham were confirmed in writing, and Englishmen were enabled thenceforward to trade without molestation at the Spanish ports. They were required only to obey the laws when on shore and to abstain—no easy matter to them—from insulting Catholic superstitions.[2] Elizabeth

---

[1] Sir John Smith's Narrative, May 19, 1577.—MSS. Spain.

[2] Quiroga, when not exasperated, could discuss these questions in an unexpectedly practical temper. An English merchant had married a

in England and Philip at Madrid were contending with all their might against the irresistible tendencies of things. Their subjects might quarrel, hate, and insult each other, but hostility, so far as they could prevent it, should not be. Doctor Sanders, who had come to Spain, in the hope of inducing the King to invade Ireland, found only indifference and discouragement. He found Philip 'as fearful of war as a child of fire.' He wrote to his friend Allen, who, like himself, considered that the welfare of Europe 'depended on the 'stout assailing of England,' that ' there was no steady 'comfort, but from God,' that they must look to the Pope and *not* the King of Spain.'[1]

Smith did not remain at Madrid. He returned after three-quarters of a year, loaded with messages of friendliness, and with every demand conceded. The diplomatic relations between the two countries were re-established, as was hoped, upon an enduring basis. The expulsion of Don Guerau de Espes was passed over as a not unfair retaliation upon Spain for its share in the Ridolfi conspiracy; and Bernardino de Mendoza, who had already made acquaintance with Elizabeth, was appointed as resident ambassador at the English court.

young Spanish lady at Seville. He had called himself a Catholic, and the marriage had been celebrated with the rites of the Catholic Church. In England, however, he was a conformist, and on his attempting to take her with him, she hesitated, and appealed to the Holy Office. She was pregnant. The husband pleaded that marriage was sacred, and that to separate his wife from him would be an affront to the English Church. Quiroga answered with singular moderation. 'The lady,' he said, 'had ascertained that in England the use of images was forbidden, and that she would be obliged to attend sermons. Being a religious woman she had applied to the church for direction, and her director considered that in going she would commit mortal sin. If she herself wished to go, it would be another matter. The Inquisition could not sanction it, but also would not interfere.'—*The Archbishop of Toledo to Cayas*, Feb. 1577. *MSS. Simancas.*

[1] Sanders to Allen, Nov. 6, 1577. *MSS. Domestic.*

Those statesmen who saw furthest did not believe that the reconciliation could last. Walsingham and Walsingham's party felt assured that in the long run the opposing forces which divided Europe would prove too strong for the efforts of politicians.[1] But that Elizabeth, with her opinions, should have struggled to escape from war, was in itself legitimate and natural, and situated as she was at home, she had good cause to dread the consequences of a more daring attitude.

Had she been secure in her own island, she might have held out a hand without fear to the struggling Protestants abroad. But the unruly elements were working together throughout all Christendom, as the ebb and flow of the Atlantic tide was felt at Richmond, under the palace windows. A sketch of the domestic history of these years will show that when once committed to forbearance and procrastination, she was all but forced to continue in the same direction. The Parliament of 1572 had petitioned for the execution of the Queen of Scots. The alternatives seemed to lie between the crown and the scaffold; and when the petition was refused, and she was not declared incapable of the succession, Mary Stuart was generally looked upon as the inevitable future sovereign. While the alarm of the conspiracy was fresh, she had been placed under restraint, and efforts were made, and continued to be made, to replace her in the hands of the Scots. But when it became clear that she must remain in England, she was soon again the guest rather than the prisoner of Lord Shrewsbury. She was treated much as Mary Tudor was treated under her brother, and as Elizabeth herself had been treated after her release from Wood-

---

[1] 'Never will there be perfect amity among any that are divided in religion. Her Majesty may dislike my plain words, but better she be angry with me than herself feel the smart hereafter.'—*Wilson to Walsingham*, April 5, 1577. *MSS. Flanders.*

stock; in some respects her position was better, for she was still called a Queen, and was allowed her Cloth of State. She was not permitted to go where she pleased, but she had all the enjoyments and conveniences which an English country life could yield. She rode, she hunted, she had change of air and scene, going from Sheffield to Chatsworth, from Chatsworth to the baths at Buxton. She was so loosely watched that she corresponded freely with her friends. The ladies of Elizabeth's household, with an eye to the future, furnished her with the secrets of the Court. She was the centre of the hopes and fears of the worldly statesmen and political intriguers; and though the Queen was often advised to remove her to some stricter guardianship, the fear of offending Shrewsbury, or of giving France or Spain a ground of complaint, combined to keep her where she was.

Her Protestant affectations were no more heard of. She had lost favour abroad by her supposed instability: she explained it away by saying, 'that when she came 'first to England she was afraid of alienating a powerful 'party in a realm which she hoped to make her own.' 'She had never communicated in the English Church,' she said, 'she had merely attended sermons; her friends 'had told her that she might listen to a preacher as she 'would listen to the barking of a dog:[1] she had talked on 'religion with the Bishop of Lichfield, but she had told 'him she could never find two clergymen agree in any-'thing except in hating the Pope, and instead of being 'converted to their opinions she had been the more con-'firmed in her own.' She ceased to be present at the prayers of the household. She obtained a chaplain from

---

[1] 'Et sur ce les plus politiques me remonstrants que j'escouterois bien un chien abboyer, me persuaderent ouir en salle lesdicts ministres et prières.'—*Mary Stuart to La Mothe Fénelon,* Nov. 30, 1571. LABANOFF, vol. iv.

abroad, who lived with her as one of her servants. His character was known, but he was not interfered with, and he had special powers granted him by the Pope. Certain Englishmen in Shrewsbury's service were useful to her, who would be sent away if known to be Catholics. They took the sacrament, by permission, in the Earl's chapel, the priest giving them absolution after each of their acts of iniquity; while for herself Mary Stuart obtained as a special grace from his Holiness, that when she prayed before the holy wafer, when she bore patiently any injury from a heretic, or if at the moment of death she repeated the words Jesus Maria, all her sins should be forgiven.[1]

She was afraid of being poisoned. She did not suspect the Queen of being likely to sanction her murder, but Shrewsbury himself hinted to her that Elizabeth might not prove implacable if she was disposed of without her knowledge;[2] and Lady Essex, Elizabeth's cousin, who was suspected afterwards of murdering her husband, was mentioned as a person of whom she would do well to beware.[3]

On the whole, however, she felt safe under Lord Shrewsbury's care. He was punctiliously honourable, and inclined, as every one knew, to favour her claims on the succession. She had great influence with him, and she contrived to entangle him in an intrigue which, implicating them both in Elizabeth's displeasure, drew him closer than before to herself. Margaret, Countess of Lennox, and mother of Darnley, had been a conspirator from early girlhood. She began her career by a secret

---

[1] Mary Stuart to Gregory XIII., Oct. 13, 1575.—LABANOFF, vol. iv.

[2] 'Que si quelqu'un sans le sçeu de ladicte Royne m'empoisonnait il sçavoit de bon lieu qu'elle leur en sçauroit bon gré de l'oster de si grande peine.'—Mary Stuart to the Archbishop of Glasgow and the Cardinal of Lorraine, March 29, 1574. LABANOFF, vol. iv.

[3] Ibid.

marriage with a brother of the Duke of Norfolk, and was sent to the Tower for it by Henry VIII. She had tried to persuade Mary Tudor to execute Elizabeth, that the crown might fall to herself. She had contrived Darnley's marriage with the Queen of Scots, to unite their titles, and had worked hard to organise the Catholic party for a rising in England in their favour.

After the catastrophe at Kirk-o'-Field, she had fallen back upon Elizabeth, believing that Mary Stuart was ruined, and expecting that the succession would be now determined in favour of her grandson James. No voice had been louder than hers in demanding vengeance on the murderers, none more emphatic in charging the guilt upon the Queen of Scots. Time, however, passed on, and Mary Stuart's star seemed again in the ascendant. There was a prevailing impression, in which Lady Lennox shared, that Elizabeth would soon die, and she began to be alarmed for the future. Early in 1573, at latest,[1] she put herself in communication with the person whom she had denounced so passionately; and Mary Stuart, as the price of reconciliation, obtained a declaration from her in writing, that she had been instigated by the Queen and Council to accuse her, and that she was fully satisfied of her innocence.[2]

---

[1] On May 2, 1578, Mary Stuart in a letter to the Archbishop of Glasgow, said that Lady Lennox and she had then been reconciled five or six years. The date is important.

[2] Mary Stuart to the Archbishop of Glasgow, May 2, 1578.—LABANOFF. This acknowledgment, which was of extreme value at the time to the Queen of Scots in assisting her to clear her reputation, has been relied upon in later times as evidence in her favour. It is worth while to observe, therefore, that Lady Lennox continued long after to speak in her old language to others. Elizabeth, suspecting the reconciliation, questioned her about it. 'I asked her Majesty if she could think so,' Lady Lennox wrote to Burghley, 'for I was made of flesh and blood and could never forget the murder of my child; and she said, Nay, by her faith she could not think that ever I could forget it, for if I would I were a devil.'— *MSS. Domestic*, Dec. 10, 1574.

Armed with this weapon, the Queen of Scots was now able to defend herself with effect, and to persuade the Catholics that she was an injured saint. The two women drew together, and began to weave fresh plots and schemes. A third cunning practitioner was added in the Countess of Shrewsbury; and after weeks of correspondence, in which De Guaras, the Portuguese Minister Fogaça, the Bishop of Ross, and other Catholics took part, it was agreed that a marriage should be made up between Lord Charles Stuart—Darnley's brother, the Countess's only remaining son—and Elizabeth Cavendish, Lady Shrewsbury's daughter by her first husband. Lady Elizabeth was passionately devoted to the Queen of Scots, and Lord Charles, who was a possible competitor against her for the English crown, would thus be made sure of. Lady Lennox took her son to Chatsworth, and all was done before suspicion had got abroad.

The secret marriage of a prince of the blood both was and is an offence against the State; had there been nothing about the match in itself objectionable, Elizabeth would have been justly offended. Lady Lennox was returned to her old quarters in the Tower: Shrewsbury was rebuked and hardly saved himself by laying the blame upon his wife; and the storm blew over only when a year subsequently Lord Charles and his bride both died, leaving as the sole result of the affair a daughter, known to history as the Lady Arabella Stuart. In itself, the matter proved of no immediate consequence; but incidentally, it occasioned a painful revelation of the hollow hearts with which the Queen was surrounded. The investigation which Walsingham had to institute, brought him on the track of half the ladies of the palace, and of more than half the courtiers, as implicated more or less in seeking favour with the lady at Sheffield. Lady

Cobham, the Queen's immediate attendant; Southampton, who had forfeited his life in the Norfolk conspiracy and had been pardoned and taken into favour again; Norfolk's brother, Lord Henry Howard; the Earl of Oxford, Burghley's son-in-law; these and many more were found to be paying assiduous court to the rising sun. Shrewsbury, it appeared, had promised the Queen of Scots that, on the Queen's death, he would himself place the crown upon her head.[1] No longer complaining of her captivity, she was well satisfied to remain where she was, her party growing daily stronger by her mere presence in the realm. When opportunities of escape were thrown in her way, she declined to use them. She said that when she left Lord Shrewsbury's charge it should be as Queen of England.[2] The eager expectation of the Queen's death was extremely likely to suggest means of hastening it. Elizabeth's behaviour, so irritating to Walsingham, was as characteristic of herself as it was perplexing.[3] She chose to encounter treason by refusing to see it; and rather to live in an atmosphere of disloyalty, than expose it and force it to

---

[1] 'La Royne d'Escosse avoit dict ou escript a quelcunque le dict Milord luy avoit promis, la morte advenante de la Royne, qu'il mettroit la couronne sur la teste de la Royne d'Escosse.'—*Note in MS. 1575.—MSS. Mary Queen of Scots.*

[2] 'Dixóme el Embajador de Escocia que a su ama le offrecian comodidad por poderse escapar de prision y que no lo quiere porque pretende salir della Reyna de Inglaterra y no de otra suerte aunque le cueste la vida.'—*Don Juan de Vargas al Rey.* TEULET, vol. v. p. 203.

[3] 'Your Majesty asks whether all or what part of the confessions shall be shown to the Council. Let your Majesty choose out those that are loyal and secret and show them all. Touching the matter itself your Majesty's delay used in resolving doth not only make me void of all hope to do any good therein but also doth quite discourage me to deal in like causes, seeing mine and your other faithful servants' care for your safety fruitless. I beseech your Majesty pardon this my plain speech proceeding from a wounded and languishing mind.'—*Walsingham to Elizabeth*, Feb. 26, 1575. *MSS. Mary Queen of Scots.*

declare itself. 'She is bent,' wrote Walsingham, bitterly, 'to cover faults rather than cure them. If she will not touch the principals, she must, of course, spare the accessories and instruments. She will not even allow the removal of the Scottish Queen to a place of more security.'[1] She continued to smile upon her false and fair-seeming courtiers. She kept her irritation, and seemingly her suspicion, for those who had never entertained an unfaithful thought towards her,[2] and she punished the Shrewsburies only by a sarcastic letter on the entertainment which they extended to Leicester when the favourite was sent down on a sanatory visit to the baths.[3]

---

[1] Walsingham to Leicester, March 2.—*MSS. Ibid.*

[2] Burghley, for instance, went over to Buxton when Shrewsbury was there with his charge. Elizabeth 'sharply reproved him, charging him earnestly with favouring the Queen of Scots.'—*Burghley to Shrewsbury,* Dec. 24, 1575. LODGE, vol. ii.

[3] This letter, unprinted so far as I know elsewhere, is one of the most curious specimens of Elizabeth's composition:

'Right trusty,—

'Being given to understand from our cousin the Earl of Leicester how honourably he was lately received and used by you, our cousin the Countess at Chatsworth, and how his diet is by you both discharged at Buxton, we should do him great wrong holding him in that place in our favour in which we do, in case we should not let you understand in how thankful sort we accept the same at your hands—which we do not acknowledge to be done unto him but to our own self; and therefore do mean to take upon us the debt and to acknowledge you both as our creditors so as you can be content to accept us for debtor, wherein is the danger unless you cut off some part of the large allowance of diet you give him, lest otherwise the debt thereby may grow to be so great as we shall not be able to discharge the same, and so become bankrupt. And therefore we think it for the saving of our credit meet to prescribe unto you a proportion of diet which we mean in no case you shall exceed, and that is to allow him by the day for his meat two ounces of flesh, referring the quality to yourselves, so as you exceed not the quantity, and for his drink the twentieth part of a pint of wine to comfort his stomach, and as much of St. Anne's sacred water as he listeth to drink. On festival days, as is meet for a man of his quality, we can be content you shall enlarge his diet by allowing unto him for his dinner the shoulder of a wren, and for his supper a leg of the same, besides his ordinary ounces. The like proportion we mean you shall allow to our brother

The Parliament of 1576 passed off without touching the succession question; and never, Mary Stuart wrote to the Archbishop of Glasgow in the summer of that year, had her prospects been fairer than they had now become. Every cloud had rolled away from the sky. Elizabeth, she said, had not dared to interfere with her pretensions. At the close of the session she had asked two of the judges, who, in their conscience, had the best right to succeed after her death: the judges had answered, that Henry VIII. had no power to change the customs of the realm; the next in blood must inherit: and Elizabeth had replied with a sigh, 'the Queen of Scots 'then is my heir.'[1] Whether she considered that she was consulting best for her own security, or for the interests of the realm, or whether she felt bound in honour to shew the same forbearance to the claims of the Queen of Scots as had been shown by her sister towards her own, her evident purpose was to humour the expectations of the Catholics, and to comfort all unquiet spirits with the hope that if she was let alone for her own time, her death would give them their desires.

On all sides her policy was the same and tended to the same end. Having been forced against her will to complete the destruction of Mary Stuart's party in Scotland, the most natural course would have been to recognise James as lawful sovereign there; and failing issue from her own person, to have settled

---

of Warwick, saving that we think it meet that in respect that his body is more replete than his brother's, that the wren's leg allowed at supper on festival days be abated, for that light supper agreeth best with rules of physic. This order our meaning is you shall inviolably observe, and so may you right well assure yourselves of a most thankful debtor to so well deserving a creditor.'—*Memorandum of Her Majesty's letter to the Earl and Countess of Shrewsbury,* June 4, 1577. *MSS.* MARY QUEEN OF SCOTS.

[1] The Queen of Scots to the Archbishop of Glasgow, May and June, 1576.—LABANOFF, vol. iv.

the English succession upon him by Act of Parliament: or, if she could not bring herself to a step so decisive, at least to have given effectual support to the government which she had assisted in establishing. Never were rulers in a more desperate plight than the successive Regents of Scotland in the minority of the young king. The crown lands were exhausted, there were no customs, no fixed revenue, no regular taxation; while they had to find garrisons for Edinburgh and Dumbarton Castles, to maintain the Court at Stirling, and to provide besides for the peace of the border, which the Marian tendencies of the Maxwells, the Kers, and the Humes, made it doubly difficult to preserve. Murray had fallen for want of help; and then Lennox. Morton had insisted on an allowance from Elizabeth as a condition of his accepting office. Elizabeth had manœuvred him into the regency without committing herself. He had submitted, but he requested that if she would give him no money for the government, she would at least distribute a few trifling presents among the other nobles, recognise his right to be in the place which she had forced upon him, and unite England and Scotland in a league 'for 'the maintenance of the common cause of religion.'[1] Liberality would have been the simplest economy. If Scotland became again disturbed, Walsingham pointed out to her, that her own expenses on the border would be increased five-fold. 'The League,' he argued, 'was 'more necessary for her than for Morton, since no one 'would assail Scotland except with a view to England.' 'The amity now offered her was one which unoffered, 'was in due policy most necessary to be sought for. It 'was a thing which her predecessors, who stood not in

---

[1] Morton to Elizabeth, Jan. 21, 1574.—*MSS. Scotland.*

'like need of Scotland's friendship, would have re-
'deemed with any treasure.' If she refused, and if
harm followed, 'the burden of the error would be cast
'upon her Majesty for rejecting the advice of her
'Council.'[1]

It will be remembered that in the first alarm after the
massacre of St. Bartholomew, there had been an intention of sending Mary Stuart home to be tried and executed for her husband's murder; the Scots had required that Elizabeth should openly share the responsibility; and 'the great matter,' as it was called in the diplomatic correspondence, passed off. The idea in its extreme form was abandoned; but she was still anxious that her guest should be removed, and that if she was not put to death, Scotland should have the responsibility of keeping her. When Morton made his proposals for a league, Philip's disposition was still dubious; France could not be relied upon, and although the Queen would not give money or commit herself openly, she sent Sir Henry Killegrew to Edinburgh, to feel his way with the Regent. She imagined that Morton and Morton's party were so circumstanced that her support was indispensable to them, and that she might make her own conditions. A few days after Killegrew's arrival, he hastened to undeceive her. If the Regent's requests were not granted, he dared not, he said, so much as enter on the special subject of his mission. The Scots told him that what his mistress had done at Edinburgh, she had done not for them but for herself; she had left them alone till she was frightened by the Paris massacre, and now she evidently cared not whether they sank or swam: the French set more value on their friendship: if Elizabeth would not help them France was ready to

---

[1] Walsingham to the Queen, March 10.—*MSS. Scotland.*

take her place, and the young king would probably be sent to Paris.[1]

Could the Queen of Scots then be exchanged for James? James to be brought up in England, and Mary Stuart to be put into the hands of the Regent, to be dealt with as he might think proper? Killegrew was empowered in his instructions to make the offer if he thought expedient. He did not think it would be accepted. He ventured a hint, and his expectations were confirmed. 'I think,' he said in a letter to Walsingham, 'that you there will never agree to the sure way of 'remedy (the execution of the Queen of Scots), and 'here they will be daunted to accept the conditions of 'the other (the delivery of James), which cannot be 'done without many a council of the matter, which 'thing, I know, would mislike your delicate ears there, 'and indeed, I think not convenient to be done unless I 'saw an assured sequel to follow.'[2]

The correspondence which followed is imperfect, and mysterious in its allusions. It is certain, however that 'an overture' was made in reply by Elizabeth, of which Walsingham disapproved, and that it contained a promise to send the Queen of Scots to the Regent, the Regent undertaking in return to give hostages. But whether hostages for the protection of her life, or hostages merely for her safe keeping either in prison or the grave, can only be conjectured.[3]

Killegrew brought the Regent's answer to London, and delivered it in person, leaving no record of its terms. Experience of Elizabeth's conduct in similar situations, permits the conclusion that she wished the Queen of

---

[1] Killegrew to Walsingham, June 17, June 21, June 23; Killegrew to Burghley, June 23; to Hatton, June 24.—*MSS. Ibid.*

[2] Killegrew to Walsingham, June 25.—*MSS. Scotland.*

[3] Walsingham to Killegrew, July 30. Cipher.—*MSS. Scotland.*

Scots to be disposed of, where she would give no more trouble, yet in such a manner that she should be able for herself, to disclaim the responsibility before the world. It is equally likely that Morton, knowing her disposition, declined the snare which was laid for him and insisted, as before, on square and open dealing.

Months now passed away. The Chatsworth marriage followed, and the discovery of Mary Stuart's correspondence at the court. 'The great matter' was at an end. But Morton still refused to be tempted by France, and continued to hold out to England the offered league. There were but two objections. In accepting it, Elizabeth would openly sanction the Queen of Scots' deposition—already it might have been thought a sufficiently established fact—and she must acknowledge in form a community of creed with Calvinists. Both of these she was determined not to do, and no persuasion could move her.

'Your Majesty,' said Walsingham to her, 'shall see
' over dangerous effects, when the trouble of the princes
' your neighbours shall be at an end, unless your
' Majesty shall, by prevention, put in execution such
' remedies as the necessity of your State requires;
' wherein if you shall not use expedition the malady
' will grow incurable, and the sparks of treason that now
' lie covered will break into unquenchable fire. For the
' love of God, Madam, let not the cure of your diseased
' State hang longer in deliberation. Diseased states are
' no more cured by consultation, when nothing resolved
' on is put in execution, than unsound and diseased
' bodies by only conference with physicians without re-
' ceiving the remedies by them prescribed. Whatever
' account is made of the Regent, there is no man of
' judgment that loves your Majesty that can imagine any
' peril that can befall you, so great as the loss of that

'gentleman, either by death or alienation. Lose not such an one negligently, whom it behoves you to keep so necessarily.'[1]

'If ever prince that possessed this crown,' Walsingham wrote to Burghley, 'had cause to desire the amity of Scotland, none can have greater than her Majesty, the corruption of her estate being well weighed, and the malice that the princes her neighbours bear to her. God forbid that no other thing should teach her Majesty to make value of the friendship of Scotland, but only the mischief that we may taste by the lack thereof.'[2]

Every word of these warnings came back in due time to Elizabeth, and many a year of anxiety, and many a million from her treasury, the neglect of them was in the end to cost her. But it will be seen that what Walsingham wished was incompatible with the course which on the whole she had determined to be best for her. After long oscillation English policy finally gravitated towards Philip and peace. She always advised the Netherlands to make no alterations in religion. Having no belief herself, she regarded Protestantism as a lost cause, and in her heart she was probably meditating how best to bring back England into communion with the rest of Christendom.

Her ecclesiastical administration at home tended in the same direction, and towards the same issue. It is evident that neither then, nor till long after, did she regard the Church of England as more than a provisional

---

[1] Walsingham to Elizabeth, Jan. 15, 1575.—*MSS. Ibid.* Killegrew also said of Morton, he was the only man who could control Scotland. 'If he were gone they could no more fill his place than England could find a successor to her Majesty.'

[2] Walsingham to Burghley, April 11, 1575.—*MSS. Domestic.*

arrangement, an Interim intended to last but while the confusions of Europe continued.

Her Bishops she treated with studied insolence as creatures of her own, whom she had made and could unmake at pleasure: the bishops themselves lived as if they knew their day to be a short one, and made the most of their opportunities while they lasted. Scandalous dilapidation, destruction of woods, waste of the property of the see by beneficial lease, the incumbent enriching himself and his family at the expense of his successors—this is the substantial history of the Anglican hierarchy, with a few honourable exceptions, for the first twenty years of its existence. At the time when Walsingham was urging Elizabeth to an alliance with the Scotch Protestants, Matthew Parker, Archbishop of Canterbury, was just dead. He had left behind him enormous wealth, which had been accumulated, as is proved from a statement in the handwriting of his successor, by the same unscrupulous practices which had brought about the first revolt against the Church. He had been corrupt in the distribution of his own patronage, and he had sold his interest with others. No Catholic prelate in the old easy times had more flagrantly abused the dispensation system. 'Every year he made profits by 'admitting children to the cure of souls' for money. He used a graduated scale in which the price for inducting an infant into a benefice varied with the age, children under fourteen not being inadmissible, if the adequate fees were forthcoming.[1] On Parker's death

---

[1] 'The late Archbishop had many occasions of wealth, the possibilities whereof are taken away from his successors. He called in all the dispensations made by Cardinal Pole, and so by faculties that year gate great sums, and every year after made a more profit than hereafter is convenient by admitting children to cures,' &c. &c. Articles touching the late Archbishop, endorsed in Grindal's hand as drawn by himself.—

these iniquities were exposed and ended. His successor, Grindal, a man of infinitely nobler character, swept clear the corrupted ecclesiastical courts, abandoned the unjust ways of collecting money, scoured away to the best of his ability the accumulated filth of eighteen years. But Grindal's zeal was less agreeable to the Queen than Parker's corruption. Grindal was a sincere Protestant, especially earnest for what was called preaching the word, and regarding the voice of a living man, whether an ordained priest or not, as having more saving grace in it than ceremonies or sacraments.

Steady to her principle of silencing speech on troublesome subjects, the Queen was inclined always to empty pulpits which she could not tune. She considered 'three or four preachers enough for a county,' and one of the Homilies decently read as better than original eloquence. The Archbishop complied with her command so far as to place the sermons under restriction, and prevent excesses which she affected to dread: but stop it altogether he would not, and Elizabeth would as little endure a prelate who was less than absolutely submissive. Leicester, it was said, had his eye on Lambeth as a pleasant London house. The Archbishop was sequestrated for contempt. The Attorney-General was instructed to take measures for his deposition, and the Queen was astonished to find that an ecclesiastical official had rights under the law of

---

MSS. Domestic. Feb. 1575-6. Compare a resolution of Council on Dispensations, evidently directed at Parker's practices, dated June 10, 1576.— *MSS. Domestic,* vol. cxxix. Among the particulars mentioned are 'dispensations for children and young men under age to take ecclesiastical promotions, the tax whereof, the party being 18 years of age or more, was 4*l.* 6*s.* 8*d.*, the tax much greater the parties being under 14 years.'

England, which even she, arbitrary as she was in such matters, could not set aside.[1]

'Thus, my good lord,' said Walsingham, writing to the Lord Treasurer, 'you see how we proceed still in 'making war against God, whose ire we should rather 'seek to appease, that he may keep the wars from us 'that most apparently approach. God open her Majesty's 'eyes that she may both see her perils and acknowledge 'from whence the remedy is to be sought.'[2]

The making war against God, in Walsingham's sense of the words, would have continued longer but for one of those sudden illustrations of the true tendencies of things which burst out from time to time, and startled even Elizabeth into doubts of her own sagacity.

The majority of the States having signed the treaty with Don John, the Prince of Orange would not give him an excuse for retaining the Spaniards by refusing to consent. He gave his adhesion at last with the rest, religion being left in suspense till an answer should come from Philip. The Spaniards departed as had been promised. Slowly, reluctantly, they evacuated the great citadels which Alva had built at Antwerp—Ghent, Maestrecht, Valenciennes, the lately won Zealand Islands,—they withdrew from them all, and made them over to the soldiers of the States. They received 300,000 crowns upon the spot; they were promised as much more on reaching Italy, and thither they went to receive it. So far, and in this most essential matter, the promise was kept. There was a party, however, among the Belgian Catholics who were loudly hostile to the connexion with Elizabeth.[3] It was observed, too, that the refugees who

---

[1] Strype's Grindal, p. 327, &c. Walsingham to Burghley, May 26, 1577. Wilson to Burghley, Jan. 23, 1578.—MSS. Domestic.

[2] Walsingham to Burghley, May 26, 1577.—MSS. Domestic.

[3] Wilson to Elizabeth, Feb. 25, 1577.—MSS. Flanders.

had been expelled by Requescens were coming back in numbers, and were well received. Sir T. Stukely, who had come from Spain, the Earl of Westmoreland, Sir F. Englefield, and several more, were 'cherished about the 'person of Don John as though they were of council 'with him.'[1] Dr. Wilson, Elizabeth's minister with the States, remonstrated, but no attention was paid to him. Secretary Escobedo was found soon after to have received a letter from the Queen of Scots,[2] and Wilson, to see how he would take it, spoke openly to Don John about the suspicion which was entertained about him with respect to that lady. Don John coloured, passed it off, and was soon after observed to be making prodigious efforts to gain the Prince of Orange. He went so far as to promise Holland and Zealand the liberty of worship which they demanded; and he even told the Prince that if his brother would not agree to the pacification, he would himself join the States and take arms in their cause.[3]

It could not be for nothing that Don John went so near committing himself to treason. 'More was meant 'than appeasing the Netherlands;' and a friend of Don John afterwards hinted to the Prince that Philip could not live for ever, and that Don John perhaps intended 'to establish his estate in the Low Countries and make 'himself master of them.'

Believing that he might be serious, the Prince consulted Elizabeth. 'The Netherlands might be made a 'kingdom, and Don John the first King.'[4] But a visit

---

[1] Wilson to Elizabeth, Feb. 25, 1577.—*MSS. Flanders.*

[2] Secret advertisements from Brussels, Feb. 22.—*MSS. Ibid.*

[3] Don John with his own mouth told Dr. Wilson that he had used these words to Orange, and Orange told him so also: 'Yet will I never the more trust Don John,' said Wilson; 'yes, I mistrust him the more. By such speech he either minds to tempt the Prince, or else he bears a false heart to the King his brother.'—*Wilson to Walsingham, May 1, MSS. Flanders.*

[4] Notes concerning the Prince of Orange, May, 1577.—*MSS. Flanders.*

afterwards from the Papal Nuncio explained the mystery. It was supposed that Orange would resent the treatment which he had received from the Queen. The Nuncio came to ask him whether if Don John made war on England he would be willing to assist, or if not assist, whether he would remain neutral.[1] A packet of letters from Escobedo to the King of Spain intercepted immediately afterwards by La Noue in France threw a yet further light on Don John's intentions. The treaty of Ghent had been accepted without the slightest purpose of observing it. The Spaniards held tenaciously as ever to their resolution to conquer the States; only in the opinion of Escobedo, and probably, therefore, of Don John, the road to their conquest lay through London.[2]

What was the meaning of words like these? Was it conceivable that Don John was flying in the face of the known intentions of the King, or was Philip himself as false as his brother? Don Bernardino, though appointed ambassador to England, was still lingering in the Low Countries, and Don John's own conduct confirmed the worst suspicions. No sooner were Escobedo's letters published than he fled from Brussels to Namur, shut himself into the castle, and sent expresses for his army to return.[3] Walsingham, supported by Leicester, repre-

---

[1] Daniel Rogers to Walsingham, July 10, 1577.—*MSS. Flanders.*

[2] 'If a miracle is to set things straight it is time for the miracle to come; if force and a stout band, your Majesty must provide what is necessary. The reduction of Holland and Zeeland is the point, and this is more difficult than the enterprise of England. Redeem England first, and the rest is ours. No great force will be needed. Let not your Majesty think I say this in the interest of Don John. I leave that aside. I mean only that your Majesty's affairs cannot be remedied otherwise. Time has proved it, and every hour will make it more clear.'—*Escobedo to Philip*, April 9. Taken with other letters to similar purpose in June 1577. *MSS. Flanders.*

[3] There is reason to think that the Prince of Orange, acting with the advice of Wilson, intended to seize

sented to Elizabeth that she was betrayed. With Don John in arms again and Guise omnipotent at Paris, her only safety lay in espousing the cause which she had trifled with. Condé and the King of Navarre had been petitioning in vain for assistance ever since the revocation of the Edicts. She now took up their request, hesitated, refused, again resolved, and, finally, decided, as it seemed, to send money to Casimir that he might raise a fresh army of Reiters and march on Paris.[1]

Everything was now for the moment changed. The friendship of Scotland became valuable, and she was ready to give pensions to the nobles there.[2] Circulars went round to compel Catholics to attend the English service. Mass-books were hunted up; scoundrels who used bad language against the Queen were pilloried and

---

Don John, and send him to England. Antonio de Guaras writes:—'He tenido información muy espantosa que los buenos officios del Doctor Wilson y de todos ellos juntamente eran para quitar á su Alteza su libertad y ponerle en mano destos, pretendiendo proceder por los terminos que usan con la Reyna de Escocia.'—*Cartas de Guaras*, Sept. 20, 1577. *MSS. Simancas.*

[1] Her fluctuations appear in a series of letters from Leicester to Walsingham. On the 10th of August Leicester wrote that she said she had promised the French King not to help Condé, and that she could not do it. He had explained to her that no other Prince would hesitate in such a situation as that in which she was placed. 'If she allowed her best friends to quail with their cause it was impossible that she could stand. She would thus have all the mighty princes of the earth against her, and not a friend left.'

On the 15th he laid before her the dangers to which she was exposed 'by the slack dealing with her friends.' He 'found her relenting.' 'God was moving her heart to consider her own and her country's wealth.' The day after he writes that 'after much reasoning he found her Majesty to be sorry that she had so slenderly dealt with her friends, and did more plainly see if they were overthrown how hardly she would be beset by her enemies. He forgot not to lay before her these counsels from time to time, and how manifestly her perils had been foreseen, and that none other remedy there was in man's policy but relieving of her friends. She was in a mind at last to repair the oversight passed.'—*Leicester to Walsingham*, Aug. 10, Aug. 13, 14, 15. *MSS. France.*

[2] Walsingham to Burghley, Aug. 29.—*MSS. Domestic.*

lost their ears, the judges shewing themselves zealous, perhaps over zealous, in catching the wind while it was blowing.[1] Leading recusants were fined, and ordered to keep their houses. De Guaras, found writing to the Queen of Scots, was arrested and sent to the Tower, and a change of guardianship was contemplated for the Queen of Scots herself. The German Protestant Princes once more invited the Queen to be the head of a reformed league. She listened, heard the arguments on both sides, and for a time seemed favourably inclined.[2]

---

[1] The judges' views on such matters are illustrated by a letter from Mr. Justice Manwood to Sir Walter Mildmay.

'Sir,—Concerning the lewd fellow, who, after his deserved punishment by pillory, did persist with more lewd and slanderous speeches towards her Majesty in the presence of the people being at the execution, his offence is thereby aggravated, and he therefore to sustain a more grievous punishment. By the late statute he is for his second offence to lose all his goods and be perpetually imprisoned during his life, whereby he shall never come out to abuse his tongue again, which imprisonment perpetual is to be executed with all extremity with irons and other strait feeding and keeping as may shortly bring him to a repentant end, an estate from which he seemeth now to be far off. Thus much by the late statute and law. And because the same statute is not in the negative restraining any former statute or common law before; by the former statute laws for slanderous rumours and speeches against the nobility and Council of the Prince, punishment was to be done by advice of the Prince's Council; the experience whereof has been by pillory and cutting of ears, as by nailing or burning the ears or such like: much more for the like offence against the Prince by the common law punishment was to be inflicted by advice of Council in discretion without limitation, but usually not to be taken to dismember the offender of any of his joints or eyes or other principal senses. As for example, the offence of the tongue in this case being so heinous, as well for the matter as for the time and place of speech, is by burning in the face with a letter or by gagging his two jaws in painful manner, and so as he cannot speak any word, and produced in public place of punishment with paper on his head, or by burning through the tongue, or perchance by cutting off his tongue, in such wise as he may eat and drink and take sustenance after. These and such like once or more often times as by her Majesty's Council may be ordered and thought necessary, I think may be done by order of the common law.—*MSS. Domestic.* Nov. 1577.

[2] Necessary Considerations for her Majesty, Nov. 1577.—*MSS. France.*

The Marquis Havré, a new envoy from the States, was received with conspicuous cordiality. A message was sent to Spain that peace must be made in earnest or England would interfere. If Guise, as report said that he intended, came to the assistance of Don John, Elizabeth decided to send over an army, and Leicester meant to be its leader.[1]

War in England was now universally looked for, and as a first object each party desired to secure the person of James of Scotland. Mary Stuart, through the Archbishop of Glasgow, endeavoured to have him carried to France.[2] De Guaras wrote again and again to Philip that it would be an advantage if he could be taken to Spain.[3] Killegrew went to Edinburgh to recover the lost opportunity and induce Morton to send him into England. Elizabeth for once was sailing a straight course. The tide might soon change, but while her alarm lasted she was really determined. The difficulty was in the temper of the States, where patriotism and religion were dragging in opposite directions. The majority of the people wished to make Orange Dictator. The Walloon nobles and the priests hated the Spaniards, but they hated Protestantism worse. England had many enemies who, as Davison wrote,[4] 'would be ready to cast the cat before our legs.' The Prince of Orange recommended Elizabeth to make sure at all risks of Holland and Zea-

---

[1] 'My Lord of Leicester comes over as general of all the men which her Majesty shall send to the Low Countries. This is his full determination, as yet unknown to her Highness. Neither shall she be acquainted with it till she be fully resolved to send, which will not be till the Prince of Orange send back again. Thus if she understand the Duke of Guyse come to assist Don John she will assist the States with 10,000 men.'—*Edward Chrrke to Secretary Davison*, Sept. 19, 1577. *MSS. Flanders.*

[2] The Queen of Scots to the Archbishop of Glasgow, Nov. 5, 1577.—LABANOFF, vol. iv.

[3] Cartas de A. de Guaras descifradas. Sept. 20, 28, Oct. 4.—*MSS. Simancas.*

[4] Davison had been sent to reside with the Prince of Orange.

land: she would then be supreme at sea, and could control the situation.

She was pausing, not from want of will but from legitimate uncertainty, when a fresh element of discord was introduced into the scene. The Catholic aristocracy, to escape Orange and an English Protectorate, threw themselves on the German Empire. They invited the Emperor's brother, the Archduke Matthias, to be their governor, in the place of Don John. They hoped that either Philip would acquiesce in the exchange, or that Rudolf, in default, would stand by them. With the Emperor's secret approval, Matthias stole away from Vienna at the beginning of October, came to Cologne, and waited there till it was certain that he would be received.

Havré was invited to explain. He knew, before he left the States, what his friends intended. He said that they had sent for the Archduke, as a Prince of the House of Austria, to govern under the King of Spain, and that he had not expected that the Queen of England would disapprove. She said that she ought to have been consulted. She would send neither men nor money, till she understood the meaning of it, especially till she knew the opinion of the Prince of Orange.[1] The Prince, to whom she wrote, answered that he had not been taken into counsel, but on the whole he did not intend to make difficulties. The Archduke, it appeared, was willing to accept the government whether Philip approved or not, and the House of Austria would then be divided against itself. The Archduke was a Papist, but 'soft and amenable,' and the States would unite more cordially under a Catholic Prince than under himself.[2]

---

[1] Walsingham to Davison, Oct. 10.—MSS. Flanders.
[2] Davison to Walsingham, Oct. 27, inclosing a letter from the Prince.—MSS. Ibid.

Elizabeth appeared to be satisfied. Havré was sent back with a favourable answer to the request for money: and not money only was promised, but an army as well, and Leicester expected to be in the field against Don John before many weeks were over.[1] A league was to be formed between England and the States on the basis of the old treaties with the House of Burgundy. On one side only her own theories continued to exert a pernicious influence over her. Havré was a Catholic like Schwegenhem, and through him she repeated her old advice, that there should be no change in religion, no liberty of conscience, no separate chapels or conventicles to divide the union.

For war with Spain she was prepared, and she had already taken one momentous step past recall, which was likely to precipitate it. The strength of Philip lay in the gold of the new world. Francis Drake had learnt, in 1572, how defenceless were the convoys at Panama. Oxenham, a Devonshire rover, had crossed the Isthmus four years later, built a pinnace in the Pacific, and made prizes among the coasters, which, dreaming of no danger in that undisturbed ocean, were bringing bullion from Lima. He had not brought home his plunder. He had wasted precious time at the Isle of Pearls, toying with a Spanish lady. Armed boats were sent after him. He was taken and hanged as a pirate, and the gold was recovered. But the ease had been again demonstrated with which some great blow might be struck in those quarters at the heart of the Spanish power, and there was a man of far higher qualities than Oxenham, who was ready to undertake the

---

[1] 'Before Candlemas, or shortly after, you shall see my Lord of Leicester well accompanied in the Low Countries.'—*Ed. Horsey to Davison*, Dec. 18, 1577.

enterprise. Some one whose signature is erased, and whose name it would be unjust to conjecture, had volunteered his services for an exploit of a less worthy kind. 'Your Majesty,' wrote this man in language curiously characteristic of the time, ' must first seek the 'kingdom of heaven, and make no league with those 'whom God has divided from you. Your Majesty must 'endeavour to make yourself strong and to make them 'weak, and at sea you can either make war on them 'openly or by colourable means;—by giving licence, 'under letters patent, to discover and inhabit strange 'places, with special proviso for their safeties whom 'policy requires to have most annoyed—by which 'means the doing the contrary shall be imputed to the 'executors' fault; your Highness's letters patent being 'a manifest show that it was not your Majesty's plea-'sure so to have it. Afterwards, if it seem well, you 'can avow the fact, or else you can disavow the fact 'and those that did it as league-breakers, leaving them 'to pretend it was done without your privity.'

Elizabeth valued much proposals of this kind. None of her subjects pleased her better than those who would do her work and save her from responsibility. It was an unusual road to 'the kingdom of heaven.' But those who would understand England in the sixteenth century must recognise that brave and high-minded men were willing to risk being condemned as pirates to shield a sovereign who would not use their services otherwise: while Catholics, since the Paris massacre, had come to be looked on as wild beasts, who had no rights as human beings, and might be deceived, played with, and destroyed like wolves or vermin. The proposal which follows had been heard of before, but had not yet taken so practical a shape. Vast Catholic fleets went every summer to the banks of Newfoundland for the food of their fasting days.

'I,' continued the same writer, 'will undertake, if you will permit me, to fit out ships, well armed, for Newfoundland, where they will meet with all the great shipping of France, Spain, and Portugal. The best I will bring away and I will burn the rest. Commit us afterwards as pirates if you will, but I shall ruin their sea force, for they depend on their fishermen for their navies. It may be objected that this will be against your league; but I hold it as lawful in Christian policy to prevent a mischief betimes as to revenge it too late; especially seeing that God himself is a party to the quarrel now on foot, and His enemy maliciously disposed towards your Highness. You may be told it will ruin our commerce. Do not believe it: you will but establish your own superiority at sea. If you will let us first do this, we will next take the West Indies from Spain. You will have the gold and silver mines and the profit of the soil. You will be monarch of the seas and out of danger from every one. I will do it if you will allow me; only you must resolve and not delay or dally—The wings of man's life are plumed with the feathers of death.'[1]

This paper is dated the 6th of November, 1577. In the first fortnight of the same month, Francis Drake had in readiness a fleet of five armed ships, equipped by a company of adventurers, among whom the Queen and Leicester were the largest shareholders. The coincidence at first suggests Drake as the possible author of the suggestion. The Newfoundland fleets contained 25,000 innocent industrious men, all of whom were

---

[1] Discourse addressed to the Queen how to annoy the King of Spain, Nov. 6, 1577. Condensed.—*MSS. Domestic.*

obviously meant to be destroyed; and if Drake it was, and if the proposal had been accepted, the naval annals of England and the fame of her greatest seaman would have been stained with a horrible crime. But the visionary audacity of the scheme, and the melodramatic imaginativeness of the closing words point to some one of a less practical temperament; nor is it likely that Drake's fleet would have been already prepared with the object of his enterprise undetermined. However this be, on the 15th of the same November, Francis Drake sailed from Plymouth Sound, nominally to search the waste of the Pacific and find openings for English commerce; but with private instructions also from the Queen, which might be shown or withheld, acted upon or not acted upon, as convenience might afterwards dictate. De Guaras had watched his preparations and suspected his real object. He was provided with a second in command, the Mr. Doughty whose fate afterwards caused so deep sensation; and Doughty was probably sent by the Spanish party in the Council to observe and embarrass his movements, and thwart his purpose if mischief was intended to Spain.

This was Elizabeth's contribution to the war of the Low Countries, bestowed while she was in the humour and happily irrevocable—a contribution more effective, measured by its results in bringing Spain upon her knees, than if she had emptied her treasury into the lap of Orange. In those five ships lay the germ of the ocean empire of Great Britain. They sailed but just in time, for the Queen's courage had passed its flood, and other help the States were after all not to receive. The appearance of Matthias upon the scene, promising as it did a quarrel between Philip and the Emperor Rudolf, relieved her when she thought about it, of an immediate necessity of action. The rupture with Philip was again put off. The pale shadow of the Archduke—his influence never amounted to a reality—soon melted away, but by that time the Queen's natural disposition had reasserted its usual influence upon her. To break a promise was never a serious difficulty with her. The subsidy which she had told Havré that she would send, remained in the treasury. The ten thousand men were left at home to plough and to dig. Instead of men and money she sent a threatening letter to Don John, and she consoled the States with saying that Don John would be reasonable when he saw 'that she was determined to 'take part against him.' But in fact, she had determined to take no part against him. Her brave purposes had evaporated in words. 'So it is,' said Walsingham's secretary, 'that such as incline more to the faction of 'Spain, than to her Majesty's safety and quiet estate of 'her crown and realm, have persuaded her that she 'cannot deal in honour to the furtherance of the States, 'either with men or money, till she have a resolute 'answer from the King or Don John, notwithstanding 'the promise that she hath made to the Marquis; which 'hath wrought such a coldness in her Majesty to hearken 'to their demands that hardly can she be moved from 'that Spanish persuasion.'[2]

Don John's English friends kept him well informed of the workings of the Queen's humour; and he saw that he had nothing to fear. His Spaniards came flocking back over the frontiers, and while Orange was away in Holland, and the Duke of Arschot, and the Walloon Catholics were busy with their Archduke Matthias, he started suddenly into the field, caught the States army unprepared at Gemblours, and shivered it to pieces.[3]

---

[1] Instructions to Mr. Leighton sent to the States and Don John, Dec. 21, 1577.—*MSS. Flanders.*

[2] Laurence Tomson to Davison, Feb. 2, 1578.

[3] Jan. 29, 1578.

Could he have followed up the blow, he might have recovered the Catholic Provinces upon the spot, so utter was their consternation. He had no reserves however, and an empty chest; and they had leisure to recover their breath and look round them. Long since they would have had France at their side, but for Elizabeth's promises.

Fiercely they demanded whether they were trifled with. Did she mean or did she not mean to keep her engagements with them? 'If her Majesty disappoint 'them now,' wrote Davison, a week after the defeat, 'it will in the judgment of the wisest bring forth some 'dangerous alteration.'[1] A month passed and they heard nothing. 'Her Majesty must say yes or no,' Davison repeated more vehemently; 'hesitation is cruel 'and dishonourable. If she say no, she will not escape 'the hatred of the Papists. If she say yes, she has still 'great advantages for the prosecution of the war; but 'it must be one or the other and swiftly.'[2]

At last the resolution came. She would send no English army, and no Leicester; but there was Casimir, whom she was to have provided for an invasion of France, and had fed with air after all. Casimir would come to the help of the States, if he could have a hundred thousand pounds. She had already lent them forty thousand. She would lend twenty thousand more, and she would lend the rest if they could not raise it among themselves. This was her last word. She would help them no further.[3] Burghley shielded her with such excuses as he could invent, still nursing their hopes that she would interfere if Casimir failed them. She sent the twenty thousand pounds. She undertook to endorse

---

[1] Davison to Walsingham, Feb. 6. —*MSS. Holland.*

[2] Davison to Walsingham, March 8. Condensed.—*MSS. Ibid.*

[3] Instructions to Mr. Rogers sent to the States and to Duke Casimir, March 9.—*MSS. Holland.*

the bonds of the States for an additional forty thousand, exacting promise of repayment both of the principal and interest of the rest of her debt; while Leicester, who had laboured with her in vain, poured out his personal disappointment to Davison. 'He had neither face nor countenance,' he said, 'to write to the Prince, 'his expectation being so greatly deceived;' 'the irre- 'solution had been dreadful, the conclusion miserable;' and 'God,' he thought, could alone now help England by miracle, seeing the apparent ordinary courses so overslipt.'

[1] Leicester to Davison, March 9, 1578.—*MSS. Holland.*

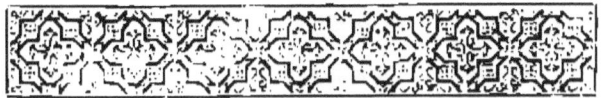

CHAPTER XXVI.

THE hesitation of Elizabeth was less unreasonable than her more eager advisers believed. The suspicions entertained of Philip were as yet without foundation. The universal impression in Europe was that sooner or later he would be forced into an invasion of England; but it is equally certain that he limited his own wishes to the reduction of his own heretical subjects. So long as there was a Catholic to succeed her, he was willing to wait till 'God should call his sister-in-law.' Escobedo, whose unlucky letters had precipitated the second revolt, was assassinated on his return to Madrid by Philip's order.[1] Money which had been promised to Don John was withheld lest he should make a dangerous use of it. The fate of the Reformation was to be decided in the end by a duel between the representative chiefs of the two faiths; but the principals hesitated equally to take their places in the field; disclaimed their obligations, and determined in spite of Papist and Protestant to remain friends. Six years had now passed since the expulsion of Don Guerau de Espes, and the experiment of a Spanish ambassador resident in London was about to be tried once more. Whatever may have

---

[1] Philip himself would have said that Escobedo was privately executed. He was held to have forfeited his life, and a public trial would have led to inconvenient disclosures.

been the reason of the delay, Don Bernardino received his
commission at last, and set out for England in the middle
of March. The selection of a nobleman of so high rank
was in itself a compliment. The house of Mendoza was
the most illustrious in Spain. Don Bernardino's father,
Don Alonzo Count of Coruña, was a favourite of Charles
V.; his mother was a Ximenez, niece of the great Cardinal. He had himself been first Philip's Master of the
Horse, and then had held a distinguished command in
the Low Countries. His instructions were profoundly
conciliatory. He brought no private directions to make
a party in England or to encourage rebellion, or lead
the Catholics to expect intervention. He was strictly
forbidden to do anything of which the Queen could
complain. He was sent to remove her alarms, to satisfy
her that she need not fear Spain unless she herself
desired a quarrel, and he was empowered to promise all
concessions in the Low Countries which she could
reasonably demand, the withdrawal once more of the
Spanish forces, the restoration of the States' privileges,
the reinstatement of the provincial governments—even
the recall of Don John and the appointment of a successor of whose designs there could be no suspicion—
provided liberty of conscience was not mentioned, and
the Catholic priests and bishops were replaced in the
churches from which they had been removed in Holland
and Zealand. It was urged at the time, and it has been
urged since, that all this was to concede nothing; that
the Inquisition itself could demand no measures against
heresy more severe than the reimposition of the edicts
of Charles V. and it is likely that in the long run the
objection would have proved well founded. With or
without a Spanish army, the bigotry of the Walloons
would probably sooner or later have interfered with the

liberties of the Batavian States, and would have forced them again into revolt. But no such result could have been looked for immediately. The only visible effect would have been the reappearance of the mass in the churches in Holland and Zealand. The edicts when they touched opinions would have been no more than words. They had remained a dead letter from the Peace of Passau to the abdication of the Emperor. They could have been enforced nowhere without the help of the local authorities: and so long as each state administered its own laws persecution would have been impossible.[1]

The state of England at the time of Mendoza's arrival was extremely critical. The Protestants were eagerly expecting war. Drake had sailed for the Pacific. Though the Queen had sent no troops to the Low Countries, the Prince of Orange was willing once more to trust to English volunteers, and Colonel Norris was already across the water with several thousand men in the service of the States. The ambassador landed at Gravesend on March 11. The question of war or peace had been before the Council incessantly during the preceding fortnight. The Queen's resolution was not yet known in the country, if it was known to herself. Antonio de Guaras was in the Tower; money had been sent to the Hague; and Don Bernardino was told that if he meant to prevent a rupture he had not a moment to lose.[2]

The storm in the Council had not yet subsided. Elizabeth's own humour was still fluctuating. Mendoza hastened to London, but no intimation was made to him that she desired his presence. He announced

[1] La commission que ha de llevar Don Bernardino para Inglaterra, Marzo 1578.—*MSS. Simancas.* Legajo 830. Segunda Instruccion, Ley 831.—*Ibid.*

[2] Declaration of Don Bernardino, March, 1578.—*MSS. Spain.*
Mendoza to Cayas, March 11.—*MSS. Simancas.*

his arrival to the Court, and requested an audience.
Five days were allowed to pass before he could obtain admission; and when he was introduced at last it seemed that he might as well have remained at Brussels. The Queen received him with formal stateliness. Without waiting to hear what he had to say, she elaborately defended the revolt of the States. She admitted and justified the assistance which she had given them. She called Don John hard names. She did not like Spaniards for near neighbours, she said, and she would not have them.[1]

When at length he delivered his message she grew calmer. She admitted that the King's offers, if they were made in good faith, were reasonable ; and then throwing off official restraint, as she usually did when she meant to be serious, she sent away the lords and ladies, sate herself down on a stool, bidding a page fetch another for Mendoza, and repeated to Leicester and four or five other councillors who remained the substance of Philip's proposals. Since his Majesty was so good and kind, she said, the States ought not to be encouraged in persisting further. Her manner became personally gracious. She told Mendoza she was delighted to see him again. People had frightened her about him, she said, pretending that he would make a revolution; but she did not believe it: and he in return assured her that it was a wicked calumny; his master had charged him to study only her pleasure; his actions should prove how sincerely he was prepared to obey.[2]

Thus the interview ended better than it began ; but the ambassador was still far from smooth water. The Council were less ready than the Queen to believe in

---

[1] 'No quería Españoles tan cerca.'
[2] Don Bernardino de Mendoza, March 19.—*MSS. Simancas.*

fair words. Don John was still pressing the States as far as his means would allow, and daily taking towns in South Brabant. Burghley and Sussex, who spoke with Mendoza afterwards, suggested a suspension of arms and spoke of the Pacification of Ghent as the sole basis of a treaty possible. The States, they said, could not trust to uncertainties. Toleration of some kind ought to be secured to them by law, otherwise they would throw themselves upon France, which England could not permit. Sussex's influence was deservedly great with the Queen in such matters. He had held aloof always from the Protestant section of the Council, and his advice if not always wise was never factious. By him and by others the incompleteness of Philip's concessions was so forced upon Elizabeth that if unconvinced she became irritated and violent, and so the ambassador found her at his next audience. She insisted fiercely on an immediate truce. She abused Antonio de Guaras, who, she said, deserved to be hanged, and then, in a loud voice and with apparent passion, she said she would have the Treaty of Ghent confirmed and observed, or an English army should try the question with Don John.

Mendoza took a high tone too; he replied that his master had a long arm; he trusted she did not mean to support rebellion. Clearing her throat and spitting,[1] she answered that the States were not rebels; they would submit to reasonable conditions. She had heard of Don John's fine schemes, she said, and the King of Spain's dealings with the Pope. She would have no French in the Netherlands, and no Spaniards either. 'By God,' she said, and three times she repeated the oath,[2] 'I will have the Treaty of Ghent allowed, or I will stand

---

[1] 'Tragando un poco de saliva.'   [2] 'Jurando tres veces.'

by the States as long as I have a man left in the realm to fight for them.'[1]

Mendoza, unused as yet to the Queen's character, took her words as serious. He told the King that both she and her Council appeared estranged from the Spanish alliance, and that Spain had no friends in England except the Catholics. But the haughty mood of the public reception was a state dress assumed for the occasion, and the expressions about the Treaty of Ghent contained a meaning other than they seemed to bear. The Treaty of Ghent had secured immediate liberty of conscience, but the ultimate settlement of that question had been referred by it to the judgment of the King, and it was with this reservation, in her mind though not on her lips, that she insisted on the acceptance of it by Don John. She held to the letter of her threat. She sent a minister to the governor to demand, as she had said to Mendoza, a suspension of arms. 'She 'would not allow these countries to be reduced to servi-'tude by him,' she said, 'nor yet be possessed by the 'French;' if the Treaty was accepted, 'the Estates were 'willing to yield all obedience and continue in the Catho-'lic faith;' and it was to the Treaty so interpreted that she required Don John to consent.[2] The London merchants exercised their powerful influence in favour of peace. At Mendoza's instigation a hint was sent from the city to the great banking houses of the Fuggers at Cologne, that they must not rely too much on the Queen's promises to endorse the bonds of the States.[3] The States in consequence could raise money only at a

---

[1] Descifrada de Don Bernardino, 31 de Marzo.—*MSS. Simancas.*

[2] Instructions to Mr. Wilks sent to Don John, April, 1578.—*MSS. Flanders.*

[3] Mendoza á su Mag^d, 5 de Mayo, 1578.—*MSS. Simancas.*

discount of 25 per cent., while the Queen insisted that the first use which should be made of the new loan was to repay her with interest the 40,000*l*. which she had originally lent them.[1]

Evidently she wished them to yield on the point, to her so indifferent, of liberty of worship. While she maintained the Act of Uniformity at home, it was impossible for her to demand toleration from Philip: and the continuance of the war was an ever present and complicated danger. France was hanging between two policies, undetermined whether to annex the Netherlands and seek a war with Spain, or go with Spain in the interests of religion, and call on England to return to conformity. Alençon, resenting the abruptness with which he had been dropped by Elizabeth, was ready for any plan or scheme which promised an opening to his ambition. The Queen-mother suggested a marriage for him with a Spanish princess 'to check the greatness of 'the houses of Guise and Bourbon.' The Duke of Guise tempted him into a confederacy with himself, to make a party in Scotland, seize Edinburgh and Dumbarton Castles, bring the young King to Paris, and demand the liberation of Mary Stuart.[3] This too, Elizabeth knew. The Count de Retz, going professedly on

---

[1] Burghley to Walsingham, July 29, 1578.—*MSS. Holland.*

[2] *Ibid.*

[3] 'Les forces estrangères, quelque grandes qu'elles soient, leur pourront peu nuyre sans l'Escosse. C'est pourquoy ils font tous leurs efforts de la remectre s'il est possible à leur dévotion; et de mesmes al messieurs mes parens MM. d'Alençon et de Guyse espèrent quelque fruict de leur desseing dont m'avez escript et sont résolus d'en venir à l'exécution, il leur est très nécessaire de haster en toute diligence le secours qu'ils déliberent d'y envoyer, affin de saisir les premiers de la personne de mon fils et des places fortes,' &c.—*Mary Stuart to the Archbishop of Glasgow*, May 9; and again Sept. 15: 'Je priray très affectueusement M. d'Alençon mon frère et M. de Guyse mon bon cousin que suyvant leur ancienne délibération ils se hastent.' —LABANOFF, vol. v.

public business to Edinburgh, was charged secretly with a message to Guise's confederates there. He passed through London, applied for a passport, and was sent for to the Queen. She received him as she had first received Mendoza. She told him she knew what he was about. He was come to disquiet England and serve the cause of a wicked woman whose head ought long ago to have been struck from her shoulders. They might do their worst, she said, but the Queen of Scots should never go free, though it cost her life and realm.[1]

Brave words, yet uttered with a faltering heart. So wearied, so perplexed was Elizabeth with the complications in which she was entangled, that a few weeks later she had half concluded to let the Queen of Scots go free, and to disarm the disturbers of her peace by yielding to them. 'She spared not to make the fault 'light, and a common fault, for which the subjects of the 'Queen of Scots had deprived her,' and she refused to recognise the Regency as a lawful government at all.[2]

---

[1] 'Esta Reyna dió audiencia á Gondi á quien no recibió con tantas ceremonias como se acostumbra á los ambajadores. Dixóle con voz alta en la sala de audiencia que bien sabia que venia á inquietarle su reyno y hacer oficios por la mas mala muger del mundo, y que merecia tener cortada la cabeça muchos años ha : á que le replicó el Gondi que la de Escocia era Reyna como ella y parienta suya y que estaba presa, á cuya causa no se espantase que tratasen de sus negocios. Respondióle con colera que en toda su vida no se verfa libre aunque á ella le costase la suya y la perdida de su reyno.'— *Mendoza á su Mag*', 5 de Mayo 1578.

[2] 'Speaking with Mr. Vice-Chamberlain (Sir T. Heneage), I asked him how her Majesty was disposed to deal with the Ambassadors of Scotland. He said it was against her heart to entertain them as ambassadors, and she spared not to make the fault light, and a common fault, for which they had deprived her. I replied that if her Majesty made a scruple in that case it were good to hold another course and persuade her to send home the Scotch Queen and set the crown on her head, and so assure herself of her friendship, and not in this sort love the one and not embrace the other. He said he had told her so much in effect, but what she would do he could not tell.'—*Edmund Tremayne to Walsingham*, July 29, 1578. *MSS. Holland.*

Alençon's inclination ultimately settled on the Low Countries. The Prince of Orange, resolute not to submit to Spain on Elizabeth's terms, was as little disposed to sit still for fear of offending her. Alençon, hoping either to turn the Netherlands into a kingdom for himself, or if his brother died without children, to take them with him and annex them to France, offered to assist at his own charge for two months, with twelve thousand men. Orange saw no reason for rejecting so seemingly generous a proposal. Secretary Davison was sent from England to entreat and to threaten. The Prince told him shortly that 'the necessities of the time' left him no choice, 'seeing her Majesty's delay, and 'the resolution of the King of Spain to destroy them.' He was sorry to displease the Queen, but it could not be helped. The Walloon provinces would revolt if Monsieur's offer was refused.[1]

Davison could not blame him; and when blamed himself for the failure of his diplomacy, he spoke out the truth with unflinching plainness. 'The Prince,' he said, 'found great fault with her Majesty's uncertainties, 'promising, and drawing back.' It was 'unwise,' 'im-'politic,' 'unjust to the States,' 'and the way to over-'throw religion.' 'If the Queen meant only practice, 'she ought to have warned them, and to have let them 'try other means for their safety.'[2]

Alençon was indisputably going, let the consequences be what they might. It was a volunteer enterprise in which the French Crown was not formally compromised; but when the Spanish ambassador at Paris remonstrated with the King, he refused to interfere. The ambassador said that he was bound to control his subjects.

---

[1] Davison to Walsingham, May 18. —MSS. Holland.   [2] Davison to Walsingham, May 11. —MSS. Ibid.

The King replied that he did not wish to quarrel with Spain, but he would prefer war with Spain to war with his brother. 'Whatever is pretended,' wrote Sir Amyas Paulet,[1] 'the King is not sorry for this enter-'prise, for any way he thinks he will be the winner. If 'Monsieur meet his master, the King is delivered of 'so many suspected subjects; if he speed well, the 'King and all his realm shall have their parts in it.'[2] Sir Edward Stafford, who was sent to remonstrate with the Queen-mother, was as unsuccessful as Davison. He could not learn what was intended; but he concluded only 'that the purpose was deep and intricate,' 'part of 'a mighty and monstrous design for the extirpation of 'religion.'[3]

The ablest of Elizabeth's ministers were now at a loss what to advise. Had an army gone over in earnest when its coming was first announced, Don John might have yielded to necessity. But the Queen had broken her word. It is likely that she thought the threat would be sufficient, and never meant to keep it; and the effect of her uncertainty had been only confusion and indignation. Walsingham so deeply distrusted Alençon, that he expected to see him take part openly with Don John. If French troops were admitted into Antwerp, he feared a second St. Bartholomew.[4] That the Duke could be really disinterested, was incredible; and annexation to France, if that were the object, was scarcely less disastrous than Spanish conquest. 'Surely,' he wrote, 'it is hard to judge whether be the greater peril: 'the second brings a present mischief, the first a future, 'that is rather to reach to our posterity than to us.'[5]

---

[1] English Ambassador in Paris.
[2] Paulet to Walsingham, May 23. —*MSS. France.*
[3] Stafford to Elizabeth, May 26.
—*MSS. Ibid.*
[4] Walsingham to Davison, May 11, —*MSS. Holland.*
[5] Walsingham to Davison, May 11.

The Council were divided, and Mendoza used the moment to weight the balance with gold. His friends among the courtiers hinted to him that among the Queen's advisers were men whose virtue was not too austere. The Controller of the Household, Sir James Crofts, ever a pernicious influence in Elizabeth's Cabinet, rose greedily at the bait. Sussex looked at it wistfully. Lord Burghley's general moderation tempted overtures to which he listened with amused curiosity, and excited hopes which it need not be said that he disappointed.[1] Ultimately Crofts and Crofts alone became a pensioner of Philip, not meaning to betray his country, but conscientiously believing in the desirableness of the Spanish alliance, and being unable as he said through his mistress's parsimony to remain longer at the Court without assistance. By other methods, not less effective, by quick perception and insight into character, the ambassador made his way with Elizabeth. He never ceased to urge on her the good will of Philip to the general repose of Europe, and his special regard for herself. Philip and only Philip, he said, had prevented enthusiastic Spaniards from passing into Ireland. Philip so loved his children in the Netherlands, that he was ready and eager to pardon their rebellion, if they would but let the outward religion be ordered by the law. Elizabeth listened with pleased ears to words reflecting so accurately her own sentiments. In the growth of Protestantism in the Low Countries, she could see only an increasing obstacle to peace.[2] She defended her own religious government on the ground that she held the Catholic

---

[1] Descifrada de Don Bernardino, 21 de Maio y 9 de Setiembre.—*MSS. Simancas.*

[2] 'That which her Majesty seems most to mislike of which is the progress of religion being well considered is the thing which shall breed their greatest strength.'—*Walsingham to Burghley*, Sept. 20. *MSS. Holland.*

creed herself, and that her differences with her Catholic
subjects were merely political.¹ She pleaded mildly
for some relaxation in favour of Holland and Zealand;
but when Mendoza answered that it did not rest with
princes to suspend the law of God, she allowed the
rejoinder to pass.² Davison being too feeble a negotia-
tor, she dispatched Sir Francis Walsingham himself,
with Lord Cobham, to compel or persuade Orange to
suspend his negotiations with Monsieur, and she persuaded herself once more that she could bring Don
John to consent to an arrangement.³ They were sent
to accomplish what in itself they knew to be impossible. The administration of Alva and the massacre at
Antwerp had dug a river of blood between Spain and the
Protestants of the Batavian Provinces, and Elizabeth's
admitted object 'was to bring about a peace, leaving
'them under the Spanish King still.'⁴ It could not be;
yet Elizabeth was determined that it should be. To
strengthen her diplomacy, she used a strange weapon,
forged in Mendoza's armoury. It was not without reason that the city merchants had warned the Fuggers to
be cautious. To prevent the States from raising more
money, she repudiated the promises on the faith of
which they had obtained their loan. The bonds had
passed the great seal; but she refused to issue them;
and as the sole fruit of their application to her for
assistance, they found themselves required, with their
ruined exchequer, to redeem obligations at par, which

---

¹ ¹ 'Me replicó que no castigaba á los
Catholicos sino por no confessarle por
Reyna. Que en lo demas creya como
ellos.'
² 'A que respondi que no estaba en
manos de los Principes el alargar ó
estrechar la religion, habiendolo dado
Dios y ley en que se habia de vivir.'
—*Mendoza al Rey*, 17 de Junio. *MSS.
Simancas.*
³ Commission to Cobham and
Walsingham, June 12.—*MSS. Holland.*
⁴ Walsingham to Davison, May 22.
—*MSS. Ibid.*

they had realised only with 25 per cent. deducted—to repay sixty thousand pounds which she had lent them —and to find wages for Casimir's ten thousand Reiters, which had been thrown upon them in exchange for the promised English army.

Accustomed as they were to her strange strokes of diplomatic art, Elizabeth's own ministers were unprepared for such a performance as this. Walsingham, ever free and frank, reported from Antwerp the language used upon the bourse there. 'It is said openly,' he wrote to Burghley, 'that if bonds which have passed 'under the great seal are not observed, no assurance 'whatever can be placed in her Majesty's promises. 'For her honour, and the honour of the realm, it had 'been better there had been given double value of them 'than this delay. We cannot excuse it. If she mean 'to desert the States hereafter, which will be a very dis'honourable and dangerous course, she ought to say so, 'and inhibit her agents from dealing with them here'after.'[1]

Burghley was equally explicit with the Queen. He told her that it was monstrous at such a time, and with the enemy in the field against them, to press the States to pay to her so large a part of what they had so hardly received. They would at once revolt to France, which would be worse to her than the loss of a hundred thousand pounds.[2] Leicester said that her honour was touched, the surety of the whole cause endangered, and Walsingham's mission condemned to certain failure. All was to no purpose. The Queen ridiculed their preciseness, and refused to hear their remonstrance. She said privately to young Edmund Tremayne, that 'the States

---

[1] Walsingham to Burghley, July 18.—MSS. Holland.   [2] Burghley to Cobham and Walsingham, July 29.—MSS. Ibid.

'ought already to have yielded to Don John.' Their attitude 'was altogether unbecoming from subjects to 'their sovereign.' Walsingham should have told them that if they persisted in such 'absurd' conduct, 'she 'would leave them in all their enterprises.' They would then have been frightened into their senses, 'and would 'have been driven by way of caution to submit.'[1]

Even this was not all, and there was yet one more strange shift behind. 'The subtle malice of the time 'obliged her to fence too much rather than too little.'[2] She wished the States to be weak; yet a power of some kind was needed in the field, to keep Don John in check; and therefore, while she had sent Walsingham expressly to prevent the admission of the French, she contrived privately to communicate to Alençon, 'that 'she would in a sort, consent to his enterprise and con- 'cur in it,' if he would act with herself and under her direction. She consulted no one. She did not even share her thoughts with Burghley: but with the intricate practice in which she so delighted, she invited the Duke to advance at the very time when she was forbidding Orange to treat with him.[3] It was like dancing on a tight rope. Her movements may have been extremely clever, but they were also extremely dangerous. She was playing with France, playing with Alençon, playing with the States, half false to all, half sincere to all. She was trifling with her own credit, and trying the patience of statesmen who, on the whole, were the wisest that ever served a European sovereign. Leicester,

---

[1] Edmund Tremayne to Walsingham, July 20.—*MSS. Holland.*
[2] Paulet to Walsingham, June 16.—*MSS. France.*
[3] 'Monsieur saith that he hath warrant from her Majesty, though to me unknown, to come thus hastily into the Low Countries as a thing that her Majesty did allow.'—*Burghley to Cobham and Walsingham, July 29. MSS. Ibid.*

whose influence with her was the strongest, who had least right to be shocked at moral improprieties, had yet intelligence enough to see the political effect of his mistress's performances. Though Alençon had engaged himself elsewhere, the Duke of Guise was intriguing with effect in Scotland. A Spanish Italian invasion, though Elizabeth refused to believe it, was impending over Ireland.[1] The most formidable enemy that she possessed was at work in the very heart of England. 'The more I love her,' wrote Leicester, 'the more fear-
'ful am I to see such dangerous ways taken. God of
'his mercy help all, and give us all here about her
'grace to discharge our duties; for never was there
'more need, nor never stood this crown in like peril.
'God must now uphold the Queen by miracle: ordinary
'helps are past cure.'[2]

Walsingham's mission was a failure as complete as Davison's had been. The Queen found fault with him for not persuading the States into submitting to Don John. On him also fell the indignation of the States at the withholding of the promised bonds, and he was tempted to withdraw in disdain from so ungrateful and unprofitable a service. 'It is given out,' he said in a letter to Randolph, 'that we shall be hanged on our
'return, so ill have we behaved ourselves here: I hope
'we shall enjoy our ordinary trial—my Lord Cobham

---

[1] 'Her Majesty will not believe in the danger. I see plainly that nothing will be done till necessity doth enforce us, and that rather to withstand harm than by any means devise the preventing of it. I pray her Majesty feel not the smart upon the sudden, when it shall be over late to repent. Security and contempt of harm are the right means to lull us to ruin, whereas foresight and provident care do preserve estates in safety. If there be a destiny, who can avoid it?—and yet because things to come are unknown to man, it were good reason so to deal with advice and counsel, as we should not in our judgment be condemned as the very causes of our own destruction through folly.'—*Wilson to Walsingham*, June 21. *MSS. Holland*.

[2] *Leicester to Walsingham*, July 10.—*MSS. Ibid.*

'to be tried by his peers, and myself by a jury of Mid-
'dlesex. I suppose I shall be forced to deal more tem-
'perately in these causes than heretofore I have done;
'and if I may conveniently, I mean, with the leave of
'God, to convey myself off from the stage and to be-
'come a looker on.'

A brief glance at the state of Scotland becomes again
necessary. The Earl of Morton had experienced at
Elizabeth's hands the common treatment of the Reformers everywhere. She had made use of him or tried
to make use of him for her own purposes. When her
negotiations elsewhere broke down, she had flattered and
caressed him. When the necessity passed away she had
shaken him off, refused to help him, refused him countenance and recognition; and had left him to hold his
own ground with his own resources. The restoration
of the Queen of Scots would form a necessary part of
the general settlement which she was labouring to
bring about; and she had as little desire to see the
Scotch Protestants inconveniently strengthened as their

' Walsingham to Randolph, July 29.—*MSS. Holland.*—Sir Francis Knollys, who understood Elizabeth thoroughly, saw deepest into the explanation of her proceedings.

'I know,' he wrote, 'that we must all give place to her Majesty's will and affections in matters that touch not the dangers of her estate; but I know also that if her Majesty does not suppress and subject her own will and her own affections to the sound advice of open Council in matters touching the preventing her dangers, her Majesty will be utterly overthrown. Who will persist in giving safe counsel if her Majesty will persist in misliking safe counsel? Her Majesty's safety consists in

'1. Preventing the conquest of the Low Countries.

'2. Preventing the revolt of Scotland to the French and the Queen of Scots.

'3. Preventing the contemptuous growth of the Papists in England.

'King Richard the Second's men (the parasites and flatterers) have hold of her Majesty. The Lord bless her from their company. The thinking thereon does so abhor me that I am more fit to die in a private life than live a courtier unless a preventing heart enters her Majesty betimes.' *Knollys to Wilson.*—WRIGHT, vol. ii.

brethren who were struggling in the Low Countries. Thus Morton had borne the odium of being a pensioner of England without the benefit of the reality, and it was infinitely to his credit that he resisted the temptations so constantly held out to him by France, and remained true to an alliance which he believed to be the best for his country. Under any circumstances his situation would have been a hard one. The Stewarts, the Campbells, the Gordons, the Hamiltons, unruly under their Kings, saw little to respect in the head of a younger branch of the house of Douglas. His natural supporters were the people and the Reformers; and the people he was driven to offend by taxation, and the Reformers more justly were shocked at the looseness of his private habits.

His character was in many ways remarkable. He was conspicuous in the young band of nobles who had listened to the preaching of Wishart; and though Knox had looked unfavourably upon his wild and lawless life, he had ever been intellectually faithful to the cause which Knox represented. It was Morton who directed the storm which drove Mary from her throne and imprisoned her in Lochleven; and when Murray was murdered, he became, by the mere force that was in him, the inevitable leader of the Protestants. They did not like him, but his firm hand secured them precious time to establish their doctrines throughout the country; and at no time in Scotland's history had order and law been more respected than during the years of Morton's Regency.

In the language of a Protestant writer, ' his regiment ' was considered as happy and peaceable as ever Scotland ' saw; he was wise, stout, and ever on the best side. ' The name of Papist durst not be heard of, nor no thief 'or oppressor durst be seen.'[1] And yet he had not pleased his party. His crime with the nobles was that he was English and Protestant; his crime with the Protestants, 'that he could not suffer Christ to reign 'freely, and that he misliked the General Assembly; 'that in conformity with England,' of which they too were jealous, 'he had put forward bishops,' in the hope of pleasing Elizabeth, 'and would have stayed the 'work of God, if God had not stirred up a faction 'of the nobility against him.'[2] 'The faction of the 'nobility' bore a worse will to the 'work of God' than Morton; as, before long, those interested in it found. He was not, like Murray or the Prince of Orange, supported by a consciousness of rectitude and unblemished integrity. His youth was spotted with blood; his middle life was very far from blameless: yet he was truer to the good cause than many a more faultless man. Surrounded by a thousand enemies, he overcame danger by despising it. He astonished the citizens of Edinburgh by appearing among them at all hours and times unarmed and unattended, and though half the Catholics in Scotland were conspiring against his life, he might be seen wandering alone with his fishing rod in the Valley of the Esk.

In the correspondence of the Queen of Scots, and in the letters of Catholic ambassadors, he appears always as the object of a peculiar hatred. He had custody of the person of the young king, and governed his education. He prevented the Catholic nobles from approaching him, and from forming parties to disturb the quiet of the realm. He was, or he was believed to be, the main obstacle which prevented France and Spain from gaining a hold on Scotland, and Scotland was the

---

[1] Calderwood.   [2] Ibid.

open gate into England. Elizabeth became aware of his value when her own safety was threatened. On the revocation of the Edict of toleration by the Estates at Blois, and the flight of Don John to Namur, she received and acknowledged with gratitude a warning which Morton addressed to her.[1] When the crusade against heretics became active, when the Catholic powers appeared to make no distinction between herself and them, she became willing to claim his assistance. She admitted ' that greater care should be had for a ' combination between the princes of the religion.'[2] She let Burghley advise her ' to stablish the King's estate ' in quietness, to spare no reasonable charges, to assure ' Scotland to herself, and to prevent the practices of ' France and Spain.'[3]

But emotions of this kind died away with the report of Philip's courtesies to Sir John Smith in Spain. The Queen of Scots believed that Elizabeth allowed Morton ten thousand pounds a year.[4] She allowed him nothing, and she allowed nothing to those other noblemen, whom the Regent, though he was himself passed over, had so often recommended to her care. The French were more liberal, and their liberality produced its effect. Contributions collected in France and Italy were freely poured into Scotland by the Duke of Guise and the Archbishop of Glasgow, and at the end of the year 1577, the Queen's party which had been broken up at the fall of the Castle, with others who preferred full to empty purses, formed themselves into a confederacy to overthrow the Regent and restore the

---

[1] Elizabeth to the Earl of Morton, Feb. 26, 1577.—MSS. Scotland.
[2] Ibid.
[3] Notes in Burghley's hand.—MSS. Ibid. 1577.
[4] Mary Stuart to the Archbishop of Glasgow, Nov. 5, 1577.—LABANOFF, vol. iv.

French alliance. Argyle,[1] who inherited his brother's dislike of England, and Athol, who notwithstanding his conformity in 1573, remained a Catholic, were its first leaders. They pretended grievances of their own without betraying their further purpose. They called their clans under arms; and when the Regent invited them to produce their complaints legally before a court of justice, they refused. Uncertain what this new movement meant, Elizabeth thought as usual of holding a balance between the two parties. She sent Morton a present of jewels. She professed herself ready to make the league which she had refused four years before.[2] But she ordered him peremptorily to make up his differences with Argyle and Athol; she threatened, if he attempted to use force against them, herself to take the part of the Earls.[3]

So ambiguous an interposition was worse than inaction. It tied the Regent's hands, and directly encouraged the revolt, although that revolt was directed not primarily against Morton, but against heresy and the English alliance; and the result expected and hoped for by the Queen of Scots and her friends was, that Morton would be disgusted at last, and would become French like the rest.[4] So far he disappointed their hopes; but he saw that he was not to be supported, and that for the present he had no choice but to yield. Ruthven, Lindsay, Dunfermline, even George Buchanan and the burghers of Edinburgh had for one

---

[1] Colin, sixth Earl, brother of Archibald, who died in 1575.

[2] 'Remembering an overture made by the Regent, A° 1574, for a mutual league between the countries for the defence of our common religion, you shall now endeavour to further the same as much as you possibly can.'—*Instructions to Randolph*, Jan. 30, 1578. *MSS. Scotland*.

[3] *Ibid.*

[4] Mary Stuart to the Archbishop of Glasgow, April 10, 1578.—LABANOFF, vol. v.

cause or another turned against him. The Earls advanced to Stirling, and took possession unopposed of the castle and the government.

It was decided that James being now twelve years old, should be held to have attained his majority, and that the Regency should cease. Morton resigned without objection, and retired to Lochleven Castle, while the anomalous confederates who had overthrown him came on with the King to Edinburgh to organise a new administration. Having accomplished the only object which they were agreed in desiring, they of course quarrelled among themselves. The General Assembly snatched the moment to vote away the bishops and make demonstrations against the Roman beast. Glamys the Chancellor was killed in a brawl by the Earl of Crawford;—as Randolph expressed it, 'all the 'devils in hell were stirring.'[1] At length a council of twelve was chosen out of the two factions. Argyle and Athol became the virtual rulers, and sent word of their success to Paris.

The opportunity so long waited for appeared to have arrived at last. To rescue the Queen of Scots, punish Elizabeth, and revolutionise England, was the sleeping and waking dream of the princes of the house of Lorraine. The Archbishop of Glasgow opened the subject with the Spanish ambassador in Paris, Don Juan de Vargas, and a few days later the Duke of Guise came in person to tell De Vargas that he had almost obtained his Sovereign's consent to his attempting 'the enterprise 'of England.' Scotland was now open. An army could be collected at Calais, and in three days landed at Leith. If Don John might co-operate, ten thousand Germans

---

[1] Randolph to Killegrew, March 20.—*MSS. Scotland.*

might be shipped simultaneously at Gravelines, and the Queen of England would receive merited chastisement for her crimes against the commonwealth of Christendom. 'The Duke,' wrote Vargas, in reporting the conversation to Philip, 'insisted much on the ease with 'which the thing might be done.' 'He was aware, he 'said, that your Majesty would have interfered long ago, 'but for France, as France would have interfered but 'for your Majesty. He trusts that you will now unite, 'and give the law—as you will be able to do—to the 'world. You can divide England between yourselves. 'His Holiness will make a third, and arrange the terms 'of partition.'[1]

The slow Philip ruminated after his fashion on the bold proposal: not liking it, yet not absolutely rejecting it. Vargas, whom Guise had inoculated with his own impatience, spurred his sluggish resolution. In successive letters, he urged that Elizabeth would interfere; that with one of her thousand tricks she would get the King of Scots into her power; that with the help of the heretics there she would make herself sovereign of the whole island, and Flanders would then be unconquerable.[2]

Philip's answer, when it came, illustrated and explained the failures of his whole career. He understood Elizabeth. He knew that he had nothing to fear from promptitude of action with her: but neither then nor ever could he understand that there were forces working in Europe beyond the pleasure of Kings and Queens and Princes. Every lost moment was a lost chance, yet he replied only that he would think over Guise's proposal. It involved grave consequences, and

---

[1] Don Juan de Vargas to Philip, April 13.—TEULET, vol. v.

[2] Vargas to Philip, August 17, 26, 1578.—TEULET, vol. v.

in a matter of such moment he must proceed with a foot of lead.¹

'I will tell you the plain truth,' said the Archbishop of Glasgow to the Ambassador, 'you are so long in 'resolving, and you apply your remedies so slowly, that 'I know not what to say to you. Affairs like these 'require expedition. Words will not conquer empires, 'you must seize the time when it comes and act.'²

The chance offered in Scotland was gone before Philip had comprehended its existence, and Guise had not dared to move without his explicit permission. The intention of the two Earls could not long be concealed, and the Protestants who had taken part against Morton soon repented of their mistake. Lindsay and Ruthven secured the Castle of Edinburgh. The King had been taken back to Stirling, in the care of Sir Alexander Erskine, the Regent Mar's Catholic brother. The head of the Erskines' house was the hereditary Chatelain, and the young Earl of Mar, a boy of twenty, devoted to Morton, made his way into the Castle, and half playfully, half by force, declared himself of age, and challenged possession of his inheritance. His uncle gave way. Morton, whose day was supposed to be over, came up from Lochleven, and once more had the King in his hands.

A parliament was called immediately. The Protestant nobles attended, and with the alarmed burgesses declared for their old leader. Argyle and Athol stayed away, not daring to show themselves, and Morton was again master of the situation. His power he well knew could be but of short duration if he was left as before; but he concluded that Elizabeth would

---

¹ 'Y como es de tanto momento y consequencia, conviene caminar en él con el pié de plomo.'—*Philip to Var-gas*, Oct. 27, 1578. TEULET, vol. v.

² Vargas to Philip, Dec. 13.—TEULET, vol. v.

have by this time learnt the importance of Scotland to her; and he sent the Abbot of Dunfermline to England on the spot, with detailed proposals for the league which, before the late change, she had desired. It was at the moment when her ill-humour with the Low Countries was at its height; and instead of welcoming Morton's recovery of power, it seemed only to increase her irritation. Several weeks passed before she could resolve whether the Abbot should be admitted to her presence; she told Heneage 'it was against her heart' to entertain as an ambassador the representative of a government of 'rebels,'[1] and meanwhile he was detained with his companions at York.

At length she made up her mind to see him. She was on her summer progress, and he came to her at Audley End, in Essex. The propositions of which he was the bearer were more favourable than any English Sovereign had ever extorted at the sword's point. 'The 'King,' for the message ran in his name, 'having as- 'sumed the government in his own hands,' was prepared to ratify at last the long debated Treaty of Leith, to unite with England in a defensive alliance against the malice of the Pope and his friends, to be the enemy of England's enemies, of all foreign powers who sought to injure the Queen, and of those among his own subjects that were lending themselves to any such designs. On the other side the Abbot explained the poverty of the Scotch treasury. The King was unable to maintain his own state, far less to support the Border police. For the welfare of the two countries, for the sake of their future friendship, for the maintenance of the common religion, and the support of the party who, through good

---

[1] Tremayne to Walsingham, July 29, 1578.—*MSS. Holland.*

and evil, had stood firm to the English alliance, the Abbot besought Elizabeth to deal liberally, and secure the King's gratitude.

There was one obvious mode in which the Queen could satisfy James's expectations at no cost to herself. Lady Lennox had died in the preceding March. The King of Scots, as Darnley's son, was the natural heir to the estates which Henry VIII. had granted to his grandfather, and which the Countess had enjoyed till her death. The rents, amounting to five or six thousand pounds a year, would cover all the demands, and supply the modest necessities of the Scotch Crown. To grant such a request as this was on the surface no more than justice. But there was more meant by it than appeared. To admit that an alien could inherit land in England, would concede one point at least on which the lawyers contested the Scotch succession, and doubtless Morton and his friends had not overlooked this particular feature in the case. By ratifying the Leith treaty, the King relinquished all claims which could be advanced either by himself or his mother during Elizabeth's life, nor did he ask for a distinct recognition of his prospective right afterwards; but it was an opportunity for her to satisfy indirectly the passionate aspiration of all parties in Scotland, and in so satisfying them remove the causes which had so often given her enemies an advantage. It would have been easy for her, without mentioning James in words, to have attached conditions of creed by Act of Parliament to the succession to the throne. If the Scotch aristocracy saw the English crown before them so conditioned, their Protestantism would be all the more assured; and James, growing to manhood, dependent for half his revenue on England, and for his prospects on his staunchness in the faith, would have been proof against all temptations from his mother and her French relations.

But the mention of a successor always drove Elizabeth frantic. Her metaphor of 'the rising sun' lost its point from perpetual iteration; while to burden the succession with the condition of Protestantism would destroy the foundation on which she most relied for her personal security. Mary Stuart claimed before her son, and Mary Stuart's rights she determined to negatively maintain. She did not mean to recognise her, but far less would she consent to religious limitation by which the expectations of the Catholics would be extinguished. She meant to keep the Catholics and Mary Stuart on her good behaviour. The request for the estates set her at once in fierce antagonism. The Abbot implored her to be reasonable. If the law was uncertain, he proposed that the lands should be sequestrated, and the rents and profits made over to the King, to maintain a guard about his person and pay the Border police. The King himself was notoriously unable to do either. He had many enemies, the Abbot said, and was exposed to violent attacks; were there no other motive for liberality, the Queen would find herself well rewarded, if she silenced those who told him that her good will never went beyond '*words*.' The estates in equity were the King's; if she would neither let him have them nor give him an equivalent, there would be serious discontent throughout Scotland.[1]

Had the Queen replied that to grant the rents would prejudge the claim, but that she would allow the King an equal sum in the name of a pension, even this offer would have been thankfully accepted. The King would have been satisfied, the profits of the lands would have been

[1] Negotiations of the Abbot of Dunfermline, July 1578.—*MSS. Scotland.*

paid into her own treasury, as in fact they were, and she would have parted with nothing that belonged to her: but she did not choose to have it said of her that she was supporting a government unrecognised by the rest of Europe. She had spent money enough on Scotland, she answered, and she would spend no more. Even her inclination to the League had once more vanished. She did not absolutely refuse it, but she rejected every one of the conditions which would make it palatable to the Scots: and she sent Dunfermline back with a reply, which was the prelude to a fresh series of revolutions, which sent Morton before long to the scaffold, and to herself brought fit retribution in years of anxiety and danger.

What she was about, what secret scheme she was herself revolving in playing thus into the hands of her enemies, the most sagacious of her advisers were unable to divine. 'We have had much ado,' wrote Burghley, 'to bring her Majesty to accept such offers from the 'Scottish King and his nobles to commit themselves to 'the protection of her Majesty, which all other Kings of 'this realm have sought by all means both fair and 'foul, and could never attain the same. A strange 'thing it is, to see God's goodness so abundantly offered 'for her Majesty's surety to be so daintily hearkened 'unto. Yet I trust her Majesty will not reject such a 'singular favour of God. I am sorry to write thus un- 'comfortably, but indeed the abundance of grief will 'not suffer my hand to stay.'[1]

'The more favours offered,' said Doctor Wilson, 'the 'greater is our negligence, and the less mind have we 'to take the benefit of occasion prescribed and laid 'open before us. Except God have ordained by His

---

[1] Burghley to Walsingham, July 29, 1578.—*MSS. Holland.*

'eternal will a necessity—a fatal destiny not to be
'avoided—things could not go as they do. *Fatum
'regit mundum*, or rather will beareth sway instead of
'reason.'[1]

To return to the relations with the Netherlands.

The bonds could not be had. No persuasion, no reproach, no picture of the dishonour which she was bringing upon herself, could move the determination of the Queen. She stood at bay, fenced in by obstinacy, like a sullen dog. Duke Casimir had come with his Reiters, as she had proposed and desired. When the English army was kept at home, it was with a distinct undertaking that she was subsidising Casimir in their place: and young Philip Sidney, beginning now to have a taste for martial glory, was going over to take service with him as a volunteer. He came to Audley End while the Scots were still there, to take leave of his mistress.

'Amongst other cold comforts, she bade him tell
'Casimir that she marvelled and was offended with him
'that he did give out that his coming was by her means;
'and that she misliked such speeches, and prayed her
'name might not be so abused since she commanded him
'not to come, and the States entertained him.'[2] Sidney refused to carry such a monstrous message, or to go to the Netherlands at all on such conditions. 'I had rather,' said his uncle Leicester, describing the scene to Walsingham, 'I had rather he perished in the sea than be
'the instrument of such discouragement. Both you
'and I, and almost all men, know the cause of Casimir's
'coming.'[3]

---

[1] Wilson to Walsingham, July 29, 1578.—*MSS. Holland.*
[2] Leicester to Walsingham, Aug. 1, 1578.—*MSS. Holland.*
[3] *Ibid.*

Sussex, an Anglican of the semi-Catholic type, conservative, Spanish, and hating revolutionists—even Sussex joined in the universal disapproval. He supposed, perhaps with justice, that Elizabeth was entertaining some crooked notion that by letting things take their course, and by giving no offence to the great powers, she might save herself for her own time, whatever ultimately came of it. 'It resteth in God,' he wrote, 'to dispose her 'Majesty's heart as shall please him. Surely whoever 'shall think by device to put over matters for a time 'for the benefit of her person, although perhaps the 'same may be hurtful to England, and thereby divide 'the good of her from the good of the realm, shall in 'the end both deceive her and the realm. It is good 'to put over time when it bringeth good effects; but to 'put over time when that only overthroweth all things 'is the most dangerous matter that may be.'[1]

The States had by this time lost patience. Casimir's troops, which Elizabeth had undertaken to pay, were breaking into mutiny. The Prince of Orange would wait no longer, and it was announced in England, that the French treaty was on the point of conclusion, and that Alençon would immediately take the field. The Queen, as we have seen, had herself privately sanctioned Alençon's movement, but about this too it seemed that she had changed her mind. She bade Burghley direct Walsingham to go immediately to him, and require him in her name to desist. The States, she said, must indemnify him by a sum of money for his trouble and expense, but go back he must. Burghley took the message from her dictation, but did not send it. The next day she enquired angrily why it was not gone.

---

[1] Sussex to Walsingham, Aug. 6.—*MSS. Holland.*

He answered that 'to move Monsieur to depart without
'some other motion than bare words was unreasonable
'and dishonourable.' She persisted, and he dared her
displeasure by speaking out a disagreeable truth. 'I
'told her Majesty with some weight,' he said, 'that the
'whole world would condemn her if the Low Countries
'should be joined to France, which by helping the
'States she might have stayed; and yet in the end
'have pleasured the King of Spain against his will
'with restoring his countries.'[1]

Elizabeth has been credited and will continue to be
credited with political sagacity, on the strength of her
general success. Political sagacity implies some positive policy, and some consistency in following it. The
policy which ultimately triumphed was that of her
Council, which she was perpetually thwarting. If she
was consistent, she was consistent only in mutability.
There was to be one more violent gyration.

On the 8th of August, she was repudiating her promises, withholding her bonds obstinately, and in every
way refusing to assist the States either against France or
Spain. On the 9th, a courier was flying to Yarmouth, carrying a message which was instantly to be dispatched to
Walsingham, that 'if they would break off their dealings
'with Monsieur, they should have a hundred thousand
'pounds upon the spot; she would send Leicester to
'them immediately with twelve thousand men.'[2] The
revolution of sentiment, as brief as it was complete, was
occasioned by the news of the battle of Rymenant. The
patriots had hitherto been uniformly unsuccessful in the
field. On the 1st of August, Don John had again at-

---

[1] Burghley to Walsingham, Aug. 8.—*MSS. Holland.*
[2] Burghley to Cobham and Walsingham, Aug. 9. Wilson to Walsingham, Aug. 9.—*MSS. Holland.*

tacked them at an advantage, expecting a second Gemblours. The States troops broke as before, but Col. Norris with three thousand English stood his ground; and after a fierce engagement, in which he had himself three horses killed under him, the Spaniards fell back, leaving a thousand dead upon the field. The courage of her subjects for a moment infected the Queen. 'Her 'Majesty became suddenly minded without all scruple 'to offer aid. So long as the Spaniards were victors, 'and were not confronted with so orderly a skirmish 'as now they have been by Colonel Norris, neither 'could her Majesty be drawn nor wholly counselled to 'offer such aid, but now it was somewhat apparent that 'the Spaniards were no such devils.'[1]

But Burghley knew his mistress too well to believe that the new humour would hold. 'Though this,' he said, 'be for the present earnestly meant, I can assure 'nothing but this only, that I am here uncertain of 'much.'[2] Walsingham shared his misgivings, and saw that there was not a moment to be lost. The treaty of the States with Alençon was signed. If the war continued, Monsieur was indisputably about to take part in it, and France itself was likely to follow. The States being now in a position to insist, refused to listen to terms which did not include liberty of worship. The English ambassadors taking advantage of the defeat of Rymenant, went to Don John to try to persuade him to acquiesce, and to save Europe from a general war. The conditions were hard; they would leave Spain in the United Provinces no more than a titular sovereignty. Walsingham reminded Don John of the Peace of Passau.

---

[1] Knollys to Walsingham, Aug. 10.—*MSS. Holland*.

[2] Burghley to Cobham and Walsingham, Aug. 9.—*MSS. Ibid.*

But Don John was at no such extremity as Charles had been at his flight from Innspruck. No one, he said, could desire peace more than he desired it, but if he was a prisoner in Brussels, he would refuse stipulations so disgraceful.[1] The interview failed. The war was to go on, and Walsingham returned to Antwerp, to find letters informing him that the hot fit of his mistress's ague had gone off. No Leicester was coming and no army. She had persuaded herself for reasons presently to be explained, that 'she could direct the course of the 'States' without spending money; and she had relapsed positively and decisively into her previous humour, amidst a chorus of lamentation from the Council. 'Fatal 'destiny,' exclaimed Doctor Wilson; 'no persuasion 'will prevail; if neither the States are our friends, and 'we do not secure Monsieur, we are to lean to our 'known enemies the Spaniards—the lamb to be com- 'mitted to the wolf.'[2]

'Neither counsel nor forecast can prevail,' said Sir T. Heneage, 'if we prosper it must be as our custom is, 'by miracle. Our old humours do not grow weak by 'age, but increase by nourishment, and he is not a 'courtier six days but can learn how to make himself 'acceptable.'

'A lamentable resolution in the end,' echoed the personally disappointed Leicester, 'to her and her poor 'realm.'[3]

One concession only was wrung from her. The

---

[1] Walsingham was much struck with Don John. 'In conference with him,' he said, 'I might easily discern a great conflict in himself, between honour and necessity. Surely, I never saw a gentleman for personage, speech, wit, and entertainment comparable to him. If pride do not overthrow him, he is like to prove a great personage.'— *Walsingham to Burghley*, Aug. 27. *MSS. Holland.*

[2] Wilson to Walsingham, Aug. 29.—*MSS. Holland.*

[3] Heneage and Leicester to Walsingham, Aug. 29.—*MSS. Ibid.*

CHAP. XXVI.
1578
August.

Cologne bankers, heavy discount as they had exacted from the uncertainty of the English security, nevertheless held Cobham and Walsingham responsible for the Queen's engagements, and they found themselves threatened with arrest. Under this pressure the bonds were issued, and were eventually redeemed. They were not sent over, however, till the States had placed the crown jewels of the house of Burgundy in Elizabeth's hands for security, nor till they had again bound themselves to repay immediately the original forty thousand pounds which she had first lent them. Burghley pleaded hard to obtain for them a longer respite; 'But though 'her Majesty shewed no reasons to move her to persist, 'she said she would have it:' 'her pleasure,' he added, writing to Walsingham, 'comes upon many evil conceits 'secretly put into her of the States there, by such as 'went over with you and are returned, that do sting 'all profession of good religion.'[1]

For the rest, all her direct dealings with the Netherlands were now closed. She no longer recognised their political existence. Her concern in their future fortunes was to depend on her influence over Alençon, and if Alençon proved unmanageable, she meant to fall back on Spain. Her resolution was formally communicated to the States: the bitter expressions with which it was accompanied Walsingham declined to deliver, 'perceiving,' as he frankly told her, 'that such 'speeches would add an increase of grief to their wounded 'minds, who, laying their necessities before her High-'ness, instead of relief should receive reprehension.'[2]

'If,' wrote Walsingham to Hatton, whom he perhaps suspected of encouraging Elizabeth, 'if it be good to 'have these countries possessed by France, and alienated

[1] Burghley to Walsingham, Aug. 11.—MSS. Holland.
[2] Cobham and Walsingham to Elizabeth, Sept. 14.—MURDIN.

'from England, then have you returned Mr. Somers,' (the Queen's messenger) 'with a good dispatch; if 'nothing can be worse than such a resolution, then you 'have committed an irreparable error. These people 'will depend no more on you and your uncertainties. 'Her Majesty will never more have the like opportunity. 'Seeing how you have acted with Scotland, I am the less 'surprised, but from both causes I have occasion to think 'there hangs over us some fearful storm.'[1]

More confidentially, in reply to a letter from Burghley, he said, 'As you write, he had need to be furnished with 'patience that shall deal in such service as we are 'employed in, being almost ashamed to shew our faces 'abroad. Besides the alienation of these people's hearts, 'which cannot but be perilous both to herself and her 'realm, it will render her Highness hateful to the world. 'To have all the world your enemies at once! It is 'greatly to be doubted you will return Monsieur's 'ministers unsatisfied; and then I know not any prince 'whose friendship you may assure yourself of. Navarre 'and Condé will learn by your dealings with the States 'here what they are to look for in the time of their 'necessity. As for Casimir he doth curse the time that 'ever he departed out of his country, finding her Majesty 'deal so coldly and grow so hateful to this people, and 'he himself for her sake the less esteemed. The mischief 'grows irreparable through distrust of the performance 'of that which hereafter may be promised for their 'relief.'[2]

Strange as Elizabeth's manœuvres appeared, they were but exaggerated specimens of her usual habits, and the explanation when it came was no less strikingly

---

[1] Walsingham to Hatton, Sept. 9.—Wright, vol. ii.   [2] Walsingham to Burghley, Sept. 9.—MSS. Holland.

characteristic. It appeared that the French ambassador, knowing that she detested the course into which events were forcing her, had suggested—unknown to Burghley or to any one—that there was a cheap and easy escape for her. The much talked of Alençon was still uncommitted to matrimony, still eager, if she would have him, to forget her ill-treatment and become the partner of her throne. The nature of him was by this time known to every one. He was an adventurer, uneasy at home, and anxious only for an independent position of some kind. He had been Huguenot after the massacre. He afterwards made his peace with the Court, and on the revocation of the Edict, he had shewn his penitence by presiding over the destruction of a Huguenot town. He had planned with Guise an invasion of Scotland. He had been a suitor since his last rejection by Elizabeth for a Spanish princess, and the Pope to further so useful an alliance had offered him a pension of 40,000 crowns, and had suggested that he should succeed Don John in the Low Countries as Philip's representative.[1] He had been trained by his mother in the art of lying,[2] and there was cause to believe that even now in his negotiations with the Prince of Orange he was playing false, that he might after all carry his twelve thousand men to Don John, assist him in the overthrow of the Provinces, and then perhaps resume his earlier project and go to Scotland with Guise.[3]

Whether Elizabeth ever seriously thought of becoming the wife of such a man was a question which those who best knew her were least able to answer. Persons at a distance, like Philip of Spain, who judged

---

[1] Sir Amyas Paulet to Elizabeth, Oct. 7, 1578.—*MSS. France.*
[2] *Ibid.*
[3] Mary Stuart certainly expected this. See her letter to the Archbishop of Glasgow, Sept. 15, 1578.—LABANOFF.

her by her past actions, pronounced unhesitatingly that she was merely pretending.[1] The ladies of the bedchamber told the Queen of Scots that she turned her lover and his expectations into ridicule. She may have been a deliberate deceiver, or she may have been one of those more accomplished artists who keep their ultimate determinations in a dark corner of their minds, which they prefer not to examine; and imagine that they mean, or may mean, or will hereafter mean, what they do not mean at all.

At any rate the last and most remarkable chapter of the matrimonial adventures of Queen Elizabeth is now about to open. It has been seen that when she seemed in greatest alarm about Alençon's entrance into the Netherlands, she had nevertheless given him leave on certain conditions; and Mauvissière had been allowed to intimate that her Majesty was not beyond his reach, and that if he would send over a confidential minister such a person would be favourably received. Accordingly on the 30th July, when her ill-humour with the States was at its height, there had arrived at Audley End 'two gentlemen from Monsieur,' one of them a Huguenot, M. de Quissey; the other a M. Bacqueville, described by Burghley as 'not malicious.' No one knew that they had been sent for. They came as if spontaneously sent by Alençon to remove Elizabeth's objections to his interference in the war, to promise that in his dealings with the Provinces he would be guided entirely by her advice—and at the same time to renew his proposals for her hand, and to tell her that if she wished to see him he would come to her from Antwerp.[2] The Court and Council were taken utterly by surprise. Nothing that

---

[1] 'Todo es embuste y entretenimiento.'

[2] Leicester to Walsingham, Aug. 1.—MSS. Holland.

they had seen in Elizabeth led them to suppose that she would listen to the Duke's suit.

'Her Majesty,' said Leicester, 'is persuaded that 'Monsieur will obey her pleasure, and she doubts not 'will return as he came. If she meant that recompense 'for his labour that his ministers sue for, there were cause 'for her to presume—but I do not perceive any such 'reward like to come from hence for anything I see yet; 'I rather fear some great unkindness to grow between 'them.'[1]

The Queen, perhaps, fancied at first that she could humour Monsieur as she had humoured him before, excite his hopes till his resources were spent, and then once more let him drop: and it may have been with this view that she dictated the message to him which Burghley refused to send. Then followed the interval of valour called out by Norris's victory, which so soon cooled again. Yet still, so far as Leicester could observe, she was no nearer 'to the satisfying of Monsieur's 'expectations.' She was 'persuaded of her ability to 'direct him to her liking,' but Leicester could not conjecture on what ground. He supposed, and Walsingham agreed with him, that at most there might be some paltry trifling between them, which would end in vapour.[2]

The matter, however, had gone deeper than Leicester, or Walsingham, or even Burghley suspected. A few weeks after the arrival of De Quissey and Bacqueville, there came a formal letter from Paris intimating the King's approval of his brother's suit;[3] and Sussex, whom the Queen took into her confidence, had a long conver-

---

[1] Leicester to Walsingham, Aug. 1.—*MSS. Holland.*
[2] Leicester to Walsingham, Aug. 19. Walsingham to Burghley, Aug. 27.—*MSS. Holland.*
[3] The Lords of the Council to Sir Amyas Paulet, Sept. 5.—*MSS. France.*

sation with De Quissey, probably at his mistress's desire. De Quissey was perfectly frank. Monsieur, he said, was ill-used at home, and it was necessary for him to seek greatness abroad, to secure his prospective interests in France. Having engaged in his present enterprise, he could not now abandon it and return home having effected nothing. He had made up his mind to marry the Queen of England, or the Low Countries, or both. The King and his mother would assist him in obtaining either or all of these objects; they desired only to be rid of him out of France: and if Elizabeth thwarted him, 'he would turn over all his forces to Don John and 'seek surety by the friendship of Spain.' This was his position, acknowledged without attempt at disguise, and Sussex formed a distinct idea that Monsieur's offer ought to be at once accepted. A marriage with him would give stability to the alliance with France, and would assure substantial toleration for the Huguenots. If children came of it, the succession would be settled, and either Philip would have to make peace with the Provinces on their own terms, or else Elizabeth and Alençon could occupy them together, and annex them without danger to the English crown. 'Thus,' Sussex said to her, 'you will give the law to the world, and 'settle your estate at home. You will be a serpent to 'the evil, and a dove to the good; you will be the 'peace-maker of Christendom, and God will bless you.'

Against these advantages were to be set Elizabeth's general dislike of marriage, and probably of Alençon in particular. Englishmen detested strangers, and especially detested the French. Alençon might become King of France, and if there was one child and no more the crowns might be united to England's injury. Possibly also, as had been suggested when Alençon's brother, the present King, had been her suitor, 'Monsieur might but 'fraudulently seek her first,' to make away with her by unkindness, and then marry her younger rival the Queen of Scots. It seemed, however, like treason to suspect a Christian prince of such a wicked purpose, 'nor was 'there sense nor likelihood,' Sussex said, 'that a prince 'possessed of her godly, virtuous, wise, beautiful, and 'peerless person would seek another so far inferior.' England stood at present in great and obvious danger, which in some way or other must be encountered. France would either annex the Netherlands, and with this vantage recover Scotland, and ultimately ruin England, or Alençon would join Don John as he threatened. The Prince of Orange would then be destroyed, and Spanish despotism become supreme.[1]

The flattery with which Sussex set aside the peril from the charms of the Queen of Scots showed his eagerness to persuade his mistress. From the beginning of the reign, he had been constant to the opinion that marriage only could save her throne. She did not pretend that she desired it. She nourished a hope that under cover of courtship, she might make some political alliance with Alençon, which would answer equally well.[2] But Sussex would not encourage what he believed to be a vain expectation. 'In regno nulla est societas,' he wrote to Walsingham. 'Alençon is said to be dealing sin- 'cerely, and looks to be sincerely dealt with;' 'he looks 'to be great by her Majesty in the Low Countries, and 'it would be dishonour and peril to him to return home 'without either one or the other. What it shall please 'her to do is in the hands of God; but for my part, I 'see no manifest surety to her Majesty, but either by

---

[1] Sussex to Elizabeth, Aug. 18, 1578.—LODGE.

[2] Sussex to Walsingham, Aug. 29. MSS. Holland.

'marriage, or by a peace, or by taking the States to her
'defence, whereby she must make herself Head of the
'Name.[1] Of peace there is little chance. To be Head of
'the Name is more than I fear she can go through withal,
'or the world will maintain. Marriage is the surest, for
'thereby she may give law to herself and her neighbours,
'and avoid perils at home and abroad, knit herself in
'amity with both kings, and keep them both in bounds.'[2]

The late variation of the Queen had been the index of her personal uncertainty, whether to marry or not. She had yielded, when she sent away the Abbot of Dunfermline. She had resisted again when Norris's success promised a safe road of escape. Then she had once more given way, glad at all events to be rid of the present necessity of spending money, knowing that a matrimonial treaty would take time, that the knot could be slipped at the last moment, as she had many times experienced, that while the negotiations lasted, and while she was believed to be sincere, she would be safe from molestation on the side of France, and that Spain would hesitate to countenance the enterprises of the Duke of Guise.

Thus on the 5th of September, M. Bacqueville was sent for to receive her answer. Burghley, Leicester, and Hatton, only were present at the reception. The Queen said she could not but thank the Duke for renewing his addresses to her, although she observed with some sharpness, as if to disclaim the fault for herself, they had been intermitted for two years. For answer she could but repeat what she had said many times to princes who had aspired to her hand. She could not promise to marry any one whom she had not first seen.

---

[1] *i.e.* Head of a Protestant confederation.

[2] Sussex to Walsingham, Aug. 29. *MSS. Holland.*

It might be that after having seen the Duke she could not accept him, and if his rejection would then be taken as an affront, she could not ask him to come over. If however, his protestations were sincere, if he intended to remain her friend at all events, whether now as Duke of Alençon, or hereafter it might be as King of France, whether as her husband or a brother sovereign, she would then be most happy to receive and welcome him in England. She bade him consult his friends, do nothing hastily, and act on mature advice. If on their becoming acquainted a liking sprung up between them, the course would then be plain. If not, no offence was intended, and no offence must be taken. These were her conditions. Should the Duke after hearing them be disposed to visit her, she wished him to come privately without noise or ostentation.[1]

'I cannot tell,' wrote Burghley, in relating what had passed, 'how Bacqueville doth understand this; but I 'know how I should understand it if I were in his place. 'I would be very loath to provoke my master to come 'over upon such an uncertain answer. The will of God 'be done to her comfort and her poor realm, that cannot 'but suffer much either by not marrying or by a 'husband.'[2]

The foreign policy of England on which the fate of Europe depended, was thus once more converted into a speculation, which, if address and management be in themselves evidence of statesmanship, entitles Elizabeth to a first place among politicians. She fed the hopes of her lover with a prospect which was for ever dancing before his eyes, receding when he tried to grasp it, yet receding so little that with the next effort he felt assured of his prize. In the art which in meaner persons is

---

[1] Her Majesty's answer to Bacqueville, Sept. 7.—*MSS. Holland.*
[2] Burghley to Walsingham, Sept. 8.—*MSS. Holland.*

called coquetry, the Queen had no rival past, present, or to come. For three years she held the heir of the French crown hanging in expectation upon her pleasure. For all that time she suspended the public action of France in the diplomacy of Europe. If the Low Countries were torn asunder, if the Belgian provinces were lost to Protestantism and freedom, if Ghent became the prey of mobs, if Maestrecht was taken by the Spaniards, and out of forty thousand inhabitants a few hundreds only escaped alive, Elizabeth laid up money for the day of her own trial, and postponed for a few years the time when she too would have to fight for her crown.

Miracles, meanwhile, such as her ministers looked for to supply her shortcomings, providences, happy accidents—events which those who profit by them trace to divine interposition, careless how they may affect the interest of other millions of mankind,—such miracles as these continued steadily to befriend her. On the 1st of October Don John of Austria died—died suddenly: poisoned, some said, either by Philip, or by the States, or by an emissary of Walsingham's; worn out as others conjectured, by anxiety, disappointment, and his brother's suspicions; killed more likely by the plague which was making havoc in his army at the time. At all events he died, and with him passed away the schemes for his marriage with Lord Shrewsbury's prisoner, which, however visionary, had disquieted England and Scotland, and had for years been the passionate dream of English conspirators. The prospects of the Low Countries were not improved, for his place was at once more ably supplied by his cousin, Alexander of Parma, who had no personal ambition to distract his activity, and who gave himself with undivided resolution to the work immediately before him.

But England was delivered from a neighbour, who was a perpetual suggestion of revolt.

As important, or even more important, was the result of a battle in the interior of Africa. Sebastian, the young King of Portugal, was at war with Abdulmelech, Emperor of Morocco. Tempted by the promises of two tributary Moorish Kings, he planned an expedition into the enemy's country, and while fitting out his fleet at Lisbon, there arrived in the Tagus, Sir Thomas Stukeley, who, finding Philip grown cold to him, had applied with better success to the Vatican, and had obtained means from Gregory for the invasion of Ireland. Stukeley had 800 Italian soldiers with him, well found and armed; but the vessels in which he brought them round from the Mediterranean were unseaworthy. He put into Lisbon for repairs, and Sebastian tempted him, perhaps with promises of further assistance on his return from Africa, to suspend his Irish enterprise and accompany the Portuguese to Morocco. Common enemies make common friends. When war was expected with Spain, in the preceding year, Elizabeth had made allies of the Moors. She sent an ambassador to Abdulmelech with presents, which were eagerly received. The questionable connexion was coloured by a good report of his Majesty's religion;[1] and Abdulmelech, fighting Elizabeth's battles as well as his own, met Sebastian at

---

[1] 'The King received me with high honour, and promises to be your Majesty's good friend. He tells me the King of Spain had sent to beg him not to receive any one coming from England; "but," said the King, "I make more account of your coming from England than of any from Spain. That King cannot govern his country, but is governed by the Pope and the Inquisition." I find the King an earnest Protestant, of good religion and living, well experimented as well in the Old Testament as the New, and bearing great affection to God's true religion used in your Highness's realm.'— *Edmund Hogan to Elizabeth*, June 11, 1577. ELLIS, 3rd series, vol. iv. p. 21.

Alcazar, on the 4th of August. The Emperor fell, but Sebastian fell also, and the Portuguese army was totally destroyed. Stukeley, when he saw the battle lost, charged desperately at the head of his Italians, and found an honourable end to a futile and foolish life. Stukeley, whether living or dead, was of small importance. Sebastian's place too might have been filled had the royal family of Portugal been more prolific. But Sebastian was childless, and was an only son: his heir was his great uncle, the Cardinal Henry, a priest and childless also; and next to him was Philip of Spain, whose succession would bring with it the union of the crowns, and the incorporation of the whole peninsula.[1] The Cardinal King was old, and the Portuguese succession became immediately an object of so much interest with Philip, that he was less than ever disposed to undertake new quarrels: while the alarm with which so great an increase of Spanish power was regarded at Paris, drew France and England closer to each other, weakened the influence of Philip's satellites the Guises, disposed Henry III. and the Queen-mother more favourably towards the King of Navarre and the Huguenots, and postponed indefinitely the alliance between the Catholic Sovereigns for which the Pope and the Church were thirsting. Another element of quarrel was thrown into the political cauldron. France was now disposed to accept Elizabeth's friendship on her own terms, and should her marriage diplomacy fail, she had less to fear from her lover's resentment.

England itself was now politically quiet. The country was prospering with the peace, agriculture was

---

[1] Philip's mother was Isabella, sister of John III. of Portugal. Antonio, prior of Crato, the only available competitor, was the son of Louis, a younger brother of John, but there was a spot upon his birth, and he was known as Antonio the Bastard.

thriving, manufactures were spreading, country gentlemen, in the contemplation of their improved rent rolls, were indulging in 'bravery of building,' raising 'fair 'houses' on the sites of grange and monastery. The complaints of the past generation were no longer heard. The looms of Flanders no longer devoured the English wool or turned the farmsteads of Hampshire into sheep-walks. The exiled Flemings had brought their arts with them across the Channel, England in moderation wove its own fleece, and the plough passed again over the old fallows. The uncertainty of the succession kept up a chronic fever, which inflamed, and was in turn inflamed by, the divisions of religion.[1] But such large questions affected principally the great families, and the yeomen and peasants were living in a golden age. The war of classes, the struggle between rich and poor, had ended.

The quiet and good order, however, was limited to the land. The pirates and smugglers, who had been checked for a time, had sprung into renewed vitality. The iniquities of the Inquisition formed a plea on one side for retaliation upon the Spaniards; the Catholics on the other had their privateer fleet in the service of Don John. But the marauders of both sorts who took possession of the Channel, made little difference between creed and country; Scotch, Spaniards, French, fell indiscriminate victims. In the Solent itself, in Southampton water, in Poole harbour, wherever traders came on their lawful calling or forced by stress of weather, the pirate lugger was on the watch to relieve them of

---

[1] Walsingham believed that at this time the establishment of the succession in a Protestant would extinguish the extreme Catholic party altogether; 'the most part of the Papists of this realm being rather of State than conscience, in respect of the hope they have of the succession.'—*Notes on the State of England*, 1579. *MSS. Domestic*, Walsingham's hand.

their cargoes. The Holy Office condemned English ships at Cadiz, if a copy of 'the Common Prayer' was found in the captain's cabin. The gentlemen of Devonshire and Dorsetshire ornamented their halls with the spoils of vessels from Corunna or Oporto; and with no police upon the seas, and with the Queen occupied as we have seen her, the efforts made to suppress these doings were merely nominal.[1] Patriotism uniting with cupidity threw a halo over the trade of a corsair, and the enthusiast who proposed to destroy the Catholic fishing fleets at Newfoundland was but a large specimen of a class who were to be found of all grades and sizes where an English flag was on the ocean. The disorder of the general world, the confused ideas of morality introduced by the conflicts of religion, and the false shows of friendship, disguising treachery and hate, may partly excuse these lawless doings; but every pillaged hulk increased the score for which Spain intended at last to apply for payment; the French alliance was sorely tried, and the shipowners of Leith and Edinburgh were alienated from England when their friendship was of first necessity, and were tempted by real wrongs to play into the hands of her enemies.[2]

---

[1] The English Government, not caring to put the pirates down, and the French and Spanish not choosing, for political reasons, to make their depredations a casus belli, the owners paid black mail to recover a per-centage of their losses. Don Bernardino writes to Philip, Aug. 15, 1579: 'Aqui han hecho y hacen cada dia piratas ingleses, presas de mercaderes españoles, vasallos de V. M⁴, y los mercaderes embian poderes á los que aqui residen, para que lo cobren; los cuales por el provecho que les viene reducen el negocio á concierto con los mismos piratas, desesperando á los proprietarios del; sino es por esta via que es ocasion de alimentarlos, como los mismos Ingleses me lo han significado, porque despues de concertada la parte aunque el que esta aqui sirviendo á V. Mag⁴, pide á la Reyna y su consejo que se castiguen los piratas, responden que no hay quien se queja dellos, por haberse acordado con las partes.'—*MSS. Simancas.*

[2] For accounts of English piracy, see the *Domestic MSS.* for the years 1577, 1578, and 1579.

In these wild ways the English sailors were educating themselves for the impending struggle. A wise and resolute sovereign might perhaps have forced their disordered energies into more honourable courses; but it suited the temper of Elizabeth's genius to leave her subjects to their own responsibilities. When Mendoza complained, she replied that England was a large island, with many ports in it. She disclaimed her corsairs as Philip disclaimed the Inquisition, and pleaded her inability to keep them in check, as Philip pleaded the independence of the Holy Office.

The Alençon marriage became now her grand occupation, and if it was intended to benefit the Low Countries, the immediate effects were anything but promising. The two months were gone for which the Duke had undertaken to serve, and nothing had been done. Elizabeth now required him as a condition of her favour to withdraw. He obeyed, and returned to France. His disbanded troops enlisted with the Hainault nobles, who were preparing to revolt to Parma; and two months later, the whole Walloon States, Artois, Hainault, Lille, Douay and Namur, finding themselves forsaken by France, gathered into a separate confederacy and submitted to Spain. The Frisian and Batavian provinces formed themselves immediately after into the union of Utrecht; and Flanders and Brabant, lying between the two combinations, were themselves divided in sympathy, and became the theatre of war. The business of Parma was to reduce the great cities of those States which still held for the patriots, Maestrecht, Mechlin, Brussels, Ghent, Bruges, and Antwerp. Elizabeth supposing the work would occupy some years, abandoned them entirely to their own resources. Walsingham, Cobham and Davison were recalled, the Prince of Orange was left face to face with his enemy, while she on her part prepared for her campaign with Alençon.

Having thrown up the Provinces at her bidding, the Duke pressed naturally for his reward. Catherine de Medici wrote to Walsingham in affected rapture at her son's prospects.[1] Elizabeth wished him to come at once to England, and he declared himself ready and anxious. But before committing his reputation, he preferred to see his way more clearly, and proposed to send first a gentleman of his household, M. Simier, to learn his real chances. The Queen did not like the change. Agents implied business; she had secured her first object, and the marriage not being so pressingly necessary, she had not the slightest intention of entangling herself further than she was obliged.[2] Mendoza one day calling on her, she asked him why he came to court so seldom. He said he had supposed that she was so pleasantly occupied preparing for her marriage, that she would not care to hear of anything else. She answered sharply, that an old woman such as she was had something else to do than think of marrying. The talk of it had effected her purpose, and had cleared the Provinces of the French.[3]

She was less at liberty however, than she had been, to indulge her own humours. The French were suspicious after their past experience. Alençon did not

[1] Catherine de Medici to Walsingham, Sept. 13.—MSS. France.

[2] 'Her Majesty was not at all willing that Simier should come, considering he is sent to conclude all things; which she liketh nothing till she had seen him that she would agree withal. I find her Majesty still with a meaning in the matter, howbeit not so earnest as before.'—Sir Edward Stafford to Burghley, Oct. 27. MURDIN.

[3] 'Replicóme que por una vieja como ella era bueno tratar de casarse; que me aseguraba que las esperanças que habia dado de poderse effectuar el suyo con M. de Alençon le habian hecho salir de los Estados; lo qual habia deseado por no verlos en manos de françeses.'—Descifrada de Don Bernardino. 1578-9. MSS. Simancas.

mean to be made ridiculous, and not perhaps anticipating a favourable effect from his appearance, wished the Queen to bind herself before she set eyes upon him. Simier indeed confessed to Mauvissière that the lovers would be better kept apart till there was no retreat for them. The interview would be but an obstruction, and might delay the entrance into the desired haven.[1]

M. Simier understood Elizabeth better, before all was over, and must have smiled at the recollection of his own precipitancy. She replied through Walsingham, that she had distinctly suspended her assent till she had seen her intending husband, that she would adhere to her resolution, and would conclude no article till she was satisfied that the matter would take effect. Simier might come if he pleased, and might arrange, should Alençon wish it, the outlines of a treaty; but he must understand that he had to do with a woman who was no fool, and did not mean to be taken in.[2]

The French Government, which had modified its whole policy in expectation of the marriage, began now to be alarmed. It was true that the Queen had made her consent conditional on Alençon's coming, but she had taken so serious a step in recalling him from the Low Countries, that they had taken it for granted, that she had resolved on accepting him.

What did the Queen of England mean? they began to ask. Could it really be that she was playing with them again? Sir Amyas Paulet was clamorously questioned, but kept a prudent silence. 'I have been baited 'here a month or more as a bear at the stake,' he wrote, 'and had nothing to say; but stood still at my defence

---

[1] Simier to Mauvissière, Nov. 3.—*MSS. France.*

[2] Walsingham to Simier, Nov. 18.—*MSS. France.* The letter was written immediately after a conversation with Elizabeth, and was evidently dictated by her.

' for fear to take hurt.'¹ Mauvissière's letters were somewhat reassuring. Elizabeth convinced Mauvissière, if she convinced no one else, that she was in earnest; and Simier came to England in January on her own terms, bringing a letter with him from Alençon, which absurd alike in form and substance, yet gratified the thirst for adulation of the 'Perfect Goddess' to whom it was addressed.² It was received with all appearance of pleasure, and the bearer of it, Simier, was charming. The small chattering voluble amusing creature became the Queen's plaything; throwing Hatton and every other favourite into the shade. She called him her 'petit singe,' her pet monkey, and cuffed or fondled him as the humour took her.

The conditions of the alliance were now gravely entered on. As a preliminary she consulted a physician on the prospect of her having children,³ and on her receiving a favourable answer, the Council set to work. Their part of the task was easy. They had only to revive the articles already fruitlessly agreed

---

¹ Paulet to the Council, Dec. 6.—*MSS. France.*

² The letter is an autograph. It begins with an assurance that his connexion with the Prince of Orange was broken off, and continues thus: 'Me proumes que metre fin asete ocquation aus negotiations depuis si lontans coumanse qui sera la chouze du monde qui me randra plus satisfet et contant; et en fesant gagnerres les heuures de misericorde restorant aune vice langisante et qui net ni sera que autant que je la pensere digne de faire chouze qui vous soit agreable, esperant que me feres met honneur de me croyre et que prandres l'affection telle coume elle est tres fidelle dans mon ame; et que ne le galleres ase maner discours confus des pations meuves de tant de bans subges et dignes de randre la plus abondante plume empeschee en le lection de tant de rares et belles vertus; qui fera pour ne tombe davantage en erreur que je vous supplie de croyre que en la seulle contanp!ation de vous, Madame, coame de la plus parfete Deesse des siens je vous baysere tres hnmblement les mins. Priant Dieu, etc.'—*Alençon to the Queen of England*, Jan. 4, 1579. *MSS. France.*

³ Descifrada de Don Bernardino, Jan. 15, 1579.—*MSS. Simancas.*

on when the suitor was Alençon's brother the present King. The question of the interview remained, and here both sides were obstinate. Alençon did not like the prospect of being looked at, and then rejected. Simier said so in sufficiently icy language.[1] His visit, if it was to be at all, he wished to be attended with public form and ceremony, that his refusal afterwards might be the more difficult. The Queen for the opposite reason desired it to be private. She wrote to him at last, suggesting that he should make his appearance unexpectedly at her Court, and she hinted at infinite favours, with which his compliance should be rewarded. On the whole, Walsingham now thought that she really intended business. 'The affair of Monsieur,' he wrote, 'takes greater foot than was looked for. She 'thinks it the best means to provide for her safety that 'can be offered, and, it is thought, she will in the end con'sent to the match, though otherwise not greatly to her 'liking.'[2] Mendoza, who was watching her with a keenness sharpened by alarm, was of opinion that if Alençon came, she would really marry him.[3] And so too, Simier inclined to believe, though he could not venture to feel sure. He was charmed with his reception, and delighted with his mistress. He described her to the Chancellor of Alençon's household, as the best and most attractive of women. Reams of paper, he said, would not suffice to dilate upon her virtues. The Duke, could he but secure the prize, would be the most fortunate of men. 'But I shall not be satisfied,' he concluded, 'till the 'curtain is drawn, the candles out, and Monsieur fairly 'in bed.'[4]

---

[1] 'Avec des mots assez gelés.'— *Elizabeth to Alençon*, March 9.

[2] Walsingham to Davison, Feb. 27.—*MSS. Holland*.

[3] Mendoza to Cayas, March 21, 1579.—*MSS. Simancas*.

[4] Simier to M. Desormeaulx, April 12.—*MSS. France*.

Among those who had the best right to advise she found slight encouragement. Sussex, as has been seen, was favourable, but Walsingham was sternly contemptuous. The friends of the Queen of Scots were jealous for the chances of the succession, and Sir James Crofts was engaged for Spain. The country received the news with universal disgust. A marriage between a woman of forty-six and a youth of twenty-three was in itself monstrous. The preacher in the Royal Chapel, on the first Sunday in Lent, said boldly in the Queen's presence that England did not need a second foreign marriage; Queen Mary's experience was sufficient.[1] Elizabeth rose in a fury, and sailed out of the church, but the same language was echoed in every pulpit in London. A French Prince, with the taint of St. Bartholomew on his family, united every party in the country in a common clamour of disapproval.

Cecil only, of all really wise men, hesitated; and Cecil hesitated only because he was desperate of the Queen ever choosing an open course and honourably following it. Notes in his handwriting, with dates of the present spring upon them, scattered through the State papers, shew how earnestly he was weighing the situation. The marriage would secure the French alliance, and would be a shield against Spain. Alençon was personally unobjectionable, and there might, perhaps, be a child. But, again, Alençon was a Papist, and would be a rallying point for the Catholics. The child was highly problematical, and parturition, at the Queen's age, was likely to be dangerous. Monsieur, too, —for Cecil could not, like Sussex, drown his fears in foolish flattery of her—Monsieur might prove an indifferent husband, 'and might mind more to obtain the

---

[1] Mendoza to Cayas, March 31.—*MSS. Simancas.*

'marriage of the Scotch Queen, seeking to establish in
'his issue the three crowns, France, England, and Scot-
'land.' Were there a hope that the Queen 'would so
'govern her realm and people, as she might be strong
'by God's goodness to withstand all attempts upon her,'
'would she but consider how the realm might succeed
'to such person as should, by the law of God and man,
'be meet to come to the same without violence and
'blood,' then 'it would be far better she should con-
'tinue unmarried, and prolong her years as God and
'nature should yield.'[1] But experience had shewn the
Queen's incurable distaste either for an open policy or
the settlement of the succession, and, in default, the
marriage with all its drawbacks seemed the only re-
source left. Simier, to reconcile the Protestants, dwelt
upon the opposition of the Nuncio at Paris, the threats
of excommunication which had been muttered against
Alençon, and the anger of the Paris populace.

Prejudice and passion, however, had taken such deep
roots that nothing which he could say availed. Sir
Nicholas Bacon had lately died. An opinion was found
in his desk, written two years before, when the matter
was last talked of, that a French marriage would be the
ruin of the realm, that the real object of it was the death
of the Queen, and the liberation of Mary Stuart.[2] The
inveterate suspicion was confirmed by the complaisancy
of the Queen of Scots, whose expectations the alliance,
if meant in sincerity, would rather tend to destroy.
She had been heard to say that 'if the marriage was
'accomplished, it would at least take the administration
'out of the hands of her enemies, and restore her friends
'among the Catholics to their places at the Court.'
She looked for Simier to communicate with her, and

[1] Notes in Burghley's hand, March 31.—MSS. France.
[2] Descifrada de Don Bernardino, April 8.

she expected Monsieur to take immediate steps for the recognition of her presumptive title.[1]

The King of Navarre and Condé did not share in the expectations of Sussex, that Alençon's position in England would be a benefit to themselves. They rather expected that it would withdraw England further from its Protestant connexion. They advised Elizabeth to avoid Catholic alliances, and prefer the Huguenots to the princes of the house of Valois. The opposition was strengthened by the adhesion of Sir Thomas Bromley, to whom the Great Seal passed on Bacon's death. Alençon, on Simier's report of the Queen's disposition, enlarged his demands. He expected to be crowned as King Consort. He asked for one of the two duchies of York or Lancaster, or an allowance of 60,000*l.* a year, and he even hinted at the occupation of an English port by a French garrison. The Council sate three days at the beginning of May to consider these singular requests. Bromley terminated the discussion by saying that the marriage was in itself preposterous, that the hope of issue from it was idle, that the French were England's hereditary enemies, and that the difference of religion was in itself an insuperable obstacle. Of all the lords present Sussex only dissented from this opinion. Simier was sent for, and was informed that his proposition could not be entertained. He ran out of the room in a rage, and complained to his mistress. The Queen swore that the Council should not thwart her thus; marry she would and must.[2] But she, too, yielded for a time to the opposition, or made use of it to escape with credit. She wrote coaxingly to Alençon: she addressed him as 'le

---

[1] Mary Stuart to the Archbishop of Glasgow, Jan. 10, 1580.—LABANOFF, vol. v.

[2] 'No pienses que he de pasar así; que yo cuarma tengo.'—Descrifrada de Bernardino, 14 de Maio. Sir James Crofts kept Mendoza exactly informed of what passed in Court or Council.

'fidel,' she assured him of her devoted attachment; yet she suggested that friendship might, perhaps, be better for them both than a closer tie.[1]

Friendship however would not answer Monsieur's object. He had demanded much, knowing that he would obtain less than he asked for. He withdrew the obnoxious requests. He professed himself willing to acquiesce in whatever arrangement the Council desired, provided only that he might have mass in the palace for himself and his retinue; and he renewed his entreaty to be allowed to visit the idol of his heart and hope.

Elizabeth was now in extreme perplexity. The net which she had made was closing round her. The actual coming of the Prince would bring her a step nearer to the matrimonial abyss than she had hitherto ventured. The Council were again assembled. She enquired whether, considering that the Duke had given way, she could honourably refuse him an interview; and whether if, after seeing him, 'there should not fall out any liking,' she could then extricate herself without offence.

She wished to be encouraged in inventing causes for delay, but it could not be. Little as the Council wished for the marriage, to trifle further might make France even forget the Portuguese succession. They replied that 'the circumstances considered of former 'proceedings, they did not see how, in honour, Alen- 'çon's visit could be denied,' nor before he had been seen 'was the time apt to consider how the matter could be 'broken off.'[2]

Simier was again called in. He said that the Duke would be ready to cross by the middle or end of August. A squadron of the Queen's ships was promised to be in

---

[1] Elizabeth to Alençon, June, 1579.—*MSS. France.* Autograph.   [2] Proceedings in Council, June, 1579. Walsingham's hand.

attendance at Calais, with passports for himself and his
suite. Sir Amyas Paulet was instructed to tell him
that if he did not fancy the Queen's person, she would
not be angry with him, and he was exhorted, on his
part, 'to brook denial with patience.'

It seemed, therefore, that he was actually coming,
and when she found that she could not escape, she
affected fervently to desire it. The pill had been
gilded with flattery, and she had been persuaded that
the mere sight of such a paragon of loveliness as herself would prove reward sufficient for him, even if she
sent him back disappointed of his hopes.[1] Yet to the
last it was uncertain what she would do. The time approached, but she had given no orders for the Duke's
reception.[2] The passports were brought to her to sign.
She could not do it. Tenderness for Leicester, tenderness perhaps for Hatton, passions of all kinds grew more
and more tempestuous as the moment approached. All
seemed uncertain again, when Simier discovered, and
was able to reveal to her, that Leicester was secretly
married to her cousin, Lettice Knollys, the false wife

---

[1] 'Desea hervorosamente la venida de Alençon; y aunque de sus consejeros se han dicho los inconvenientes que dello podrian suceder, han podido mas los de la parte contraria, y con ella no poco el parecer de que se entiende que sus partes y hermosura son tan grandes que por solo ellas huelga de venir a su reyno, sin estar asegurado de que sera su marido.'—*Descifrada de Don Bernardino*, 24 de Junio. *MSS. Simancas*.

[2] 'It is given out that Monsieur will be here at the time limited, and yet her Majesty gives no order for the receiving of him, which maketh us to muse what will become of the matter; and therefore it is suspected that between her Majesty and Simier —for few others are made acquainted with the cause—it is concluded that he shall come over shortly in secret manner. I am of opinion that the wise men of France will never assent thereto, but matters of love and affection be not guided with wisdom. God send the cause better success than I hope after, for I am more afraid of the event hereof than of James Fitzmaurice's attempt' (alluding to a landing in Ireland to be related in the next chapter).—*Walsingham to Burghley*, Aug. 6. *MSS. Domestic*.

and widow of Walter, Earl of Essex. The scandals of that bad story concern only the curious in human wickedness. It is enough that the only man that Elizabeth ever loved was the husband of another woman. It had been done without seeking her permission, for permission, it was well known, would never have been granted. Hatton, too, it was said, had formed a similar secret connexion; and after a struggle of three days, in an indignant agony of tears, and rather forced at last than convinced that it was necessary, she subscribed the document which was to bring Alençon to her feet.[1]

If she was playing an idle game the sport was dangerous, but it rather seems that she had no formed, no fixed resolution. She varied in earnest from day to day, flashing up into violence when contradicted, and desponding when the opposition ceased. It had been her own work from the beginning. She had made the first advances in her eagerness to break her connexion with the Low Countries, and the alternative which she then preferred was knocking at her door, and she had to meet it as she could. Alençon came—came without ostentation, hardly stirred beyond the palace, and remained but a few days—but the objection behind which she had shielded herself hitherto was removed. She had seen him, and that excuse for indecision existed no longer. He was a small, brown creature, deeply pock-marked, with a large head, a knobbed nose, and a hoarse croaking voice, but whether in contradiction, or from whatever

---

[1] 'Leicester and Hatton are married secretly, which hath so offended this Queen; it is thought she has been led upon such miscontentment to agree to the sight of the Duke of Alençon. Notwithstanding, she had differred three whole days with an extreme regret and many tears afore she would subscribe the passport, being induced thereunto, and almost forced by those that have led this negotiation, in spite of Leicester.'— *The Queen of Scots to the Archbishop of Glasgow*, July 4, 1579. LABANOFF, vol. v.

cause, she professed to be enchanted with him. She, who was accustomed to the stately presence of the Dudleys and the Sidneys, declared she had never seen a man who pleased her so well, never one whom she could so willingly make her husband.[1] For him too as for Simier she had a name of endearment. Simier was her monkey. Alençon became her 'grenouille,' her frog, a frog prince, beneath whose hideousness lay enchanted, visible only to a lover's eye, a form of preternatural beauty.[2]

In seriousness the impression which he left was believed to have been favourable, and the marriage to have been made many degrees more likely. An uneasy and angry murmur began to be heard like that which had risen when Queen Mary was to marry Philip, only deeper and more unanimous. Antipathy to France was stronger in England than difference of religion. Though Alençon was a Catholic, and though his presence was expected to produce a change in their religious position, the prospect did not even reconcile the Romanists; and Mendoza consoled himself with thinking that if the Queen took him it would be a judicial blunder permitted by God to punish the apostasy of England and to bring it back under the bondage of the Church again after a bloody civil war.[3]

Philip Sidney, in the name of the Protestants, told her that it was too late to separate herself now from the party with which her fortunes were bound up. He

---

[1] Mendoça á su Mag⁴, 25 de Agosto. —*MSS. Simancas.*

[2] Alençon accepted the name, and in the long love correspondence, which is preserved at Hatfield, he thus pathetically signed himself.

[3] 'Se pueda creer que es permission divina para reducir este reyno á la religion Catolica, y castigalla del haberse apartado della con una muy intestina guerra.'—*Don Bernardino al Rey,* 9 de Noviembre. *MSS. Simancas.*

denounced with a fiery invective the false brood of Catherine de Medici;[1] and while the Queen herself was holding a ball at the palace, and exhibiting her dancing to her lover, who was gazing at her from behind a curtain with emotions which have been left unrecorded, Sidney's father, Sir Henry, with Pembroke, and the other Puritan leaders, were sitting in Leicester's house to consult how best to defeat the monstrous alliance in Parliament.[2]

The rage of the people found expression at last in a pamphlet, written by a Puritan lawyer, brother-in-law of the celebrated Cartwright, named John Stubbs. It was no time for polished phrases. The genuine loyalty of Protestantism refused to garnish itself in euphuistic compliments, preferring plain words as the most becoming dress for plainness of thought. The pamphlet told the Queen that she was too old to think of marriage. The hope of children might have reconciled the country to an alliance which it did not otherwise like, but at forty-six she was unlikely to produce a living child. The marrow of Monsieur's bones had been eaten out by debauchery. Monsieur was not Satan in the form of a serpent, but the old serpent himself in the form of a man, come a second time to seduce the English Eve and ruin the English Paradise.

Rhetoric, which seems extravagant to colder eyes, was mere statement of fact to a generation so near a St. Bartholomew. Wherever a Valois set his foot the 'Paris nuptials' were expected to follow. Yet the language was indecorous and certainly injudicious. The Queen's natural hatred of the Puritans found an excuse for indulging itself. Her vanity had been wounded,

---

[1] Sidney's spirited letter is printed in the Cabala.

[2] Don Bernardino al Rey, 15 de Agosto.—*MSS. Simancas.*

her guest insulted, and the French nation insulted also in his person. The writer and the printer were arrested. She flung them into the Tower, she swore she would hang them, and she tried to do it. She put out a proclamation indignantly denying the insinuations against Alençon's character. 'She was touched in honour,' she said, 'that having so long loved her, and having ventured into England to visit her, he should be so falsely and unjustly reproved. Her subjects had persuaded her to marry; she was endeavouring to gratify them, and was met with an unworthy reward.'[1]

The proclamation and the arrest of Stubbs caused fresh exasperation, and it was feared that violence might be attempted against the French residents in London. The multitude knowing nothing of European politics, could not appreciate the reasons which recommended the marriage. Proud of England and proud of their sovereign, they imagined themselves able to resist the united efforts of the world. The Council too had confidence in England, if England was wisely guided. De Quadra had long ago described Burghley as having a faith in the resources of his country, which seemed to himself like insanity. But the Queen would not guide, nor would she allow others to guide for her. Determined only to go her own way, she did not know for two months together what that way was to be. In mere desperation Cecil had submitted to a necessity as painful to him as it was to Walsingham, and he made one more appeal to her nobler nature.

The temper of the people could not be trifled with. There was again a call of the Council, and on the 2nd of October, after a long day's sitting, they 'agreed to present to her Majesty,' as an alternative for Alençon, 'the

---

[1] Proclamation by the Queen, Sept. 27, 1579. *MSS. Domestic.*

'following resolutions':—'The country was in great and 'increasing danger. Much might be hoped for from 'God, but God would not help them if they neglected 'ordinary means. Her Majesty must continue to de-'serve the love of her people. She must be zealous for 'God's honour, and maintain the laws for religion; and 'then it might be expected that the number of her at-'tached subjects would increase, and the uneasy humour 'would die away; the Papists would dissemble or amend 'for fear and would be less able or willing to maintain 'the English rebels on the continent.' Further, the loose disordered administration required to be amended, and godly and learned men appointed as magistrates to do justice without partiality. The present practice of pardoning notable crimes, of pardoning piracy especially, ought to cease, and 'penal laws not to be dispensed 'with for private men's profit, a matter greatly misliked 'of all good people.' Malcontents and recusants should be disarmed. Special fines should be imposed on them, and all authority in the realm carefully taken from them, and it should be generally understood through the country that if disturbances were attempted in favour of the Queen of Scots, she would be herself the first to suffer.[1]

So much for the realm; and the recommendations throw light on the slipshod character of Elizabeth's internal government.

Abroad, the Council invited her to abandon her hesitating courses and make up her mind once for all

---

[1] A precaution extremely necessary. On the 29th of September Don Juan de Vargas told Philip that the Queen of Scots, 'desesperada de ver el poco socorro que halla y la mala firma que tiene de salir de captividad, ha dado orejas y empesado á tratar con algunos particulares Ingleses que se han venido á offrecer; y que podria ser que se aventurasen á tentar la fortuna, y que se viese alguna gran solevacion en aquellas partes.'—*Vargas to Philip*, Sept. 29. TEULET, vol. v.

to assist the struggling Protestants in France and the Low Countries. In defending them she would really be defending herself. Condé, Navarre, and the Prince of Orange were fighting England's battles as much as their own. She should make herself strong at sea, and not be afraid to apply to her subjects for money. Being childless too she might sell lands of her own for so great a purpose. Above all she should not neglect Scotland. There lay her greatest peril. Some part of the large allowance now made to the Queen of Scots might be reasonably transferred to her son if she could not otherwise afford to help him. In other words the Council advised her to adopt the policy to which Sussex thought her resources unequal, become 'The Head of the Name,' and with the glory, risk the perils. They did not press their recommendations; they offered them merely as the only visible means of escape from the marriage, and they concluded with desiring that 'intercession should be made to 'God to direct her Majesty's heart, as should be most to 'His honour, her comfort, and the weal of the realm.'[1]

It is needless to say that the advice was not accepted. Burghley reported two days later 'that the remedies 'proposed to her Majesty had misliked her.' He, therefore, for his own part, was of opinion that the marriage must go forward.

Yet so unfavourable still was the general feeling, that only Sussex went with him. The rest of the Lords waited in a body on the Queen, and represented to her that the objections of the nation to Alençon amounted to abhorrence, and that it would be unsafe for her to persevere. It would be a sufficient excuse to France that the people reasonably or unreasonably declined to receive the Duke among them. Bromley, who with Bacon's office had inherited his freedom of

[1] Report of Proceedings in Council at Greenwich, Oct. 2.—MURDIN.

speech, added another argument, which he knew would tell. If she married, Parliament would insist on a settlement of the succession. With the door opened to their hereditary enemies the nation could not and would not remain any longer in uncertainty.[1]

Worried, harassed, imagining now that she desired the marriage above all things, when her people most objected to it, she ordered Walsingham out of her presence in a rage, telling him he was fit for nothing but to be a champion of heretics. She turned pathetic. In a flood of tears she asked 'if there could be any doubt that the 'best surety to her and the realm was to marry and have 'a child and continue the line of her father.' 'She con-'demned herself of simplicity in committing the matter 'to be argued by the Council. She thought rather to 'have had a universal request to proceed in the mar-'riage than to have made a doubt of it.'

'Conceiving by this,' wrote Burghley, 'her earnest 'disposition in the marriage, the Council held one more 'consultation.' Walsingham and Leicester, since she chose to have it so, withdrew their opposition. They agreed, all of them, to do the best they could to gain the consent of Parliament, and to reconcile the country. They went again to her the next day. They told her that her pleasure should be theirs. They would die at her feet rather than offend her, and as she wished it, they would make Alençon welcome. This ought to have been enough; but she was in a humour which nothing would satisfy. She refused to allow Hatton to come near her. She told Sir Francis Knollys that before all was over 'his zeal for religion would cost him dear.'

---

[1] Descifrada de Don Bernardino, 16 de Octubre,—*MSS. Simancas.* The Ambassador, describing the effect of Bromley's words on Elizabeth, speaks of her 'pusillanimidad y miedo en cualquiera adversidad' as something which everybody knew.

'She was very sharp in reprehending such as had argued against her marriage.' Yet when all was said she left them ignorant what she really desired. 'Her Majesty 'thought it not meet to declare to the Council whether 'she would marry Monsieur or no; yet she looked at 'their hands that they did so much desire her marriage 'and to have children of her body as they should with 'one accord have made special suit to her for the 'same.'[1]

If, as is sometimes said, Elizabeth was the greatest of English sovereigns, one is tempted to suppose that the average stature cannot have been excessive. Her whole conduct was saturated with artifice, and the performance was as poor as the object was paltry.[2] Her exasperation with the opposition was assumed to persuade France that she was herself sincere; and as the two Dutch Anabaptists had been sacrificed to propitiate Spain, so two other victims were offered now to appease the displeasure of Monsieur and his brother. Walsingham, Sidney, Bromley, were too great persons to be meddled with. Elizabeth, when she stooped to strike, preferred to choose a humble quarry. Stubbs who had written the offensive pamphlet, Page, the bookseller, who had sold it, and Singleton the printer of it, were tried for felony, and she wished to hang them. The jury refused to find a verdict. The law could not be manipulated to touch their lives. They were then indicted for conspiring to excite sedition, under an act which had been passed in the late reign for the protection of the Queen's husband.[3] 'The Queen's husband'

---

[1] Notes of Proceedings in Council, Oct. 7 and 8. Burghley's hand.— Mendex. Descifradas de Don Bernardino, Oct. 16.—*MSS. Simancas.*

[2] 'Puede se hacer mal juicio si es todo artificio.'—*Don Bernardino to Cayas,* Oct. 16. *MSS. Simancas.*

[3] 1 & 2 Philip and Mary, cap. ii.

was construed liberally to cover the Queen's suitor. The act had been continued for the protection of Elizabeth herself,[1] and she translated the insult to her lover into an insult to the Crown. 'Lawyers murmured that 'the proceedings were erroneous.' Mounson, one of the judges of the Common Pleas, resigned, rather than be a party to an unrighteous sentence.[2] Mauvissière interceded, but the Queen was the more determined not to be outdone in generosity. Singleton was acquitted; but on the 3rd of November, Stubbs and Page were brought from the Tower to a scaffold before the palace at Westminster, and 'their right hands were 'struck off with a cleaver driven through the wrist with 'a beetle.' Page, as the bleeding stump was seared with a hot iron, said proudly, 'I have left there a true 'Englishman's hand.' Stubbs waved his hat with the hand remaining, cried 'God save Queen Elizabeth,' and fainted from loss of blood. Camden, who was himself present at the scene, saw the surrounding multitude 'altogether silent, either out of horror at this new and 'unwonted punishment, or else out of pity to the men, 'being of most honest and unblameable report, or else 'out of hatred to the marriage, which most men pre- 'saged would be the overthrow of religion.'

The same morning when the butcher's work was over, the Queen again summoned the Council, and condescended this time to tell them her resolution. Her mind was made up. Monsieur was to be her husband; and the preliminaries were to be completed with all haste.[3] She had given so fierce a proof that she was in earnest, that the Council ceased to mistrust her. The

---

[1] 1 Elizabeth, cap. vi.   [3] Don Bernardino al Rey, Nov. 9.
[2] Camden.

treaty was drawn out and signed by Simier at Greenwich on the 24th of November;[1] and nothing now remained but the sanction of Parliament before Monsieur might return to England for the concluding ceremony. The meeting of Parliament, however, could not be avoided, and the late cruel doings had not made the prospect of it more agreeable. It was the old Parliament of 1572, which the Queen had not ventured to dissolve, saturated though it had proved to be with Puritanism. The circulars had been issued for the members to be in their places in November; but the temper of the spectators round the scaffold had been so evidently dangerous, and it was so likely that the House of Commons would reflect the general discontent, that Elizabeth controlled her impatience. Mauvissière wrote to the Court of France that the marriage must be postponed till the irritation had subsided. Attached to the treaty was a note by Simier agreeing to allow two months' delay 'to allow time to her Majesty to persuade her 'subjects' to conformity. Parliament was put off till January. The Queen promised to write to France when the time was come for the final ratification, and if the letter was not sent within the two months prescribed, the treaty, with all that had been done, was to be considered ' null and void.'[2]

Those who hold the traditionary belief in Elizabeth's profound ability and equally profound insincerity, will consider that this was a loophole deliberately contrived for her escape. Her deception, if such it was, imposed on her ministers, and probably imposed on herself. Parliament did not meet after all. She found or affected to

---

[1] Treaty with M. Simier, Nov. 24, 1579.—*MSS. France.*
[2] *MSS. France*, Nov. 24.

find it necessary to yield to the continued aversion of her subjects. The two months passed and she had not written, and the negotiation so strangely followed up was as strangely supposed to be at an end. The natural interpretation must be that her ministers were her accomplices, that she had again entangled herself deeper than she intended, and that the objection of the country was an excuse of which they enabled her to avail herself. If this was the truth, and possibly it was the truth, she had allowed two honourable men to be mutilated to blind the eyes of the French Court to her own deliberate fickleness. But if there were members of her Government who, careless of what happened to herself, were betraying her into rash and dangerous courses; there were others too sincerely attached to their mistress to feel anything but shame and dismay. Chief among these was the ever loyal Cecil. 'While your 'Majesty desired the marriage,' he wrote on the 28th of January, 'I was myself in favour of it, and so am 'I now persuaded it would be your best security; but 'the matter being as it is, I am your servant, and will 'do my best for you in this and all conditions. You will 'find me more ready to defend you from the hurt when 'it comes, than those of your Council who have been the 'occasion of its coming. Your marriage is now broken 'off, and no hope left of the good that was thereby 'expected. Alençon having been brought by your 'Majesty's means to be the author of trouble in his 'own country, having by you been drawn from his late 'enterprise in the Low Countries, and by you hindered 'of his marriage treated of with the King of Spain's 'daughter, having now lately come hither to see you to 'be by you rejected, it may be taken as quite certain 'that he will now seek to be revenged upon you. You

'have no hope of an heir, and all eyes will be turned
'upon your successor. Alençon will probably marry
'where we feared. France and Spain will then unite
'against us. Our trade will be destroyed. Foreign
'soldiers will be landed in Ireland, and in all likelihood
'there will be a rising at home, supported from abroad,
'in favour of the King and Queen of Scots. The
'Crown revenues will not enable you to encounter this
'combination, and when civil troubles have broken out
'subsidies cannot be raised.

'In the face of these dangers, so far as I understand
'them, what your Majesty must do is this. You can-
'not prevent your people from considering who is to
'be their future sovereign. They have too much at
'stake. It is against reason to expect otherwise.
'Perilous as it may be, you must now encourage
'Alençon to take possession of the Low Countries, if
'only to separate him from the Papists. You must
'arm your realm, call out the musters and have them
'trained; strengthen your navy, and fortify your har-
'bours; make a league with the Protestant princes;
'abridge your excessive expenses; attach the nobility
'and chief persons of the realm to your service by
'those gifts and attentions which have hitherto been
'cast away upon others who in time of need will fail
'you. You must seek new markets for your merchants,
'and invite strangers to you from all parts of the world,
'that if your trade is stopped in one quarter, it may be
'open in another. You must conciliate Ireland; allow
'the chiefs to continue their ancient greatness; take
'away the fear of conquest lately grafted in the wild
'Irish, and wink at disorders which do not offend the
'Crown; make as strict laws as can be devised to terrify
'into quiet the competitors for the crown; place the

'Queen of Scots in surer custody, and by a wise
'liberality to the King and the lords, prevent them
'from seeking more profitable alliances with France
'and Spain.'[1]

The wheel had made its full round. The situation of England was again what it had been when the Queen listened at Audley End to the whispers of Mauvissière, save only that her master-piece of policy had recoiled upon herself, and that her danger was aggravated by the affront which she had passed upon Alençon. The wisest of her ministers could recommend nothing better than what he had recommended before. The obligation which of all others had once been most incumbent on her, she had neglected the fulfilment of till it had become useless. Queens do not reign for their own pleasure, and the ignoble passion which had prevented her from making an honourable marriage when she was young, with a prospect of children, was no justification of her barren age which now threatened the realm with convulsions. Individuals may trifle at their foolish will with character or fortune; sovereigns, on whom depends the weal of empires, contract duties from their high places, which their private humours cannot excuse them for neglecting. To expect her to do what Cecil advised was to expect her to change her nature. Incurably convinced of her own supreme intelligence she would take no more of his counsel than such fragments as necessity enforced upon her, and these fragments, backed by the energy of a splendid nation, carried England, and Elizabeth with it, clear at last of the threatening breakers. The calamities of unprosperous reigns are charged upon sovereigns; and sovereigns therefore, it is but just, should be credited with their people's successes; but the personal

---
[1] Burghley to the Queen, Jan. 28, 1580. Abridged.—MURDIN.

contribution of Elizabeth to the final victory of Protestantism, was but in yielding at last to a stream which she had struggled against for thirty years. She believed in kings and she possessed skill to hoodwink kings less able than herself; but there was a volcanic energy in Europe, as she was about to feel, beyond the reach of her diplomacy, passions deep as the hell which the Popes mistook for heaven, which were proof against paltry artifices, and could be encountered only with other passions preternatural as themselves. Philip might 'loiter in 'the ford'' or halt upon his foot of lead. The Valois Princes and their mother might play with Huguenot and Papist, and fish for fortune or safety in the troubled waters; but the European Catholics were no longer to be trifled with. The first growth of the Reformation had been made possible only by the quarrel between Francis and the Emperor Charles. The political energies of the great powers were still hampered by their traditional jealousies; but the priests and those who believed in priests were free, and they determined, before it was too late, to act while their kings diplomatised. Acute as Cecil was, he did not see the precise form in which the danger was approaching. He expected political coalitions; he had to encounter an invisible influence stealing into the heart of the realm; a power which, when it took earthly form, appeared in the shape of pale ascetics armed but with their breviaries, yet more terrible than the galleons of Philip, or the threatened legions of the Duke of Guise. England was considered on the continent to be the heart of heresy. It was in England that French, Flemings, Germans, Italians, Spaniards, fugitives for religion, found home and shelter. It was in England that the patriot armies

---

' ' Meando en vado.'

recruited themselves; and the English Protestant congregations supplied the money that supported them. So long as England was unconquered, the Reformation was felt to be unconquerable, and it was the more exasperating because the English Catholics believed that, had they received the smallest practical assistance at Elizabeth's accession, they could have compelled her to remain in the Roman communion. Every year that had been allowed to pass had made recovery more difficult. Of the Catholic nobles some were dead, some were landless fugitives. The creed survived as a tradition, but the exercise of it was dying out. The more impetuous of the priests had gone abroad. Many had conformed; many had adhered to the faith, and said mass with the connivance of the Government in private houses. But they were dropping off, and the vacancies were not replenished. The old ceremonial was not yet forgotten, but was more and more faintly remembered. The longer the invasion was delayed the fainter the support which could be looked for in England itself, and the refugees, sick of pleading with Philip, had appealed with more success to the Pope and the Church. A new and passionate impulse had been given to the Catholic creed by St. Teresa and Ignatius Loyola. The Carmelite and Jesuit orders had revived something of the fervour of ancient Christendom, and personal and family ambition came to the help of religious enthusiasm. The Guises, as the leaders of the French Catholic aristocracy, intended, if the house of Valois failed, to snatch the crown from heretic Bourbons. The Guises' chance of success would be multiplied a hundred fold if they could revolutionise England in the interests of Mary Stuart; while the singular fortune of that world-famed lady, her wild story, her exile, her imprisonment, her constancy to the faith of which she was the supposed martyr, set on fire the imaginations of half the youths in Europe. Philip it seemed would do nothing till the ground had first been broken by others. Well then, others should break it. The refugees at Rheims were in the closest intercourse with Guise. Sanders and many others of them were for ever on the road between Brussels, Paris, Madrid, and the Vatican. A beginning had been made in Scotland. It had failed, but it could be attempted again, and the secret Catholic correspondence of the time reveals henceforward a connected and organised scheme, in which many different constituents were part of a single movement, the last issue of which was to be the entrance of the Duke of Guise into England over the Scotch Border. The objections of Philip to French interference would, it was hoped, be found inapplicable to the house of Lorraine, for the house of Lorraine were pensioners of his own. The Duke of Guise would act, not as a Frenchman, but as the executor of the Papal decree, and neither France nor Spain would then have cause to dread the ambitious projects of the other.[1]

---

[1] A passage in a letter from Don Bernardino de Mendoza to Cayas explains exactly the difficulty which had so long paralysed the action of the great powers, and how delicately it would be obviated by the employment of Guise. Mendoza was speaking of an application made by the Archbishop of Glasgow to Philip for money to raise a force to assist Argyle and Athol. He agreed with the King, he said, that it was a case for great caution. What was the force to consist of? If of foreigners, England, and probably France, would send troops to Scotland also, and there would be a general war. If of Scots, who was to be their leader? and what security could be given for the constancy of that most inconstant people? Further, he could not see in the manifestoes of the two Earls any symptoms of being sound in religion. The party opposed to Morton were of all sects and creeds. Some were Catholic, some were Protestant: some had quarrels of their own. In such a combination there was no element of success. 'And even suppose,' Don Bernardino continued, 'that the Catholics had direction of the enterprise, there would still be

The approaches were made on three separate lines of action. Ireland was sound in the faith; missionaries therefore were not required there, but only directions from the Pope with substantial help in men and money. It was decided that Doctor Sanders, with a commission as Legate, and Sir James Fitzmaurice, whom Perrot, since he could not hang him, hoped to convert into a St. Paul, should land in Kerry with a few ship-loads of Italians and Spaniards. The Irish were expected to rally to the Papal banner from Dingle to Dunluce. Money, ever potent in that country, could be provided without stint, for the Pope was liberal, and enthusiastic Catholics everywhere made it a cause of conscience. Arms, too, there would be for as many of the nation as needed them. If Ireland was not absolutely conquered, which it easily might be, yet Elizabeth's attention would be distracted by the insurrection, her treasure would be wasted and her soldiers consumed, while the real attack was made elsewhere. A young Scot, Esme Stuart, the King's cousin (son of a brother of the Earl of Lennox), called in France, where he had been educated, Count d'Aubigny, applied for and obtained permission to return to Scotland. His ostensible object was to pur-

---

many inconveniences. Nor is the Archbishop of Glasgow a fit person through whom to treat on such matters. He is sound in religion, and faithful to his mistress, but he is pensioned by France. He will take the French into the secret, and either they will turn the movement to their own advantage, or else throw obstacles in the way. The French are the natural enemies of the crown and greatness of Spain. How little they regard religion may be seen from the state of their own realm; much less do they care for what becomes of it in England, where they have always prevented us from interfering, both now, lately, and in the time of the late Emperor. Here, in my opinion, lies the great difficulty of helping the poor Queen of Scots. The French have no concern about her. All that can be done is to bring her friends in Scotland and England to act together, to watch their opportunity to set her free.'—*Don Bernardino to Cayas*, Feb. 8, 1579. *MSS. Simancas.*

sue his claim for some lands of his father's. In reality he was acting under the direction of the Duke of Guise. He was a brilliant fascinating youth, accomplished in all arts, whether of grace or villany, which France could teach, and his mission was to wind himself into the favour of the King, to lavish money among the hungry nobles whom Elizabeth declined to satisfy, to persuade, to corrupt, to reconstruct the party of France, and destroy Morton. He was a Catholic, but to disarm suspicion he was allowed to pretend to be a Protestant. His plan was to suggest toleration after the French pattern as a just and humane concession, and to obtain permission, secret if not avowed, for the exiled Catholic priests to return, reanimate the creed, and if possible convert the King. The traditional hatred of England was one sure ground to work on; the sympathy with Mary Stuart was another; and Scots of all persuasions were determined not to be defrauded of the English succession. These motives, skilfully handled and backed with money, would open the road to the entry of the Duke of Guise. A demand would be preferred for the release of the imprisoned Queen, and if it was refused, a united army of French and Scots would enter Northumberland and raise the northern counties.

And there was yet a third branch of this conspiracy, and not the least notable one. There was to be another preparative mission directed immediately at England; not this one of armed men, but of lads fresh from college, fugitives from Oxford, who nurtured at Oriel and Baliol on Catholic interpretations of the English formularies, had developed, before the down had stiffened upon their cheeks, into converts to the old faith. Half the colleges had fallen into the hands of High Churchmen, and had thus become training schools for Rome. The neophytes, when their conversion was completed, were drafted off to Douay or Rheims, were admitted, most of them, while their imaginations were still fevered, into the order of Jesus, and were sent back again in one or two years to carry their master's message through the English homesteads. They were charged with no commission to teach rebellion. Their orders were but to quicken into life the dying embers of the faith, to recall the wavering, to establish the faithful, to reconcile the lapsed, to preach, teach, provoke and bear at last the fate which the Government might order for them.

The heads of the order knew better than to waste such metal as this in practising conspiracy. Those who were reconciled to a Church which declared Elizabeth deposed might be safely trusted to play the parts expected of them when Guise should give the signal from Scotland. Devoted and single-hearted youths, inspired with zeal for their religion, were the most perfect missionaries of disaffection, though no word on politics ever issued from their lips. If the Government could be provoked to punish them, the odium of persecution would be fastened upon the Queen; the cause would triumph in their martyrdom; and the victims themselves were eager to share the cup which their Saviour had drunk before them.

The conspiracy was skilfully planned and boldly executed. The fortunes of the separate parties will be told in turn. The storm broke first in Ireland.

CHAPTER XXVII.

THE administration of Ireland, from Elizabeth's accession to the period at which it was to be the scene of a sanguinary religious rebellion, presents, year after year, a series of recurring features—severity ineffectually sustained, and attempts at conciliation, which were a fresh temptation to rebellion. In Ireland, as elsewhere, the Queen's personal desire was for moderation and forbearance, but a ruling power can be gentle only when it is strong. The English were a conquering race, and were therefore objects everywhere of suspicion and dislike. They had purchased in the past an imperfect toleration by adopting the habits of the conquered, but the Reformation had introduced new elements of animosity. The Parliament of the Pale had changed the religion of the country. As the circle widened over which English law was extended, an alien and intrusive creed went along with it, and the cause of Irish independence became sanctified by the obligations of piety. The native opposition grew more combined and determined; while the false economy of the Queen maintained the garrison at a strength too low to support her authority, even while the chiefs were disunited and quarrelling among themselves. She defeated her immediate object. Her thriftiness was more wasteful in the end than her father's expenditure. For the revenue of the country could not rise till rebellion was suppressed, and the suppression of rebellion cost more than the sustained police garrisons which would have prevented it. At the same time, she made impossible the forbearance which she enjoined: she talked of mercy, and she made violence inevitable. Her Deputies and her Presidents, too short-handed to rule with justice, were driven to cruelty in spite of themselves. It was easier to kill than to restrain. Death was the only gaoler which their finances could support. While the Irish in turn lay in wait to retaliate on their oppressors, and atrocity begat atrocity in hopeless continuity.

When the failure of the intended settlement of the Earl of Essex in Ulster was known in London, it produced, as usual in Elizabeth, 'a great misliking of the 'whole matter.' She blamed Burghley and Leicester 'for having advised it.' She drew directions to Essex to compose his differences with the chiefs of the O'Neils, to apologise—for it could mean nothing else—for having attempted to dispossess them of their lands; to withdraw any English holders or colonists out of the Northern Provinces, except a handful who were to be left in the castle at Knockfergus, and then to return to England.[1]

To the Earl this order was a sentence of disgrace and ruin. He had embarked honour and fortune in the enterprise. To force him to abandon it thus, at the end of a few months, was held at once unjust to himself and dangerous to the realm. His friends represented to her, that he had failed so far only from his anomalous position, and from the jealousy of the Deputy, Fitzwilliam. If Essex was made Deputy himself, his own energy, supported by the Queen's authority, would overbear opposi-

[1] Burghley to Essex, March 30, 1574.—*MSS. Ireland.*

tion. The conquest of Ulster, the conquest of all Ireland, presented no real difficulty. The Irish Lords, Ormond, Desmond, O'Neil, O'Donnell, Clancarty, O'Brien, and Clanrickard maintained among them twenty thousand armed vagabonds, who were the obstacle to the pacification of the country. The same cost and the same land which supported an army of anarchy, would support, at no cost to England, at least half the number of English police; and 'the idle kerne could then be set to their 'work or to the gallows.'[1]

This might be true in itself: but to make the kerne work, and to replace them with police, implied that the backs of the chiefs should be first broken, an exploit which might be called easy, but had hitherto proved to be hard. Elizabeth, however, partially yielded. Essex had shown many noble qualities; but a capacity for independent command had not been one of them. She made him Governor of Ulster, with a direct commission from the Crown; but she kept Fitzwilliam at his post till Sir Henry Sidney, the most successful Deputy Ireland had ever had, except Bellingham, could be prevailed on to take his place. Fresh companies were sent over with money and stores; and though the plans of confiscation and settlement were suspended, she prepared to make one more effort to bring the chiefs upon their knees.

Munster, Connaught, and Ulster were in open revolt. To carry on the war in the three provinces at once was thought impossible. Tirlogh Lenogh and Sir Phelim O'Neil (Sir Brian MacPhelim, as he was called in Ireland) were the most immediately dangerous; and she directed the Dublin authorities to make a temporary compromise with the leaders in the south and west. The

---

[1] Reasons for my Lord of Essex's preferment to be Deputy of Ireland, Feb. 19. Essex to Burghley, Feb. 9. —*MSS. Ibid.*

Earl of Desmond had promised, when he was in England, to further the Reformed Church in Cork and Kerry, to bring the bishops to obedience, complete the suppression of the monasteries, and introduce the Anglican Prayer-book.[1] He considered himself released from his engagements, if he had ever meant to keep them, by his second arbitrary arrest; and after his escape from Dublin, and his return to his own country, his first act was to replace the friars in the abbeys from which they had been expelled. No defiance could have been more open and deliberate. But Elizabeth or her Council thought it prudent to conceal their resentment, and to leave this part of their policy for the present unenforced. They meant to insist on the restoration of the two fortresses Castlemaine and Castle Martyr, which the Geraldines had surprised at the outbreak of the last rebellion; but Fitzwilliam was directed to tell Desmond, and to tell Clanrickard also, that 'if they would acknowledge their obedience as in 'former times,' they might have their own way in other matters. Terms short of unreserved submission might be offered also to the O'Neils. 'It was thought a hard 'matter to subvert the customs of the people which they 'had enjoyed to be ruled by captains of their own 'nation.' The Irish might have peace, and be governed still after their own manner; and the Queen agreed to permit Tirlogh Lenogh to retain his signories, his body-guard, his captaincies, and feudal supremacies, but she required him also to sue for pardon, to surrender his lands to the Crown, and to receive them back again under an English tenure.[2]

Essex, who had been in the deeps of despondency, brightened with the prospect of work. The men who

---

[1] *i.e.* the Latin translation of it. April 20, 1574. Burghley's hand.
[2] A memorial of Irish causes, —*MSS. Ireland.*

came to him from England were not undisciplined
emigrants, like those which had accompanied him in the
preceding autumn, but 'soldiers trained in the wars of
'the Low Countries.' Instantly on their arrival, he
marched from Belfast into Clandeboy, flung himself on
his old enemy Sir Brian MacPhelim, and in a week
brought Sir Brian on his knees, a penitent suppliant for
mercy.[1] Tirlogh Lenogh upon this promised to be a
good subject, and the O'Neils being thus submissive,
Essex turned next to the Earl of Desmond. He had
probably known him in England, and he wrote to him
as a friend, inviting and even entreating him to accept
the hand which was now held out to him. The Queen,
he said, so far from desiring to injure the Irish nobility,
wished only to strengthen them; and if he would but
assure her of his general loyalty, she would not interfere
with his rights of sovereignty. Desmond's attitude had
been so menacing that the English Council had half
resolved to send Sir William Drury with a second army
into Munster. Edward Waterhouse, a correspondent
of Walsingham, then and always insisted that the
smooth policy would fail with the Geraldine chief, that
nothing but force would hold either him or indeed any
other Irish leader in permanent subjection. Even the
bishoprics Waterhouse wished to see bestowed, for the
present, on soldiers of experience. There was no work

---

[1] Sir Brian wrote on the 8th May to the Queen, 'That he had gone wickedly astray, and wandered in the wilderness like a blind beast.' He threw himself at her Majesty's feet, imploring her clemency, and making lavish promises of good behaviour for the future. He renounced all his rights. He professed himself desirous only to live at her Majesty's hands, and petitioned only in conclusion that he might be the farmer of his own estates.—*Sir B. MacPhelim to the Queen*, May 8, 1574. *MSS. Ireland*. It is noticeable that Sir Brian, the head of the second branch of the O'Neils, from whom the present family descends, signed with a cross, being unable to write his name.

for bishops, as ministers of religion, and 'no room for 'justice till the sword had made a way for it.'[1] The liberal offers of Essex, however, found Desmond naturally willing to listen. He proposed an interview, to which Essex acceded, and Essex, accompanied by the Earl of Kildare, went to Waterford to see him. He was told that he must go through the form of surrendering to the Deputy; he made no objection, and under the protection of a safe-conduct, he returned with Essex and his cousin to Dublin. On his arrival, he found that the Queen had sent a new order, that he was to repair immediately to her presence. Remembering his long captivity, he did not choose to risk a repetition of it. He refused to go to England; and Fitzwilliam dared not disobey the letter of the Queen's instructions. The negotiation was suspended. Essex, who had pledged his honour for Desmond's safety, conducted him to the frontier of the Pale; and followed him, a month later, with Fitzwilliam and Ormond and some companies of English soldiers. A fortress on the Suir was destroyed and the garrison executed; the conditions of compromise were so far modified that the repair to England was dispensed with; and Desmond then signified his readiness to submit. He ascribed his past faults to bad advisers, whose names he was exhorted to reveal if he wished to recover perfectly his mistress's confidence.[2] He surrendered Castlemayne and Castlemartyr, which were again occupied by English garrisons, and in other respects his authority was undisturbed. He was left supreme over his feudal principality, and passed for a loyal subject.

It was again Ireland for the Irish, and the two

---

[1] Edward Waterhouse to Walsingham, June 14.—*MSS. Ireland.*
[2] The English Council to the Earl of Desmond, October, 1574.—*MSS. Ireland.*

southern provinces were left to be governed by their
own laws and their own rulers, in return for a nominal
allegiance. The same or hardly different conditions
were offered to and accepted by Tirlogh Lenogh. But
it was the curse of the English rule that it never
could adhere consistently to any definite principle.
It threatened, and failed to execute its threats. It
fell back on conciliation, yet immediately, by some
injustice or cruelty, made reliance on its good faith
impossible.

Sir Brian MacPhelim O'Neil was owner, by the Irish
law of inheritance, of the grant which Essex had received
from the Crown. The attempt to deprive him had been
relinquished. He had surrendered his lands, and the
Queen at Essex's own intercession, had reinstated him as
tenant under the Crown. It seems, however, as if Essex
had his eye still upon the property. Report said that
during the expedition against Desmond, Sir Brian had
held a suspicious conference with Tirlogh Lenogh and
the Scots of Antrim. It was assumed that he was again
playing false, and Essex determined to punish him.
He returned to Clandeboy, as if on a friendly visit.
Sir Brian and Lady O'Neil received him with all hos-
pitality. The Irish annalists say that they gave him
a banquet; he admitted himself that they made him
welcome, and that they accompanied him, afterwards,
to the Castle of Belfast. Had Sir Brian meditated
foul play, he would scarcely have ventured into an
English fortress, still less would he have selected such a
place for a crime which he could have committed with
infinitely more facility in his own country. Essex,
however, was satisfied that he intended mischief. He
had been deceived by Sir Brian once before, and 'for
'avoiding a second folly by overmuch trust,' as he ex-

pressed it, 'he determined to make sure work with so
'fickle a people.' A high feast was held in the hall.
The revelling was protracted late into the night before
Sir Brian and his wife retired to their lodging outside
the walls. As soon as they were supposed to be asleep,
a company of soldiers surrounded the house, and prepared to break the door. The O'Neils flew to arms.
The cry rang through the village, and they swarmed
out to defend their chief; but surprised, half armed, and
outnumbered, they were overpowered and cut to pieces.
Two hundred men were killed. The Four Masters add
that women were killed. The chieftain's wife had
probably female attendants with her, and no one was
knowingly spared.[1] The tide being out, a squadron of
horse was sent at daybreak over the water into the
'Ardes,' from which, in a few hours they returned with
three thousand of Sir Brian's cattle, and with a drove
of stud mares, of which the choicest were sent as a
present to Fitzwilliam. Sir Brian himself, with his
brother and Lady O'Neil, were carried as prisoners to
Dublin, where they were soon after executed.

This exploit raised Essex high in the estimation of
the Anglo-Irish of the Pale. The taint of the country
was upon him. He had made himself no better than
themselves, and was the hero of the hour. The example found, as was natural, immediate imitators.
'I may say of Ireland,' wrote Sir Edward Fitton a few
weeks later, 'that it is quiet; but if universal oppression
'of the mean sort by the great, if murders, robberies,
'burnings, make an ill commonwealth, then I cannot say

---

[1] Annals of the Four Masters, A° 1574. Essex to Fitzwilliam, Nov. 14. Essex to the English Council, Nov. 24. In the report to the Deputy the number killed was said to be a hundred and twenty-five, in the report to England to be two hundred.

'we are in good case.'[1] Public sentiment at Dublin, however, was unanimous in its approbation. Essex was the man who would cauterise the long standing sores. There was a soldier in Ireland at last who understood the work that was to be done and the way to set about it. Beloved by the soldiers, 'admirable alike for 'religion, nobility, and courtesy,' 'altogether the Queen's, 'and not bewitched with the factions of the realm,' the governor of Ulster had but to be armed with supreme power, and the long wished for conquest of Ireland would be easily and instantly achieved.[2] Fitzwilliam, who had been waiting impatiently for Sidney's coming to relieve him, was not more reconciled to his place by the popularity of Essex, or by Essex's performances. He 'was made the packhorse,' he said, ' for reproof and 'disgrace.' He was ruined in fortune. He was blamed for all that went wrong. He complained piteously that 'his fate would be to be buried in Ireland and slandered 'in England.'[3]

He and Essex could not work healthily together; but as Sidney's reluctance was not yet overcome, the Queen could not resolve to recall either of them. She was not displeased with the massacre of the O'Neils. Her occasional disapprobation of severities of this kind was confined to cases to which the attention of Europe happened to be especially directed. She told Essex that 'he was a great ornament of her nobility; she 'wished she had many as ready as he to spend their lives 'and fortunes for the benefit of their country.'[4] Taking courage at the overthrow of Sir Brian, she was half

---

[1] Fitton to Burghley, Jan. 5, 1575. MSS. Ireland.
[2] Waterhouse to Walsingham, Jan. 1.—MSS.
[3] Fitzwilliam to the Council, April 26.—MSS. Ireland.
[4] The Queen to Essex, April 12. MSS Ireland.

persuaded into allowing Essex to follow up his success, and break the power by similar means of all the northern chiefs. She empowered him to levy the forces of the Pale, and rebuked Fitzwilliam for want of forwardness in giving him assistance. She encouraged him to continue his preparations till the intended invasion of Tirlogh Lenogh was on everybody's lips. Then suddenly, either alarmed at the expense, or for some other reason, she changed her mind. Essex, she said, might be surprised, that having so lately desired him to resume his enterprise, she should so soon be of another opinion; but she had been afraid of a general revolt if it had been suddenly known to be abandoned, and in fact had never meant the conquest to be seriously resumed at all: she had found occasion to look more earnestly into her estate at home, and had discovered causes which made an Irish war at that time undesirable, and Essex was ordered to make peace with the Ulster leaders on the least dishonourable terms which he could obtain.[1]

There would be no occasion to dwell on these vacillations, so universal as they were in every department with which the Queen interfered, but for their consequences to the miserable Irish: the English officers distracted by change of purpose, encouraged in acts which roused the fiercest exasperation, and then forbidden to carry out their severities to conclusions which would have formed the sole justification of commencing them, employed their forces in murderous raids where they were not strong enough to conquer. The order to make peace gave Essex discretionary power as to the means of effecting it. A reproach of cowardice had been thrown out against him by Leicester. He had a few

[1] The Queen to Essex, May 22, Instructions to Mr. Asheton sent to the Earl of Essex, May 22.—MSS. Ireland.

hundred soldiers ready to march, and he preferred to negotiate in the field. Before the news of the change of policy could reach Ulster he made a rapid march into Tyrone, carried off twelve hundred of Tirlogh's cattle, defeated him in action, and all but took him prisoner, and then exacting an oath of him for his future good behaviour, he left him in possession by treaty of all his lands, privileges, and royalties, and of all the estates of the religious houses between the Bann and the Blackwater, Lough Foyle and Lough Erne.[1] The sovereignty of the O'Neils remained unimpaired, and the attempt to introduce English law or English religion was not pursued. The attack therefore had been simply gratuitous; a few more Irish had been killed without provocation, and the rest was left as before.

From Tyrone the English army turned into Antrim—again not to conquer, but to hunt; to chastise as it was called Surleyboy Macconnell, and the Scots.[2] To him too he read a sharp and worse than useless lesson on the 22nd of July. After slaughtering many of his people, he reported that Ulster was now at peace, and that the Queen could resolve at leisure what next she would do, and then he returned to Dublin.

The work of the expedition, however, was not over. It had yet to receive its crowning distinction. Ulster, as Essex admitted, was quiet; but quiet or not quiet, wolves were still wolves to be exterminated wherever they could be caught.

---

[1] 'Item habebit omnes terras monasteriorum, abbatiarum, et aliarum ædium spiritualium intra dictum præcinctum.' Essex adds in a note, 'Upon examination what monasteries and other spiritual lands there were in the circuit of land now appointed to Tirlogh, it was proved that there were neither abbeys nor any religious houses at any time in those parts save priories wherein the friars do yet remain.'—*Articles of Peace with Tirlogh*, June 17, 1575. *MSS. Ireland*.

[2] Surley boy, otherwise spelt Sarley boy or Sarle boigh: meaning Sarley or Charley the yellow-haired.

On the coast of Antrim, not far from the Giant's Causeway, lies the singular Island of Rathlin. It is formed of basaltic rock, encircled with precipices, and is accessible only at a single spot. It contains an area of about 4,000 acres, of which a thousand are sheltered and capable of cultivation, the rest being heather and rock. The approach is at all times dangerous; the tide sets fiercely through the strait which divides the island from the mainland, and when the wind is from the west, the Atlantic swell renders it impossible to land. The situation and the difficulty of access had thus long marked Rathlin as a place of refuge for Scotch or Irish fugitives, and besides its natural strength it was respected as a sanctuary, having been the abode at one time of Saint Columba. A mass of broken masonry on a cliff overhanging the sea, is a remnant of the castle, in which Robert Bruce watched the leap of the legendary spider. To this island, when Essex entered Antrim, Macconnell and the other Scots had sent their wives and children, their aged, and their sick for safety. On his way through Carrickfergus, when returning to Dublin, the Earl ascertained that they had not yet been brought back to their homes. The officer in command of the English garrison (it is painful to mention the name either of him or of any man concerned in what ensued) was John Norris, Lord Norris's second son, so famous afterwards in the Low Countries, grandson of Sir Henry Norris executed for adultery with Anne Boleyn. Three small frigates were in the harbour. The summer had been dry, hot, and windless. The sea was smooth; there was a light and favourable air from the east; and Essex directed Norris to take a company of soldiers with him, cross over and kill whatever he could find. The run up the Antrim coast was rapidly and quietly accomplished.

Before an alarm could be given the English had landed,[1] close to the ruins of the church which bears Saint Columba's name. Bruce's castle was then standing, and was occupied by a score or two of Scots, who were in charge of the women. But Norris had brought cannon with him. The weak defences were speedily destroyed, and after a fierce assault, in which several of the garrison were killed, the chief who was in command offered to surrender, if he and his people were allowed to return to Scotland. The conditions were rejected; the Scots yielded at discretion, and every living creature in the place except the chief and his family, who were probably reserved for ransom, was immediately put to the sword. Two hundred were killed in the castle. It was then discovered that several hundred more, chiefly mothers and their little ones, were hidden in the caves about the shore. There was no remorse, not even the faintest shadow of perception that the occasion called for it. They were hunted out as if they had been seals or otters, and all destroyed. Surleyboy and the other chiefs, Essex coolly wrote, had sent their wives and children into the island, 'which be 'all taken and executed to the number of six hundred.' Surleyboy himself, he continued, 'stood upon the main-'land of the Glynnes and saw the taking of the island, 'and was likely to have run mad for sorrow, tearing 'and tormenting himself, and saying that he there lost 'all that ever he had.'[2]

The impression left upon the mind by this horrible story is increased by the composure with which even the news of it was received. 'Yellow-haired Charley' might tear himself for 'his pretty little ones and their dam,' but in Ireland itself the massacre was not specially

---

[1] July 22.
[2] Essex to Walsingham, July 31. 1575.—*MSS. Ireland.* Essex to the Queen, July 31.—*Carew Papers.*

distinguished in the general system of atrocity. Essex described it himself as one of the exploits with which he was most satisfied, and Elizabeth in answer to his letters bade him tell John Norris, 'the executioner of his 'well designed enterprise, that she would not be unmind-'ful of his services.'[1] But though passed over and unheeded at the time, and lying buried for three hundred years, the bloody stain comes back to light again, not in myth and legend, but in the original account of the nobleman by whose command the deed was done; and when the history of England's dealings with Ireland settles at last into its final shape, that hunt among the caves at Rathlin will not be forgotten. It is some satisfaction to learn that an officer and forty of the soldiers, who had been concerned in it, were cut off three months after, near Carrickfergus. Essex himself went back in the autumn to England, to gather together what remained of his property and arrange for the payment of his debts.

A short interval of better days was now approaching. Sidney, who for many reasons was liked by the Irish, was prevailed on at last to accept what he called his thankless charge. Tirlogh O'Neil congratulated the Government on his appointment, 'wretched Ireland 'needing not the sword,' but sober, temperate, and humane 'administration.'[2] The hot summer had been followed by the plague. Dublin and the neighbouring villages were infected, and not choosing to go near the pestilential atmosphere, the new Deputy landed, accompanied by his son Philip, at Drogheda, and though in the dead of the winter, commenced a progress round

---

[1] The Queen to Essex, Aug. 12.—*Carew Papers.*
[2] Tirlogh O'Neil to the Queen, to Burghley, and to Walsingham, Nov. 1575.—*MSS. Ireland.*

the four provinces. Going first into Ulster he saw Surleyboy, to whom at his earnest entreaty he restored Rathlin, perhaps that he might collect and bury his dead. On leaving the Scots he paid a friendly visit to O'Neil, who gave him assurance of his loyalty, and intimated that if he was well treated he would accept an earldom and adopt English manners. Referring him to Elizabeth, Sidney crossed rapidly through Leinster, which he reported as being for the most part waste, burnt up, and destroyed, and then went on through Waterford, Dungarvan, and Youghal, to Cork. Everywhere he was received with acclamation. The wretched people, sanguine then as ever in the midst of sorrow, looked on his coming as the inauguration of a new and happier era. Three earls, Desmond, Thomond, and Clancarty, attended him with their retinues. The intriguing restless James Fitzmaurice, disappointing utterly Sir John Perrot's expectations of him, had left the country, and was now alternately in France and Spain, preaching the wrongs of Ireland. His relations and the other Munster chiefs appeared to be weary of disaffection, and willing to be loyal if their religion was not interfered with. M'Carties, O'Sullivans, O'Carrolls, M'Teigues, Roches, came to the Viceroy's levées, 'detesting their barbarous lives,' 'willing to hold their lands from her Highness, and 'promising rent and service.' The past was wiped out. Confiscation on one side, and rebellion on the other, were to be forgotten and heard of no more. A clean page was turned. The Irish were ready to be quiet if they might manage Ireland their own way; and England was eager to receive them on their own terms.

Strange figures appeared to pay their homage. Among them Granny O'Malley, a famous virago of Connaught, came round from Achill with her three pirate galleys, and two hundred men, to Cork harbour. This woman was wife of 'the MacWilliam,' chief of the second branch of the Burkes. Sidney says expressively, 'she 'had brought her husband with her;' 'by sea and land 'being more than Mrs. Mate with him.'[1] She and her galleys were to be at Sidney's disposition if he pleased to use them, and a close acquaintance sprung up as was natural between herself and young Philip.[2]

Then too at Cork, writes Sidney, 'there came to me 'three or four bishops of the provinces of Cashel and 'Tuam, which bishops, albeit they were Papists, sub-'mitted themselves to the Queen's Majesty, acknow-'ledging that they held their temporal patrimony of her 'Majesty, and desiring to be inducted into their eccle-'siastical prelacies.'[3]

It was a grand and imposing reception, filling even Sidney's unsanguine mind with hopes of brighter days for Ireland. So changed had the people become, so

---

[1] Sidney to Walsingham, March 1, 1583.—*Carew Papers.*

[2] Sir Wm. Drury mentions this singular woman two years later. 'Granny O'Malley,' he says, 'a woman that hath impudently passed the parts of womanhood, and been a great spoiler and chief commander and director of thieves and murderers at sea, to spoil this province, having been apprehended by the Earl of Desmond this last year, his lordship hath now sent her to me to Limerick, where she remains in sure keeping.'—*Drury to the Council*, March 24, 1578. *MSS. Ireland.*

[3] 'There was some hold,' Sidney continues, 'between the bishops and me too long here to be recited; for they stood still upon mero suo ordine, and I of the Queen's absolute authority.' He does not say how the dispute terminated, which it is likely that he would have done if he had brought them to submission. But the passage any way requires explanation from those who maintain that all the bishops in Ireland, except those of Meath and Kildare, took the oath of supremacy at Elizabeth's accession, and conformed to the Reformation. Here in Munster, after she had been Queen eighteen years, were three or four bishops described by the Viceroy as Papists, unsworn as yet, and in actual possession of the temporalities of their sees. Who and what were they? Bishops still surviving who had been appointed by Mary, or bishops since appointed by the Pope? one of the two they must have been.—*Sidney to Walsingham*, March 1, 1583. *Carew Papers.*

willing to do all that was reasonable to please him, that he records of Cork, 'We got good and honest juries 'there, and with their help twenty-four malefactors 'were honourably condemned and hanged.' The gallows everywhere was the perhaps much needed but the unfortunate symbol of each advance of English authority. It might have worked better had justice been even-handed, and had scoundrels of both nations been hung upon it indifferently.

From Cork the progress was continued to Limerick and Galway, where the same ovation attended the Deputy. There were grievances to be redressed, and crimes to be punished, 'plenty of burnings, rapes, 'murders, sacrileges, besides such spoil in goods and 'cattle as in number might be counted infinite and in 'quantity immeasurable.' The citizens at Galway, 'if 'their report was to be believed, had lost more than four 'times the whole value of the county.' Sir Henry satisfied them as he could, used the rope again freely for the hanging of rascals, and so in April came at last to Dublin, from which he sent over his reports with reflections on the general condition of the country. He insisted, as when he was Deputy five years before he had urgently advised, that Connaught and Munster must be made into presidencies. The experiment might have failed once, but it must be tried again at all costs. If England, for its own convenience, found it necessary to occupy Ireland, England was bound to make its government a reality. It was bound to protect the poor from the oppression of the chiefs, who under an affectation of loyalty to the Crown, were now securing an immunity to tyrannise in their own counties.[1] 'Munster was

---

[1] Then and always the difficulty with Ireland has been that the peasantry prefer ill government by their own people, to the most intel-

'in towardness to be reformed,' said Sidney, but notwithstanding the display of good will, 'if James Fitzmaurice came back, and there was no English governor 'in the province, he would have the whole country at 'his feet.'[1] He was not deceived by the smoothness of the surface. The causes of disaffection were vigorous as ever. The momentary peace had been bought by the abandonment of effort for the real regeneration of the country. Most distressing, and most pregnant with future disaster, was the condition of the Church, which had been flung out like a carcase to be the prey of the wolf and the kite. Elizabeth's latest orders were to establish peace, and leave creeds and doctrines to settle themselves. Sidney saw clearly that nothing permanent could be arrived at on that road; and his opinion was the more important, as he was one of those statesmen who had hesitated long and gravely on the prudence of the revolution in England which had been made at the Queen's accession. 'Preposterous it seems to me,' he wrote, 'to begin reformation of the politic part and 'neglect the religious; and the Church here is so spoiled 'as well by the ruin of temples and the dissipation and 'embezzling of patrimony, as so deformed and over-'thrown a Church there is not, I am sure, in any region 'where Christ is professed.'[2]

Enthusiastic defenders of the Irish Establishment have maintained that during the first eleven years of the reign of Elizabeth the prelates and clergy were working cor-

---

ligent and most just administration of the Saxons. Yet it is interesting to find a confession even in an Irish annalist, that the difference was felt and perceived. When Sir John Perrot left Munster, the Four Masters scornfully say, 'his departure was lamented by the poor, the widows, the feeble, and the unwarlike.'

[1] Sidney to the English Council, April 27.—*MSS. Ireland.*
[2] *Ibid.*

dially and successfully on the new paths which had
been opened to them. The truth is rather that the old
creed had been shaken to its base, while carelessness or
atheism were revelling among its ruins. In the three
Irish provinces the religious houses had fallen to the
chiefs. About half of them were still occupied by friars.
The lands were annexed to the patrimonies of the
O'Neils, the Desmonds, the O'Briens, and the O'Don-
nells, who allowed the old occupants to remain in
possession; but the monks had lost for the most part
even the outward show of religion, and were little better
than organised bands of freebooters. In the Pale the
suppression had been complete. The houses were
destroyed or given to laymen. The benefices which
had been attached to them were impropriated to the
Crown, and farmed at the best prices which speculators
would offer for them, the Queen being eager only to
wring from Ireland some driblet of revenue to meet its
enormous expenses, and troubling herself apparently
not the least about the spiritual condition of the
people.

But the Irish were constitutionally religious. They
could not long remain without some kind of spiritual
sustenance, and a strong Catholic reaction was now setting in. Young men of family were going to Louvaine,
or to the Spanish universities, to study, and were returning filled with the passions of the counter-reforma-
tion. The Irish dioceses began to be of concern to the
Pope, and the sees, as they fell vacant, to be supplied by
Papal nominees. So dangerous a movement could be
encountered only by the teaching of the so-called purer
creed, and Sidney felt it his duty to lay before his mistress the condition of one single diocese inside the Pale,
the best managed, as he affirmed it to be, in all Ireland,

and therefore conveying, in the most striking form, the lesson on which he wished to insist.

There were in Meath, he said, two hundred and twenty-four benefices, of which one hundred and five belonged to the Crown. In these hundred and five parishes there was not a single resident clergyman. The roofs of the churches had fallen in, the windows were broken, the doors were off their hinges. No effort had been made to provide educated Protestant ministers. A curate, whose duties were distributed between three or four parishes, went occasionally through the form of what he called a service. He had been a priest in the Roman times, and so far as he was anything he was a priest still; but in reality he was nothing better than 'an Irish rogue.'¹ The parishes in the hands of the

---

¹ It has been stated with much positiveness, that the Reformed liturgy, either in English or Latin, was in use in Ireland, and the Reformed religion taught at the beginning of the reign of Elizabeth. Besides the memorable letter of Sidney, other evidence survives on this curious subject which cannot be impugned. In the year 1584, eight years, therefore, after Sidney's remonstrance, the prebendaries of St. Patrick in Dublin wrote thus to the Council: 'There is not one in that land which can or will preach the gospel, four bishops and the prebendaries of St. Patrick only excepted. There is an infinite number of impropriated churches in Ireland, all being in her Majesty's hands or her farmers. There is not in any one impropriation a preacher—there is scant a minister to be found among them, but rather a company of Irish rogues, and Romish priests teaching nothing but traitorous practices, all in a manner enemies by profession to God's true religion. This comes of the covetousness of her Majesty's farmers, who for the most part allow not the ministers above forty shillings or three pounds by the year, and therefore seeketh a priest that will serve his cure the cheapest, without regard to person or quality, and then this curate to make his stipend as he may live upon it, travelleth like a lackey to three or four churches in the morning, every church a mile or two miles asunder, and there once a week readeth them only a gospel in Latin, and so away, and so the poor people are deluded.'—MSS. Ireland, Dec. 1584.

Three years later an English resident in Ireland writes:—

'There is no divine service in the country—all the churches are clean down, ruinous, and in great decay. The ministers will not be accounted ministers but priests. They will have no wives. If it would stay

Anglo-Irish owners were in scarcely less disorder. And if this was the state of the best governed county in the realm, Sir Henry left the Queen to infer the condition of the rest. The children were growing up unbaptized, the churches were falling to pieces, 'the arch-'bishopricks and bishopricks pilled and ruined, partly by 'the prelates themselves, partly by the potentates, their 'noisome neighbours.'[1]

The Crown was most immediately to blame. Sir Henry entreated that in the Crown benefices at least care should be taken to provide competent ministers. Elizabeth listened, but did nothing. It was no policy of hers that two opposite creeds should grow up together to generate hatreds and quarrels; and since she would not put down the Catholics, she did not wish the Protestants to become strong. Lord Burghley replied for her that no doubt 'a sound state of religion 'was the foundation of civil government, so necessary 'as without it no commonwealth might stand.' He said that if two members of the Irish Council would come to London, her Majesty would consult with them.[2] But the consultation, if they went, remained barren. Three years

---

there it were well; but they have harlots, which they make believe it is no sin to live and lie with them, but if they marry they are damned. With long experience and some extraordinary trial of these fellows, I cannot find whether the most of them love lewd women, cards, dice, or drink best, and when they must of necessity go to church, they carry with them a book in Latin of the Common Prayer, set forth and allowed by her Majesty, but they read little or nothing of it, or can well read it; but they tell the people a tale of Our Lady, or St. Patrick, or some other saint, horrible to be spoken or heard of, and do all they may to dissuade and allure the people from God and their prince, and their due obedience to them both, and persuade them to the Devil the Pope.'—*Andrew Trollope to Walsingham*, Oct. 16, 1587.—*MSS. Ireland.*

[1] Sir Henry Sidney to the Queen, April 28, 1576.—*MSS. Ireland.*

[2] Burghley to Sidney, July 10.—*MSS. Ibid.*

later Sir William Pelham reported that in the immediate neighbourhood of Dublin, there were sixteen benefices in one block belonging to the Queen, in no one of which was there vicar or minister;[1] and as a commentary on the value of the established ecclesiastical organisation, Sir William Gerrard, the Irish Chancellor, recommended that Archbishop Loftus should be translated to some English see, the see of Dublin sequestrated, and the revenues applied to the maintenance of circuit judges, and to the better execution of the laws within the Pale.[2]

As usual, there were two possible policies, and neither one nor the other was consistently followed. Sidney wished to reform the church and country, and conceived 'that he worked but waywardly when the latter was 'preferred before the former.' Waterhouse, the advocate of military despotism, advised the Queen, as has been already said, to bestow her bishoprics on soldiers, 'there 'being no room for justice till the sword had made a 'way for the law.'[3] Elizabeth, halting between two opinions, concluded upon the course which would be least immediately troublesome. She left the establishment standing, and continued to squeeze a miserable revenue out of the neglected benefices; while for religious reformers, who wished to impart some life to it, she had but one answer, that there should be no persecution and no straining of conscience. If the Irish were to become Protestants, they were to be won by time and instruction; and Sidney had to acquiesce in the same resolution which, with equal emphasis, was enforced afterwards upon his successors. 'The miserable state of the Church 'of Ireland,' wrote Walsingham a few years after, 'grieves

---

[1] Carew Papers, Dec. 7, 1579.
[2] Sir Wm. Gerrard to Walsingham, Oct. 19, 1576.—Carew Papers.
[3] Waterhouse to Walsingham, June 14, 1574.—MSS. Ireland.

'me much to think upon, the rather for I see no help of
'remedy to be applied to it. The Lord Deputy's mind to-
'wards the reformation of the country is very honourable,
'but it has not been agreeable to our humours. He might
'have lived in better season in the time of King Henry
'VIII., when princes were resolute to persist in honour-
'able attempts; but our age has been given to other
'manner of proceedings, whereunto the Lord Deputy
'must be content to conform himself as other men do.'[1]

The recommendations for civil government were more favourably attended to. Sir William Drury was appointed President of Munster, and signified his accession to office by vigorous operations of the usual kind. In the autumn which followed Sidney's progress, he too held an itinerant justice court in the southern province. At an assize at Cork, according to his own report, he hung forty-three notable malefactors. One he pressed to death as declining to plead to his indictment, and two traitorous M'Sweenies from Kerry were drawn and quartered.[2] At Limerick he disposed of twenty-two more. In a subsequent sessions at Kilkenny he executed thirty-six, among which, he says, with laudable satisfaction, were 'some good ones.' Two he hanged for treason, and three others, 'a blackamoor and two witches,' he put to death 'by natural law, for that he found no law to try 'them by in the realm.'[3] But on the whole he thought it necessary to apologise for his moderation. 'I have 'chosen rather,' he wrote, 'with the snail slenderly to 'creep, than with the horse swiftly to run.'[4]

Notwithstanding the calamitous failure of Sir Edward Fitton as President of Connaught, Col. Malby, who was

---

[1] Walsingham to the Archbishop of Armagh, Dec. 1585.—*MSS. Ireland.*
[2] Drury to Walsingham, Nov. 24. *MSS. Ireland.*
[3] Carew Papers, p. 144.
[4] Drury to Walsingham, Nov. 24, 1576.—*MSS. Ireland.*

knighted on his appointment, was sent to Athlone in his place. The re-establishment of the Presidencies was an intimation to the chiefs that after all, their jurisdictions were to be superseded; and if Drury's executions were to be regarded as creeping, they had cause to fear for themselves when he began to move in earnest. They held their compact with the Deputy to be broken, and they prepared once more to try conclusions in the field. The two sons of the Earl of Clanrickard, Ulick and John, who had distinguished themselves in the rebellion against Fitton, were the first to appear as the champions of their father's rights. Before Malby could arrive they broke out. Sidney hastened in person to Athlone. The country had been slow in answering to their call, and old Clanrickard, afraid of consequences to himself, came trembling to him, protesting his innocency, and begging pardon on his knees in Athlone Church for his boys' indiscretion. Sidney sternly told him that 'the bastard 'brats' must be brought to him, dead or alive, or the Queen would seize his lands and extirpate his house from Connaught. He promised the humblest obedience for them, and on the occasion of Malby's instalment, they presented themselves under a safe-conduct at Athlone, and undertook to serve under the President if he would guarantee them the Queen's pardon.

'Her Majesty,' reported Malby, 'having charged me 'to win the Irish if possible by gentle methods, I agreed 'to this.' The Burkes 'swore fearful oaths' that they meant loyally; and having, as they supposed, thrown the President off his guard, they made a sudden attempt to seize him. Missing their mark, they attacked a few outlying companies of English soldiers who were billeted in the adjoining farmhouses, and destroyed them. It was the middle of the winter, when they considered themselves safe from immediate retribution. Malby sent to Dublin for reinforcements, and proceeded to show them that they were mistaken.

'At Christmas,' he wrote, 'I marched into their coun-
'try, and finding courteous dealing with them had like
'to have cut my throat, I thought good to take another
'course; and so with determination to consume them with
'fire and sword, sparing neither old nor young, I
'entered their mountains.[1] I burnt all their corn and
'houses, and committed to the sword all that could be
'found, where were slain at that time above sixty of their
'best men, and among them the best leaders they had.
'This was Shan Burke's country. Then I burnt Ulick
'Burke's country in like manner. I assaulted a castle
'where the garrison surrendered. I put them to the
'misericordia of my soldiers. They were all slain. Thence
'I went on, sparing none which came in my way, which
'cruelty did so amaze their followers that they could
'not tell where to bestow themselves. Shan Burke
'made means to me to pardon him and forbear killing of
'his people. I would not hearken, but held on my way.
'The gentlemen of Clanrickard came to me; I found it
'was but dallying to win time; so I left Ulick as little
'corn and as few houses standing as I had left his
'brother, and what people was found had as little
'favour as the other had. It was all done in rain and
'frost and storm, journeys in such weather bringing
'them the sooner to submission. They are humble
'enough now, and will yield to any terms we like to
'offer them.'[2]

Where the people were quiet there was the rope for

---

[1] The Slievh Droughty Mountains over Lough Derg.
[2] Sir Nicholas Malby to Walsing-ham, March 17, 1577.—MSS. Ireland.

malefactors, and death by 'natural law' for those whom the law written would not touch. Where they broke out there was the blazing homestead, and death by the sword for all, not for the armed kerne only, but for the aged and infirm, the nursing mother, and the baby at the breast. These, with ruined churches, and Irish rogues for ministers—these, and so far only these, were the symbols of the advance of English rule; yet even Sidney could but order more and more severity, and the President of Munster was lost in wonder at the detestation with which the English name was everywhere regarded. Clanrickard surrendered. He was sent to Dublin, and the Deputy wished to hang him, but he dared not execute an earl without consulting his mistress, and Elizabeth's leniency in Ireland, as well as England, was alive and active towards the great, though it was dead towards the poor. She could hear without emotion of the massacres at Rathlin or Slievh Broughty, but the blood of the nobles, who had betrayed their wretched followers into the rebellion for which they suffered, was for ever precious in her sight. She forbade Sidney to touch him.

Shortly before these horrors the Earl of Essex had died. After he had set his affairs at home in some order he had returned in the past September to Dublin, and it was perhaps intended that he should take Sidney's place. Three weeks after he landed he was dead. Lady Essex was generally believed to have intrigued, during his first absence, with the Earl of Leicester. She married her lover immediately that she was free, and the sudden deaths of husbands at convenient times throw suspicion upon wives who are in haste to profit by them. Whether Essex was poisoned must remain uncertain. The symptoms were those of violent dysentery. Nothing wrong was detected when the body was examined; but the analytical skill of the Dublin surgeons was not great, and Leicester's antecedents do not entitle him to a charitable construction of the doubt. The circumstances of the death were singularly touching. Notwithstanding Rathlin, Essex was one of the noblest of living Englishmen, and that such a man could have ordered such a deed, being totally unconscious of the horror of it, is not the least instructive feature in the dreadful story.

His bearing, when he learnt that he was to die, was described by a bystander 'as more like that of a divine 'preacher or heavenly prophet than a man.' 'He never 'let pass an hour without many most sweet prayers.' 'He regretted that of late he had lived but a soldier's 'life, thinking more of his Prince and of his duty than 'of his God.' 'He prayed much for the noble realm of 'England, for which he feared many calamities.' His opinion of the religious character of his countrymen was most unfavourable. 'The Gospel had been preached to 'them,' he said, 'but they were neither Papists nor 'Protestants; of no religion, but full of pride and in-'iquity. There was nothing but infidelity, infidelity, 'infidelity; atheism, atheism; no religion, no religion.' With which gloomy iteration, breaking out spasmodically as his breath ran short, Walter Devereux, father of the more famous but far meaner Robert, passed away; the Archbishop of Dublin, Edward Waterhouse, and young Fitzwilliam, standing round his bed and watching him die.[1] It was perhaps well for him that his career was cut short. Had he lived through the events which were now fast approaching, he might have

---

[1] Narrative of the Death of the Earl of Essex, September 22, 1576.— *MSS. Ireland.*

reaped bloody laurels: but he had too much blood upon his head already.

The symptoms of an approaching explosion could no longer be mistaken. The angry spirit was as universal as it was deserved. The Deputy, straitened as he had been for money, had been driven into a severe exaction of the cess, a tax in kind on every ploughland for the support of the army; and the gentlemen of the Pale were as discontented as the O'Neils and the Burkes. The police duty for which the army was maintained was left undone: the cattle were not safe in the fields under the walls of Dublin. Complaints being unheeded, the landowners of Meath and Kildare refused at last to allow the cess to be levied, and it was found necessary to arrest half of them, and fling them into Dublin Castle. They were all Catholics, and loathed the mockery which was offered them in lieu of their own ritual. The bishoprics had been made prizes for the scrambling of scoundrels. Ross Carberry, and Kilfenoragh were occupied by laymen.[1] The Bishop of Killaloe was a boy at Oxford.[2] In some sees there were bishops nominated from Rome,[3] whom the Government recognised or did not recognise as their humour varied. The Bishop of Cork sold the livings in his diocese to 'horsemen' and 'kerne,' and when called to account, defended himself in a sermon, preached before the Lord President in the cathedral, saying 'that except he sold 'the livings of his collation he was not able to live, his 'bishopric was so poor.'[4]

At Waterford, where the English service was estab-

---

[1] Answer of the Commissioners, Garvey and Ackworth, to the complaints of the Archbishop of Dublin, Jan. 2, 1579.—*MSS. Ireland.*

[2] Sir Wm. Fitzwilliam to the Council, August 16, 1574.—*MSS. Ibid.*

[3] Answer of the Commissioners.

[4] *Ibid.*

lished with some regularity, the citizens refused to attend, but took possession of their churches early in the mornings, and heard mass there. They would accept none of the rites of religion from the Reformed clergy. Their own priests married them in private houses. They buried their dead in spots of their own selection, avoiding the churchyards, which they now regarded as profaned, and consecrating these new resting-places 'with prayers and flowers and candles and ringing of 'bells.' The gallows was the only effective English preacher of righteousness. Sir William Drury, in the second year of his office, reported that he had hanged four hundred persons 'by justice and martial law.' All sorts suffered that he held to be dangerous, and taking especial pains to exasperate Irish sentiment, he hanged a friar in his habit, whom he caught attempting to fly the country; and he hanged a Brehon 'who was 'much esteemed among the common people, and taught 'such laws as were repugnant to her Majesty's.'[1]

If the Irish would have submitted, if they would have relinquished, without a struggle, their habits, their language, their laws, and their creed, England would have bestowed upon them, in return, her own better laws, her own better religion, and the orderly and just government which they had been unable to provide for themselves. The poor would have been protected from plunder, the weaker chiefs from the swords of their stronger neighbours. There would have been no confiscation, no oppression, no wrong of any kind. The object of England was to extend to her wayward sister every blessing which she most valued for herself. She desired nothing but the true genuine good of the Irish people, and because they did not recognise her kindness,

[1] Sir William Drury to the Council, March 24, 1577-8.—*MSS. Ireland.*

she thought herself justified in treating them like wild beasts. The triumphal progress of the Deputy, the levees at Cork and Galway, the policy of conciliation, had ended in vanity. To leave Ireland to be governed by the Irish was to give it over to anarchy, and the system had invariably failed whenever it was tried. The appointment of the presidents, and their hard and cruel rule, shewed the chiefs that the fine speeches at Sidney's reception had been but an affectation to delude them into quiet while English authority was establishing itself; and the signs of an approaching rebellion were visible to the blindest eyes.

Sidney, who saw the storm coming, made haste out of the country before it broke: perhaps unable to encounter the expense which the acceptance of all office under Elizabeth entailed, and which a war would make trebly burdensome to him.[1] The sword of justice was left to the President of Munster, who had been so successful in inspiring hatred; and while the country was outwardly quiet, communications had been passing close and thick with the courts of France and Spain. Long before, a Spanish force would have been landed in Munster but for Philip's reluctance to quarrel with Elizabeth, and his just distrust of the Irish temperament. While English volunteers were in the pay of the Netherlands, no fair complaint could have been raised if a few hundred or thousand Castilians had come to the help of their fellow Catholics in Ireland. Philip, however, had formed no good opinion of Irish constancy, and his distrust was painfully justified. Tirlogh O'Neil, and Hugh O'Donnell wrote to him for help in 1575-6, after

---

[1] 'Three times her Majesty has sent me as her deputy to Ireland. I returned from each of them three thousand pounds worse than I went.' *Sidney to Walsingham*, March 1, 1583.—*Carew Papers.*

Essex's murderous campaign. Their first messenger was taken by the English and hanged. The second, a friar, made his way to Madrid and presented his supplication.[1] O'Neil, however, had been under the influence of his wife, the famous Scotch Countess who had undergone so many fortunes, and who hated England and all belonging to it for the sake of Mary Stuart. Philip's final answer was, as usual, slow in coming, and O'Neil finding Sidney inclined to keep the peace with him, wrote privately to say that if England would help him to destroy the Scots in Antrim, he would send his Countess about her business.[2]

Little confidence could be placed in allies so fickle, but another figure was now to be introduced upon the scene. Doctor Nicolas Sanders has been already mentioned in this history as the most energetic of the English Catholic refugees. He was now just turned fifty. He had been educated at Winchester, and was afterwards Fellow of New College, where he had resided till the accession of Elizabeth. He had witnessed the anarchy under Edward, the restoration of order with Mary, and had been probably present at the burning of Cranmer. He went abroad with the next revolution. He attended the Council of Trent, and afterwards, being a man of great practical force and energy, he became the ruling spirit among the refugees, and the most enthusiastic preacher of a Catholic crusade against England. When Philip, to his bitter disappointment, made peace with Elizabeth, he turned to the Pope; and he employed his leisure, till Gregory saw his way to interference, in helping forward the Catholic cause by the most venomous

---

[1] La suma de la commision y cartas que Fray Donato Irlandes traxó de los señores de Irlanda, 1576. — *MSS. Simancas.*

[2] Sidney to the Council, March 17, 1576.—*MSS. Ireland.*

and most successful of libels. In a history of 'The
'English Schism,'[1] he collected into a focus every charge
which malignity had imagined against Henry VIII. and
his ministers; and so skilful was his workmanship
that Nicolas Sanders, in the teeth of Statute and State
Paper, in direct contradiction of every contemporary
document which can claim authority,—except the invectives of Pole, which he appropriated and exaggerated—
has had the shaping of the historic representation of
the Anglican Reformation. Sanders 'On the Origin and
'Progress of the English Schism' has governed the impressions of millions who have least believed that they
were under his influence. Not a scandalous story was
current at the time of the revolt from the Papacy but
Sanders took possession of it and used it—used it so
adroitly that he produced a book which eclipsed Buchanan's 'Detectio,' and made Mary Stuart's doings appear
pale and innocent beside the picture of rapine, lust, and
murder, which he held up before the eyes of Europe.

Having delivered himself of his book, Sanders spent
his time between Rome and Madrid, ever watching his
opportunities, supplying Philip with information from
England, and never ceasing, in spite of discouragement,
to press the claims upon him of the suffering Catholics.
An acquaintance with Sir T. Stukeley, which he formed
at Rome, and with Fitzmaurice, whom he met in Spain,
drew his attention specially towards Ireland. Here was
a distinctly Catholic people, trodden under foot by the
English harlot, troubled by no scruples of loyalty like
his own countrymen, but ready with the smallest help
from abroad to fight for the good cause. Here then
was an opportunity like no other for striking Elizabeth
at her point of least advantage.

---

[1] De Origine ac Progressu Schismatis Anglicani Liber.

At the end of the year 1577, the moment so long waited for appeared to have come. Drake had sailed from Plymouth. The war party on the councils of both Spain and England were clamorous for an end of uncertainty, and a powerful insurrection in Ireland might perhaps decide Philip's irresolution. Fitzmaurice obtained money from the Pope, and a commission as general in the Pope's name, with power to raise troops in all Catholic countries for the service of the Church. Sanders was chosen to accompany him as Legate, and applied to the King of Spain for assistance. 'The Irish 'people,' he said, 'were unanimously well affected to 'Spain. They were Catholics, they were themselves of 'Spanish descent,[1] and they loathed and abhorred the 'Saxons. In all the island there were not more than a 'thousand English soldiers. They were dispersed over 'the country in garrisons, and the Irish would long 'since have expelled them had they not been divided 'among themselves. But these divisions would instantly 'disappear if the Pope interfered, and if war was de-'clared against England for the defence of the faith 'against heresy. Not one of the chiefs would oppose a 'papal general, and the English, deserted by their friends, 'would at once be overwhelmed and destroyed. His 'Holiness,' as Sanders represented to Philip, 'had there-'fore nominated a nobleman of the house of Desmond to 'this office, an accomplished soldier, whose name in Ire-'land was worth an army. Men were not needed. There 'were men enough in the country itself, hardy, brave, 'resolute, trained by poverty to bear hunger, thirst, and 'exposure. The Scots of the Isles, good Catholics all of 'them, were also prepared to join. They wanted only

---

[1] 'Quieren mucho á los Españoles de los cuales se precian tener su origen y descendencia.'

'guns, powder, and a little money, and if Fitzmaurice
'could bring these, and if a ship or two with stores and
'a few thousand ducats were sent to him three or four
'times a year from Spain, the whole country would soon
'be at his feet. The presence of a few English Catholics
'would be also useful, and he himself, therefore, and two
'or three others, were about to accompany the expedition.
'Their friends at home, already impatient to rise, would
'hear of it. The Queen would not dare to reinforce her
'own army, for half the men that she would send would
'probably be Catholics, and would turn against her;
'and Fitzmaurice, having swept Ireland clear, would
'then cross the channel with his victorious hosts and
'strike the usurper to the ground.'[1]

It is certainly singular that Philip resisted the temptation to countenance an experiment, the failure of which would involve to him nothing more than the loss of a few thousand ducats. But Philip, Sanders bitterly said, was as afraid of war as a child of fire, and had a kingly dislike of countenancing rebellions. Stukeley, independent of Fitzmaurice, procured ships and men for a private expedition of his own, and was on his way to Ireland, as has been already told, when he was diverted by Sebastian at Lisbon, and exchanged his expected Leinster dukedom for an African grave. Another year passed away. The cloud between Spain and England again cleared: Mendoza came to London, and the Council, who had been seriously afraid for Ireland, were beginning to be reassured, when news came from across the Atlantic—first vague and indefinite, then sharp, clear, and formal—that Francis Drake was plundering the Spanish colonies on

---

[1] Apuntamientos que dió el Doctor Sanderus en Madrid á 16 de Deciembre, 1577.—*MSS. Simancas.*

the Pacific, burning churches, profaning the sacred vessels, and seizing the King's bullion. The history of Drake's expedition will be told in another chapter. It is enough to say at present that Mendoza could obtain no satisfaction from the Queen. She first questioned the fact, then denied that Drake was acting by orders from herself, and to nothing which the ambassador could say could she be brought to give serious attention. The patience of Spain, already tried severely, was almost exhausted. Fierce expressions of indignation were heard in court and country at the King's remissness. An alliance was now formed between the Guises, the refugees at Rheims, and the Pope, and without waiting further on Philip's pleasure, and with the avowed approbation of the Spanish people, Fitzmaurice and Sanders prepared to sail. Sanders had bought a ship at Lisbon. His companions, with the help of the Governor of Galicia, had procured two others at Ferrol. The first was detained by order from the King.[1] The vessels at Ferrol escaped, and the little party who were to conquer Ireland set sail in May 1579 for Kerry. The party consisted of Fitzmaurice, the general of the army which was to be raised as soon as they landed; his wife, Lady Fitzmaurice; Sanders, who had joined him as Legate; two Irish bishops; a few friars; a handful of English refugees; and some five-and-twenty Italians and Spaniards. That was all. Their strength lay in Fitzmaurice's name, which was itself a firebrand, in their being representatives of the Pope, and in the precious banner blessed by his Holiness's hands, on which was emblazoned a Christ upon the cross. Off the Land's End they fell in with a Bristol trader, took it, and threw crew

---

[1] Examination of Friar James O'Hay, August 17, 1580.—*Carew Papers.*

and captain into the water.[1] From another barque they carried off some English sailors as prisoners. On the 16th of July they were seen from Berehaven. On the 17th all Ireland was shaken as with an earthquake at the news that Fitzmaurice and a Legate from the Pope had actually arrived. The landing was at Dingle, a harbour at the south-western angle of Kerry, and was performed with a solemnity befitting the greatness of the occasion. Two friars stepped first on shore, a bishop followed, mitre on head and crosier in hand; their Sanders, with the consecrated banner, and after him Fitzmaurice. The first business was to build a fort to deposit their stores. Dingle harbour being inconvenient and difficult in case of extremity to escape from, they crossed the peninsula to Smerwick, a bay four miles to the west, opening on the Atlantic, and there, having selected a spot which suited them, they set their prisoners to work in chains trenching and building.[2] Messengers meanwhile went out, carrying a letter from Fitzmaurice and the Legate to Desmond, with a proclamation in Irish, signifying the purpose of their arrival. The letter to Desmond was as follows:

'After due and hearty commendation in most humble manner premised. For so much as James Fitzmaurice, being authorised thereto by his Holiness, warfareth under Christ's ensign for restoring of the Catholic faith in Ireland, God forbid the day should ever come wherein it might be said that the Earl of Desmond has forsaken his kinsman, the lieutenant of his spiritual father, the banner of his merciful Saviour, the defence of his ancient faith, the delivery of his dear country, the safeguard of his noble house and posterity. Whereas King Henry VIII. left behind him one son and two daughters,

---

[1] Don Bernardino á Cayas, 20 de Junio, 1579.—*MSS. Simancas.*

[2] Mr. Gold to the Mayor of Limerick, July 22, 1579.—*MSS. Ireland.*

how came it to pass that none of them all could have lawful issue of their own bodies, but because even as King Henry had overthrown many houses in England which bare the name of God and represented God's majesty and mercy towards us, even so God hath determined to root up all them by whom King Henry's name and blood might have been maintained and preserved in the world? Insomuch that, although Queen Mary was a builder up of God's house for her own part, yet for the revenge of her father's fault, whose person she by nature represented, she left no heir of her own body behind her. If, therefore, you are resolved, me [sic] dear cousin, to make an end of our noble house and blood in your days—which God forbid—then dissemble with God's honour a little, bear with them that pull down God's houses and destroy his monasteries, forsake the banner of Christ, and profess yourself the soldier of antichrist. But if as well the punishment to come as the present infamy of such an act ought to make your honourable heart to abhor all such counsel and advice, then resolve to be the first that shall stand for God's honour, for the health of our country, and for the restoring of the Catholic faith. He that defendeth God's honour shall be defended and honoured of God. He that doth it first and chiefly shall have the first and chief reward for that his service. God forbid that any Geraldine should stand in the field against the cross of Christ, which is the ensign of our salvation. As we live now because our ancestors were builders up of God's house, so let not our lack of courage in restoring God's house hinder the seed that hereafter may spring out of our children. And indeed how can their seed flourish that will defend Elizabeth, a woman that is hated of all Christian princes for the great injuries which she has done them, hated of her own subjects as well for compelling them to forswear the Christian faith, as also for not publishing the heir apparent to the crown; a woman that leaveth no issue of her own body either to reward them that fight for her or revenge them that fight against her—nay rather a woman that is surely hated of her successor whoever he be—and, therefore, they that seek to please her cannot but be unpleasant to the next heir of the crown, whose right she so tyrannously forbiddeth to be published. I cannot tell what worldly thing would grieve me more than to hear not only that your honour would not assist Christ's banner, but also that any other nobleman should prevent you in this glorious attempt. All that I write is spoken also to me good lady, your bedfellow, and to me good uncle,[1] [and] your brothers,[2] to all whom I commend myself, and also me bedfellow most heartily doth the like; trusting in Almighty God that as his Holiness has made me Captain-General of this holy war, so your honour being head of my house will be the chief protector and patron of their no less than me quarrel.'[3]

This letter shewed that Fitzmaurice understood the Earl's character, distrusted his courage, and doubted his principles, and, moreover, that as yet there was no clear understanding between them. Desmond had no reason to love England; but he had sense enough to know that unless the support from abroad was more than nominal, England would prove too strong in the end for Irish rebellion. He was in a strait between the two parties. If the invasion failed, and he had compromised himself, he could not hope for a second pardon. If it

---

[1] Sir John of Desmond, brother to the late Earl.
[2] Sir John of Desmond the younger, and Sir James.
[3] Sir James Fitzmaurice to the Earl of Desmond, July, 1579.—*MSS. Ireland.*

succeeded, and he had not joined it, the earldom would pass to his kinsman. He sent Fitzmaurice's letter to Drury, with an assurance of his own loyalty, and he promised to take the field for the Queen. Had he exerted himself he might have captured the insignificant force at Smerwick, but he left them unmolested; and he lay still at his castle at Ashketyn, waiting to see whether the rest of Ireland would move.

But Fitzmaurice could not afford to delay, and it was necessary to force Desmond's hand. Relying on his promises to the President, two English officers, Henry Davell, and Carter the Marshal of Munster, attended only by two or three servants, ventured down to Tralee, to learn what was going on. They were the guests of the Earl's brother, Sir John, who knew Davell, and was indebted to him for protection in some previous scrape. Sir John, impatient at his brother's remissness, and knowing that a murder of two Englishmen, aggravated by treachery, would compromise the Geraldines beyond forgiveness, stabbed Davell in his bed with his own hand, while Carter and the rest were dispatched by his companions.[1] A party of Spaniards from Smerwick was secretly in the house. 'Let this,' said the murderer, plunging in among them covered with Davell's blood, 'let this be a pledge of my faithfulness towards you 'and this cause.'[2] At dawn the Desmond battle cry

---

[1] Mendoza says distinctly that Davell was the guest of Sir John, and speaks of the murder with honourable disapproval.—*Draifrada de Don Bernardino*, Agosto 15. Fitzmaurice regretted that he had been killed in his bed. Sanders thought otherwise. 'This fact,' says Camden, 'Sanders commended as a sweet sacrifice in the sight of God.' Sir Wm. Gerrard heard from one of the English prisoners at Smerwick that the Legate 'persuaded all men it was lawful to kill any English Protestant; that he had authority to warrant all such from the Pope, and to give absolution to all who could so draw blood.'—*Sir Wm. Gerrard to Burghley*, Sept. 16, 1579. MSS *Ireland*.

[2] Camden.

was raised. Three thousand of the clan sprung to arms. Before the week was out all Kerry and Limerick were up, and the woods between Mallow and the Shannon were swarming with howling kerne. 'The rebellion,' wrote Waterhouse, 'is the most perilous that hath ever 'begun in Ireland. The Lord Justice[1] is resolute, and 'so are all the English; but nothing is to be looked for 'but a general revolt.'[2]

Elizabeth had persisted in her disbelief of danger. She had jested at the remonstrances of Mendoza. She had regarded her desertion of the Low Countries as securing her from Spanish interference in Ireland, and now it seemed as if Walsingham had been right after all, as if she had sacrificed her friends and had not disarmed her enemies. She complained to Mendoza that Spaniards had landed in Ireland. Mendoza answered coldly, that they had not been sent by the King. When the King declared war against her, they would come in something more than boatloads. The reply was not reassuring. The report that Sanders had landed threw, as he expected, the English Catholics into a ferment. An insurrection was looked for at home. A courier, therefore, was dispatched in hot haste to Drury, to bid him make peace on any terms, and if the public exercise of the Catholic religion was insisted on, to grant it.[3] A thousand men, however, were sent at the same time from Chester, and in a few days the Irish post brought news which in a degree relieved the anxiety. The English

---

[1] Sir Wm. Drury, so appointed on Sidney's departure.
[2] Waterhouse to Walsingham, August 3.—*MSS. Ireland.*
[3] 'Ha despachado á Irlanda el Consejo con ultima resolucion de que procure el Virrey acordarse con los que se han levantado; y cuando no puede ser de otra manera, les otorgue publicamente el ejercicio de la religion Catolica, si quieren reducirse con esto á la obediencia de la Reyna.'—*Descifrada de Don Bernardino,* Agosto 15, 1579. *MSS. Simancas.*

commanders understood perfectly that hesitation would be fatal to them, that at any odds they must face the insurgents in the field, or all Ireland would be in arms. Sir Nicholas Malby had a few hundred English soldiers at Athlone, and he was fortunately able to avail himself of a feud between the Geraldines and the Connemara and Mayo Burkes. Granny O'Malley had been taken and imprisoned by Desmond, and had probably died, as her name appears no more in Irish story. Her husband, the MacWilliam, cast his fortunes with England, and sent his retainers with his son Theobald to Malby's assistance. With their and his own troops he plunged into the Limerick woods, came up with the rebels, and forced them into action. Fitzmaurice, at the beginning of the fight, was struck by a ball in the breast. As he staggered in his saddle, Theobald Burke rode at him and cut him down, being himself at the same moment struck dead by a blow from a Geraldine. Fitzmaurice's body was taken after a desperate scuffle by the English. His head was cut off and sent to Dublin. The Papal standard, which had been unfolded in the battle, was almost captured also, and the figure upon it, as Malby scornfully said, 'was of 'a new scratched about the face, for they carried it 'through the woods and thorns in post haste.'[1] Des-

---

[1] Sir N. Malby to ——, Oct. 12, 1579.—*MSS. Ireland*. This banner was apparently never taken by the English, unless indeed it is referred to in the following curious passage from a note of the services done by James Meagh. 'Upon a time the said James made a journey to Desmond: he took from certain of the traitor John of Desmond's men a painted cloth, 40 yards long, which cloth the traitors James Fitzmaurice and Dr. Sanders brought from Rome, in the midst of which cloth was sumptuously drawn the said traitor James's arms, with the red dragon and many other ceremonies about it, as the picture of two angels upholding the said arms, and over it the figure of the cross, with the portraiture of our Lord and the pictures of two women, images about it also; and under the said arms, in great Roman letters, the poesy written—

mond, who had been hovering in the neighbourhood with six hundred horse, retired to Ashketyn again. His brothers, Sir John and Sir James, fell back with the Spaniards to Dingle, where in revenge for their kinsman they murdered some of the poor English prisoners.[1]

The blow to the rebellion was serious, and decided the waverers to waver longer. The Pope's general had been defeated and killed in his first action, and the loss of Fitzmaurice, who was a man of resolution and ability, was most unfortunate. Sanders, however, found an explanation of the disaster in his theory of Providence. He told the Geraldines it had been so ordered that 'the noble 'Princes of France and Spain' might see that the cause did not hang upon one man's life; that others would spring into the place of the lost leader better able to advance the cause than he was.[2] He promised legions of Spaniards, who were already, he protested, on their way. He called on Ulick Burke to restore the honour of his house, to repair to him with the galloglass of Clanrickard, and to come at once if he would have God reward him. 'When our aid is come,' he said, 'which 'daily we look for, when the Scotch and English nobility 'are in arms, and when strangers invade England itself, 'it shall be small thanks to be of our company.'[3]

Fortune seemed to encourage his hopes. Sir William Drury, though so ill that he could scarcely sit upon his horse, took the field in October, to follow up Malby's success. He too attempted to penetrate into the great

---

[1] 'In omni tribulatione et angustiâ spes nostra Jesus et Maria.
'This cloth at every mass or sermon that Dr. Sanders had in the field was set up and spread abroad upon stakes in the face of all the people.'—*MSS. Ireland*. July, 1586.

[2] Sir William Gerrard to Burghley, Sept. 16.—*MSS. Ireland.*
[3] Drury to Walsingham, Sept. 14, —*MSS Ibid.*
[4] Dr. Sanders to Ulick Burke, Sept. 24.

wood,[1] but with less skill or less fortune than Malby he entangled himself among bogs and rocks. The Irish set upon him at an advantage, killing several officers and three hundred men. He was himself driven into Kilmallock, from which he returned to Cork to die.

Ireland was thus left without a governor, but Malby, without waiting for instructions, snatched the command of Munster, gathered together the remains of Drury's troops, attacked the Geraldines again, killed an English Jesuit who had accompanied Sanders, destroyed a monastery where the rebels had concealed their wounded, and dispatched them all. He then ordered Desmond to come to him, and when Desmond hesitated, he marched to Ashketyn to look for him, burning farms and villages on his way, and killing all that he met. Unprepared for these vigorous measures, the Earl had admitted his brothers and Sanders himself into the castle, where they were all together when Malby arrived under the walls. The castle was too strong to be taken without cannon. The English commander had none with him, and the season did not allow him to keep his troops long exposed. He burnt the town to the gates therefore. He destroyed the abbey under the Earl's and the Legate's eyes, and broke in pieces the tombs of the Desmonds;[2] and then after wasting the whole country round and leaving a small garrison in Adair, he returned to his own command in Connaught.

But the example was far from producing its expected

---

[1] The wood so often spoken of covered the whole country between Mallow and Limerick; Kilmallock lay in the middle of it. It extended east to the foot of the Galtee mountains, and west to the long chain which divides the county of Limerick from Kerry.

[2] Ashketyn or Askeaton as it is now called, stands at the head of a creek running into the Shannon, fifteen miles below Limerick. The ruins of the abbey are still to be seen as Malby left them.

effect. The Queen, who by this time had learnt the smallness of the force which had arrived at Dingle, believed that she had been deceived. She complained angrily of the expense into which she had been betrayed in sending troops which were not needed, and she required that they should be immediately disbanded.[1] The consequence, as usual, had been foreseen by every one but herself.

Notwithstanding Malby's vigour, there was too much fuel in Ireland ready to kindle. Desmond conceiving that he was now committed beyond hope of pardon, sent a messenger to Spain, to announce that he had risen, and every Catholic in Munster made up his mind to stand by him.

When the Desmond was in the field, rebellion had grown serious. Stealing out of Ashketyn on Malby's departure, the Earl crossed the country, and starting up where he was least looked for, one Sunday night in the middle of November, broke at low water into Youghal, which was then an English town. All Monday and Tuesday the Geraldines revelled in plunder. The houses of the merchants were sacked, and their wives and daughters violated and murdered. Every one who could not escape was killed, and on Wednesday the houses were fired, and not a roof was left standing.

From Youghal, their force daily increasing, the insurgents marched upon Cork, and Sir Warham St. Leger, who was in the city, looked for no better fate. The citizens were at heart with their countrymen. 'Here is no Englishman but myself with forty of my 'family,' he wrote. 'We owe God a death, and her 'Majesty our service, and we have put on resolute

---

[1] Walsingham to Waterhouse, Nov. 8, 1579.—*MSS. Ireland.*

'minds to yield ourselves a sacrifice to God before the traitors shall have their purpose.'¹

Elizabeth, when the bad news arrived, became as usual furious and abusive. Lord Ormond happened to be in London when the rebellion broke out. She sent him back with a commission as military governor of Munster, and with directions to restore order instantly; but she expected him to do it with his own resources, for further assistance she could not be brought to supply. He hurried over to find everything in confusion, Drury's soldiers scattered or dead, Malby overawing Connaught from Athlone, but unable to spare a man; and Sir William Pelham and Sir Henry Wallop, who were in temporary command at Dublin, equally helpless. He looked round him in despair. 'The Queen,' he wrote to Walsingham, 'mislikes that the service goes no 'faster forward; but she has suffered all things needful 'to want. If I could feed soldiers with the air, and 'throw down castles with my breath, and furnish naked 'men with a wish—if these things might be done, the 'service should go as her Highness would have it. 'This is the second time I have been suffered to want 'all these things in the charge I have. There shall not 'be the third. I would sooner be committed prisoner 'by the heels than thus be dealt with again.'²

The supplies ordered for Dublin had been stopped, but none the less the blame was flung on Pelham and Wallop. In exigencies like that which had arisen, Elizabeth never moved till weeks or months had first been spent in cavils. Pelham complained that 'the detestable 'service of Ireland was the grave of every English 'reputation.' He was doing his best, 'but only to be

---

¹ St. Leger to Burghley, Nov. 19.—MSS. Ireland.   ² Ormond to Walsingham, Jan. 4, 1579-80.—MSS. Ibid.

'misrepresented and blamed.' Wallop said plainly that if the Queen would not provide what was necessary, the country could not be held. The Irish were longing for a change, and the few English bands remaining were powerless. For each pound which she had just saved in cashiering the last instalment of troops she had to spend five in replacing them, and of course she held every one to blame except herself. Burghley had to encourage the English officers in Dublin as he could. He prayed Pelham to go on in God's name, and not be discouraged 'by the Queen's usage of him.' 'He himself, with 'others of the Council, sustained undeservedly some 'reprehension.' 'With the land on fire, and the Pope 'and his faction ready to bring coals,' they must all, he said, do what they could. The Queen would gradually become reasonable, and supplies would be sent.[1]

After a month's wrangling she yielded grudgingly and angrily. Men, money, ammunition, all was dispatched at last. A larger force was thrown into Ireland than had been assembled there for a century. Ormond was given supreme command as the Desmonds' hereditary foe. He was directed to prosecute to the death the Earl, his brothers, the murderers of Davell, and especially 'the viper Sanders.' 'So now,' concluded Burghley, in conveying the Queen's last order, 'I will 'merely say Butler aboo, against all that cry in a 'new language Papa aboo, and God send you your 'heart's desire to banish and vanquish those cankered 'Desmonds.'[2]

Meanwhile Cork had escaped. Desmond for some unknown reason had fallen back into the 'wood.' He

---

[1] Burghley to Pelham, Dec. 30, 1579.— *MSS. Ireland.*

[2] Burghley to Ormond, Jan. 26.— *MSS. Ireland.*

attempted, unsuccessfully, to recover Adair,[1] but with this exception he held the whole country lying west of a line drawn from Cork to Limerick, with all the rest of Munster at his secret devotion, and the strength of its population in the field with him.[2] Fresh supplies came in from abroad, if not so amply as the Irish looked for.[3] Two Italian vessels with powder arrived at Dingle in January, bringing the news that a large force might soon be expected.[3] There was a general impression that unless the rebellion could be extinguished in the spring, the O'Neils, and probably the Earl of Kildare, would revolt also.

It was not till the beginning of March that the English could move. At length, however, the promised stores had all arrived. Sir William Winter, with a heavily armed English squadron, came round to the mouth of the Shannon, and Pelham and Ormond started simultaneously, each at the head of a division of the army, from Dublin and Kilkenny, proposing to meet near Limerick. 'We passed through the rebel countries,' wrote Pelham, 'in two companies, consuming with fire 'all habitations, and executing the people wherever we 'found them.' Alone of all English commanders he expressed remorse at the work, but he said that the example was necessary. Fitzmaurice's widow and her two little girls were discovered by the way, concealed

---

[1] He sent 'a fair young harlot' as a present to the Constable, hoping by her means to corrupt him. The Constable, not being open to such advances, fastened a stone to the young woman's neck and flung her from the walls into the river.—*Pelham to the Council*, Jan. 16. *Carew Papers*.

[2] St. Leger to Burghley, Jan. 25,

—*MSS. Ireland.*

[3] Desmond had written to Philip to say that he had taken arms at the request of the Pope, and relying on Spanish assistance. He had supported the weight of the war for four months, and looked for immediate help.—*Desmond to the King of Spain*, Jan. 12, 1580. *MSS. Simancas.*

in a cave. They are heard of no more, and were probably slain with the rest. The Irish annalists say that the bands of Pelham and Ormond killed the blind and the aged, women and children, sick and idiots, sparing none.[1] Pelham's own words too closely confirm the charge.

Uniting their forces at Adair, the two commanders went on to Tralee, when, hearing that the English fleet was in the Shannon, they doubled back to attack the hitherto impregnable castle of Carrigafoyle, which was occupied by the Italians and Spaniards who had landed with Fitzmaurice. The fortress stood upon a rock, divided from the shore by a channel, which was dry only at low water during spring tides. An Italian engineer, Captain Julian, had added to the natural strength of the position. The keep rose ninety feet above the water. The cracks in the rock were filled with masonry, presenting a smooth front of stone on every side. If attacked only from the land, and by the old methods, it might have stood a siege for a hundred years. But times were changed. The ships lay outside at anchor to prevent the garrison from escaping in boats. Half a dozen heavy guns were landed and placed in position, and a fire was opened so terrible to the unpractised Irish ear, that the annalists say there was not a glen from Killarney lakes to the far parts of Clare where the roar of these unknown and wonderful cannon was not heard. Down fell the barbican, down fell the walls of the keep, forming in heaps against the side of the rock, and opening a road to a storming party. A hundred English soldiers waded over when the tide fell, carried the castle in an hour, and slew every one that they found in it, Julian only being

---

[1] Annals of the Four Masters, A° 1580.

allowed a few hours' shrift to tell who he was and whence he came.¹

Ashketyn was to have been taken next; but Desmond's people, terrified at the fate of Carrigafoyle, blew it up with powder and fled. Mutterings of dismay began to be heard among them. Where was the promised help? Why were the Spaniards so slow? A little more delay, and their friends, when they came, might find them all dead. Pelham, at Elizabeth's order, wrote to Lady Desmond, offering a pardon to herself and the Earl, if Sanders and Davell's murderers were given up. The proud lady's spirit was not yet subdued. She sent Pelham's letter to Sanders, 'scorning 'the matter.' Had the English been able to follow up their success on the spot, they might perhaps have stamped out the fire, or taken Desmond and the Countess prisoners. They were stopped short, however, for a time by want of money to pay their soldiers. Elizabeth, conceiving that she was unfairly dealt with in the accounts, had again suspended a second instalment of the promised remittances; a pause followed, and gave the Geraldines time to recover breath.

The fleet remained on the coast; as long as it stayed there no foreign transports would venture near; and Malby, who had been in Clare on the opposite bank of the Shannon during the operations at Carrigafoyle, found leisure to make a circuit through Mayo.² The

---

¹ Pelham to the Queen, from the camp at Carrigafoyle, April 6.— *MSS. Ireland.*

² Pictures of quiet industry appear unexpectedly amidst the horrible scenes which chiefly make up Irish history. Malby in the course of his progress went to a place called Burrishoole, on the shores of Clew Bay, now black desolate moor and mountain, at that time clothed with a magnificent forest, and possessing rich iron mines; 'the best fishing place for herring and salmon in Ireland; where a ship of 500 tons could ride close to the shore, and fre-

rebels dispersed through the forest, and scattered in parties over the open country of Cork and Tipperary, murdering English settlers, or any of their own people who had adopted English habits. The lords and gentlemen of Munster looked on approvingly, especially when any one was killed who had dared to occupy confiscated lands. 'The young horse,' wrote Justice Meagh, 'is not more loathsome of the snaffle than the 'chieftains are grieved with the yoke of justice.'[1]

At length the Queen was coaxed into good humour again. Remittances came, and as it was known that ships and men were actually waiting at Coruña to come over when the coast should be clear, Pelham determined on another raid into the south-west. Small detachments of men were sent by different routes to distract attention, with orders to meet at Buttevant.[2] Desmond, his wife, and Doctor Sanders, were at the Castle of the Island,[3] in Kerry, and Pelham hoped to surprise them by a rapid march over the mountains. He had almost succeeded, but the watch was too good, and the summer nights were short. His companies were seen stealing through the defiles at the foot of Knockadunne, and a breathless herdsman secured the Earl an hour's notice to escape. Sanders and the Countess fled on ponies; the Earl, unable to sit a horse, was carried by galloglass; and Pelham when he arrived found his prey had escaped him. The habits of an Irish Earl in the sixteenth century were much like those of the modern Irish peasant. The same roof sheltered man and beast, and 'the Island,' a 'huge

---

quented annually by fifty Devonshire fishing smacks, the owners of which payed tribute to the O'Malleys.' —*Narrative by Sir N. Malby*, April, 1580. *MSS. Ireland*.

[1] Meagh to Walsingham, June 2, —*MSS. Ibid.*

[2] A town on the great wood, ten miles from Mallow, on the Kilmallock road. The name indicates that it was an ancient Norman outpost, Boutez en avant.

[3] Now Castle Island.

'monstrous castle full of many rooms,' was at the same time 'very filthy, and full of cow dung.' It was given over to plunder. The soldiers took possession of 'the 'Earl's provision of aqua vitæ.' Some 'women's hand-'kerchiefs' were found, a cloke or two, and the Legate's 'masking furniture,' 'Sanctus Bulls, crucifixes, vest-'ments and chalices.' This was all which the palace of the Prince Palatine of Kerry yielded in the shape of household spoil. His wealth was in his cattle, which were driven in and devoured by the troops. The next day they went on to Castlemayne, where Ormond joined them, having in his train MacCartymore, who, believing Desmond's day to be done, hoped by making himself useful to secure a share of the plunder. Again dividing, Pelham marched on to Dingle, destroying as he went, with Ormond parallel to him on the opposite of the bay, the two parties watching one another's course at night across the water by the flames of the burning cottages. The fleet was in the harbour at Ventry, and Winter and the other officers came on shore for a pleasant meeting with their friends.[1] 'Here,' says Sir Nicholas White, 'my Lord Justice and I gathered cockles for our supper.' Fulke Greville and Captain Bingham 'climbed a crag 'to fetch an eagle from its nest,'—light episodes of entertainment to relieve the monotony of destruction. Sir Edward Fenton, another of Pelham's party who records the daily proceedings, regrets that on their way from the Island the sport had generally been bad. They had hanged a priest, whom from his Spanish dress they had

---

[1] The harbours of Ventry and Dingle are but two miles apart. Sir N. White, who accompanied the expedition, gives the following account of them. 'Ventry,' he says, 'is called in Irish Coon Fyntra or Whitesand Haven; Dingle is called Coon Edaf Derick or Red Ox Haven; it took that name from the drowning of an ox in the haven at the first coming over of Englishmen from Cornwall, who brought cattle with them.'— *Diary of the Expedition of June,* 1580, *by Sir Nicholas White.*

conceived at first to be the Legate. 'Otherwise,' he says, 'we took small prey, and killed less people, though 'we searched many places in our travel.'[1]

Dingle itself, so lately the scene of the landing, was an absolute desert; not a creature, human or other, was found in it. The officers crossed the peninsula to survey the deserted fort at Smerwick, which the Spaniards who had been killed at Carrigafoyle had begun to build, and which was so soon to be the scene of a world-famous tragedy. They were struck with the singular want of judgment which had been shewn in the selection of the spot—'a 'very small neck of land joined to the shore by a bank 'of sand.' The bank had been cut through, but the trench was necessarily filled in by the sand in a few tides. The place had no feature of natural strength about it, and there was no fresh water within a mile.[2] They looked at it, however, merely with curiosity, as a thing of the past. The flames at Valentia, shooting over the bay, told that Ormond's work was finished, and they and he retraced their steps to Castlemayne. Ormond, more fortunate than Pelham, had to report a satisfactory tale of slaughter. He brought back with him Lord Clancarty, the two O'Sullivans of Berehaven, and other chiefs who had been hiding among the mountains. If rebellion was a crime, they were more guilty than their followers who had been killed. But they had promised obedience, and their submission and pardon might be a useful example.

The work was done. The farthest corners of Kerry had been searched and swept clean, and the English could now return at their leisure. On the 26th of June Clancarty entertained them at 'the Palace'—'a name,'

---

[1] Fenton's Narrative, 1580.— MSS. Ireland.

[2] So Fenton reported, but there is now a considerable stream of water within a quarter of a mile.

says Fenton, 'very unfit for so beggarly a building, not
'answerable to a mean farmer's house in England.' 'On
'the 27th,' says Sir Nicholas White, we marched by the
'famous Lough Leyne.[1] The Lough is full of salmon,
'and hath in it forty islands. In one of them is
'an abbey, in another a parish church, in another
'a castle, out of which there came to us a fair lady,
'the rejected wife of Lord Fitzmaurice. The lake is
'in circuit twenty miles, having a fair plain of one side,
'and fair woods and high mountains of the other.'[2] It
was midsummer, and even the soldiers were struck
with the singular loveliness of the scene on which they
gazed. 'A fairer land,' one of them said, 'the sun did
'never shine upon—pity to see it lying waste in the
'hands of traitors.' Yet it was by those traitors that
the woods, whose beauty they so admired, had been
planted and fostered. Irish hands, unaided by English
art or English wealth, had built Muckross and Inisfallen
and Aghadoe, and had raised the castles on whose walls
the modern poet watched the splendour of the sunset.

From Killarney the army passed through Glenflesk
to the Blackwater, whence Ormond's men, who were
barefoot from their long marches, were carried on to
Cork to refresh themselves. On them the burden of
destruction had chiefly fallen. Ormond, in a report of his
services, stated that in this one year 1580, before and
after, but chiefly during, this expedition, he had put to
the sword forty-six captains and leaders, with eight
hundred notorious traitors and malefactors, and above
four thousand other people.[3] Pelham turned back to

---

[1] Killarney. The days of tourists were not yet, and it is a pity that White did not explain in what sense he called it 'famous.'

[2] Diary of Sir N. White.

[3] Services of the Earl of Ormond, A° 1580.—*Carew Papers.*

Ashketyn to glean a second harvest of the Geraldines, and he too, on the 30th of July, reported 'great 'execution.' Penitent rebels began privately to apply for pardon. In all cases the price exacted for forgiveness was the head of some friend or leader,[1] and it was a price which was often paid. Sanders, accused of having betrayed them by false promises, was nearly murdered by the despairing wretches, who were now starving in the wood, and Desmond's personal interference barely sufficed to save him. The Earl's own person was sacred; no one ventured, as yet, to conspire against the chief of the Geraldines, but no such devotion protected his brothers. Sir James, the younger of the two, was surprised, wounded, and taken by Sir Cormac Mac Teigue, the sheriff of Cork. Sir Cormac, whose conduct had been suspicious, made his peace by surrendering his prisoner to Ormond, by whom he was immediately executed. The garrison of Kilmallock fell in one night with Sir John of Desmond and Sanders. They spoke English, and escaped in the dark, being mistaken for officers of Pelham. Sir John not wishing to run a second risk, communicated privately with Sir Warham St. Leger. He was promised pardon if he would betray the Earl, his cousin Fitzgerald of Imokelly, and the Legate; but before he could consent or refuse, fortune took a momentary turn, and the prospects of the insurrection brightened again.

The Barons of the Pale, who had resisted the payment of the cess, remained for a year in Dublin Castle. They gave way at last, but they went home in bitter humour, and the rebellion in the south was a sore

---

[1] 'I do not receive any but such as come in with bloody hands as executioners of some better person than themselves.'—*Pelham to the Council*, July 30, 1580. *Carew Papers*.

temptation to them. Had they risen when Desmond rose, the resources of English power would have been severely tried. Had they risen later in a mass together they might have revenged terribly the destruction of the Geraldines. But they were disorganised by the remissness of their natural leader. The feudal chief of the English Pale, who in past generations had exercised sovereign sway there, was the head of the elder branch of the Fitzgeralds, the Earl of Kildare. The present lord was as Irish at heart, and as true a Catholic as his forefathers, but he lacked the vigour of his race, and was afraid to risk his skin. Sanders had sent letters round the Anglo-Irish houses, and the younger generation of Plunkets, Dillons, Aylmers, Brabazons, and Nugents, most of whom had been educated at Louvaine, was enthusiastically eager to join him. Their fathers' hearts were in the same place, and they had their personal grievances to complain of also. But many of them remembered the fate of Silken Thomas and his uncles, and like Kildare they hung back, at least till something more definite was heard of the force coming from Coruña. The excitement, however, and the massacre of so many of their friends in the south, overtired the patience of the more impetuous or bigoted. Rowland Eustace, Viscount Baltinglass, was one of those who had been imprisoned for the cess. He was a passionate Romanist; but besides his creed he was connected in blood with the marauding tribes of the Wicklow mountains. He was the owner of Glenmalure, the scene of the murderous performance of the Naas garrison, and the victims of that remarkable atrocity were dependents of the House of Eustace. There were, therefore, special causes peculiarly prompting him to rebellion. After vainly endeavouring to persuade Kildare to rise with him, in the middle of July, while Pelham was still at Ashketyn, he threw off his allegiance, and sent circulars to the nobles and officers specially connected with England, explaining that he had drawn the sword at the command of the highest power upon earth, and inviting and expecting them to imitate his example. 'A woman 'incapable of orders,' he said, 'could not be head of the 'Church—a thing which Christ did not grant to his 'own mother,' and Elizabeth by usurping the title had forfeited her sovereignty.[1]

The messenger who carried one of these letters to the Mayor of Waterford was immediately hanged for his pains, but from all parts of the Pale highborn young men hastened to Baltinglass's side. The Wicklow hills offered a shelter and a rendezvous to the disaffected, and Sir John of Desmond, changing his mind about surrendering, and taking Sanders with him, shifted his quarters out of Munster, and stole up across the country to his new allies.

At this moment Lord Grey de Wilton arrived in Dublin to relieve Pelham and Wallop of their command. He came, as all other deputies came, bitterly against his will, and his unwillingness had been hardly overcome at last by the urgent entreaties of Burghley. In many respects he was well fitted for the post. He was a soldier and a Puritan. He conceived that the misery of Ireland had been caused mainly by an unstable and uncertain policy towards it, and believing the Catholic religion to be false, he regarded the conversion of the country to a purer faith as a necessary preliminary of its improvement. He came, however, with his hands tied. The Queen strictly prohibited him from meddling

---

[1] Baltinglass to the Mayor of Waterford, July 18. To the Earl of Ormond, July 30.—*MSS. Ireland.*

with religion in any way, and she sent him to his post already desponding of good results. He landed at Dublin, on the 12th of August, bringing six or seven hundred soldiers with him, and being told that no time was to be lost in dealing with Baltinglass, and being dependent in his inexperience of the country on the opinions of others, he marched at once into the mountains.

The rebels lay in Glenmalure;[1] the same spot at which the English officers being offered *kine* or *killing*, had preferred the last. It was an appropriate scene for the retribution now to be inflicted. Kildare, who accompanied the expedition, had doubtless sent notice to his friends to be on the watch. The Deputy, with Kildare and Colonel Wingfield, held the mouth of the gorge, to prevent escape, while young Sir Peter Carew, Colonel Moore, and a distinguished officer named Cosby, advanced with the body of the troops. They went unmolested up the narrow valley for some distance, seeing no one, when suddenly the crags and bushes on either side, before and behind, became alive with armed men, and amidst yells and shouts they were assailed with a storm of shot, and stones, and arrows. The new comers in their bright red and blue uniforms found themselves especially aimed at, and the unearthly howling, and the wild figures glancing among the rocks, made sudden cowards of them. 'Amazed,' 'terrified,' they crowded together, threw down their arms, and tried to fly. But the trap had closed upon them, and all the officers and almost all the men were destroyed.

A disaster at such a moment was unusually dangerous. Two thousand Scots had just landed in Antrim;

---

[1] Not Glendalough, as Camden says.

the famous Countess threatening to occupy the entire north-east corner of Ulster, in the name of James or his mother.[1]

Malby, who was hastening to Dublin on the news of the defeat at Glenmalure, was recalled by disturbances in Roscommon. Shocked at last by the report of the cruelties in Munster,[2] and discovering from the demands upon the exchequer that they were not producing the effect which might have excused them, Elizabeth was now thinking once more of trying the effect of a pardon, accompanied, as Mendoza said that she had intended before, with religious toleration, when at the back of the other bad news came authentic tidings that the ships from Coruña had arrived at last, and that Dingle and Smerwick were again occupied by a Papal force. Eight hundred men, Italians chiefly, with a few Spaniards among them, had actually landed, and Philip, though not actively consenting, had not allowed them to be interfered with.

They had sailed from a Spanish port, and the eager Irish imagination saw in their coming the fulfilment of

---

[1] 'I find she is wholly bent to make a new Scotland in the north parts of Ireland, and falling in further communication with her she told me plainly that if God should call the Queen's Majesty, England and Ireland were and should be the King of Scotland's own.'—*Captain Piers to Walsingham*, Aug. 12. *MSS. Ireland.*

[2] Malby considered that the Irish had been dealt with too leniently. 'I perceive by your letter,' he wrote to Walsingham, 'that Irish complaints have good hearing there. I am sorry for it. And hard it is for us that serve, when rebels' tales and the surmises of such as be friends to rebels, shall work us disadvantage and misliking, for so often adventuring our lives, which we do only in respect of our duty to her Majesty. No man can hold it for a pastime; neither will any man of discretion desire to govern by fighting if it may be done by honest policy; but my hap is worst of any man's in that I hear it said I use the sword over severely. I am sorry I have spared it so much, and if it be not used more sharply than hitherto it has been, her Majesty is like to lose both sword and realm. It is now a quarrel of religion, and the expectation of foreign aid doth much further it.'—*Malby to Walsingham*, Sept. 7. *MSS. Ireland.*

Sanders's promise. They would have been in Ireland long before, except for the fleet. But Admiral Winter finding himself short of provisions, with the autumn weather coming on, his ships' bottoms foul with weed, 'unable to go from such as might be an overmatch for 'him, nor to overtake any that he should chase,' and further believing that the insurrection in Munster was crushed, had returned home without waiting for orders.[1] Notice of his intention must have been sent to Coruña before he left, for the two fleets met upon the seas and crossed each other unseen or unrecognised.

Thus the peninsula of Dingle was again the focus of Irish interest. The new comers entrenched themselves in their predecessors' fort at Smerwick without noticing its defects. They landed four thousand stand of arms, which they had brought for the Irish, in addition to six months' provisions, and three hundred of them at once went inland to look for Desmond. How many had arrived, or how many more might be coming, the Council at Dublin were for several days unable to learn. The roads were beset, and messengers detected carrying news to the English were cut to pieces. On the Irish the effect appeared at first most serious. The young Clanrickards seized Loughrea Castle, raised King's County, and threatened Malby in Athlone. Baltinglass and the rebels in Wicklow came down into the Pale, and swept the country to Dublin, and as if the elements were taking part with the insurrection, two hundred English soldiers, coming over from Chester, were drowned.

Ormond, as governor of Munster, went with four thousand of his own people into Kerry to encounter the strangers. He was set upon on the skirts of the

[1] Explanation of Sir Wm. Winter, Sept. 23.—*MSS. Ireland.*

wood, and though he repulsed the attack, he suffered more loss than he could inflict. He went on as far as Smerwick and surveyed the fort, but retired without meddling with it; and in the universal panic and suspicion, there were not wanting those who whispered that even Ormond's loyalty was wavering. But expectation was singularly at fault. Again, as when Fitzmaurice and Sanders landed, the first impulse with Elizabeth was to concede everything that the Irish demanded.[1] Her alarm would have been less if she had seen a letter which the leaders of the rebellion sent from Smerwick a month after their arrival. A quarter of a year of bitter experience had taught the Legate that the 'enterprise of 'Ireland' was less easy than he had believed; and the devotion of the people to the Holy Cause more lukewarm. Tirlogh O'Neil described himself as occupied with the Scots and unable to move. Kildare, notwithstanding the victory at Glenmalure, was still afraid; and the gentlemen of the Pale would not move without Kildare. The sanguine Legate had imagined that the Irish generally would rush to the Pope's banner; and that they needed only arms. Arms in plenty had arrived, but no one could be found to use them, or permit himself to be trained as a soldier, till he had received four gold crowns in advance. The chiefs it was true hated England, but they would not commit themselves till they were certain of success, and the Legate who said a few months before that a crucifix, a consecrated flag, and the name of James Fitzmaurice would suffice to drive the English out of Ireland, was now obliged to confess that if the Spaniards wished it done, they must themselves do it with their own hands. They must send eight thousand men fully provided with heavy guns, powder,

---

[1] Descifrada de Don Bernardino, 30 de Octubre.

shot, stores, waggons, horses, muskets, lead, and match, two hundred pipes of wine at least, and food for six months for the army; the whole of Munster being wasted, and the cattle destroyed.

This remarkable acknowledgment was signed by Sanders himself, by Desmond and Baltinglass, and by two officers of the Spanish-Italian force.[1] It was sent to Spain through a priest, who went back thither in the swiftest of the Spanish ships, and Desmond wrote by the same messenger to Philip, that he was himself a homeless wanderer. Every town, castle, village, farmhouse, belonging to him or his people had been destroyed. There was no longer a roof standing in Munster to shelter him.[2]

So terribly, so effectively Pelham and Ormond had done their work in the preceding summer. Those who had escaped alive had lost faith in their cause or their chiefs, and would now serve only with gold dollars in advance, to desert with them at the first opportunity; and the strangers, now all collected again, sate idly at Smerwick, intending if no further reinforcements were to be sent over, to re-embark and go home.

But the chance was not allowed them. Orders were sent to Winter to return instantly to the coast of Kerry. The fleet left Portsmouth on the 13th of October. It was caught by a gale off Portland. The admiral, with most of the ships, ran in for shelter under the Bill. Captain Bingham in the Swiftsure, having been parted from his consorts, and believing, as his ship was the slowest in the squadron, that Winter was before him, held on down Channel; and after looking in vain into Falmouth made straight for Valencia. There he waited ten hours,

---

[1] Letter from Smerwick, Oct. 19, 1580.—*MSS. Simancas.*
[2] *Ibid.*

and having learnt where the Italians were and the extent of their strength, he then sailed again for Smerwick, and brought up within falcon shot of the fortress, exactly sixty hours after he had left St. Helen's.[1] There entirely alone he lay for three weeks. Coming off in a hurry he had but half his complement of men. He had scarce hands enough to weigh his anchor. A fort with seven or eight hundred men in it, and the vessels in which these men had come were within a few cables' lengths of him. Fresh arrivals might any day apppear from Spain, yet he preferred risking all chances to giving the Italians an opportunity of escape unfought with.

Meanwhile Grey having recovered, as well as he could, from his first calamity, and being reassured by a victory of Malby's over the Burkes and the unexpected quiet of the rest of Ireland, gathered all the soldiers that he could raise, and set off, with a small but, from its composition, unusually interesting force, to attack the invaders by land. Ireland had become to young Englishmen of spirit a land of hope and adventure, where they might win glory and perhaps fortune; and among the names of the officers who accompanied Grey are found those of Burghley's kinsman, 'young Mr. Cheke,' of Edmund Spenser, and of Walter Raleigh.

They reached Dingle by the end of October. Bingham came on shore to meet them, and, after a survey of the fort, it became clear to every one that nothing could be done till the arrival of the rest of the fleet; the troops having come away ill provided and depending on Winter for their supplies. For eight days, therefore, they lay encamped between Dingle and Smerwick, in 'penury of victuals,' and amidst the howling of the Atlantic gales. On the 5th of November a few droves

---

[1] Bingham to Walsingham, Oct. 18.—*MSS. Ireland.*

of cattle, for which they had sent back to Castlemayne, were seen approaching, to relieve them of the fear of actual and immediate famine. Almost at the same moment, the yet more welcome news came in that the fleet was in Ventry harbour, and if the wind held would be at Smerwick the following morning. Winter was old and cautious, and forgetful of everything but the safety of his ships, had felt his way from harbour to harbour in the intervals of moderate weather. He had arrived at last, however, and past troubles were forgotten. Grey galloped down to Ventry sands to welcome him. On the 7th, at daybreak, he was by the side of Bingham in Smerwick bay, and instant preparations were made for the attack. A reconnoitring party approached the fort in the afternoon. Some skirmishers came out and drew the English within range of the Italian guns. The ships replied, and the last hours of daylight were spent in loose firing, which did little harm on either side. At night the English cannon were brought on shore. Trenches were dug, and they were placed in position three hundred yards from the sand-hills which formed the outer line of defence. A heavy bombardment was kept up all the next day, and the second evening the batteries were advanced till within a cable's length. The Italians too had heavy guns, and the fire of the fort on the second day was severe, doing little hurt however beyond killing young Cheke, who exposing himself on the parapet of the trench to watch the effect of a shot, was struck down at Grey's feet, and died a few hours after.[1]

[1] Grey's account of Cheke's death, in a letter to the Queen, is characteristic of himself and the times. 'Truly Madam he was so disposed to God and made so divine a confession of his faith, as all divines in either of your Majesty's realms could not have passed it if matched it. So wrought in him God's spirit, plainly declaring him a child of his;

At last a ball, aimed by Sir Wm. Winter himself, dismounted the largest piece which the garrison had, and destroyed the men who were serving it, and after another round an Italian sprang on the wall, waved a handkerchief, and demanded a parley. The firing ceased, and two officers, an Italian and a Spaniard, came over to the English lines. On being asked who they were, and for what purpose they had landed in Ireland, they said that they had been brought over 'upon fair speeches and great promises, which they 'had found vain and false,' and their only desire was to be allowed to depart as they had come. Lord Grey asked the Spaniard if he had a commission from his King. He confessed that he had not. He said that Don Martinez de Recalde, the Governor of Bilbao, had told him to raise a company of soldiers and join the Italians at Santander. He had obeyed 'as a blind man,' not knowing where he was going. The Italians, to a similar question, replied frankly that 'they were sent 'by the Pope for the defence of the Catholic faith.' The right of the Pope to levy war was what the English could not recognise. Grey said that it was not uncommon for men to take in hand unjust actions at the command of their natural princes, but that gentlemen of birth and breeding should allow themselves to be sent on such an enterprise by a person who had no authority from God or man, but was 'a detestable shave-'ling, the right antichrist and patron of the doctrine 'of devils,' did indeed surprise him. He declared that he could regard them only as pirates. He could promise them no terms. They must surrender at discretion and

---

elected, to be no less comfort of his good and godly friends than great instruction and manifest motion of every other hearer that stood by, of whom there was a good troop.'— *Grey to Elizabeth*, Nov. 12, 1580. MSS. Ireland.

take their chance. They begged hard for a promise of
their lives, but the Deputy was inexorable. They
carried his answer back to the fort, and the general,
Don Bastian de San Josepho, then came in person, and
consented to surrender in the morning if he could be
allowed one night's respite. To this Lord Grey agreed
on condition of his sending in hostages, and at daybreak
the following day the gates were opened. Don Bastian
with the officers came out with ensigns trailing, and
gave themselves up as prisoners. The men piled their
arms outside the walls, and waited defenceless to learn
the pleasure of their conquerors.

They were strangers and by this time alone. Sanders,
Desmond, Baltinglass, had taken themselves off when
they heard that Grey was coming down. The officers
were reserved for their ransom. Common prisoners
were inconvenient and expensive, and it was thought
desirable to read a severe lesson to Catholic sympathisers
in Ireland. 'The Lord of Hosts,' wrote Grey, 'had
'delivered the enemy to us, not one of ours being hurt,
'Mr. Cheke only excepted. Then put I in certain bands
'who fell straight to execution.'[1] A certain number of
the original party had fallen sick, and had been sent back
to Spain. With the exception of these and of the officers
the entire party was slaughtered. A few women, some
of them pregnant, were hanged. A servant of Sanders's,
an Irish gentleman, and a priest were hanged also. The
bodies, six hundred in all, were stripped and laid out
upon the sands—'as gallant and goodly personages,' said
Grey, 'as ever were beheld.' To him it was but the

---

[1] Captain Bingham, writing from the spot two days after, said that the execution had not been intended, but was the work of certain mariners who had gone in to plunder. Grey equally close upon the event took the responsibility on himself, evidently supposing that he had done nothing which required explanation or apology.

natural and obvious method of disposing of an enemy who had deserved no quarter. His own force amounted barely to eight hundred men, and he probably could not, if he had wished, have conveyed so large a body of prisoners in safety across Ireland to Dublin.[1] Camden says that Grey shed tears, and that Elizabeth wished the cruelty, though necessary, undone. It is possible that some pity was felt for subjects of the King of Spain which was refused to the wives and babies of the Irish chiefs, and some traces of compunction may be read in Grey's description of the row of bodies. Elizabeth, however, if she may be judged by the letter which she wrote on the occasion, regretted only that the officers had not shared the punishment which had been extended to the rank and file. She paid the Deputy the compliment which she reserved for the rarest occasions. To the official letter of thanks she prefixed a gracious sentence in her own hand.[2] She promised to respect the indulgence which had been extended to Don Bastian and the gentlemen, but she said that she would have been better pleased if the choice of justice or mercy had been reserved to herself; and she left no doubt for which alternative she would have decided by adding, that their treatment 'would,' in that case, 'have served for a ter-
' rour to such as might hereafter be drawn to be the
' executioners of so wicked an enterprise, when they
' should hear that as well the heads as the inferiors had

---

[1] Grey to Elizabeth, Nov. 12. Sir Geoffrey Fenton to Walsingham, Nov. 14. W. Smith to Burghley, Nov. 28. Captain Bingham to ——, Nov. 12.—*MSS. Ireland.*

[2] 'By the Queen, your loving Sovereign, Elizabeth R. The mighty hand of the Almightiest power hath showed manifestly the force of his strength in the weakness of feeblest sex and mind this year, to make men ashamed ever hereafter to disdain us; in which action I joy that you have been chosen the instrument of his glory, which I mean to give you no cause to forethink.'—*The Queen to Lord Grey*, December, 1580. *MSS. Ireland.*

'received punishment according to their demerits.'[1] The execution was not complained of by Mendoza. The incapacity with which the enterprise had been conducted, and the miserable defence which the unfortunate wretches had made for themselves, rendered him indifferent to their fate as a soldier, while their absolute destruction relieved Philip of further concern for their fate.[2]

So ended the grand expedition, the subject of so many prayers, the first effort made by the Father of Christendom in his own behalf for the recovery of his lost dominions. The blessed banner had been scratched by the thorns in the woods of Limerick. The Legate was thenceforward to be hunted like a wolf among the mountains, cursed at heart by the people whose superstition still protected him. The soldiers of the cross possessed no more of the land which they had come to conquer than the soil which covered their bones. The Irish branch of the great enterprise concerted at Rheims had broken in the hands of its projectors. There remained nothing of it but a catalogue of horrible memories, and bands of outlaws who had lost hope, but were mischievous and murderous in their despair. It was to the credit of the Irish, that deceived as they had been, their houses burnt, their wives and children massacred, they still spared Sanders, who had been the instrument of their ruin. Desmond was once more offered his own pardon if he would surrender him, but he honourably refused. Some other chiefs might ere long perhaps have been less scrupulous, had not death taken him under a more sure protection. The hard wild life, the exposure in all seasons to wet and cold and hunger, did their work upon a frame too old to encounter so severe a trial. English rumour said

---

[1] The Queen to Lord Grey, Dec. 1580.—*MSS. Ireland.*

[2] Descifrada de Don Bernardino, 11 de Deciembre.—*MSS. Simancas.*

that he was lost in a bog, and died of starvation.[1] O'Sullivan Bere, perhaps desirous of clearing Ireland of the stain of such neglect, says in his memoirs, that the Legate was attacked by dysentery in a peasant's cabin, that he received extreme unction from the Bishop of Killaloe, and was buried by O'Sullivan's own father and three other gentlemen.

The embers of the rebellion smouldered for two years more. Desmond and his brothers continued roving through the Munster forests; while scores of young Irish gentlemen, in passionate hatred of the English dominion, preferred a wild life of outlawry at his side to submission to the oppressors, and one after the other were killed, or captured and executed. The history of their deeds and their fate need not be related in detail. A few scenes will represent the rest. The English commanders were now only anxious to restore order. The plans of appropriation and confiscation were postponed till happier times. Those who were now in office, Grey, Malby, and Bingham, who after his service at Smerwick continued to be employed in Ireland, had no desire to enrich themselves on the spoils of the chiefs. They had come to serve their country and to do their duty as soldiers, to the ruin rather than the advancement of their private fortunes. They were honourable, high-minded men, full of natural tenderness and gentleness to every one with whom they understood themselves to be placed in human relations. The Irish, unfortunately, they looked upon as savages, who had refused peace and

---

[1] Mendoza confirms this version of Sanders's end, but mentions it confessedly only on English authority. 'Tienen aqui,' he wrote, 'por cosa asegurada ser muerto de frio y mal pasar en Irlanda, y que hallaron su cuerpo en un bosque con su breviario y Biblia debaxo su braço.' —*Don Bernardino al Rey*, 1 Marzo, 1581. *MSS. Simancas.*

protection when it was offered to them, and were now therefore to be rooted out and destroyed.

They regarded the Irish nation as divided into two classes, the Kernes, or armed followers of the chiefs, and the Churles, who were the tillers of the ground. The kernes were marked for death wherever they were found. The churles they wished to befriend, but the churles who accepted their friendship were killed by the kernes as traitors to their country; and, therefore, it seemed as if on one side or the other the same fate impended over all. At times misgivings rose that there had been enough of slaughter. In a discourse on the reformation of Ireland in 1583, it was suggested that 'all Brehones, carraghs, bards, rhymers, friars, monks, 'Jesuits, pardoners, nuns, and such like should be exe-'cuted by martial law;' and that with this clean sweep the work of death might end, and a new era be ushered in, with universities and schools, a fixed police, and agriculture, and good government.[1]

The destiny of the country however was too strong for these excellent intentions. The people declined to separate their fortunes from those of their priests and poets, and they all drifted on together through blood and misery.

On the return of the Deputy from Smerwick, Kildare and the Baron of Delvin were arrested and thrown into the castle. Clanrickard's sons lay out among the hills in Connemara and could not be caught, but their cousin Oliver Burke was brought into Limerick, put on his trial, and declining to plead, was pressed to death with the peine forte et dure.[2] No second good fortune came

---

[1] Discourse for the Reformation of Ireland, 1583.—*Carew Papers.*

[2] Grey describing his execution, adds tenderly, 'the which, as I am informed, he accepted with great humility, acknowledging his evil life

to the Wicklow insurgents. Feagh MacHugh O'Toole and his brother were killed in an incursion into the Pale. Their wounded followers were tracked by their blood into the mountains and killed also. Garrot O'Toole, and two Eustaces, brothers of Baltinglass, and many of their companions were overtaken a few weeks later, and their heads forwarded in sacks to Dublin.¹ Baltinglass himself escaped abroad and joined the English exiles. Four more distinguished Burkes were accounted for in Connaught by Malby's officers, with three hundred kerne and their families, men, women, and children. O'Rourke of Roscommon, who had married Clanrickard's daughter Lady Mary, was out with his brothers-in-law Ulick and Shan. His house was burnt, and his son, 'a child 'being but five or six years old,' was 'slain,' so it was hoped, 'with the rest,' 'for his coat was brought away 'among the spoils.' On the whole, Malby reported in April 1581, that since the preceding November, subsequent therefore to his campaign of the winter of 1579-80, he had killed seven hundred of Clanrickard's people, of whom two hundred were of the Earl's 'kinsmen and best 'men of war.'²

Lord Grey, if Elizabeth had allowed him, would have now made a Mahometan conquest of the whole island, and offered the Irish the alternative of 'the Gospel' or the sword.

'Your Highness,' he wrote to her, 'gave me a warning 'at my leave taking for³ being strict in dealing with 'religion. I have observed it, how obediently soever 'yet most unwillingly I confess, and I doubt as harm- 'fully to your and God's service: a canker never re-

---

to have deserved a worse death.'— Grey to Walsingham, Jan. 15, 1581-2. MSS. Ireland.
¹ Briskett to Walsingham, April 21.—MSS. Ibid.
² Malby to Walsingham, April 11, 1581.—MSS. Ireland.
³ i.e. against.

ceiving cure without corrosive medicine.'[1] Elizabeth would not respond to his zeal. He lost hope at once of doing good, and was eloquent in his disapproval to Walsingham. 'The wrong end is begun at,' he said. 'Rebellion and disobedience to the Prince's word are 'chiefly regarded, and reformation sought of God's cause 'is made a second or nothing at all. I have received 'many challenges and instructions for the civil and 'politic government and caretaking to the husbandry of 'worldly treasure, where there is one article that concerns 'the looking to God's dear service, seeing his Church 'fed with true food, and repressing of superstition 'and idolatry. Nay, rather have I not been watch-'worded that I should not be too eyefull therein. And 'I confess my sin. I have followed man too much in 'it, and this is the cause—that neither the chief can 'hearken to that that concerns both honour and safety 'most, nor you that persuade the truth can be believed; 'nor I that desire the right can be satisfied. Baal's 'prophets and councillors shall prevail. I see it is so. 'I see it is just. I see it past help. I rest despaired.'[2]

The cause of Lord Grey's despondency is the one ray of light which falls on the records of this horrid time. Elizabeth's government, fierce as it was, did not quite sink to the level of the Catholic continental tyrannies. Human creatures of all ages and both sexes were massacred in thousands, but the blood that was shed was not allowed to besmirch a name which in such connexion is better left unwritten. Ormond, Protestant as he was, grew weary of killing. In pity for the wretches who were still his countrymen, he pleaded that enough had been done, and that it was time for mercy; and the

---

[1] Grey to the Queen, Dec. 22, 1580.—MSS. Ireland. [2] Grey to Walsingham, April 14.—MSS. Ibid.

Queen, at his instigation and Walsingham's, sent over a general pardon, from which only Desmond and his brothers were excluded. 'The Irish,' she said, 'were 'misled by a fear that she meant by a conquest to deprive 'them of their lands and liberties. She had no such 'thought or intention;' 'the realm of Ireland was hers 'already,' and 'if the people would show themselves 'obedient she would take them as her loving subjects.' In the opinion of Lord Grey, the turn to clemency was premature. 'If there be issue of a pardon now,' protested he, in a letter to Walsingham, 'farewell all. I 'marvel, sir, that you are so earnest in it as to think it 'can do no hurt. To have pardon offered when none is 'sought, will show the chiefs that her Majesty is weary 'of the war.'[1] 'Your Majesty considers,' he wrote to the Queen, 'that the results of the war are not equal to 'its cost.' 'If taking of cows, killing of kerne and 'churles had been worth advertising, I would have had 'every day to have troubled your Highness.' 'If we 'make peace now, it will be a peace where your High-'ness's laws are answered by none but a handful of 'the English Pale.'[2] Elizabeth, either from economy or good feeling, adhered to her view, but neither her hopes and Ormond's, nor the Deputy's fears, were realised. The Irish would not submit. The iron had entered too deep into their souls, and desperate as were the fortunes of the rebellion, the young lords of the Pale, and the sons of the half reclaimed families of Munster, the Barries, the Roches, the Fitzgeralds, the MacTeigues, and the O'Sullivans, choose rather to live as 'Robin Hoods' with Desmond, than to enjoy their properties in peace under the rule of an English Deputy.[3] In answer to

---

[1] Grey to Walsingham, April 14, 1581.—*MSS. Ireland.*
[2] Grey to the Queen, April 26, 1581.—*MSS. Ibid.*
[3] Sir Warham St. Leger to Burghley, 1581.—*MSS. Ibid.*

the proclamation of pardon, Desmond dashed into the hitherto unspoiled country of his cousin Fitzgerald of Decies, who had sent in his submission to Grey, burnt thirty-six villages and swept off or destroyed seven thousand cattle.[1] Lying in the mountains between Waterford and Cork, he made the Butlers suffer in turn what the Butlers had inflicted upon Kerry. Ormond roused again into fury took the field in turn. Backwards and forwards the tide of havoc swayed, and at last so wretched, so desolate became Munster, 'that the lowing 'of a cow, or the voice of the ploughman was not to be 'heard that year from Dingle to the Rock of Cashel.'[2] To kill an Irishman in that province was thought no more of than to kill a mad dog; and small distinction was made at last between friends and enemies. Not only, says Mendoza, 'do the English make organised in-'roads upon them, killing men, women, and children, 'but I understand one of the Council has a letter from 'Ireland, in which it is related that an English officer, a 'favourite of the Viceroy, invited seventeen Irish gentle-'men to supper, and when they rose from the table had 'them all stabbed.'[3]

Of the neighbourhood of Dublin there is a curious account at this time in a letter of an English lawyer named Trollope, who appears to have been sent over by Walsingham, to learn the real condition of the country. The pardon had been rejected in Munster; the O'Tooles and the O'Birnes of Wicklow, who had escaped killing, had taken advantage of it, but only to gain time to secure their harvests. The mingled wretchedness, savagery, and defiant audacity which Trollope describes, show how desperate the Irish problem had by this time become.

---

[1] St. Leger to Burghley, June 3, 1581.—MSS. Ireland.
[2] Annals of the Four Masters, A° 1581.—MSS. Simancas.
[3] Mendoza to Philip, August 13, 1581.—MSS. Simancas.

'They desire now to get in their corn,' he wrote, ' and
'then they will break out again. Meanwhile, they
'murder privately any one who was loyal to the Queen
'during the rebellion. They have had a dozen pardons
'a piece. Every Irishman who gets a pardon, makes
'his account to be pardoned again as often as he wishes,
'let him murder, burn, and rob whom he list. They
'never did or will delight in anything else than murder,
'treason, theft, and mischief, which their countenances
'now at this instant at their coming in make apparent—
'for if they meet an Englishman or two walking in the
'streets, they shake their heads, they rouse themselves
'in their lowsy mantles, and advance themselves on tip-
'toe, as who should say, We are those who have done
'all this mischief; what say ye to us?'[1]

Lord Fitzmaurice and the Earl of Clancarty came to stay in Dublin with their ladies, 'in all their bravery,' while Trollope was there. The full dress of an Irish nobleman of the period, as he describes it, was a russet mantle, a hat, a leather jerkin, a pair of hose, and a pair of brogues, the whole equipment 'not worth a noble.' 'My lord and my lady,' with men servants, women servants, pages, horsemen, and all, slept in a single room, 'not so good as many a hogscote in England.' 'When 'they rose in the morning they shook their ears, and 'went their ways without any serving of God, or other 'making of them ready.' The common people, says the same authority, ' ate flesh if they could steal it,' if not, they lived on shamrock and carrion 'with butter 'too loathsome to describe.' ' They never served God ' or went to church.' The churches being roofless, they had perhaps no opportunity. They had no religion, and no manners, 'but were in all things more barbarous

---

[1] Andrew Trollope to Walsingham, Sept. 12, 1581.—*MSS. Ireland.*

'and beastlike than any other people.' The population
'was not half a quarter that of England,'[1] yet was
perpetually on the edge of starvation, though 'the soil
'was naturally as fertile as any in the world.' The
only policy for England in Trollope's opinion was evidently to exterminate the native Irish altogether. 'No
'governor shall do good here,' he said, 'except he shew
'himself a Tamerlane. If hell were open, and all the
'evil spirits abroad, they could never be worse than
'these Irish rogues—rather dogs, and worse than dogs,
'for dogs do but after their kind, and they degenerate
'from all humanity.'[2]

The quiet, as Trollope had foreseen, was of short continuance. The overthrow of the churches, the total absence of all instruction, the character of the administration, which had abolished the native Irish laws, yet was too weak to enforce order of its own, had turned the people generally into wild beasts. The Anglo-Irish of the Pale, if retaining vestiges of civilised humanity, yet in their sympathy with the inhabitants of their adopted country had become deliberately disloyal. The Wicklow Highlanders broke out as was expected when they had got in their harvest. A conspiracy was formed at the same time in which one or other member of almost every family in the Pale was implicated, to seize Dublin, force the Castle, and liberate Kildare and the Baron of Delvin. The plot was betrayed, the leaders were arrested, and those who had no property were hanged as usual by martial law. Nineteen others, Nugents, Sherlocks, Eustaces, and Neutervilles were brought to trial; and Grey having cause to fear that being men of family,

---

[1] England cannot have contained at this time more than five millions. Trollope's guess therefore, gives Ireland about 600,000.

[2] Trollope to Walsingham, Sept. 12, 1581.—*MSS. Ireland.*

Elizabeth would interfere in their favour, told Walsingham 'that he would make small stay in giving them 'their deserts.'[1] 'The jurors, by a secret power of God 'working in their consciences, proceeded very uprightly.' They were all found guilty of high treason and executed at once. A certain tenderness was shewn for their souls: they were Catholics, and an English clergyman[2] tried to convert them on the way to the scaffold. 'Is it not enough,' said a young Eustace to him, 'that 'you have our lives, but that you must seek to draw us 'from our religion?—Vade post me, Satana—Get thee 'behind me.'[3]

Kildare was sent to England. Confessions of accomplices shewed that he had been in close correspondence with Baltinglass. He escaped trial, however, and died in the Tower three years after. Col. Zouch fell in with Sir John of Desmond, the murderer of Davell, one misty morning on the Avonmore river, killed him at last and sent his head to Dublin, while his body swung like a mountebank's, in chains on the top of a tower in Cork, 'his legs upwards, his arms down; so high hanging he 'might be seen a mile off: a terrible sight to the rest of 'the rebels, a comely funeral and end of an earl's son, 'but too good for such a murderer and traitor.'[4]

Sir Nicholas Malby being recalled to England on business, committed Connaught to Captain Brabazon, whose administration left behind even that of his leader and instructor. 'Neither the sanctuary of the saint, nor of the 'poet,' write the Four Masters, 'neither the wood nor the 'forest valley, the town nor the bawn, was a shelter from

---

[1] Grey to Walsingham, Nov. 6.—MSS. Ireland.
[2] Thomas Jones, father of the first Lord Ranelagh.
[3] Notes of executions in Dublin, Nov. 1581.—MSS. Ireland.
[4] John Meade to Walsingham, from Cork, Feb. 8, 1581-2.—MSS. Ireland.

'this captain and his people till the whole territory was
'destroyed by him.' The condition of Munster was
beyond imagination frightful. The herds had been
swept away, the ground had not been tilled, and famine
came to devour what the sword had left. 'This
'country,' wrote Sir Warham St. Leger from Cork in
the spring of 1582, 'is so ruined, as it is well near un-
'peopled by the murders and spoils done by the traitors
'on the one side, and by the killing and spoil done by
'the soldiers on the other side, together with the great
'mortality in town and country, which is such as the like
'hath never been seen. There hath died by famine
'only, not so few as thirty thousand in this province in
'less than half a year, besides others that are hanged
'and killed.'[1]

The outlaws still clung to the forests. Of the once
brilliant house of Desmond, the Earl and his little son
who was in England were all that now were left. His
brothers' heads were rotting by the side of their cousin's
James Fitzmaurice on Dublin Castle. But the clans-
men held passionately to their chief and his lost cause.
Four Geraldines who had flinched and applied for their
pardons were taken at night from their cabins and
carried into Desmond's camp. They were arraigned as
traitors and hewn in pieces by their kindred, 'every
'sword in the band taking part in their deaths.' 'So,'
said the Earl, 'shall every Geraldine be served who will
'not follow me.' In their despair they were still
dangerous, and had their snatches of fierce revenge.
Half the garrison of Adair were surprised and massacred. Fitzgerald of Imokelly took Youghal, and sacked
it a second time. Six English soldiers were caught

[1] Sir Warham St. Leger to Sir John Perrot, April 22, 1582.—*MSS.
Ireland.*

alive in a fort there. Fitzgerald 'caused them to be
'held before him stark naked, till he with a halbert
'dashed out their brains.'[1]

Desmond himself bore a charmed life. Captain Zouch had all but surprised him once at Aghadoe; another time a party from Kilmallock were guided at night by traitors to a hut in the wood, where he and the Countess were sleeping. The guides mistook the path. Alarm was given, and the Earl and Lady Desmond escaped in their mantles; but escaped so narrowly, that the soldiers found the bed warm where they had been.[2]

In Ireland it had become a struggle of mere brute ferocity on both sides. In England the shame and disgrace began to be seriously felt.

Lord Burghley, who possessed the rare quality of being able to recognise faults in his own countrymen, saw and admitted 'that the Flemings had not such cause 'to rebel against the oppression of the Spaniards,' as the Irish against the tyranny of England.[3] Sir H. Wallop, to whom Burghley addressed his remonstrance, tried to defend the Irish Government. 'The causes of rebellion, 'my good lord,' he says, 'as I conceive them are these— 'the great affection they generally bear to the Popish 'religion which agreeth with their humour, that having 'committed murder, incest, thefts, with all other exe- 'crable offences, by hearing a mass, confessing themselves 'to the priest, or obtaining the Pope's pardon, they 'persuade themselves they are forgiven; and hearing

---

[1] Sir Warham St. Leger to ——, Jan. 16, 1582-3.—*MSS. Ireland.*
[2] Fenton to Walsingham, Jan. 16, 1582-3.—*MSS. Ibid.*
[3] 'Your lordship writes that, as things be altered it is no marvel the people have rebellions here, for the Flemings had not such cause to rebel by the oppression of the Spaniards, as is reported the Irish people.'—*Sir H. Wallop to Burghley,* June 10, 1582.

'mass on Sunday, or holyday, they think all the week
'after they may do what heinous offence soever, and it
'is dispensed withal. They also much hate our nation,
'partly through the general mislike or disdain one
'nation hath to be governed by another; partly that
'we are contrary to them in religion; and lastly they
'seek to have the government among themselves.'[1]

They wished 'to have the government among them-
'selves.' That was the only part of Wallop's explan-
nation which admitted of being acted upon. It might
be possible to revert to the old practice, when one or
other of the great Irish nobles ruled as Viceroy, and
Ireland was administered by Irishmen as a dependency
of the Crown. Grey was recalled at his own request.
The sword of justice was left as before to two of the
council, Archbishop Loftus, the Chancellor, and Sir H.
Wallop. But this arrangement could be only temporary, and the difficulty returned of finding some one
to undertake a post which entailed nothing but failure
and disgrace. Success seemed impossible to an Englishman. Should Ormond be tried then? The allegiance
of the house of Butler had been tried for centuries,
and had never failed. The present Earl had stood with
his countrymen against confiscation and appropriation.
His share in the massacre of the Geraldines was partly
recognised as legitimate, the Butlers being their hereditary foes, partly attributed to the English viceroy at
Dublin, whose officer Ormond was. Who then could be
found fitter than he to heal the wounds of the unhappy
people? There had been enough and too much of
slaughter; the superior strength of England was written
in characters too conspicuous to be mistaken. Kildare,
Delvin, perhaps Desmond, might now be pardoned

---

[1] Sir H. Wallop to Burghley, June 10, 1582.

safely, and the long waited for Irish millennium begin. So wished and so hoped Elizabeth; but from every English officer serving in the country, every English settler, every bishop of the Anglo-Irish Church, there rose one chorus of remonstrance and indignation. To them it appeared as a proposal now would appear in Calcutta to make the Nizam Viceroy of India.

'If the Earl of Ormond shall have the government of 'Ireland,' wrote Sir Henry Wallop in cipher to Walsingham, 'there will be no dwelling here for any English-'man, nor Ireland long be quiet. Ormond has written 'that so long as the Lord Justice is in Dublin,[1] he will 'never come thither. No harm will grow by it if he 'never do. Ormond is too great for Ireland already.'[2] The objection prevailed so far, that Ormond was not appointed Viceroy, but he was reconfirmed in the military government of Munster. Fresh troops were sent over to him, and he was directed to make an end of the remains of the insurrection at once, in the coming summer. Elizabeth trusted him—others it appeared did not trust him. While Ormond, therefore, held public authority, those who believed that his Irish sympathies would overcome his duty to his sovereign, were allowed to pursue independent of him their separate schemes for a pacification. The question was, whether it was better to destroy Desmond or preserve him. There was a suspicion that if the Geraldines were entirely uprooted, the Butlers having no rival to hold the balance against them would become sovereigns of Munster; and the Queen permitted Sir Warham St. Leger to open a private communication with the Earl and persuade him to surrender. No absolute promise was to be made to him, not even that his

---

[1] Archbishop Loftus was now Lord Justice in the absence of a Viceroy.
[2] *MSS. Ireland*, July 1581.

life should be spared, but hopes might be held out obscurely of far more than life. 'After so long and bloody 'a rebellion, her Majesty thought it would not be 'honourable to continue him in his earldom, and restore him to his former estate. But if his life might 'be saved, and liberty either in England or Ireland to 'live as a private person until she should think meet 'to give him some better state, her honour might then 'be preserved.'[1]

Elizabeth was not revengeful, and her troubles at home at this time made her unusually anxious that the Irish wars should be ended. It is singular that on this one occasion she resisted Burghley's advice to give Desmond a more distinct promise. 'Her Majesty 'would not consent.' Some private communication had passed between herself and Ormond, and to Ormond she insisted that the decision should be ultimately referred. While St. Leger was throwing out his bait of pardon to Desmond, other means were being tried to kill him.

'I was told,' wrote Secretary Fenton to Walsingham, 'at my being with the Earl of Ormond, to remember 'him that in a war of this nature practice and subornation is as necessary as force; and, therefore, as I knew 'there were in all places where Desmond had his haunt 'many poor and needy gentlemen who could and would 'for money draw some assured draught upon him either 'for taking of his head or delivering him prisoner to 'his lordship, so if his lordship could shorten the war 'by that means without dwelling upon the changeable 'and uncertain end by arms, I told him I thought it 'would be holden for right good service, not doubting 'but there will be found some who will undertake 'that service for the hire of a thousand pounds, with

---

[1] Burghley to Loftus and Fenton, Dec. 9, 1581.—*MSS. Ireland.*

'some farther small gratification of Desmond's lands.'[1] Either the attempt was not made or failed if it was tried, but neither Ormond nor any one would have been scrupulous on the lawfulness of such a deed in itself. 'Lord Ormond means well,' said St. Leger, 'but he will 'make but a patched piece of business. He would end 'the war by receiving traitors to mercy, and granting 'them protection for life, lands, and goods.'[2] If Ormond was too merciful what would St. Leger have been? His instructions from England were that before receiving any men of better quality to mercy he should exact substantial pledges for future good behaviour, one pledge especially, that as a condition of pardon 'they 'should embrue their hands in the blood of their wicked 'confederates that stood disloyal.'[3] It will be seen that Ormond faithfully observed these orders, and that so far at least the suspicions of his overleniency were undeserved.

The spring was now passing. The days were growing long and the ground hard, and the preparations were all complete for the closing campaign. Desmond himself was in the Kerry mountains. Lady Desmond, conscious that the end was coming, went in person to Ormond before he took the field to sue for her husband's pardon. Ormond could but reply that he had no power to grant her request, that nothing could be accepted but an unconditional surrender. This being so the Countess desired to remain in Ormond's hands; but her presence, it was thought, would embarrass Desmond's movements, and she was therefore forced to return to him. He too was weary of his miserable hunted life. He was a poor

---

[1] Fenton to Walsingham, March 17.—MSS. Ireland.

[2] St. Leger to the Queen, May 8.—MSS. Ibid.

[3] Memorandum to the Earl of Ormond by Walsingham, March 24, 1853.—MSS. Ireland.

creature at heart, with no quality of the Geraldines except
their pride. The enchantment of the name, the feudal
sacredness of the person of the chief, alone had made
him formidable. But his pride at the crisis of his fate
would not allow him to save himself. Never, he said,
would he stoop to a Butler, 'whose blood he would
'drink like milk but for the English churles.'[1] In the
vanity of chieftainship he spoke out stoutly from his
mountain stronghold, and imagined that he could still
treat with Elizabeth as an independent prince. Addressing himself no more to Ormond, he wrote in regal
style to Sir Warham St. Leger:—

'Where I understand that the Earl of Ormond giveth
'forth that I should submit meself before him as attor-
'ney to her Majesty, you may be sure he doth report
'more thereof than I have sent him either by word
'or writing. But this I have offered in hope to prove
'the unreasonable wrongs and injuries done to me by
'her Highness's officers in this realm from time to time,
'unguilty in me behalf as God knoweth. I am contented
'upon these conditions, so as me country, castles, pos-
'sessions, and lands, with me son, might be put and left
'in the hands and quiet possession of me council and
'followers, and also me religion and conscience not
'barred. With a pardon, protection, and passport for me
'own body to pass and repass, I would have gone before
'her Majesty to try all those causes just and true on
'me part, as still I do allege if I might be heard or have
'indifferency, and likewise hoping I might have more
'justice, favour, and grace at her Majesty's hands when
'I am before herself than here at the hands of such her
'cruel officers as have me wrongfully proclaimed. And
'so thereby thinking that her Majesty and I may agree,

---

[1] Gold to Burghley, April 13.—*MSS. Ireland.*

'if not that I may be put safe in the hands of me
'followers again, and I to deliver me son and me said
'possessions back to her Highness's officers. At Abbey
'Feale, April 28, 1583.

'GERON DESMOND.'

No one save Desmond himself could have imagined that such conditions as these would be entertained by the Queen. There was nothing left but for Ormond to draw the sword once more, and the campaign was commenced by an execution at Cork. Fitzgerald of Imokelly, who had killed the Englishmen at Youghal, was the most dangerous of the rebels next to Desmond. His mother, Lady Fitzgerald, 'that devilish witch,' as Ormond calls her, was supposed to have been the instigator of his cruelties. She fell into Ormond's hands, and he tried and hanged her. Then without more delay he set once more about his old work. A few days after he was in motion he reported himself as having killed or executed a hundred and thirty-four insurgents, while the chiefs, to whom he had made known the terms on which they might earn their pardon, were bringing him sacks full of heads.[1] By measures of this kind the county of Cork was speedily pacified. He then pushed on into Kerry to finish the work. Desmond, he said, would have long since been captured, but that the soldiers in garrison at Castlemayne and Ashketyn had made acquaintances among the Irish women, who had seduced them into negligence. A few necessary changes and moderate diligence would place 'the archfool' in his power.[2]

It appears that Desmond still clung to the hope either of a fresh rebellion in the Pale, or of a rising in Ulster,

---

[1] Ormond to the English Council, May 28, 1583.—*MSS. Ireland.*
[2] *Ibid.*

or of the interference in his favour of Philip. Every one in Ireland, high and low, in the Pale as well as out of it, was a Catholic openly or inwardly. Annexation to Spain had become a universal passion, and the people could not believe that Spain would leave them to be destroyed.[1] But the summer went on, and the O'Neils lay still, and the Catholic chivalry of the Pale were rotting on the gallows. No Spanish sail came again to the harbour at Dingle: and Desmond, gulping down his pride, wrote at last to Ormond in abject humility asking an opportunity to explain how he had been misled. Ormond had but one answer. He must surrender and plead his excuses at his trial. Lady Desmond, the companion hitherto of all her husband's adventures, forsook him now, perhaps by his own desire. She again came to Ormond. He would have sent her back a second time, but she would not go unless by force, 'lamenting 'greatly the folly of the Earl, whom wisdom could 'never rule.'[2]

Free from the encumbrance of her presence, the

---

[1] Wallop to Walsingham, June 18. The temper to which even the Anglo-Irish of the Pale had been brought, was curiously illustrated by a declaration of Walter Eustace, Lord Baltinglas's brother, who had hitherto escaped capture, but had been betrayed by a comrade.

'Being examined he confessed himself a Catholic. He said that he had done no offence against the Queen's Majesty, for that she was no Catholic; but what he had done, he had done it for God's cause, and by authority from the Pope. And that touching the robbing and murdering of her people, God did not forbid it, but rather commanded him to kill and rob all such as were out of the Catholic faith and religion of the Pope, who also had given him and the residue authority so to do; that he saw no cause to repent him of anything done against her Highness, for that he had done nothing against her as a lawful Queen, being no Catholic. That this doctrine had been taught him from the beginning, and that he would die in this opinion.'— *Loftus and Wallop to the English Council*, June 14. *MSS. Ireland*.

A theory of this kind, professed and acted upon by a whole people, does certainly go near to justifying extermination.

[2] Ormond to Burghley, June 18. —*MSS. Ireland*.

last of the Geraldines wandered from glen to glen, and mountain to mountain, attended only by a priest and three or four faithful followers who would not leave him. The wildest enthusiast had abandoned his cause as hopeless. Every chief had made his peace by a bloody offering to Ormond. Even Fitzgerald of Imokelly had earned forgiveness and been received to grace, and not a hand by the end of the summer was raised against Ormond's rule. Loftus, St. Leger, and Wallop hated him and disparaged his success. They insisted that the pardoned insurgents would revolt again with the winter, and they persuaded the Queen to bid Ormond revoke his protection and seize them unprepared. Ormond's answer was worthy of his name. 'My lord,' he proudly wrote to Burghley, 'the clause in the 'Queen's letter seems most strange to me. I will never 'use treachery to any, for it will both touch her High-'ness's honour too much and mine own credit; and 'whosoever gave the Queen advice thus to write is fitter 'to execute such base service than I am. Saving my 'duty to her Majesty, I would I were to have revenge 'by my sword of any man that thus persuaded the 'Queen to write to me.'[1]

To Ormond the Irish were human beings, with human rights. To the English they were vermin, to be cleared from off the earth by any means that offered. Desmond, unhappily for himself, was beyond even Ormond's concern or pity. A price was set upon his head; one by one the remaining companions of his misfortunes were taken from him. The priest was captured first, brought handcuffed to Cork, and hanged. MacSweeny of the Kenmare mountains fell next.

MacSweeny was the best friend that he had left, and had sheltered him and fed him through the summer; and

---
[1] Ormond to Burghley, Sept. 10.—*MSS. Ireland.*

when MacSweeny was gone, killed by an Irish dagger, the Earl's turn could not be distant. He was hunted down into the mountains between Tralee and the Atlantic. Escape was impossible either by sea or land, and the reward offered for his head was a temptation which the savages among whom he had taken refuge were not likely long to resist. One of these, Donell Macdonell Moriarty,[1] had been received to grace by Ormond on his last visit to Tralee, and had promised to deserve his pardon. One night, a fortnight after the dispatch of MacSweeny, this man came to the captain of Castlemayne, and informed him that the Geraldine chief was at that moment in a cabin at Glanquichtie, five miles up the river. The captain, with half a dozen English soldiers and a few Irish kerne, stole in the darkness along the path which followed the stream, and this time no friendly scout gave warning of the enemy's approach. The house was surrounded, the door dashed in, and the last Earl of Desmond was killed in his bed, as his brother had killed Henry Davell four years before in Tralee.

So ended a rebellion which a mere handful of English had sufficed to suppress, though three-quarters of Ireland had been heart and soul concerned in it, and though the Irish themselves man for man were no less hardy and brave than their conquerors. The victory was terribly purchased. The entire province of Munster was utterly depopulated. Hecatombs of helpless creatures, the aged, and the sick, and the blind, the young mother and the babe at the breast, had fallen under the English sword, and though the authentic details of the struggle have been forgotten, the memory of a vague horror remains imprinted in the national traditions.

Had no Saxon set foot on Irish shores, the tale of

---

[1] The name Moriarty still hangs about those parts of Kerry.

slaughter would have been as large or larger. To plunder and to kill, to massacre families of enemies, and to return to their dens with the spoil, while bards and harpers celebrated their triumphs, was the one occupation held in honour by the Celtic chiefs, and the Irish as a nation only began to exist when English rule at last made life and property secure. But England still pays the penalty in the hearts of an alienated race for the means by which it forced them into obedience. Millions upon millions of Celts have been enabled to exist, who, but for England, would never have been born—but those millions, not wholly without justice, treasure up the bitter memories of the wrongs of their ancestors.

Desmond's body was taken to Cork, where it was swung by the skeleton of his brother. The head went to Dublin Castle to be shipped for London and moulder upon a spike on London Bridge. The Council at Dublin, true to their policy of death, again urged the execution of Fitzgerald of Imokelly, and of others who had been Desmond's companions. Ormond had pardoned them, but the Lords Justices had not pardoned them, and the confiscation of their lands was held out as a bait to tempt the Queen to severity.[1] But Ormond pleaded successfully 'that it could not but be honour-'able to her Majesty after so much bloodshed to grant an 'indemnity,' 'and it could not stand with her honour to 'stay her mercy from those to whom he had himself 'given his word by virtue of her Majesty's authority.'[2]

---

[1] Wallop to Burghley, Nov. 10.—*MSS. Ireland.*

[2] Ormond to Burghley, Nov. 28.—*MSS. Ireland.* Sir Warham St. Leger, who had received large grants in Munster, and wished to make himself secure from his Irish neighbours, was still an advocate of severity. Ormond spoke contemptuously of him as 'an old alehouse knight, malicious, impudent, void of honesty; an arrogant ass that had never cou-

The south of Ireland had been made a desert; the last
gleanings of the harvest had been gathered, and it was
called peace. The insurgents of the Pale were dead or
in exile. Tirlogh Lenogh, unable to move on account
of the Scots when Fitzmaurice landed, and distrusting
afterwards the chances of the insurrection, had spared
his own people till Spain would speak out more clearly.
Submission was the order of the day. Connaught had
been scourged into quiet by Malby and Brabazon. Clanrickard died, and his sons, united hitherto in evil,
quarrelled over his inheritance. The younger brother,
John, was the favourite of the clan. He was a rol-
licking, marauding scoundrel, 'beloved by all the bards,
'and rhymers, and women,' and setting a fair example
of morality by living in incest with his sister, Lady
Mary, the wife of O'Rourke of Roscommon. Ulick
the elder, fearing his too successful rivalry, marked him
down one night when he was out on an expedition for
plunder, broke into the castle where he was sleeping, and
murdered him. The service was well received, and
well rewarded. Ulick, with Elizabeth's consent, was installed at Portumna in the earldom.[1]

One more cruel melodrama at Dublin concluded the
tragedy of the Desmond rebellion. It had arisen from
the direct action of the Pope. Fitzmaurice had landed
with a Papal commission and an accredited Legate. The
rebels everywhere pleaded Elizabeth's deposition as the
ground of the war, and in England as well as Ireland
the Pope was trying the question of allegiance, with
conspiracy and attempts at force. But for the incapacity
of the Irish leaders he would have driven the English

---

rage, honesty, or truth in him, nor
put him on a horse one hour in the
field to do any service.'

[1] Connaught correspondence, Nov.
1583.—MSS. Ireland.

out of the island; and when the revolt of Ireland had been accomplished the train was laid for an answering movement across the Channel.

A Papal emissary, whatever he might be, therefore, landing on the Irish coast was a fair object of suspicion, especially if commissioned to some permanent employment; and if born a subject of the Crown of England, was liable to prosecution for high treason. No person bearing a commission from an open enemy and coming to a country which through that enemy's instigation was in a state of deadly civil war could be allowed to plead innocence of unlawful intention.

In September 1583, two months before Desmond's death, there appeared suddenly in Drogheda an Irish priest named Hurley. He had been for some time resident at Rome, where he had been a member of the Inquisition, and had been closely connected with the English Catholic College. He had brought with him letters of induction from Gregory XIII. as Archbishop of Cashel, and he had arrived to take possession of the see. He was making his way in disguise across the Pale, intending to go to Kilkenny, of which he was a native, and claim the protection of the Earl of Ormond. Unfortunately for himself he had also secret letters of commendation with him, undirected, but seemingly addressed to Catholic noblemen of the Pale who had given cause of distrust. He was seized, searched, and his papers found, and he was carried to Dublin before the Lords Justices, Archbishop Loftus and Sir H. Wallop. He refused to give an account of himself, maintaining an obstinate silence on all points on which he was examined. The Irish Council wrote for instructions to London, and he was told that unless he would speak they must apply torture. There was no ' rack or other 'engine' in Dublin, and the justices, wishing perhaps to be rid of the responsibility, or doubting how far the rest of the Council would support them, suggested that he should be sent to London. It was considered, however, that a sharp example would produce a salutary effect in Ireland, and after a few months' delay, the intended archbishop was brought again before Loftus. Proof had been obtained, he was told, that his letters were for Desmond and Baltinglass, that they were in the hands of the Government, and that denials would be to no purpose; if he would deal frankly and discover all that he knew, her Majesty's mercy would be extended towards him.

Walsingham must share with Loftus the responsibility for what ensued, for the substitute for the more regular engine was suggested by Walsingham himself.

'Not finding,' wrote Loftus to him, 'that easy 'method of examination to do any good, we made com- 'mission to Mr. Waterhouse and Mr. Secretary Fenton, 'to put him to the torture, such as your honour advised 'us, which was to toast his feet against the fire with 'hot boots.'¹ Yielding to the agony he confessed something, probably less than the truth. The letters proved 'how deeply he was overtaken with treason,' though it does not appear that they contained matter plain enough to ensure conviction on a trial, unless the presentation to the see by the Pope was ruled to be treasonable in itself. It was proved that he had been intimate at Rome with the English refugees; it was not shewn that he had come to Ireland with a distinct insurrectionary purpose; and like the Jesuits in England, he insisted loudly that his mission was purely religious. Loftus consulted the Dublin lawyers, who being Catholics

---
¹ Irish tradition says that melted rosin was poured into his boots.

themselves, 'found scruple to arraign him for that his
'treason was committed in foreign parts.' It was
thought, too, that his 'clamorous denials' in open court
would produce a bad effect on the people. To allow
him to escape would be a manifest failure of justice;
both Loftus and Wallop, therefore, considered that,
with the Queen's approval, it would be well to execute
the unfortunate wretch 'by martial law,' 'against which
'he could make no just challenge, for that he had neither
'lands nor goods.'[1] Elizabeth took a month to consider,
and then answered, 'that the man being so notorious
'and ill a subject as he appeared to be, the Lords
'Justices should proceed to his execution by ordinary
'trial first;' but that 'if they found the effect of that
'course doubtful, through the affection of such as
'should be of the jury, or the interpretations of the
'lawyers, or the Statute of Treasons,' 'they might then
'take the shorter way' which they had proposed. No
further confession being expected, the torture was not
to be repeated; 'for what was past her Majesty ac-
'cepted in good part their careful travail, and greatly
'commended their doings.'[2]

The Irish judges persisting in their opinion that
there was no case for a trial, the second alternative was
taken. Sir John Perrot had been appointed at last to
succeed Grey as Viceroy. He had arrived in Dublin,
and was ready to begin his duties; but Loftus and
Wallop were permitted to conclude the work which

---

[1] Loftus and Wallop to Walsingham, March 7, 1584.—*MSS. Ireland.* Forfeiture of property could only be enforced after a legal trial and conviction. Martial law therefore, was confined to the poor, but the inverse argument of Loftus that because a man possessed no property he was to be expected himself to acquiesce in being arbitrarily executed could hardly have been used out of Ireland.

[2] Memorandum to the Lords Justices, April 18.—*MSS. Ireland.*

they had commenced, and finish with the archbishop before they delivered up the sword. 'On the 19th of June, they wrote, 'we gave warrant to the Knight 'Marshal to do execution upon him, which accordingly 'was performed, and thereby the realm rid of a most 'pestilent member.'[1]

Thus with one more barbarity, of all the deeds connected with the suppression of the insurrection perhaps the least excusable, the chapter of executions closed. The chain of English authority was once more riveted on Ireland, and the rule of the sword superseded by the rule of law. Sir John Perrot, in taking office, made a speech to the people in which he endeavoured to soothe their apprehensions, and give them hopes of better days. He told them that as 'the natural born subjects 'of her Majesty they were as dear to her as her own 'people,' and that they should have no more cause to complain of English oppression.

'In this particular,' reported Secretary Fenton, 'the 'Deputy was universally noted most acceptable to all 'men, that he wished to be suppressed and universally 'abolished throughout the realm the name of a churle 'and the crushing of a churle; affirming that how-'soever the former barbarous times had devised it and 'nourished it, yet he held it tyrannous both in name 'and manner, and therefore would extirpate it, and 'use in place of it the titles used in England, namely, 'husbandmen, franklins, or yeomen. This was so plau-'sible to the Assembly that it was carried throughout the 'whole realm in less time than might be thought 'credible if it was expressed.'[2]

---

[1] Loftus and Wallop to Walsingham, July 9.—*MSS. Ireland.*
[2] Sir Geoffrey Fenton to Walsingham, July 10.—*MSS. Ireland.*

CHAPTER XXVIII.

WHILE the Irish insurrection was in its infancy, a few weeks after Sanders landed at Dingle a second emissary charged with a similar mission appeared at Holyrood. Esmé Stuart, Count d'Aubigny, who had been selected to play over again the game which Queen Mary had begun and lost, was now twenty-three years of age. He had been trained by the Jesuits, and was an intimate friend of the Duke of Guise. As heir of the Regent Lennox, he was near in blood to the crown of Scotland, and was entitled to dispute the succession after the King with the house of Hamilton. He was not too old to be James's companion. He had qualities of mind and body calculated to give him influence and ascendancy, and he had been drilled with the utmost care for the part which he was to play.

To the world generally it was represented that he was going to Scotland to reclaim the Lennox lands there. Catherine de Medici and Henry were made to believe that his object was to restore the French party in the Scottish councils. The Queen of Scots herself was not admitted to a secret of which her knowledge would be useless till the conspiracy was further advanced, and the Pope, the Duke of Guise, the Archbishop of Glasgow, and the English at Rheims, were the only persons in Europe who were acquainted with the real purpose.

The opportunity was singularly favourable. The Earl of Morton had fallen. He had recovered power again, but he knew that without Elizabeth's assistance, he would be unable to maintain himself.

He had asked her to give the rents to the King of estates which were really his own, and to distribute a few trifling pensions among the Scotch peers. She had met his request with a violent, passionate, and insulting refusal. The party which had dethroned Mary Stuart were the only friends that she possessed in Scotland; yet it suited her to plead to the world that she had no connexion with them. To grant the King the rents of his grandmother's estates would prejudge, she was pleased to maintain, the question of the succession. Thus the Abbot of Dunfermline was sent back empty-handed, and the patience of the Scots was worn out. They would have preferred the most insignificant assistance from Elizabeth to the profuse offers which were pressed on them from abroad. But when, in return for their service, they found nothing but hard words, and when the King's claims in England were implicitly denied which they were enthusiastically bent on maintaining, all those who had wavered between the two parties, and would have gone with Morton, if they could have received any kind of reasonable encouragement, fell away from an ungrateful service, to employers who promised to be more open-handed. Argyle, Maxwell, Montrose, with another Maitland, brother of the more celebrated secretary, secretly reorganised their party. It was easy to persuade James that Elizabeth was insulting and robbing him, while Maitland and Sir Robert Melville worked on his natural feelings as he grew older, by dwelling to him on his mother's injuries. His kinsmen in France affected an earnest interest in his welfare; and smarting under a sense of ill-usage, he had listened eagerly to Guise's advice to invite over his cousin, and to confer on him the Lennox title which Elizabeth had denied his right to dispose of.

The sudden death of the Earl of Athol after a banquet at Stirling had, about the same time, occasioned fresh suspicions of Morton. His administration had been unpopular with all parties. He had alienated the Calvinists by supporting bishops to please Elizabeth. He had made his policy English in its faults as well as its merits, and when England threw him over, the dissatisfaction which had murmured in secret broke into open hostility. Thus it was that when the young Gallicised Scot landed at Leith in September 1579, he found the country, or at least the nobles, and all who were under their influence, prepared to receive him with open arms. Rumour said indeed that before leaving Paris he had been closeted with the Archbishop of Glasgow, and that the Duke of Guise had accompanied him to Calais; but in their existing humour the people would believe nothing but good of their brilliant and accomplished countryman; especially when he was found to have forty thousand crowns in gold to distribute among those whom Elizabeth had refused to relieve. The few who murmured danger to religion were easily silenced. D'Aubigny admitted frankly that he had been brought up a Catholic, but professed himself willing to be taught a purer faith. The Scotch Parliament was held at Edinburgh at the end of October, where James took his place as King regnant. The Acts of Religion were confirmed, and the Kirk of Scotland once more formally recognised. The earldom of Lennox was then conferred on the new comer, and it was understood that he would be declared next in blood to the Crown as soon as his conversion should be completed.[1]

D'Aubigny's easy success so far, coupled with the report of the rebellion which had broken out as they had hoped in Ireland, worked on the impatience of conspirators. The time had come, they supposed, for the next step in the game. The Archbishop of Glasgow waited on Don Juan de Vargas, Philip's ambassador in Paris, pointed out to him the opportunity which was opening, and asked him to use his influence with his master to bring Spain at last to declare itself. The Queen of Scots acting in concert with the Guises had broken, the Archbishop said, with the French Court, and had placed herself and her cause unreservedly in the hands of the Catholic King. Her fondest hope, in which the Duke of Guise shared, was to see her son carried off to Spain, converted to the true faith there, and married, if the King so pleased, to a Spanish princess. The present circumstances of Scotland would permit his capture if the King would receive him, and for herself, the Queen of Scots could now also, if she wished it, effect her escape, but she thought it better to remain, to run all risks, and to leave her prison only as Queen of England.[2]

Don Juan, who like most of the Spanish nobles was impatient to see the King exert himself, transmitted the

---

[1] Mauvissière, though no party to d'Aubigny's secret mission, suspected that his appearance in Scotland had more meaning in it than was acknowledged, and imagined that he was aiming at the throne. 'L'on dict,' he says, 'que ce seroit avec une clause qu'il se feroit de leur religion. Ceux qui veuillent regner il fault qu'ils scaichent dissimuler.' — *Mauvissière au Roy*, Oct. 29. TEULET, vol. iii.

[2] 'Dixóme assimismo que á su ama le offreriran commodidad para poderse escapar de prision, y que no lo quiere, porque pretende salir della Reyna de Inglaterra y no de otra suerte, aunque le cueste la vida.' — *Don Juan de Vargas al Rey*, Hebrero 13, 1580. TEULET, vol. v.

Archbishop's communication in the most favourable colours. He had himself, he said, been acquainted in early life with the Queen of Scots, and he knew her to be a person of courage and ability. She was furious with the French Court for having so long neglected her; being a woman, she would not forgive, and longed to be revenged on them.[1] The movements in Ireland and Scotland were already exciting the Catholics in England. The Queen of England felt herself so weak, that she was in terror if a cat stirred—and if d'Aubigny succeeded in overthrowing Morton, and the English Catholics took up arms, the mere appearance of a Spanish fleet upon the coast would make a revolution certain. France could not interfere while the Duke of Guise was on the side of the movement, and the overthrow of Elizabeth would bring with it the submission of Flanders. The Guise family would then probably partition France, the brothers would take each a portion, and Spain would be relieved for ever of all danger from French rivalry.[2] In conclusion, he begged Philip, whatever he might resolve, to be secret. A bold stroke was being played, and if the suspicions of the French Court were once excited the game would be spoilt.

It is hardly necessary to say that Philip was not to be tempted. He replied generally that he was well pleased with the zeal of the Catholic party. He would entertain the King of Scots, he said, if he came to Madrid, and would endeavour to reclaim him to the truth. But he had himself his eye on Portugal, and he had no intention of meddling with England till the annexation

---

[1] 'Esta indignada con estos grandemente, y como muger no perdona y desea vengarse dellos.'

[2] 'Por ventura descubrirían occasion que los hiciese resolver de emprender cada uno su pedaço desta corona y salir con el, dexandola tan debilitada que no se hubiese que temer de ella.'

was completed. Others, however, were inclined to
move if Philip would not. The Knights of Malta had
taken up the cause at the Pope's instigation as another
crusade. The Grand Master was in correspondence
with the College of Cardinals, on the dispatch of a fleet
to the support of Sanders, and the public feeling of
Europe was expected to compel the King of Spain to
take a share, whether he desired it or not, in so saintly
an enterprise.[1]

However De Vargas might insist on secresy, it was
impossible, when the plot began to take form, for the
nature of it to escape the English Government. In the
Cabinets of Cardinals and Kings, in the cells at Rheims,
in the purlieus of the Paris legation, or hanging about
the posthouses in France, Walsingham's spies were
everywhere. As soon as ever the plans of the conspirators became entrusted to letters, transcripts found
their way to London, and the meaning of d'Aubigny's
presence in Scotland, which Walsingham suspected from
the first, ceased to be a mystery.

Elizabeth as usual fell into a passion of alarm. She
had herself caused the mischief: she was ready now to
promise anything to repair it. Lists of noblemen were
drawn out who were to be 'entertained' with pensions,
when there was no longer a chance that the pensions
would be received. The Calvinists, so lately despised
and hated, became objects of new interest; and Captain
Errington was sent down to Scotland 'to incense the
'ministers and others well affected in religion against
'd'Aubigny, assuring them that he was a most danger-
'ous practiser against the King's government, under

---

[1] Copie d'une lettre mandée al evesque de Glasgow, 1580.—*MSS. Mary Queen of Scots.*

'colour of renouncing his Catholic religion.'¹ Every day information came in more and more unfavourable. Sir Robert Bowes wrote from Berwick that he had learnt on certain authority that Morton's death was determined on. He was to be tried and executed on a charge, which Elizabeth's conduct about the Casket letters had alone made possible, of being privy to the murder at Kirk-o'-field. It was true that Bothwell had consulted Morton. It was true that Morton had concealed his knowledge that the murder was intended. By weaving together fact and falsehood, it was possible to give colour to the pretence of the Queen of Scots that the crime had been Morton's own, and at once vindicate her innocence before a still suspicious world, and revenge her on the most dangerous of her enemies.

Errington reported that he could do nothing; and increasingly alarmed, Elizabeth sent Sir Robert Bowes after him as a more competent person on the same errand, to warn the King that there was a plot to carry him abroad, to bribe the Captains of Edinburgh and Dumbarton Castles to hold them for England, to terrify the ministers, to do anything and to promise anything 'to 'abase the credit' of the formidable stranger. Between herself and d'Aubigny letters passed of false politeness. D'Aubigny assured her that he was the most harmless of men, and in her answer she pretended to be satisfied; but she bade Bowes speak plainly in secret to Morton, warn him of his peril, and concert measures with him which would best meet the emergency.²

Edinburgh was in a wild state. 'I find right strange 'humours here,' wrote Bowes when he arrived, 'and 'matters standing in doubtful condition; the nobility

---

[1] Mission of Captain Errington, 1580.—MSS. Scotland.

[2] Instructions to Sir Robert Bowes, April 17, 19.—MSS. Scotland.

'no less in division than the people in fury, and ready to
'take part according to their affections.' The Protestant leaders had planned a second seizure of James's person. They intended to decoy him into the Castle and close the gates upon him.[1] But James, as Bowes expected, was not to be caught so easily, nor did the Queen's message to him when it was delivered produce much effect. A hint that if he lent himself to d'Aubigny's intrigues his hopes in England might be cut short by Parliament, for a moment seemed to alarm him. 'He appeared much perplexed; he said he would follow 'her Majesty's advice, and require her counsel in all his 'affairs.' But his young cousin had 'won his affections' so completely, that the ambassador 'dared not assume 'any long continuance of his promise.' With James himself there was nothing to be done. 'The wise,' however, with whom Bowes took counsel, 'considered the 'matter though hard not desperate to be recovered.' Though 'Morton was fallen from his high estate,' the 'experienced' thought that he might again be restored. 'The better sort made no difficulty of the matter, offer'ing to adventure themselves and their friends if they 'might be assured of her Majesty's support and back'ing.' Morton himself 'was ready to execute any plot 'that should be devised;' but he knew by this time the person with whom he was dealing, and he would not risk his life and fortune at Elizabeth's bidding, without secu-

---

[1] 'The King will be moved to visit the Castle of Edinburgh, and I think it is either done or will be done this night, but I look it shall not take effect to the desire of the movers.'— Bowes to Burghley and Walsingham, April 27. MSS. Scotland. It is noticeable that Elizabeth only half trusted Burghley in Scotch matters. Walsingham bade Bowes direct his general letters to himself and the Lord Treasurer; but if there was 'any specially private matter,' he was to write it in cipher to Walsingham singly, 'to be by him conveyed alone to the Queen.'— Walsingham to Bowes, May 3. MSS. Ibid.

rity that this time she would take up in earnest the cause of which he was the representative. Offers, he said, had been made to him from the other side, which would enable him to provide for his own safety. He could not trust to an uncertainty. The Queen of England must identify herself with the Protestants of Scotland on the one side, and satisfy James's just demands on the other. She 'must declare publicly her care for the common 'cause of religion, and divide the King from foreign prac-'tices by relieving him with some good liberality.'[1]

In other words, Morton not unnaturally required Elizabeth to commit herself, and in fact as well as promise, part with some little money. He pressed for a speedy reply, and as might have been expected, he could not have it. Walsingham, earnest as he was himself in the cause, 'was unable to draw from the Queen such 'answer as the necessities of the time required,'[2] nor could anything more be wrung from her, though Bowes again said that unless she could resolve a revolution was 'imminent and inevitable.' There was a party still well inclined to England, but they would run no risks without knowing her Majesty's 'resolute purpose.' And so little hope had Morton from his past experience, that after a few weeks' delay, he told Bowes that ' he looked ' not for any seasonable resolution from her,' and must provide for his own safety.

Such words could bear but one meaning. He implied that he must desert England altogether, and throw his weight and name into the other scale. Bowes, more faithful to his mistress than to Morton, continued to keep him in play by promises which he knew would never be fulfilled; so 'handled the matter' that the difficulties

---

[1] Bowes to Walsingham, May 23, May —.—*MSS. Scotland.*
[2] Walsingham to Bowes, June 1. —*MSS. Scotland.*

seemed rather to be raised on his side than the Queen's.¹
He tried, and Elizabeth herself tried, to tempt him into
some dangerous enterprise, either the seizure of James's
person, or the sending d'Aubigny out of the world, into
something in which when once involved he would be
compelled for his own sake to persevere. She wrote to
him in her own hand, professing to warn him of a conspiracy for his own destruction, begging him to lay his
mind frankly open to her, and promising that 'upon in-
'telligence received from him, she would not fail to put
'in execution whatever should by him be thought
'meet.'² Morton saw the snare and declined to be
caught. He 'took the letter in very evil part.' 'He
'thought it devised by some that loved him not,
'invented to delay time as had been done often before.'
'Words without deeds,' he said, 'should not prevail
'with him.' He saw clearly that her Majesty intended to
'be at no charge, nor yet would maintain and stand to
'such as would adventure themselves.'³ He replied to
Elizabeth that he did not see how a single nobleman
could lay plans before another sovereign for a change
in the government of his own country. If he obeyed
her, he feared that she would not herself 'allow' him
in so doing; and he invited her to invert the situation
and to consider what she would feel if he was a
member of her own Council 'solicited by strangers.'⁴
He knew that his life was in danger; he had no ambition for martyrdom; and though he preferred the English

---

¹ 'If Her Majesty please not to lend any money as is desired, then the matter must be handled with expedition and some cunning to persuade that the lets and impediments thereof may arise and come from themselves.' —*Bowes to Walsingham*, June 15. *MSS. Scotland.*

² Elizabeth to Morton, June 11, 1580.—*MSS. Ibid.*

³ Bowes to Walsingham, August 1 and 10.—*MSS. Ibid.*

⁴ Morton to the Queen, July 16. —*MSS. Ibid.*

alliance as the best for his country, he confessed that Elizabeth might drive him to seek his safety by means which would not be eventually profitable to her.[1]

The government of Scotland meanwhile rapidly passed to d'Aubigny. Edinburgh Castle was given in charge to one of his adherents. Dumbarton was made over to him as an appanage of his earldom, and he had thus the key in his hand to open Scotland to the French or the Spaniards; while he won the hearts of the General Assembly by subscribing the confession of faith, by petitioning for a minister to reside with him to perform the offices of true religion, and by throwing himself on the wisdom of the Kirk to choose a fitting pastor for him.[2] Bowes came up to London to tell Elizabeth what could not be safely committed to letter. She sent orders to Lord Shrewsbury to keep a vigilant eye on Mary Stuart, and she dispatched Bowes again to Scotland, with instructions to demand an audience from which d'Aubigny should be excluded, to insist to the King that whatever d'Aubigny might pretend he was 'a professed enemy to the Gospel,' that he had come to Scotland to carry out a plot which had been devised at Rome for the overthrow of religion, and to entreat at all events that he should not be left in possession of a place of so much importance as Dumbarton. If the King paid no attention, it appeared as if Elizabeth had made up her mind at last to the other alternative. Bowes was empowered 'to confer with the Earl of Morton 'and other enemies of Lennox,[2] how the matter might 'be helped, either by laying violent hands on the said 'Lennox and his principal associates, or in any other 'way which by the Earl of Morton should be thought

---

[1] Bowes to Walsingham, August 1.—*MSS. Scotland.*

[2] So d'Aubigny will henceforth be called.

[1] Calderwood.

'meet;' her Majesty giving a positive assurance 'that
'the Earl should not lack any assistance that she could
'give him,' and 'express commandment' having been
sent to the governor of Berwick to put himself and his
force at Morton's disposition.[1]

Sir Robert had himself seen and spoken with Elizabeth, and, notwithstanding past experience, believed that she was really in earnest. He galloped back to Edinburgh. He asked for a private interview, which Lennox prevented him from obtaining. He then turned to Morton as he had been told to do, and Morton, trusting to an engagement from which he believed that Elizabeth could not now retreat, committed himself at once to a plot for Lennox's destruction. The haste was fatal. A panting courier came in two days later from London with news that all was undecided again. 'Her Majesty,' Walsingham wrote to Bowes, 'desires you to follow the way of 'persuasion, and forbear to enter into any conference 'with them of force to be used, or promise of assistance 'from her Majesty.' 'You perceive,' he added, in bitter despondency, 'how uncertain we are in the course of 'our doings. I am afraid our unthankfulness to God, 'which in justice ought to receive some severe punish-'ment, will not suffer us to put off by timely prevention 'the approaching mischiefs that hasten towards us, which 'I fear are to receive their beginning from that realm. 'Be not hasty to promise much from hence for we take 'no care to perform.'[2] Unfortunately Bowes had promised. Morton had involved himself in schemes at Elizabeth's instigation which were distinctly treasonable, and which, if unexecuted, could not fail sooner or later to be discovered by his enemies. He might still have saved himself, powerful as these enemies were, if he had

---

[1] Walsingham to Bowes, August 11.—*MSS. Scotland.*
[2] Walsingham to Bowes, Sept. 1. —*MSS. Ibid.*

acted on his first impulse, and dropped thenceforth all connexion with England and its Sovereign. But Morton, though unprincipled as a man, was singularly steady to his political convictions. He was firmly convinced that the interests of Scotland lay in an alliance, not with France, but with England. He believed that Elizabeth could not now desert him, and he continued to listen to her wavering messages till he too, like every other Scot who had run her fortune, perished in his confidence.

She had not absolutely decided on deserting him. Had she decided anything and given him timely notice of it, he might have fled. Her infirmity of purpose unfortunately took shape in language as violent as her action was weak. She thundered out threats at James that 'if he would not follow her counsel she would work 'him more prejudice than in his young years he could 'understand.'[1] In the morning in the Council Chamber she made up her mind to be brave. Her resolutions were undone at night by the whispers of the ladies of the bedchamber, sworn friends of Mary Stuart. All would go well, wrote Bowes, if she would be but firm, 'while drifts and faintness would utterly overthrow 'the cause.'[2] Every one but Elizabeth saw through the situation. The Council dreaded, not unjustly, that the patience of the loyal Scots would be tried too far, that the English party among them would fall in pieces, and that England would then inevitably be invaded.

The Council represented to her that if 'Lennox were 'suffered to continue in his greatness,' he would destroy her friends one by one. He would 'nourish troubles' on the Border, and for every hundred pounds that she

---

[1] Walsingham to Bowes, Sept. 10.—*MSS. Scotland.*
[2] Bowes to Walsingham, Sept. 12.—*MSS. Ibid.*

had saved by refusing the requests of the Abbot of
Dunfermline she would have to spend a thousand on
the garrisons of the Marches. He would find a wife for
the King in France or Spain, and, when opportunity
served, would make 'present title' to her crown, as his
mother did when she married the Dauphin. And 'the
'King would have more help than she, because he was
'a young man in whom both kingdoms would seem to
'be knit to avoid peril by uncertainty of succession:'
while 'he would have the comfort also of all discontented
'persons in England, whereof the number was now far
'greater than at the beginning of her Majesty's reign.'[1]
She was recommended to send 'an embassy of weight'
to Edinburgh—Lord Hunsdon, Lord Scrope, or some
other great person whose presence 'would encourage
'those who liked not Lennox,'—and to intimate clearly
and decidedly that if her remonstrances were not attended to, she would declare war. She yielded as usual.
Instructions in this spirit were drawn out for Lord
Hunsdon and Sir Walter Mildmay; but they were no
sooner written than they were repented of. Lennox
plied her with deprecating letters, which she allowed to
influence her, though she did not believe their sincerity.
She recalled Bowes, bidding him tell the King that she
was deeply displeased with his ingratitude, but that as
he would not listen to her he must go his own way;
while to Morton again, 'for fear he should think him-
'self forsaken and given over as a prey to Lennox,' she
sent a message that she did not really mean to leave
things thus; that very soon, if not immediately, she
would send up 'persons of greater quality to put in
'execution the advice by Morton given, assuring him

---

[1] A purpose of Council at Richmond, Sept. 18, 1580.—*MSS. Scotland.* Burghley's hand.

'for the great constancy she had always found in him 'for the maintenance of amity between the two nations 'she would never see him abandoned.'[1]

The value of the promise was now to be seen. There were persons about Elizabeth who tempted her into vacillation and betrayed her weakness. Lennox was given to understand from England that he had nothing to fear, and that he might venture safely on the next step of the revolution. Morton had till now been titular President of the Scotch Council, while Angus, Mar, and others of the Protestant leaders had remained members of it also. On the departure of Sir Robert Bowes the King informed them that their services would no longer be required, while a charge was brought publicly against Morton that he had held treasonable dealings with England. Everything which he had done, all his correspondence with Bowes, had been discovered. Lennox knew that his own life had been in danger, and he had entirely made up his mind to take Morton's life in return. Yet he paused after the first step to see whether Elizabeth was as weak indeed as he was given to believe. She roused herself into a passing fury. She dictated an order for Lord Hunsdon, who was now at Berwick, to go to Holyrood and tell James once more that she saw through his purpose, and that she would use the power which God had given her to prevent it. She bade Hunsdon take money with him, bribe Argyle if possible to leave the Lennox faction, form a party among the Protestants, and hold himself ready to advance to their support if they found it necessary to take arms. But Elizabeth's politics ran for ever in a single groove. The order was drawn at her words; but it was no sooner ready than it was qualified with additions which made

---

[1] The Council to Bowes, Oct. 7.—*MSS. Scotland.*

it meaningless.[1] Finally her purpose evaporated, and she recalled it altogether.

The next step followed as matter of course. To destroy Morton had been d'Aubigny's first object. So long as Morton lived the reaction could never be safe. His talents, and his experience, backed by help which sooner or later might come from England, would bring him back into power. He was now at Lennox's mercy. It would have been easy to try him for his late treason and to execute him with a show of fairness. But the House of Guise, under whose directions Lennox throughout was acting, had a subtler purpose, and Bowes had early ascertained the charge on which Morton would be brought to trial. To kill the Protestant chief and to stain him with the murder of Darnley would at once remove the main obstacle to Lennox's policy and the blot upon the Catholic cause; and those who, like all passionate Catholics, imagined Scotch Protestantism to be an accidental creation of a few intriguing nobles, could believe that the disgrace of the leader would be the death-blow of the creed.

James Stewart, the second son of Lord Ochiltree, famous or infamous afterwards as Earl of Arran, a youth little older than Lennox, was selected for the execution of the arrest. The King had consented, and the first plan was to send for Morton to the presence chamber, when he would necessarily be alone and unarmed, and seize him in the King's presence. Either James's courage failed him however, or his better nature prevailed. On the day agreed upon (December 26) he took Morton hunting with him. He called him his father. His manner was unusually affectionate, and in the course of

---

[1] Instructions to Lord Hunsdon, with her Majesty's additions, Nov. 1580.—*MSS. Scotland.*

the chase Lord Robert Stuart, possibly at James's instigation, told him what was intended, and advised him to fly. He had long known that he was in danger, but for some cause he was unable to believe that it would approach him in the form of an arrest. He neglected the warning, he would not even retire to his own castle at Dalkeith, but returned to Edinburgh with the Court. When informed that he was to be accused of the murder of Darnley he laughed at the thought of it, and went as usual to his apartments in Holyrood, 'confident in the 'King and in his own innocency.'[1]

The name of Sir James Balfour will be remembered as one of Bothwell's confederates. Balfour, like many others who had been concerned at Kirk-o'-Field, had profited by the general disinclination to look deeply into the history of the murder, but he had found it prudent nevertheless to remain chiefly on the Continent. It happened that he, and only he, was in a position to prove the communication which had passed between Morton and Bothwell. He had a quarrel of his own with Morton, which he had long watched for a chance of settling. He had been in communication with Lennox—it was believed in England that he had been at Madrid, and had obtained money from Philip to assist Lennox's enterprise,[2] and he had now secretly returned to Scotland to give his evidence. The arrest was effected on the last evening of the year in the Earl's own room in the Palace.[3] That night and the next

---

[1] Bowes to Burghley and Walsingham, Jan. 1, 1581.—MSS. Scotland.

[2] 'Avisan asimismo que este Sir James Balfour habia estado en España, que V. M* le habia mandado dar quantidad de dinero con que habia ganado algunas voluntades en Escocia para conseguir la execution del negocio.'—Bernardino de Mendoza to Philip, Jan. 15, 1581. MSS. Simancas.

[3] Bowes to Walsingham, Jan. 1.— MSS. Scotland. Calderwood says er-

day, which was Sunday, he remained there under a
guard, and it was said that he might have escaped had
he tried. On Monday morning Captain Stewart carried
him up to the Castle with a strong escort, which appeared, however, not to have been required. Morton
had but few friends. The Catholics hated him as the
champion of Protestantism; the Protestants, for having betrayed the liberties of the Kirk by maintaining
bishops to please Elizabeth; and both, for having been,
as they considered, too subservient 'to the auld enemy.'
The crowd saw him pass in silence; and when the Castle
gates closed behind him there was neither regret nor
sign of displeasure. The news flew to England, to
France, and over France to Spain and Rome, and the
exultation of the Catholic world was a singular tribute
to Morton's greatness. The Queen of Scots heard of
it at Sheffield, and though as yet ignorant of all its
meaning, she knew that her most detested enemy was
in the power of her friends, and had but one fear, that
the English might interpose to save him. She wrote to
Mauvissière charging Morton with having been the
cause of all her misfortunes, and the most disloyal of
mankind.[1] She wrote to the Archbishop of Glasgow at
Paris bidding him explain to the King the enormity
of Morton's offences;[2] and the King little dreaming
that the overthrow of the late Regent was the first act
of a scheme of which one of the results contemplated
by its authors was the dismemberment of the French
Empire, addressed a request to Elizabeth at Mauvissière's
entreaty to abstain from interference. The English

---

roneously, that it was in the Council
chamber, where Morton had ceased
to sit.

[1] Mauvissière to the King of France, Jan. 11.—TEULET, vol. iii.

[2] The Queen of Scots to the Archbishop of Glasgow, Jan. 12 and March 4.—LABANOFF, vol. v.

Catholic nobles—Mendoza does not specify which among them but speaks generally of all—let Lennox know that by them the death of his prisoner would be received with entire satisfaction, and Mendoza himself in sending his congratulations to the Queen of Scots pressed upon her with superfluous eagerness the importance of his execution, if the Catholic faith was to be restored.[1]

The meaning of the charge on which he had been arrested was perfectly understood in England. It was to verify to the world the Queen of Scots' allegation that those who had accused her of her husband's murder were themselves guilty of it.[2] The obligation of Elizabeth to protect him, was, it is needless to say, at least as great as the eagerness of the Catholics for his destruction. She it was who had prevented Morton and Murray originally from publishing the Casket letters, and making a defence of the Queen of Scots impossible. She it was who had forced the Regency of Scotland upon him against his will, and had used him ever since for her own convenience, while she had withheld from him the support which she had promised. She had herself under her own hand invited him to concert measures with her for the coercion of his own sovereign. She had entangled him in a dangerous intrigue by engagements of the most solemn kind; and at the last moment, when he could have provided otherwise for his personal safety, she had bound him to her side by reiterated assurances that come what would she would never abandon him.

Lightly as obligations of this kind sate upon Elizabeth,

---

[1] Don B. de Mendoza to Philip, Jan. 15, 1581.—*MSS. Simancas.* Philip wrote on the margin of the decipher, 'Fué muy bien,'—'It was very well done.'

[2] 'Queriendo proceder en esta manera el Rey con Morton porque se clarificase mas la innocencia de su madre, y falsedad de que le han querido culpar.'—*Ibid.*

she did in some degree recognise that she could not safely let Morton die. She was herself, as she well knew, the real object of the conspiracy, and interest as well as honour required that Lennox should not suppose that he could defy her with impunity. He had gathered courage from her vacillation; he should see that she could be provoked too far. She sent the Earl of Huntingdon to York to raise levies of men, with directions to make choice especially of men 'well affected 'in religion,' and to join Hunsdon at Berwick with as large a force as he could collect; while Thomas Randolph, grown old now, but with long experience in Scotch politics, went back to the scene of his early labours to take part in a later act of the same play, to tell the King in Elizabeth's name that her forbearance was exhausted, and that he must retrace his steps and release Morton, or prepare for the consequences. He carried with him copies of a correspondence between the Archbishop of Glasgow and a Cardinal at Rome, procured by an emissary of Walsingham, which revealed the meaning of Lennox's presence in Scotland, which exposed the connexion of the invasion of Ireland, the inroad presently to be described of the Jesuits and seminary priests into England, and the Guisian intrigue at Holyrood. The young lord by whom James was allowing himself to be directed had come over, as Randolph was able to prove, merely and only 'to overthrow religion' in Scotland first and in England after; 'a thing which would not be accom- 'plished without the bloodshed of infinite numbers, and 'the irrecoverable dishonour of the King's name.' The Queen required that the charges against Morton should be examined, not by Lennox, but by indifferent judges, and she desired James to understand that if the story of Kirk-o'-field was reopened, the accusations pressed against one should be pressed equally against all who had been concerned.[1]

If this remonstrance produced no effect, 'you will then,' so Randolph's instructions concluded, 'seek out 'the party opposed to Lennox, who wish well to the 'King and to England; you will find what strength they 'can make, if her Majesty send a power to preserve the 'Earl and the realm from foreign practices; and you will 'tell them that we have ordered the Earls of Huntingdon 'and Hunsdon to put a power in readiness to be sent 'forward forthwith in case a milder course will not be 'taken by the King. If you find nothing can be 'obtained but extremity against Morton and his friends, 'you are immediately to send for such forces as the 'Lord-Lieutenant shall have prepared in such number 'and at such time as you shall think meet.'[2]

In recommending Elizabeth to take a determined attitude, the whole Council were for once heartily agreed. The nature of the conspiracy was so patent, the danger so serious and so widely spread, that minor differences vanished before the general necessity of self-defence. The cautious and moderate Sussex was at one with the impetuous Walsingham. 'He was sorry,' he said, 'that her Majesty had overslipped her best oppor-'tunity,' 'that it had not pleased her to enter sooner into 'the execution of matters fit for her surety.' 'If his 'own blood would stop the gap that had been opened 'he would gladly give it.' But it was now too late for regrets. Courage was wanted—courage 'in deed and 'not in words,' and what her Majesty would do she must do quickly.'[3]

---
[1] Commission to Thomas Randolph, Jan. 7. Walsingham to Randolph, Jan. 8.—*MSS. Scotland.*
[2] Commission to Randolph.
[3] Sussex to Walsingham, Jan. 7.—*MSS. Scotland.*

Her Majesty it seemed was herself of the same opinion. Huntingdon flew to York to collect troops, while Randolph made haste to Edinburgh. Morton's friends had not been idle. The Earl of Angus, his cousin, had two thousand of the Douglases under arms. The ministers had begun to see that worse might be before them than Tulchan Bishops. Ruthven, who had gone with Lennox from a private grudge, had gone back to his party. Lindsay was true as steel to the cause for which he had stood by Morton at Carberry and at Lochleven; and all the Protestants in Scotland, peers and commons, were ready to take arms when the first English soldier had stepped out from Berwick upon Scotch soil. Should Huntingdon and Hunsdon move they would blow Lennox back to France again, with more ease by far than Sir Wm. Drury had taken Edinburgh Castle. Yet he was indifferent to his danger, and his friends in Elizabeth's household must have told him that he need not be alarmed. The day before Randolph reached Edinburgh Morton was carried off to Dumbarton. To the Queen's message, the King replied that he was sovereign in his own realm, that he meddled not between her and her subjects, that he must request her to leave him to deal with his own as they had deserved. This answer was to have been the signal for the advance of the Earls from Berwick. Unhappily either Randolph had secret and separate orders from Elizabeth, or age had dulled his courage and his intelligence. The Marian spirit with which he had once contended so bravely was again in the ascendant. The old situation was repeated with no substantial difference, yet he allowed himself to be drawn into a private correspondence with Lennox, and yet worse allowed himself to become his dupe. This true pupil of the Jesuits pretended that no harm was meant to

Morton, that the supposed correspondence was a forgery, and the suspicions against him baseless as a dream; that he was a sincere Protestant, devoted to his King, his country, and the Queen of England. Instead of sending for troops to Berwick, therefore, Randolph, to the astonishment and dismay of every loyal English statesman, wrote to say that force would not be needed, and that Lennox's character had been mistaken. Huntingdon tried to open his eyes. The Scotch Commons were the true friends of England, he said, and no good could come from d'Aubigny.[1] 'By your letter to the Earl of 'Leicester,' wrote Walsingham scornfully to him, 'you 'seem to conceive hope that Lennox may be won to be 'at her Majesty's devotion, which we suppose you 'deliver by way of mirth. We cannot be persuaded that 'any sure foundation can be made that way, though it 'may stand him to great purpose to entertain us with 'that alluring hope. I pray you harp no more on that 'string.'[2] 'I am sorry,' wrote Walsingham again to Lord Huntingdon, 'I am sorry Mr. Randolph should 'suffer himself to be carried into an opinion that 'Lennox may be won. I know that both he and those 'that put that conceit in his head will find themselves 'deceived in that man. I beseech your lordship concur 'with me in seeking to divert Mr. Randolph from such 'a belief.' Huntingdon sending on these words to Randolph added of his own: 'You already know my 'opinion, whatever he offers will prove but dissimulation 'in the end. You build on sand to accept him in 'any such credit. I can but repeat the sentence of St. 'Paul, Qui stat, videat ne cadat, chiefly a warning in 'matters of faith, but it may serve our turn in matters

---

[1] Huntingdon to Randolph, Jan. 25.—MSS. Scotland.
[2] Walsingham to Randolph, Jan. 31.—MSS. Scotland.

'of policy, especially when religion and policy are so knit
'together as in this action.'[1]

Their anxiety was but too justly founded, and if Randolph's conduct was not the work of some private order from the Queen, hopes like those which he was holding out were the straws which she for ever caught at to escape the necessity of action. The Council remained determined, and she did not openly oppose them. The Earls at Berwick held themselves ready to march, and ships hung on the coast to intercept James if an attempt was made to send him to Spain. Orders went again to Randolph to insist that Morton should be removed from Dumbarton and placed in neutral hands, that his trial should be open without practice or corruption, and with due regard to time and place. If these demands were refused, Randolph was instructed 'undelayedly to call in the English army.' 'Morton,' said Walsingham, 'was not put at for the 'slaughter of the King, but for the putting down of the 'young King's mother;' and he sent Lennox word that if 'by foul play he touched one hair of Morton's head 'it should cost the life of the Queen of Scots.'[2]

Threats unluckily were not actions, and Walsingham was not Elizabeth. Randolph's eyes continued mysteriously dim. He continued to hold intercourse with Lennox; he continued his favourable reports to the Court. The King, he said, had no thoughts of leaving Scotland. Morton would have a fair trial, and there was not the faintest purpose of altering religion. Lennox 'after conference with the ministers had embraced 'the true Evangile.' He was in Scotland only because

[1] Huntingdon to Randolph, Feb. 8.—MSS. Scotland.
[2] Walsingham to Randolph, Feb. 9.—MSS. Ibid.

he was the King's nearest relation. He was devoted to England and the English alliance.[1]

The young nobleman who had been trusted with so great an enterprise, was doing ample credit to his instructors. To blind Randolph, to pacify the alarms of the ministers, and as an answer to Elizabeth, a confession of faith of the most extreme Protestant kind, running through the whole gamut of Calvinist doctrines, and cursing the Roman antichrist, was subscribed at Holyrood, on the 2nd of March, by the King, by Lennox, by Lord Seton, by the master of Grey, by all the party who then, and in the years which followed, were the leaders or instruments of the Jesuit faction. To so audacious a stroke what reply could be given? It deceived the English Parliament, which was then in session. It appeared incredible that if Lennox meditated mischief against England, he should have taken a step which would alienate the great Catholic powers. It deceived for a time even Mendoza himself, who described the confession as the vilest composition ever committed to words, which he could only hope to be a forgery.[2] But it answered its purpose in Scotland. It broke up the party which would have taken arms not out of love for Morton but in fear of Popery, and to Elizabeth it was a fresh excuse for inaction. Rumours were studiously spread, to which the troops at Berwick gave appearance of truth, that the independence of Scotland was threatened. Morton's correspondence with Bowes was published. He had been betrayed by his secretary, who charged him with having intended to send the King to England. Angus, Mar, Ruthven, Glencairn,

---

[1] Answer of the King of Scots and Council, Feb. 7.—*MSS. Scotland.* Enclosed by Randolph to Walsingham.

[2] Don B. de Mendoza to Philip, March 17, 1581.—*MSS. Simancas.*

Montrose, and Lindsay, held together, prepared to rise till the end of February, but 'jealousies and sus-'picions changed the state of the cause, and altered 'the minds of many;'[1] and half of those who in January would have welcomed the English as allies, in March would have encountered them as their 'auld enemies.' Huntingdon still longed to go forward. The Douglases could be counted on at all events; the cause was God's, and God would fight for justice. But influences were at work with Elizabeth which made Huntingdon a special object of suspicion. The French ambassador had protested, under directions from Paris, against English interference in Scotland. Burghley told him that France was as much interested as England in suppressing Lennox, who was entirely Spanish; that the party now in power about James intended to send him to Madrid, where he was to be made a Catholic of and married, and that Spain would then give the law to the world. The ambassador, scarcely knowing whether to believe Burghley or not, advised Elizabeth to end her difficulties not by taking part with Morton, but by making friends with Mary Stuart. He told her that by recognising the Queen of Scots as her successor, she might secure herself from danger either from Scotland or the Continent; while he dwelt on the danger of entrusting Huntingdon with an army, who was her most formidable competitor, considering the temper of the Puritans, of whom he was the leader and idol, and their notorious objection to female sovereigns. This chord never failed to wake a response in Elizabeth. The Puritans, whatever their abstract theories about monarchy, were passionately loyal to herself, but the blast against the monstrous regimen of women which Knox and Good-

[1] Bowes to Walsingham, Feb. 14.—MSS. Scotland.

man had blown so loudly in the Marian persecution had never been forgiven or forgotten.¹ The remains of her purpose disappeared. To obligations of honour long practice with Murray, Orange, Condé, and Morton himself, had rendered her remarkably indifferent. To use the Protestant leaders for her convenience, to tempt them by promises to commit themselves, and if they failed to leave them to their fate, had been either her deliberate policy or her custom a hundred times repeated.

A custom 'dangerous and dishonourable' always, but never more dangerous, never more dishonourable than now. Murray and the Prince of Orange belonged to that supreme order of men whom it does not rest with kings and queens to injure. Morton's character was spotted with much that was ill. His one virtue was his fidelity to England, and for that he was left to die. On the 7th of March, Walsingham reported Elizabeth to be 'very doubtful and irresolute,'² so doubtful that as she would go no further he regretted that she had gone so far. The Council strove hard to save her from herself. When insensible to shame she was amenable at times to arguments of prudence. They told her that she must either encounter Lennox now, when he was comparatively weak, or try conclusions with him

---

¹ 'Je me suis aussy aidé, Sire, d'un argument que nul de ses conseillers et subjects ne luy a osé dire, et qu'elle a bien reçeu, qu'elle aura toujours beaucoup meilleur compte de la dicte Royne d'Escosse et de son filz, puisque ils luy sont si proches et en sa puissance que des aultres plus esloingnez de son sang, pretendants la succession par moyens illicites et factions illicites, en tenant du tout le party Puritain, et qui vouldrait se delivrer du puissance superieure et principalement du regne des femmes s'il estoit possible—chose que je luy ay si bien faict sentir qu'elle a eu ce propos agreable et cognoit que c'est la verité.'—*Mauvissière au Roy*, Fevrier 10. TEULET, vol. iii.

² Walsingham to Randolph, March 7.—*MSS. Scotland.*

later, when he would have a Spanish army at his back, and half England in insurrection, when the question would no longer be of the life of Morton, but of the English crown. She replied that she could not invade Scotland, merely because the King had called to his services one of his near relations. They told her she was not asked to invade Scotland. Her soldiers would go there as friends to all Scots that were good and honest, and whether or no, if she valued her throne she must not leave James in the hands of Lennox. She gathered up her courage again. On the 15th Walsingham wrote that after all he had hopes that she would yield.[1] But Randolph's letters again overthrew her half-formed purpose. He cast doubts on the probability of success in an armed movement. He still insisted that there would be no danger to Morton if Lennox was not unwisely irritated. Walsingham told him angrily that the Queen had given her word and must keep it. Huntingdon said that it was 'madness to hope for good from a Guisian 'and a Romanist.' Lennox 'might dally and speak 'fair till he had things fit for his purpose, and then he 'would shew himself a man of the Holy League.' Assassination had been hinted at as a means of getting rid of Lennox. Huntingdon flung such means from him with scorn, and desired only to see his mistress take the place that belonged to her at the side of the Protestants of Scotland. 'Perhaps you will think I would have 'England make war with Scotland,' he wrote. 'No, no; 'not so. Nor above all things can I consent to murder. 'Absit. Accursed be he, say I, that either deviseth or 'executeth any such device; for non est faciendum 'malum ut inde veniat bonum; but if that you desire in 'the name of your sovereign cannot be obtained, as I

---

[1] Walsingham to Randolph, March 15.—*MSS. Scotland.*

'look it will not, why may not some of the nobility, ad-
'vised and assisted by England, say to the King, Your
'Grace is young, you cannot judge of your own State,
'and we therefore pray you not to lean to the advice
'of one only. Why may not such a course be taken
'to encounter Lennox? And then if he reply with har-
'quebuz and not with reason, then let the nobility say
'he must put up his forces and submit to hearken to
'what is fit for the King and country. If he will not
'yield to this let them disarm him, and to this I wish my
'Sovereign to give aid.'[1] It was to no purpose, and
Randolph was soon forced to own that he had been mistaken, and 'that nothing now could save Morton's life.'
Had there been hopes otherwise, the discovery of his
negotiations with Sir Robert Bowes would have sealed
his fate. 'No councillor dared open his mouth for him.
'All his friends were appalled; courage and stomach
'quite overthrown.' The mask was thrown away, and
so fierce a feeling had risen up in Edinburgh among
the retainers of Lennox and his adherents against England, that Randolph was himself shot at through his
window, and was obliged to fly to Berwick.[2]

Two days after, a messenger came in from the Earl
of Angus to know whether England would interfere,
and demanding a definite answer. Hunsdon was obliged
to say that it was not to be, and at once the relics of
the Protestant combination dissolved. Mar made his
peace with Lennox; Angus retired into Northumberland; and the troops selected so carefully to revolutionise
Scotland were dismissed to their homes. Mauvissière
reported to his master that his remonstrances had been
successful, that the Queen would meddle no more in

[1] Huntingdon to Randolph, March 24.—MSS. Scotland.
[2] Randolph to Walsingham, March 25.—MSS. Ibid.

Scottish politics, and that Morton would be left to his fate;[1] and the Queen of Scots, who, so long as Elizabeth's conduct was uncertain, had played into Mauvissière's hands, had besieged her with protestations of affection, and 'had sworn by the Eternal God that she 'would never undertake anything to the prejudice of 'her sister of England or her estate,'[2] sent a message to Philip through the Archbishop of Glasgow, that now was the time for him to step in. The King her son was about to return to the true Catholic faith; his next step would be to declare war against England in revenge for her own imprisonment; and he would not hesitate for a moment were he assured of support from his Majesty. She pressed Philip for his own sake to snatch the opportunity. Through her friends in Scotland she endeavoured to drive James into hostilities, believing that when once the work was commenced the Spaniards would be compelled to assist.[3] An army of them might land first in Ireland and after establishing Desmond and Sanders and expelling the English, they could then cross over into Scotland.[4]

The Catholic powers had been embarrassed hitherto in dealing with James, because no ambassador could be received at the Scotch Court who was not accredited to him as King; and the Queen of Scots had protested against a recognition which would imply that she had

---

[1] 'A la fin j'estime avoir gaigné ce point que la dicte Royne laissera faire la justice du comte de Morton et ne se meslera plus.'—*Mauvissière au Roy*, Avril 9. TEULET, vol. iii.

[2] The Queen of Scots to Elizabeth, May 2, 1580.—LABANOFF, vol. v.

[3] 'Exortandole que pase adelante con lo comencado contra la Reyna de Inglaterra.'—*Don Juan B. de Tassis al Rey*, Abril 10, 1581. TEULET, vol. v. De Tassis had succeeded De Vargas as Spanish Minister at Paris.

[4] 'Pide la Reyna de Escocia que en toda diligencia V. M⁴ mande embiar el socorro que fuese servido dar á su hijo, y que case acuda á Irlanda y alli se esté á la mano para entrar en Escocia quando sea llamado.'—*Ibid*. Mary Stuart to the Archbishop of Glasgow, March 4, 1581.—LABANOFF, vol. v.

herself been legally deposed. She proposed now to remove the difficulty, preparatory to the great move which was in contemplation, by associating James with herself in a united sovereignty. A correspondence had been opened with the happiest promise between mother and son, having this for its aim; and Mary Stuart told the Archbishop of Glasgow that she was in haste to put James in lawful possession of all the greatness to which he could aspire. He would continue King, but King by her own free grant and consent, and no longer by usurpation and violence.[1]

There remained only the knitting up of the Morton tragedy for the first act of Lennox's work to be satisfactorily completed. The mad Earl of Arran, the heir of the House of Hamilton, once thought of as a husband for Elizabeth, was still living in confinement. He had been in charge of his cousin Colonel Stewart, Morton's accuser, and to this Stewart his title had been transferred. The new-made earl was sent to Dumbarton to bring Morton back to Edinburgh. Morton looking over the commission, and seeing a name which he did not know, enquired the meaning of it. On receiving his answer he said that his doom was decided. There was a prophecy that the bloody heart of the Douglas should fall by the mouth of Arran. The young King had shown much natural hesitation in consenting to the death of a man who had been in the place of a father to him. His scruples had been overcome by the prospect of clearing the reputation of his mother.[2] The promise given to Elizabeth that Morton should be tried

---

[1] Mary Stuart to the Archbishop of Glasgow, May 26, 1581.—LABANOFF, vol. v.

[2] Mendoza to Philip, June 15, 1581.—*MSS. Simancas.*

by his peers was observed to the letter and broken to the sense. Argyle, Seton, Lochinvar, Maxwell, Eglinton, Sutherland, and half a dozen others, the leaders all of them of the faction which had been held down under the Regency, were impanelled. Morton challenged some of them, but his objections were overruled, and his fate was decided on before the court opened. The indictment charged him with foreknowledge of the murder of the King's father. Balfour's evidence was heard and accepted. No defence was permitted. The bare fact was true and could not be denied, and after a rapid consultation the Lords declared him guilty 'art and 'part.'¹ 'Art and part,' said Morton, striking the ground with his staff as the verdict was declared, 'art and part; 'God knows the contrary.' His share in the crime had been that he knew that it was about to be committed, and that he had stood apart and let Bothwell do his work. But the technical guilt was sufficient for the present purpose. Short shrift was allowed. The trial was on the 1st of June: the next afternoon was fixed for the execution, and in the morning two of the Edinburgh ministers came to prepare the late Regent for death. No one till that moment knew the part that he had actually taken in the murder. A shadow had hung over him. He had been looked askance upon even by the party to which he belonged, and there was the most earnest hope among the Protestants that before he died he would say something to dispel the mystery which still hung over that horrible transaction.

He had slept soundly, being, as he said, 'at the end of 'his trouble.' The ministers ' telling him to be of good ' comfort, he said that he was rather willing to render

---

¹ Pitcairn's Criminal Trials of Scotland, vol. I. part 3.

'his life than live.' 'God had appointed a time for his 'death, and had appointed the manner of it, and seeing 'that now was the time and this the manner, he was 'content.'

He was then reminded that it was his duty while he had yet the means to make a clear confession. Knox had asked him on his death-bed if he had been acquainted beforehand with the murder, and he had then denied all knowledge of it. To Scotland and to his own soul he owed now a frank acknowledgment if he had anything to tell. He made no difficulty. Very simply he related the overtures which had been made to him by Bothwell, and the answer which he had given. He had not consented, but he knew that the deed was to be done. His cousin Archibald Douglas had been present, and he knew this also, and had taken no steps to punish him. The ministers asked him why he had not put Darnley on his guard. He replied that he had not dared, and he admitted that he was justly condemned. He had no new light to throw on the manner of the murder. Whether Darnley had been strangled or was alive at the explosion, he was as ignorant as the rest of the world. Of the death of the Earl of Athol he declared himself wholly innocent.

The ministers obviously bore him no good will. They charged him with having been a pensioner of Elizabeth, of having intended to put James into her hands, and of having betrayed the Kirk by maintaining the iniquitous bishops. He could afford to smile at the charge of having received money from the Queen of England. He had asked her for money certainly, but for the King and not for himself, and his requests had been uniformly refused. Bishops or no bishops he had been a true friend

to the Kirk of Scotland, and the ministers, of all men in
the world, had least cause to reproach him. They 'bade
'him not stand upon his innocence.' 'God,' they said,
'always did justly, and men never suffered more than
'their deeds had deserved.' The admonition might
have been spared. He made no complaints. 'God,' he
admitted, 'had not only dealt justly with him, but merci-
'fully, for he had been a sinner overmickle given to the
'world and the pleasures of the flesh. Had his life been
'spared he meant to have cast away such vain delights
'and dedicated himself to God's service in quietness and
'simplicity, but as God was pleased to take him he was
'satisfied.' 'As to his sentence,' he remitted his judges
to their consciences; 'but it had been alike to him if
'he had been as innocent as Stephen or as guilty as Ju-
'das; the authors of his death had purposes on hand
'which could not be done except he was taken away.'
'Tell the King from me,' he said, 'I admonish him in
'the name of God to beware of them; the estate of
'religion was never in such danger.'

'Then,' continue the narrators of this singular scene,
'then he prayed, and asked us to show him arguments of
'hope on which he could rely; and seeing flesh was weak
'that we would comfort him against the fear of death.'

'We told him of the promises of mercy in the Word,
'on which it behoved him to lean, the example of mercy
'towards God's servants who had been sinners, of David,
'Magdalen, and Peter, and the experience of mercy
'which he had found himself.'

'He answered: I know all that to be true. Since I
'passed to Dumbarton I have read all the five books of
'Moses, Joshua, and Judges, and now I am in Samuel.
'I see the mercy of God wonderful, and always inclined

'to have pity on his people; for howbeit he punished them oft, yet when they turned to him he was merciful again.'

The Old Testament had not been Morton's only study. Lady Ormiston, when he was first arrested, had given him an ominous present, Bradford's 'Meditations on Death;' and the stern sad man, sitting caged upon the rock above the waters of Clyde, had made ready for his end by patient thought upon it. A few passages from this book were read to him; and then, as it was still early, he was called to his 'dishine,'[1] 'which he ate with great cheerfulness, the ministers and he drinking to each other,' and 'promising to drink bye-and-bye together in the Kingdom the immortal drink which would never suffer them to thirst again.'

He had a weary morning, for others of the Edinburgh clergy came to see him, and to prevent false reports from going abroad, the confession was repeated to them from the beginning. At two o'clock he dined, and immediately after one of the keepers entered to say that the preparations were complete, and that his presence was waited for in the Grass Market.

He did not know that the time was so near. 'They have troubled me overmuch this morning with worldly things,' he said; 'I supposed they would have given me a night's leisure to have advised myself with God.'

The keeper intimated that it could not be: the scaffold was ready, and the officers could not stay.

'I am ready also, I thank God,' he said. He muttered a short prayer, rose and followed the guard down the stairs. At the door of the Tolbooth he encountered the Earl of Arran, who brought him back to his room, and desired him to write his confession and sign it.

---

[1] Déjeuné.

Having begun his journey he was impatient till it was over. He could not confess again, he said. The ministers knew all. He was pressed no further. Arran asked for his forgiveness. 'It is no time to reckon 'quarrels,' he answered; 'I forgive you and all others.' That there might be no misconception he repeated from before the block to the crowd the real character and extent of his crime, and then added in proud consciousness of his general rectitude, 'The King shall 'lose a good servant to-day; as I have professed the 'Evangile now taught in Scotland, so I am content to 'die in it; and albeit I have not walked therein as I 'ought, yet God will be merciful to me, and I bid all 'good Christians pray for me.' With these words he prepared for the end. Many remarkable men have attitudinised on the scaffold, concealing agitation under a mask of coolness. Morton perfectly simple yielded to the awfulness of the moment. One of the clergy, Mr. Lawson, said a prayer. While he was speaking, 'the Earl 'lay on gruife[1] on his face before the place of exe-'cution, his body making great rebounding with sighs 'and sobs, evident signs of the mighty inward work-'ing of the Spirit of God.'

'Then,' says a spectator, 'he shook hands with us 'all round and bade us farewell in the Lord. So con-'stantly, patiently, humbly, without fear of death, he 'placed his cruig under the axe, his hands being un-'bound, and crying continually, Lord Jesus receive my 'soul; Into Thy hands, Lord, I commend my soul, the 'axe fell, and whatever he had been before, he died the 'true servant of God.'[2]

---

[1] Grovelling.
[2] Narrative of the Confession and Execution of the Earl of Morton.
—*Illustrations of Scotish History*, p. 493.

'So,' reported Mendoza to Philip, 'all is well over, 'and blessed be God the event is far better than a few 'days since we feared. The King was then hesitating, 'but we see now that it was only from a sagacious 'desire to compass his end more effectually, to make 'clear the innocence of his mother, and throw the guilt 'of his father's murder on Morton and the heretics. 'This is a grand beginning, from which we may look 'soon for the recovery of that realm to Christ; God 'being pleased that so pernicious a heretic should be 'removed out of the way by a chastisement so signal 'and so exemplary.'[1]

The victory of Lennox had been complete. He had destroyed the Protestant champions, broken up the English party, sown divisions among themselves, and made shipwreck of Elizabeth's honour. A little more, and Scotland, at its present rate of progress, would be ready to lend itself to the Duke of Guise, and to open its ports to the armies which were to avenge the wrongs of Mary Stuart. The Irish part of the great Jesuit conspiracy had failed, though at this time had not yet failed obviously, and Munster and Wicklow were still in flames. The Scotch part of it had been absolutely successful. The story must now turn to the third division of the confederates, the soldiers of Christ, whose scene of action was England itself. An account given by one of them of a visit of himself and a companion to the Vatican, will serve as a fit introduction to the invasion of Parsons and Campian.

It was towards the close of the Pontificate of Gregory

---
[1] Mendoza to Philip, June 15, 1581.—*MSS. Simancas.*

XIII. that two young English Jesuits, Anthony Tyrrell, who tells the story,[1] and Foscue or Fortescue, better known as Ballard, and concerned afterwards in the Babington conspiracy, set out upon a journey to Rome on a noticeable errand. Their object was to learn from the lips of the Pope himself whether 'any one who, for 'the benefit of the Church and the delivery of the 'Catholics from their afflictions, attempted to destroy 'the Queen of England, should have for the fact his 'pardon.' They halted on their way at the Seminary at Rheims, where they found the fraternity occupied with the same subject as themselves. The preacher of the Easter-day sermon, an English convert, called Elizabeth 'the monster of the world, worthy of deposition,' and he said from the pulpit that 'Pity it was there could 'not be found any of that courage to bereave her of her life.' Father Allen, the principal, spoke afterwards in the same strain, 'inveighing most heinously against 'the Queen, saying that her law exceeded for cruelty 'both heathen and Turk, and that she sought nothing 'but blood.' Language of this kind was congenial food for Tyrrell and his companion, and they went on upon their way greatly strengthened and comforted. Tyrrell was not a stranger in Rome. He had been educated at the English College, and thither he went on his arrival, taking Ballard with him. He explained to the rector, Father Alfonzo Algazari, the object of his coming. The rector 'being rejoiced to hear of priests of that mind,' consulted Everard Mercuriano, the general of the order to which the Englishmen belonged. Mercuriano sent for Tyrrell, and enquired who Ballard was, 'whether

---

[1] Confessions of Anthony Tyrrell, made in the Tower, Aug. 30 and 31, 1586.—*MSS. Mary Queen of Scots.*

'he was of credit in England,' 'whether he was wise and fit for any great action;' and the answers being satisfactory, he procured for them the interview which they desired with the great person whom they had come to consult. Gregory received them in his cabinet. They prostrated themselves, kissed his foot, and remained kneeling, while Algazari, as their spokesman, described their errand.

'May it please your Holiness,' he said, 'here be these 'reverend priests lately come from the hot harvest in 'England, who have come hither partly to gain strength 'to give the enemy a new encounter, but chiefly to 'obtain such spiritual graces from your beatitude as the 'nature of their country doth require. One thing I 'am to move your Holiness in their behalf—for without 'the fulness of your apostolical authority they dare 'attempt nothing—if any person moved with zeal 'should take out of this life their wicked Queen, whether 'your Holiness would approve the action.'

The Pope—it was the same Pontiff who had sung Te Deums for the massacre of St. Bartholomew—turned to the kneeling pair, and said: 'Children, beloved in the 'Lord, we embrace you in the bowels of Christ. We 'have always had a fatherly and pastoral care of you 'and your country. We have opened the bowels of our 'compassion upon you, and have long bewailed your 'miseries. As touching the taking away of that im- 'pious Jezebel, whose life God has permitted thus long 'for our scourge, I would be loath you should attempt 'anything unto your own destruction, and we know not 'how our censure on that point amongst her subjects 'which profess themselves our children would be taken; 'but if you can wisely give such counsel as may be 'without scandal to the party or to us, know you we do

'not only approve the act, but think the doer if he
'suffer death simply for that to be worthy of canonisa-
'tion. And so with our Apostolic benediction we dis-
'miss you.'[1]

This interview took place four years later than the events which are now to be described, when the passions of the priests had been exasperated by the persecution as it was termed of the Jesuit missionaries, and when the hopes of regicides had just been stimulated by the accomplished assassination of the Prince of Orange. When allowance has been made, however, for these influences, the story throws a definite light upon the character of the men with whom Elizabeth and her ministers had to deal. The disposition of an organised party is not changed in a day or a year. The Pope who had blessed the murder of Coligny, who from the day of his accession had laboured unremittingly to stimulate a crusade against England, who had landed a Nuncio and an armed force commissioned from himself

---

[1] Tyrrell was twice examined, and gave two accounts of this conversation. Both are preserved, one of them being endorsed by Burghley. They vary very little, one being merely rather fuller than the other. The shorter confession adds a few interesting words on the disposition towards regicide of the English Catholic laity. 'We were warned,' says Tyrrell, 'to be very cautious of the Pope's censure to our country Catholics, for it might be it served not for all men's appetites, and therefore we were to use great discretion.'

Falling afterwards into the hands of the priests, Tyrrell published a recantation, and wrote to the Queen to say that his story was an invention. See Strype, *Annals*, vol. iii. part 2, p. 415. The following year he reasserted what he had before stated; withdrew his recantation 'wherein he had repeated for falsehood that which he had bonâ fide uttered,' and promised so to confirm the original narrative, 'that neither fear nor flattery should cause him to deny it again.'—*Annals*, vol. iii. part 1, p. 698.

The words which he places in the Pope's mouth, agree exactly with the message sent from Rome to Dr. Parry, through the Cardinal of Como. See Parry's trial. *State Trials*, vol. I.

in Ireland, and who, when his efforts had all failed, gave his sanction to the darker method of cutting through the difficulty, cannot be credited with more innocent intentions in the interval; and the Jesuits were but spiritual soldiers bound to execute his bidding whatever it might be.

Elizabeth boasted with justice that no Catholic had as yet suffered in England for his religious opinions. The laws against the Catholic services were technically severe; but for twenty years they had been evaded with the frank connivance of the authorities. The Queen had repressed sternly the persecuting zeal of her own bishops. Priests of the old sort were still to be found in every part of England, though in diminished numbers, saying mass in private houses, while justices of the peace looked away or were present themselves. Nuns were left unmolested under the roofs of Catholic ladies, pursuing their own devotions in their own way, and were denied nothing but a publicity of worship which might have provoked a riot. Whatever had been the Queen's motive, she had refused to let the succession be determined, and the Catholics could look forward to seeing again a sovereign of their own creed. She required nothing but political obedience and outward submission to the law, and with the average Englishmen of native growth and temperament, loyalty was an article of faith which the excommunication had failed to shake. The rebellion of the north had elicited few signs of practical sympathy, and the Duke of Norfolk and the Earl of Northumberland had been executed without increasing the existing disaffection.

The truce between the two parties, which might have lasted otherwise till Elizabeth's death, was ended by the impatience of the converts. The Pope in his spiritual capacity had put out his thunders in vain. The Pope as a temporal prince, at the instigation of Sanders and Allen, had fallen back therefore on the arm of flesh. He was making actual war upon her in Ireland. His agents had revolutionised Scotland, and the most short-sighted eyes could not but see that England's turn was to follow. The forbearance which had been extended to the old priests was not unnaturally suspended when from the seminaries at Rheims and at Rome, which had become notorious as nests of conspiracy, and from the Order of Jesus, which recognised no obligation but the will of its General and of the Pope, a flight of spiritual immigrants appeared suddenly on the English shore. They were subjects who had left their country without leave, and had sworn allegiance to a power which was then at war with their sovereign. Primâ facie they were fair objects of suspicion: the confession of Tyrrell proves that no wrong was done them when they were credited with a more dangerous character. They presented themselves as innocent lambs, apostles of a spiritual creed; and there was something lamb-like in the disposition of more than one of them. But to suppose them ignorant of intentions which were avowed in the pulpits, and formed the common talk at the tables of the seminaries to which they belonged, does over great injustice to their equally undoubted ability. Even the lamb when infected by theological fanaticism, secretes a virus in his teeth, and his bite is deadly as a rattlesnake's.

A more particular account must be given of the men who were strong enough to alter in their own disfavour the policy of Elizabeth's Government.

Sanders, Allen, Harding, Dorman, Phillips, and the other protochampions of Catholic orthodoxy, who established the celebrated seminaries at Douay and Rheims, had been persons in authority in Oxford in the reign of Queen Mary. They had witnessed the execution of the martyrs. They had shared in the enthusiasm of the reaction and the reconciliation with Rome, and when Mary died childless and Elizabeth succeeded, they fled abroad anticipating a counter persecution. But Elizabeth, tolerant towards Catholics everywhere, was especially tolerant at the Universities. Catholic fellows retained their offices unmolested. Catholic students were admitted to degrees without being required to take the oath of supremacy. It was only as the Heads of the Colleges dropped off that care was taken to put Anglicans in the vacant places, that the universities might be tranquilly metamorphosed without violent change. Cambridge, which had been the nursery of the Reformers, retained their spirit. When Cambridge offended the Government it was by over sympathy with Cartwright and the Puritans. The genius of Oxford, then, as always, for some singular reason inclined equally to the opposite extreme. While Whitgift could hardly succeed in forcing the scholars of Trinity into surplices, Allen was able to return to Oxford and preach Popery without interference; and the professors' lecture halls, the College common rooms, and the students' parties among themselves, were saturated with sentimental devotionalism.

In this element grew up Edmund Campian and Robert Parsons. Campian was born in 1540, the son of a bookseller in London. Parsons was a few years younger. The first became a fellow of St. John's, the other of Balliol. They were dear friends, both 'sound

'Catholics at heart, and utterly condemning the Queen's
'and Council's new religion,' and both distinguished
by a large following of pupils and admirers. Campian
was the more shewy of the two; he was patronised by
Leicester, when Leicester was coquetting with de Quadra
and Rome, and in 1560, when he was twenty, he made
an oration at Amy Robsart's funeral, stuffed with high
compliments to Lord Robert's virtues. In 1566, when
the Queen came to Oxford, he was one of the disputants
who had been selected to amuse her, and he gained
favour by the skill with which he distributed his compliments between her Majesty and her lover. The
arrival of Mary Stuart, and the rebellion of the north,
put an end to these halcyon days. Leicester went over
to the ultra-Protestants, and being made Chancellor of
the University gathered up the reins, and enforced the
Act of Uniformity. The English service was introduced into the College chapels; the oath of allegiance
and subscription to the Articles was exacted of the
fellows, and those who refused to comply were removed. Allen, foreseeing the coming troubles, had
already fled a second time, and gone back to Belgium,
where with Philip's help and sanction, he opened a
seminary at Douay, for the education of English
Catholics. Thus he had a home ready prepared for the
exiles to take refuge in, and his ranks were daily
recruited by priests and scholars, who preferred their
creed to their country. Parsons, whose conscience was
elastic, took the oath, but was discovered and expelled
with some discredit. The house of Rimmon was the
favourite illustration of those who tried to compromise
between God and their fellowships, but the Council of
Trent and the Pope refused to sanction the subterfuge.
Campian saw his way less clearly, and his conduct was

less open to reproach. He had speculated out the Anglo-Catholic theory for himself, and in 1567 was ordained deacon in the Church of England. 'Extraordinary mental anguish' followed. He shrunk from being examined by Leicester's commissioners. The imposition of hands by a heretic bishop he felt as a brand of infamy. He left Oxford and went to Ireland, to reside with Stanihurst the Recorder of Dublin, and the father of one of his pupils. Here he occupied himself in writing a short but valuable history of Ireland—valuable especially as containing a lucid account of things which in that curious time he saw there with his own eyes. Afterwards, being for some cause suspected, he came back in disguise, witnessed the trial of Doctor Story in Westminster Hall, and feeling that his own country was no longer a home for him he followed Parsons and joined him and Allen at Douay.

The establishment at Douay was broken up, as will be remembered, by Requescens, and the seminary was removed to Rheims; but its prosperity continued unabated. The pupils whom Campian and his friends had trained at Oxford had caught and retained his spirit. They grew from boys to men. They took their degrees and became fellows, and Holt of Oriel, Arden of Trinity, Garnet, Bryant, Sherwin, Emerson,[1] and many more, wandered together by Cherwell and Isis, brooding over their masters' teaching, and resolving one by one to break the ties of home and kindred and devote their lives to the cause of the Catholic faith. Those who had been born Catholics continued cool, collected, and moderate. The Anglican converts developed the Catholic theory among themselves to its most extravagant conclusions.

---

[1] Ralph Emerson, namesake of Ralph Waldo Emerson the great American, and probably of the same blood with him.

'Those who are seminary priests,' wrote one to Walsingham, in 1585, 'learnt not their papistry abroad, but 'carried it with them from their colleges at Oxford.'[1] The sum of life to them became the triumph of the Church, and they themselves longed to become the Church's soldiers. Thus Oxford became a perpetual recruiting ground from which year after year flights of students passed over to Rheims or to another college which the Pope had erected at Rome, filled with a passionate hatred of the Church of their country, whose orders were a mark of the beast, and which itself was the Antichrist of prophecy. To profess the Catholic creed and to become themselves priests was not enough for them, and the subtle politicians into whose hands they fell understood how to utilise their enthusiasm.

To dreamers such as these, the Order of Jesus became an object of ecstatic admiration. The Jesuits had come into existence to combat the Reformation, as the Templars and the Knights of St. John to be the warriors of the Cross against the Crescent. Their discipline and their devotion were absolute alike. They had no law but the will of their superior, no purpose but what they called the cause of God. They appeared a legion of angels, with weapons tempered in celestial orthodoxy, sent down to earth to smite the hydra of heresy. In this order, therefore, the choicest of the English converts instantly enrolled themselves. Campian and Parsons went first, and the best of the rest were allowed to follow them. Through the lax police system of England and the connivance of secret friends in high places, they corresponded with their companions whom they had left behind at the university. They visited their old haunts when they pleased, undiscovered by officials who did not

[1] *Domestic MSS.* April, 1585.

wish to see them; and whenever a new man was wanted Oxford could always supply some young enthusiast, eager to venture his life in the service of God and Mary Stuart.

From these sources, as the Marian priests died off, Allen supplied their places. 'The number of Catholics,' wrote Mendoza, on the 28th of December, 1578, to Philip, 'increases daily, the instruments being mission-
'aries from the seminary which your Majesty founded at
'Douay. A hundred of those who went to study either
'there or at Rome have returned in this past year. They
'travel disguised as laymen, and young as they are, the
'fervour with which they throw themselves into their
'work, and the cheerful fortitude with which they accept
'martyrdom when occasion offers, are entirely admirable.
'Some have already suffered with the utmost calmness,'
'following in the steps of the saints who had gone before
'them. Till lately there were but few priests left in
'England, and religion was dying out for want of
'teachers. None called themselves Catholics but the
'few to whom God had given grace to persevere out of
'pure zeal for his service. But now, by means of those
'who have come over, it has pleased God to provide a
'remedy.'[2]

These first comers, however, were but the rank and file of the converts: mere secular priests who, unless they gave other cause for suspicion, had not as yet

---

[1] Mendoza perhaps alludes to Cuthbert Mayne, who was discovered in Cornwall in November, 1578, having about him copies of the Bull of Pope Pius. He was tried for treason and hanged at Launceston. This and similar executions are now held to have been needless cruelties. But were a Brahmin to be found in the quarters of a Sepoy regiment, scattering incendiary addresses from Nana Sahib, he would be hanged also.

[2] Mendoza to Philip, Dec. 28, 1578.—MSS. Simancas.

drawn on themselves the special animosity of the Government. But in connexion with the great efforts which were being made to overthrow Elizabeth, something was needed more vigorous, more publicly effective. The Church, so Allen deliberately calculated, required martyrs to set off against the victims of Queen Mary. Catholics should shew that they could suffer pain as well as inflict it, and if Elizabeth could be forced into a confessed religious persecution, it might rouse the Catholic powers out of their apathy. As a preparation further for the intended invasion from Scotland, men were wanted of authority and intelligence to stimulate everywhere a powerful Catholic revival. In other words the Jesuits were wanted, and as yet no Jesuits had been allowed to go to England. Their lives were precious, and the English mission was considered likely to be the most dangerous which they had yet undertaken.

To the young spiritual knights-errant, however, the peril was an additional temptation, and the consent of the General of the order had at length been obtained. When Sanders sailed for Ireland Allen went to Rome to arrange the plan of the campaign, and Campion, who had been for some years working at Prague, was selected with Parsons to make the first adventure. Mercuriano sent for them to Rome to receive their instructions, and they arrived there in the spring of 1580, just at the time when d'Aubigny had secured his footing in Scotland. The principle of the Jesuit organisation was absolute despotism. Parsons, now about five and thirty, cool, clearheaded, and not given to emotions or sensibilities, was made head of the mission. He was trusted with the inner secrets of the Papal policy, and was left to rule himself and his companions as occasion or opportunity required.[1] Campian and the rest of the party had no such discretion. It was essential that the mission should bear the character of a purely religious crusade, that those who became martyrs should appear as martyrs for their faith, without note or taint of treason on them. To make converts would be entirely sufficient for the purposes of the intended insurrection. Enthusiastic Catholics (and converts were always enthusiastic) could be relied on with confidence when the army of liberation should appear. Campian, therefore, was directed to keep strictly to the work of conversion, not to mix himself with politics, to avoid all mention of public matters in his letters to the General, and never to speak against the Queen except in the presence of persons of known and tried orthodoxy.

Absolute adherence to such a programme was impossible. The great difficulty of the English Catholics, which they felt more keenly the more their consciences were aroused, was the Bull of Deposition. They had been absolved from their allegiance. They were themselves implicated in the censures of the Church if they continued to regard Elizabeth as their

---

[1] Mr. Simpson, the latest and most candid biographer of Campian, endeavours to believe that Parsons was ignorant of Sanders's expedition to Ireland, that he and Campian only became acquainted with it, and were embarrassed by the knowledge, when on the eve of entering England. Sanders had landed openly at Smerwick, with a commission as Legate, in July 1579, nine months before Parsons and Campian left Rome. He had published circulars to the Irish chiefs immediately on his arrival, announcing that his coming was to be followed by a Papal army. James Fitzmaurice, the Pope's general, had been killed. The progress of the insurrection was being watched with the greatest eagerness in France and Spain, and yet we are to suppose that at Rome itself, the head-quarters of the enterprise, nothing was generally known about it. Mr. Simpson is too intelligent a person to defend so preposterous an hypothesis.

sovereign, and the alternative of disloyalty or infidelity had been harshly forced upon them. The Jesuits, therefore, were commissioned to tell them in the Pope's name that the Bull only remained in force as it regarded the Queen and the heretics, but that it was so construed as not to touch the Catholics. It left them free to profess themselves loyal until circumstances would allow the sentence to be executed. Catholic English gentlemen, that is, were to be allowed to call themselves good subjects of Elizabeth, to disclaim all disloyal intentions, to lead the Queen to trust them by assurances of devotion and fidelity, until the Spaniards or the French or the Scots were ready to invade the country, and then it would be their duty to turn against her.[1]

The poison of asps was under the lips of the bearers of such a message of treachery. It could not be communicated, as Burghley fairly argued,[2] without implied treason. No plea of conscience could alter the nature of things. To tell English subjects that they might continue loyal till another sovereign who claimed their allegiance was in a position to protect them, was to assert the right of that sovereign, as entirely and essentially, as to invite them to take arms on his side. And if the Pope erected his pretensions to dispose of kingdoms into an article of faith, a government which flung back his insolent claims into his teeth was not likely to allow priest or layman to make a conscience of disloyalty.

After receiving their instructions, the forlorn hope of Popery, Parsons, Campian, and seven of their Oxford pupils, now Jesuits like themselves, commenced

---

[1] Facultates concessæ PP. Roberto Personio et Edmundo Campiano, pro Angliâ, die 14 Aprilis, 1580.—*MSS. Domestic.*

[2] Execution of Justice, London, 1583.

their journey from Rome on the 18th of April. They were received at Milan with distinguished honours by Carlo Borromeo, who gave them fresh exhortations to constancy. They made a second halt at Rheims, where Campian preached a sermon which shewed that he had not forgotten his command of English, and threw the college into an ecstasy of enthusiasm. In the beginning of June they went forward again, and at St. Omers they were met by a warning, that if they valued their lives they would go no further. A number of inflammatory briefs scattered by Sanders about Ireland had been sent over to the English Council; alarming reports had come in of Spanish preparations; a declaration of war was not unlikely—in return, as will be presently told, for the depredations of Drake; and one of Sanders's papers declared positively that a Spanish fleet was on the point of sailing for Kerry. Elizabeth shewed it to Mendoza, and enquired whether his master had authorised Sanders to use such language. Mendoza's answer did not mend matters. He declined to say whether assistance would or would not be sent from Spain to Sanders. He looked on the Pope, he said, as undoubtedly God's vicar, and head of the Roman Catholic world. For that confession he would lose a hundred lives if he had them. What his rights were as a temporal prince he did not know; but this he would say, that the tyranny of the Pope was the eternal subject of declamation with the English clergy. Caricatures were sold publicly in London of the Pope, Nero, and the Grand Turk, as the three tyrants, and the Queen ought not to be surprised if the Pope used such power as he possessed to restore Ireland and England also to their old condition.

She was alarmed, and not without reason. She had

just broken with the Duke of Alençon, as Burghley supposed definitively, and had thus affronted France. An uneasy humour was spreading among the English Catholics, and Mendoza represented to Philip that if he would take advantage of the existing confusion, and send his fleet to the Channel, he would probably find an easy victory. A commission had been sent out to the Bishops bidding them look more sharply after the Catholic families. Elizabeth pretended to Mendoza that it had been issued without her consent. She recalled it. She said her bishops were a set of knaves,[1] and she would not have the Catholics ill-used. But her hesitation was ill-timed, and could not be maintained. Reports of the Jesuit mission came in from Rome with exact information of its nature, and of the new construction of Pope Pius's Bull. Briefs identical with those dispersed by Sanders in Ireland, declaring the Queen a schismatic, and Queen no longer, were found lying about the streets in London; and Elizabeth, in spite of herself, had been driven back upon severity. The statutes against the Catholics were put in force, and gentlemen detected in hearing mass were thrown into loose confinement:[2] Two proclamations were issued, one requiring every one who had sons or relations abroad to recall them to England, and declaring that whoever harboured Jesuits and seminary priests would be prosecuted as a maintainer of rebels;[3] the other, a noble appeal from the Queen to her well affected subjects, to judge between her and those who were now seeking to overthrow her throne. Confident in the just moderation of her past government, she told them that she relied upon their

---

[1] 'Diciendo por su misma boca que eran unos bellacos.'—*Don B. de Mendoza al Rey*, 6 13 Marzo, 1580.

[2] *Mendoza to Philip*, June 26. Mendoza says they were imprisoned. The meaning of the word will be presently seen.

[3] Camden.

CHAP XXVIII

1580 June or July

loyalty, to support her against her enemies domestic or foreign.[1]

' 'The Queen's Majesty findeth the continuance or rather increase of traitorous and malicious purposes, labours and solicitations of such rebels and traitors as justly have been condemned by law, and do live in foreign parts, and the joining to them certain others that are fled out of the realm, as persons refusing to live here in their natural country like natural subjects; both which of long time have wandered from place to place, and from one prince's court to another; but specially to Rome; and there have falsely and traitorously slandered the good government of the realm by the Queen's Majesty, who in very deed, and that most notably to be recorded, hath so graciously, favourably, and with that [indifferency (MS injured)] ministered justice to all her subjects, high and low, as [in no] age by any history can be recounted such a long and peaceable continuance of quietness and rest as in her time hitherto hath been. And if the foresaid traitors and their complices had not for their private ambition and rancour sought at one or two times to have interrupted the same in one or two corners of the realm, it might have been pronounced of her Majesty's quiet government, by the goodness of God for these twenty years, that could not have been recorded by any history for these thousand years, either of England or any kingdom in Christendom. And yet, it may be truly said, notwithstanding their said interruptions at home by their open rebellion, and their traitorous labours, practices, and solicitations to many great princes to procure sedition in the realm, yea, to have the realm invaded by foreign force as lately they have begun in Ireland, whereof by God's goodness their attempts are likely to be frustrate. But now to add some matter to serve their wicked purpose they have caused to be put in writing that the Pope, the King of Spain, and other princes are accorded to make a great army to invade England, and to dispose of the Crown, and the possessions of the subjects of the realm at their pleasure, thereby intending to move the people of the realm to a discord in their minds, as some to be bold to permit in their undutifulness, some to be afraid to continue dutiful. But her Majesty considering the goodness of God, how hitherto she and her whole realm have been preserved by his godly and special protection, and that she ought not only to be most thankful for the same, and to maintain his glory and honour by retaining her people in the true profession of the gospel, and to keep them free from the bondage of the Romish tyranny, but also she ought and must use those means which God hath given to her and put into her hands, that is power over an infinite number of godly, dutiful, faithful, manlike, and able people, her loving subjects through all parts of the realm; with which and by whose ready help, with their bodies, lives and substance, by God's grace she is and shall be able to withstand, both by sea and land, all foreign power how mighty soever the same may be procured or intended against her and her realm.

At this moment Parsons and his party reached Calais. They were prepared for danger, and had come to seek it. Half the country, at least, they believed to be at heart in their favour. They had friends everywhere, from the palace at Westminster, to the village alehouse; and to issue proclamations was more easy than to execute them. To avoid suspicion they crossed in separate parties. Parsons went first,[1] disguised as a volunteer officer returning from the Low Countries. He found no difficulty. His buff uniform, his gold lace, his hat and feather, and well appointed servant, were passport sufficient for the Dover searchers. He made his way to Gravesend, and up the river to London; and as the readiest means of finding a friend, he went openly to the Marshalsea to look among the Catholic prisoners.

—And to that end she hath of late caused the universal strength of her subjects to be viewed, prepared, and arranged, and the same she doth mean to have still continued in a readiness to withstand all hostile attempts, as well by sea with her own navy and the navy of the realm, as by land both on horseback and on foot; whereby, through God's goodness, she hath such a strength as, in comparison, never any king of this realm hath had the like, to overcome all foreign malice to her and to the state of true Christian religion, for the profession and maintenance whereof her Majesty knoweth that both herself and her realm is maligned. So she thinketh it good to admonish her good people that they continue in the dutiful and humble service of Almighty God, manifesting by their honest conversation, their Christian profession, and also do remain constant in courage with their bodies and substance to withstand any enterprise that may be offered to this realm; and that whatsoever rumours by speech or writing they shall hear of as maliciously dispersed by traitors abroad or by their secret compliers and favourers at home, that they not only be not moved therewith to alter their duties and courage, as by God's grace there shall be no just cause, but that they cause all such spreaders of like rumours to be apprehended, and speedily brought to such justices as they shall know to be faithful professors of true religion, and dutiful and faithful ministers under her Majesty, by them to be chastised according to their demerits as sowers of sedition, and aiders and abettors of foreign traitors.'—*Admonition for the People*, Burghley's hand. *MSS. Domestic.*

[1] June 11.

His reception there shows with what extreme laxity the word 'prison' must be understood as applied to recusants who could pay for good treatment. They were no more prisoners than law students at an Inn of Court. They went in and out at their pleasure, complying only with the rules of hours. They had apartments to themselves, where Parsons dined with them, and they introduced him to a young Catholic gentleman of fortune, a Mr. Gilbert, who invited him to his house in Fetter Lane.

Campion came next. He crossed on the day of St. John the Baptist, his patron saint, as he observed, to whom he had commended his cause and his journey. His pretended calling was that of a jewel merchant, and Ralph Emerson, 'his little man,' followed him with his box and his pack. Campion wanted the cool adroitness of his superior. He was suspected and carried before the mayor, who took him for Allen himself. Allen, he could safely swear that he was not. The mayor, however, was on the point of sending him to the Council, when God and St. John introduced an old man in some authority, who overruled the magistrates and dismissed him. Believing himself thus under the special guardianship of heaven, he too went to London, and made his way to the friend in Fetter Lane. The rest came in one by one, and found a hearty welcome from Gilbert, who, with other young Catholics of family, had formed themselves into an association for the protection of the Jesuits as soon as they should arrive. In the list of its members may be read the names of Charles Arundel, Francis Throgmorton, Anthony Babington, Chidiock Tichbourne, Charles Tilney, Edward Abington, Richard Salisbury, and William Tresham, men implicated all of them afterwards in plots for the assassination of the Queen. The subsequent history of all these persons is a sufficient indication of the effect of Jesuit teaching, and of the true object of the Jesuit mission.

London was the stronghold of English Protestantism. Yet even in London the Government was singularly feeble. Campian was known everywhere to have arrived. His reputation for eloquence caused such an eagerness to hear him preach, that Lord Paget hired a hall near Smithfield, and on the 29th of June, a Jesuit missionary, under the ban of the Council, and liable, if arrested, to be tried for treason, preached publicly in the middle of the city to a vast audience. A warrant was, of course, issued for Campian's apprehension, but 'great persons at court' sent him warning. The constables were Catholic, and conveniently blind. The fathers agreed that if taken, they should swear all of them that their errand was purely a spiritual one: they then dispersed to visit every English county, to hear confessions, administer the sacraments, reconcile the lapsed, encourage all Catholics to persevere in the faith, and wait for the good time that was in store for them. Gilbert and his friends provided money. Each father had two horses, a servant, a variety of disguises, and sixty pounds in cash. They dressed as occasion required, sometimes as officers, sometimes as gentlemen, sometimes as Protestant clergy, sometimes as bailiffs or apparitors. Campian himself, in a letter to the general of the order, sketches his adventures and his success.

'I came to London,' he wrote, 'and my good angel
'guided me unwittingly to the same house that had
'harboured Father Robert[1] before, whither young gentle-
'men came to me on every hand. They embrace me,

[1] Parsons.

'reapparel me, furnish me, weapon me, and convey me
'out of the city. I ride about some piece of the country
'every day. The harvest is wonderful great. On horse-
'back I meditate my sermon; when I come to the house
'I polish it. Then I talk with such as come to speak
'with me, or hear their confessions. In the morning,
'after mass, I preach. They hear with exceeding greedi-
'ness, and very often receive the sacraments, for the
'ministration whereof we are well assisted by priests,
'whom we find in every place. The priests of our country
'being themselves most excellent for virtue and learn-
'ing, yet have raised so great an opinion of our society,
'that I dare scarcely tell the exceeding reverence all
'Catholics do to us. How much more is it requisite
'that such as are hereafter to be sent for supply, where-
'of we have great need, be such as may answer all men's
'expectation of them. Specially let them be well
'trained for the pulpits. I cannot long escape the
'hands of the heretics. The enemies have so many
'eyes, so many tongues, so many scouts and crafts. I
'am in apparel to myself very ridiculous. I often
'change it, and my name also. I read letters some-
'times myself, that in the first front tell news that
'Campian is taken, which noised in every place where I
'come, so fills mine ears with the sound thereof, that
'fear itself has taken away all fear. My soul is in my
'own hands ever. Let such as you send, make count
'of this always:—The solaces that are intermeddled
'with the miseries are so great that they not only
'countervail the fear of what temporal government so-
'ever, but by infinite sweetness make all worldly pains
'seem nothing. A conscience pure, a courage in-
'vincible, zeal incredible, a work so worthy—the
'number innumerable of high degrees, of mean calling,

'of the inferior sort, of every age and sex. Among
'the Protestants themselves that are of milder nature,
'it is turned into a proverb that he must be a Catholic,
'that payeth faithfully that he oweth; in so much that
'if any Catholic do injury, every body expostulates
'with him as for an act unworthy of men of that calling.
'To be short, heresy heareth ill of all men, neither is
'there any condition of people commonly counted more
'vile and impure than their ministers, and we worthily
'have indignation that fellows so unlearned, so evil, so
'derided, so base, should in so desperate a quarrel
'overrule such a number of noble wits as our realm
'hath.' Threatening edicts come forth against us

---

¹ There was too much justice in Campian's description of the Protestant clergy. The bishops seemed determined to deserve the name which Elizabeth was so fond of bestowing on them. The House of Commons had many times remonstrated in vain against their commutations of penance, their dispensations for pluralities, their iniquitous courts, and the class of persons whom they ordained to the ministry. The Crown at length took up the complaint, and at an interview between the Queen and Council, and a number of the bishops in February 1585, there was the following singular dialogue:—

'Then spake my Lord Treasurer to my Lord of Canterbury. Truly my lord, her Majesty has declared unto you a marvellous great fault that you make in this time of light so many lewd and unlearned ministers.

'Well, quoth her Majesty, draw articles, and burden them that have offended.

'I do not burden, quoth my Lord Treasurer, them that be here; but it is the Bishop of Lichfield that I mean, who made seventy ministers in one day for money, some tailors, some shoemakers, and other craftsmen. I am sure the greatest part of them are not able to keep houses.

'Then said the Bishop of Rochester, That may be so, for I know one that made seven in one day. I would every man might bear his own burden. Some of us have the greatest wrong that can be offered. For mine own part, I am sure I never made above three in one day. But my lord, if you would have none but learned preachers admitted into the ministry, you must provide better livings for them.

'To have learned ministers in every parish is, in my judgment impossible, quoth my Lord of Canterbury. Being 13,000 parishes in England, I know not how this realm should yield so many learned preachers.

'Jesus! quoth the Queen; 13,000

'daily; notwithstanding by good heed and the prayers
'of good men, we have passed safely through the most
'part of the island. I find many neglecting their own
'security to have care of my safety.... The persecu-
'tion rages most cruelly. At the house where I am, is no
'other talk but of death, flight, prison, or spoil of their
'friends. Nevertheless they proceed with courage,
'many even at this present being restored to the
'Church; new soldiers give up their names, while the
'old offer up their blood, by which holy hosts and obla-
'tions God will be pleased, and we shall, no question,
'by him overcome. There will never want in Eng-
'land men that shall have care of their own salvation,
'nor such as shall advance other men's. Neither shall
'this Church here ever fail, so long as priests and
'pastors shall be found for these sheep, rage man or
'devil never so much.'[1]

It was characteristic of Campion that he failed to discover where the strength of the Reformation lay. It appeared to him to be a question of this or that opinion. It was in fact a question of national life, a question whether the ecclesiastical system of which the Pope was the head was to continue to rule without appeal over the entire destinies of mankind. To the Jesuit the temporal and spiritual power of the Papacy were related to one another as soul and body, one incapable of existing without the other. He did not see that the thing which he called heresy had a body also, the body of the State,

---

is not to be looked for. I think the time has been, there hath not been four preachers in a diocese. My meaning is not you should make choice of learned preachers only, for they are not to be found, but of honest, sober, and wise men, and such as can read the Scriptures and the Homilies well unto the people.'— *Brief effect of her Majesty's speech to the bishops,* Feb. 27, 1585. *MSS. Domestic.*

[1] Edmund Campian to Everardo Mercuriano. — *MSS. Domestic,* Nov. 1580.

which represented justice, which represented law, which represented those rights of conscience which ecclesiastics denied, and considered it a crime to claim. Campian saw the Catholic Church agreed upon a body of doctrine which had the prescription of ten centuries in its favour, which had been taught by the Fathers, and had shaped the spiritual thought of Christendom. He saw the heretics split into a hundred sects, staggering like men walking on quicksands, and over their confusions and uncertainties he anticipated an easy victory. Heresy appeared to him in extremity of death, without defence of reason or authority of age. He wrote from his concealment to the Council offering to dispute in public with any Protestant or Protestants who would encounter him. He published a book which he and his admirers considered to have closed the controversy. It was as if an adversary of the Newtonian astronomy had thought to overset the modern theory of the celestial motions by an appeal to Ptolemy or Hipparchus; or as if Julian or Porphyry had imagined that they had disproved Christianity by shewing that it was not to be found in the Theogonies or in the Zend Avesta. Time and accumulation of knowledge, and the mental expansion which came with it, had shewn intelligent men that things which their forefathers had believed to be true were not true. That a priest, by muttering a few words, could convert a cake into Almighty God, had become for ever incredible to them. The Church had said, You shall believe it or we will kill you; and the State had interposed with the stern intimation that the Church should do nothing of the kind. You priests and bishops, the English Parliament had said, shall have stake and gibbet at your disposition no more. You had power once, and you abused it, and we shall not trust you again. For these abstruse questions we cannot absolutely say what is true, nor do we believe that you can say. Within the limits of reverence and piety we will allow men to think for themselves. Our own laws are politically sufficient for us. Your master the Pope has no authority in this island, and shall not meddle with us. If you will obey the law and live peaceably, you shall have the same protection from us that others have. If you will not obey, if you choose to persist in claims which we deny, and conspire with strangers against the Government of your country, your so-called sacred character shall not save you. We will hang you as we would hang any other traitor.

This was the position which Campian had really to assail, and keener arguments were needed to overcome it than were to be found in the patristic armoury. It became daily more and more clear that mischief was intended, and Elizabeth, against her will, was compelled to see that the laws must be enforced, and these itinerant incendiaries be put down before the whole realm was on fire. They were protected for the first six months by the Queen's extreme aversion to severity. When Walsingham was permitted to exert himself, large captures were rapidly made. At the beginning of December seven or eight of the younger priests, Sherwin, Bryant, Pascal, Harte, Johnson, Kirby, and one or two more were arrested in various places and taken to the Tower. Harte's courage failed him; he recanted and saved himself by becoming a spy. The rest when examined said frankly who and what they were—English subjects in the service of the Pope, who was levying war against the Queen in Ireland. They were required to give the names of the gentlemen at whose houses they had been received, and to reveal the place of concealment of their leaders. They refused, and it was thought just and necessary to use other means to force them to speak. The Tower rack stood in the long vaulted dungeon below the armoury. Under a warrant signed by six of the Council, and in the presence of the Lieutenant, whose duty was to direct and moderate the application of the pains, they were laid at various times, and more than once, as they could bear it, upon the frame, the Commissioners sitting at their side and repeating their questions in the intervals of the winding of the winch. A practice which by the law was always forbidden could be palliated only by a danger so great that the nation had become like an army in the field. It was repudiated on the return of calmer times, and the employment of it rests as a stain on the memory of those by whom it was used. It is none the less certain, however, that the danger was real and terrible, and the same causes which relieve a commander in active service from the restraints of the common law, apply to the conduct of statesmen who are dealing with organised treason. The law is made for the nation, not the nation for the law. Those who transgress do it at their own risk, but they may plead circumstances at the bar of history, and have a right to be heard.

This also is to be said of the torturing of these Jesuits. 'None was put to the rack that was not first by 'manifest evidence known to the Council to be guilty of 'treason, so that it was well assured aforehand that there 'was no innocent tormented. Also none was tormented 'to know whether he was guilty or no; but for the 'Queen's safety to know the manner of the treason 'and the accomplices.'[1] 'Nor was any man tormented 'for matter of religion, nor asked what he believed of

---

[1] Thomas Norton to Walsingham, March 27, 1582.—*MSS. Domestic.*

'any point of religion, but only to understand of parti-
'cular practices against the Queen for setting up their
'religion by treason or force. If any one of them did
'say that he would truly answer to such things as he
'was demanded on the Queen's behalf, and would by
'oath or without oath, seriously and upon his allegiance
'say that he did know or believe his answers to be true,
'he was never racked. Neither was any of them racked
'that had not both obstinately said, and did persist in
'that obstinacy, that he would not tell truth though the
'Queen commanded him.'[1]

Allen and his friends had now the confessors which they desired. Where eye could not reach, imagination penetrated, and the scenes in the Tower dungeons were painted in the gorgeous colours of the Catholic martyrologies. The Government published no details of these dark transactions, and the Church had the field to itself. Only here and there is it possible to check with certainty the facile pen of the describer. The imprisonment was made intentionally severe. The cells were underground, lighted by tunnels sloping upwards, and closely grated to prevent communication. The prison diet was bread, beer, salt fish, and water not the freshest.[2] The alarm had extended beyond the influence of its immediate cause. Old Abbot Feckenham and the surviving Marian bishops, who had lived hitherto in country houses, under loose restraint, were confined more strictly in the castles of Hull, Wisbeach, and Banbury. They suffered from the change of lodging, and some of great

---

[1] Thomas Norton to Walsingham, March 27, 1581.—*MSS. Domestic.*

[2] 'Ad vitæ victusque sustentationem aliud non habent præter panem et cerevisiam et modici salsi piscis sustentationem. Tum, quod valde inhumanum est, aqua ad eorum necessitates supplendas illis denegatur, nisi ejusmodi quæ putrida sit velint acceptare.'—*Letter from a Priest in the Tower,* July 1581. *MSS. Domestic.*

age died of it. Those whose estimate of probabilities will allow them, may believe if they please that debauched women were introduced into the rooms of Feckenham and Watson the Bishop of Lincoln, to tempt these aged and broken men to acts of impurity.[1]

Bryant, a youth of twenty-four, was known to be aware of the hiding-place of Parsons. He refused to reveal it, and the Commissioners who had been sent to examine him threatened that 'if he would not tell truth 'for his duty to God and the Queen, he should be made 'a foot longer than God had made him.' He defied them, and they kept their word, and the Catholics exultingly reported that by special miracle he had felt no pain. He had laughed upon the rack, and had asked his tormentors if that was all that they could do. Thomas Norton, one of the examiners, when the story was published conceived that he would be touched in honour if he was believed to have done his work so ill. He admired Bryant's courage. He 'lamented that the Devil should have so 'possessed him in so naughty a cause.' But 'as to the 'setting forth of the miracle that he was preserved 'from feeling of pain,' he said, 'it was most untrue, for 'no man of them all after his torture made so grie- 'vous complaining and shewed so open signs of pain

---

[1] 'Erat non multis abhinc diebus meretrix quædam quorundam opera in reverendi Episcopi Lincolniensis cubiculum inverecunde introducta, quæ, omni muliebri pudore abjecto, hunc, senem virum senio pœnis confectum, ad nequitiam et turpem libidinem omnibus modis solicitavit. Præ verecundiâ taceo quibus illecebris hæc virago usa est quæ cum a perpetuæ castitatis constantia deduceret; cui senex fortiter resistens dum hanc impudicam belluam foras expellere totis viribus operam dedit, nebulones pessimi qui istam adduxerunt reverendissimo seni verbera minitabantur. Alia quoque meretrix ad Feckenhammum pari arte intromissa fuit.'—*Ibid.* Both Feckenham and the Bishop of Lincoln were a hundred miles from London. The priest in the Tower, therefore, could have learnt these stories only at second hand.

'as he.'[1] Harte's constancy was loudly boasted of,[2] but his suffering was merely imaginary. He was a traitor to his friends, and he was put on the rack that the report of his endurance might gain him credit and confidence with his order. 'There is nothing,' said this wretch, in a letter to Walsingham, 'that can please 'Doctor Allen better than to hear of his scholars' stout-'ness in suffering for the Catholic faith. It is a wonder 'to see how he will rejoice at hearing thereof, which 'thing maketh me to think that whereas I who was before 'this so dear to him that he made some account of 'me, and was not willing that I should depart when I 'did, if he shall now hear of my stoutness, that it has 'been such as to abide a whole year's close imprison-'ment, and that in the Tower, the only name whereof 'is terrible abroad, yea, and much more, to have been 'at the rack—although I endured nothing thereon, but 'that is unknown to him—to have been indicted, ar-'raigned, and condemned for the same, as both he and 'his fellows I know are fully persuaded, and now stand 'at her Majesty's pleasure for my life—without any 'speeches as I suppose yet openly known that I am so 'minded as I have professed to your honour to reform 'myself according to her Majesty's good and virtuous 'proceedings—if I were now with him in this case I 'should be so much made of as I cannot express it in 'words, and I think verily he would now make me privy 'to many things which hitherto, mistrusting my con-'stancy, he has kept secret from me, imparting them to 'very few of the chief seniors of the house.'[3]

---

[1] Thomas Norton to Walsingham, March 27, 1582.—MSS. Domestic.

[2] 'Dominus Hartus per tres horas in tormento expansus jacebat.'—Letter of a Priest from the Tower, July, 1581. MSS. Domestic.

[3] John Harte to Walsingham, Dec. 1, 1581.—MSS. Domestic.

From these specimens the condition generally of the Jesuit prisoners may be easily pictured. Campian and Parsons meanwhile were still at large, and more successful than ever. The account of his friends' endurance added fire to Campian's oratory, and trebled the rate of conversion. Lord Oxford, Burghley's ill-conditioned son-in-law; Sir Francis Southwell; Lord Vaux; Lord Henry Howard, the Duke of Norfolk's brother; Philip, Earl of Arundel, Norfolk's eldest son, to whom Elizabeth was endeavouring by special kindness to compensate for his father's death; these and many more of high blood were early 'reconciled,' either by him or his companions.[1] 'The heretics,' wrote Campian to the General, 'brag 'no more of their martyrs, for it is now come to pass 'that for a few apostates and cobblers of theirs burned, 'we have lords, knights, the old nobility, patterns 'of learning, piety, and prudence, the flower of the 'youth, noble matrons, and of the inferior sort innu-'merable, either martyred at once,[2] or by consuming 'prisonment dying daily.'[3]

There must have been something at the bottom vulgar in Campian. It was at once the glory of the Reformation and the disgrace of Pole and Mary that the Protestant confessors were mainly taken from mechanics' workshops. Galilean fishermen were the first to die for the Gospel, and a burnt cobbler did as much honour to Protestantism as an executed noble to Rome. But the conversion of so many men of rank was politically of extreme importance. The spirit of the Ridolfi con-

---

[1] Deposition of Charles Arundel, Dec. 1580.—*MSS. Domestic.*

[2] The only martyrs of distinction whom the Church could as yet boast of were the Duke of Norfolk and the Earl of Northumberland, who had been executed for palpable treason.

[3] Ed. Campian to Everardo Mercuriano, Nov. 1580.—*MSS. Domestic.*

spiracy was evidently reviving. It was a question of life and death, and the Government determined to be masters. Jesuits and seminary priests continued to arrive in tens and twenties. The Earl of Westmoreland received a summons to Rome from the Pope, and brought back a pile of bullion to Flanders. 'The 'Papists said openly they hoped to see Westmoreland 'and the Duke of Alva in England before the coming 'Midsummer.'

The Catholics, for the first time, refused generally to attend the Anglican services, and one of Walsingham's spies in England warned him that 'the times were peri-'lous, the people wilful and desirous of change, 'with 'greater danger on hand than was provided for.'[1] Walsingham, with Burghley at his side, accepted the challenge. Attendance at Church was made a test of loyalty, and Lord Paget and other suspected nobles were required to hear the service at Paul's Cross at their peril.[2] Parliament was called to grant extraordinary powers, the same Parliament which had been returned in 1572, in the excitement which followed the rebellion. The Protestant majority was valuable, and there had been no dissolution.

The Houses met on the 16th of January. The Queen was absent and there was no speech. The attendance of peers was ominously small. Elizabeth had intimated that the session was to be a short one, and that she would have no meddling under any circumstances with the government of the Church. Sir John Popham, the Speaker, endeavoured to meet her wishes, and recommended the Commons to be discreet and brief. It was easier to ad-

---

[1] —— to Walsingham, June 5, 1581.—*MSS. Domestic.* [2] Paget to Walsingham, Jan. 10, 1581.—*Ibid.*

vise than to secure compliance. The Lower House had already shown signs of restlessness under the Queen's dictation, and English Protestant gentlemen were as resolute as the Jesuits, and no less conscious of the goodness of their cause. When Popham sate down, Paul Wentworth[1] moved that there should be 'a Fast of the 'House,' and that every morning at seven, before business 'commenced, there should be a sermon, 'that so begin- 'ning with the service and worship of God, he might the 'better bless them.' The House was favourable to both proposals. Sir F. Knollys objected the Queen's orders, but was overruled. A Fast of the Commons House was carried by a majority of fifteen, and Sunday the 25th was named for it. The Privy Council were requested to select the daily preachers, 'that they might be discreet per- 'sons, who would keep a convenient proportion of time, 'and meddle with no matter of unquietness.'[2]

Elizabeth, determined as she was to put down the Jesuits, was equally resolved to treat them merely as traitors, and to keep religion out of the field. Anything which would give a Protestant character to the measure about to be proposed she looked upon as specially objectionable. She sent for Popham, who the next day told the House that she was greatly displeased and that she required them to recall their resolutions. When they hesitated Knollys rose again and addressed them in the Queen's name. She was splenetic even when she was wise. She knew that she could depend on their loyalty, but she liked to treat them as schoolboys. She desired them to understand that 'she did not disallow 'fasting and prayer, using the same in her own person.'

---

[1] Brother of Peter Wentworth, member for Tregony, who had been distinguished in the past session.

[2] Proceedings of the House of Commons in the matter of the Fast, Jan. 1581.—*MSS. Domestic.*

'She acquitted them of malice but condemned them of 'errour and unadvisedness.' After 'her lenity to the 'brother of the man who had made the motion, that a 'second Wentworth should be heard and followed she 'interpreted to be great unthankfulness.' They were still inclining to be mutinous when Sir Nicholas St. Leger opened a way for them to yield with dignity. He spoke of 'the great affection' which the House bore to the Queen, the imperfection of all estates, and chiefly 'the faults of the bishops who had suffered the duty of 'fasting and humiliation to go out of use.' He considered, however, that they would do well to submit in the present instance, with the hope 'that both her Majesty and 'others would repent all defaults and humble themselves 'to God in sackcloth and ashes.'[1] So expressed, the House accepted his advice without a division, and Knollys was empowered to tell the Queen that her will should be obeyed. Sir Walter Mildmay then rose for the Council. He spoke of the moderation of the Government, of the prosperity which England had enjoyed under the Queen while the rest of Europe was in flames. He dwelt on the successive attempts which had been made by the Popes to destroy her, the northern rebellion, the Bull of Deposition, the Irish revolt, and the secret countenance given to the disaffected by Spain. So far the Queen had been able to encounter these plots against her at her own cost. The country had been called on for little or no assistance. The few subsidies for which she had asked had not covered half her expenses, and without loans or benevolences she had carried on the government out of her private revenues. England

---

[1] Proceedings of the House of Commons in the matter of the Fast, Jan. 1581.—*MSS. Domestic.* Compare D'Ewes' Journals, 1580-81.

under her moderate rule enjoyed more freedom than any
nation under the sun. She had been personally a virtuous princess, unspotted in word or deed, merciful,
temperate, a maintainer of peace, of justice. She had a
right, therefore, to call upon her subjects now to stand by
her against the malice of the Pope and his confederates.

'The enemy sleeps not,' he said. 'The mischievous
'purposes will be renewed. They are determined to
'root out the Gospel and set England on fire. The obstinate and stiff-necked are not converted, but are
'bolder than they were. A sort of hypocrites, Jesuits
'and vagrant Friars, have come into the realm to stir sedition, and many of those who used to come to church
'have fallen back and refuse to attend. We must
'therefore look to it. Our Church, compared to the
'persecuting Papal Church, has been lenient and merciful, but when fair means have done no good, and behind our tolerance there come in these emissaries of
'rebellion and sedition, it is time to look more strictly to
'them. They have been encouraged so far by the
'lenity of the laws. We must shew them that as the
'Pope's curses do not hurt us, so his blessings cannot
'save them. We must make laws to restrain these
'people, and we must prepare force to resist violence
'which may be offered here or abroad.'[1]

With this preface a bill was introduced, 'to restrain
'her Majesty's subjects in their due obedience.' On the
publication of the Bull of Pope Pius, an act had been
passed making the introduction of this or any other
Papal rescript into England treasonable; but it had been
proved inadequate, and Parliament was now therefore
requested to enact 'that all persons pretending to any

---

[1] Speech of Sir Walter Mildmay.—*D'Ewes' Journals*, 1580-81.

'power of absolving subjects from their allegiance or 'practising to withdraw them to the Romish religion, 'with all persons after the present session willingly so 'absolved or reconciled to the See of Rome, should be 'held guilty of high treason;' and 'that those who 'abetted or concealed such persons should be held 'guilty of misprision of high treason;' that the saying mass in private houses which had been winked at for twenty years should be permitted no longer, that whoever should say or sing a mass should be fined 500 marks and imprisoned for a year, and that those who refused to attend the service of the Established Church should pay 20*l.* a month for their exemption.[1]

It was a serious step. The last clause especially was equivalent to the confiscation of the estates of the Catholics; and although the Commons did not hesitate to pass a measure which was felt to be necessary, yet they felt also that if the nation was to be coerced into conformity the Established Church must be made worthy of its position. In the last session they had complained of the revival by the bishops of the worst practices of the unreformed system. The Queen had promised improvement, but her injunctions had been evaded or despised. 'Were there any honesty in those prelates in whom 'honesty should most be found, said one, 'we should 'not be in our present trouble.' Notwithstanding her order to abstain from such subjects the Commons by committee renewed their petition. The Queen thought it prudent to yield, and six of the bishops were appointed to confer with the Commons to devise means of redress. The discussion which followed appears to have been extremely acrimonious. The bishops were told that they

---

[1] Statutes of the Realm, 23 Eliz. cap. 1.

were unfit to be trusted with the charge of the Church.
'They had filled the pulpits with unlearned and unfit
'ministers whom they had admitted into orders, and
'the number of Papists and Anabaptists had increased
'by their remissness.'

'The bishops,' in reply, 'spake most or only for
'jurisdiction, in so much as one great bishop said that,
'rather than he would yield that private schoolmasters
'should acknowledge their conformity in religion before
'justices of the peace, he would say Nay to the whole
'Bill.'[1] At length, not without bad blood on both sides,
the dispute was compromised. The bishops promised
amendment. The Commons withdrew the additions
which they had meant to attach, and the Bill was passed.
A large subsidy was voted for the defence of the realm.
Another act was passed also levelled intentionally
against pamphleteers like Stubbs, but made double-
edged to strike Papist as well as Puritan, raising into
felony the publication of rhyme, book, ballad, letter,
or writing to the defamation of her Majesty.[2]

The remaining business was hurried over. The Crown
had obtained money, and the Council their increased
powers. On the 18th the Queen came to the House of
Lords, thanked the Parliament for their services, 'not
'including such members of the Commons House as
'had during the session dealt more rashly in some things
'than was fit for them to do;' and declared it pro-
rogued.[3]

The passing of the Treason Act obliged the Catholics
to review their position. Almost all among them who

---

[1] Note of proceedings in Parliament. Mr. Norton's defence against Mr. Hampton's report, March 1581.—*MSS. Domestic*.

[2] Statutes of the Realm, 23 Eliz. cap. 2.

[3] D'Ewes' Journals. This Parliament never met again. It was continued by prorogation till April 19, 1583, and then dissolved.

were Catholics by descent were patriotic Englishmen. They had no desire either to lose their lands or be forced into disloyalty, and could they be permitted would gladly continue to attend the Church services as before. But they dared not resist the Jesuit authorities. Their wishes were referred to Parsons and Campian, who though they could not sanction what the Council of Trent had forbidden, yet allowed them to use their best ingenuity to evade the statute.

'No Catholic Christian,' it was said, 'could go to 'church without danger of damnable schism.' The Anglicans might claim the name of Catholic, but their ministers 'were some Protestants, some Puritans, some 'holding other plain heresies.' 'He that was a Protestant 'to-day would to-morrow be a Puritan, or some other 'sectary.' 'No Catholic, therefore, ought to pray with 'them or hear them preach.' 'Christians were bound 'fully and wholly, and not by pieces and patches, to keep 'the Catholic faith, which was impossible to be done if 'they went to church and prayed and communicated 'with heretics and schismatics, Puritans, Anabaptists, 'Brownists, or the Family of Love.' When, however, they were asked whether they would or would not go to church, they need not answer. No one by English law was bound to criminate himself, while a general refusal might lead 'the simple' 'to repute them Atheists or 'Godless.' Before they could be indicted there must be proof of fact or facts. A B, it would have to be said, being of the age of sixteen years, for the space of many months had not frequented church or chapel, not having lawful excuse. And of this no jury could possibly be assured. That a man had not attended his parish church did not prove that he had attended no church. Nor was there any definition of the words 'lawful ex-'cuse.'

Should these exceptions be disallowed, however, the Jesuits concluded that a true Catholic must confess his faith and brave the consequences. If he was required to say distinctly whether he would attend church or not, he must in that case, 'making protest that he spoke under 'compulsion, and not to impeach any law or statute,' say out plainly and honourably why he could not obey. The service was not Catholic, and he dared not, for the peril of his soul, go near it. The laws and statutes of a Christian country could not compel a man to damn his soul.[1]

The Catholics were now in hard case, and they had to thank for it the fanatics who had erected the right of the Pope to depose princes into an article of faith. The letters of Mendoza to Philip throw an interesting light on the despair of the better part of them. 'The leading 'Catholics of this country,' he wrote on the 6th of April, 'have signified to me that, besides the troubles and 'miseries which they have undergone in the two last 'years, a persecution now awaits them of which the 'first was but a shadow. They must not depart from 'the realm; and unless they will forget God, and profess 'the errors which are here established, they will not only 'lose lands, liberty, and perhaps life, but, through these 'laws now passed through Parliament, they may leave 'tainted names to their children.[2] They place them-
'selves in the hands of God, and are willing to sacrifice 'life and all in the service, but scarcely with that burn-
'ing zeal which they ought to show.[3] They feel as men

---

[1] Papers endorsed 'Catholics going to Protestant churches, 1581.'—*MSS. Domestic.*

[2] This could be said only of converts — or of those who chose to entertain the Jesuits. The statute touched no one who had been born and bred a Catholic, if he offended in an other way, further than by a fine if he was recusant.

[3] The uncertainty of the English Catholics, placed between two duties,

'the shame of figuring before their descendants as traitors
'to their Prince; yet they see also that these unjust
'and rigorous laws may be the means of extirpating the
'Catholic religion out of the land, unless in some way
'the execution of them be prevented. It is to effect this
'purpose that the heretics have pressed them on the
'Queen. They have made her believe that the Catholics
'will not be contented with liberty of worship, but
'desire a change of sovereigns. They have pretended
'that her life is in danger, the independence of the
'country threatened, with other lies and fictions; and
'although the Catholics did their utmost to prevent these
'laws from passing, and offered the Queen at last a hun-
'dred and fifty thousand dollars if she would refuse con-
'sent, they could not prevail upon her. They address
'themselves, therefore, to your Majesty as the pillar and
'defender of the faith. They ask your pity, and they
'ask your help: and they beseech your interest with
'his Holiness, if the tares of heresy are not entirely
'to choke the good seed which God has planted by the
'seminary priests, to appoint some English cardinal,
'such as Father Sanders or Father Allen. If they have
'no head or no leader, they will crumble away under
'these statutes. A cardinal only can help them; and

---

was acknowledged by a seminary priest in the Tower. 'For preparation,' he said, ' to be made here before our coming, who were priests sent to win men home again to our society and fellowship, I knew none other but that it was chiefly to be made by our own labours, hoping that if there were any great number of such, when any power were once set on land—though how that should be done we likewise knew not—they would all join together to make a reformation. And yet, I tell you true, there were more that did doubt hereof than did affirm it, because they thought all generally, of what religion soever they were, would jointly bear arms against a foreigner.'—*Depositions. MSS.* MARY QUEEN OF SCOTS, 1582.

'one gentleman has offered a thousand dollars annually
'for his support.'[1]

'God,' wrote Mendoza again, in a second letter a few
weeks later, 'for our sins, permits the spirits of the
'Catholics to sink more and more, while with the
'heretics, whatever happens inspires them only with
'fresh courage to maintain their delusions.'[2]

The confession of the Spaniard was in singular contrast to the dream of Campian that heresy was dying. During the session of Parliament the latter was hiding in London, printing his 'Ten Reasons for being a Catho-'lic,' which were to complete the conversion of England. He had a friend living on the Harrow Road, whom he often visited. His walk led him past the Tyburn gallows,[3] and instinct telling him what might one day befall him there, he touched his hat to the ugly thing whenever he went by. The 'Ten Reasons' came out, throwing Oxford, among other places, into an ecstasy of enthusiasm; and Campian and Parsons, who had been in London also, then went into the country to the house of Lady Stonor, near Henley. The publication of the book had increased the determination of the Government to disarm and punish its author; but the persecution had created much general pity for the hunted Jesuits. Notwithstanding the threatened penalties, some Protestants were found, of the milder sort, who concealed them from their pursuers;[4] and the care of their friends and

---

[1] Mendoza to Philip, April 6, 1581.—MSS. Simancas.

[2] 'Parece que habia de hacer caso en los Catolicos. Por nuestros pecados permite Dios que les anichilen mas los animos, viendose el contrario en los hereges que cualquiera novidad les da á los corage para sustentar su cequedad.'—Mendoza to Philip, May 14. MSS. Simancas.

[3] Where Connaught Terrace now stands.

[4] 'Con todo esto permite Dios que se vea lo que se vió en la primitiva Iglesia, habiendo gente de todas suertes que con ser hereges son tan

the wilful blindness of the country gentlemen had hitherto served to screen them. But the search was now growing hot, and greater precaution had become necessary.

At Lyford, near Abingdon, twenty miles from Henley, there was an ancient 'moated grange,' the abode of a Mr. Yates, a Catholic who was in confinement in London. His wife was at home, and with her were eight Brigittine nuns, who had gone to Belgium on the death of Queen Mary, but had returned on finding that they had no persecution to fear, and were now lingering out their lives and their devotions in this Berkshire manor house, with the knowledge and consent of the Queen. The ladies, hearing that Campian was in the neighbourhood, were extremely anxious to receive the communion from him. They had two priests in constant attendance. They were not in want of the sacraments, and the house being notorious and likely to be watched, his appearance there was thought unnecessary and imprudent.

Parsons had resolved to return alone to London. His companion he proposed to send to Norfolk, where the Catholics were numerous and concealment would be easy. The nuns, however, were pressing, and Campian was anxious to please them; and Father Robert gave a reluctant consent, on condition that his stay should not be protracted beyond one day and night.

To Lyford therefore he went, on Wednesday the 12th of July. He was received with tender enthusiasm. The long summer evening was passed in conferences and

fieles á muchos de los clerigos que andan aqui escondidos, que por solo acariciarles postponen hijos, muger y haciendas, diciendo que son buena gente sin haberse hallado jamas hombre destos que los acuse hasta agora con conocerles por Catolicos, ayudandoles con lo que tienen.'— *Mendoza al Rey*, 4 de Julio, 1581. *MSS. Simancas.*

confessions, and absolutions and pious tears. Mass was
said at dawn, and the devotions were protracted through
the morning: an early dinner followed, and the dangerous visit was safely over. Campian and Emerson
mounted and rode away across the country. Their road
led them near Oxford. It was hard for them to pass
the place to which so many memories attached them,
without pausing to look at it. They lingered, and put
up their horses at an alehouse, where they were soon
surrounded by a crowd of students. The same afternoon some Catholic gentlemen happened to call at
Lyford, and hearing that they had so nearly missed
Campian, one of them followed, and overtook him and
begged him to return. The students added their entreaties. If Campian would but remain at Lyford on
Sunday, half Oxford, they said, would ride over to hear
him preach. The temptation was strong. Knowing
his weakness, Parsons had placed him under Emerson's
authority: but Emerson wanted strength, and clamour
and entreaty prevailed. He gave the required permission, and himself went on upon his way; while Campian
'turned again by the road that he came,' promising to
follow in the ensuing week. The expected sermon
became of course the talk of the University. An agent
of Leicester, named Eliot, was in Oxford at the time
with a warrant in his pocket for Campian's apprehension.
He gave notice to a magistrate, collected a posse of
constables, and on Sunday morning early concealed
them in the neighbourhood of the grange; whilst he himself went boldly to the gate, and pretending to be a
Catholic requested to be admitted to mass. The nuns
and the Catholic visitors had for two days enjoyed to the
full the presence of their idolised teacher. The Sunday
only remained, and then he was to leave them indeed.

The students had crowded over as they promised, and Eliot passed in as one of them. Mass was celebrated. They all communicated; and then followed the last sermon which Campian was ever to preach.

The subject was the tears of Jesus at the aspect of Jerusalem, Jerusalem that murdered the prophets and stoned them that were sent to her. England was that Jerusalem, and he and his fellows were the prophets. The Protestants on their side could sing the same song. Campian, though not past middle age, could remember the martyrs at Oxford, and the burning of those four hundred mechanics at whom it pleased him to scoff. Who was to choose between the witnesses? But the dreams of hysteria are to the dreamers the inspiration of the Almighty. He was never more brilliant, his eloquence being subdued and softened by the sense that his end was near. Eliot—Judas Eliot as he was afterwards called—glided out before he had ended. A few minutes after, a servant rushed into the assembly, to say that the doors were beset by armed men.

Those who are acquainted with English manor houses must have seen often narrow staircases piercing the walls, and cells hollowed out in the seeming solid masonry. These places were the priests' chambers of the days of the persecution, where in sudden alarms they could be concealed. Into one of them Campian and the two chaplains were instantly hurried. The entrance, scarcely to be detected by those who knew where to look for it, was in Mrs. Yates's room behind the bed curtains. The constables with Eliot at their head were admitted, searched every place, and could find nothing. The magistrate who was in attendance apologised to Mrs. Yates, and was about to withdraw his men, when Eliot, who had seen Campian there with his own eyes,

and knew that no one had left the house, produced
the Council's warrant, and insisted on a further search.
It was continued till dark, but still without success.
The brave Mrs. Yates showed no anxiety, begged the
constables to remain for the night, entertained them
hospitably, and dosed them heavily with ale. Sound
slumber followed; Campian and his two companions were
brought out of their hiding-place, and at that moment
might have easily escaped, but enthusiasm and prudence
were ill companions. A 'parting of friends' was necessary, and 'last words,' and tears and sobs, at Mrs. Yates's
bedside. The murmurs of voices was heard below stairs,
and disturbed the sleepers in the hall. The three priests
were again hurried into the wall, and at daybreak the
search was renewed. Again it was unsuccessful. The
magistrate, an unwilling instrument throughout, was
about to depart with a sarcastic remark to Eliot on the
accuracy of his information; they were descending the
staircase for the last time, when Eliot, striking the wall,
heard something unusual in the sound. A servant of
the house who was at his side became agitated. Eliot
called for a mattock, dashed in the plaster, and found
the men that he was in search of lying side by side
upon a narrow bed. They had confessed their sins to
each other. They had said their *Fiat voluntas tua*.
Three times they had invoked St. John as Campian's
patron saint. But St. John had left them to their fate.
Campian was taken out without violence, and was carried first to Aldermaston, the house of Humfrey Forster,
the Sheriff of Berkshire. Forster, who, like most English gentlemen, was more than half a Catholic, received
him rather as a guest than a prisoner, but was obliged
to communicate with the Council, and received orders
to send him up at once. The sympathy which protected

him in the country did not extend to London. He was brought into the city in his lay disguise, wearing cap and feather, buff jerkin, and velvet hose, his feet tied under his horse's belly, and his arms pinioned behind his back. A placard was fastened on his head, with the words, 'Campian, the seditious Jesuit.' He was led along through a yelling crowd to the town gate, where Sir Owen Hopton received him, and his lodging for the night was ' Little Ease '—a narrow cell at one end of the torture chamber, underground, entirely dark, where he could neither stand nor lie at length.

The next day the Council directed that some better lodging should be provided for him. Neither the Queen nor Leicester had forgotten the brilliant youth who had flattered them at Oxford. The Earl sent for him; and being introduced into a private room, he found himself in the presence of Elizabeth herself. She wished to give him a chance of saving himself. She asked whether he regarded her as his lawful sovereign. The relaxation of the Bull allowed him to say that he did. She asked whether he thought that the Bishop of Rome could lawfully excommunicate her. A distinct declaration of loyalty, a frank repudiation of the temporal pretensions of the Pope, were all that was required of him. He would not make either. He said that he was no umpire between parties so far above him, he could not decide a question on which the learned were divided. He would pay her Majesty what was hers, but he must pay to God what was God's. He was returned to the Tower with directions that he should be kindly treated; but Burghley's determination prevailed over Elizabeth's good-nature. Morton had just been executed. A spy at Rheims procured and sent over a copy of a letter from Allen to Father Algazzari, boasting of Campian's successes, of the multitude of priests who were at work in England, of the ease with which they baffled the searchers at Dover, and of the unnumbered converts whom they were reconciling to the faith. Two expressions in the letter, underlined either by Burghley or Walsingham, justified the worst interpretation of the Jesuit's objects. Allen spoke of a young Catholic of good family as having come over to him *ut se servaret ad illud tempus*, that he might keep himself safe till *that time*—the time of the insurrection and invasion. Another piece of information was that Parsons was in continual conference with several noblemen, and even with certain members of the Privy Council.[1]

Everard Hurte, a seminary priest, perhaps the traitor's brother, who had defied the Government, and declared himself the Pope's subject, was hanged and quartered under the late act at Tyburn, on the 31st of July. 'He 'died,' says Mendoza, 'with invincible resolution, to 'the wonder of the heretics and the great edification of 'the Catholics. Two nights after, there was not a par- 'ticle of earth which his blood had stained, that had not 'been carried off as a relic, and infinite sums were given 'for his shirt and other clothes.'[2] The same 31st of July, Campion was questioned at the Tower, first on his allegiance, and afterwards, since his answer was still equivocal, as to the houses which he had visited, the families which had received him, and the whereabouts of the printing press from which his books were issued. He would confess nothing, and he was racked two days suc-

---

[1] 'Continuas interpellatur a nobilibus etiam et a quibusdam consiliariis propter necessaria consilia.'—*Allen to Algazzari*, June 23. *MSS. Domestic.* Opposite to the words in italics either Burghley, Walsingham, or Elizabeth—for no one else saw these papers—has drawn a finger ☞

[2] Mendoza to Philip, August 4, 1581.—*MSS. Simancas.*

cessively.[1] His courage was not absolutely proof. He gave up a few names; and his bearing was contrasted unfavourably with Bryant's, who had suffered far more severely. Additional arrests followed, and greater strictness with the ordinary prisoners. Their friends were no longer admitted indiscriminately into the Marshalsea, and indulgences were taken away which they had been allowed to purchase. Relations of those who lay under charge of treason, or who had gone abroad without leave, were forbidden to send them money. The Spanish ambassador became a general banker for the families of the distressed, and through his servants some few conveniences were smuggled into the prisons notwithstanding the Council's vigilance.

Filled as they had been with visions of 'a good time' soon coming, the Catholic leaders now became wild with impatience. The arrest and torture of Campian were too horrible to be borne, and they besieged Mendoza with entreaties that Spain and the Duke of Guise should delay no longer. D'Aubigny had succeeded brilliantly in Scotland; Morton was dead; the English party gone; the friends of the Queen of Scots in power. Now, if ever, was the time for their allies to come over and interfere between them and destruction. Unfortunately, Guise was not France, and d'Aubigny, though he had destroyed

---

[1] Mendoza says that when the rack failed, needles were run under the nails of the fingers and toes of the Jesuits—a mode of torture, he tells us, which the Spaniards expected to form one of the worst atrocities of the Kingdom of Antichrist. 'Aprecian á los clerigos que aciertan á prender con diversissimos y terribles generos de tormentos, y entre otros uno uno que en España se imagina la gente que como el mayor de todos ha de obrar el Antichristo, que en el meter hierros entre las uñas y la carne, y con este han sido atormentados dos clerigos que tienen en la Torre, siendo uno dellos Campian.'—*Mendoza al Rey*, 4 de Agosto. *MSS. Simancas.* Such exceptional barbarity could hardly have escaped the knowledge of the Catholic martyrologists. Mendoza had probably heard some confused account of the thumbscrew.

Morton, had not destroyed Protestantism. James was still Protestant; d'Aubigny had been obliged to profess himself Protestant; both he and the King had recently signed a vehemently Calvinistic confession; and Philip, anxious always to find excuses to put off interference, could not think of compromising himself by an alliance with a non-Catholic power.

'I have let them know in Scotland,' wrote Mendoza to him, 'that before anything can be done, the King
'must be reconciled to the Church. It is not an easy
'matter, for the Scotch Council are declared Protestants,
'and would send word of it to this Queen. The
'Catholic nobles here have been the means of com-
'munication. I shewed them that, in the present state
'of Europe, a change on the part of the King of Scots
'was the indispensable preliminary to a movement in
'England. For your Majesty to employ your forces in
'the Low Countries in the immediate service of the
'English Catholics, would only lead to war between
'your Majesty and France; and when the war had
'once begun, the French Government would declare,
'in self-defence, for heresy and heretics. I told them
'that France could not, for its own sake, allow your
'Majesty to make yourself sovereign of England under
'colour of religion.

'They saw the reason of this. They acknowledged
'that, ground down as they had been, they could do
'nothing for themselves, unless your Majesty sent a
'fleet and more than fifteen thousand men—unless, in
'fact, you were yourself prepared to undertake the con-
'quest. I pointed out, however, that Ireland, although
'it could do no more than embarrass the Queen and
'prevent her from sending troops to Flanders, could
'still distress her for men and money; and if the King of

'Scots could be converted, the war could then be begun 'by him—which for a number of reasons would be the 'most desirable plan. This, in fact, was the foundation 'for them to build upon. I advised them to lose no 'time in setting about it, and I recommended such of 'them as had acquaintances in Scotland, and understood 'the humours of the people there, to feel their way 'through their friends upon the border. They entirely 'approved of what I said. Six of them—six noblemen 'of the highest rank—have now combined for the liberties 'of their country. They will reveal their plans to no 'one but myself, but they have sworn to stand by 'one another with their lives and lands. They will 'send a priest to Edinburgh, to obtain if possible a 'private interview with d'Aubigny, and let him know 'that if the King will return to communion with the 'Holy See, the English peers and gentlemen, supported, 'as they may reasonably expect to be, by the Pope, by 'your Majesty, and also by France, will demand the 'release of his mother and his own nomination as next 'heir to the Crown. Otherwise, d'Aubigny must not 'deceive himself. The King, if he persists in remaining 'Protestant, will find them more determined enemies 'to his succession than the heretics themselves.

'Supposing d'Aubigny to listen, and the King to show 'a disposition to comply, a brother of one of them will 'then repair to his Holiness, and entreat his good 'offices with your Majesty.

'I committed myself to nothing beyond observing that 'their object being the conversion of their country, and 'therefore purely disinterested, I recommended them to 'have as little as possible to say to the French. In 'this view of mine they coincided fully. They have all 'Catholic and Spanish hearts, and will be guided wholly 'by your Majesty's wishes. The King of Scots having

'become a Catholic they will send their sons to Rheims
'to be out of the way; and when the Scotch army is
'over the border, they will rise with the whole North in
'his favour. If your Majesty will then help them, they
'know that their force will be irresistible. The Queen,
'being now forty-nine years old, can no longer hope for
'children, and the entire realm will join with them in
'insisting on the settlement of the succession. If she
'refuse to allow the restoration of the Catholic religion,
'she can be deposed. I do not mention the names of
'these six noblemen.[1] They made me promise that I
'would neither write nor speak of them to any one till
'we see how things turn in Scotland. Of course, if
'they can do nothing, they would then prefer to remain
'unknown. But I am personally acquainted with all
'of them. They are zealous in God's service and your
'Majesty's. Their plans are reasonable and well laid.
'The first object being the winning of souls, God can-
'not but desire their success; and besides the service of
'God, it will be in the interest of your Majesty and
'your realm to give them all the help that you can.'[2]

The Jesuit leaven was working to some purpose. The
six noblemen had all been 'received' in course of
the past year, and their dread of disloyalty had been
washed away in the waters of their baptism. Proof
multiplies on proof that Walsingham was right in his
estimate of the character of the mission, and that no
injustice whatever was done the seminary priests or the
Order of Jesus, in regarding and treating them as traitors. They had served their cause vigorously by their
teaching, they were to serve it now in their deaths.

---

[1] It is easy to supply them. They must have been the Earl of Northumberland, the Earl of Arundel, Lord Henry Howard Arundel's uncle, Lord Paget, Lord Lumley, and either Vaux or Morley.

[2] Mendoza to Philip, Sept. 7, 1581. —*MSS. Simancas*, abridged.

Campian had challenged the Protestant divines to a public discussion. He was indulged in his desire. The Tower chapel was fitted up for the engagement, and the Deans of St. Paul's and Windsor, Nowell and Day, were selected to enter the lists with him. A stage was raised for the Council and the courtiers; seats were placed for the Catholic prisoners that they might benefit by the defeat of their chief, and free access was allowed to the public. Campian was brought in under a guard. He stood for six hours arguing intricate divinity. It was a false issue, and the Government gained nothing by it. He could make a case which to Catholics appeared unanswerable; but the real question was not a theological one; it was rather was he or was he not a loyal English subject, was he or was he not engaged in recruiting soldiers for the Pope, *ad illud tempus*, for the time when the King of Scots should cross the border? To permit a controversy was to sanction his own defence that his crime was not treason but religion, and his pale face and tottering limbs showed painfully that his case had been removed already beyond the arguments of the learned deans. Thrice the adversaries engaged; thrice they failed to work conviction on each other. The appeal was not to reason any more, but to that dread arbiter to which nations refer their differences when reason fails. England had revolted from the Papacy. The Pope had reclaimed his subjects, and the God of battles was to try the issue between them. The discussion was found impolitic, and the case was remitted to the secular judges, from whose hands it ought never to have passed. The Queen was still eager to save Campian. He was promised pardon and liberty if he would consent to appear once in church. When kindness failed torture was again tried, but nothing more could be wrung from him; and the Council then determined to bring him and the other priests to trial. Some delay was necessary, for the last racking had dislocated his limbs, and he could not at once be moved.[1] At last on the 14th and 15th of November true bills were found before the grand jury of Middlesex against Campian and fourteen others, for having conspired to deprive the Queen of her style and dignity, with having come to England to seduce her subjects from their allegiance, and with having attempted to induce strangers to invade the realm. On the 20th they were brought to the bar in Westminster Hall and arraigned, Sir Christopher Wray sitting as Chief Justice. Campian was no longer in his secular masquerade dress, but in a priest's cassock, with his beard close shaven, and his face half buried in a black cap. The prisoners pleaded all Not Guilty. Campian being unable to raise his arm, two of his companions raised it for him, first kissing the broken joints.

Anderson, the Queen's Serjeant, stated the case for the Crown. Her Majesty, he said, from the day of her accession had been a merciful and tolerant princess. She had given her subjects no legitimate cause of complaint, but Pope after Pope had endeavoured to disturb the quiet of the realm. Pope Pius had caused the rebellion of the north, and had declared the Queen deposed. Pope Gregory had invaded Ireland, and now, lastly, English fugitives, who had left the country without permission, and had become the Pope's subjects, had come back to persuade others to follow their example. They had entered the country secretly. They had travelled in disguise, and under false names, pretending

---

[1] Mendoza writes on the 7th of November to Philip, that the indictment was then complete, but that the trial had been postponed.
'No habiendo sacado á juicio a Campian por estar descoyuntado y no poderse mover.'—*MSS. Simancas.*

to be laymen. The very concealment which they practised proved that they were engaged in something which they dared not acknowledge. They were charged with treason, not under the new statute, but that there might be no pretence of religious persecution, under the usual statute of Edward III.

It was equally the object of Campian to prove that they were to suffer, if condemned, not for treason but for religion. They were allowed no counsel. Campian spoke for the rest.

'We are charged with treason,' he said. 'We are no 'traitors. We are Catholics, and what is that to the 'purpose? We persuaded the people—but what then? 'We seduced no subjects from their allegiance. We 'had nothing to do with their allegiance. We are men 'dead to the world, and we travailed for the salvation 'of souls. We touched neither state nor policy. We 'had no such commission. We were told that if we 'would attend church and hear sermons we should be 'released, and it is therefore impossible that we could 'have committed treason. Our religion and our religion 'only is our crime.'

He was asked why he had gone about disguised if he had meant no harm. He admitted that it was to escape arrest. The Clerk of the Crown produced copies of an oath found in Catholic houses, disclaiming obedience to the Queen. Campian protested that he had administered no such oath; but he declined to swear to the supremacy, nor would he give a direct answer on the effect of the Papal excommunication upon the duties of Catholic subjects. He repeated the answer which he had given to the Queen, and he argued 'that the jury, 'being laymen and temporal, were unfit to decide so deep 'a matter.'

In these words he had touched the exact point at

issue. It was precisely this which the priests were to learn, that laymen were fit to decide and would decide. The national life and independence of England turned upon it, and though all the learning of the clergy, from the beginning of time, might be on the Pope's side, it was to avail him nothing.

The English Reformation was a lay revolt against clerical domination in all its forms. The clergy, from highest to lowest, were divorced from political authority, and consigned to the sphere of opinion. Evidence was produced of language used by the Jesuits to their penitents, preparing them for the time when tyranny would end and the Church would enjoy her own again. Campian, in his address, put out all his power of moving eloquence, but he was addressing bearded men, not women and excited students. A verdict of Guilty was returned against the whole party, and Wray pronounced sentence in the usual form.

'Te Deum laudamus,' exclaimed Campian; 'Te Deum confitemur.'

'This is the day which the Lord hath made,' said Sherwin; 'let us rejoice and be glad in it.'

Five days' shrift only was allowed. The execution was ordered for the 25th.

The Duke of Alençon, as will presently be seen, was again in England. The Protestants were once more violently agitated at the prospect of the Queen's marriage with him. It was considered that the punishment of the Jesuits during his stay in London would quiet the apprehensions of the country, that it would shew the Protestants that they had nothing to fear from him, and the Romanists that they had nothing to hope.[1]

---

[1] 'El apresurar la execucion destas cosas es porque se hagan en el tiempo que esta aqui M. de Alençon, y que con esto se aseguren los Pro-

A French abbé, at Mendoza's instigation, besought Alençon to intercede for Campian's life. The Duke was in a tennis court, on the point of commencing a game, when the abbé came to him. He hesitated, stroked his face for a moment, and then turning abruptly away, exclaimed, '*Play*.'

For some cause, probably Elizabeth's reluctance, the execution was deferred for a week. She could order Yorkshire peasants to be hung in batches with undisturbed composure. She could read without distress of the wholesale slaughter of Irish mothers and their babes, but each death-warrant which she signed for a person that she had herself been acquainted with cost her poignant anguish.

At length, on the 1st of December, Campian, wearing the gown which he had worn at his trial, was brought with Sherwin and Bryant out of the Tower. They had suffered their last miseries there, and Little-ease, and the scavenger's daughter, and the thumbscrew, and the rack, and the black cells, and the foul water, were parted with for ever. Peace at any rate, and, after one more pang, a painless rest lay now before them. The torture chamber brought one blessing with it—Death had ceased to be terrible.

The morning was cold and wild. They were lashed on hurdles, their hollow faces transparent with the beauty of highly wrought enthusiasm. As they were dragged along the road they were spattered with showers of mud from the horses' hoofs. Notwithstanding the weather the streets were thronged, and familiar

tratantes Ingleses y Escoceses, y descaescan los Catholicos, y que todos entiendan que el no atiende á cosas de religion, sino solo seguir la voluntad de la Reyna.'—*Don B. de Mendoza al Rey*, 7 Noviembre. *MSS. Simancas.*

as these dreadful scenes had become, the crowd was unusually excited. At Tyburn, round the gallows, more than three thousand gentlemen were assembled on horseback, and every spot of vantage ground was covered with knots of citizens. Sir Francis Knollys, Lord Charles Howard, and Sir Henry Lee, attended officially with pardons ready if the prisoners would but consent to hear a Protestant sermon, or would acknowledge in plain words that the Pope could not depose their Sovereign.

Campian, as the eldest, was allowed the privilege of dying first. He ascended the cart and spoke a few words. Criers had proclaimed that the crime was not religion but treason. 'We are come here to die,' he said, 'but we are no traitors. I am a Catholic man and 'a priest. In that faith I have lived, and in that faith 'I mean to die. If you consider my religion treason, 'then I am guilty. Other treason I never committed 'any, as God is my judge.'

'Once more then,' said Sir Francis Knollys. 'How 'do you regard the Bull against the Queen?' 'The 'Bull has been mitigated,' Campian answered, 'so that 'Catholics may regard her as their Sovereign.' 'Do 'you renounce the Pope?' said Knollys. He replied, 'I am a Catholic:' and a bystander cried out, it must be admitted, justly, 'In your Catholicism all treason is 'contained.' That false-meaning mitigation, that suspension of the Bull, *ad illud tempus*, when the invader should have come, was but to arm the rattlesnake with deadlier venom.

He began his prayers. Some one bade him pray in English. He smiled faintly, and said, 'I will pray to 'God in a language we both understand.' They told him to pray for the Queen. 'He had not offended the

'Queen,' he said, 'and he would and did pray for her.' 'For which Queen?' said Lord Howard; 'for Elizabeth the Queen?' 'Yea, for Elizabeth,' he answered, 'your Queen and mine, to whom I wish a long quiet reign and all prosperity.'

The cart was then drawn away. The executioner was about to cut him down alive according to the form of the judgment, but some one in authority bade him 'hold till the man was dead.' He was then quartered. A drop of blood spirted on the clothes of a youth named Henry Walpole, to whom it came as a divine command. Walpole, converted on the spot, became a Jesuit, and soon after met the same fate on the same spot.

Sherwin's turn came next, and then young Bryant's, and their innocent faces called out general emotion. Knollys made an earnest effort to save them. 'We know,' he said, 'that you are no contrivers and doers of treason; you are traitors by construction.' Could they but have admitted that Pope or no Pope they were Elizabeth's temporal subjects, they might have preached Catholicism till they were in their dotage, but it could not be. Sherwin explained Campian's prayers for the Queen, by praying for her conversion. Then they too had to die, and a few days later all the rest had to die who had been tried and sentenced with them.

Through the Catholic population of England there rose one long cry of exulting admiration. An arm of Campian was stolen as a relic from the place where it had been hung.[1] Parsons secured the halter, and died with it about his neck thirty years after at Valladolid. The Pope had the passion of the martyrs painted on the walls of the English College at Rome, to stir the emulation of the rising students.

---

[1] Simpson. Mendoza, Dec. 4. 1581, says a finger only.—*MSS. Simancas.*

'In their sufferings,' said Mendoza, 'they shewed
'the graces which God reserves for his most favoured
'servants. Their words, before they died, were fragrant
'of Heaven. They declared their innocence, and they
'forgave their murderers. After Campian's death it
'was seen that they had torn away his nails. The ad-
'mirable lives of these priests, and their constancy in
'bearing such cruel tortures, give them a place among
'the great martyrs of the Church of God—and that God
'permits the Catholics to be thus afflicted, and so much
'saintly blood to be shed in the realm, is a sign that ere
'long he will be pleased to restore England into the fold.'[1]

The continent rung with the story as forty-four years before it had shrieked over the deaths of More and Fisher, and the Charterhouse monks. Then too the constancy of the martyrs was a sign that the straying flock would be recovered. The flock had been brought back, but had strayed again, and was still in the wilderness. The modern reader will find it hard to judge fairly the men that ordered these things. Abhorrence of deliberate cruelty provokes abhorrence also of those who were guilty of it, and the long impotence of the Catholic clergy in England renders us incredulous of the dangers that were to be feared from them. For the rack, the thumbscrew, the Tower dungeons, and the savage details of the execution, no detestation can be too strong, no gratitude too vehement that we have left them, with stake and wheel, and red-hot pincers and the ferocious refinements of another age, long and for ever behind us. But there is a common level of humanity among contemporary civilised nations, from which there is seldom any large deviation for good or evil; and Protestant England, notwithstanding the cruel-

---

[1] Mendoza to Philip, Dec. 4.—*MSS. Simancas.*

ties to the Jesuits, was not below but above the average continental level. The torture chambers of the Inquisition were yet more horrible than the cells of the Tower, and the use of torture in England, though forbidden by the law, was inherited by the Council, through a long series of precedents. Protestant prisoners had been racked by Mary, as Catholics were racked by Elizabeth. We condemn Burghley and Walsingham, not because they were worse than Pole and Gardiner, but because they were not better, while the atrocious sentence for treason was repeated for two more centuries from the bench whenever rebel or conspirator was brought up for justice. The guilt of judicial cruelty to criminals must be distributed equally over the whole contemporary world. The mere execution of these Jesuits, if political executions can be defended at all, was as justifiable as that of the meanest villain or wildest enthusiast who ever died upon the scaffold. Treason is a crime for which personal virtue is neither protection nor excuse. To plead in condemnation of severity, either the general innocence or the saintly intentions of the sufferers, is beside the issue; and if it be lawful in defence of national independence to kill open enemies in war, it is more lawful to execute the secret conspirator who is teaching doctrines, in the name of God, which are certain to be fatal to it. The Catholics throughout Europe had made war upon Protestants. They had taught as part of their creed the duty of putting heretics to death. England had shaken off their yoke, but it had not retaliated, and although the professors of such an accursed doctrine might have been treated without injustice as public enemies, Elizabeth had left her Catholic subjects to think as they pleased so long as they would remain quiet under the law. They refused to accept her forbearance. They availed themselves of her lenity as a shelter. They conspired behind it against her throne and life, and they brought down upon themselves at last with overwhelming force the heavy hand of justice.

They imagined that the persecution would efface the memory of the Marian cruelties. Persecution was to be the beginning of their triumph. The blood of martyrs was the seed of the Church.

'What greater comfort can there be,' wrote one of them, ' than to see God work these strange wonders in ' our days, to give such rare grace of zeal, austerity of ' life, and constancy of martyrdom unto young men, ' learned men brought up in the adversaries' own ' schools, and to whom if they would have followed the ' pleasures of the world it had been lawful to have lived ' in favour and credit? This cannot come of flesh and ' blood, when the tenderest and frailest flesh passeth ' valiantly to heaven through rackings, hangings, draw- ' ings, quarterings, and through a thousand miseries.

'The cross appears, Christ doth approach,
 A comfort to us all,
For whom to suffer or to die,
 Is grace celestial.
' Be therefore of good courage now,
 In your sharp probation,
Which shall you bring to glory great,
 And mighty consolation.
' If you persevere to the end
 Of this sharp storm indeed,
You shall confound both foe and friend,
 And Heaven have for meed.'[1]

'We must think,' wrote another, 'more modestly, ' yet not less hopefully, that we have deserved a great

---

[1] MS. endorsed, 'Letters from a Jesuit to a friend on Campian's condemnation, 1581.'—*MSS. Domestic.*

'deal more punishment for our faults. Nevertheless,
'when God suffers us to receive punishment and wrong
'for his sake, it is a manifest token that he intends
'to forget our faults; and no doubt one day's suffer-
'ance here of so small grief in this behalf doth dis-
'charge a whole year's of intolerable punishment in the
'world to come. We have lost the chief pearl of Chris-
'tendom, yet we are to hope that by the shedding of
'his innocent blood God will the sooner appease his
'wrath against us; and all men are of that opinion, that
'the offence and negligence of our forefathers were so
'great, and our own sins so many, as they must needs
'be redeemed by the blood of martyrs.'[1]

When Latimer was about to die, he said that a fire would that day be kindled in England which would never be put out. That fire is burning now, not in England only, but wherever the English tongue is spoken; and the warmth of it is felt in countries where the names of the Reformers are still held in detestation. Romanism may seem to revive, but every year cuts shorter its practical power to hurt. Its hand is disarmed. It forgets and tries to deny the blood that rests upon it. A faith which is alive thrives by persecution. To trample on a decaying superstition wins sympathy for particular sufferers, but will not and cannot make that superstition live again. So far as it could pretend to be an innocent evangelisation the mission of the Jesuits was effectively ended. Stripped of disguise, it appeared thenceforward in its true colours, and lent itself avowedly to plots for assassination and rebellion. The courage of the Government brought the question to a decided issue, and every English subject now saw distinctly that he must choose between his

[1] — Eyermann to his brethren, Feb. 6, 1582.—MSS. Domestic.

country and the Pope. Campian had not failed. Catholic disaffection had obtained shape and consistency, and attainder ceased to have terrors for the knots of determined men who regarded Elizabeth as a usurper, and the Queen of Scots as their legitimate sovereign; but an increasing number of waverers fell off the national side, and even Catholics themselves can now command sufficient temper to understand and half defend the Jesuit prosecution. The latest of Campian's biographers says with a candour infinitely creditable to him:

'The eternal truths of Catholicism were made the 'vehicle for opinions about the authority of the Holy 'See which could not be held by Englishmen loyal to 'the Government; and true patriotism united to a false 'religion overcame the true religion wedded to opinions 'that were unpatriotic in regard to the liberties of Eng- 'lishmen, and treasonable to the English Government.'[1]

The vitality of a belief is measured by its practical strength. Men will make willing sacrifices for a truth of which they are firmly convinced. They will not make sacrifices for opinions which are either inherited and held without meaning, or are inconsistent with duties which they recognise as of higher obligation. The English Catholics had hitherto supported by subscription the seminaries at Rome and at Rheims. Money was wanted for these, and was wanted also for a Jesuit mission to Scotland in connexion with the general conspiracy, and for neither of these purposes was money any more to be obtained. Father Allen boasted of the lords and gentlemen whom Campian had converted. The story had another side. 'The persecution ruins us,' wrote Mendoza. 'The Catholics are crushed by the

[1] Life of Campian, by R. Simpson, p. 343.

'fines which are levied on them if absent from church.
'Some have relapsed to escape payment. Their alms
'have fallen off and scarce suffice for the prisoners.
'The cost of the seminaries grows with the increasing
'number of students. The subscriptions used to be
'large. Two gentlemen only on one occasion gave me
'300*l.* to remit to Rheims. Now the supplies have
'sunk to almost nothing, and while the stream has
'dried up, new demands rise for the priests who are to
'go to Scotland, and if they are to make themselves
'acceptable must pay their own expenses.'[1]

To the clamorous complaints which the Jesuits poured out over Europe Lord Burghley, for the satisfaction of England, condescended to reply. England first and Ireland after, he said, had rebelled at the instigation of the Papacy. Plots had been formed to assassinate the Queen, and she and her advisers had been made the objects of venomous libels. Priests, commissioned by the Pope, had stolen into the realm to seduce subjects from their allegiance, and some of them had justly suffered death for maintaining and adhering to the Queen's capital enemy. Every one of them had been spared, who, after condemnation, would consent to admit that the Pope had no right to deprive her, 'such 'was her Majesty's unwillingness to shed blood.' They pretended that they had been sent by their superiors to inform men's consciences on points of religion, but their real object was to win them to allow the Pope's authority, that 'when they should be thereto called,' 'they might hold themselves warranted to take arms.' The priests might colour their proceedings with professions of devotion in religion, but the Queen's duty was to maintain the peace of the realm, to prevent the

[1] Mendoza to Philip, Nov. 19, 1581.—*MSS. Simancas.*

torrents of blood which were always shed in civil war, and she had a right therefore to impeach their practices by sword and law. Many of her subjects entertained and openly professed opinions which were not those of the Established Church, but being loyal to her Majesty and ready to resist any foreign force, though sent by the Pope himself, they had not been interfered with. Those only had suffered who had maintained the Bull of Pope Pius, and the libels against the Queen for religious persecution were therefore false and scandalous. If Popes might absolve subjects from their allegiance, no kingdom could stand but with the Pope's pleasure. The Queen intended to maintain her lawful authority, and England, which had survived the excommunication of Henry VIII. would survive the repetition of it against his daughter.[1]

Allen answered Burghley. At the very time when Elizabeth's assassination was advocated publicly in the Rheims pulpits, he ventured to make a distinct denial of the charge of treason. He insisted that his missionaries had been innocent preachers of a religion of peace, and that those who had suffered were martyrs in the holiest sense. The persecution of the Protestants under Mary he defended as agreeable to law, while the punishment of the Jesuits was murder. He declared the Papal supremacy to be a point of conscience, and he was safe in saying therefore that they had confined themselves to teaching religion. He omitted what alone would have given weight to his argument, a frank confession that Catholics were the subjects of the prince under whom they were born, and that neither Pope nor Council could absolve them from their obligations of obedience.

[1] Execution of Justice, condensed.

He overshot his mark. Denunciation could not alter fact, and religion was not permitted to consecrate rebellion. The hostility of the English people, which was originally confined to the temporal pretensions of the Roman bishop, became extended to his creed; and if one result of the mission of the Jesuits was the formation of a dangerous conspiracy, another was the alienation and wafting over into Protestantism of many a knight and gentleman who had continued Catholic, till to be a Catholic was to cease to be an Englishman.

CHAPTER XXIX.

WHILE the Prince of Parma was recovering the Low Countries town by town; while d'Aubigny was destroying the English party in Scotland; while Ireland was in flames and the Jesuits were undermining Elizabeth's throne at home,—she was herself following a policy exclusively her own, in which she was encouraged only by those who secretly desired her destruction—a policy which in the opinion of every one of her loyal ministers was as perilous as it was discreditable, and had but one merit, that it cost nothing to the treasury.

So long as France could be prevented from allying itself with Spain, she considered that she was safe from invasion; and Burghley and Sussex had desired a close and permanent combination between France and England, cemented by the much talked of marriage. Walsingham, on the other hand, who had witnessed the massacre of St. Bartholomew, and shared the horror with which the English Protestants regarded the house of Valois, preferred a frank and honest league with the Princes of the Reformation, with legitimate and open war. He would have sent a hundred corsairs to the sea to sweep up Spanish commerce, lent money to the King of Navarre, landed an army in the Netherlands, and helped Morton to expel d'Aubigny.

Between two honourable courses Elizabeth chose a

third, as better suited to her circumstances and her temperament. She left Morton and the Prince of Orange to their fate. She declined to offend the French Government by assisting the Huguenots, and she fell back once more on her old schemes. Once more, she set herself to amuse Catherine de Médici with the hope that she would marry the Duke of Alençon, to play with him, to advance, to draw back, and meanwhile to use the chances of the political game, to tempt France, by the prospect of securing her, into open hostility with Philip. Her ministers, who were the instruments of her diplomacy, told her in unconcealed disgust that they would rather be sent to the Tower;[1] but she went her own way, dragging them with her through honour and dishonour; and her singular fortune saved her after all from consequences which to every one but herself appeared inevitable.

In January 1580 Lord Burghley believed, as has been seen, that the marriage was to be mentioned no more, and he had addressed to his mistress a sad but earnest letter of advice in the isolation to which he believed that she had reduced herself. Alençon had come and gone. A provisional treaty had been drawn and signed. M. Simier and his brother commissioners had returned to Paris, and it had been arranged that if after two months the treaty remained unratified, the negotiation should be considered at an end. The two months had gone and the Queen had given no sign. She herself, it is possible, then regarded the game as played out; but she wished to throw, if possible, the blame of the rupture upon France. She wrote herself to Alençon. She sent

---

[1] 'I told her Majesty when she chose to employ me in this way that I should repute it a greater favour to be committed to the Tower, unless her Majesty may grow more certain in her resolutions. Instead of amity I fear her Highness shall receive enmity.'—*Walsingham to Burghley*, Aug. 21, 1581. Printed in Digges.

Sir Edward Stafford to Paris with fresh conditions, and the French Court, to her extreme embarrassment, accepted everything.[1]

A special cause had arisen, which made an affront to France at that moment peculiarly dangerous. News had arrived of the performances of Francis Drake in the Pacific, which might render nugatory all Elizabeth's efforts to avoid war with Spain. It is time to return to the history of the extraordinary expedition which laid the foundation of the naval empire of England. It had been undertaken as part of a general policy which had been immediately afterwards abandoned. Spanish interference in England was supposed to be imminent, and the Queen, who dreaded the cost of war, yet believed that it was about to be forced upon her, had been brought in a moment of resolution to consent to a preliminary act of indirect hostility which promised to be enormously lucrative.

Intellectually vacillating, yet delighting in enterprise and energy, she had found in Drake a man after her own heart, whom she could disown without fear that he would resent her affected displeasure. She herself and the Earl of Leicester provided the larger part of the funds; a company of adventurers found the rest. The first object was to show Philip that he was vulnerable where he held himself most secure, and frighten him into consenting to a general peace;[2] the second to seize some

---

[1] 'I find there shall be no shew of breach made of their parts. They think they have the Queen at an advantage, and there they will keep her.'—*Stafford to Walsingham*, Jan. 28, 1579-80. *MSS. France.*

[2] 'Le aseguraba ol Drake que pondria en estado las cosas de la carrera de las Indias que V. M⁴ le embiase, como dicen aqui, le blanche signet, para que ella acordase las condiciones que quisiese en el capitular sobre esto y las demas cosas que á ella y su corona le pudiesen estar bien.'—*Don Bernardino de Mendoza al Rey*, Enero 15, 1581. *MSS. Simancas.*

handsome store of plunder, to be useful in itself, or at any rate as a material guarantee. If excuse was wanted for sending ships into the South Seas it could be alleged that America was no patrimony of Spain, that all the world had a right to share in its treasures; and that the mere fact of the Spaniards having compelled Indian slaves to dig the gold out of the earth gave them no exclusive right to the possession of it. There was no clause in the treaties between Spain and England which prohibited English subjects from trading or cruising in those waters. The laws of Europe had no place in the western hemisphere, and Sir Christopher Hatton gave his first recorded legal opinion, that, although privateers might go there at their own risk and might be sent to the bottom if the Spaniards could catch them, yet if they returned safe the Spanish Government could make no legal claim on the Queen, either for their punishment or the restitution of their spoils.[1]

To Drake himself, all that he might do appeared more than justified. He was the avenger of the English seamen who had perished in Mexican dungeons, on the Cadiz galleys, or had been tortured or burnt to death at Seville. The Inquisition had too often evaded its promises, and had treated the engagements of Philip and Alva as not more binding on them than things of air. To a Spanish ecclesiastic, to be suspected of heresy was in itself sufficient to deserve death. Poor wretches who had fallen into their hands had been tortured into madness, had

---

[1] 'Han tratado Leicester y Hatton que para no castigar á Drake en su persona ni hacer restitucion del robo, tienen una buena escusa, que V. Mag.^d no tiene prohibido por ningun aliga ny intercursos que tiene con esta corona que no vayan los Ingleses á las Indias, por lo cual pueden hacer el viage, poniendose el riesgo que corren si los toman alla, pero que volviendo libres por no haber contrato sobre ello. no se puede pedir á la Reyna los castigue.'—*Don B. de Mendoza al Rey*, Octubre 23, 1580. *MSS. Simancas.*

hung themselves or hurled themselves out of their windows, and been dashed in pieces.[1] This was sufficient motive for Drake, and was a better excuse for retaliation than ambiguous theories of property in the Indian seas.

The reader will desire a more particular account of the person who was to play so large a part in the approaching struggle for the sovereignty of the ocean.

Francis Drake was born near Tavistock in the year 1545.[2] His father was a tenant of the House of Bedford, occupying lands which had belonged to the Abbey of Tavistock, and was related by marriage to the Hawkinses of Plymouth. He was a Protestant, and must have been held in favour by the Russells, for the young Francis was godson of the second Earl, after whom he was named. Trouble rising in the neighbourhood under the Six Articles Act, the Drakes were driven out of Devonshire, and went to Chatham, where, on the accession of Edward, the old man, having a gift that way, became a preacher among the sailors of the King's fleet, and afterwards taking orders, was made Vicar of Upnor, on the Medway. Being brought up among seafaring people Francis took early to the water. He served his time as an apprentice in a channel coaster, and his master, who had been struck with his character, left the vessel to him in his will when he died. He was then twenty-one. His kinsman, John Hawkins, was fitting out his third expedition to the Spanish main, and young Drake, with a party of his Kentish friends, went to Plymouth and joined him. The adventure ended in the disaster at St. John de Ulloa; Hawkins, Drake, and a handful of their

---

[1] Relacion del punto que toca á los Ingleses que estan presos en Santorcas, 1579.—MSS. Simancas.

[2] Drake's early history soon became mythical. Every variety of account is given of his origin. Camden, whom I follow, says that 'he relates no more than was told him by Drake himself.'

comrades, barely escaped with their lives, and Drake at least lost all that he possessed.

He was soon upon his feet again. In 1572, as has been already related, 'he made himself whole with the 'Spaniards,' by seizing a convoy of bullion at Panama, and on that occasion having seen the South Pacific from the mountains, 'he fell on his knees and prayed God 'that he might one day navigate those waters,' which no English keel as yet had furrowed.

The time and the opportunity had come. He was now in the prime of his strength, thirty-two years old, of middle height, with crisp brown hair, a broad high forehead; grey steady eyes, unusually long; small ears, tight to the head; the mouth and chin slightly concealed by the moustache and beard, but hard, inflexible and fierce. His dress, as he appears in his portrait, is a loose dark seaman's shirt, belted at the waist. About his neck is a plaited cord with a ring attached to it, in which, as if the attitude was familiar, one of his fingers is slung, displaying a small, delicate, but long and sinewy hand. When at sea he wore a scarlet cap with a gold band, and was exacting in the respect with which he required to be treated by his crew.

Such was Francis Drake when he stood on the deck of the Pelican in Plymouth harbour, in November, 1577. The squadron with which he was preparing to sail into a chartless ocean, and invade the dominions of the King of Spain, consisted of his own ship, of a hundred and twenty tons, the size of the smallest class of our modern Channel schooners, two barques of fifty and thirty tons each, a second ship as it was called, the Elizabeth, of eighty tons, not larger than a common revenue cutter, and a pinnace, hardly more than a boat, intended to be burnt if it could not bear the seas, which had brought from London a Puritan minister who could talk Spanish.[1] These vessels, with a hundred and sixty-four men, composed the force. The object of the expedition was kept as far as possible a secret. Some of the party believed they were going to the Mediterranean. Others supposed that it was to be a voyage of discovery into the southern hemisphere. But the armament betrayed that danger was looked for of some kind. The Pelican carried twenty brass and iron guns. She had others as ballast in her hold, with heavy stores of cartridges, 'wildfire, chainshot, guns, 'pistols, bows, and other weapons in great abundance.'[2] Curiosity was provoked by preparations so unusually warlike, and it was not long before the traitors at the Court penetrated the mystery. The refugees sent warning to Philip,[3] and Mendoza, having discovered that the squadron was going certainly to the coast of Peru, bade his friends at Madrid set the Viceroy on his guard, and direct him to sink every vessel that he could catch, with every living thing on board. If there was any mercy shewn the Indies would never be at peace.[4]

---

[1] Mendoza considered this minister the most pernicious feature in the expedition. 'En los naos,' he wrote, ' que he scripto que partiéron á robar á la carrera de las Indias he venido á descubrir que embió una muy pequena un consejero desta Reyna, grandisimo bellaco y Puritano terrible, por solo embiar en ella un ministro que hablaba la lengua española, con intencion de que se quemase á las armadas, armando el hereje para solo este efecto el navio. No he podido entender el nombre del predicante, lo qual procuraré con toda la diligencia, pues es de tanta importancia atajar el passo para que no entre semejante pestilencia en aquella tierra.'—*Mendoza á Cayas*, 7 Junio, 1579. *MSS. Simancas*.

[2] Deposition taken by a Spanish officer in the Indies touching Mr. Drake. Contemporary translation.—*MSS. Spain. Rolls House*.

[3] N. Sanders to Philip, July 15, 1578.—*MSS. Simancas*.

[4] 'Convendria que mandase V. M⁴ resolutamente que cualquier navio que se tomase se eche á fondo sin escapar cosa viviente; porque si se usa de misericordia con ellos, jamás dexaran de intentarlo, y las fuerças que van no son tan grandes que no se pueda hacer esto.'—*Descifrado de Don Bernardino*, Julio 20, 1578. *MSS. Ibid.*

Drake well knew the fate which awaited him if he was taken. His small vessels were swift sailers, and he trusted to his skill and speed. It was lucky for him, however, that Mendoza's counsels were neglected, and that the officers of the New World were allowed to sleep on in security. On the 15th of November,[1] the expedition sailed from Plymouth Sound. It was encountered immediately by a storm, in which the Pelican lost her mainmast. She ran with her consorts into Falmouth, put back to Plymouth to refit, when the weather moderated, and cleared away once more on the 13th of December. The second time all went well. A rapid run of twelve days brought them down to Mogador, and after staying four weeks at the Cape de Verde Islands, trading with the natives, and picking up and rifling a few vessels from Spain and Portugal, they struck across the Atlantic and made the coast of South America on the 5th of April in latitude 33° south. Thence following the shore they entered the Plate River, finding fresh water to their astonishment at the ship's side in 54 fathoms. Not caring to waste time in exploring, they put to sea again, and immediately after one of the barques disappeared.

It has been mentioned that the officer second in command was a Mr. Thomas Doughty. Whenever the veil that overhangs Elizabeth's Court is lifted, treacherous influences are seen invariably at work. Mary Stuart, Philip, and the Jesuits had each their instruments in the Council or the Privy Chamber. The struggle between the two great parties in the State was nowhere hotter than in the immediate neighbourhood of the Queen, and every ambassador sent to a foreign Court, every general in command of an expedition, found some one attached to him whose business was to tie his hands and thwart his

---

[1] The 25th, as we at present reckon.

enterprises. It is likely, though there is no proof of it, that Doughty was one of this venomous breed. His brother was involved afterwards in Catholic conspiracies. He himself had a grudge against Leicester, whose fortune was largely embarked in Drake's venture. At any rate, from some cause the man had become discontented and mutinous, and on leaving the river slipped away from the rest of the fleet. The example was extremely dangerous. The four remaining vessels dispersed in search of him. He was overtaken, and transferred with his crew to the Pelican. His ship was fired and left behind. The mischief, however, was not over. The offender gave new cause of suspicion, and success in such an adventure as Drake's being desperate without unity and discipline, he found it necessary to use prompt measures. On the 20th of June he put into Port St. Julian, a harbour on the coast of Patagonia. The first object which met the eye on landing was a gibbet, left there by Magellan, and the skeletons of a party of mutineers who had met their fate there. In that wild scene, in the dead of winter, a court-martial was extemporised on the shore. 'The 'crews of the ships were called together, and acquainted 'with the particulars of the cause.' Doughty himself confessed to something, and evidence was produced of more. The desertion was a palpable fact which could not be denied.

'Which when our general saw,' wrote an eyewitness,[1] 'although his private affection to Mr. Doughty, as he 'then in the presence of us all sacredly protested, was 'great, yet the care he had of the state of the voyage, of 'the expectation of her Majesty and of the honour of his 'country, did more touch him, as indeed it ought, than 'the private respect of one man: so that the cause being

[1] Hakluyt, vol. iv. p. 232.

'throughly heard, and all things done in good order,
'as near as might be to the course of our laws in
'England, it was concluded that Mr. Doughty should
'receive punishment according to the quality of the
'offence. He, seeing no remedy but patience for him-
'self, desired before his death to receive the communion,
'which he did at the hands of Mr. Fletcher, our minister,
'and our general accompanied him in that holy action.
'Which being done, and the place of execution being
'made ready, he having embraced our general and taken
'leave of all his company with prayers for the Queen's
'Majesty and our realm, in quiet sort laid his head to
'the block where he ended his life. This being done our
'general made divers speeches to the whole company,
'persuading us to unity, obedience, love, and regard of
'our voyage, and for the better confirmation thereof
'willed every man the next Sunday following to pre-
'pare himself to receive the communion as Christian
'brethren and friends ought to do, which was done in
'very reverend sort; and so with good contentment
'every man went about his business.'[1]

---

[1] 'There wanted not some,' says Camden, 'who gave out that Drake had a charge from Leicester to make away Doughty by any colour whatsoever, for that he had reported abroad that the Earl of Essex was made away by the cunning practices of Leicester.' The infamous character of Leicester gave occasion and presumptive credibility to many dark suggestions about him. Mendoza, however, who inquired minutely into every particular of Drake's voyage, mentions the execution and the causes of it, making no allusion to the favourite, but saying merely that the men were terrified by the storms near Cape Horn; and that there was a mutiny of which Doughty was the leader. He adds, on the authority of Winter, that Drake himself was the executioner:—'Á la entrada del entrecho empeçáron á tener grandes tormentos, que fué ocasion de amotinarse los mas marineros, no queriendo proseguir el viage. El Drake entendió ser la principal causa dello un gentilhombre ingles que iba en su nao, y le prendió y puso cargo, haciendo juezes á los propios marineros, que le condenáron á muerte, y no queriendo ninguno darselo, fué el propio Drake el executor, cortandole por sus manos la cabeça, y proseguió

The perils of the voyage were now about to commence. No Englishman had as yet passed Magellan's Straits. Cape Horn was unknown. Tierra del Fuego was supposed to be part of a solid continent which stretched unbroken to the Antarctic Pole. A single narrow channel was the only access to the Pacific then believed to exist. There were no charts, no records of past experiences. It was known that Magellan had gone through, but that was all. It was the wildest and coldest season of the year, and the vessels in which the attempt was to be made were mere cockleshells. They were taken on shore, overhauled and scoured, the rigging looked to, and the sails new bent. On the 17th of August, answering to the February of the northern hemisphere, all was once more in order. Drake sailed from Port St. Julian, and on the 20th entered the Straits, and felt his way between the walls of mountain 'in extreme cold with frost and snow continually.' To relieve the crews who were tried by continual boat work and heaving the lead in front of the ships, they were allowed occasional halts at the islands, where they amused and provisioned themselves with killing infinite seals and penguins. Everything which they saw, birds, beasts, trees, climate, country, were strange, wild, and wonderful. After three weeks' toil and anxiety they had accomplished the passage, and found themselves in the open Pacific.[1] But they found also that it was no peaceful ocean into which they had entered, but the stormiest they had ever encountered. Their vessels were now reduced to three; the pinnace had been left behind at Port St. Julian, and there remained only the Pelican, the Elizabeth, and the thirty-ton cutter. In-

---

su viage del estrecho.'—*Descifrada de Don Bernardino*, 10 Junio, 1579. *MSS. Simancas.*   [1] Sept. 6.

stantly that they emerged out of the Straits they were caught in a gale which swept them six hundred miles to the south-west. For six weeks they were battered to and fro, in bitter cold and winds which seemed as if they blew in those latitudes for ever. The cutter went down in the fearful seas, carrying her crew with her. The Elizabeth and the Pelican were separated. The bravest sailor might well have been daunted at such a commencement, and Winter recovering the opening again and believing Drake to be lost, called a council in his cabin and proposed to return to England. They had agreed to meet, if they were parted, on the coast in the latitude of Valparaiso. The men, with better heart than their commander, desired to keep the appointment. But those terrible weeks had sickened Winter. The way home lay temptingly open, and if lost a second time might never be recovered. He overruled the opinion of the rest, re-entered the Straits, and reached England in the following June. Drake meanwhile had found shelter among the islands of Tierra del Fuego. He waited there till the advancing season brought milder weather, and amused himself meanwhile with studying the habits of the natives, who swarmed about his ship in their canoes stark naked, men and women, notwithstanding the terrible climate.

At length spring brought fair winds and smooth seas, and running up the coast and looking about for her consort, the Pelican or Golden Hind—for she had both names—fell in with an Indian fisherman, who informed Drake that in the harbour of Valparaiso, already a small Spanish settlement, there lay a great galleon which had come from Peru. Galleons were the fruit that he was in search of. He sailed in, and the Spanish seamen, who had never yet seen a stranger in those waters, ran up their flags, beat their drums, and prepared a banquet for their supposed countrymen. The Pelican shot up alongside. The English sailors leapt on board, and one 'Thomas Moore,' a lad from Plymouth, began the play with knocking down the first man that he met, saluting him in Spanish as he fell, and crying out 'Abajo, 'perro'—'Down, dog, to ——.' The Spaniards, overwhelmed with surprise, began to cross and bless themselves. One sprung overboard and swam ashore; the rest were bound and stowed away under the hatches while the ship was rifled. The beginning was not a bad one. Wedges of gold were found weighing four hundred pounds, besides miscellaneous plunder. The settlement which was visited next was less productive, for the inhabitants had fled, taking their valuables with them. The chapel, however, yielded something. Mr. Fletcher's provision for the sacrament was enriched by a chalice, two cruets, and an altar cloth. A few pipes of wine, some logs of cedar, and a Greek pilot who knew the way to Lima completed the booty.

Leaving Valparaiso to recover from its astonishment, the corsairs, as the Spaniards termed them, went on and landed next at Tarapaca, where silver bullion was brought down from the mountains to be shipped for Panama. It was as when men set foot for the first time on some shore where the forms of their race have never before been seen, and the animals come fearlessly round them, and the birds perch upon their hands, ignorant as yet of the deadly nature of the beings in whom they trust so rashly. The colonists of the New World, when they saw a sail approaching, knew no misgiving, and never dreamt that it could be other than a friend. The silver bars lay piled at the Tarapaca pier;

by their side the weary labourers who had brought them from the mines were peacefully sleeping, or if they heard the clash of the moving metal supposed that their comrades had arrived for their lading. There was no gratuitous cruelty in Drake; he was come for the treasure of Peru, and beyond seizing his plunder he did not care to injure the people. As the last bars were being stowed away in his boats a train of llamas appeared bringing from the hills a second freight as rich as the first. This too was transferred to the Pelican. Four hundred thousand ducats' worth of silver were taken in one afternoon.

Arica came next—Arica, the port of Potosi, where fifty-seven blocks of the same precious metal were added to the store; and from thence they made haste to Lima, where the largest booty was looked for. They found that they had just missed it. Twelve ships lay at anchor in the port without arms, without crews, and with their sails on shore. In all of these they discovered but a few chests of reals and some bales of silk and linen. A thirteenth, called by the seamen the Cacafuego, but christened in her baptism 'Our Lady of the 'Conception,' had sailed for the Isthmus a few days before, taking with her all the bullion which the mines had yielded for the season. She had been literally ballasted with silver, and carried also several precious boxes of gold and jewels.

Not a moment was lost. The cables of the ships at Lima were cut, and they were left to drive on shore to prevent pursuit; and then away sped the Pelican due north, with every stitch of her canvas spread. A gold chain was promised to the first man who caught sight of the Cacafuego. A sail was seen the second day of the chase: it was not the vessel which they were in pursuit of, but the prize was worth the having. They took eighty pounds' weight of gold in wedges, the purest which they yet had seen. They took a great gold crucifix set with emeralds as large as pigeons' eggs. They were carrying off the ship herself, but the delay had given time to two half-armed Spanish cruisers to overtake them, which the Viceroy of Callao, as soon as he had recovered from his amazement, dispatched in chase. Not caring, therefore, to keep their prize, they left it to join its friends. The cruisers, not liking the report which they received, went back to Lima for more guns and men, and then came slowly up the coast again, but too late to overtake the English rover.[1]

For eight hundred miles the Pelican flew on. At length, one degree to the north of the line, off Quito, and close to the shore, a look-out on the mast-head cried out that he saw the chase and claimed the promised chain; she was recognised by peculiarities in her sails, of which they had received exact information at Lima. There lay the Cacafuego; if they could take her their work would be done, and they might go home in triumph. She was several miles ahead of them; if she guessed their character she would run in under the land, and they might lose her. It was afternoon: several hours remained of daylight, and Drake did not wish to come up with her till dark.

The Pelican sailed two feet to the Cacafuego's one, and dreading that her speed might rouse suspicion, he filled his empty wine casks with water and trailed

---

[1] 'Sabido esto por el dicho Virrey, envió tras él dos navios armados, y habiendose estos vuelto con el navio que el dicho Ingles llevava robado por no ir bien aderescados para poderle seguir, los tornó á aderescar y enviar en su seguimiento hasta Panama.'—*Relacion de lo que se sabe del Corsario Ingles por cartas del Virrey de Peru, de 18 de Hebrero y 21 de Março, 1579. MSS. Simancas.*

them astern.[1] The chase meanwhile unsuspecting, and glad of company on a lonely voyage, slackened sail and waited for her slow pursuer. The sun sunk low, and at last set into the ocean, and then when both ships had become invisible from the land the casks were hoisted in, the Pelican was restored to her speed, and shooting up within a cable's length of the Cacafuego, hailed to her to run into the wind. The Spanish commander, not understanding the meaning of such an order, paid no attention to it. The next moment the corsair opened her ports, fired a broadside, and brought his mainmast about his ears. His decks were cleared by a shower of arrows, with one of which he was himself wounded. In a few minutes more he was a prisoner, and his ship and all that it contained was in the hands of the English. The wreck was cut away, the ship cleared, and her head turned to the sea; by daybreak even the line of the Andes had become invisible, and at leisure, in the open ocean, the work of rifling began. The full value of the plunder taken in this ship was never accurately confessed. It remained a secret between Drake and the Queen. In a schedule afterwards published, he acknowledged to have found in the Cacafuego alone twenty-six tons of silver bullion, thirteen chests of coined silver, and almost a hundredweight of gold. But as will be seen by and by, this was only so much as the Spaniards could prove to have been on board. There was a further mass, the amount of which it is im-

---

[1] 'Y porque su nao yba algo delantero y no navegarse tanto, echó cables por popa con botiguas llenas de agua.' *Relacion del viage de F. Drac, Corsario Ingles, cual dió el Piloto Nuño de Silva. MSS. Madrid.* Hakluyt obtained a copy of this curious narrative, but the translator was a bad Spanish scholar, and imagined that the water casks were hung overboard 'as a pretty device to make the ship sail more swiftly' — an indifferent compliment to Drake's seamanship.

possible to guess, of which no account was ever rendered, and 'a great store' besides, of pearls, emeralds, and diamonds, supposed to have been of enormous richness. The Spanish Government roughly estimated their loss afterwards at a million and a half of ducats, which Elizabeth did not pretend to be exaggerated.[1] The total treasure appropriated was perhaps, therefore, considerably greater.

Leaving part of his crew in possession, and removing the master of the Cacafuego on board the Pelican, Drake, being 'greatly satisfied,' did not care to remain longer in the neighbourhood of the scene of his exploit. The two ships sailed leisurely northward side by side. San Juan de Anton, so the master was named, remained with his captor till he had recovered from his wound, and making the best of his misfortune, spent his time in studying the character of the corsairs into whose hands he had so strangely fallen.

One of the Englishmen—the heretic minister, probably, whose presence in the expedition so distressed Mendoza —spoke excellent Spanish. Drake must have known something of the language also. They conducted San Juan over the ship, which, though shewing signs of rough service, he reported as being admirably appointed, thoroughly seaworthy, provided with all kinds of arms, and not with arms only, but with mattocks, pickaxes, smiths' tools, everything that would be needed either on land or water. The crew were reduced to eighty-five all told; some had been drowned, some had gone back with Winter, some had died; of those remaining, fifty were 'men of war,' the rest, 'young fellows, ship's boys, 'and such like.' He observed that Drake 'was greatly

---

[1] The gold ducat was equal to about nine shillings and sixpence.

'feared and reverenced by all on board.' A sentinel stood always at his cabin door. He 'was served with 'sound of trumpets and other instruments at his meals.'

No mystery was made of the plunder which had been taken elsewhere. The minister shewed San Juan the great crucifix with the emeralds, and asked him if he could seriously believe it was God, or if it was God, why it had made no resistance to being taken. 'God,' he said with instructive solemnity, 'was a spirit in heaven, 'and images and ceremonies were idle mockery.' Drake too spoke freely of his voyage, telling the Spaniard where he had been, and the adventures which he had encountered on the way. San Juan asked how he intended to return to England. He pointed to a chart of the globe. There was the way he had come, the way by China and the Cape of Good Hope, and there was 'a third way,' but that San Juan said 'the captain 'would not acquaint him withal.'

The Spaniard enquired whether his master was at war with England. Drake answered evasively, that he had the Queen's commission for what he had done, that the spoil which he had taken was for her, and not for himself. But he said afterwards that the Viceroy of New Spain had robbed him and his kinsman Hawkins, and that he was but making good his losses; and then touching the sore to the quick, he added:

'I know the Viceroy will send for thee to inform 'himself of my proceedings. Thou mayst tell him he 'shall do well to put no more Englishmen to death, and 'to spare those four that he has in his hands, for if he 'do execute them, they shall cost the lives of two 'thousand Spaniards, whom I will hang and send him 'their heads.'[1]

---

[1] Depositions taken in the West Indies by the King of Spain's Ministers. — *MSS. Spain*, 1580. *Rolls House.*

After a week's stay in the Pelican, San Juan was restored to the empty Cacafuego and allowed to depart, with an ironical protection against further molestation, should he fall in with Winter. On his way back he met the two Spanish cruisers who had followed up from Lima. They had been ordered if they could not take Drake to convoy San Juan. They had come too late. They were now armed to the teeth, they had two hundred men, picked Spanish sailors, and a consort had joined them from Panama. They went in chase, and the Pelican being under easy sail they came up with her, but though three to one their courage failed when within gunshot. The indifference with which Drake allowed them to approach frightened them. They turned about and 'returned for more aid.'

The Viceroy, furious at their cowardice, put the officers under arrest and sent the ships in pursuit once more with peremptory orders to fight. A special messenger was dispatched across the Atlantic to Philip, and couriers carried the alarm along the coast of the Isthmus. The third route which Drake had hinted at was guessed to be no sea route at all. It was thought that he meant to leave his ship and transport his plunder over the mountains, and either build some vessel in Honduras to carry him to England, or find a consort which had been sent out to meet him.[1]

Drake's own views were more original. He imagined, like most other English seamen, that there was a passage to the north corresponding to Magellan's Straits, of which Frobisher conceived that he had found the eastern entrance. He went on, therefore, at his leisure towards the coast of Mexico, intending to follow the shore till he found it. Another ship coming from China crossed

---
[1] Relacion de lo que se sabe del Corsario Ingles.—*MSS. Simancas.*

him on his way loaded with silks and porcelain. He took the best of the freight with a golden falcon and another superb emerald. Then needing fresh water he touched at the Spanish settlement of Guatulco. His proceedings were humorously prompt. The Alcaldes were in session trying a batch of negroes. An English boat's crew appeared suddenly in the court, tied the judges hand and foot and swept them off to the Pelican, where they were held as hostages till the water casks were filled, and the houses of the principal citizens had been inspected and rifled. The prisoners were then set on shore with a Portuguese pilot who had been picked up at the Cape de Verde Islands, and for whom there was no further use.

The work of plunder was nearly over. Again sailing north, the Pelican fell in with a Spanish nobleman who was going out as governor to the Philippines. He was detained a few hours and relieved of his finery, and then, says one of the party, 'Our general thinking 'himself both in respect of his private injuries received 'from the Spaniards, as also their contempt and indigni- 'ties offered to our country and prince in general, suffi- 'ciently satisfied and revenged, and supposing her 'Majesty would rest contented with this service, began 'to consider the best way for his country.'[1]

The first necessity was a complete repair of the Pelican's hull. Before the days of copper sheathing, the ships' bottoms grew foul with weed; the great barnacles formed in clusters, and stopped their speed, and the sea-worms bored holes into the planking. Twenty thousand miles of unknown water lay between Drake and Plymouth Sound, and he was not a man to run idle risks. Running on till he had left the furthest Spanish station far to the south, he put into the Bay

---

[1] Printed by Hakluyt.

of Canoa in Lower California. There he laid his ship on shore, set up forge and workshop, and refitted her with a month's labour from stem to stern.[1]

Leaving him thus occupied, we must glance for a moment at the effect produced in England and Spain by the news of his performances. The fastest vessel at Portobello carried the messenger of the Viceroy of New Spain to Cadiz, and before the summer all Europe was ringing with the fame of the English freebooter. The Viceroy's letter found Philip intensely occupied with the annexation of Portugal. The Cardinal King was at the point of death, and the available force of Spain by sea and land was being held in readiness to use the opportunity.

Terribly agitated, yet unwilling to add a war with England to his other responsibilities, Philip enclosed the letter to Mendoza. Beyond the insult to the Spanish nation, the loss of so much treasure was at the moment particularly inconvenient. The corsair who had pillaged the Indies might repeat his insolence on the coast of Spain itself, where wealthy towns lay open and unguarded. 'It is a most extraordinary proceeding,' Philip wrote; 'learn all that you can about it. The spoil 'it is likely will be brought to England. Advise me 'instantly when you hear that the pirate has arrived.'[2]

England was as much surprised and almost as much disturbed as Spain. The London merchants trading to Cadiz expected that their ships and goods would be arrested in reprisal, and went in alarm to the Council. The Council told them that Drake was a private adventurer, and that the King of Spain could not hold them responsible because a single English subject had

---

[1] March 14 to April 16, 1579.   [2] Cayas to Mendoza, Aug. 1579.

committed piracy. They were but half satisfied, and the rate of insurance rose heavily.[1] No such incisive measures, however, were to be feared from Philip. Slow and decorous always, he was especially unwilling to act hastily with Portugal on his hands. He wrote again saying that he had sent ships to watch Magellan's Straits, and that there was a chance that Drake's career might be ended before he could reach England. If this should be the case, nothing further need be said. Otherwise, and if he came back in safety, Mendoza was instructed to lay a formal complaint before Elizabeth, of whose complicity the King affected to have no suspicion, to dwell upon the enormity of the proceeding, and firmly, but gently,[2] to require the restoration of the stolen property and the punishment of the offender. 'He understood,' the King continued, 'that English 'adventurers gave securities for good behaviour before 'sailing on their voyages, and he felt assured that the 'Queen would assist in enforcing their obligations. For 'himself he had done everything in his power to facili- 'tate commerce between England and Spain. English 'seamen still complained that their boxes were searched 'by the Inquisition, but it was merely to prevent the 'introduction of forbidden books. Their other griev- 'ances had been all removed, and they had nothing to 'fear, notwithstanding the present provocation, but 'might come and go as usual.'[3]

Nothing could prove more clearly how anxious Philip was to avoid a quarrel. The Inquisition, however, was less innocent than he pretended. Great naval preparations had notoriously been made at Cadiz. The Cardinal

---

[1] Mendoza to Cayas, Sept. 13, 1579.—*MSS. Simancas.*

[2] 'Haga con la Reyna muy encarecidos officios.'—*Puntos para responder á Don B. de Mendoza*, Dec. 1579.—*MSS. Simancas.*

[3] *Ibid.*

King of Portugal was not yet dead, and by some persons the Portuguese succession was supposed to be a mere pretence to cover an intended invasion of England and Ireland. Until Drake returned Mendoza was ordered to avoid appearance of menace, but his moderation upon a subject so notorious was in itself suspicious. England was arming also. The fleet was being set in order at Chatham. The musters and trainbands were drilling in town and country. Elizabeth was elaborately polite to Mendoza, but her conscience telling her how deeply she was implicated in Drake's performances, she determined to wheedle out of him the secret of his master's intentions. She invited him to a bear-bait.[1] She talked politics to him in the intervals of the performance. She spoke of France, Italy, Germany, of all the world. At length after circling about the real subject she came to the great fleet at Cadiz. 'She understood,' she said, 'that six thousand additional seamen were taken up, 'and that no sovereign in Christendom had ever had so 'powerful an armament afloat. Ut quid tot sumptus!' she exclaimed, turning suddenly upon him; 'what can 'such an expense be for?' 'Nemo novit nisi cui Pater 'revelavit,' replied Mendoza, ironically: 'of that know-'eth no man save he to whom the Father has revealed 'it.' 'Ah,' said the Queen, 'I see you have been some-'thing more than a light dragoon;[2] they tell me you 'have views on these countries, but I don't believe it; 'if your King come here it will be as my good brother, 'and I will go myself to welcome him.'

Mendoza's composure was not to be disturbed. 'I 'have not the gift of inspiration,' he coolly replied. 'I 'can give your Majesty no information.'

---

[1] Mendoza to Philip, Jan. 13, 1580. MSS. Simancas.

[2] 'Me replicó que yo habia sido mas que caballo ligero.' Mendoza was Philip's Master of the Horse.

He saw that the Queen was afraid, and he did not wish to relieve her anxiety. His blood was hotter than Philip's, and he was provoked at the effects produced in London by the message to the merchants. The men who had lately been so alarmed at Philip's probable displeasure now thought that he was pigeon-livered. In the most insolent language they disclaimed all gratitude for his forbearance.[1] Spain, they said, could not live without the English; and it was true, as Mendoza admitted, that the entire trade of the north with Spain and the Mediterranean was carried on in English vessels. The ignorant Andalusians and Gallicians could not cope with the superior energy of the British islanders. They were becoming the sovereigns of European commerce. Their fleets were growing every day and their wealth increasing. For the general good of the Peninsula, as well as for their present delinquency, Mendoza advised Philip to close his ports against them[2] and ruin them. The securities given by the adventurers, he said, were in all cases a form; the names were either fictitious, or represented persons not worth a ducat; while men like Drake, who were supported by the Court, gave none at all. The single fear in the City was lest letters of marque should be issued to those who had been plundered by the corsairs, permitting them to indemnify themselves, and Mendoza advised Philip at least to threaten that this would be done unless full restitution was made. The merchants would not submit to loss to enrich the Queen's favourites, and would then support his own remonstrances.[3]

---

[1] 'Con una insolencia terrible.'
[2] 'Fabrican cada dia muchos mas navios . . . . navegandolos ellos mismos, con que vienen á ser casi señores del comercio en muchas partes, teniendo en sus manos la navegacion, gozando de todos los fletes.'—*Don B. de Mendoza á Su Mag'*, 10 Hebrero, 1580. *MSS. Simancas.*
[3] Descifrada de Don Bernardino, 10 Hebrero.—*MSS. Simancas.*

Elizabeth herself clearly expected the worst, and the ambassador went beyond his instructions in frightening her. 'I found her,' he said, giving an account of an interview with her in the beginning of February,—' I found her in such alarm of your Majesty's fleet, and so conscience-stricken for her own complicity, that when I entered her cabinet she bounded half a dozen paces from her sofa to receive me. Before I could say a word she enquired if I was come as a king-at-arms to declare war. I said I gathered from her own preparations that she herself meant war, war with all the world. She said she did not mean to be caught sleeping, but there would be no war unless your Majesty began it, and she could not think you would trouble the peace of your own sister, who had ever sought your good, and had saved your Low Countries from the French.

'She was so manifestly uneasy that I thought it as well to alarm her further. I said that we found no fault with her, but I could not say as much for her Ministers, who had sought only to maintain your Highness's rebels in Flanders. Beyond wasting her treasures, and shaking the alliance between Spain and England, their labours had been entirely thrown away. The rebels had shown their gratitude as usual by biting the hand that fed them; yet even now there were English corsairs plundering your Majesty's subjects on the coast of Spain and in the Indies, and say what I would, I had never been able to obtain satisfaction either from herself or her Council.

'She asked if I knew of any corsairs having returned from the Indies. I said I did not. Your Majesty's officers I was confident had given them their deserts and sent them to the bottom. If any such person contrary to expectation should return, I hoped it would be unnecessary for me to insist upon his punishment. For her own sake I felt assured that she would make an example of such men, considering how foul and pernicious their example had been, and the grave inconveniences which would arise if they were tolerated. The Queen herself, I said, had received far different treatment from your Majesty. You had given her life and crown, and as yet no Spanish sword had been drawn against her,[1] although I myself had many a time encountered English in the field who were fighting by the side of the Flanders rebels. In Spain her subjects had nothing but kindness from your Majesty, entirely out of consideration for herself.

'She did not dispute the truth of my allegations. She said she valued your friendship much. She trusted that she would never lose it; and then again for three hours she laboured to extract from me the destination of your Majesty's fleet.

'I studiously encouraged her uneasiness. In pregnant and ambiguous language, I told her that she must not be surprised if I could give her no information. Your Majesty had the infidel at your door as a constant enemy. Your provinces were in rebellion, and many others had done you an ill turn. Your resources were so great that you could either concentrate your force or divide it upon more enterprises than one. It was impossible to say, therefore, what your intentions might be.

'Finding she could' extract nothing from me by direct questions, she tried her gipsy tricks,[2] and said in a wheedling way that it was impossible I should have

---

[1] Julian, who came with Fitzmaurice to Ireland, was an Italian. There were Spaniards with him, but only in a subordinate capacity. The second detachment had not yet arrived.

[2] 'Acariciandome con grandes gitanerias.'

no guess where the fleet was going. I told her that great princes, as she was well aware, treated their ministers as the stomach treats the other members of the body, giving each no more nutriment than would enable it to fulfil its functions. Your Majesty had been pleased to reserve your secret in your own breast.

'With this I left her more frightened than before, and more conscious of her obligations. Thus my presence here is of some service to your Majesty. She gives me audience freely. By talking to her I discover her own and her Ministers' dispositions, and after she has been conversing with me she speaks very differently to them.'[1]

Drake, meanwhile, had brought his ship into condition again to encounter the seas. Among the spoils which had fallen into his hands, he had not forgotten sails and cordage, which he had found in abundance and excellent. By the 16th of April 1579, the Pelican was once more in order, and started on her northern course in search of the expected passage. She held on up the coast for 800 miles into latitude 43° North, but no signs appeared of an opening. Though it was summer the air grew colder, and the crew having been long in the tropics suffered from the change. Not caring to run risks in exploring with so precious a cargo, and finding by observation that the passage, if it existed, must be of enormous length, Drake resolved to go no further, and expecting, as proved to be the case, that the Spaniards would be on the look-out for him at Magellan's Straits, he determined on the alternative route by the Cape of Good Hope. The Portuguese had long traded with China. In the ship going to the Philippines he had

---

[1] Descifrada de Don Bernardino, 10 Hebrero, 1580.—MSS. Simancas.

found a Portuguese chart of the Indian Archipelago, and with the help of this and his own skill he trusted to find his way.

Running back to San Francisco, he landed and made acquaintance with the Indians there. A native chief came to visit him with a number of his tribe. He distributed medicines and ointments among them, and they in turn mistook him for a god, and offered sacrifice to him. The King, as the chief was called, resigned crown and sceptre, and made over California with its buried treasures to the use of her Majesty of England.

He remained long enough to discover the gold with which the soil was teeming; but time pressed, and setting sail again, and avoiding the dangerous neighbourhood of the Philippines, he made a straight course to the Moluccas, where he again halted at the little island of Ternate, south of Celebes. The ship was again docked and scraped. The crew were allowed another month's rest, when they feasted their eyes on the marvels of tropical life, then first revealed to them in their luxuriance —vampires 'as large as hens,' crayfish a foot round, and fireflies lighting the midnight forest. Starting once more they had now to feel their way among the rocks and shoals of the most dangerous waters in the world. They crept round Celebes among coral reefs and low islands scarcely visible above the water line. The Malacca Straits formed the only route marked in the Portuguese chart, and between him and his apparent passage lay the Java sea and the channel between Borneo and Sumatra. But it was not impossible that there might be some other opening, and the Pelican crawled in search of it along the Java coast. Here, if nowhere else, her small size and manageableness were in her favour. In spite of all the care that was taken, she was almost lost. One evening as the black tropical night was closing, a grating sound was heard under her keel: another moment she was hard and fast upon an invisible reef. The breeze was light and the water calm, or the world would have heard no more of Francis Drake and the Pelican. She lay immovable till morning; 'we were out of all hope,' says the writer already quoted, 'to escape danger,' but with the daylight the position was seen not to be utterly desperate. 'Our general,' he continues, 'then as always 'shewed himself most courageous, and of good confi- 'dence in the mercy and protection of God; and as he 'would not seem to perish wilfully, so he and we did 'our best endeavour to save ourselves, and in the end 'cleared ourselves of that danger. We threw overboard 'three tons of cloves, eight cannon, and certain meal and 'beans, and then at four o'clock in the afternoon, the 'wind happily changing, we hoised our sails and were 'lifted off into the sea again, for which we gave God 'the thanks.'

Almost every one on board, though with death before his eyes, had behaved excellently. There had been but one exception, Mr. Fletcher the chaplain. He, it seems, having uneasy recollections of the scene at Port Julian, had been found wanting when his services were most needed; and instead of encouraging the rest, had hinted at judicial retribution for the execution of Thomas Doughty. When off the rock they found clearer water, and coasting westward along Java they found Drake's conjectures verified, and passed through the Straits of Sunda into the open sea. Meeting here the great ocean swell they knew that their perils were over. Thenceforward they were on a travelled course, and they breathed freely for the first time for many months. In high spirits and half in jest, they proceeded to do judgment on the offending chaplain. An English captain, representing the person of his Sovereign, was head on his own deck of Church as well as State. Mr. Fletcher was brought to the forecastle, where Drake, 'sitting 'on a sea chest with a pair of pantoufles in his hand,' pronounced him excommunicated, 'cut off from the 'Church of God, and given over to the devil,' and left him chained by the ankle to a ring bolt in the deck till he had repented of his cowardice. In the general good humour no punishment could be of long duration. After a day or two the chaplain was absolved and returned to his duty. The Pelican had no more adventures; and sweeping in clear fine weather close to the Cape of Good Hope, and touching for water at Sierra Leone, she sailed in triumph into Plymouth harbour in the beginning of October, having marked a furrow with her keel round the globe.

Eighteen months had passed since Drake had last been heard of. His return had ceased to be looked for, and politicians had congratulated themselves on having escaped from an awkward complication; yet here he was once more, with a monarch's ransom in his hold. The national sympathy of England with an extraordinary exploit successfully performed is always irresistible. A shout of admiration rose over the whole country. The Protestants exulted in the blow which had been dealt to their enemy, careless whether it was fair or foul. Elizabeth could not conceal her delight at the greatness of the prize, and she had a genuine enjoyment of daring actions. She sent for Drake to the Court, and received him with the most distinguished honour, while London rung with his praises.

A few statesmen, however, and especially Burghley, could not share in the general satisfaction. If there was to be war with Spain he would have preferred war in a better cause than the defence of what the law of nations could only call buccaneering, and he knew Elizabeth too well to hope that she could be brought to part with money on which she had once closed her hands. The moment was particularly critical. The second detachment of Italians and Spaniards had landed three weeks before at Smerwick, and assuming that they could not have sailed from a Spanish port without Philip's cognisance, if not with his direct sanction, the Queen had declined to see Mendoza or listen to his excuses and explanations. She was standing so far on honourable ground, and Burghley was extremely reluctant that she should forego her advantage.

The ambassador on the other hand determined either to make Elizabeth restore the spoil, or force her to appear before the world as the avowed protectress of piracy. He sent word into the City that unless reparation was made they must look for immediate war. Leicester, whose interests were deeply involved, told him that if he forced a quarrel the Queen would marry Alençon immediately, and make an offensive alliance with France. Mendoza insisted on seeing and speaking with her himself. He was a soldier, he said, more accustomed to use his hands than his tongue. She must do as she pleased about her marriages and alliances, but he recommended her not to provoke his master too far. Spain was not afraid of England and France combined, and he insisted peremptorily on being admitted to her presence.

One resolution only had been definitely formed by Elizabeth. She disliked 'paying back' as heartily as Falstaff, and would not hear of it. For the rest she decided to face out the matter first with a general denial, and if driven from her ground to go off upon the Irish rebellion. She sent a secretary to Mendoza to say that she understood he resented the reception which had been given to Drake. She had called him to her presence, as she was bound to do, to learn the particulars of his voyage, and she had ascertained that he had done no injury to any subject of the King of Spain in any part of his dominions.[1] If she was misinformed she promised to see justice done, but she must be guided by the behaviour of the King to the Irish insurgents. Until the Irish question was settled she could give Mendoza no audience as a public ambassador, 'but his behaviour in 'England,' she said, 'had generally pleased her, and if 'he would visit her as Don Bernardino, she would 'be happy to receive him.'

Mendoza replied to her messenger with quiet sarcasm, that he regretted she should have thought it necessary to tell him what he could prove so distinctly to be untrue. Besides burning and destroying ships, and robbing towns, Captain Drake was believed to have brought home a million and a half of money belonging to his master or his master's subjects; he could say no more till he had received instructions from home. With respect to the rest of her message, he was highly honoured, and would have been delighted to kiss her Majesty's hands, but as long as he was in England he could not divest himself of his office, and was obliged to decline.

'I have thought it my duty,' he continued in relating what he had done to Philip, 'to answer their large talk 'with some choler. I have given out that unless com- 'plete restitution be made of all that has been taken,

---

[1] 'Hallaba que no habia sido haciendo daño á vasallo de V. Mag.^d ni en tierras de su dominio.'—*Descifrada de Don Bernardino*, Oct. 21. *MSS. Simancas.*

'there will be perpetual war with Spain: and I have
'tried to make men feel here that if they break with us
'they are lost.'

For once the Spanish Ambassador found powerful support in many loyal members of the Queen's Council. In the opinion of Burghley, Clinton, Sussex, and several others, who had no interest in the plunder, to force on a quarrel upon such a ground was to play into the hands of the Jesuits. If Philip ceased to interfere with Ireland they strongly advised restitution, insisting meanwhile that the treasure should be brought to the Tower, and an exact account be taken of it. Elizabeth's genius did not fail her. When remonstrance came from such a quarter as this it was evidently possible that she might have to yield. She could not refuse to allow the booty to be registered. The examination must be made in form before some public officer or officers, and she would be bound afterwards by her own return, and could not pretend that the amount was overstated. Yet she meant for all this to indemnify herself for her own outlay, to keep something handsome besides for her favourites, and to reserve ten thousand pounds for Drake himself and his company. As yet everything remained as it had been brought home in the hold of the Pelican. She sent Drake back to Plymouth to superintend the landing of it. The registration was entrusted to Edmund Tremayne, who was a magistrate living in the neighbourhood, on whose discretion she knew that she could rely; and she directed him in taking charge of the cargo not to be too inquisitive, and to give Drake an opportunity of removing an unknown portion of the treasure before an inventory was made.

A letter from Tremayne to Walsingham explains the instructions which he must have received, and the steps which he took in consequence.

'To give you some understanding,' he said, 'how I in particular proceeded with Mr. Drake, I have at no time entered into the account, to know more of the very value of the treasure than he made me acquainted with. And to say truth I persuaded him to impart to me no more than need, for so I saw him commanded in her Majesty's behalf, that he should reveal the certainty to no man living. I have only taken notice of so much as he has revealed, and the same I have seen to be weighed, registered and packed, to be carried according as the counterpass thereof be or shall come to your hands. And to observe her Majesty's command for the secret delivery on leaving of the ten thousand pounds to remain in his hands, we agreed that he should take it to himself out of the portion that was landed secretly, and to remove the same out of the place before my son Henry and I should come to the weighing and registering of that which was left; and so it was done, and no creature living by me made privy to it but himself, and myself no privier to it than as you may perceive by this.'[1]

The secret and unconjecturable deductions being thus

[1] Tremayne to Walsingham, Nov. 1580.—*MSS. Domestic.* Tremayne adds one or two more interesting particulars about Drake.

'And so,' he continues, 'by offering to do more than this I might show myself a busy officer to go beyond my commission to lead me, so in the matter general I see nothing to charge Mr. Drake further than he is inclined to charge himself; and withal I must say, as I find by apparent demonstration, he is so inclined to advance the value to be delivered to her Majesty and seeking in general to recompense all men that have been in this case dealers with him, as I dare take an oath with him he will rather diminish his own portion than leave any of them unsatisfied. And for his mariners and followers, I have been an eyewitness, and have heard with mine ears upon the shutting up of these matters such certain show of goodwill as I cannot yet see that many of them will leave his company wheresoever. His whole course of his voyage hath shewed him to be of great valour, but my hap has been to see some particularities, and namely in this discharge of his company, as doth assure me that he is a man of great government, and that by the rules of God and his Book. So as proceeding upon such a foundation, his doings cannot but prosper.'

accomplished, a return was given to the ambassador of twenty tons of silver bullion, five blocks of gold, each eighteen inches long,[1] and a quantity of pearls and other precious stones. The chests were first stored in Saltash Castle, from whence they were removed to London, and were formally deposited in the Tower.[2]

The seizure of the Spanish treasure in Plymouth and Southampton Water twelve years before, an act in many respects similar to that which had been accomplished by Drake, had been sanctioned and perhaps advised by Burghley for reasons of state. It was going to Alva to pay his army at a moment when if that army had been able to move it might have crushed the Prince of Orange for ever; the English Catholics, instigated by Don Gueran de Espes, were at the same time on the eve of insurrection, and Elizabeth was unable to resolve to condemn Mary Stuart. The money itself was formally the property of Genoese bankers, to whom the Crown of England was ready to answer. Even then perhaps, ending as that matter had ended in lies and equivocation, Cecil would have hardly counselled a repetition of the experiment; while Drake had been plundering private individuals, compromising, as Cecil thought, the honour of the country, and dishonouring the cause of which he wished to see his mistress the open and acknowledged champion.

Far different was the opinion of Sir Francis Walsingham. Walsingham, like Burghley, would have preferred open courses could Elizabeth have been brought to consent to them, but he knew that it could not be. She had baffled his policy, disappointed his hopes, and with her broken engagements had made herself 'hateful to the world.' In Scotland, in France, in the

---

[1] Depth and breadth not mentioned.
[2] Doscifrada de Don Bernardino, Octubre 30.—*MSS. Simancas.*

Low Countries, she had allowed him to pledge her good faith, to tempt the friends of the good cause to risk their lives and fortunes in reliance on her word; and one by one she had left them to be defeated in the field, to die on the scaffold, or to hold on in despairing self-defence, with no genuine intention of interposing between them and destruction. Walsingham was persuaded that her own turn would come at last, and he thought it better for her that the issue should be tried out while she had friends still strong in the field. If he could force her into a bolder position he was not scrupulous about the means, and as he could not influence her by persuasion he was content to play upon her weakness. She shrunk from war, because war was costly, but he taught her to see by Drake's exploit that war might give her the wealth of the Indies.

Drake therefore when he returned to London a second time was received with undiminished favour. He was continually closeted with the Queen, or was seen walking with her in her garden or in public. She gave him a second present of ten thousand pounds. The Pelican was brought round to the Thames, and drawn up on shore at Deptford to be preserved as a remembrance of the voyage. A banquet was held on board, at which Elizabeth was present, and the occasion was used to give Drake the honour of knighthood. Philip sent orders to Mendoza to make a positive demand for restitution. Twice he requested an audience, and twice he was refused. He made no third application, and waited for his letters of recall. Elizabeth between her opposing counsellors drew her own profit from their differences. Burghley and Sussex recommended that the treasure should remain untouched in the Tower; Walsingham that it should be given to the Prince of Orange and the Huguenots; while Leicester and the other adventurers thought that in justice it ought to be divided among themselves, and made proposals to Mendoza to share the spoil with him if he would consent to some private arrangement. Mendoza haughtily answered that neither that nor any such overture would tempt him a hair's breadth from his duty to his Prince; he would himself give twice the sum they offered him to chastise such a bandit as Drake.[1] With opinions thus divided the Queen concluded on keeping the bulk of the prize to herself. She gave the adventurers a hundred per cent. on their shares. The rest she reserved.

The crew of the Pelican, besides Elizabeth's bounty to them, were allowed perquisites out of the secondary spoil, and London was astonished at the splendour in which these heroes of the hour lounged at St. Paul's and Westminster. Drake feeling keenly the censures which were flung on him by men whose good opinion he valued, attempted to propitiate opposition by lavish presents. To the Queen he gave a diamond cross, with a crown set with enormous emeralds. To Lord Chancellor Bromley he gave eight hundred dollars' worth of wrought plate, and almost as much to other members of the Council. To Burghley he offered ten bars of curiously chased gold, and to Sussex vases and fountains of gold and silver intertwined. The Queen wore her crown on New Year's day. Sir Thomas Bromley and most of the rest were contented to decorate their sideboards at the expense of the Catholic King. But

---

[1] 'Se resolviéron en este medio de tentarme por algunas vias, diciendome que si yo templaba parte del rigor que mostraba en el viage del Drake, podria tener de la mia ó á quien quisiese darsela mas de 50,000 ducados de provecho. Esperaba en Dios que él me daria gracia para que esta ni otra ninguna offerta me biciese faltar un cabello en cosa del servicio de V. Mag⁴, respondiendoles que cuando yo tuviera mucho mas que los 50,000 ducados les diera por hacer castigar tan gran maldad y ladron como Drake.' —*Don Bernardino al Rey*, 9 de Enero, 581. *MSS. Simancas*.

Burghley and Sussex put aside the splendid temptation. Burghley said he could not see how in conscience he could receive presents from a man who had nothing but what he had made by piracy, and Drake had to content himself with wealth, fame, and the favour of his sovereign, and the approbation of at least one good man in Walsingham.[1]

With a cause of probable quarrel with Spain, which Philip's real desire to keep clear of interference in Ireland rendered none the less serious, Elizabeth had good reason to avoid adding France to the number of her enemies. Her diplomacy had been baffled by the completeness of the French acceptance of every condition on which she had insisted. Mauvissière told her that if she again threw Alençon over, the Duke, for his own character's sake, would have to publish the letters which she had written to him.[2]

'What shall I do?' she said one day to the Archbishop of York. 'I am between Scylla and Charybdis. Alen-'çon grants all that I ask. If I do not marry him

---

[1] 'Ha dado á Milord Burghley diez barras de oro labradas que valia cada uno 300 Δ""; pero él no las quiso tomar, diciendo que no sabia con que consciencia podia acceptar cosa que se le diese Drake, habiendo sido robado todo quanto traya; y al Conde de Sussex 600 Δ"" de jarros y fuentes labrados, que no quiso, respondiendo lo mismo que el Thesorero.'—*Don Bernardino al Rey*, 9 Enero. MSS. Simancas. Camden says that 'Drake being now returned, nothing troubled him more than that some principal men at the Court rejected the gold which he offered them as being gotten by piracy.' It is noticeable that Walsingham's name does not appear among the recipients of Drake's bounty; Walsingham being absolutely without reproach in such matters, receiving nothing from Crown or subject, and lavishing his own fortune on the business of the State.

[2] 'Concluyendo el Embajador con decille que quando no se casase no podria dexar Alençon de publicar las cartas que ella le habia escripto sobre este negocio, que servirán de disculparle de haber venido en este reyno, y que la gente entendiesse que no habia sido ligereza suya.'—*Don B. de Mendoza al Rey*, 28 Hebrero, 1580. The reader must remember that Sir James Crofts, the Controller of the Household, was in Philip's pay, and that Mendoza's information came therefore from a credible authority.

'he will be my enemy, and if I do, I am no longer mis-
'tress in my own realm.'

The Archbishop said that her subjects only wished
her to consult her own pleasure.

'And what say you, my lord?' she said to Cecil, 'you
'have not been at Council these three days.'

'If you mean to marry, Madam,' said Burghley, 'do
'it; no ill can happen to the realm. If you do not
'mean it, undeceive Alençon at once.'

'Other of my advisers do not agree with you, my
'lord,' she answered; 'they would have me entertain
'him with half promises.'

'Madam,' Cecil replied, 'I have heard men say that
'those who would make fools of princes are the fools
'themselves.'[1]

The trifling policy prevailed, however, and the death
of the King of Portugal and the immediate steps taken
by Philip to make himself master of the country rendered the English alliance of more importance than
ever to France, and enabled Elizabeth to have it on her
own terms. It was not Portugal, not the sovereignty
of the entire Peninsula only which would fall to Philip,
but the Portuguese East Indies, the Azores, and an
enormous trade; and all the world had cause to fear the
addition of such vast resources to the already over-
powering strength of the Spanish monarchy. The ease
with which the annexation was effected increased the
alarm. Don Antonio, Prior of Crato, attempted an opposing claim. The Duke of Alva marched on Oporto,
and in a single battle annihilated all resistance. Don
Antonio fled, with a price upon his head, carrying nothing with him but the Braganza jewels; and Philip, by

---

[1] 'Á que le replicó Cecil que siempre el habia oydo decir que quien
burlaba á los Príncipes se burlaba
á si mismo.'—*Ibid.*

the summer of 1580, found himself with his immense preparations unexhausted, the resources of Portugal added to his own, and his fleet and army free to move in any and all directions

It was impossible either for France or England to look with calmness on so large an increase to their rival's power. It was no time to stand on nice punctilios, and the Alençon coquetry was renewed with no certain idea how it was to end. Letters and presents were interchanged. The Duke was told that if he continued faithful he should have his reward at last, and he on his side fed himself with the hope that if not King of England he might, with Elizabeth's help, become King of the Netherlands, or even wrest from the House of Hapsburg the imperial crown itself.[1]

So passed the spring, amidst interchanges of diplomatic coquetries; Alençon looking wistfully at the Low Countries, and the French and English Governments each trying to persuade the other to take an open part in the war. Mauvissière advised the Queen to send Leicester with an army against Parma; Elizabeth hinted to Alençon that she objected no longer to the entry of the French into Flanders; while the marriage treaty grew and dissolved and was put together and ravelled out again, like the web of Penelope.[2] Indecision, however, could not last for ever. The Catholics and the patriotic party were so nearly balanced in France, that slight causes were continually turning the scale. The annexation of Portugal had discredited the Duke of Guise;

---

[1] 'Que el blanco al que mira Alençon en ser elegido por Rey de Romanos, y por este desea el casamiento y procura tener á sud devocion á los Protestantes de Alemania con ayudar á los rebeldes de Flandes.'—*Don B. de Mendoza al Rey*, 27 Hebrero, 1581. *MSS. Simancas.* Opposite to this passage Philip wrote 'Ojo.'

[2] 'Quieren que sea la tela de Penelope.'—*Mendoza al Rey*, 21 Maio, 1580. *MSS. Simancas.*

religious disturbances threatened to restore him to ascendancy; and so critical was the condition of things at the Court that a revulsion of policy was always on the cards with a Spanish marriage for Alençon. The Queen-mother, who hated Philip with Italian malignity, was more than willing to hold on to Elizabeth. She was ready, and the King with her, to make a league with England in favour of Don Antonio, to invade Flanders, to declare war against Spain, to do anything and everything that Elizabeth might wish, could they but have a guarantee that Elizabeth would stand by them; but they knew their good sister of England too well to run the risk of committing themselves alone; they feared, and with good reason, that when France was entangled in war, Elizabeth would snatch the opportunity to arrange her difficulties with Spain.

How much in her conduct was deliberately insincere, how much arose from legitimate uncertainty, the surviving historical materials make it difficult to decide. The enquirer is beset on all sides with contradictions, with demonstrations of one kind made in public, and explanations and retractations in private. Elizabeth's pleasure was to swim in the backwater of the main stream, and to shift her front in the continual eddies.

A paper, dated the 10th of July, in the handwriting of Lord Burghley, places us for a moment on firm ground.

Elizabeth had led Alençon to believe that she would not object to his interference in Flanders. The Prince of Orange, finding that she had entirely deserted him, finding that she would not even redeem the bonds which had been issued on her credit,[1] had invited

---

[1] 'Her Majesty has not made payment to the Italian merchants, Pallavicino and Spinola, for money which they lent to the States at Her Majesty's request and on her bonds.'—*Note in Burghley's hand*, July 10. *MSS. Holland.*

Alençon to become sovereign of the Low Countries. It was understood that the offer would be accepted, that the King would support his brother, and that those countries would be annexed to the Crown of France. The day when France became possessed of Holland and Zealand, Lord Burghley considered, would be the last of English independence. Yet how was the difficulty to be met? The Queen would not say whether she would marry Alençon or not. The Prince of Orange could not be forbidden to seek help from France, and France would not give it except on one or other of those conditions.

Even now, Lord Burghley said, it was not too late for the Queen to take up the cause of the Prince of Orange. The Prince still infinitely preferred her protection to that of France; 'and it was likely that the realm of 'England in Parliament would consent to the charge 'rather than for want of aiding those countries with 'men and money see them fall to the crown of France.' If she could bring herself to consent it would be her duty at once to communicate with Philip, and to tell him that her interference was intended only to preserve the Provinces for Spain. 'She would offend Mon- 'sieur, whom she might now have for a husband to her 'great advantage,' but 'she would be considering less 'her private gain than the public interest.' In return Philip must be pressed to concede 'liberty of conscience, 'on which point the whole difficulty stood,' and without which no peace was possible.[1]

It was an open and honourable course, and Burghley's recommendation so far prevailed that Mendoza was sent for. The Queen said in the presence of the Council

---

[1] Questions to be considered, July 10, 1580. In Burghley's hand.—*MSS. Holland.*

that she had learnt that his master had entered into confederation to dispossess her of her crown. A party from Spain had already landed in Ireland, and a second expedition was in preparation at Ferrol. Her own support of the insurgents in Flanders was neither a precedent nor an excuse. She had refused the offer of the States to attach themselves to England, and had interfered only to prevent their occupation by France. She had no wish to quarrel, and if attacked would know how to defend herself. But the state of Flanders admitted of no delay. She knew for certain that the French meant to possess themselves of those countries, and unless Philip would conciliate them by making concessions, which he had hitherto refused, 'she would be 'forced, contrary to her liking, to set in foot and make 'herself a party.'[1]

The emphasis with which she spoke provoked a doubt of her sincerity. When Elizabeth meant what she was saying her voice was always low, thin, clear, and unimpassioned. She had already sent privately to France, to tell the King that if he would go to war with Spain she would furnish him underhand with the means.[2] Alone afterwards with Mendoza she told him that she had spoken so strongly only to please the Council, that at bottom she desired nothing so much as to preserve her friendship with the House of Burgundy, or draw closer to it by a renewal of the league;[3] while

---

[1] Heads of speeches delivered to the Ambassador of Spain, July 10.—*MSS. Spain.* A Spanish translation is at Simancas.

[2] Instructions to Mr. Middlemore, June, 1580. Sir H. Cobham to Burghley, August 1.—*MSS. France.* Mendoza to Philip, July 4.—*MSS. Simancas.*

[3] 'Despues se apartó sola conmigo, y me dixó que ella habia hecho este oficio para cumplir con sus consejeros; y que no dixesen que faltaba en lo que tanto le iba: que no deseaba sino conservar la antigua amistad que habia tenido siempre con la casa de Borgoña, y si necesario fuese estrecharla, ratificando las ligas de nuevo.'—*Mendoza al Rey*, 16 Julio.

again a few weeks after, on the news of the landing at Smerwick, she directed Cobham, her ambassador at Paris, to propose a joint expedition of French and English into Portugal, to establish Don Antonio.[1]

As to sending a force to the Netherlands she never seriously thought of it. Instead of men and money she sent only reiterated demands for the payment of her old debts, with a schedule of the interest which had accumulated since they first became due.[2] The States in consequence persisted in their application to Henry and Catherine. On the 29th of September St. Aldegonde presented Alençon with an offer of the crown of the Low Countries, and Alençon paused over his answer till he could see whether the fear of his acceptance would overcome Elizabeth's objection to matrimony.

When on the back of the already existing uncertainties Drake returned with his prize, war with Spain seemed all but inevitable. The Queen was in sore trouble, for marriage appeared now the only alternative left. The brown, blotched face of the Frog Prince had not become more agreable to her in his absence; it was pleasanter far to listen to the innocent homage of the faithful Hatton.[3]

---

[1] Walsingham to Sir H. Cobham, Sept. 18, 1580.—MURDIN.

[2] Holland Correspondence, August 1580—April, 1581. MSS.

[3] Hatton's letters to Elizabeth are the caresses of an affectionate spaniel. One of these came to soothe her in the middle of her perplexity. It is addressed to the Queen's Most Excellent Majesty, and prefaced with four triangles of unknown cabalistic meaning.

'I most humbly,' it runs, 'with all dutiful reverence, beseech your sacred Majesty to pardon my presumption in writing to your Highness. Your kingly benefits, together with your most rare regard of your simple and poor slave, hath put this passion into me to imagine that for so exceeding and infinite parts of unspeakable goodness I can use no other means of thankfulness than by bowing the knees of my own heart with all humility to look upon your singular grace with love and faith perdurable. I should sin, most gracious Sovereign, against the Holy Ghost most damnably if towards your Highness I should be found unthankful. Afford me the favour, therefore, most dear Lady, that your clear and most fair

Time pressed, however; Mendoza's menaces continued; and on the 20th of October she told Mauvissière that if Alençon still wished it, and the King approved, she was ready to let the marriage take effect without further delay.[1] Perhaps she was never so near to serious consent as at this moment. Between the Low Countries, the relapse of Scotland, the Irish rebellion, the English Jesuits, and the fear of Spain, her difficulties were so many and so complicated that it seemed as if no other escape lay open to her. She bade Cobham, as if she were struggling with her destiny, try once more to persuade the French to accept instead a political alliance, but they told him it must be the marriage or nothing. 'We will not break 'with Spain alone,' said the Marshal de Cossé significantly to Cobham; 'there would be many that would 'be contented to see two others in a quarrel whereby

eyes may order and register these my duties which I beseech our God to requite you for.

'The poor wretch, my sick servant, receiveth again his life, being as in the physician's opinion more than half dead, through your most princely love of his poor master, and holy charitable care (without respect of your own danger) of the poor wretch. We have right Christian devotion to pray for your Highness, which God for His mercy's sake kindle in us for ever, to the end of our lives.

'I should not dissemble, my dear Sovereign, if I wrote how unpleasant and froward a countenance is grown in me through my absence from your most amiable and royal presence; but I dare not presume to trouble your Highness with my not estimable griefs, but in my country I dare avow this fashion will fall evil become me. I hope your Highness will pardon my unsatisfied humour that knoweth not how to end such complaints as are in my thoughts ever new to begin, but duty shall do me leave to cumber your beamlike eyes with my vain brabblings. And as most nobly your Highness preserveth and royally conserveth your poor creature and vassal, so shall he live and die in pure unspotted faith towards you for ever. God bless your Highness with long life, and prosper you to the end in all your kingly affairs. At Bedford, this Wednesday morning. Would God I were worthy to write,

'Your bounden slave,
'CH. HATTON.'

—*MSS. Domestic.*

[1] 'Laquelle m'a asseurée vouloir et s'accorder au marriage sans aulcun longueur ny remise, si voz Majestés et Monseigneur vostre frère n'en faictes de vostre part.'—*Castelnau de Mauvissière au Roy*, Oct. 20, 1580. TEULET, vol. iii.

'they being the third might live more safely.'[1] Nor would Alençon consent to suspend any longer his reply to the offer of the States.

In the convention of Bordeaux, on the 23rd of January, he accepted the sovereignty of the Netherlands. Elizabeth recognised the necessity, and seemingly submitted to it. She appeared willing to take part in what she could not prevent. She had already promised Mauvissière that she would supply Alençon with means to equip his army;[2] and as the marriage treaty which had been drawn with Simier a year and a half before required revision, she professed herself willing to receive a second set of commissioners whenever it might please the King of France to send them. She wrote to Henry with some dignity, excusing her past irresolution as a weakness for which he ought to pardon her, since she had herself been the chief sufferer by it; and she said she would pray to God so to crown the long negotiation as neither the King should have cause to regret her decision, nor his brother the choice which he had made. She confessed that she still looked on marriage as too much happiness for an old woman like herself, for whom paternosters were more fitting than a bridal. If the Duke was dissatisfied with her, the King, who had so long pressed the marriage, would alone be to blame.[3]

---

[1] Cobham to Walsingham, Jan. 6, 1581.—MSS. France.

[2] 'Ha dado la Reyna esperanças al Embajador de Francia que como vengan los ciudadanos dará 200 mil ducados á Alençon de los que ha traydo Draques para hacer en compañía del de Berne y Conde, la jornada de Flandes, y juntamente que hará que Casimiro entre al mismo tiempo con ejercito por la parte de Gueldres, asegurando aquel Estado y divirtiendo las fuerças de V. Mag⁴; y aunque para semejante empresa no les faltan dificultades, la Reyna alimenta á Alençon con estas esperanças, de las cuales se imagina, y assimismo los Francesses, que les han de ser aseguradamente de gran fruto, lo cual creen con facilidad por lo mucho que lo desean.'—Don B. de Mendoza al Rey, 9 Enero, 1581. MSS. Simancas.

[3] 'Pour donner fin à ceste cy

This letter really looked like business. But as M. Simier had said long before, nothing but the candle being out and the happy pair established together behind the bed-curtains, would be really conclusive. The royal family of France had already been made sufficiently ridiculous, and before the appointment of another commission Alençon's secretary, M. Marchmont, was ordered over to ascertain if the Queen was serious at last. His task was not likely to be an easy one. 'Our disposition here,' wrote Walsingham to Sir Robert Bowes, 'is to prosecute nothing either throughly or season-'ably;' and on the same day to Sir John Wallop, 'We 'shall continue our lingering and irresolute manner of 'proceeding, and blame others though the fault be in 'ourselves.'[1]

Marchmont came. She received him with the most ardent demonstrations of friendship. There was nothing, she said, which she now so keenly desired as the arrival of the commissioners; every hour which they tarried was a thousand years. Courtesy would not permit Marchmont to doubt her sincerity. He hurried back with the happy news to Paris, and she charged him with a letter to her lover and the significant present of a ring. Sussex, Crofts, even Burghley believed now that her mind was made up, and that the marriage was to be after all.[2] Only Walsingham remained contemptuously

---

longue demeure, je impetreray de Dieu ceste seule grace, qu'il pourra couronner toute l'œuvre, de sorte que Vous mesmes n'ayez jamais pensée de regretter ceste sentence, ny Monsieur tienne oncques cause de repentir son election de ma part. Je suys en ferme foy que ma solicité sera que trop bonne pour une vieille à qui les Paternosters suffiront au lieu des nopces; et non obstant je seray toujours preste à recevoir les commissaires quand il vous plaira à les m'envoyer.'—*Elizabeth to the King of France*, Jan. 1581. *MSS. France*.

[1] Walsingham to Bowes and to Wallop, March 17, 1581.—MURDIN.

[2] Mendoza to Philip, Feb. 17.—*MSS. Simancas*.

incredulous — Walsingham and the Spanish ambassador.

France, eager to be convinced, at once appointed an embassy to England, and an embassy splendidly composed. France evidently was now prepared, with England at its back, to strike effectively for the overthrow in Europe of the Spanish supremacy; and once committed to the war, a liberal internal policy would have followed by inevitable necessity, and the influence of the Guises and the Jesuits would have been at an end. The first commissioner was a Prince of the blood royal, Francis, son of the Duke of Montpensier. He was accompanied by the Marshal de Cossé, La Mothe Fénelon, Chasteauneuf, Brisson President of the Parliament of Paris, Pinart Chief Secretary of State, and many others of the noblest French houses. Two points, at least, were made clear by so marked a selection: the first, that the Court of Paris at once desired the marriage, and was satisfied that it was about to take effect; the second, that if Elizabeth had been in earnest, a cordial alliance was possible between two of the leading powers in Europe which, before the ardour of the Reformation had cooled down, would have broken the remaining power of the Roman Church, and shut up Spain in her own peninsula.

No fears of this kind disturbed the repose of Bernardino de Mendoza. He knew Elizabeth too well to believe for one moment that she meant to place Alençon beside her on her throne. He did not credit either her or her brother of France with sufficient sagacity to inaugurate a powerful policy. He had watched her alienating the Hollanders, trifling away her hard-won advantages in Scotland, and leaving her truest friends to be murdered, while she was toying with a phantom at

which in private she jested among her women. With
a chuckle of satisfaction, he described to Philip the
splendid ceremonies with which she was preparing to
receive the embassy.

'What will come of it,' he wrote, 'I cannot pretend
'to tell your Majesty, but the Queen is chiefly occupied
'in providing the pageantry. There are serious questions
'at stake, such as Alençon's relations with the Low
'Countries. But she is thinking less of these than of
'tournaments and dancing rooms, pretty women to make
'a shew at court, and things of that kind. The peers
'have been required to bring their families to London.
'A magnificent gallery is being erected in the palace at
'Westminster. Fourteen carriages have been built for
'the ladies, and ten thousand pounds' worth of Drake's
'plunder have been laid out. . . . She has desired
'the merchants to sell their silks and velvets and cloth of
'gold at a quarter less by the yard than the usual price,
'that the Court may appear to better advantage.[1] Ob-
'viously she means nothing but vanity and idle trifling.'

Elizabeth was as innocent as Mendoza believed her
to be of greatness of purpose, but he gave her insufficient credit for cunning and small sagacity.

The ambassadors came; they were received by Lord
Cobham at Dover, on the 17th of April, and conducted
to Gravesend, where the Earls of Hertford and Northumberland and thirty other lords and gentlemen, were
waiting with the royal barges. They were carried up
the river amidst acclamations from shore and ship, and
two hundred guns were fired from the Tower as they

---

[1] 'Ha mandado que todos los mercaderes vendan al cuarto menos cada vara de lo que solian, así de tela de oro como terciopelo y otras sedas, diciéndoles que quiere que lo hagan este servicio para que con mas commodidad se puedan aderezar y vestir las damas y gentiles hombres del Reyno.'—*Don B. de Mendoza al Rey,* 6 y 16 Avril. *MSS. Simancas.*

passed under London Bridge. Somerset House had been fitted up in splendour for their reception. Dinners, balls, bear-baits, bull-fights, and music parties were lavished upon them day after day, as Mendoza had foretold. When they spoke of business they were put off with flattering excuses. 'No one,' the Queen said, 'was 'more grieved at the delay than she was; an hour lost 'to her was of more consequence than a year to Monsieur; 'but she had written to him on a private matter, and 'could not enter on the treaty without his answer.' They forced her at last into a serious conversation. She mentioned objections. They admitted them, but they said that so intelligent a person must have weighed them before, and it was to be assumed that she had made up her mind. They were not sent, they said, to discuss the general question, but to conclude the arrangements for the ceremony. She fell back on Monsieur and her correspondence. After all, she said, the object of the marriage was political. Why would not a league answer the purpose equally well? Why could not the defensive treaty which already existed be made comprehensive for a common course of action in Europe?

It was the old language over again. When France was willing to make a league, she preferred the marriage. When the marriage came close to her, she fell back on the league. The French were not to be caught. The marriage, said Pinart, is the surest league; the political alliance shall be made the first article of the treaty. They held her close to the point. She answered that she could determine nothing till she had heard from Monsieur, and when one letter came it was not sufficient, and she wanted another.[1]

---

[1] Dispatches of the French Ambassadors sent to England in April 1581. Printed in the Egerton Papers.

The Council gave them as little satisfaction as the Queen. Walsingham said that when Parliament was sitting in the winter, the temper of the House of Commons had been felt about the marriage. There was still found to be a fear that it might further the designs of the Jesuits, and a fear also that Monsieur having embarked in the cause of the Low Countries without open support from his brother, the realm might be brought into a war of which it would have to bear the exclusive cost.[1] The English Government expected that the commissioners would have brought power to treat for a league, and they required a distinct explanation about it before they could proceed with the marriage treaty. Would the King pledge himself to help his brother in the Low Countries or not?[2]

The question had been already answered by Pinart, but it was referred to Paris, and a reply instantly came, that if the marriage proceeded, 'the King would 'not only assist in the enterprise of the Low Countries, 'but would also make a league with England, offensive 'and defensive, on any reasonable conditions the Queen 'would propound.'[3] This objection being disposed of, the Queen consented to name a commission on her part, and to allow a marriage treaty to be drawn; insisting, however, still that the execution of it was to remain contingent on a private understanding between Monsieur and herself. The ambassadors might have refused to proceed on a reservation, the effects of which had been experienced already; but they too, perhaps, on their side desired to entangle Elizabeth. No one, now, not Burghley, not Walsingham, not even

---

[1] Speech to be delivered to the Commissioners, April 30. Walsingham's hand.—*MSS. France.*
[2] Causes of delay, May 16. Burghley's hand.—*MSS. Ibid.*
[3] Instructions to Mr. Somers, June 20.—*MSS. France.*

Hatton and Leicester, knew exactly what she meant—possibly she did not know herself. Grave Councillors submitted to be the playthings of her uncertainty, and once more the conditions on which she was to be the wife of the Duke of Alençon were elaborately argued and agreed upon, down to the form of the ceremony. The articles were formally subscribed; the treaty was to become binding when Elizabeth and Monsieur respectively pronounced themselves satisfied, and the ambassadors took their leave.

She was playing evidently for time. She believed that she could wait longer than France, and that, league or no league, France would be compelled to commit itself. Alençon had accepted the charge of the Low Countries. The Duke of Parma was besieging Cambray on the frontier of Picardy, and this place from its situation it was Alençon's especial duty to relieve. The French Court had kept him inactive while they were waiting for the result of the English negotiation. Elizabeth, who knew the weak stuff of which her lover was composed, had in the private correspondence that she spoke of, continued to play upon him. She sent him money and promised him more. She persuaded him to act independently of his brother; and she made him believe that if his brother resented it he might still rely upon her support.[1] France swarmed with disbanded soldiers, and an army for short

[1] 'Assimismo para cualquiera de los designos que él tenga de la invasion de los Payses Bajos ó alterarse contra su hermano, no se puede hacer sin dinero; y que la Reyna lo daria con mayor facilidad, pidiendose lo el por su persona, á título de que hacia la empresa por complacerla, principalmente que el Marchmont lo habia advertido que cuando el Rey de Francia respondió que de ninguna manera queria declarar guerra á V. Mag^d, le dixó la Reyna que si él lo hiciera, ella le ayudaria con 500 mil libras esterlinas; que aunque son palabras que dice con artificio, moverian á Alençon para esperar sacar fruto dellas.'—*Don B. de Mendoza al Rey*, 6 Junio. *MSS. Simancas*.

service was easily brought together. Alençon collected a few thousand men with Elizabeth's help, and moved on Cambray. Parma, unwilling to fight an action which might force France into the field, raised the siege; and Alençon, having strengthened the garrison, thrown in supplies, saved his credit with the Low Countries, and at all events, compromised himself, fell back into his expecting attitude, waiting for Elizabeth to reward him.

She, on her part, had no sooner seen the ambassadors turn their backs, than she commissioned a political agent, a Mr. Somers, to go to Paris to undo their work, and by exacting more and more concessions make the marriage impossible. The King had said that he would make a league with her on reasonable conditions. She wished to know what those reasonable conditions were. Would France follow up the war in the Low Countries effectually without putting her to expense? Otherwise 'she 'could not without offence to her realm consent to the 'marriage.' The King would probably say that he could not go to war unless he was assured that she would join with him; that without the marriage there could be no assurance; and that, as his brother must marry somewhere, he might look to Spain if she refused him. Or again, he might say that the treaty had gone so far that it could not be broken off without discredit, and that if the marriage was dropped the enterprise in the Low Countries must be abandoned. Somers was directed to combat these arguments. Mutual interest, he could argue, was as good a foundation as marriage, and great causes were subject to great impediments. The Queen would not hear of the abandonment of the Low Countries. It would be so dangerous every way, that sooner than Monsieur should desert them, she would help him *underhand*,

and if the King was forced into a war with Spain, she would contribute also *underhand* 'in reasonable sort.'[1]

Somers, before speaking to the King, communicated his errand to the friends of England in the French Council of State. '*They were appalled at it*, looking for a far other answer.'[2] 'The matter of the Low Countries,' they said, 'was yet a body without a soul, and would turn to 'dust unless some one breathed into it.' 'Nothing would 'be hearkened to from her Majesty till they might know 'her Yea or No. If *Yea*, she should have what she de-'sired, to break with Spain, or otherwise as should please 'her.' A league, if she wished, might be made at once offensive and defensive, with a proviso 'that the marriage not 'happening it should be void.' If *No*, the present alliance might continue, but it would be nerveless and barren. Alençon being heir to the crown must immediately marry elsewhere, and 'the King would have to respect those with whom his brother should match.'[3]

The private opinion was confirmed officially a few days later. 'Mr. Somers,' Henry said, 'had brought a 'message that unless the war in the Low Countries might 'be prosecuted without cost to her Majesty, she could 'not without offence to her realm assent to the mar-'riage. That was as much as to say, that the King being 'involved in war, her Majesty could be content to be a 'looker on.' It was absurd, out of the question, and not to be thought of. Somers, tied to his orders, hinted at help *underhand*. The King said 'he would do nothing '*underhand*. Hitherto he said he had prohibited his 'brother's proceedings altogether. Since the marriage 'was agreed upon he had altered his mind, and as soon

---

[1] Instructions to Mr. Somers, June 20.—*MSS. France*.
[2] Somers to Burghley, July 3.

The words in italics were underlined by Burghley himself.—*MSS. France*.
[3] *Ibid.*

'as it was completed, or when Monsieur had gone to
'England for the purpose, he would put his army in
'the field.' But England must stand at his side; 'her
'Majesty must declare herself openly along with him.'

'Her Highness,' Somers said, 'could not marry a hus-
'band and a war together after so long and happy peace.'
There need be no declaration on either side; 'the King
'might let his brother alone, and himself not seem to
'meddle, but by aid underhand, as her Majesty might
'also do.'

The French Council repeated that this was not possible. If France was to take a part it should be an open
and avowed part. 'The marriage was the base of the
'rest.' The Queen had promised, the Duke had promised, the contract was drawn and signed. If after all
that had been done and said in England the treaty was
now turned to air, France would be profoundly astonished, and as profoundly hurt. Time pressed: they
required a distinct answer in ten days.[1]

Sickened with the insincerity, and frightened at the
danger, of the course which Elizabeth was pursuing, her
ministers were looking eagerly for anything which would
force her into an honourable position. Marriage or no
marriage, if she would go to war with Spain, she would
now have France for an ally. Her sharp practice, if she
persisted with it, was but too likely to recoil upon herself, and to leave her without a friend to the united
vengeance of Catholic Christendom. A characteristic
incident of the period came to her help. The Dutch
governor at Flushing had laid a trap for Parma by offering to betray the town to him for a sum of money.
Notice was given to the Prince of Orange, and the

---

[1] Somers and Cobham to Walsingham, July 12.—*MSS. France*. Somers to Walsingham, July 12.—
MSS. Ibid.

Spanish force which came to take possession was to be set upon and destroyed. The governor, to do his work completely, required and obtained beforehand his promised bribe. He had given his son in return as a hostage, but with a condition that the boy should be sent to England to be kept by Don Bernardino. The plot was discovered by Parma. The governor, uneasy for the fate of his child, sent word to the English Council, and one evening when Don Bernardino was at supper with the French Ambassador, a party of men in the employ of Walsingham entered Mendoza's house and carried him off.

Mendoza was furious; the law of nations had been broken, he said. An ambassador's house was a sanctuary, and the boy was a Spanish subject; he demanded the instant restitution of his prisoner, and the execution of the instruments of the outrage. Except for Philip's strict injunctions to him to avoid a rupture, he declared that he would have applied for his passports.[1]

A worse offence threatened to follow. The Azores had been less submissive to the Spanish conquest than the mother country. Terceira declared for Don Antonio, and Terceira, if there was to be war with Spain, was the best imaginable position from which to intercept the gold fleets on their way from Panama to Cadiz. Don Antonio's agents had been busy in London and Paris, and Catherine de Medici wished the island to be immediately occupied by a united expedition from England and France. Elizabeth, refusing to commit herself openly, half consented to allow Drake and Hawkins to go with the French as privateers under the flag of Don Antonio. Sir James Crofts at the beginning of June gave information to Mendoza that a squadron was in preparation,

[1] Castelnau au Roy, Juin 20.—Teulet, vol. iii. Mendoza á su Mag.d, 24 Junio, 1581.—MSS. Simancas.

among others a very fine vessel of 500 tons, which the ambassador innocently said that the Governor of Cadiz had coveted for her beauty when she was lately in harbour there, and had fired upon and endeavoured to take.[1]

Mendoza arrived with his double complaint, presented himself at the palace, and required admission to the Queen. She sent him word that she was about to see the French Ambassador, and begged that he would have the goodness to call at another time. He refused to be put off. The Council, he said, wished to drive him from the realm. It was the third time that he had been sent away, and he would not bear it. She yielded. He was allowed to enter; and knowing, he said, how 'timid 'and pusillanimous'[2] she was when alone, he told her that he was surprised she should treat him with so little ceremony. The French could wait as well as he, and if he was to be put off for any trivial excuse, he might as well return to his master. Elizabeth mildly answered, that princes seldom demanded favours as she had done of Don Bernardino. She, too, was surprised that he, a Spaniard and a Mendoza, should have refused the request of a lady. But he was in no humour for soft

---

[1] Sir James Crofts was the same person who did his best to betray his mistress at the siege of Leith, 'going,' it was said, 'as near to treason as any man ever did without falling over the edge.' He was now in Philip's pay, yet Elizabeth clung to him with an odd perversity. A few years later she permitted him to lead her and the realm to the very brink of ruin, and at this moment he was secretly advising Mendoza.

'He tells me,' continues the ambassador, 'that if your Majesty wishes to prevent these ships from sailing, and to hinder the Queen from interfering further in Flanders, you cannot do better than send two thousand men to Ireland, colouring them under the name of the Pope. This will be the best of bridles to her. She will then be afraid to allow man or vessel to leave her ports. I should be wanting in my duty to your Majesty if I did not tell you what zeal Sir James displays, how instantaneously he advises me of all that passes, and how sound a Catholic he is at heart.'—*Mendoza to Philip*, June 6. *MSS. Simancas.*

[2] 'Quan pavorosa y pusillanima.'

speeches. He said that since it was her pleasure he would wait four days, and for the time consented to withdraw. But he was sick of the work on which he was employed, and as eager to break the diplomatic meshes as Walsingham could be. He told Philip, that surrounded as he was by malice and falsehood, he could do little more good by remaining at his post. He wanted skill to steer his way among such quicksands. He had tried to place himself in the hands of God, the matters with which he was occupied being chiefly such as concerned Him. But he was so great a sinner that he feared God would not use his service.[1]

The squadron was still in active preparation, when the Portuguese pretender appeared in person. He had been in Paris and had seen the Queen-mother, and Catherine and Henry had sent him on to London. Greatly disturbed at his coming, Elizabeth at first affected to be indignant that a rebel to his sovereign should dare to approach her presence. She was afraid of provoking Philip further, and Walsingham expected that he would be shuffled in haste out of the realm. He lay concealed at Stepney, the Queen refusing to see him till he had let her know that he was not come to ask for money.

But Don Antonio had brought with him the Braganza jewels which he wished to dispose of, and was ready to pay with the proceeds for the equipment of the ships. Elizabeth was fond of jewels. The diamonds of the House of Burgundy were already in the Tower. She had wrung them from the States as security in triple value for the sums which she had advanced. The diamonds of Portugal, the property virtually, like the others, of the King of Spain, would look well in companionship with them. And it would be well also if the cost of the

---

[1] Mendoza to Philip, June 15.—*MSS. Simancas.*

privateer fleet, which otherwise she was to have furnished
herself, could be thrown on the exiled Prince. On the
other hand, to entertain Don Antonio publicly, to give
him leave to make use of England and English seamen
to fit out an armament against the Crown of Spain, was
an act of which she could not evade the responsibility,
and which might be taken as a declaration of war. At
the end of the month he was allowed to come to London.
On the 1st of July he applied for permission to buy
ships, and was put off with an evasive answer.[1] In a few
days, by some curious manœuvre, the jewels were in the
treasury. A sum of money had been paid over by which
Don Antonio had purchased what he wanted. He had
gone down the Thames with the Portuguese flag flying,
and had made for Plymouth to join Drake. He had sent
secret word to Paris, and orders had been issued by Catherine
to Bourdeaux for the French contingent to proceed
at once to Terceira. She had assumed from Don Antonio's
report that the joint enterprise was to go forward,
and that she was to depend on Elizabeth's co-operation.
It was the first step towards war, and had made the message
brought by Somers doubly irritating. Walsingham,
though imperfectly in his mistress's secrets, was convinced
that, notwithstanding the preparations at Plymouth,
she had no intention of countenancing Don
Antonio.[2] It was with a feeling, therefore, approaching
disgust, that he found himself suddenly selected to take
Somers's place at Paris, entangle France in the war with
Spain, and extricate Elizabeth both from a share in it and

---

[1] Walsingham to Cecil, July 1.—*MSS. Domestic.* Walsingham to Cobham, July 1.—*MSS. France.*

[2] 'However France shall incline to assist Don Antonio, I see some cause to judge that there will be nothing done in his favour or assistance, or rather in the assisting of her Majesty's self by the abating of the pride and force of that Prince who desires nothing more than her ruin.'—*Walsingham to Cecil, July 7. MSS. Domestic.*

from her promise of marriage also. He told the Queen he would rather she sent him to the Tower. His task was an impossible one. He would fail and would be held responsible for failing.[1]

His instructions, as they were drawn up by Burghley, were 'so to deal as to acquit her Majesty of the mar-'riage,' drag her any way out of the mess into which she had plunged, and to bring France to agree to a league against Spain, in which England should not be committed to go to war. Monsieur, being of softer materials than Secretary Pinart, was to be the first object of his arts. He was to 'tell Monsieur that the Queen loved him dearly, but was embarrassed by self-willed subjects. Being, as he was, at open war with Spain, the English people would not allow her to marry him; yet, as it was of great consequence that he should go forward with his enterprise in the Low Countries, she would help him privately with money. He would perhaps say that he would prefer to abandon the enterprise and marry instead; but this could not be heard of. He might say that secret help would be valueless, that his brother would either go to war openly or not at all, and that she must follow his example. In this case, if it was clear that the mind of France was made up and there was no remedy, Walsingham was by his first instructions empowered to consent. He was directed to speak to the King as he had spoken to Monsieur; to put off the marriage without committing her otherwise if he could, but at any rate to put it off; if secret assistance was refused, he was then 'to yield to the open sort of 'aiding, and declare frankly that England would stand 'by France in a war with Spain.'

So Elizabeth thought on the 21st of July. On the

[1] Walsingham to Somers, July 19.—*MSS. France.*

22nd she had advanced on one side and receded on the
other. The first instructions were cancelled. In the
second she dwelt long and pathetically on her affection
for Monsieur's person. Cruel circumstances had hitherto
interfered with their union, but her love, she said, was
not subject to change, and in time might still be brought
to perfection. In time but not at present. She could
not ask him to sacrifice his prospects in the Low Countries; she could not marry her realm to a war; and she
loved her Prince too ardently to expose him to the dislike of her subjects. For the present therefore she must
postpone the accomplishment of her dearest wishes, and
must beg him meanwhile to rely on the certainty of her
attachment. The sentimental portion of the message
was thus mixed more strongly; the practical portion
was equally weakened. She now said that under no
circumstances would she agree to go to war, or 'give aid
'against Spain except underhand and indirectly.' In the
first message she was to be extricated from the marriage
at all hazards; in the second she preferred marriage to
war, and if 'it appeared that she was to be left alone
'without aid, subject to the malice of Spain, not free from
'the evil neighbourhood of Scotland, and uncertain of
'the good will of the French King or his brother, or
'both,' then she allowed Walsingham 'to renew some
'speech of the matter of marriage.' 'If it could be ob-
'tained that the Duke should prosecute his enterprise
'without open appearance that England should give him
'aid, so as English subjects should not think themselves
'burdened in consequence of the marriage,' he was to say
that 'then her Majesty would not think but the marriage
'should content both her and her realm.' 'She could be
'content to promise to marry, and that without unneces-
'sary delay, according to the treaty already made, if the

'French King and his brother would devise how she should not be brought into a war.'[1]

Orders so contradictory, following so close one upon the other, would in themselves have been sufficient to madden the minister that was to act upon them; but twice more, before Walsingham could depart, the pendulum of Elizabeth's resolution swung from extreme to extreme. A third set of instructions was a repetition of the first. She was to be delivered from the marriage at all hazards, even by a promise of going to war; and finally when Walsingham waited on her personally to take leave, she told him that she was not prepared to go to war, and that he was not to commit her to it.[2]

Well might Walsingham consider a lodging in the Tower preferable to going to Paris on such an errand. His own expectation was that unless something definite was done, the King and the Duke, feeling themselves trifled with, would revolt to the Catholic faction, and revenge themselves for the imbecile caprices which were making them ridiculous before the world.[3] But it was not a time when a loyal minister could afford to throw up his office. Walsingham had taken his place beside Elizabeth to do his best for her and the realm, and her own humours were among the unhappy conditions of the service. He went. He saw Monsieur first as he was directed, and Monsieur received his

---

[1] Instructions to Sir Francis Walsingham, July 21. Second instructions, July 22.—*MSS. France.*

[2] 'My Instructions, in case the King insist on assistance, and without it will not move, give me authority to yield thereto. But her Majesty's own speech since the signing of those instructions has restrained me in that behalf. Let me therefore know her Majesty's pleasure; lest if, upon my denial of yielding to open assistance, there ensue a breach of the treaty, the blame hereafter might be laid on me.'—*Walsingham to Burghley,* July 28, 1581. Digges.

[3] *Ibid.*

message precisely as he expected. 'After his long pursuit publicly known to the world,' the Duke said, 'his repulse would be greatly to his dishonour.' The war in the Low Countries was no new matter. He had consulted the Queen in every step which he had taken, and she had never hinted that his engaging in it would be a hindrance to the marriage. The King would not move a step till the marriage was completed, being persuaded that otherwise 'her Majesty would withdraw her neck 'out of the collar when once he had broken with Spain.' His connexion with Flanders would be terminated to his own and her Majesty's dishonour, 'and the King of 'Spain, having none to oppose him, would become 'absolute conqueror.'

Turenne, to whom Walsingham spoke afterwards, used the same language, hinting, however, that a large sum of money paid down might perhaps make a difference.[1]

The King was the most irritated of all, having been betrayed into sanctioning the expedition to Terceira,[2] and it became certain that if unsupported by Elizabeth, he would disentangle himself from all connexion with Don Antonio.

Walsingham, at a distance from the Court, could write what it was difficult to say. He told his mistress that she had only to throw away her reservations and declare freely and frankly that she was willing to make a political alliance with France against Spain, and the marriage would not be pressed upon her. The French Court insisted upon it at present, only from a legitimate distrust which she had provoked by her changes. If, on the other hand, she was determined not to go to war,

---

[1] Walsingham to Burghley, Aug. 6.—*MSS. France.*
[2] Cobham to Burghley, Aug. 9.—*MURDIN.*

she must interfere no further. 'To give them occasion to think,' he said, 'that your Majesty dallies with them both in marriage and league, cannot but greatly exasperate them against you; and how your Majesty shall be able to bear alone the malice of Spain, France and Scotland—for such a concurrence against you is to be looked for—I do not see. You have to consider whether you had not better join with France against Spain, than have them both with Scotland to assail you, and whether it were not better to convey the wars out of your own realm by associating with this crown, than have this crown with the rest of your ill-affected neighbours to assail you in your own realm. The solution is very easy. The only difficulty rests upon charges. It were hard your treasure should be preferred before safety. For the love of God, Madam, look to your own estate, and think there can grow no peril so great to you as to have a war break out in your own realm, considering what a number of evil subjects you have. Your Majesty cannot redeem the peril at too dear a price. Bear with my boldness, and interpret the same to the care I have of your Majesty's preservation.'[1]

By the same post he wrote to Burghley, to say that the King was deeply hurt, but would not take the Queen's message as final. If she would contribute a hundred thousand crowns, France was ready to make a league on her own terms, and he could but hope that so good a purpose would not fail for so small a sum. He had ventured to put them in hope that it would be conceded, and if it fell out otherwise he would have done ill service.

'For my own part,' he said, 'though my estate be

[1] Walsingham to Elizabeth, Aug. 10.—*MSS. France.*

'very poor and my debts great, yet rather than the
'yielding of the support should not take place, I would
'myself sell anything I have to contribute a thousand
'pounds towards the same, so greatly do I see it import
'her Majesty's safety.'[1]

The general success of Elizabeth passes for a sufficient answer to doubts cast upon her ability. Effects must have had causes equal to them, and that she left England at her death the first of European powers is accepted as proof that she was herself the first of Princes. It was not, however, the ability of Elizabeth, it was the temper of the English nation which raised her in her own despite to the high place which she ultimately filled. The genius and daring of her Protestant subjects, of whom Walsingham was no more than a brilliant representative, formed the splendid pedestal on which her own small figure was lifted into dignity.

When Walsingham's letter came she was alternately hysterical and furious. She cried like a child, sobbing out that she knew not what to do. She had sacrificed herself for Leicester, she said; Leicester had persuaded her to her ruin. Then she raged at Walsingham. Walsingham had done his message ill, and had betrayed her. Monsieur wanted her for her money. The King of France wanted her for her money. She would keep her money, and they should have none of it.[2] Burghley, reasoning vainly with her passion, told her 'that great 'matters could not be managed without charge.' 'If she 'had no need of help to withstand her perils, there was 'no occasion to send to Paris at all.' 'Walsingham had 'done no more than he would have done himself.' Her

---

[1] Walsingham to Burghley, Aug. 10, 11.—*MSS. France.* [2] Mendoza to Philip, Aug. 12.—*MSS. Simancas.*

last injunctions to him were 'to acquit her of the mar-
'riage,' and 'if she would not marry she must spend.'[1]
She answered in her old tone that if she gave money
it should and must be underhand. Burghley objected the
determination of France not to accept assistance underhand. Then she shifted her ground, and said that if she
was to have open war, 'she would rather marry with the
'war than have the war without the marriage:' but
Burghley saw that she was persuading herself that the
King had gone too far both in the Low Countries and in
Portugal to recede. A squadron, with the French flag
flying, was already at Terceira, and she herself was so far
uncommitted. Don Antonio's fleet was ready to sail
from Plymouth. Twelve thousand pounds, raised upon
his jewels, had been spent upon it. The Queen had first
promised an additional 2,000*l.* and then had refused. It
had been subscribed by Drake and Hawkins, and only her
permission to depart was waited for. She now said that
the ships should not sail at all. She professed to fear
that she would be left alone with a war with Spain upon
her hands,—her real hope being that France was implicated already, and that now she could escape altogether.

And France was so far really implicated that the King
declared himself ready to accept one of the alternatives
first offered by Elizabeth. If she would marry his
brother he was willing to take his chance for the
future, to declare war and send an army into Flanders,
and bind himself to ask for nothing either in ships,
men or money from England.[2] Elizabeth, just then in
anguish for her money, once more considered Monsieur
preferable, and sketched a letter which she was on the
point of sending to Mauvissière, intimating that if the
King would confirm this promise under the Great Seal

---

[1] Burghley to Walsingham, Aug. 10, 11.—DIGGES. [2] Walsingham to Elizabeth, Aug. 16.—DIGGES.

of France she would hesitate no longer, and the marriage should forthwith be completed.¹ But again the mood changed. She flattered herself that by stopping Don Antonio's ships she had diverted Philip's anger from herself upon France. Once more she said she could not marry into a war; nor could she permit Monsieur to throw up the Netherlands. She therefore promised to give him money, but privately only, and she refused to specify the sum. And meanwhile d'Aubigny had brought the Jesuits into Scotland, and Morton being gone the English party was broken to pieces, and to every one but the Queen herself it appeared more than likely that France would be irrecoverably affronted; and that, using Scotland as a base to operate from, the united Catholic powers would invade England before another year had passed over their heads. 'A doom predestined' could alone explain to Walsingham the infatuation of his mistress. 'There is no one thing,' he sadly wrote to Burghley, 'that does so assuredly prognosticate that 'some unavoidable mischief is to grow out of Scotland 'against her Majesty, as that her Highness of late has no 'power to put anything in execution that tends to the 'prevention thereof. Such as do love her Majesty can but 'lament it, and pray to God to open her eyes to see and 'do what may be most for her salvation. . . I see 'her Majesty not disposed to redeem her peril otherwise 'than necessity shall lead her; who is one of the most 'dangerous pilots that can take helm in hand, for where 'necessity rules, election and consent can take no place.'²

¹ 'La quelle promesse et asseurance nous estant faicte par ledict S' Roy en forme que dessus, et le traicté de marriage negociée conclu pareillement ratifié, vous luy pourrez donner la parole de nostre part qu'il peult tenir ledict marriage pour parfaict et conclu.'—*Copy of her Majesty's letter intended to have been written to the French Ambassador*, Aug. 1581. *MSS. France.*

² Walsingham to Burghley, Aug. 20.—*MSS. France.* Sept. 13.— Digges.

'What may move her hereafter,' replied Burghley, no less mournfully, 'I know not; but I see it common 'to great and small not to think of adversity in time of 'prosperity, and so adversity comes with double peril.'[1]

Once more the faithful Walsingham, 'beknaved' as he was whenever her pleasure was crossed, attempted to rouse her to a more just perception of her situation.

'I will not deny,' he said, 'but that I have been 'grieved to see my desire to do your Majesty service so 'greatly crossed. For your marriage, if your Majesty 'mean it, remember that by the delay your Highness 'uses therein, you lose the benefit of time, which, if 'years be considered, is not the least to be weighed. If 'you mean it not, assure yourself it is one of the worst 'remedies you can use, however your Majesty conceives 'it may serve your turn. If a King of Scots, pretending 'a title to the crown of England, was like by matching 'with Spain to have wrought that peril towards your 'Majesty's father as the present King is towards you, he 'would not then have stood upon generalities, as your 'Majesty now doth. Sometimes when your Majesty 'beholds in what doubtful terms you stand with foreign 'princes, you wish with great affection that opportu-'nities offered had not been slipped; but when they are 'offered to you, if they are accompanied with charges, 'they are altogether neglected. The respect of charges 'has lost you Scotland. I would to God I had no cause 'to think it might put your Highness in peril of the 'loss of England. The cause that moves them here at 'Paris, not to weigh your Majesty's friendship, is that 'they see you fly charges otherwise than by doing 'something underhand. We are now specially instructed 'by you to yield to nothing that may be accompanied

---

[1] Burghley to Walsingham, September.—DIGGES.

'with charges. The General League must be without
'certain charges; the Particular League with a volun-
'tary and no certain charge. Your Majesty's pre-
'decessors in matters of peril did never look to charges,
'when their treasure was not so great as your Majesty's,
'nor subjects so wealthy or so willing to contribute. I
'pray God the abatement of the charges towards the
'nobleman that hath the custody of the bosom serpent,
'hath not lessened his care of keeping her.[1] Morton
'is taken away, the King alienated, a general revolt
'threatened in religion. Nothing being done to help
'this is a manifest argument that the peril is so fatal
'as can no way be prevented if this sparing and im-
'provident course be held still. I conclude therefore
'in the heat of duty that there is no one that serves
'in the place of a councillor, that either weighs his own
'credit or carries that sound affection to your Majesty
'that he ought to do, that would not wish himself in
'the farthest part of Ethiopia rather than enjoy the
'fairest palace in England. The Lord God direct your
'Majesty's heart to take that way of counsel that may
'be most for your honour and safety.'[2]

The diplomacy at Paris came at last to a feeble end. Ungraciously, because without it, France would have broken from her altogether, the Queen sent Monsieur privately two hundred thousand crowns; and Henry in return renewed, with slight amplifications, the defensive league which Charles IX. had made with her at Blois. Monsieur's connexion with the Low Countries was continued on his own responsibility; and war with Spain was left conditional on the marriage, or on the

---

[1] The allowance made by the Queen to the Earl of Shrewsbury had been largely reduced.

[2] Walsingham to Elizabeth, Sept. 2.—DIGGES.

consent of Elizabeth to share its cost. It fared the worse with Don Antonio. The King disclaimed the ships which had gone to Terceira, and left them to be dealt with as pirates by the Marquis of Santa Cruz, who had gone in search of them. Elizabeth came to a final resolution to detain the squadron at Plymouth. Don Antonio applied again for leave to sail. She said she could not offend her good brother the King of Spain. He asked for 30,000*l*., which it appears she had promised to lend him upon his jewels. She replied that she could not furnish him with means to make war upon her ally. He requested that his jewels should be restored to him. She said he must repay first the instalment which had been advanced on their security. He flung away in desperation. He cursed the day when he came to England. He offered his unlucky ships for sale again, and demanded his passports to begone. Leicester's intercession at last prevailed so far, that four out of the ten which had been equipped were allowed to go, the jewels being left as a pledge that Don Antonio should do no injury to any sovereign with whom Elizabeth was at peace. Twelve thousand pounds were advanced to him by the London merchants, from which his debt to the Queen was deducted; and a vague hope was held out to him that the rest of his fleet might eventually follow. An order, some months later, went to Plymouth for their release. A Council warrant followed to detain them. At length, in the usual fashion, the responsibility was cast on Don Antonio's friends. The order for the detention was outwardly sustained, while Walsingham, in a private letter, told Edmund Tremayne to let the ships slip out; and Tremayne, with no little fear that he might be called to account, contrived their escape. They sailed half manned. Neither Drake nor Hawkins was allowed to accompany them. They came too late to strengthen Terceira, or prevent the catastrophe which presently followed there, while Don Antonio, one more victim of Elizabeth's shifting politics, remained in England to starve.[1]

The current of her own humour was setting again towards marriage. She imagined, or pretended, that she now wished definitively to purchase economical safety by the sacrifice of her person. Alençon volunteered to come again to England, and, after some hesitation, his offered visit was accepted. He came down to Calais, to correspond with her before he crossed, while Sion House was put in order for his reception.[2] The substance of the letter which the Queen had written for Mauvissière and withdrawn, was revived in a dispatch to Sir Henry Cobham. She bade her ambassador tell Henry that if he would send her a formal promise that Monsieur's expenses in the Low Countries should be borne by France, and that if Spain attacked England she might count on his assistance, 'he might be assured 'that she meant to proceed to a full and absolute con-'clusion of the said marriage.'[3]

Mendoza was incredulous as ever; but he could not conceal from himself that France and England were for the present closely united, and that together they might declare war against Spain was at least a possibility. He desired to submit Elizabeth's disposition to some deciding test. Hearing that Don Antonio was fitting out a fleet at Plymouth with the crown jewels of what

---

[1] Burghley to Walsingham, Aug. and Sept. 1581.—DIGGES. Mendoza to Philip, Sept. 7 and Sept. 17, 1581.—*MSS. Simancas.* Edmund Tremayne to Walsingham, Feb. 19, 1582.—*MSS. Domestic. Rolls House.*

[2] Mendoza to Philip, Oct. 9.—*MSS. Simancas.* Opposite the name of Sion House Philip wrote, 'solia ser un muy hermoso monasterio.'

[3] The Queen to Sir H. Cobham, Nov. 1581.—*MSS. France.*

was now his own realm, Philip had directed Don Bernardino to present a remonstrance. Uncertain of the tone which it would be desirable to assume, the King of Spain wrote three letters to his sister-in-law of graduated severity, leaving his ambassador to choose between them. Don Bernardino selected the sharpest, which contained a demand for the arrest and extradition of Don Antonio's person, requested an audience, and, with some difficulty, obtained it. The Queen was at Richmond, and received him in the chamber of presence, sitting under the cloth of state in a satin chair. Usually, when Don Bernardino came to see her, she rose from her seat; on this occasion she sate still, with a cold excuse that she had rheumatism. The ambassador apologised for troubling her when she was unwell, but she said nothing, and, after allowing him to stand for some time uncovered, she asked for his master's letter.

Don Bernardino gave it. She ran her eye over the contents, and then said that Don Antonio had left England, and that if she had cared to help him, the Indian treasure fleet would not at that moment have been safe in Cadiz harbour.

Mendoza knew that Don Antonio had not left England, and was otherwise irritated at her tone.

'It is easier to talk of taking fleets than to take them,' he answered; 'we Spaniards can hold our own, and those 'who seek us may have the worst of it; and as for Don 'Antonio, Madame, you have certainly given him assis-'tance: you have supplied him with men, arms, and 'money; the ships which he bought in the river sailed 'past your Majesty's windows at Greenwich, with the 'flag of Portugal at the mast-head; he received stores 'out of the Tower, and money upon his jewels out of 'the City.'

Having broken ground thus, he went on with his catalogue of grievances:—the meddling in the Low Countries, the plunder of Spanish merchant-ships, the piracies of Drake, for which he could have no satisfaction. Retribution, he said, must come at last, and the King of Spain's forbearance be worn out.

Elizabeth was brave while she had her Court behind her. She answered, that had she chosen, she and her subjects could have helped Don Antonio to some purpose, and she probably would help him. As to the rest of his speech, she knew not what he was talking of.

'She spoke so insolently,' Mendoza said, 'that I re-
'plied that I had now been in England three years and
'a half, and for the whole of that time I had been able
'to obtain no redress, either from her Council or from
'herself, for any wrong that had been done. Your
'Majesty, I said, will not hear words, so we must come
'to the cannon, and see if you will hear them.'

'Quietly, in her most natural voice, as if she was tell-
'ing a common story, she said, that if I used threats of
'that kind she would fling me into a dungeon.'

'I replied, that I was not threatening, but was giving
'her my master's message. She must do as she pleased,
'but if she made me prisoner, God had given me a
'sovereign who, if I were merely his subject instead of
'an ambassador, would come and fetch me out.'

But Mendoza had ascertained what he wanted to know. The Queen was no longer afraid, and then and always he had strict orders not to provoke her too far. She called the Earl of Sussex and Lord Clinton to her. 'My lords,' she said, 'Don Bernardino affirms that 'since I will not listen to his words, we must come to the 'cannon. I told him he need not think to frighten me.'

'I replied,' wrote Don Bernardino, 'that I was not so

'foolish; princes did not endure to be menaced by 'private persons; and the Queen, being a lady also, and 'so beautiful a lady, might well throw me to the lions.'

'Her countenance cleared at the compliment, so absurd 'a person is she. She began to boast of the kind things 'that she had done for your Majesty. She had saved the 'Netherlands from France for you, she said, and you in 'return had invaded Ireland, and pensioned her rebels; 'Don Guerau de Espes had stirred disaffection in England; 'and I had tried to bribe a man to kill Don Antonio.'

'I answered that subsidising Alençon was a singular 'way of keeping the French out of the Netherlands; that 'I had many times told her that your Majesty had not 'meddled with Ireland, and that for Don Antonio, I was 'only sorry that, after so long an acquaintance, she had 'not known me better.'

'Sussex said that a serious wrong had been done in 'Ireland. The Queen grew loud again, and added that 'your Majesty had not made a sufficient acknowledge-'ment of your fault; and to conclude, and as my final 'answer about the affairs of Drake, she said she would 'make no restitution till your Majesty had given her 'full satisfaction about Ireland. She had first received 'offence; she must first receive reparation. Afterwards 'she would see what could be done.'

'I replied that I would report her words to the Board 'of Trade at Seville; that more than a million and a half 'of ducats had been stolen, and that if your Majesty was 'content to forget your own share of the loss, you could 'not neglect the claims of your subjects. She herself, I 'said, issued letters of marque when her people had been 'wronged, and redress could not be had for them; and 'I did not doubt that, when her answer was known 'in Spain, your Majesty would empower the merchants

'of Seville to indemnify themselves out of English pro-
'perty in our harbours.'

'She repeated that she had been the first offended,
'and would have the first satisfaction; and so, with
'much composure, told me that I might retire.'

'I said I must speak further with her Council.'

'She turned away, and I heard her say, with a deep
'sigh, "Would to God we could each have our own,
'" and be at peace!"'[1]

Mendoza had assumed a bold front, but he was painfully aware that he would not be supported by his
master. The last direction of Charles V. to his son had
been to cherish always, and especially if threatened by
France, the alliance with England; and Philip, unless
he could overthrow Elizabeth by internal revolution,
believed himself compelled to be her friend. Nor were
political interests the only links which religious antagonism found it hard to dissolve. The English trade was
as important to Spain as to England itself. For several
years there had been short harvests in Gallicia, Portugal, and Andalusia, and the maritime provinces of the
Peninsula had been fed by English wheat. France, distracted by civil war, could hardly supply her own necessities; the soil of America was cultivated as yet only
for its gold and silver; and but for the surplus produce
from Norfolk and Hampshire, there would have been
famine. So long at least as Henry and Elizabeth were
in alliance, it was certain that Philip would not venture
upon violent measures; and Elizabeth's language had
satisfied Mendoza that for the present she felt sure of
her ground. The London merchants, learning that re-
prisals had been threatened, had applied to Walsingham

---

[1] 'Volesse a Idio che ognuno habesse il suo e fosse in pace.'—Men- doza to Philip, Oct. 20, 1581. MSS. Simancas.

for an explanation. Walsingham had told them that the Queen meant to make use of Drake's treasure to pay the expenses which Philip had caused her in Ireland. If their ships were seized at Cadiz, there were goods enough in London belonging to Spain to reimburse their losses.

The honour of Spain was at stake. To have demanded reparation—to have been unable to obtain it—yet not to venture to resent the refusal, was a confession of weakness or cowardice. 'Many of their ships,' wrote Mendoza, ' I
' understand to be on their way home, and beyond the
' reach of arrest. Had they remained in our harbours the
' seizure might have still been impolitic in the present
' attitude of affairs at Terceira. I have therefore tried to
' frighten the merchants in another way. This treasure
' of Drake's is the bait which keeps the French at the
' Queen's devotion. We must recover it if we can. I
' therefore have forged a letter from the Board of Trade
' at Seville to the Anglo-Spanish Company in London,
' in which the Board intimate that they are waiting
' earnestly for the Queen's resolution. If the plunder be
' not restored, they will be obliged, to their extreme
' regret, to close the intercourse between the two coun-
' tries, and lay an embargo on English property. They
' recommend the company, therefore, to press on the
' Government the necessity of doing justice. I gave this
' composition to the masters, by whom it was translated
' and presented to the Council. The Council, I under-
' stand, said that it was moderate and reasonable, and
' they would give it their best consideration.'[1]

The consequences were extremely curious. The Council might consider, but their thoughts were not likely to take form in action, till Spain used sterner

---

[1] Mendoza to Philip, Nov. 7.—*MSS. Simancas.*

weapons than forged letters. Mendoza, like most other Spanish statesmen and soldiers, was weary of intrigue and subterfuge, and recognising the indisputable fact that England was the representative power of Protestanism, wished most heartily to cross swords with it, and try out the question in fair and open fight. To men like Mendoza and the Duke of Feria and Juan de Vargas, the dilatoriness of Philip was no less irritating than the artifices of Elizabeth to Walsingham and Burghley. Yet Philip could not forget his father's injunctions or the political traditions which he had inherited, and since he could not be forced into war, and his existing relations with England were productive only of ignominy, Mendoza, as a second alternative, not in irony, but in deliberate seriousness, recommended his master to make up his quarrel with Elizabeth *bonâ fide* and with no reservations. The attempt to recover England by revolution had failed hitherto, but there was again hope of success. The Jesuits were busy; the conversions had been large; the state of Scotland was promising; the leading English nobles had promised to rebel. To make a league with the excommunicated Queen was to defy the Pope, to fling over the eager instruments of insurrection with as much indifference as Elizabeth had flung off Morton. It was the very moment when Campian and his comrades were winning their martyrs' crowns at Tyburn. Yet Mendoza considered notwithstanding that if Spain was not to assume an open and honourable attitude it would be better to risk these minor inconveniences and renew the league which Charles V. had made with Henry VIII. It could not now be re-established without the introduction of a clause against the Queen of Scots.[1] Yet

---

[1] 'Agora cuando se le tratase á la Reyna lo de renovar las confederaciones, en demas, en las primeras platiras, indubitadamente creo que lo primero que se propornia seria se haga liga contra la de Escocia por

notwithstanding, so weak, so ineffectual, so discreditable, had been Philip's diplomacy, that Mendoza advised him to submit to necessity—to offer his hand cordially and frankly to his sister-in-law, and to leave the Queen of Scots to her fate.[1] He promised to observe the utmost caution — to feel his way with the lead-line in his hand; but, after all, he said that the Queen had done but little for Don Antonio, and he expressed a serious hope that Philip would empower him to make the offer, should an opportunity arise.[2]

Philip's answer is not among the Spanish archives, but in his well-known hand he has scrawled his approbation on the margin of the decipher of his ambassador's letter.[3] Mendoza himself was writing evidently in perfect good faith, and in the tone of his letter there is as evident an acknowledgment that substantial justice had hitherto been on Elizabeth's side. It came to nothing, but the course of history turns upon slight accidents. A little more and Spain and England would have been friends again on free and fair conditions, with immeasurable consequences to Europe for good and evil.

Alençon meanwhile was again in England without the knowledge and against the wishes of his brother, who did

---

ser de quien ella mas se recela, teniendo que con el titulo de Catolica y augmento de la verdadera religion, ha de ser ayudada y favorescida para su demanda de V. Mag^d con mas calor que de otro ningun Principe Christiano; por ser esta maxima que tienen concebida ella y sus consejeros y hereges, y sobre la cual se afirman en inquietar por todas vias á V. M^d, para impedir que no pueda volver los ojos á la reduccion deste Reyno; de manera que no siendo servido V. Mag^d condescender en semejante punto, el presentarles no serviria sino hacerlos cierta su sospecha.'—*Don Bernardino al Rey*, 20 Nov^{bre}. *MSS. Simancas.*

[1] 'Por cuyo respecto supplicando á V. Mag^d perdone tan gran atrevimiento, seria de parecer que ya que algunas otras consideraciones que yo no puedo alcançar pidan se trate desto, se le se aclarase con la Reyna quando quisiese mayor seguridad que el decirle V. Mag^d le hará amistad, correspondiendo ella con la misma llaneza y verdad, ofrecelle el ratificar las ligas pasadas.'—*Ibid.*

[2] *Ibid.*

[3] 'Dice bien en mucho desto.'

not wish to be made increasingly ridiculous. He slipped across in disguise from Dieppe. An escort waited for him at Rye, and at the beginning of November he appeared in London. The enchanted frog of the fairy tale was present in all its hideousness, and the lovely lady was to decide if she would consent to be his bride. Walsingham, who detested the whole business, concluded now, like Burghley, that having gone so far she must carry it to the end. He praised Monsieur to the Queen. He said that he had an excellent understanding; his ugly face was the worst part of him. 'Then thou knave,' she said, 'why hast thou so many times said ill of him? 'Thou art as changeable as a weathercock.'[1] The analogy suited better with herself. On his first arrival little seems to have been said about the marriage, the Queen trying to lay him under obligations to her in other ways, which could not be spoken of in treaties. He was heir to the French crown. The Guises and the enemies of religion interfered with his legitimate influence and threatened to obstruct his succession. If he would maintain the edicts, 'her Highness promised all her 'power to support him and impugn his contraries.' He had 'taken on him the protection of the Low Countries.' 'Her Majesty would aid and succour him as far as she 'might with the contributions of her realm and people.'[2] But if this would satisfy Alençon it would not satisfy France. Since the Duke had chosen to come to England, the French Government desired to be informed of the probable results of his visit, and three weeks after his

---

[1] 'Walsingham decia estos dias atras muchos bienes á la Reyna de las partes y entendimiento de Alençon, sin tener falta sino la fealtad del rostro. Respondióle pues "Knave," que es una palabra muy injuriosa en Ingles, porque me has dicho tantas veces lo contrario y males del, que te vuelves como belita'—*Mendoza al Rey*, 7 Noviembre. *MSS. Simancas.*

[2] Note in Burghley's hand, Nov. 14.—*MSS. France. Rolls House.*

arrival Mauvissière waited on the Queen to learn what he might write to his master.

It was the 22nd of November. She had settled for the winter at Greenwich. She was taking her morning walk in the gallery with Alençon at her side, and Leicester and Walsingham behind, when Mauvissière was introduced. He put his question with a Frenchman's politeness. 'Write this to your master,' she answered: 'the Duke will be my husband.' With a sudden impulse she turned upon Monsieur, kissed his brown lips, took a ring from her finger and placed it herself on his hand. She sent for the ladies and gentlemen of the household and presented Monsieur to them as their future master. She dispatched a messenger to tell Burghley, who was confined to his bed with the gout. He drew a long breath of satisfied relief. 'Blessed be 'God,' he exclaimed; 'her Majesty has done her part; 'the realm must complete the rest.' Letters were sent out to summon Parliament immediately. Couriers flew to Paris with the news, and for a few days every one believed that the subject of such weary negotiations was settled at last.

But Burghley and all others were once more deceived. Not only was nothing settled, but Elizabeth neither meant anything to be settled nor even believed at the time that she meant it. Hatton, her 'sheep,' as Mendoza ascertained, came to her afterwards with tears running down his cheeks: well as he knew her, the gift of the ring had frightened him, and he bleated about the grief of her people. Leicester asked her sarcastically whether they were to consider her as betrothed. She

[1] 'Ella le respondió podreis scribir esto al Rey que el Duque de Alençon será mi marido, dandole al momento al Alençon un beso en la boca y un anillo que sacó de su mano en señal de ser cierto.'—*Don B. de Mendoza al Rey*, 14 Noviembre, 1581. *MSS. Simancas.*

assured them both tenderly that they had nothing to
fear.[1] She meant to demand concessions to which the
French King would not consent. Leicester thought she
had gone dangerously far. Hatton asked how she would
extricate herself if the King did consent. 'With words,'
she answered, 'the coin most current with the French:
'when the field is large and the soldiers cowards there
'are always means of creeping out.'

She had need of her skill. Henry instantly sent over
Secretary Pinart to congratulate and to conclude the
settlements. Walsingham, who had too well-founded
misgivings, asked him how much money the King
would look for as damages if no marriage came off after
all. Pinart enquired with wide eyes if there were still
doubts about it. He soon learnt that he had come
across on a fool's errand. Elizabeth first demanded the
dissolution of the Seminary at Rheims. Pinart intimated that this would be conceded. The abolition of
the Scotch league was next asked for, and after that
the restitution of Calais. Leicester, frightened for what
might follow, proposed to raise 200,000*l*. by privy seals,
give them to Alençon to buy off his displeasure, and to
set him up on his own account in the Netherlands.
Elizabeth, ridiculing the very thought of throwing
away such a sum, announced that if Alençon would
truck her affection for money he should have neither

---

[1] 'Hatton la habló con muchas lagrimas, diciendole que cuando quisiere casarse, tuviese cuenta quanto lo sintia su Reyno, etc. Ella le respondió con gran ternura.'—*Don Bernardino al Rey*, 4 Deciembre, 1581. 'Hatton dixó á un confidente suyo que él no habia temido jamas el casamiento sino cuando la Reyna dió el anillo á Alençon, pero en hablandola le habia asegurado.'—*Al Rey*, 1 Noviembre, 1581.

[2] 'Preguntando Hatton en que manera pensaba eximirse si el Rey de Francia embiaba el scripto, dixóle, con palabras, que es la mejor moneda que corria entre Franceses; y cuando la campaña era larga, y medrosos los soldados, nunca faltaba lugar para descabullirse.'—*Ibid*.

the one nor the other, and might go where he pleased.¹ She had to lower her tone before many weeks were over. The humour at Paris had become really dangerous. The Duke of Guise was recalled to Court, received with studied favour, and was present at the audiences of Sir H. Cobham, hanging like a threatening portent over the king's shoulder. Though his brother might submit to be trifled with, Henry said the honour of France was touched and the nation would not bear the reproach. The request for Calais he treated as an insult. To entertain the proposal, he said, might cost him his crown.

At this moment came the unwelcome news that the Prince of Parma had taken Tournay. The States had trusted to Alençon, and Alençon was idling in England, and France was rendered motionless by Elizabeth's uncertainties. An impression spread among the Netherlanders that they were betrayed, and a cry rose at Bruges that it would be better to make terms with the enemy while they had still something to lose.² Events would not wait while Elizabeth was amusing herself. After a week of confusion and quarrel the Council met, and Cecil, desperate of any good resolution in the Queen, supposing now that she would only exasperate France, and in Walsingham's words, 'for amity find 'enmity,' said that there was but one course open. They must make peace with Spain, securing the best terms they could obtain for the Netherlands and restoring Drake's plunder. No one could any more believe that the Queen would marry. It was equally certain that Alençon would resent the idle impertinence to which he had been subjected.

Leicester and Hatton clamoured against the restitu-

---

¹ Mendoza to Philip, December 11. —MSS. Simancas. ² Th. Stokes to Walsingham, Dec. 24.—MSS. Holland.

tion. Walsingham, bitterly as his worst fears were confirmed, still advised that the treasure should be used to subsidise Casimir and the King of Navarre and to help the struggling States. But Burghley adhered to his opinion, and Sussex, Bromley, and Clinton stood by him. They had disapproved from the first of Drake's expedition. They considered that if not at once yet by instalments everything ought to be given back; and Mendoza saw with delight that the most powerful English statesman was moving on the course which he had himself recommended to Philip, while he was spared the mortification of making the first advances. Burghley went so far as to feel his way with him and hint his wishes; and Mendoza, with a slight suspicion that perhaps he might be played off against the French and made use of to frighten Henry, yet admitted temperately the pleasure with which he would regard a restored alliance between Spain and England.[1]

But how to shake off Alençon? The Queen had brought him over, and now both with herself and the Council the first object was to rid the realm of him. It was represented to him that his honour was suffering through Parma's conquests, that the marriage at all events could not take place immediately, and that his presence was required at Antwerp. The Queen promised him unlimited supplies of money, a promise however which, if Simier was to be believed, she hoped to escape from keeping.[2] In public she affected the deepest sorrow at

---

[1] Mendoza to Philip, Dec. 25, 1581.—MSS. Simancas.

[2] Simier was in England, in as high favour as ever with the Queen, but no longer as devoted as he had been to the interests of his master. Elizabeth, Mendoza says, told Simier that Alençon pretended that he had gone into the war to please her and that she must give him money to carry it on. 'Not having other means to shake him off, she had offered him a large monthly allowance.' 'But as soon as he was across the sea,' she said, 'I mean to represent to him that the Council will not

the Duke's compelled departure. In private she danced for joy at the thought that she would see him no more. Struggling and complaining, the victim of her caprices submitted to be pushed along. He said it was but too clear that she did not love him, and that his own devotion deserved a better return. She swore that her desire that he should go rose only from her anxiety for his welfare. He said he could not go. He had her word, her letter, and her ring, and he would not leave her till she was his wife. She set Cecil upon him, who for very shame was as earnest for his departure as herself. She availed herself of the Spanish leanings of the Council. She thought, according to Simier, of declaring publicly that she was going over to the Spanish side in the hope that Alençon would be recalled at once by the French Court. He was told that he had better go before the 1st of January or he would have to make a New Year's present to the Queen.[1] Anything to be quit of him. That was the necessity of the present hour; the next might care for itself.

Her changes had been so many and so violent that Burghley once more asked her if she was really and finally decided. She said she would not be Alençon's wife to be empress of the universe.[2] If this was true, the longer he remained the greater the danger; and Burghley again urged him to begone. He said he had only meddled with the Provinces in the hope of marrying the Queen; if she would not have him, he would concern himself no further with them; he would

---

consent; that the realm cannot afford him so large a contribution, without too much weakening the home defences, and that this cannot be suffered.'—*Mendoza to Philip*, Dec. 25.—*MSS. Simancas.*

[1] *Mendoza to Philip*, Dec. 25.— *MSS. Simancas.*

[2] ' Al 25, en la noche, estando hablando con el Tesorero sobre esto, le dijó que aunque pensaba ser Emperatriz de todo el mundo, no se casaria con Alençon.'—*Don Bernardino á su Mag*', 29 Deciembre, 1581. *MSS Simancas.*

complain to every prince in Christendom of the wrong which he had suffered, and his brother would see him avenged. Burghley could prevail nothing. The Queen took him in hand herself. She said she could not marry a Catholic. He swore he loved her so that he would turn Protestant for her sake.[1] She told him she could not conquer her disinclination; she was sorry, but such was the fact. Might she not be a friend and sister to him? In a tumult of agitation he declared that he had suffered anguish from his passion for her. He had dared the ill opinion of all the Catholics in Europe. He had run a thousand risks for her, and sooner than leave England without her, he would rather they both perished.

The Queen, agitated or professing to be agitated in turn, exclaimed 'that he must not threaten a poor old 'woman in her own kingdom; passion not reason spoke 'in him,' she said, 'or she would think him mad. She 'begged him not to use such dreadful words.'

'No, no, Madame,' croaked the poor Prince, 'you 'mistake; I meant no hurt to your blessed person. I 'meant only that I would sooner be cut in pieces than 'not marry you and so be laughed at by the world.'

With these words he burst into tears. The Queen gave him her handkerchief to wipe his eyes with, and in this charming situation the curtain drops over the scene.[2] He would perhaps have been driven out of the country with some discourtesy but for the arrival a second time of Secretary Pinart. Pinart had gone back to Paris to

---

[1] 'Poniendole delante cuan gran inconveniente era para poder vivir con contento ser él de diferente religion, Alençon le aseguró con juramento que él dexaria la suya por su amor.'—*Mendoza al Rey*, 19 Deciembre. Opposite these words Philip writes 'Ojo.'

[2] 'La Reyna le dió un lienço para enjugarse, consolandole con algunas palabras de mas ternura que las que antes habian pasado.'—*Ibid.*

report his disappointment, and had been again dispatched upon the spot to tell the Queen that unless she shewed more consideration for the honour and interests of France, a league would be immediately formed between France and Spain, and demands would be made upon herself, which she would probably find unpleasant. Pinart spoke so sternly, so seriously, that it cost her a night's rest and a fever in the morning. She sent for Sussex to her bed-side. She said she had reconsidered her situation. The danger was too great. She would accept her fate and marry after all. Again the wretched Council was forced to assemble and travel once more over the dreary road of argument. The two favourites as before were vehemently hostile. Sussex repeated his opinion that the marriage would give peace to Europe, and that nothing else would save England from calamity.

The comedy would perhaps have been played over once more; but Cecil, after the meeting, was closeted for an hour with the Queen, and convinced her that to trifle further at that moment would probably cost her her crown. An order was issued to prepare a squadron to take Alençon to the Low Countries. Pinart, in the Queen's presence, forbade him to go—forbade him in his brother's name to prosecute the enterprise further—unless in the capacity of her husband. Every point which had been originally raised, every rational condition which had been added, the King was ready to concede. So anxious was he to leave her without excuse, that although he said he could not restore Calais to her, which she might use against him in some future combination, he was willing to give her hostages for the performance of his own part of the treaty; but he could not consent that his brother and the heir of his crown should place himself defenceless as a mere adventurer in the hands of the Hollanders.

What was to be done? 'The tricks which the Queen 'is playing to get rid of Monsieur,' wrote Mendoza, 'are 'more than I can describe.' Messengers came one after another from the Prince of Orange entreating Alençon's presence. They had been sent at Elizabeth's instigation. She bribed his companions to tell him that if he let the Low Countries escape him, he could not show his face in France again. She told him herself that she had been reflecting on her relations with Spain, that she regretted the wrongs which she had done to an old ally; that she must repair them and recover his friendship. She ridiculed to Pinart the pretence that France could be reconciled to Philip. She told him, with a slight exaggeration, that Mendoza was at her feet, entreating an alliance with England.[1]

Alternately worried and cajoled, the unfortunate Prince at last consented to go, on condition that the Queen would so far compromise herself as to give him money to pay an army of Germans; that Leicester and Howard should accompany him to Holland, and that he might look forward to returning in a few months to claim her hand. Words cost her nothing. She promised faithfully to marry him as soon as circumstances allowed. To part with money was a hard trial, but she dared not refuse. She gave him thirty thousand pounds, with bills for twenty thousand more; the bills, however, were not to be immediately cashed, and she left herself time to cancel them if she altered her mind.[2]

She accompanied him to Canterbury, lavishing freely, as he was really going, her oaths and protestations

---

[1] Mendoza to Philip, Jan. 27, 1582.—*MSS. Simancas.*

[2] 'Entiendo que le han dado 20,000 ducados en letras de mercaderes para la leva de la caballeria Alemana, y otras de la misma suma para la de los Esquyzaros; las cuales van con restriccion por si la Reyna mudare de proposito, ser á tiempo para que no se cumplan las letras.'— *Don Bernardino al Rey*, 2 de Hebrero, 1582. *MSS. Simancas.*

that she would be his wife, Lord Sussex listening with disgust to what he knew to be falsehood and absurdity.[1] She bade him write to her, and address his letters as to his wife the Queen of England;[2] while to France she sung the same tune, swearing that she would do anything that Henry wished when immediate fulfilment could be no longer demanded of her. The English lords conveyed their charge to Flushing, where they left him, as Leicester scornfully said, stranded like a hulk upon a sandbank.[3] He was installed as Duke of Brabant, and the States took an oath of allegiance to him, Leicester jesting at the ceremony as a pageant and idle illusion. The Prince of Orange intimated that he was accepted by the States only as a pledge that England would support them; if England failed them, they would not trust their fortunes to so vain an idiot; while in affected agony at his loss, she declared that she could not bear to think of her poor Frog suffering in those stagnant marshes, and that she would give a million to have him swimming in the Thames again.[4]

Having disposed of her lover, and naturally ill pleased with her own performances, the Queen fell into one of her violent fits of ill temper, quarrelling with every one about her, and angry, above all, with the Earl of Leicester. She had herself sent him to the Low Countries; but rehearsing, as it were, her subsequent resent-

---

[1] 'Dixó que por mas que hiciese, eran todas fictiones y disparate.'—*Dn B. de Mendoza al Rey*, 19 Hebrero.

[2] 'Esta Reyna dixó á Alençon á la partida que le scribiese de Flandes á mi muger la Reyna de Inglaterra.'—*Ibid.* 1 Marzo.

[3] 'El de Leicester ha dicho que dexaba á Alençon, plantado como nao vieja que habia tocado, que sin gran marea y viento no podria salir del banco donde se habia sentado.'—*Ibid.* 6 Marzo.

[4] 'Dixó en publico que diera un millon porque su Rana, que asi llama al Alençon, nadara en el Tomise y no en las aguas estantias de los Payses Bajos.'—*Ibid.* March 1.

ment with him for the same cause, she suspected that
he was using her name to obtain the Low Countries for
himself. She blamed him for having been present when
Alençon was installed, as implicating her with the Spanish King. She charged him with conspiring with the
Prince of Orange. She called Leicester traitor. She
beknaved Walsingham for having carried off her Prince
to a place where he could gain nothing but dishonour.[1]
She sent for Burghley. He was again confined with gout,
but she would admit no excuses. Her relations with
France were grown precarious, she said. The Spaniards
were ready to make up their quarrel with her, and she
had resolved to return to her old friends. Burghley
raised no objection: he reminded her, however, that
there was such a thing as honour: she must not desert
the Low Countries, which had struggled so long and so
bravely, after using them for her own convenience.
She must make conditions for them as well as for herself, and must secure them liberty of conscience at least.
Mendoza, to whom the Queen's words were immediately
reported, was ready to encourage her; he ascertained, however, that Leicester, notwithstanding her
violence, was the only person that had influence with
her. Leicester told her that if she allied herself with
Spain, every town in the Netherlands would at once be
garrisoned by the French; and his own ambition, which

---

[1] Some scandalous secret connected with the Alençon business had
a narrow escape of falling into wrong
hands, as appears from a curious note.
I do not find what the secret was,
but on the 11th of February Burghley
wrote to Walsingham:—

'Of late M. Marchmont's lodging
in Cannon Row was robbed, and in
a trunk his writings also were em-
bezzled, and the trunk conveyed into
a garden, where the persons that
found it, perceiving French writings,
brought to me the very papers between D. and you, written in your
name, the discovery whereof made
me ready to blush to see by that accident such secrets made common.'—
MSS. Domestic.

it was to be feared that she might be tempted to indulge, was to obtain the Netherlands for himself.

The humour of France, meanwhile, was becoming really dangerous. The fanatical faction was at no time easy to control. If the politicians and the Huguenots were ready for a war with Spain, the Guisians and the Catholics had an equal detestation for England; and had any other sovereign been on the throne than the weak and vicious Henry of Valois, the English treaty would have been torn in shreds and flung in Elizabeth's face. But Henry, like Philip, inherited the traditions of his race. Elizabeth had out-manœuvred him, and he had a Spanish quarrel on his hands. Experience had shown that an alliance between Catholic Spain and schismatic England was not impossible. Francis I. had forced Henry VIII. into a combination with Charles; and the result had been an invasion of France, and a war which ended in the loss of Piedmont and Milan, in the defeat of St. Quentin's and the destruction of French influence in Scotland. Henry hated the house of Guise too cordially to risk at their side a repetition of the same misfortunes.

Yet he did not care to conceal his resentment. Sir Henry Cobham, when he waited on him for the first time after his brother had been shouldered out of England, found him sullen and cold. He said that the Queen, by her humours and changes, had brought dishonour on his family. She had plunged Alençon into a war from which misfortunes only could be looked for. For himself he washed his hands of the affair, and would have nothing more to do with it. The ambassador reported his words to Elizabeth. Instantly she sung over again her old strain. If France would bear the cost of a war with Spain, she was ready to marry at any time. She bade Sussex send for Marchmont, Alençon's secretary, and tell him so. Sussex answered coldly that her aversion to marriage was evidently too strong for her to overcome. She had better say no more about it; and give France no fresh offence. From Sussex she went to Cecil, who was now unable to leave his bed, and she found Cecil equally unwilling to meddle further. He reminded her that every difficulty in the way of the marriage had been removed; her own people had been reconciled to it; France had yielded to the most extravagant conditions; Alençon had twice risked his credit to visit her; and the result had been that at the last moment she had altered her mind, with infinite peril to herself and the realm. The Council could say no more. The decision must rest with herself.

Yielding to her immediate impulse, she summoned Marchmont to her presence. If Monsieur would leave the Low Countries and come back to her, she said she was now ready to become his wife.[1] She did not even leave it to Marchmont to communicate with his master. She commissioned a gentleman of her household to carry the flattering message to him from her own lips. Walsingham, hearing what she was doing, cautioned her that if Monsieur took her at her word, and she again disappointed him, every Catholic Prince in Europe would set upon her.[2] She hesitated for a moment, but she imagined or she pretended that she was resigned to the sacrifice. She sent for Mauvissière, and gave him her solemn word of honour, that if he would bring

---

[1] Mendoza to the King, March 19, 1582.—*MSS. Simancas.*

[2] 'La Reyna despachó un gentilhombre de su camera, pidiendo á Alençon se partiese al momento de los Estados. Pero Walsingham, entendida esta resolucion, le dixó mirase lo que hacia, porque cuando Alençon viniese era forçoso casarse con él, y cuando no, venir las armas de todos los Principes Christianos sobre ella.'—*Don Bernardino al Rey*, 1 Avril. *MSS. Simancas.*

Monsieur back she would marry him. Mauvissière, like her own ministers, had heard the same song too often to be deluded further. To herself he answered that she had made him write what she did not mean so often, that he must decline to take a further part. To others he said, that if she intended to continue her tricks she must use paper and ink of her own.[1]

Even Leicester and Hatton were now frightened. One more affront to France might be the last which would be borne. Sussex wished to see something done as well as talked of, towards the reconciliation with Spain. Cecil, touching yet more dangerous ground, told the Queen that the time was come when she must settle the succession; her subjects could not permit a matter which concerned them so nearly to remain longer in uncertainty. The hint of a successor was uniformly maddening. Again, openly in Court, she swore she would marry. Again, she bade Sussex write to Monsieur, and not only gave him her word as a Queen that she was sincere, but her oath as a Christian woman. But neither her word nor her oath would convince Sussex. He refused to let her use him again as an instrument to wound her reputation.[2]

Alençon, in his letters to her, had ceased to allude to the marriage. She began now to fear that Henry and Alençon, being finally alienated from England, might take the Netherlands for themselves, and annex them to the French Crown. She flew out at Walsingham and told him that he deserved to lose his head, for having advised that Alençon should be sent thither.

But the impassioned lover was still faithful to his

---

[1] 'Diciendo en publico que pues la Reyna queria continuarse en engañar al mundo, que aun tenia papel y tinta para hacello.'—*Don Bernardino al Rey*, 1 Avril. *MSS. Simancas.*

[2] *Ibid.* April 15.—*MSS. Simancas.*

vows. No sooner had he received her message, than he poured out his eloquent delight: he loved her better than his life, he said; he would fly to her side; he would go back to England like a swallow with the summer, and make his nest for ever in her realm.

At once she sent for Marchmont and Mauvissière; she told them that Alençon was coming; but before the ceremony could take place, she must receive an instrument from the French King binding him to go to war with Spain at his own cost. They answered that she had used the same words to them before; they had believed her, and had been blamed for their credulity. She replied that these were not words but oaths, which she had sworn as a Queen and a Christian. She called God to witness that she was speaking truth. Then, as if the blame for past miscarriages had rested not with her but with France, she pretended that if, after so long a negotiation, the instrument was not sent, she must suppose she was trifled with. Unless Alençon was her husband, neither the King nor he should have a foot in the Low Countries while she had a man left to fight, or a shilling to spend. 'You think I want friends,' she said; 'you fancy that if your King abandon me, I am 'lost. At this moment the King of Spain is courting 'my friendship at my feet, swearing that he will stand 'by me against every Prince in Christendom, if I will 'leave France and renew my league with the house of 'Burgundy. Say to your master that if there is more 'delay and the marriage is again postponed, I will not 'be cheated with words; I will accord with the King of 'Spain.'[1]

The King of Spain being at Elizabeth's feet was a somewhat bold figure of speech. It was true that

[1] Mendoza to Philip, May 4, 1582.

he was anxious for the English alliance. It was true that he was willing to forget the Queen's excommunication and the persecution of the Jesuits; but he intended at the same time to exact complete reparation for his own secular wrongs, and had sent fresh instructions to Mendoza to make another demand for the stolen treasure. The Queen, instead of being continually closeted with Philip's ambassador, as she pretended, listening to his entreaties for a reconciliation, had refused to see him. He had written without effect to Sussex and to Walsingham; and now, hearing what she had said to Marchmont and the ambassador, he used the opportunity to write to herself. That she might be under no mistake about Philip's real position towards her, he told her that peace between the two countries was hanging on a thread; and that if she again declined to give him an audience, he would take her answer as final, and immediately leave the realm.[1]

Reduced to their true dimensions, Elizabeth's Spanish prospects were extremely moderate. She could have Philip for an ally, but she must repay first a million and a half of ducats; and to part with a large sum of money was worse than death. She continued, therefore, to play upon her solitary string. Mauvissière told her that his master had gone far already, that it was impossible for him to give her the instrument which she desired without better security than her word. In affected indignation she invoked the most fearful maledictions on herself, if she did not marry immediately that it was granted. She called Cecil, who was present, to bear witness to her promise, swearing so fearfully that even Mauvissière shuddered to hear her. The Lord

---

[1] Mendoza to the Queen of England, May 18.—*MSS. Spain. Rolls House.*

Treasurer, on leaving the presence chamber, whispered to Lady Stafford, that if the King consented and she did not marry after all, God would surely send her to hell for such awful perjury.[1]

---

[1] 'Se enojó mucho la Reyna, protestando con terribles juramentos y maldiciones que le viniesen, si luego que el Rey acordase lo que ella le pedia no se casase, llamando el Tesorero que se halló ally, para que fuese como testigo de su Intencion, y de la promesa que hacia; y esto con juramentos tan temerosos que el mismo Embajador afirma que le ponia grima el oyrles, y en conformidad desto dixó al Cecil á la salida á Milady Stafford, Camarera Mayor, que cuando él de Francia viniese en lo que se le pedia y no se casase la Reyna, la castigaria Dios, embiandola al Infierno, por las juras hechas.'—*Don Bernardino de Mendoza al Rey*, 15 Noviembre, 1581. *MSS. Simancas.*

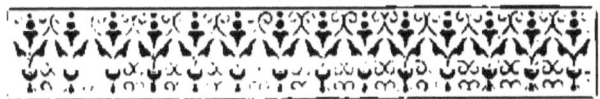

CHAPTER XXX.

'SUCH is the course of all our proceedings,' wrote Walsingham of the policy of his mistress, 'that when we want the friendship and amity of the Princes our neighbours, we do then lament that we have not sought it. When it is offered unto us, we make little account of it.'[1] With a temperament so constituted that she could feel neither sustained interest in the questions which divided Europe, nor sustained anxiety for herself, Elizabeth floated with the stream of the revolution, trusting to the goodness of her intentions and to the fortune which had borne her so long unharmed, supposing that she was secured by the jealousies of the rival powers, and only roused to energy when threatened by the combinations which she had provoked, or when Burghley forced her to see that causes which might protect the independence of England need be no protection to herself.[2] While she was jesting in private with Hatton at the pretensions of Alençon, and in

---

[1] Walsingham to Sir H. Cobham, June 20, 1582.—*MSS. France.*

[2] 'It is most likely that Monsieur will now marry in some place where the Queen's Majesty shall not have cause to like, and if it be with Spain then her Majesty must look to receive unkindness both from Spain and France, a matter hardly for her Majesty to bear, and yet so to be used by either of them as the crown of England shall take no hurt but only the person of her Majesty and her government.'—*Notes in Burghley's hand*, 1582. *MSS. France.*

public calling down the vengeance of God upon herself
if she did not mean to marry him, danger was approaching
her—the most serious to which she had yet
been exposed—from the quarter in which her wisest
ministers had anticipated its appearance.

With the death of Morton, her influence in Scotland
had gone.[1] D'Aubigny was rewarded with a dukedom
and with Dalkeith Castle. The second instrument in
Morton's destruction, Colonel Stewart, had ascended
through infamy to almost equal greatness. The Earl
of Arran, who still survived in a state of idiotcy, had
been for some years in charge of Lord March. The
house of Hamilton had been crushed by Morton. Lord
John and Lord Claude were in exile, and the Hamilton
estates were a tempting prey. Colonel Stewart was
appointed Arran's tutor. He first used his opportunities
to seduce Lady March, who, when she found herself
with child with him, obtained a divorce from her husband,
on the ground of impotence, and married her
lover. He then raised a plea of illegitimacy against his
ward, preferred a claim to his estates and title in the
right of his mother, Lady Margaret, sister of the Duke
of Chatelherault; and according to the easy methods of
Scotch justice courts when the Marian faction was in
power, he obtained his suit without difficulty. The
largest private estates in Scotland were made over to
him, and he figured thenceforward with the Arran
coronet, while the true owner was left to languish in a
prison. Careless and fearless of God and man, Stewart
had perilous stuff in him, which was not long in coming
out after his advancement. For the present he
continued a useful dependant of Lennox, and was employed
to prepare James's mind for conversion to Rome,

---

[1] Henceforth he will be called Duke of Lennox.

by debauching his mind, surrounding him with loose women, 'provoking him to the pleasures of the flesh, 'and fostering him in foolish talk.'[1]

Lennox himself, meanwhile, proceeded in the development of the great conspiracy, which he had commenced so successfully. In religion, he was still obliged to wear his mask. The King, boy as he was, had opinions of his own which were not easily shaken. In other respects, everything combined to throw him into the groove in which it was Lennox's object that he should move. He hated Elizabeth as cordially as he knew that Elizabeth hated him.[2] She had refused to help him with money. She had robbed him of his grandmother's inheritance. She would not acknowledge his claims on the succession. His mother's imprisonment was a continual challenge to his resentment; and though he could have borne it philosophically had Elizabeth adopted him in her place, it was a ground of quarrel which he could not but recognise, so long as he was treated as an alien and enemy. England was associated in his mind with Morton's despotism, with his dreary childhood at Stirling, with the austere discipline which had denied him all amusement. Lennox and Lennox's friends had broken his fetters, changed his schoolbooks for the hunting-field, and emancipated him from the lectures with which the ministers had dosed him from their pulpits. It was but natural that he should look to Lennox and his kinsmen in France, both for the enjoyment of his present freedom and the realisation of his expectations for the future.

---

[1] Calderwood.

[2] 'Voyant que le Prince ne se soucioit pas beaucoup de la Royne d'Angleterre, la quelle d'aultre part le hait plus qu'elle ne feist jamais la Royne d'Escosse sa mère, et estime ung jour sa ruyne de ce côté là, si ellemesme ne ruyne le dict Prince d'Escosse: ils sont les ungs et les aultres pour en venir en extremités.' —*Mauvissière au Roy*, 10 Juillet, 1582. TEULET, vol. iii.

The English alliance being gone, the next step was to renew the traditionary league with France. The conspirators would have preferred Spain, had circumstances permitted; but an alliance between Scotland and Spain would have driven the French Court more absolutely upon England. The Duke of Guise being a knight of the order of St. Esprit, which Henry III. had founded, affected to shrink from acting against his sovereign, and considered that Scotland judiciously handled might be the cement of the union between the Catholic powers, which the Pope so passionately desired, and which Guise, for the sake of France as well as of the general cause, was so eager to promote. France, it was perfectly certain, could not, and would not permit Spain to act alone either in Scotland or in England. Spain might possibly permit the Duke of Guise to act on the part of Catholic France if he could obtain the sanction of his own Crown; and the Scotch alliance, which the French King wished to recover as a bridle to Elizabeth, was the natural road towards the resolution of the problem.

Since the deposition of Mary Stuart, France had received no public Minister from Scotland, nor had any Frenchman been permanently in residence at Edinburgh. The Archbishop of Glasgow, Mary Stuart's ambassador, was the only accredited Scot acknowledged by the Court of Paris. France had never yet recognised James as King; and Scotland would enter into no formal relations with any power which persisted in giving him a lower title. A punctilio of this kind could no longer be allowed to stand in the way of the interests of Catholic Europe. George Douglas, who had contrived the escape of Mary Stuart from Lochleven, and was now about the person of James,[1] had been employed to feel the disposition of the French King towards a renewal of the league. Henry was as eager for it as Lennox; but not to offend the Queen of Scots, both he and the Queen-mother thought it proper first to consult her pleasure and to ask her permission to entitle James King of Scotland in connection with herself.[2]

It was a subject on which Mary Stuart was particularly tenacious. To call James King, was to admit the validity of her own deposition at Lochleven. It was to reduce her into the position of a subject, and to deprive her of those sovereign rights on which she most relied for the safety of her own person. The proposal, it was true, went no further than to acknowledge him as ruling jointly with herself;[3] but the reservation would be inadequate so long as the title of her son to share the throne with her originated with any authority but her own. She professed herself willing to associate James with her by her own act, leaving her rights unimpaired, and holding herself free, should James continue a Protestant, or otherwise oppose her wishes, to interfere in the government of Scotland, and to resume her throne when she could obtain her liberty. But if the Scotch sovereignty was once recognised abroad as existing in her son independently of herself, she knew well that she would cease to be an object of interest to the European powers; that her virtual deposition would be construed to extend to her expectations also; and that from the heir presumptive of the throne

---

[1] George Douglas was called by James 'his little ape,' 'Mon petit singe,' as M. Simier had been Elizabeth's.

[2] The King of France to Mauvissière. The King and the Queen-mother to the Queen of Scots, Sept. 1, 1581.—TEULET, vol. iii.

[3] 'Conjoinctment avec vous,' 'ensemble avec vous.'

of England, she would sink into a cipher. In reply, therefore, to the King's and Queen's letters, she begged them earnestly to do nothing directly or indirectly, until a deed of association, proceeding from herself, had been accepted by the Scotch Parliament. The acknowledgment that James was a lawful king under other conditions, she said would be utter ruin to her; and instead of accrediting a minister to Edinburgh, she desired the French Court to return George Douglas with the answer that they would make no treaty with her son except with her consent, and that no foreign prince would show him countenance or friendship except as he was her representative.[1]

The difficulty was an awkward one. Mary Stuart understood too well the sandy nature of the ground she stood on to part with any solid legal right to which she could pretend; while on the other hand such an association as she desired, even if it could be accepted by the Scots, might provoke the premature interference of England. Reluctant as Elizabeth had shown herself to meddle in arms with Scotland, yet she had done it twice and might do it a third time. Lennox had felt the temper of the leading nobles, and except from a few fanatical Catholics like Seton and Fernyhurst, he had found extreme objections to Mary Stuart's plan. 'It was 'thought very dangerous, both for the mother and son; 'by reason there was a despair entered into the hearts 'of the people if the King should grant himself un'lawfully crowned.'[2] Every Act of Parliament, every grant of land, which had passed under the Great Seal of Scotland for thirteen years, would be made invalid if he

---

[1] Mary Stuart to the Archbishop of Glasgow, Sept. 12.—LABANOFF, vol. v.

[2] Lennox to George Douglas, Sept. 1581.—*MSS. MARY QUEEN OF SCOTS.*

was reduced but for a single hour to the rank of Prince.[1]

But the reasons which made the Scots unwilling determined Mary Stuart to insist. If an ambassador's credentials contained her name as well as her son's, France would be committed to a positive act in her favour, and Scotland, in accepting such an ambassador, would acknowledge the illegality of her deposition. She clung to her formula, excited by Lennox's victory over Morton, and by the vacillation and timidity of the English Queen. She sent a message to James that the time was come for him to declare himself her champion, and to appeal in her behalf to the Princes of Europe. She forwarded a draft of the proposed association to Paris, with a request to the King to support her in persisting with it; and she wrote to Elizabeth, telling her that the question of her son's title having been publicly raised must now be publicly decided. With her usual adroitness, she turned the position to her own advantage; and with fierce complaints of her captivity, she threatened, if she was detained longer, to resign to her son every right which she possessed or to which she pretended. Her enemies, she said, when she had thus denuded herself, would have but a feeble woman to work their cruelty upon; and she would relieve her party of the embarrassment which her captivity had caused. They might continue to hold her prisoner if they pleased, or they might kill her if they dared; but a competitor for the crown of England, claiming by unquestionable descent, would still be at large, and with the world before him.[2]

This was dangerously true. One chief cause of the

---

[1] Lennox to George Douglas, Sept. 1581.—*MSS. Mary Queen of Scots.*

[2] Mary Stuart to Elizabeth, Oct. 10.—LABANOFF, vol. v.

forbearance of the Catholics, both in England and abroad, had been the fear that on the first sign of disturbance, the person in whose interest they would move might at once be put to death. George Douglas's papers and the correspondence in connection with his mission was seen by a spy of Walsingham's in Paris. It was pervaded by a tone of deep hostility to England;[1] but in the course of it there appeared symptoms of rising differences between Lennox and the Earl of Arran, and Elizabeth tried to avail herself of the clue to divide the Queen of Scots' party. She commissioned Captain Errington, a skilled practitioner in Northern diplomacy, to go down to Edinburgh to bribe Arran, to work on the Protestant fears of Argyle and Gowrie, to advise and, if desirable, to threaten the King, to protest especially against any act which might discredit the legality of his coronation—a legality which she herself, when it suited her purpose, had been the first to deny.[2]

But Elizabeth had sent too many such messages to Scotland, and they could serve her turn no longer. Errington arrived at Berwick, but he met an intimation there that he would cross the border at his peril, and he was obliged to return to London. The ladies of the Court watched the effect of the failure upon the baffled Queen. She stood alone in a window of her room muttering between her teeth, 'That false 'villain of Scotland! That villain for whom I have 'done so much! The night before Morton was taken 'he could call him father! He could say that he had 'no friend like Morton who had brought him up, and

---

[1] —— to Walsingham, Sept. 1581, misdated 1580 in the arrangement of the MSS. MARY QUEEN OF SCOTS. Rolls House.

[2] Secret Instructions to Captain Errington, Oct. 26, 1581.—MSS. Scotland. Notwithstanding the extreme care which was observed with these instructions, the Spanish Ambassador was exactly informed of their purport. See his letter to Philip, Nov. 7, 1581.—MSS. Simancas.

'that he would protect him! and the next day he had him seized and cut off his head. What must I look for from such a double-tongued scoundrel as this?'[1]

Her answer to the letter of the Queen of Scots had been drawn up before Errington came back; and Beale, Walsingham's brother-in-law, the Clerk of the Council, had his foot in the stirrup to start with it for Sheffield. Confident of succeeding in Scotland, she had meant to tell her prisoner that the association was full of difficulties, that her letter was menacing and strange, and that 'if she thought to terrify her she would find herself abused.' 'If other Princes had been as ready to execute the Queen of Scots' intentions as she was to provoke them, she had said she well knew that she would ere this have tasted of her malice; but if those princes meddled with her she would know how to make head against them'—the Queen of Scots trusted to a disaffected party in England, but she could tell her that the people were loyal to their Sovereign; she had deserved their love by governing wisely and justly; and 'if the Queen of Scots had held the same crown, neither England nor Scotland would have been troubled by her'—it pleased her to say that she would resign her title to the crown of Scotland to her son; but it was a question if she had any title to resign; and for the crown of England, unless her son altered his conduct, she said 'she would take order to cut off all hope by ordinary course of justice, that he

[1] 'Han me advertido que la Reyna estuvó sola en una ventana, diciendo entre sí con enojo (lo cual oyéron unas damas), Que aquel Rapaz de Escocia tan falso—aquel por quien yo he hecho tanto—que dixese á Morton la noche antes que le hiciese prender, l'adre, yo no tengo otro que me aya criado sino vos, y como á tal os he de defender de vuestros enemigos, y que debaxo desto otro dia lo mandase prender para cortarle la cabeza. Que se puede esperar del doblez de semejante rapaz?'—*Don Bernardino al Rey*, 7 Noviembre. *MSS Simancas.*

'might have hereafter to attain to the crown'—the imprisonment of which the Queen of Scots complained had risen from her own misbehaviour; by assuming the arms and title of England 'she had given just cause 'to the Queen to make profit of her repair thither;' she had received more honourable treatment than many princes would have yielded to pretenders to their crown, and in return she had been ungrateful and treacherous; she had been used better than she deserved, and if she continued her past practices, the Queen would take some other course, such as her own safety and the Queen of Scots' ingratitude might require.[1]

Among the least agreeable features in Elizabeth's character was the rapidity with which she could alter her language to the same person with a slight alteration of circumstances. Mary Stuart's conduct was not changed by the repulse of Captain Errington, but the dignified severity of the intended message was altered at once into a cringing affectation of friendliness. Her diplomacy having failed in Scotland, Elizabeth's next idea was to play off the mother against the son, and terrify James's adherents by a threat of replacing her by force on the Scotch throne.[2] Mr. Beale was dispatched, not to defy or reprove, but to endeavour to convince the Queen of Scots of Elizabeth's tender affection for her, to complain of the imprudence of Lennox in breaking off the English alliance, on which her own and her son's future depended, and to invite the Queen of Scots to co-operate privately with her in restoring the Hamiltons,

---

[1] Instructions to Mr. Beale, Nov. 1581.—*MSS. Mary Queen of Scots.*

[2] 'Offrece ella á la de Escocia que la quiere sostituyr con su braço y fuerças en la corona de aquel Reyno, viniendo por este medio á enquedejarla con su hijo.'—*Don Bernardino al Rey*, 7 Noviembre. *MSS. Simancas.*

in overthrowing the favourites in whose favour they had been dispossessed, and in drawing up some scheme of reconciliation by which Scotland could be quieted, she herself restored to liberty, and her expectations in England directly or indirectly recognised. Every sentence breathed confidence and concession. So far Elizabeth went in her seeming frankness as even to consult the Queen of Scots on the European policy of England; and to treat her as if personally interested in the prosperity of the country. She pointed out to her how she might hereafter have cause to regret the overgreatness of Spain—how imprudent she might hereafter find it, to have encouraged the designs of the Spanish King, either in England, Ireland, or Scotland. She invited her rather to become her own friend, that they two united might defy the world.[1]

The Queen of Scots received these advances with as much sincerity as Elizabeth felt in making them. She was so confident in the turn in her favour which events appeared to be taking, that she had waited rather with curiosity than anxiety for the answer to her letter; and when Beale arrived at Sheffield she sent for him to come at once to her room. He found her in bed, with the room darkened. She said she was ill and unable to bear light, but he ascertained afterwards that the candles had been extinguished immediately before he was admitted. She revived rapidly when she learnt the character of his message. He remained a fortnight with her, and she talked to him repeatedly with apparent frankness and the blandest cordiality. She discussed the politics of the world. She told him that she had felt from the first it would never be well with Scotland or England, while she and her dear sister were at

---

[1] The Queen of Scots to Meadows, Jan. 14, 1582.—*MSS. Simancas.*

variance. The welfare of the island, she said, depended on the union of the realms, which she, for her own part, was warmly desirous to further. She swore almost as vehemently as Elizabeth herself to the honesty of her intentions. She declared that she had no correspondence with the Catholic powers, none especially with the Catholic King, and that she was not seeking to trouble her sister with foreign practices. She was herself a Catholic, and she confessed she would be glad to see her son a Catholic; but she disclaimed all wish to see the forms established in either realm violently overthrown. 'God,' she said, 'must frame men's hearts to religion, 'and not violence or the force of man;' she had always opposed and always would oppose a religious revolution.

She had acquainted Mendoza with her plan of association, and she had desired him to communicate it to Philip. It has been seen that she had herself written to the Court of France about it. Yet she declared with an oath to Beale that no prince or potentate, except her Majesty, was acquainted with her purpose; and that her desire was to be guided in all her actions by the advice of the Queen of England. Again and most particularly she denied that she had dealings with Spain.

Accomplished as the Queen of England often showed herself in the art of lying, her genius paled before the cynical proficiency of her rival. When Mary Stuart had done with Beale, she sent an exact account of her conversation with him to Mendoza. She described scornfully the advances which had been made to her, how she had met them, and how Elizabeth was counting without her host.[1] While she had sworn to Beale

---

[1] 'Voilà le compte qu'elle me faisoit, comme on dict, sans son hoste.'—*Queen of Scots to Mendoza,* Jan. 14, 1582.—*MSS. Simancas.* Cf. Beale to Walsingham, November 14 and November 28, 1581.—*MSS. MARY QUEEN OF SCOTS.*

she had no views for herself or James in connexion with Spain, and no wish to revolutionise the Church, she told Mendoza in the same letter that all her hopes lay with Philip; that she looked to Philip to put down heresy in Scotland, and that her warmest hopes for her son were to see him married to a Spanish Princess. She had herself long felt—the Pope had told her, and her Catholic friends in England had told her— that Spain was the power on which she must rely; but James's conversion was the first step, without which all else would fail. He had promised her, she said, to give a hearing to any one whom she would send to teach him. Her desire was, therefore, that the Archbishop of Glasgow should return to Scotland, taking with him some learned French divines. They would encounter, and of course triumphantly defeat, the ministers of the Kirk, and all would be done.[1]

Six English noblemen, it will be remembered, had resolved to represent to James that his prospects in England depended on his reconciliation with Rome. Arran had been sapping his morals with loose women at Dalkeith; while Lennox, with cautious dissimulation, had destroyed the political combination which had supported the Kirk, and had brought him into violent hostility with Elizabeth. His mother and his Guise cousins were now going to work upon his soul. All these separate influences were set playing like converging batteries on the unfortunate boy. They had been hitherto acting independently. The Jesuit mission was now to be the instrument to bring them into harmonious co-operation.

Among the Scotch Catholics who had been educated at the seminary at Rome, there was a youth of unusual

[1] The Queen of Scots to Mendoza, Jan. 14.—*MSS. Simancas.*

promise, named Crichton. The Pope, to whom he was
introduced, had talked often to him of the prospects of
his country; and confounding, as many others did, the
Scotch nobility with the Scotch nation, Crichton had
assured his Holiness that the heretics were but a miserable handful of base people, who, but for the help of the
Queen of England, would have been long since trampled
out. The Pope sent him to London to remain there
under Father Parsons' orders, but with an understanding
that if an opportunity offered itself, he was to go to
Scotland, and tell the Catholic leaders that if they could
recover the King, and re-establish the faith, he would
undertake that, either by himself or by Spain, they
should be protected from the interference of the Queen
of England. The Queen of Scots, the English Catholic
lords, and the Jesuits were now acting cordially together. Mendoza was in all their secrets—ready to use
them if the present aspect of affairs remained unchanged;
ready to fling them over, if Philip and Elizabeth
were inclined to make up their quarrels—and meanwhile feeding their enthusiasm with vague expectations
of help. Crichton was selected to carry the message of
the six noblemen to Scotland. The Jesuits always
hunted in couples, and Parsons assigned him one of
the Oxford converts, named Holt, who had been a
Fellow of Oriel. Crichton travelled as an itinerant
dentist,[1] with Holt as his servant. Holt fell ill on the
border, and was left behind, and Crichton went on alone.
He saw Lennox, he saw Eglinton, Huntly, Seton, Caith-
ness, Fernyhurst, and others of the anti-English faction.
Not knowing at first whom he could trust, he felt his
way with extreme caution. He enquired whether, under
the new Government, the Jesuits would be allowed

---

[1] 'Sacamuelas.'

to preach and administer the sacraments, and whether Scotland would now be an asylum to persecuted English Catholics. On both these points the answer was satisfactory. The Jesuits might come freely, and the King would hear what they had to say, and English refugees would find welcome and protection. With Lennox, he dared not go further. Lennox still pretended to be a Protestant; and it was not for Crichton to disregard his disguise. To Lord Seton, however, whose orthodoxy was unimpeached, he spoke out the message with which the lords had charged him.[1] The first motive for the King's conversion was, of course, the salvation of his soul; but his worldly and his spiritual interests closely coincided; and if he aspired to be King of England and Ireland, he could obtain his object only by the support of the English Catholics, and the King of Spain. He must not quarrel with France, but he must not be too intimate with it. He must keep before his eye the old league with the House of Burgundy, and rely first on Spain.[2]

Seton, after twelve years' unsuccessful diplomatising at Paris, was perfectly ready to exchange France for the Catholic King. He entered heartily into Crich-

---

[1] 'Alargandose mas con el Seton á causa de hallarle con mucha voluntad, diciendole que para aficionar al Rey que se reduxese á la santa Religion Catolica Romana, ningun medio habria mejor, fuera de ser el verdadero camino de su salvacion, como representarle assimismo que era solo por el que podria aspirar á ser un gran Rey con juntar á su corona las de Inglaterra y Irlanda, lo cual no podria conseguir sino fuese grangeando á un tan poderosisimo monarca como V. Mag^d, ligandose con el, que seria desta manera, con renovar entonces las ligas que la casa de Borgoña tenia con Inglaterra,' &c.—*Don Bernardino al Rey*, 19 Noviembre. *MSS. Simancas.*

[2] The reader will observe the single eye with which Mendoza regarded the interests of Spain. He was at this very moment advising Philip to renew the league with Elizabeth. He had been taken into counsel in drawing the message of the Jesuit, so that whether Elizabeth held her ground or was overthrown by a revolution Spain could still secure the English alliance.

ton's suggestions. He promised to speak to his master, and explain to him the benefit to his prospects which he might expect from his conversion. He undertook that the Jesuit preachers, when they came, should find the soil prepared for them.

With this answer, Crichton went back to London, to find Campian and many more of his friends executed, and the Jesuits generally in hysterical exhilaration at the testimony which had been given to the faith. He communicated with Parsons and Mendoza, and then crossed the Channel with Parsons, to arrange the details of the Scotch mission. It was thought at first that Parsons should go: but Parsons could not be spared from England, nor would Englishmen be otherwise the best qualified to convert Scots—especially as, in the words of Mary Stuart, who was consulted, they could not speak the language. So it was decided that Crichton should go again.

Meanwhile Holt had recovered his health, and had proceeded by himself. He was received as favourably as his companion had been. Seton entertained him at his house, and introduced him to Lennox, who for some cause was more open with him than he had been with Crichton, confessed that he was a Catholic, and discussed the entire situation with him. Lennox said that he knew James thoroughly, and that he doubted whether either interest or argument would effect his conversion. The Jesuits might try what they could do with sermons and admonitions. If they failed, however, as they were likely to fail, Lennox said that he was prepared to seize the government in the Queen of Scots' name, and either force James to act with him; or send him out of the realm to some place where the truth could be impressed upon him; or, finally, declare him deposed as long as his mother lived, and make his future re-accession contingent on his becoming a Catholic. He was unwilling to move, however, without the Queen of Scots' permission. He therefore desired Holt to consult her wishes through Mendoza, and inform him of her pleasure. Should she consent, he said that he must have assistance from abroad, and he seemed to have no doubt that, for her sake, and in her interests, either France or Spain would spare him a few thousand men.[1]

Mendoza had more responsibility thrown upon him by this communication than he liked. He was delighted that the English and Scots should conspire among themselves, but he had been strictly ordered to keep clear of complicity, and to avoid committing his master by indiscreet promises. The leading Catholics were under arrest, or under severe surveillance; the management of the party was therefore inconveniently thrown upon himself; and his embarrassments were increased by the time which was lost in writing to and hearing from Madrid. He sent Lennox's message to the Queen of Scots, and received in return her hearty approbation. She was in high spirits, and more confident than she had been at any time since her coming into England. Her interview with Beale had answered well. Elizabeth having, as was supposed, given mortal offence to France by her treatment of Alençon, and having failed to recover a party in Scotland, even Walsingham considered that nothing was now left but a compromise with the lady at Sheffield. Her detention hitherto, he said, had been made possible only by the state of parties on the Continent; the division between France and Spain was not likely to endure longer;

---

[1] Mendoza to Philip, Feb. 9, 1582.—*MSS. Simancas.*

something would probably be attempted in the Queen
of Scots' favour; and 'it was therefore convenient that
'her Majesty should proceed with the treaty not long
'since begun with the said Queen.'[1]

Mary Stuart understood her advantages. A treaty being allowed to be possible, the terms of it presented no difficulty. According to the threadbare formula, the treaty of Leith must be confirmed. She must abandon for herself and her son their pretensions to the English crown during Elizabeth's life; Elizabeth binding herself on her side not to interfere with the Queen of Scots' prospective rights. She thus, as before the discovery of the Norfolk conspiracy, held the strings in her hands of two separate negotiations. There was a promising plan for a revolution. There was the treaty on which she could fall back if the revolution came to nothing. With one hand, therefore, she was writing letters to London, to Paris, and to Edinburgh; she was corresponding with Mendoza; she was directing Lennox; she was communicating with the Archbishop of Glasgow, with the Pope, the Duke of Guise, and the Jesuits; she was the soul of the conspiracy, ordering and guiding everything.[2] With the other she was playing with Elizabeth; manœuvring to escape committing herself by writing, while she obtained, as a result of her more amicable relations with the English Government, the removal of restrictions which had embarrassed the movements of her messengers.[3]

---

[1] Reasons to move her Majesty to proceed in the treaty with the Scotch Queen, April, 1582. Walsingham's hand.—*MSS.* MARY QUEEN OF SCOTS.

[2] 'La Reyna virtualmente gobierna estas materias . . . . es virtualmente ella la que mueve la guerra, sin cuyo parecer y consentimiento el de Lennox y los demas no quieren tratar de nada.'—*Mendoza al Rey*, 1 Avril, 1582. *MSS. Simancas*.

[3] Elizabeth required a promise from her either in writing or by word of mouth to Lord Shrewsbury that

Holt, meanwhile, had carried back to Scotland her consent to any measures which Lennox might consider necessary. Crichton, after an interview with the Duke of Guise, joined him in Edinburgh, and brought word that Philip had yielded to the entreaties of the Pope, and had promised, as soon as Lennox had secured the person of the young King, to send an army of liberation to Scotland. The Rheims priests in the vehemence of their eagerness had turned their wishes into facts, and arranged everything. Lennox was to take the command, and after restoring the Church at home, was to cross into Northumberland, where the entire Catholic population would rise to join him. The rest of England would follow, the usurper would be deposed, and the Queen of Scots be carried in triumph from Sheffield to the throne. Whence this brilliant vision of the Spanish invasion rose, Mendoza, when he heard of it, was at a loss to conceive. He supposed that either Crichton had invented the story out of his own head, or had construed into a certainty some vague promise of the Pope.[1] 'These holy fathers,' he said, 'though most saintly per- 'sons, are unfit to deal in affairs of state. They can be 'trusted in nothing unless they have their message by 'heart.'[2] He had, in fact, to tell them that they must

---

while the treaty was in progress she would meddle no further in Scotland. She preferred the verbal promise as more easy to escape from. 'Sur ce d'aultant que par escript de main ou signé d'icelle je demeurerois plus obligée à l'observation des dictes promesses qui se pourroient estendre bien loing, n'estant que generales, j'ai advisé pour ne me laisser surprendre de les confirmer seulement de bouche au Conte de Shrewsbury.' —*Mary Stuart to the Archbishop of Glasgow*, April 7, 1582. LABANOFF, vol. v.

[1] 'Yo no dudbo sino que el buen hombre lo habia de suyo, pareciendole que con el haberle asegurado Su S^d por el mes de Mayo del año pasado que estuvó en Roma que assistiria con la gente que fuese necessaria el offreceria á bulto aquel numero.'—*Don Bernardino al Rey*, 26 Avril, 1582. *MSS. Simancas.*

[2] 'Los cuales aunque tienen honoroso celo en lo de la religion, on

attend for the future to their own business of saving souls, and leave wars and conspiracies to men of another profession.[1] So it was, however, that Crichton definitely promised that 15,000 Spaniards and Italians should be landed in Scotland. A letter of credit which Mendoza had given to Holt was construed into a confirmation from head-quarters. The Jesuits, with febrile and feminine impatience, believed, like Pompey, that armies would spring out of the earth at a stamp of the foot. Lennox, who knew better, could not suppose that they would have spoken so positively without authority, and wrote to tell the Queen of Scots that he accepted the charge, and would deliver her or die.[2] The two priests, after leaving Lennox, instead of going to England, crossed directly to France, and heaping indiscretion on indiscretion, wrote to Mendoza to ask him to cross the Channel, and meet them and the Duke of Guise at Rouen; 'as if,' Mendoza said with provoked contempt, 'it was to be supposed that I could leave my post without orders, or could disappear suddenly without

---

hay entender materia d'estado, sino es haciendolos capaces ad rerbum de lo que han de decir.'—*Don Bernardino al Rey*, 26 Avril. *MSS. Simancas.*

[2] *Ibid.*

[3] 'Madame, depuis mes dernières est venu vers moi un Jésuite nommé Guillaume Crichton, le quel avec lettres de creance de vostre ambassadeur m'a faict entendre que le Pape et le Roy Catholique avoyent deliberé de vous secourir d'une armée pour le restablissement de la Religion Catholique en ceste Isle, vostre delivrance hors de captivité et la conservation en vostre endroict à la couronne d'Angleterre; et qu'il a esté mis en avant que je sois chef de la dicte armée. Depuis ay receu une lettre del Ambassadeur d'Espaigne qui reside à Londres pour ce mesme effect par un aultre Jésuite Anglois. Quant à moy, Madame, si c'est vostre volunté que la chose se face, et que je la entreprenne, le ferai, et ay esperance que si ils tiennent promesse et que les Catholiques d'Angleterre facent aussy ce qu'ils promettent, que l'entreprise viendra à bonne et heureuse fin, et perderais la vie ou je vous delivrerois hors de vostre captivité.'—*The Duke of Lennox to the Queen of Scots*, March 7, 1582. *MSS. Simancas.* The Duke sent the letter through Mendoza, who forwarded a copy of it to Philip.

'exciting suspicion.' He was extremely embarrassed. He was afraid of encouraging expectations which he knew to be vain. He was afraid equally of revealing the disagreeable truth that his master was thinking of nothing less than sending his troops on any such service.

Had Philip had it in him to use the opportunity, he might have done much—perhaps everything—but he lost not a moment in correcting the mistake, and so correcting it as to show not only his inability to assist, but his disapprobation of the project in itself. It was his most ardent desire, he said, to see Scotland brought back to the truth, but the only sound and safe way of accomplishing it was by preaching. Other means were dangerous, and could not be tried without consideration. Lennox and his friends might find it less easy than they expected to get possession of the government. To depose the King during his mother's life might be hard also, and was, moreover, contrary to the oath which they had sworn to him;[1] while to send him out of the realm to be converted would be equally to take the crown from him, and leave his conversion uncertain after all. The Catholics, he said, must not be so impatient. They must wait and hope. As soon as Flanders was conquered he would take up their cause, and perhaps sooner, if he saw a convenient opening.[2]

The 'leaden foot' of the King of Spain was as fatal to his friends as the irresolution of Elizabeth to hers—and those who wait for convenient seasons do not use them when they present themselves. Mendoza explained matters as well as he could. He laid before the Queen of Scots the certainty that if a Castilian force

---

[1] 'Deponerle de la corona mientras viviere su madre, caso que no fuere Catolico, es de muy gran dificultád y contra lo que le han jurado.'—*El Rey al Bernardino de Mendoza*, 13 Avril. TEULET, vol. v.
[2] *Ibid.*

was landed in Scotland, France would declare war against Spain. He promised her that not 15,000 men only, but a far larger force should be sent when circumstances were favourable; but the re-opening of a general war at that moment, he said, was not to be contemplated. He sent back Holt to his place in Scotland, with a charge to confine himself to his preaching. He wrote to Lennox, not telling him that Crichton's promises were things of air, but with vague encouragement to look forward to ultimate success, and urging him meanwhile to forward the association of the King with his mother, and to organise his party into a more harmonious and manageable shape.[1] With Allen he was more severe. He lectured him on his imprudence in meddling with the business of statesmen. He charged him to confine himself for the future to his spiritual duties, and it was a lesson which Allen was particularly unwilling to receive.

The Jesuits and the Pope had taken in hand the recovery of England, because, as they thought, the statesmen were neglecting their duties. It was not to be sneered down in this way that they had sent Sanders to perish in an Irish bog, and Campian to be quartered at Tyburn. Holt declared that the English Catholics were prepared for rebellion. The Jesuits, he insisted, had confessed too many of them to be unaware of their condition and resolution.[2] Mendoza being so cold, Holt, and Allen, and Crichton referred themselves to Baptista de Tassis, the Spanish ambassador in Paris, who from the first had taken a warmer interest in them. Lennox

---

[1] Mendoza al Rey, 26 Avril.—MSS. Simancas.

[2] 'Preguntandole yo qué seguro tienen de todo esto, y si algunos principales se han confederado para este affecto y dado entre si algunas seguridades de firmas como se suele. Respondióme que todo esto se sabia por lo que muchos dellos se habian declarado, tratando de sus conciencias con ellos.'—J. B. de Tassis al Rey, 18 Mayo, 1582. TEULET, vol. v.

had written to De Tassis when he wrote to the Queen of Scots, telling him that he was ready to risk life and fortune in the invasion of England.[1] Crichton testified in return to Lennox being a genuine Catholic.[2] Holt undertook for the insurrection of the northern English counties; and afterwards, in secret council, the Duke of Guise and the Archbishop of Glasgow laid their views in detail before De Tassis. Crichton's random promises were explained away as a mistake—neither did they think that the hand of Spain need be visible in the matter at all. If Philip would secretly supply money, the Pope would undertake the open responsibility, as he had done already in Ireland. Five or six thousand Italians and Germans could be raised in Italy, as if for a campaign against the African Corsairs. They could be run through the Straits of Gibraltar, and taken direct to Scotland. A proclamation would be issued on their landing that they had been sent by his Holiness for the delivery of the Queen of Scots. Lennox could take the command, and march immediately for England; while the Duke of Guise would make a diversion by throwing himself, with a few thousand French, into Sussex. In the most earnest manner they deprecated delay. Delay meant feebleness of purpose, and feebleness of purpose, discovery. It was now May. The expedition ought to be undertaken by the end of the summer at latest. The interval could be employed in carrying money and stores into Dumbarton and Blackness.[3]

De Tassis, like Mendoza, was tied by his instructions; but he was more sanguine of success, and more gene-

---

[1] Lennox to De Tassis, March 7.—TEULET, vol. v.
[2] 'El qual sabia ser Catolico.'—
Tassis to Philip, May 18. Ibid.
[3] Tassis to Philip, May 18 and May 29.—TEULET, vol. v.

rally encouraging. The decision, however, he said, must rest with his master; and while Crichton went to Rome to report progress to the Pope, Holt, with another companion from Rheims, prepared to go into Spain, and exert their eloquence upon Philip.

Mendoza, who had sufficient difficulty in controlling the Jesuits in England, found his task made all but impossible when they were made acquainted with the conference in Paris. In their impetuous imaginations, the Pope's legions were already in the field, and the armies of the Philistines flying before the blast of the Archangel's trumpet. In the phrase so common in Catholic mouths, it was God's cause, and who could resist? Campian's blood cried from the ground, and the intercession of the saints below the throne had been heard, and would now be answered. Parsons had intended, after all, to go to Scotland and convert James, but the heat of the confederates infected him. He proposed to accompany Holt, to plead with the Spanish King; and Lennox and Seton determined, if Philip could not be persuaded, to seize James's person at any rate, and send him into France. Mendoza was in distraction. He was himself convinced that a movement of Lennox upon England, or a general Catholic insurrection, would be unsuccessful without Spanish support, or, if successful, would be mischievous to Spanish interests. In the Queen of Scots alone he found assistance. The Queen of Scots had learnt wisdom by suffering. Her religious faith was tempered with the understanding that the right side did not conquer without adequate means, and she gave what help she could to bridle the impatience of her friends.[1] But the plot would have boiled over prematurely, and, in the opinion of Mendoza, the recovery of England and

---

[1] Mendoza to Philip, May 15.—*MSS. Simancas.*

Scotland would have from that moment become impossible, had not the Spanish post been more expeditious than usual.

Invariably, when Philip was called upon to act, he found that the moment for action had not arrived. On hearing of Crichton's proceedings from England, he wrote in the tone which Mendoza himself had adopted. He discouraged every overt movement. He insisted that Lennox should remain quiet. As scornfully as his ambassador he bade the Jesuits keep to their spiritualities and leave politics alone. When the letters of De Tassis reached him, he expressed his displeasure yet more emphatically; he absolutely prohibited the repair of either Holt or Parsons, or any other of the crew, to his court. Money he was willing to give, but only in small quantities, to support the priests of the Scotch mission; and, after three months' consideration, he allowed a few thousand additional crowns for the fortification of Dumbarton.[1] Nothing more could be extracted from him in the way of practical help; only he encouraged Lennox, vaguely, to hope that a time might come when the Queen of England should be really punished.

Even this cold answer might not have sufficed to repress the fever of the conspirators. The Duke of Guise had at his back the great Catholic party of France, which, ready always to take arms against heresy, was at that moment peculiarly irritated. The national pride had been wounded by the heretic Queen. The King was ill and not expected to live. If he died, the crown would fall, first, by the law of succession, to Alençon, who was supporting the Calvinists in the Low Countries; and, failing Alençon, to Henry of Navarre. A brilliant blow

---

[1] Philip to Mendoza, May 10.— June 11 and Sept. 16. — TYTLER, MSS. Simancas. Philip to De Tassis, vol. v.

struck by Guise in England, might not only place his cousin on the throne of Elizabeth but give him paramount influence over the destinies of his own country. Lennox was burning to begin, prepared to place restraint upon James, and to colour his apparent rebellion with the name of the Queen of Scots.[1] And Guise might perhaps have declined to sacrifice his opportunity to the timidity of Philip. With the support and in the name of the Pope, he would probably have crossed into Scotland, in the course of the summer, but for the power of a party there whom the great world of Europe had not yet learnt to take into account.

The story turns from the secret chamber of conspirators to the keen air of the Presbyterian General Assembly.

Although James showed unexpected objections to be made a Catholic, it was more easy to teach him to detest the Kirk. His sister of England kept her clergy in order with the help of bishops in dependence upon herself. He admired the example and was eager to imitate it. Morton, it has been seen, had preserved the spectre of an Episcopate partly to gratify Elizabeth, partly as a means of supplying the necessities of the exchequer. Refractory cows in Scotland were induced to yield their milk by calfskins stuffed to deceive them. The mock calves were called Tulchans, and the creatures of Morton were nicknamed Tulchan Bishops. They collected the revenues of the sees and handed them over to their patron. The assembly had lately resisted the appointment of these imaginary dignitaries. The King found them financially convenient, and desired rather to give them a more substantive existence, as Crown officers for the control of the Church. It was an opportunity for

---
[1] Lennox to Mendoza, July 1582.—*MSS. Simancas.*

Lennox to strike a blow at the organisation of the Kirk, which had survived unexpectedly the fall of Morton. To establish bishops would be to divide Protestantism against itself, and make its ultimate overthrow the more easy. The see of Glasgow was considered vacant. The true archbishop was in Paris. His restoration as a Catholic would have created an immediate outbreak; and Mr. Robert Montgomery, minister of Stirling, whose pliancy had been tried and could be depended on, was named to take his place. The Glasgow Presbytery refused to receive him, Lennox and the King insisted, and the struggle began between the prerogative and the independence of the Church of Scotland.

The Earl of Arran, already uneasy in the second place which had been assigned him, was inclined at first to bid for popularity, and take the Presbytery's side. But the Presbytery did not value their champion. Arran had seduced his friend's wife, and married her when on the point of her confinement. The Kirk had compelled the profligate pair to do public penance in Edinburgh, and made enemies of them for ever. The Catholics might make a heroine out of Mary Stuart. The Kirk did not choose to purchase a patron by flattering adultery, and preferred to fight their own battles with their own weapons. The contention about the bishopric of Glasgow was going on through the winter and spring of 1581–82, at the very time when Lennox was plotting with the Jesuits, and laying his plans for the coming in of the Duke of Guise. It seemed comparatively but a contemptible matter, yet it was the more necessary for the Duke to prove his strength by carrying his point. The General Assembly threatened Montgomery with excommunication. The King said they should be proclaimed traitors if they dared. They told him, as Knox had told his mother,

that they must obey God rather than man, and that
his own welfare lay in the maintenance of the Kirk,
although he was not old enough to understand his position.
The bishop elect attempted to take possession of
Glasgow Cathedral pulpit. He was taken by the arm,
lifted from the stairs, and ejected out of his church.
Whispers had been heard of the coming in of Jesuits,
and though Lennox's true character had been concealed
under his Protestant oaths, a feeling was beginning to
spread that he was not altogether what he seemed.
A messenger sent to him by the Duke of Guise was
recognised as a person who had been concerned in
the massacre of Paris; and one of the Edinburgh ministers,
John Durie, denounced both Lennox and Arran
in a sermon as corrupters of the King's mind. Durie
was summoned to answer for himself at Dalkeith, where
Lennox was now established in the castle which had
once been Morton's. The rabble of the household was
set on to insult him. 'The Duke's French cooks came
' out of the kitchen with spits and great knives to invade
' him.'[1] Lennox called him[2] 'a little devil,' and ordered
him to leave Edinburgh instantly, with seventy of the
chief persons of his congregation. He thought it prudent
to obey; but none the less, on the Sunday following,
Mr. Robert Montgomery was excommunicated;
the sentence was publicly read in every Lowland pulpit;
and it was intimated in no very vague terms that Lennox's
own turn should follow. Father Holt, who was
with Lord Seton at the time, attributed the courage of
the ministers to the intrigues of Elizabeth. 'The Queen
' of England,' he informed Mendoza, 'has instigated the
' ministers to preach against Lennox, and, finding it impossible
' to shake his credit with the King, is now

---

[1] Calderwood.   [2] 'Un petit diable.'

'seeking to have him cut off from their diabolical con-
'gregation, and rendered thus incapable by law of hold-
'ing office in the country. As a step towards it, they
'have excommunicated a person whom the King, at the
'instance of Lennox, had appointed Bishop of Glasgow.
'Their religion, they pretend, does not permit men to
'call themselves bishops. They will have no Papistry,
'they say, but will be ruled by superintendents, after
'the fashion of Geneva.'[1]

The Assembly required no prompting by Elizabeth, and had she interfered it would not have been in defence of Presbytery; but the dispute gave her a chance of re-establishing the party which she had so lightly allowed to fall to pieces, and of which she had felt the loss bitterly. She put herself in communication with Lord Angus, who was still in Northumberland, and through Angus with the old English party. Money was sent down. Lord Henry Howard[2] discovered that as much as three thousand pounds had been delivered to Angus in August. One of those dangerous associations, so common in Scotland, was formed either to kill Lennox or force him out of the country, and Lennox believed that a large reward had been offered to any one who would stab or poison him.[3]

Familiarity with perils of this kind rendered the

---

[1] Mendoza to Philip, July 12, 1581.—*MSS. Simancas.*

[2] Lord Henry Howard was the brother of the Duke of Norfolk, and possessed with a passionate hope of revenging the wrongs of his house. He was more useful than even Sir James Crofts to Mendoza, who in many letters mentions his services, and recommends Philip to reward him. The House of Howard, Mendoza says, meant the English aristocracy, and Lord Henry meant the House of Howard. Elizabeth treated him with exceptional confidence, and he used his advantage to communicate state secrets to Mendoza twice in every week. Walsingham and Burghley both guessed that he was treacherous, but, true to her general endeavour to overcome disloyalty by trusting it, Elizabeth could not be persuaded to send him from the Court.

[3] Mendoza to Philip, August 14, 1581.—*MSS. Simancas.*

native-born Scot indifferent to them; but Lennox had been bred where he at least had been in no such danger. He now imagined that a thousand poniards were aimed at his heart. He dared not stir from his apartments unless surrounded by guards whose bodies would intercept a pistol shot.[1] No actual effort was made to kill him, nor was there need of any, for the mere menace of it sufficed to kill his reputation, and convinced his friends and convinced himself that he was unequal to the post into which he had pushed himself. In cunning and adroitness he was without a rival. He could take life when there was no risk to his own, but in the nervous courage which could face death without flinching he was entirely deficient. He was terrified and longed to fly.[2] No more serious calamity could have befallen the conspirators. Arran was biding his time to snatch the leadership at the Court; but Arran was only known as an ambitious, unscrupulous soldier, eager for his own advancement, and careless of all besides. Lennox alone was in the confidence of the Duke of Guise; and if Lennox failed, there was no one to be found in the faction which had destroyed Morton who could hold his ground against Arran's rivalry.

---

[1] 'No sale jamas de su aposento que no sea rodeado de gente, porque si le quieren tirar arcabucaço no passe sin herir primero á otro.'—*Don Bernardino al Rey*, 12 Julio. *MSS. Simancas*.

[2] 'Intentan con grueso sierro de dinero por todas vias que maten al Aubigny y apoderarse de la persona del Rey. De lo qual le advierten por infinitas vias al de Lennox; y ofrescen premio aqui á quien le hechizare, atosigare, ó matare, y finalmente echarele del Reyno; por manera que de razon ha de tener cuantos puñales hay en Francia, que no solo estan avisados por livianas causas en bañarse en la sangre de particulares, pero en la de sus mismos Reyes: y desea verse fuera de tan manifiesto peligro, el cual no es pusible que no haga mas horrible el miedo, viendose combatido y al ojo la muerte para abraçarle en tan miserable estado—cosa que necesariamente le ha de tener confusissimo como yo entiendo que lo esta fuera del decirlo la Reyna en su carta.'— *Don Bernardino al Rey*, 14 Agosto. *MSS. Simancas*.

Meanwhile the battle with the General Assembly raged more fiercely than ever. Andrew Melville, the moderator, preached on the 27th of June, in the new Kirk at Edinburgh, against those 'who would pluck 'the crown from Christ's head and wring the sceptre 'from his hand'—the politicians who would raise in Scotland a counterpart of the Anglican supremacy. The supremacy of the Crown meant bishops, and bishops meant Popery in a disguise, which it would drop as soon as Protestantism was killed. Lennox, afraid of bullets and daggers, kept Montgomery with him at Dalkeith; but to try his strength with the ministers, he one day sent him into Edinburgh with a company of men-at-arms, and attended by a pursuivant, who declared that, excommunicated or non-excommunicated, bishop he was, and bishop he should be. The Assembly gathered in force, and announced stormily that they would resist to death. Lennox enquired whether they or the King were the rulers in Scotland. They replied with a protest against the King's misgovernment and violation of his oath. The supremacy of the Kirk was Christ's, not his. He was subverting the law of God by arbitrary force. They drew up a list of their grievances. Their synods, they said, were broken up, God's enemies were protected, and the ministers of Christ suspended or expelled from their offices. Excommunicated persons were supported and encouraged, and the ordinances to which the King had sworn were trodden under foot. Andrew Melville, with a deputation of the Presbytery, carried the document, when it was finished, into James's presence.

'Who dares subscribe these treasonable articles?' said the Earl of Arran, who was at the King's side.

'We dare,' answered Melville, taking a pen from a

clerk and writing his name at the foot of the paper—
'We dare, and will render our lives in the cause.'

Again a demonstration was attempted in Edinburgh in favour of Montgomery. A second time he was brought into the town. The streets were thronged with scowling faces. The artisans and apprentices turned out with their bats, and as taunts and gibes began to fly, the escort was frightened and made their way to the Tolbooth, intending to shelter their precious charge there. But the burgesses had carried off the keys; the gates could not be opened; and as they halted and hesitated the crowd set upon them. The Grassmarket was an arsenal of missiles; eggs, cabbage-stalks, fish, stones, street filth, anything that came to hand, flew like hail over the heads of the guard in the face of the miserable bishop; and amidst howls of 'False thief,' 'Mansworn thief,' he was hustled back along the street and out of the gates.

At the news of this outbreak Lennox lost the little courage that remained to him. Three-quarters of the nobility were on his side, but the nobility were no more the Scotch nation. He wrote to Mendoza to say, that unless help came quickly he must leave the realm. The King's conversion was no longer to be thought of. He dared not for his life introduce a priest into his presence; and he and Seton prepared to fly, taking James with them.[1]

Mary Stuart, whose spirit rose with danger, and knew not what fear meant, was in despair at her champion's poltroonery. She sent him orders to remain at his post at least till she could hear again from Philip. Guise was ready. Ten thousand disbanded soldiers trained in massacre and rapine, could be gathered at a moment's notice to Guise's standard, and in that fair

[1] Mendoza to Philip, July, 1582.—*MSS. Simancas.*

summer weather the fishing fleet of Normandy could be impressed to carry them into Scotland. Her son, she believed, so hated the ministers and so dreaded England that he would welcome any one who would rid the land of them. She wrote imploringly to Mendoza of the confusion which had fallen on her party at home; and she refused to part with the hope that Philip would strike in for her while they had still possession of the Government.[1]

'I had formed such expectations of this enterprise,' she said, 'that I had resolved not to go forward with a
' treaty with the Queen of England. I would not bind
' myself by the conditions which were offered me, that
' I might be free to use my own advantage without in-
' curring a charge of breach of faith. I know, of course,
' how many things the King my brother has on his
' hands. I know what work these people here are
' providing for him. There are now plans on foot for
' the re-conquest of Navarre. But this enterprise, I
' fancy, would be the best remedy which he could apply.
' It would paralyse England, and England is the foun-
' tain from which other troubles are fed.

' Then, too, his Holiness is at an advanced age. He
' may be succeeded by a pontiff who will not inherit his
' zeal. My own health is broken. My son is infected
' with this accursed heresy. The Duke of Lennox is
' now all-powerful, but if he is obliged to resign the go-
' vernment Scotland will be lost. My cousin the Duke

---

[1] 'Vous pouvez considerer par le change en Ecosse dont je pense que vous avez entendu les particularités, quel avantage pourroit avoir une bonne armée arrivant; et temps, et toutes choses estant ya si bien preparées, et mon filz mesme pourant estre persuadé de le recevoir, main- tenant qu'il a découvert la malice de ceste canaille de ministres, et qu'il craint aucunement d'estre par leur menée en trouble, tant par nos subjects propres que de colé de deça.'— *Mary Stuart to Don Bernardino*, July 29, 1582. *MSS. Simancas.*

'of Guise will turn his thoughts elsewhere, and the Eng-
' lish Catholics, given over to oppression, will be less and
' less able to help themselves. I fear, therefore, that if
' we allow the present opportunity to escape us of re-
' establishing religion in this island, it may be long before
' such another returns. The French King is given over
' to indulgence. His brother is entangled with the
' heretics. We have little to expect even from them:
' how much less should the crown fall—as God forbid
' it may—to the King of Navarre. I beseech you, lest
' so good a work should come to nothing, hasten the
' execution with all possible speed, and pray your mas-
' ter meanwhile to supply fifteen or twenty thousand
' crowns to fortify a few castles and positions where our
' friends, if pressed, can maintain themselves.'[1]

This letter, coupled with the news from Scotland, was not without its effect upon Mendoza. Nothing more could be expected from Lennox. The preachings and discussions from which Philip had formed so high expectations would be evidently barren. The Jesuits might be entertained in the castles of the noble lords, but would be torn in pieces if they appeared in public; Lennox was likely to be killed or expelled, the King to remain a heretic, and the ground which Lennox had recovered to be altogether lost. The Queen of Scots might perhaps be right, and the present might be the most favourable moment which Philip was likely to find. He altered his tone, and sent word to Lennox that as soon as certain present difficulties with France were got over and adjusted, his master would take their cause in hand, and they might rely on his helping them.[2]

[1] Mary Stuart to Mendoza, July 29.—*MSS. Simancas.*

[2] 'Yo he hecho como lo apunta la Reyna de Escocia, dandoles esperanças de socorro para entretener la platica y alentar el negocio; y esto debaxo de poner á los ojos las ocasiones que en Francia á conten-

It is possible that Philip might have been persuaded also but for a too complete success of the Spanish army at Terceira. So long as the Duke of Alençon was not publicly supported by his brother, the King of Spain had made up his mind to endure his presence in the Low Countries. He regarded him as in the service of the States—to be encountered in the field like any other enemy, but not as necessarily implicating the French Government. The ships which had gone to the Azores were similarly considered as privateers, but their occupation of those islands was more mischievous than Alençon's bad generalship in the Low Countries; and when Elizabeth had backed out, and it was clear that France was not going to war, strong means were taken to extirpate them. Don Antonio, having extricated the remains of his property from the Queen's clutches, found his friends in Paris more generous. Elizabeth had used him for her own purposes, plundered him, and flung him off. Catherine de Medicis, who had already sent out an expedition from Bordeaux in his favour, had equipped a second at Belleisle. The veteran Philippo Strozzi was in command of it, with the Huguenot De Brissac, and they had sailed for the Azores, having Don Antonio with them. Being joined by the other ships, and by the half-dozen small privateers which had come from Plymouth, they attacked and took St. Michael's. Don Antonio landed in state, and was proclaimed king in the town. The Castilian flag was struck on the castle, and the keys made over to the rightful sovereign. It was a first, but it was also a last success. They had been seen by an armada sent out from Cadiz to look for them; and on

placion desta Reyna buscaban para occupar á V. Mag^d por termino que se diessen á entender que cuando cessassen estas aseguradamente V. Mag^d les assistiria.'—*Don Bernardino al Rey*, 14 Agosto, 1582. *MSS. Simancas.*

the evening of the same day, the Marquis de Santa Cruz, with a force double their own, anchored in the roadstead. The sea was running high, but the French, who were on shore, re-embarked in good order, leaving Don Antonio on the island. The two fleets lay for five days looking at each other — the French exposed to the weather, and rolling heavily, but unable to remove into a better anchorage without a battle; the Spaniards under shelter, and waiting for Strozzi to get under weigh.

The wind would not moderate, and rose at last into a storm. One of the French ships drove on the rocks, and all on board perished. Strozzi found that he must fight or be destroyed. He called a council of war. The officers generally were out of heart and hopeless; and, wild as the weather was, he went round the fleet in a boat, trying to inspirit the crews. He had small success, however. The ship's companies were discontented and desponding. In laying out a plan for the battle he had placed himself in the centre. He was reproached with cowardice, and was told that he must himself lead or none would follow.[1] Thus was nothing left to him but to fall with honour. It was the morning of the 26th of July. The breeze had shifted, giving him a slight advantage. He was in a small vessel of 350 tons. Singling out the galleon San Martin, which was three times his size, and carried the flag of Santa Cruz, he bore down into the middle of the enemy. Only De Brissac and two other vessels followed, and the Spanish line closed behind them and cut them off. Missing the San Martin, Strozzi ran into the San Matteo, which was almost as large. Both his and

---

[1] 'Quoi, Monsieur!' said an officer to him, 'au lieu d'approcher voulez-vous reculer? Ne sçavez-vous que si vous n'allies pas le premier, vostre armée, quoy qu'elle vous aye promis, n'approchera. Voulez-vous aujourd'huy perdre l'occasion de remectre la couronne de Portugal?'—*How Strozzi was slain. MSS. France*, July, 1582.

Brissac's ships were immediately surrounded. Brissac, after fighting desperately for an hour, forced a way through into the open sea and escaped. Strozzi had given a good account of the San Matteo, and had almost escaped also, when the San Martin, coming close alongside, poured in a broadside which brought down his masts, and killed and wounded three quarters of his crew. Santa Cruz sprang on board. The old admiral lay bleeding on the deck, and died at the Spaniard's feet. Of the remaining ships some had made away after Brissac; the rest fell into the hands of Santa Cruz, and were treated as pirates. The officers were all beheaded, the crews were hanged; not a man was spared. Strozzi himself, had he been taken alive, was to have been drawn asunder by four boats—a horrible travesty of the ferocious dismemberment by horses.[1]

Neutralised as it was by theological mania, there was still a national feeling in France which was roused by this extravagant cruelty. It was reported that some of the gentlemen had been tortured, and the gallantry with which four ships—for only four had been engaged—had faced and encountered an enemy six times as numerous touched the pride and the indignation of the country. The King sent money at once to his brother; a fresh squadron was ordered at Belleisle, and a declaration of war seemed immediately imminent, when news came that Don Antonio had fled, that St. Michael's was recovered, Terceira taken, and that the Portuguese flag floated no longer on land or water. Further views in this quarter were abandoned, but a sore feeling remained, which rendered it for the time impossible for Guise to co-operate with Philip, and made it certain also that France would instantly resent the interference of the Spaniards in Scot-

---

[1] Cobham to Walsingham, Sept. 17 and Sept. 18.—*MSS. France.*

land. Even Guise himself was a Frenchman as well as a Catholic, and, notwithstanding the entreaties of the Queen of Scots, it was felt by all parties that nothing could be done till the immediate exasperation had abated.

Thus the stars in their courses were fighting for Elizabeth, even the successes of Spain turning for the moment to England's advantage. Some slight exertion was now all that was needed for the Protestants to recover their ascendency in Scotland. The Earl of Angus had offered to expel Lennox at the beginning of the summer, if the Queen would express her approval openly, but he had required money, and Elizabeth was half frightened and half unwilling to spend. Walsingham tried to drag her into some straight road of policy, but with indifferent effect. 'All remedies,' he complained to Sir Henry Cobham, 'are rejected and found 'unpleasant that bring any charge with them—Provi-'dence is esteemed prodigality; Necessity is here presi-'dent of the council.'[1] A ciphered letter from James to the Queen of Scots being intercepted, however, and read by Walsingham's secretary, there appeared so clear indications of intended mischief of some kind,[2] that she had been induced, as has been seen, to send Angus a few thousand pounds, and to give him other promises which encouraged him to proceed. After the affair in Edinburgh, the Assembly had determined, as Holt foretold, to strike at Lennox boldly, and excommunicate him. Seton, Maxwell, and a party of the Kers attempted to seize and carry off some of the

---

[1] Walsingham to Cobham, June 17, 1582.—*MSS. France.*
[2] Letter endorsed in the hand of Phillips, Walsingham's confidential secretary, from the Scotch King, in cipher, May 28, 1582.—*MSS. Mary Queen of Scots.*

leading ministers, but they missed their mark. It was discovered, at the same time, that Lennox had asked the Duke of Guise for five hundred men to garrison Dumbarton. The ferment, already violent, became ten times hotter. The Earl of Gowrie, from some private quarrel, had assisted in the overthrow of Morton, and the feud which had risen in consequence between the Ruthvens and the Douglasses had been one chief cause of the disintegration of the Protestant party. English friends interposed and made up the quarrel. During an altercation in the Council, the Duke of Lennox had called Gowrie poltroon; Gowrie withdrew in anger from the court, and with Angus, Lindsay, Glamys, the Earl of Mar, and the younger Maitland, who had inherited something of the genius of his brother the secretary, concerted measures to seize the government, and take the King out of Lennox's hands, for fear he might be carried off abroad.[1] Elizabeth had signified her approval; and it was hinted, in confirmation of Lennox's fears, that if both he and Arran were sent the way of Rizzio, slight enquiry would be made into their deaths by England.

James had been hunting in Athol; he passed through Perth on his way to Falkland in the middle of August; and when riding out of the town, on the morning of the 22nd, he was surrounded by a party of men-at-arms, taken, and carried back to Gowrie House. Lennox, who intended to have joined him, received notice and kept out of the way at Dalkeith; Arran was away in Fife, but was captured the same day, not far from Kinross,

---

[1] James himself was supposed to be not unwilling to go, and it was thought that he might imitate his grandfather and marry a daughter of the House of Lorraine.—*Note on the affairs of Scotland*, May 30. *MSS. Scotland.*

and would have been killed but for the entreaties of
Lady Gowrie. He was spared to make her repent her
interference, and was given in charge to his secret
friend the Provost of Edinburgh.

The formalities of respect continued to be observed
to the King; a remonstrance, however, was presented
to him by the confederate lords, and he was required to
conform his government to the wishes of the country.
He was told that two insolent and upstart adventurers
had troubled the commonwealth. Papists and murderers had been brought back from exile and restored to
their honours; a conspiracy had been on foot for the
overthrow of the Evangel, and there had been secret
dealings with Papal nuncios, Spanish ambassadors, and
other enemies of the truth. Scotland would not part
with the freedom which had been so hardly won, and
the lords declared quietly but sternly that they owed
a duty to God as well as the King; and must preserve his Majesty from the treasons of his corrupted
favourites.[1]

Had Lennox been equal to the occasion, he would
have thrown himself at once at the head of all the force
which he could raise, and have flown to the King's rescue.
The Kers and the Maxwells had been preparing the
border marauders for the expected invasion of England;
many hundreds of them had but to spring into their
saddles to be ready for the field; and everywhere, even
in the Lothians, there were loose gentlemen and their
retainers who had no love for the discipline of the Kirk,
and had no wish to see the days of Morton come back
again. But the confederate lords were less united than
they seemed; and the secrecy with which Lennox had
worked told against him in the suddenness of the emer-

---
[1] Calderwood.

gency. He was himself feeble and frightened; his friends had no immediate purpose or rallying point. Arran, by far the ablest of them, had not been trusted, and had separate aims of his own.

Gowrie and his friends, giving their adversaries credit for more energy than they possessed, carried James at once to Stirling for security. He cried for anger, and refused to eat; respectfully, however, he was compelled to sign a proclamation, in which Lennox and Arran were charged with having conspired to destroy religion, to corrupt his own morals, to break the alliance with England, and betray the country to the Pope.[1]

Arran for himself protested that he was maligned and slandered, and neither entertained nor ever had entertained any of the designs ascribed to him; Lennox, fearing to be outdone, and false as he was cowardly, protested before God, 'that it never entered his mind to 'subvert religion as was falsely alleged upon him—God 'having given him grace to embrace that religion, he 'would not desist to profess and maintain it.'[2]

Mary Stuart alone from her prison at Sheffield retained her courage and presence of mind. She, when she heard the news, sped away one messenger to the Pope, and another to the Duke of Guise: the first to implore all the influences of the Vatican to rouse Philip; the second to beg Guise to make haste for his life, if he would save her son from being murdered. She threw herself at his feet; she threw herself at the King of France's feet. He might call her son King, Prince, or what he pleased, if only he would allow Guise to rescue him from destruction, if only he would save the party of France in Scotland from being broken up for ever. All was prepared. Her friends in England

---

[1] Calderwood.   [2] Ibid.

she said were ready. Her own escape was arranged. Help only must be sent to Lennox without an hour's delay.[1]

Had Mary Stuart been a man, or woman as she was had she been free, she might have changed the history of the world. Unluckily for the Catholics, Shrewsbury was true to his trust, and her cause was again trampled into ignominy. Lennox, afraid of remaining at Dalkeith, came into Edinburgh under the protection of the Provost. The expelled ministers were brought back to their flocks; one of them, James Lawson, preached at St. Giles's on the Sunday which followed the revolution; and Lennox, to maintain his character for orthodoxy, was obliged to be present. The Provost had prayed Lawson to be moderate; he said he must speak what the Lord put in his mouth, 'and he preached upon the 6th of Zacharie, and opened 'up upon the Hills of Brass.' The instincts of these men had pierced the secret of the conspiracy, shrouded as it lay in hypocrisy, and the imagery of the Hebrew prophets gave their tongues superhuman eloquence. Durie, 'the little devil' whom the French cooks at Dalkeith had 'invaded,' addressed the King from the pulpit at Stirling. On the 4th of September he too was restored in triumph to his congregation at Edinburgh. He landed at Leith. Two thousand people met him at Gallows Green, escorted him back to the city, and replaced him in his church; the vast throng as they went along chanting the 124th Psalm, 'Now may Israel say, 'if the Lord himself had not been on our side, they had 'swallowed us up quick when they were so wrathfully 'displeased at us: our help is in the name of the Lord, 'who made heaven and earth.'

---

[1] Instructions to De Buisseau, September 1.—*MSS. Mary Queen of Scots.* Mary Stuart to the Archbishop of Glasgow, cipher, Sept. 10. Intercepted October 14, and deciphered by Walsingham's secretary.—*MSS. Ibid.*

'The Duke,' it was said, 'was more afraid at that 'sight than at anything that he had ever before seen in 'Scotland, and rave his beard for anger.' He might curse it as heresy, he might scorn it as fanaticism—but there visibly present before him was a power which had baffled his plots, and which neither he nor his Jesuits could exorcise. He stole away out of the town, and never rested till he was among his own people at Dumbarton, with the highway of the sea open before him. 'If these news be true,' wrote the old Randolph when he heard what had happened, 'we may see what it is to be 'true followers of Christ in earnest preaching and con- 'stant persevering in the setting forth his word: now 'is the time for the Queen to do service to God.'[1]

The conspirators were scattered, and their secrets were swiftly ravelled out. Arran told all that he knew. George Douglas was caught going to or coming from Paris. He was tortured, Mendoza says, at the instigation of Elizabeth, and confessed part if not all of his negotiations with the Duke of Guise.[2] The Queen of Scots' correspondence was watched; a letter, in cipher, to the Archbishop of Glasgow fell into Walsingham's hands, repeating what she had said to her cousin, dwelling on Guise's fitness to conduct the invasion, as reconciling the interests of France and Spain, and furnishing an instructive comment on the oaths of innocence which she had sworn so lately to Elizabeth.[3] Now, as

---

[1] Randolph to Walsingham, Sept. 2. Randolph, like an old hunter hearing the cry of the hounds, was anxious to be in the field again. 'If any are to be sent to Scotland,' he said, with more emphasis than decorum, 'let me not be cast out of the cart's arse, and others reap the glory of that for which I have adventured my body and spent of my own almost to extreme beggary.'

[2] 'A la peticion desta Reyna le daban tormentos.'—*Mendoza al Rey*, 1 Noviembre, 1582.

[3] Mary Stuart to the Archbishop of Glasgow, Sept. 10, 1582.—*MSS. MARY QUEEN OF SCOTS*.

Randolph said, was Elizabeth's time; but it was necessary to keep up appearances with France, and if possible to come to an understanding with the French Court. Henry and his mother were really anxious to maintain their influence in Scotland. The Lennox faction was the French faction, and, had Henry dared, he would have gladly assisted them. But he was most unwilling also to offend Elizabeth.[1] Mauvissière told him that if France interfered, England would interfere, even if war should come of it; and Mauvissière, therefore, was left to do what he could by diplomacy. Elizabeth conceived that as long as France was neutral, she was obliged to abstain from the appearance of intervention herself. On hearing of James's capture, she sent down Sir George Carey to the lords with a message half approving and half in blame. She did not mislike what they had done in itself, she said, but she disapproved the manner of the execution, the time and the other circumstances, 'which carried shew as though it had 'been intended purposely to her Majesty's disgrace.' She hoped, however, 'to find at their hands all good 'offices tending to the amity between the realms,' and she was content therefore to leave them to themselves.[2]

Her secret feelings were far less agreeable; much had been done, but more had been promised, and she had expected a more complete return for her money. All the mischief had arisen from Arran and Lennox; their deaths had been part of the programme which Angus had arranged with her; and Lennox was at large and apparently unsought after, and Arran had been in Angus's hands, and had been spared. Leicester wrote

---

[1] The King and the Queen-mother, Sept 5, 1.—TYTLER, vol. iii.

[2] Instructions to Mr. Carey by the Queen, Aug. 30.—*MSS. Scotland.*

privately to complain. 'Her Majesty,' he said, 'wondered
'Angus could be so slack in a matter which required
'prompt and severe execution of justice, and did not
'know what to think.'[1] The original intention, so far as
Mendoza heard it whispered in London, had been to kill
or expel Lennox, and appoint Angus Regent; to poison
the King and his mother, and then nominate the Earl of
Huntingdon heir to the English Crown.[2] To the latter
part of the scheme Elizabeth at least must have been no
consenting party. But it may possibly have occurred to
Leicester, and to others whose worldly fortunes depended
on the Protestant succession. If the persons of English
sovereigns were sacred, no lives were more precarious
than those of princes or princesses who had inconvenient
pretensions in virtue of royal blood. It seems, however, that the Gowrie's party did not choose to commit
themselves to severe measures till they knew on what
support they might calculate. Without money the force
which they could command was after all extremely
small. The strength of Protestantism lay among trades-
men, artisans, and peasants, who were a fine material for
soldiers, but were unorganised, untrained to arms, and too
poor to fight at their own expense, unless on an immediate
emergency. The few noblemen among them had estates
to lose, but were disinclined to gratuitous risks. If

---

[1] Leicester to Angus, Sept. 7.—*MSS. Scotland.*

[2] 'El designio con que inflamáron, fuera de las pensiones dadivas y dineros, al de Angus, fué con que echado del reyno ó muerto á Aublgny, él sería Gobernador del como fué su tio Morton, y por haber sido el medio el Conde de Huntingdon de assistir al de Angus, y ser despues de la reyna de Escocia el que piensa tener derecho á esta corona, es de temer que no maten ó den venedicos al Rey como se empieça á rugir desde agora; acabando juntamente á su madre, con lo cual él de Leicester y toda la parcialidad de los hereges entienden á segurar el derecho de Huntingdon que les es grandísimo, y en que tiene puesta la mira.'—*Mendoza al Rey*, 1 Setiembre, 1582. *MSS. Simancas.*

Elizabeth expected them to hold their ground with their own resources, some kind of compromise with the other side could not be avoided. The Gordons, the Kers, the Setons, the Grahams, the Humes, the Maxwells, representing as they did the historical genius of Scotland, had a popularity and a strength of their own. They were Catholics at heart, determined enemies of the Reformation and all belonging to it. Their feudal authority enabled them at all times to bring a swarm of personal followers into the field. France and Spain were as liberal as the Queen of England was niggardly; and it had been proved, over and again, that although the Protestant leaders could keep the Government in their hands with a small annual contribution from England, they were no match alone for three quarters of the peers of Scotland backed by the Catholic treasuries. They did not choose to try the experiment again, and Angus and Gowrie declined to widen the gulf between themselves and the other nobles to please Leicester or Huntingdon, till they were satisfied that they might not themselves be flung into it.

The state of things was now precisely what it had been when the Earl of Morton recovered power after his first deposition. The lords of the English faction, as they were called, had the King in their hands, and for the present the control of the situation. On the same conditions which the Abbot of Dunfermline had vainly offered at Audley End, and the rejection of which had been the cause of all the subsequent troubles, Elizabeth might secure the continued supremacy of her friends. James, angry and bitter as he was, might be reconciled to the change, if she would but allow him the rents of his grandmother's estates. A few pensions, and five thousand pounds a year to maintain the court, and a handful of men-at-arms, would place Angus and Gowrie out of all risk of overthrow; and the Queen would have no more need of lying diplomacy. The unanimous opinion of the times was that England could not be successfully invaded as long as it had Scotland for a friend.

So plain was this to all statesmen that they would not believe the opportunity would again be thrown away.

'I shall be sorry in my heart,' wrote Sir Walter Mildmay to Walsingham, 'if anything is omitted now that 'should be done here. To let slip such an opportunity 'to make sure of that realm, the assurance whereof is 'more for us than both the others, might be counted a 'marvellous oversight, and sparing of charge that way 'a small point of husbandry. I pray God it may be 'considered in time, as the weight thereof deserves. 'The lords should be comforted and advised effectually, 'whereof I am sure that you will take care.'[1]

'All depends on England now,' Sir James Colville wrote from Scotland. 'The Queen's interest is as much 'at stake as ours. She must not stint her liberality 'if she wishes the lords success.'[2]

The circumstances were the same as they had been. The Scotch Protestants had once more snatched their country out of the hands of a faction whose chief aim was England, whose manœuvres in Scotland were solely undertaken that it might be used for the general invasion. Elizabeth, untaught by experience, acted in precisely the same manner. She had wished Lennox and Arran to be killed. She would have been rid of two dangerous enemies at a trifling cost to herself, and she would have paraded to the world her horror at the atrocity of their assassination. But they had fallen from

---

[1] Mildmay to Walsingham, Sept. 14.—*MSS. Scotland.*
[2] Colville to Randolph, Sept. 28. —*MSS. Ibid.*

power—the immediate danger was passed, and the ordinary humour again interposed. The Kirk was the chief buttress of her throne, and she hated it in proportion to its value to her. She had sent Sir Robert Bowes with a thousand pounds to Gowrie after the capture of the King, but even this miserable sum she had forbidden him to give if Lennox could be got rid of without it.

'I lament,' wrote Bowes, prudently committing his opinion to a friend,[1] 'I lament to behold such untimely
' sparing in cases where most cost ought to be employed
' to purchase the fruit that might yield both security for
' her Majesty's estate, and avoid expenses in time
' coming. I am inwardly afraid that God's determined
' judgment will not suffer us to repair the ruins of our
' house before it fall on our heads, and that this present
' husbandry shall be found like the huswifry of Calais.
' You see the towardness of the King, easy now to be
' carried into such courses as by her Majesty and
' Council shall be found best. The lords, with the
' King and all the religious, earnestly press the same.
' If the work be at this time stayed or fail, the build-
' ing, I think, will never hereafter prosper, for our
' credit, broken so far, shall be unable to repair the
' breach; and the loss of the good instruments to be now
' cast away will not suddenly be recovered.

' Because that I perceive my labours herein shall bring
' forth great discomfort to good men that in the end are
' like to be abandoned, and also more disgrace to my-
' self, that have no power to perform the effects meet to
' be promised them that may work contentation and
' commodity to her Majesty, for whom I am ready to lay

---

[1] Bowes to Walsingham, Oct. 17. Cipher.—*MSS. Scotland.*

'down my life, therefore I see it high time to stay my
'further progress in these matters, and right humbly
'do pray you that I may be speedily called away to live
'at my charge in such poor estate as shall please God
'and her Majesty to appoint me. The thousand pounds
'I received for these purposes remain entirely with me,
'and ready to be returned or bestowed as shall please
'her Majesty to direct me. I beseech you procure me
'directions, that I may know what to do therewith,
'being loath to touch the same or hereafter persuade
'the opening of her Majesty's purse, but rather to choose
'for the present a heavy burden on my weak back, to
'answer all things for her Majesty's service in my
'charge.'

Not only might it be said of Elizabeth that none but herself could be her parallel, but she was able to eclipse herself, and suggest expedients in her difficulties which could have occurred to no imagination but her own. She was still swearing, and she meant to continue to swear, that she intended to marry her French Prince;[1] but, more wonderful than this, she allowed a report to be spread that she would marry the young King of Scotland, and ensure herself against danger from him by being his wife.[2]

---

[1] 'Those that weigh the matter indifferently, considering her Majesty's years and their necessity in France to be provided of a successor, either by the King or Monsieur, do judge they have good reason not to be hasty in this matter. Notwithstanding it is meant that the negotiation shall still be entertained whereof we have hitherto taken more hurt than good.'—*Walsingham to Cobham*, November 8, 1581. *MSS. France.*

[2] 'J'ay veu par la lettre qu'avez escripte à la Royne ma Dame ot mère la negotiation que l'on mect en avant de marier la dicte Dame d'Angleterre avec mon nepveu le Roy d'Escoce. Cette nouvelle practique le pourra encores quelque temps entretenir en esperance en Angleterre et en Escoce, ne doubtant pas qu'icelle Dame Royne, selon qu'elle a accoustumée, ne soit bien contente que le brulet en soit, car cela ne peult que servir à ses affaires.'—*Le Roi à Castelnau de Mauvissière*, Jan. 17, 1583. TEULET, vol. iii. 'Aquella Reyna no puede estar sin platicas de casa-

Money, at any rate, she would not part with, neither from her own treasury nor the Lennox rents, and among the possible consequences there was one extremely serious, which those who knew Scotland best were afraid might follow. The King had been partly reconciled to his fate by promises of what England would do for him. When he found England would do nothing, he began to grow restless himself, and meditated escape. One day he asked to be allowed to ride, and when he was refused permission, he cried that he would not bear it, and would appeal to his subjects. Gowrie scornfully bade some one bring him a rocking-horse.[1] He made a rush at the door. Gowrie striding before him put his boot across the opening, and James swore he would make him pay for the insult with his life. Gowrie and Angus were situated with him much as Morton and Lindsay were with Mary at Lochleven. They knew that if he lived, and Elizabeth did not help them, they could not keep him for ever; he would recover his power, and be revenged on them; and it was extremely likely that they would avoid a repetition of the previous weakness, and make sure of him while he was in their hands.[2]

Another possibility was that James would dissemble, tempt them into a reconciliation with Lennox, and afterwards destroy them. Elizabeth had been premature in revealing her intention to break her promises, and in exasperation as just as it was natural, the lords were already listening to overtures which were tentatively

---

miento, y ahora las tiene con el Rey de Escocia por asegurarse de donde mas teme.'—*Mendoza á Don Juan de Idriaquez*, 2 Marzo, 1583. *MSS. Simancas.*

[1] 'Una áca.'—*Mendoza al Rey*, 2 Noviembre, 1582. *MSS. Simancas.*

[2] This was Walsingham's opinion:

'Entiendo que Walsingham, relatando esto á un consejero, le afirmo que su opinion era que romperia en breve aquello, porque los conjurados ó atosigarian al Rey, ó él se les haria de suyo para cortarles despues las cabezas.'—*Ibid.*

made to them. Lennox had actually sailed from Dumbarton at the beginning of October, but he was driven back by stress of weather, or overtaken by news which induced him to return. The lords had asked Bowes categorically whether his mistress would make the King an allowance, and Bowes had been unable to give them the answer which they had a right to expect. Mary Stuart, meanwhile, having waived her scruples about James's title, French agents, well supplied with money, had made their appearance at Edinburgh. An ambassador was promised, and was said to be coming immediately, bringing in his hands proposals for a new organisation of parties, the dissolution as well of the English alliance as of the new connection with Spain, and the union of all factions in the interests of the French Court. Gowrie and Angus, weary of their ungracious patron, and delighted to make her feel that they were not in her power, had all but consented to let Lennox stay, and to be reconciled to him. Ker and Seton and Maxwell had joined Lennox in the Western Highlands after he had relanded, and were threatening a march on Stirling. They had hesitated only from a fear that either the King would be murdered, or that Elizabeth, in spite of herself, would then be forced to send troops from Berwick:[1] and French diplomacy would thus have solved the situation by a reconciliation of all parties, to the ruin of the English connexion, had not the ministers of the Kirk held the secular politicians in check.[2]

---

[1] 'El no hacer demostraciones es por no obligar á que la Reyna entre con mano armada en favor de los conjurados; ó en ultima desesperacion que los fuerçe á matar al Rey, confundiendo lo todo.'—*Mendoza al Rey*, 1 Noviembre. *MSS. Simancas.*

[2] 'Escribe Sir Juan Foster que los conjurados se hubieran acordado con Aubigny sino fuera por los ministros que lo habian impedido.'—*Mendoza al Rey*, 1 Noviembre. *MSS. Simancas.*

The Queen of Scots, after her first burst of energy, finding Guise motionless, Lennox shut up in Dumbarton, and Mendoza's encouragement to look for help from Philip unrealised, had again begun to despond. M. de Fontenay, the brother of Nau, her French secretary, had been at Sheffield, and had been allowed to see her. She bade him go to Madrid, and try once more to move Philip, while she wrote to Don Bernardino to say that her affairs would not bear any further procrastination, and that if the King would not or could not assist her, she must come to terms with Elizabeth. She was prepared, she said, to consent to any conditions which would restore her to liberty; and she proposed to retire to some place where she could spend the rest of her life in devotion, and no longer fret away her life in fruitless efforts.[1] She addressed one of her long passionate appeals to Elizabeth, in which eloquence gave falsehood the effect of truth. Now upbraiding, now tender and pathetic, she sung again the old tale of her ill-usage. Through the weary years of her imprisonment, she vowed that she had laboured to please, and her sincerity had been doubted, her motives misrepresented, delay had been piled on delay, and injustice on injustice. If she was supposed to have done wrong, and to have conspired to trouble the peace of England, she begged the privilege of the meanest criminal. Let the proofs be produced, let her be heard in answer in a public court, and if found guilty let her be punished as she deserved.

---

[1] 'Je desire infiniment avoir de une façon ou aultre quelque resolution; car si mes ouvertures ne sont pour reussir, j'ay deliberé de rechercher par tous moyens et à quelques conditions licence de me retirer en quelque lieu de repos, pour y passer le reste de ma vie avec plus de liberté de ma conscience, sans me consumer ici davantage inutilement.' —*The Queen of Scots to Don Bernardino*, Oct. 12, 1582. MSS. Simancas.

She was not troubling the world, she said; Elizabeth's own agents rather were filling Scotland with misery, and seeking the life of her child. For herself she was near the end of her pilgrimage. She could not last much longer—only let not Elizabeth think she could be tamed by harshness. Dispositions like hers would not yield to violence. If she was to be won, she must be won by kindness. She was innocent of all that she was charged with, and she prayed as a favour, and demanded as a right that she might have better servants to wait upon her in an illness which she expected would be her last, and a priest to prepare her for her end.[1]

The letter was sent open through the French Ambassador that a copy of it might move the compassion abroad, but at the unlooked for turn of things in Scotland, her spirits rose again, and from despair she sprung back to confidence. Messengers from Dumbarton and from the Duke of Guise continued to evade the watchfulness of Lord Shrewsbury's guard at Sheffield. Guise reported that French influence was reviving, and that it would soon be re-established, and that Scotland would then be his to deal with as he pleased. He was ready as ever to cross over; he waited only for the permission of his own Sovereign and the King of Spain: and Mary Stuart again pressed on Mendoza the peculiar qualifications which Guise possessed—his courage, his brilliant ability, and those exceptional conditions which, while they endeared him to the French Catholics, made him not unacceptable to Spain. Evidently both she and Guise considered that the chance which had been almost lost had been thoroughly recovered, and that the only result from the Raid of Ruthven, as the enterprise at Perth had come to be called, was, that the King hated more intensely than before the lords who held

[1] Mary Stuart to Elizabeth, Nov. 8.—LABANOFF, vol. v.

him in thraldom, and would give the French when they came a heartier welcome.[1]

The move which had been made by the French might or might not mean all that Mary Stuart expected of it. Scotland might be useful to Henry and Catherine, either to punish Elizabeth, or as a bridle to hold her with. Walsingham believed that the disposition of the French Court towards a genuine alliance with England could not have survived the trifling with Alençon, and that whatever influence France could recover in Scotland would be used in the interests of the Catholics. The dowry of the Queen of Scots being paid by settlement out of several different estates, required a continual correspondence. Many of her letters had thus passed and repassed unwatched, and had gone regularly in the bags of the French Ambassador. It was discovered that Mauvissière had allowed her to abuse her privilege, and had transmitted papers for her connected with the conspiracy. This was taken as another evidence of the bad faith of the French Court. Walsingham bade Cobham keep his eyes open. 'If,' he said, 'the Ambassador here has proceeded by direction 'of the French King and his mother, then are we to 'think that their protestations of amity are but abuses; 'for if they desire unfeignedly an association against 'Spain, they would be careful to preserve the quiet of 'England, and advise Scotland to depend upon her 'Majesty.'[2]

While the uneasiness was at its height, La Mothe Fénelon, the late Ambassador in England, came over suddenly with a request that the Queen would allow him to proceed to Edinburgh. His conduct while at Eliza-

---

[1] Mary Stuart to Don Bernardino, Nov. 1581.—*MSS. Simancas.*

[2] Walsingham to Cobham, Sept. 26, 1581.—*MSS. France.*

beth's Court had been eminently conciliatory. All parties had liked him, and nothing could be more friendly than the professed object of his mission. He represented the French King as still extremely anxious for the Queen's marriage with his brother, and as being ready to make all concessions for it, short of giving up Calais: or if the marriage could not be, there was still room for a league offensive and defensive. The Queen-mother professed an intention of continuing her privateering war with Philip. She had commissioned La Mothe to ask Elizabeth to sell her ships for a fresh expedition to the Azores.[1] She wished them to be manned with English officers and seamen, and she promised that if Philip resented it, Elizabeth might count on France to stand by her.[2] As regarded Scotland, his objects, as La Mothe described them, were equally plausible. He said generally that he had come to help England in pacifying the feuds with which that unhappy country was distracted; and his principle of pacification was one which was likely to be seductive to Elizabeth, however unsafe it might appear to Walsingham. 'The Queen of Scots,' La Mothe said to her in a private conversation, 'must either be held 'prisoner for life, or released under hard conditions, or 'lastly Elizabeth, like a true friend and loving sister, 'might replace her on her own throne. To condemn 'her to perpetual captivity would provoke the anger of 'God, the enmity and perhaps the interposition of man. 'Her Majesty was too honourable and too wise a 'Princess to take a course so unjust and so hazardous. 'The second alternative, if less cruel, was even more 'dangerous. Hard conditions would, of course, be resented. They might be imposed, but circumstances

---

[1] Walsingham to Cobham, Dec. 13.—*MSS. France.*
[2] Don Bernardino to Philip, Dec. 16.—*MSS. Simancas.*

'might change. Elizabeth might be without power to
' enforce them, and the end might be convulsion and
' violence. To impartial observers the most prudent
' course appeared to be to gain the Queen of Scots'
' gratitude by a frank and generous clemency, and restore
' her to the station which she had lost. Past unpleasant-
' nesses would then be forgotten. The treaty of Leith
' could be ratified, and the two Princesses, rivals no
' longer, might reign in peace and good-will to the end
' of their natural lives.'[1]

The sentiment of all this was as little likely to have touched Elizabeth as to have been meant in earnest by La Mothe; but the presence of the Queen of Scots in the realm was a fact which did not allow itself to be forgotten, and the question of what to do with her was as necessary to solve, as it was still far from solution. The Queen had all along preferred the mother to the son, and if France would become a guarantee for Mary Stuart's future behaviour, La Mothe's proposal had, after all, much to recommend it. Connected with the restoration of Mary Stuart, he had brought plans for a general policy in Europe, a close alliance between France and England, the liberation of the Low Countries, the toleration of the Huguenots, and the fine picture—so often shaped by imagination, to fade as soon as it had been drawn—of a world restored to order and peace on broad principles of moderation and justice.

Was France sincere?—all turned on that,—or was the French Court France? and might not La Mothe be after all an agent of the Guises? Sir Henry Cobham discovered that among La Mothe's secret instructions there was one to keep Lennox in Scotland, another to arrange

---

[1] Paper endorsed 'Advice of M. de la Mothe,' Jan. 1583.—*MSS. France. Rolls House.*

a marriage between James and a daughter of Lorrayne.[1] He had been also ordered to encourage Mary Stuart's plans for the associate sovereignty of herself and James; to prevail on the Estates of Scotland to declare the Lochleven abdication null, and to obtain, if possible, a public act acquitting her of the Kirk-o'-Field murder. Again, and it was a curious instance of Mary Stuart's revengeful memory, a charge had been given him to procure the execution of Ker of Faldonside, who had held a pistol at her breast when Rizzio was assassinated, and of George Douglas, who had stabbed him with Darnley's dagger.[2]

It was possible that Lennox might be ruled by La Mothe, and be no longer dangerous. The Lorrayne marriage might be an improvement on the contemplated match with Spain. If Mary Stuart was to be restored, Elizabeth's own policy had been always to throw a veil over the Darnley tragedy. But the tone of these purposes, as they were discovered by other means, did not harmonise with La Mothe's language to Elizabeth. Without proving that he had been playing false, they suggested unpleasant suspicions, and the Queen could not tell whether she would let him proceed to Scotland or not. The Council sate upon it from morning till night without coming to a resolution.[3] Elizabeth said

---

[1] Cobham to Walsingham, Nov. 19. Cipher. Walsingham to Cobham, January 4.—*MSS. France.*

[2] 'Aura soing de faire par tous moyens verifier l'innocence de la dicte Royne sa mère pour la calomnie que luy a esto imposée touchant le meurtre du feu Roy son mari. Il fera justice exemplaire de ceulx qui ont autrefois attempté à la personne d'icelle Royne comme Andrew Kerr de Faldonside, et George Douglas, lesquels demeurent hors de toute abolition generale ou pardon particulier à l'advenir.'—*Articles presented by La Mothe*, Jan. 10, 1582-3. *MSS. Mary Queen of Scots.*

[3] 'Se juntáron,' says Mendoza, as if it were a fact of great importance, 'se juntáron los de su consejo, estando en el desde la mañana á la noche.' Philip, remembering his English experiences, wrote on the margin, 'No es mucho, porque comen alli muchas veces y estan en conversacion.'—*Don Bernardino al Rey*, 16 Deciembre, 1582. *MSS. Simancas.*

that when La Mothe was in England as ambassador he was a lamb, and that now he was a vixen,[1] but he might gain less by his cunning than he looked for. She tried the marriage on again. La Mothe declined to dip his fingers in the pitch with which he had defiled them already. If the Queen wished to reopen that subject, he said, she must write herself to Alençon. Secretary Pinart hinted to Cobham, that if she objected to take a husband for her own person, she might give Alençon the little Arabella Stuart, and settle the crown on them.[2] Mendoza was told that she parried Pinart's suggestion by pretending that she had powers from Parliament to appoint any one that she pleased to succeed her, and that if France would declare war against Spain and send an army to the Low Countries, she would name Alençon, married or unmarried.[3]

Leicester, it seems, had an eye on Lady Arabella for his own son. Mary Stuart's life was thought a bad one, and James ran a fair chance of destruction among the Scotch nobles. In default of these, the lawyers were inclining to think that the Lady Arabella's claims stood next, and the house of Dudley might arrive after all at the sceptre which Leicester's father had perished in grasping, and which he himself had so narrowly missed.

With toys of this kind Elizabeth amused the time

---

[1] 'Una raposa.'
[2] 'Pinart pretending to understand the meaning was not to suffer the Scotch King to become successor to the Crown.'—*Cobham to Walsingham*, Dec. 19.—*MSS. France*.
[3] 'La Reyna scribió una carta de propia mano, en la cual dice que cuando el Rey de Francia publicamente quisiere romper guerra con V. Mag^d y asistir á su hermano para los negocios de los Payses Bajos, ella declararia á Alençon por heredero desto Reyno en virtud del consentimiento que en un Parliamento le dieron de aceptar por tal á cualquiera que ella señalase. Entiendo que él de Leicester tiene la mira de casar su hijo con la nieta de la Condesa de Shrewsbury, juzgando los mejores letrados y mas cuerdos que en defecto de la Reyna de Escocia y su hijo es la mas propinqua heredera de todos.'—*Mendoza al Rey*, 16 Deciembre. *MSS. Simancas*.

while she struggled with her perplexities. One day La Mothe was to be allowed to go. The next day she was positive that he should not go. At last his passports were sent to him, and he started on his journey. Immediately after there came a message from the Earl of Gowrie, that a letter had been intercepted addressed to Lennox, in which there was information that a French army was coming over ; that the Duke of Guise and his brother the Duc de Mayenne were to lead, that the King of Spain had consented, and that the Pope was to supply the funds.[1]

Secretary Davison was instantly sent galloping down the north road to overtake and stop La Mothe, when again news came that, in consequence of his long detention, Henry had sent a second ambassador, M. de Mainville, to Edinburgh by sea. To arrest the first would be therefore a gratuitous affront, and a second courier galloped after Davison with orders that La Mothe was to go forward, and that Davison himself should accompany him.[2]

'Mr. Bowes,' wrote Walsingham sadly, 'had once 'brought things to so good a pass, and prepared the 'King's mind so well to depend upon her Majesty, as if 'it had pleased her to have been at some charges to con- 'tinue him in that good devotion, she might have had 'the disposing of him in marriage, the saving of which 'charges now will breed peril hereafter.'[3]

Both La Mothe and de Mainville came too late to prevent the departure of Lennox. Encouraged by his letters from France, and by the evident irresolution of

---

[1] Mendoza al Rey, 16 Deciembre.—*MSS. Simancas.*
[2] Letters from Walsingham to Davison, Dec. 12-14.—*MSS. Scotland.*
[3] Walsingham to Cobham, Jan. 4.—*MSS. France.*

the confederate lords, he had communicated with James
and had arranged to carry him off from Stirling. The
plot was discovered by a servant[1] the day before it was
to have been executed, and Gowrie snatched up his
royal prisoner, and secured him in the safer quarters
of Edinburgh Castle. Lennox having missed his mark,
made a feint of attacking Edinburgh Castle, and actually
threw supplies into Blackness; but matters had now
become extremely critical, and in the panic at the expected French interference James's murder had become
a seriously probable contingency. The English Puritans would have made no very curious enquiry into
the end of a boy from whom they anticipated nothing
but mischief; the politicians who wanted the succession for Huntingdon or Lady Arabella would have been
still less scrupulous; and Elizabeth herself would undoubtedly have breathed more freely had she understood that he was dead. Mendoza believed that on La
Mothe's first coming to England orders were sent from
London to Gowrie to have him poisoned, and that one
cause of La Mothe's detention had been that Gowrie
might have time to get it done.[2] Whether this suspicion
was just or false, James was in as much danger as his
mother had been at Lochleven, and no similar intervention in his favour was to be looked for from England.
He scrawled on the wall of the room in which he was
confined a feeble lamentation over his captivity;[3] the

---

[1] 'Un porrero,' the keeper of the King's dogs.

[2] 'Luego que llegó aquí La Mota, despacháron un correo en Escocia con orden que procurase avenenar al Rey. ... El de Ruthven ha scripto una carta de propia mano en las de la Reyna, que no se puede entender que le diga, mas de ser por discursos del atosigar al Rey, porque luego que tuvó la dicha carta, la Reyna dizó que era la ocasion del detenerse tanto La Mota tras tener pasaporte suyo.' —*Don Bernardino al Rey*, 10 Deciembre, 1582. *MSS. Simancas.*

[3] 'A prisoner I am and liberty would have.'—*Advertisements out of Scotland*, Nov. 30. *MSS. Scotland.*

next morning he saw written by some fierce hand under his words:—

> A Papist thou art and friend to a slave;
> A rope thou deservest, and that thou shalt have.

It was full time for Lennox to be gone. All along and when his power was at its highest, he had wished to retire to France till Guise was ready to cross over. He was afraid for his own skin in such a boiling element, with no better protection than his own skill and courage. Guise, Mendoza, the Queen of Scots, Philip himself, had insisted that he should remain, and he had obeyed; but now he had an adequate excuse. The Protestant party was disorganised and divided, and without the help which Elizabeth would not give, it could not readily gather form again; his friends undertook to keep Dumbarton, and to hold themselves prepared to move when the opportunity returned.

James himself contrived to send him a letter assuring him of his constant affection, promising to receive him again when he was out of Gowrie's hands, but meanwhile begging him,[1] for his own sake, to leave Scotland. Arran gave the same advice. Until Lennox went, he said, the King's life was in danger. Permission was sent to him to pass through England, and an intimation that Elizabeth would see him on his passage through London, and by the end of December he was gone.

Elizabeth regarded his departure as the victory of her

---

[1] 'I enquired of the Master of Livingstone the cause of the Duke's departure. He answered the Duke mistrusted not his power nor did he doubt of the King's good will, but the King mistrusted very much his own life so long as the Duke continued in Scotland, being sharply threatened by the Lords that if he would not cause the Duke to depart he should not be the longest liver of them all. The Duke therefore at the private and special request of the King departed, nothing less assured of his Majesty's favour. Arran wrote to the King that unless the Duke departed there could be no surety for his life nor peace for the country.'—— to Walsingham, Jan. 5, 1583. MSS. Scotland.

own diplomacy. Sir Robert Bowes, who understood how wildly she was deceiving herself, made another effort on behalf of Gowrie and Angus. 'I wait,' he said, 'to see what will be done towards the support of 'the lords and their contentment, without which the 'King and this realm will not be kept long in this 'course, wherein if they again slide and fall I shall 'utterly despair of their recovery. The offer of them 'is once more presented frankly to her Majesty, who at 'some charge may have them. If we will needs save 'our money we must of force lose their friendship, be-'cause necessity doth press them to provide for their own 'standing. Her Majesty has to choose, to have Scotland 'at her devotion or to save her money.'[1]

Her Majesty preferred both to have Scotland as she wished and to save her money also, and she refused to believe that the two things were incompatible. She bade Bowes to cram the lords with the chameleon's dish, with expectations which she had predetermined to disappoint. Lord Burghley would have preferred, since this was her resolution, that at least there should be no more lying. 'Seeing,' he wrote to Bowes, 'that 'we are no better disposed to lay hold of the amity of 'that realm, I see no cause why either yourself should 'be continued there, or any other appointed to supply 'your place.'[2] But the Queen chose to play her game in her own way, and having deceived the lords she prepared to deceive Lennox. The latter, on his way from the border, encountered La Mothe and Davison at Topcliff. La Mothe was surprised and 'discontented' to see him, but after a long private conversation Lennox satisfied him that he had sufficient reason for going, and

---

[1] Bowes to Walsingham and Burghley, Dec. 15, 29.—*MSS. Scotland.*
[2] Burghley to Bowes, Jan. 4, 1583. —*MSS. Scotland.*

that his departure would be no injury to the cause.[1] La Mothe went on, carrying with him a portmanteau full of gold crowns to weigh against Elizabeth's words. Lennox came to London, and the object of so many anxious thoughts and against whom so many daggers had been sharpened, found himself in the Queen's presence.

He too had his game that he was playing. Deficient as he was in nerve and daring, at cool falsehood he had not his match in the world. Elizabeth received him graciously, and bade him wear his cap while speaking to her in consideration of his rank. She then told him that he was suspected of having gone to Scotland at the instigation of the Duke of Guise, with a view to making a religious revolution and of destroying the alliance with England; that he was said further to have introduced Jesuits there, whom he had seen, talked to, and consulted with. Every word of this was literally true: yet he swore that it was nothing but a dream. His return to Scotland was at the King's invitation, he said. He had no connexion with Guise, and had never spoken to a Jesuit. He was a true Protestant. He had always insisted to the King that the Queen of England was his surest friend; and the cause of his unpopularity had been nothing but a difference with the ministers about church government. He preferred the Anglican system to the Scotch, and he had wished to introduce the orderly institution of bishops.

Elizabeth allowed him to believe that she thought him sincere. She should hear, she said, how he behaved in France, and if she was satisfied with the accounts of him she would allow him to return to Scotland. He imagined that he had succeeded in blinding her, and afterwards, that his friends in England might

---

[1] Davison to Burghley, Jan. 3, 1583.—*MSS. Scotland.*

not be led astray about him by a report of his words, he
gave an account of himself and his intentions to Mendoza. He did not think it prudent to appear at the
Spanish embassy in person, but he sent his confidential
secretary, and the substance of his message was forwarded by the ambassador to Philip.

'The secretary,' wrote Mendoza, 'brought me two
'lines in the cipher which I used with his master, bidding me give full credit to what the bearer would say
'to me. The Duke, I was then told, had been forced to
'leave Scotland because the King had promised that he
'should go, and because a plan had failed to take the
'King out of the hands of the confederate lords. His
'party was still far superior in strength, but it was
'thought imprudent to use force in the face of the
'Queen of England. His friends had agreed that he had
'better retire. The King would then probably recover
'his liberty without trouble or tumult. The Master of
'Graham, through whom the King and Lennox cor-
'responded, with the rest of the Catholic noblemen,
'had bound themselves under their hands and seals to
'procure his release. Lennox had himself signed with
'the rest, and as soon as he was in France, the rest, if
'other means failed, intended to take arms, and would be
'glad of any help which could be furnished them. As
'soon as the King was free, Lennox was to return and re-
'sume his place at the Court. The bond was every day
'receiving fresh adhesions, and the King himself meant
'to affix his name when the time came. The Master of
'Graham had wished him to do it before Lennox left,
'but the King had feared that a premature signature
'might lead to an immediate explosion. He had given
'his word to the Queen of England that Lennox should
'go to France, and he must keep his promise. But to

'go to France need not mean to remain there, and in
'six months at latest he might be again at Edinburgh.

'I asked the secretary if the Duke meant while he
'was in Paris to attend the Protestant services. He
'said that he did, and the Duke had particularly charged
'him to tell me so, that his Holiness and your Majesty and
'the Queen of Scots might be under no false impression
'about him. He was forced to dissemble that obstacles
'might not be raised to his return. If he avowed him-
'self the Catholic which he really was, the King could
'not conveniently recall him, and the Queen of England
'would certainly interfere. He wished me to be satisfied
'that nothing should prevent him from taking arms in
'the great cause, when a Catholic army was once landed
'in Scotland. The King he undertook should then be
'reconciled to the Church. He would make him under-
'stand that his prospects in England depended on his
'compliance, and on the help of the Catholic powers.

'The secretary assured me further of the great affec-
'tion which the King felt for Lennox. I was aware
'of it already, and it appears plainly in two notes
'which the King wrote to him before his departure. He
'gave me a letter further from his master to the Queen
'of Scots, referring her to me for further information
'about him, with which he begged me to furnish her.

'I replied with generalities. It appeared to me that
'in desiring the recovery of these realms to the Church,
'the Duke, instead of thinking like his Holiness and
'your Majesty, of the salvation of souls, might perhaps
'be looking rather to the succession to this crown, to
'which it was the readiest road, and to the interests of
'himself and his family; and that for this reason he
'wished to know your Majesty's decision about the inva-
'sion. I hesitated therefore to enter into particulars
'till I had heard what had been arranged between

'Baptista de Tassis and the Duke of Guise; but not
'wishing that he should think me indifferent, I referred
'him to Guise, from whom he would soon hear all.'[1]

Whatever might be the faults of the Spaniards, to dissemble their religion was never one of them; and Mendoza's opinion of Lennox, already unfavourable, was not raised by the secretary's account. But Lennox was not Scotland; or if the objects of his whole party were less pure than they ought to have been, they might be turned notwithstanding to purposes of good. Philip was coming very slowly to a consciousness that he would be obliged to interfere. The French succession was becoming as momentous as the English. Henry III.'s health had been destroyed by debauchery. Alençon's was little better, and Alençon in the Netherlands was at open war with Spain. Next after him was the King of Navarre. The Duke of Guise was the only hope of the orthodox Catholic party in France, and Philip was keenly alive to the necessity of strengthening the Duke's influence and securing his friendship. Already he had bidden de Tassis tell him that he might count on Spain to stand by him in preventing the accession of a heretic sovereign: already de Tassis had all but promised that Philip would support him in an expedition to Scotland.[2]

The Archbishop of Glasgow indeed, who had meant to rush to Madrid to entreat, had been sharply rebuked by de Tassis and been told to remain at his post.[3] The veneration of Philip for priests in chapel and confessional was equalled, though it could not be excelled, by his contempt for them as politicians. But none the less he had given his confidence to Guise,

---

[1] Mendoza to Philip, Jan. 16, 1583.
[2] Philip to de Tassis, Sept. 14.—Teulet, vol. v.
[3] Philip in his usual form scribbled approval on the margin: 'Ilisóbien.'—Tassis to Philip, Dec. 19. Teulet, vol. v.

and professed a willingness to be guided by his advice. Dumbarton was still open. The Lords of Lennox's faction had promised to hold the castle against all comers till the following summer. Lennox had sent word to the Queen of Scots, and his opinion was confirmed by Walsingham,[1] that Elizabeth's latest infidelity to her promises had left her party there weaker and more estranged than when the King was first seized by Gowrie; and that an invading army would find everywhere an enthusiastic welcome. The Queen of Scots was once more all fire, animation, and hope.

'I am more assured than ever,' she wrote to Mendoza, 'of the devotion of my child to me. My nobles also are 'more earnest for the enterprise than ever. They assure me that with the slightest countenance from abroad 'they will destroy the English faction in a fortnight. 'They would have destroyed it already but for fear my 'son might be killed or carried to England. For myself I am preparing to escape. If I succeed you may 'tell his Holiness and your master that there will then 'be immediate war. We shall look for present help, 'and as the struggle may be a protracted one there must 'be reserves. The Duke tells me that before anything 'considerable is done he will himself bring over part of 'the force for the reception of which he has arranged at 'Dumbarton.'

Mendoza had many times petitioned to be recalled. He was a brave soldier, and out of his element in lying intrigues. The climate disagreed with his eyes. They

---

[1] 'They have been often fed with fair promises, and therefore it is not likely that words shall prevail before deeds. The French bring crowns and we give words, our success will be thereafter. I hold Scotland for lost unless God be merciful to this poor island. How unseasonably the same is likely to fall out, or rather dangerously, all the world may see if the state of things at home and abroad be duly looked unto. God open her Majesty's eyes to see her peril and not prefer treasure before surety.'— *Walsingham to Burghley*, Jan. 30, 1583. *MSS. Domestic.*

were affected with a disease of which he became ultimately blind, dying long afterwards, at a great age, a monk in a convent at Madrid. The Queen of Scots, who knew what he was feeling, besought him to stay if only till the great event had been consummated. He was the one person, she said, in whom she had implicit confidence. She considered his presence essential to success; she relied on him for qualities of prudence not to be found among English conspirators.

'I agree with you,' she added, 'that there must be no 'talking beforehand. If, however, his Holiness and the 'King Catholic are really resolved, you must give notice 'to a few of the leading nobles to prepare in secret. I 'have myself as yet sounded none of them, nor till the 'Catholic powers are actually moving in this cause are 'they likely to pledge themselves at all. The fine promises, they say, which were made to them at the rising 'of the North were never fulfilled. Those who made 'the venture were destroyed in consequence, and they 'will undertake nothing till they are quite certain of the 'help of his Holiness and your master.'[1]

Meanwhile Lennox in Paris sustained the farce of being a zealous Huguenot, and he carried his hypocrisy and falsehood—falsehood any way, whatever was its purpose—so far that but for his letter to the Queen of Scots and the distinct intimation of his secretary that he intended to play a double part, it might be doubted whether after all the Queen of Scots herself was not the person that was deceived, whether he had not changed sides like his grandfather and been converted by his interview with Elizabeth. Three weeks after his arrival there came a Scot named Smollet to the English Ambassador, Sir Henry Cobham, to say that if it was

[1] Mary Stuart to Mendoza, Feb. 28, 1583.—MSS. Simancas.

made worth his while 'he could assure Lennox to the 'Queen's Majesty in such sort as he should altogether 'abandon France.'[1] A few days later Smollet came again with a message from Lennox himself, that he wished to devote himself for the future to the service of the Queen of England, that he was ready to put her in possession of the secret plots of the Duke of Guise, and that if she distrusted him he would send his son to her as a pledge of his good faith. 'The King of Scots,' Lennox said, 'was a deep dissembler. The King had 'many times requested him to transport him into France, 'and but the other day had written to him to return as 'quietly as he might and all things should come to pass 'to his desire.' By the same messenger Lennox begged Cobham 'to bestow a Bible on him,' and sent a declaration in writing that 'his religion being the same with 'the Queen's Majesty's, the zeal which he had for the 'same might command him further than any worldly 'interest.'[2]

The ambassador knew not what to think. The Bishop of Ross had been seen at Lennox's house. Guise and Guise's adherents were there continually. Lady Lennox had been closeted with the Queen-mother, and it was not to be supposed that such persons would trust him with their confidence unless they were certain of his devotion. His overtures, the religious cant especially, tallied exactly with his declarations to Mendoza; but his next message seemed to indicate that Mendoza was right about his character, and that he contemplated genuine treachery. He did not mean to give his services gratuitously. The Queen, he said, must make a distinct agreement with him. 'If she refused, he would

---

[1] Cobham to Walsingham, March 11.—*MSS. France.*   [2] Cobham to Walsingham, March 21.—*MSS. France.*

'in religion and always run the course of France and
'would adventure his life into Scotland, well and
'strongly accompanied. Sufficient force was promised
'him as soon as the lords of their party would pass
'assurance to rise on their parts.'[1]

The Queen, who had seen through him sufficiently to
recognise at any rate that he was a scoundrel, treated
his advances at first as attempts on her credulity. She
bade Cobham hear what he had to say, be on his guard
against deception, and commit her to nothing. But she
did not feel quite certain. The bottom of a base nature
is difficult to probe. 'On second thought, she enter-
'tained a hope that the offer might be sincere;' and Walsingham told Cobham that he was to close with the conditions, whatever they might be.

The result was extremely curious, though conjecture
is still free to choose its own conclusion. Had Lennox
asked for an immediate sum of money, his conduct would
be intelligible. He would have put it in his pocket and
laughed at his dupes. He asked, indeed, to be restored
by the Queen's means to Scotland; he promised to use
his influence there to promote English interests; and
this too might have been mere illusion. But as a proof of
sincerity he gave in a list of the nobles who had signed
the bond with himself; he gave details of the plan to
which Mary Stuart alluded, for her rescue from Sheffield, and he added that there was a second conspiracy,
into which, out of revenge for their neglect by England,
the Earls of Angus, Gowrie and Glencairn had entered
with La Mothe Fénelon for the transport of the young
King into France. He described all the particulars.
He named the vessel in which the King was to be
brought over. It belonged to himself. It was fitting

---
[1] Cobham to Walsingham, March 18.—*MSS. France.*

in a French port as if for trade, and was really going to Kirkcudbright. He advised the Queen to send a ship secretly to cruise on the coast, when without fail she would secure her prize.[1]

This too is explicable if we suppose Lennox to have wished to sow distrust between Elizabeth and the confederate lords. It is less easy to understand what appears like a deliberate betrayal of the Queen of Scots and of her friends at Elizabeth's own Court. He expressed a wish to go in person to London and deal with the Queen at first hand. 'The Duke proposes,' wrote Cobham, 'to shew at his repair to her Majesty a letter 'written to him from the Queen of Scots, directed to 'Dumbarton, wishing him to stay in those parts; offering 'that her friends in Scotland should join their forces 'with his: her confederates in England would then shew 'themselves in his favour. And since his being in this 'place the Queen of Scots has written again, declaring 'that she understood by her friends about her Majesty 'the conference he had passed with her whereat he 'quitted himself honourably, assuring him that the 'Queen of England should intend nothing against him 'but she should be advertised thereof. Which letter he 'keeps to deliver to her Majesty, intending to write to 'the Queen of Scots to discover the names of her as-'sured accomplices in England, if her Majesty findeth it 'good.'[2]

The character of Lennox is of little moment to history. It is waste of labour to look among the masks which he assumed for the true face of so insignificant a wretch. The probability perhaps would still be that by an affectation of revealing what Elizabeth already knew he was

[1] Cobham to Walsingham, May 1. —MSS. France.
[2] Cobham to Walsingham, May 1, 1581.—MSS. France.

attempting to steal into her confidence, or by false lists of names to conceal the real conspirators. There is one circumstance, however, which points the other way, and seems rather to indicate that he was false to his Catholic friends. In the midst of his negotiations with Cobham he suddenly died. Again, it may have been no more than coincidence. But if he was really treacherous he possessed secrets which would have cost Mary Stuart her life; and if Guise discovered him to be false the dysentery which was said to have killed him may be easily explained. Any way, he may serve for an illustration of the training of the Jesuits, and is perhaps the only conspicuous person in the sixteenth century whose basenesses were unredeemed by any one single virtue.

In the meantime the remonstrances of Walsingham and Burghley and the letters of Sir Robert Bowes so far prevailed with Elizabeth that she was brought to reconsider her resolution to do absolutely nothing. She consented that the confederate lords should send representatives with their own and the King's demands, that she might consider them at leisure. Sir John Colville and Col. Stewart were chosen commissioners, and were expected in London in the spring.

She had been hard to persuade, and remained violently suspicious. 'She had entered into a jealous conceit that reports of French promises and offers of 'pensions to the King and the lords were devices to 'prepare the way for Col. Stewart's arrival that he might 'have the better market.' She did not see that James's marriage concerned her. Let him marry where he would, 'her Highness was persuaded that nothing would be 'attempted during her life for attaining the interest 'which the King pretended to the English crown.'[1]

---
[1] Walsingham to Bowes, Feb. 27, 1583.—*MSS. Scotland*.

Walsingham believed her to be mistaken. 'He feared 'she would learn by dangerous effects the error of her 'own judgment.'¹ 'He saw no disposition in her to 'deal with Scotland as she ought.' She fancied that a smooth letter to James would now keep him straight. Walsingham knew that neither James nor the lords would be cheated any more with words. 'They would 'look for deeds,' which, as he said, 'we are slow enough 'to perform.'² She desired Burghley and Walsingham, with the Lord Chancellor and Sir Walter Mildmay, to consult and report to her what they considered that she ought to do. They concluded that with ten thousand pounds a year she might purchase the permanent quiet of Scotland, and that the price was not excessive. Half of it would be paid as a pension to the King, and would cost her nothing, for it was in fact his own. Four thousand pounds might be given in the form of pensions to the lords of the English party, and one thousand would maintain a permanent English minister at Edinburgh. It was a cheap bargain. Every pound so expended would in the long-run have saved ten. But the Queen 'utterly misliked the casting of her into 'charges.' She would not listen to any such proposal. She said she would sooner marry James than give him so much money. 'What further determination she 'would grow to,' Walsingham was unable to guess.³

For direct measures then and always Elizabeth had an incurable dislike. She resented the perpetual efforts to extort money from her. Experience had proved more than ever that in extremity the Protestant party had been able by themselves to take the control of the

---

¹ Walsingham to Bowes, Feb. 27, 1585.—*MSS. Scotland.*
² Walsingham to Bowes, Feb. 6. —*MSS. Ibid.*
³ Walsingham to Bowes, March 2. —*MSS. Ibid.*

government. She believed that they could hold it without help from her treasury, if a certain number of waverers could be detached from the opposite faction, and if by skilful manœuvres she could force them to rely upon themselves. They were now playing France against England. She conceived that she could turn their position by playing the mother against the son. She had ascertained during the winter that whatever the Queen of Scots might pretend, there was not only a general objection in Scotland to the Queen of Scots' plan of association, but that it was shared by James himself, and by the Earl of Arran, by whom, after Lennox's departure, the King was principally influenced. They were willing to consent to an informal permission from the Queen of Scots that her son should be called King, but to pass an Act of Association through the Scotch Parliament, or to allow the Queen of Scots' name to appear in the Acts of the realm by the side of her son's was on every ground, political and personal, a thing which very few of them could bring themselves to think of.

The King had tasted the pleasures as well as the pains of sovereignty, and did not fancy receding into a second place. Arran was in possession of the Hamilton estates of which he was afraid that a change might deprive him. The return of the Queen even to nominal power threatened a revolution, by which every one who had gained anything in the convulsions of the past fifteen years feared that he might be made to disgorge his spoil. They had raised difficulties which Mary Stuart was known to resent. She had determined not to recede from her own demands. The treaty which Elizabeth had opened with her in the preceding year had been suspended, but had not been broken off. Her release would produce extreme confusion in Scotland, while, if the French Government would make themselves a party to the treaty, as they had repeatedly promised, the dangerous effects might not be extended to England. Elizabeth determined to make the hungry Scotch lords feel that she was less in their power than they imagined.

Before the promised commissioners arrived, Secretary Beale was again dispatched to Sheffield with an answer to the passionate reproaches which Mary Stuart had addressed to her in the past November. That letter has been regarded by the Queen of Scots' admirers as a masterpiece of power and beauty; the reply, as an English composition, was more than its equal. It bore Elizabeth's name, and may have been written by herself, but in the nerve and sinew of its sentences, it presents no feature of resemblance to the tortuous affectation of her ordinary personal style, and is the most complete defence which exists of her past behaviour towards her prisoner.

'We have delayed our answer,' so ran Mr. Beale's instructions, ' not for want of matter, having sufficient for
' our defence before God and the world, but from respect
' to herself though not deserved on her part, for that
' we could not justify ourselves without renewing the
' memory of horrible acts of hers which we wish were
' rather buried in silence than revived to her infamy.
' You shall let her understand that if she was as free
' from the guilt of those horrible acts that in the open
' eye of the world she has been publicly noted withal, as
' we with reason rest free from remorse of any extremity
' that we have ever offered to her, she should enjoy
' more peace and quietness than presently she doth.
' . . . And seeing she deeply charges our conscience,
' we think ourselves bound in conscience to let her
' know that if anything towards herward may justly

'breed in us remorse, it is the care we have had for the
' safety of such an one, whose preservation has since
' brought the ruin and overthrow of infinite numbers
' in both realms. All this passion has been provoked
' by the alterations in Scotland, to which she would have
' done well to have reconciled herself. The King had
' been led away into ill practices, as the taking the life
' of the Earl Morton, a worthy and well-deserving ser-
' vant. Had this course been a little continued, it would
' have brought her son to the same ruin which she has
' brought upon herself. How far forth the prosecution
' of those violent counsellors of the death of Morton,
' under pretence that he was privy to the death of her
' husband, might in the end reach unto herself—if prin-
' cipals are not to be spared when accessaries come in
' question, her own judgment, or rather her own con-
' science, can best judge; and we fear she shall feel,
' unless she shew some other remorse of conscience than
' hitherto she hath done. And where she wishes by
' way of invocation that God would retribute unto us
' at the time of his last judgment according to our
' deserts and demerits one towards another, putting us
' also in mind that all disguisement and counterfeit
' policies of this world shall not then prevail, you shall
' tell her, that if that severe censure should take place, it
' would go more hardly with her than we (whatsoever
' cause she hath given us to the contrary) can in Chris-
' tian charity wish unto her. For howsoever she is bold
' with men who can judge but of things outwardly, she
' ought to beware how she dallyeth with God.'

As she had presented her grievances at length, so
Beale was to present her in return with a list of her
own misdoings, her plots at her first return from France,
her hatred of the Earl of Murray, her intrigues with the

disaffected English Catholics, her husband's death, her marriage with the murderer, the rebellion in the North which followed her flight into England, her correspondence with the Duke of Norfolk, her transactions with the Bishop of Ross and Ridolfi, and again with a ciphered letter that had been intercepted, in which she had slandered the nobility as being ready to take arms in her behalf, in which she had invoked the Catholic powers to maintain and revenge her cause, in which she had described Elizabeth as a tyrant, faithless antichrist, usurper of titles, maintainer of rebels, and enemy of all good princes, for the cutting off of whom she had a way made by her Holy Father, both for their and her relief.[1]

Opposed to all this, there were on the side of Elizabeth acts of kindness which it pleased her to forget. While she was in France, proposals had been made to her Majesty by Maitland of Lethington to deprive her of her kingdom, 'which we utterly rejected.' When she was in Lochleven, the lords had determined to take her life: 'the same was stayed by our mediation, not 'without difficulty.' 'When the noblemen repaired to 'England, furnished with sufficient matter to justify 'their proceedings against her, her Majesty herself 'was the only impediment and stay, that there was no 'further proceeding in that matter;' 'for that we saw '(by the view of her own letters which we sought by 'all means to conceal), the proofs fall out so sufficient 'against her (as both Norfolk and Arundel did declare 'unto us, howsoever they were after drawn to cover her 'faults and pronounce her innocent), as the said nobility 'of Scotland intended to urge us that without our mis-

---

[1] 'Out of a letter written in cipher by her to the Bishop of Ross, April 30, 1578.'—*Note on the margin of Mr. Beale's instructions.*

'like, having so apparent matter to charge her withal
'they might have proceeded against her.'

Lastly, when the Parliament moved her Majesty to proceed judicially against her after the rebellion of the North, her Majesty was the only stay that it was not done. If the case were fairly weighed, the princes whom she now sought to raise against her Majesty would not have dealt with equal leniency.[1]

The stern and serious tone of these instructions was no agreeable introduction to the reopening of a treaty; but it was a better evidence of true meaning than smooth and vague phrases, and no one understood better than the Queen of Scots the difference between the sincere and the plausible, was a more accomplished mistress of the second or had a keener appreciation of the first. Her first question, on hearing of Beale's arrival, was whether he had brought her a letter from the Queen. Finding that he had only a message, she at first stood upon her dignity and refused to hear him. Her own letter of November, she said, should remain as a testimony between the Queen of England and herself, and she would never trouble her further. This, however, was only acting; she produced the tears which were always at her command, she called God and her conscience to record, that she had never meant harm to her Majesty's person or estate, and then allowed him to proceed.

When she learnt the quality of his communication, she was instantly attentive, and heard it patiently to the end. It was clearly a prelude to something which he had yet to say to her, and of which she was anxious to be put in possession. When he had finished, she said

---

[1] Commission to Mr. Beale, April 4, 1583. Abridged.—*MSS. Mary Queen of Scots.*

that if she was charged in writing with the murder, she would put in a reply. The Queen it was true had at first kept back her letters, 'but the worst had been done 'that could be done, in the printing Buchanan's book,' and for her complicity, she appealed to Lady Lennox, whom she had convinced of her innocence. Towards Elizabeth herself, too, she insisted that she stood perfectly clear; she had never plotted against her, never corresponded with Jesuits, or any other of her enemies, never placed on paper a single word of which Elizabeth could justly complain.

The secretary, not perhaps without a smile, produced a bundle of her intercepted letters which had fallen into Walsingham's hands; letters to Father Allen, letters to the Bishop of Ross, to the Archbishop of Glasgow, to others of her secret agents in Paris and elsewhere. He began to read, and 'she changed countenance,' saw that denial was useless, and allowed that part of them might be her own. Beale completed her confession, intimating that they knew all to be her own. She affected to throw the fault upon her secretary, but said at last frankly, that she had been hardly treated, and under severe provocation impatient words might have escaped her.

It was not Beale's object to press her further. It was enough that he had shewn that Elizabeth possessed dangerous matter against her, and was aware, at least in some degree, of the present conspiracy. Then passing to herself, he asked her what she desired. She said at once, that she desired liberty, an end of her imprisonment, and permission to go where she would. To obtain this, she was ready still to accept all the conditions which had been before submitted to her. She would ratify the treaty of Edinburgh for herself and her son, her son possessing no rights save those which he derived from herself. She would bind herself never in any way to molest her Majesty, never to deal with Pope, Jesuits, or seminary priests, or attempt to change the established religion; and she would give any other assurance which her Majesty desired. She was ready to engage also, that if the Queen died leaving the succession undetermined, she would not seek her right by force, but would leave it to be orderly settled by Parliament.[1]

Her manner was so warm that Beale was really satisfied of her sincerity. In a letter to Walsingham, he intimated his conviction that she had ceased to be ambitious, that she wished only to live in quiet for the rest of her life, and that he thought her offers were not to be neglected.[2]

Beale's insight was not so acute as he imagined. She had grown restless at the inexplicable delay of the long talked of invasion. M. Fontenay, her secretary's brother, had hinted that the Duke of Guise was less earnest than he pretended.[3] A fear was beginning to rise, that the French Government might be gaining too much influence in Scotland, and that a French expedition, however Guise might endeavour to direct its action, might lead to France obtaining a stronger hold there than Spain could allow.[4] Mary Stuart

---

[1] Beale to the Queen, April 16, 1583.—*MSS. Mary Queen of Scots.*

[2] Beale to Walsingham.—*Ibid.*

[3] 'Par les lettres de Fontenay il me mecte en toute bonne esperance de la part du Roy Catholique mon dict Sieur et frère pour l'execution de l'entreprise, et me mande tout plainement que l'on n'attend que apres la resolution de mondict cousin de Guise, la quelle je trouve merveilleusement estrange,' &c. — *Mary Stuart to Mendoza,* May 15, 1583.

MSS. Simancas.

[4] This was Mendoza's fear. 'No es cosa ninguna mas prejudicial segun lo que yo puedo entender asi para la reduction desta Isla como para el servicio de V. Mag.⁴ que dan lugar á que Franceses por el medio de Escocia metan las manos en ella, teniendola totalmente á su devocion.' —*Mendoza al Rey,* 6 Mayo.

Philip, who had been taught that Guise might be trusted though France could not, writes on the

felt uncertain whether the present overtures to her were not merely blinds to lead her off from present designs.[1] But liberty was precious, and conditions after all were but words. She wrote to consult Mendoza. She would conclude nothing, she said, without his consent; but wishing probably to force Philip to a more rapid decision, she described the terms on which she now believed that she could be released, and enquired if he would advise her to close with them.

Mendoza's answer was long and elaborate. Many questions were raised by her letter, he said. The first was the place to which she was to go, if she could recover her liberty. Neither France nor Spain could offer her an asylum, for reasons which could easily be understood.[2] Their mutual jealousies forbade it. If she went elsewhere, it must be to some place at a distance, where her friends would soon forget her, and the great purpose of the recovery of England to the faith by her means would be utterly defeated. There remained, therefore, Scotland and England itself. Could the association be passed Scotland would be an excellent position for her. She would of course have the exercise of her religion, and her personal influence, her example, and the changes which she could introduce into the Government, would soon make an end of heresy there. If, however, either the Queen of England would not countenance the association, or her son accept it, she must in

---

margin, 'No sé si es esto por lo de Hercules que seria de consideracion.' Hercules was Philip's name for the Duke of Guise.

[1] 'Je crains beaucoup que tout ce remuement ne soit seulement une artifice pour me entretenir á faire laisser et interrompre mes aultres disseyns.' — *Mary Stuart to Mendoza*, May 15. MSS. Simancas.

[2] 'El tener V. M^d libertad fuera de la Isla puede ser en España ó Francia, partes donde hay los inconvenientes que se dexan entender.' — *Carta de Mendoza á la Reyna de Escocia*, Maio, 1583. MSS. Simancas.

some shape or other, make up her mind to remain in
England. Under what conditions, depended on circumstances with which he was imperfectly acquainted, the
number of her friends, their resources and their general
resolution. All the Catholic nobles, all the schismatics,
and some of the Protestants were known to be well disposed towards her, but so far as he could see himself,
they were diffident, distrustful of one another, and disinclined to move, unless supported by a force strong
enough to conquer the country single-handed. Supposing this to be a true account of them, her best plan
would then be to accept any terms on which the Queen
would release her. Liberty and health were, next to
the welfare of the soul, the most precious of human possessions. If she could keep those, time would cure all
else. She could remain in the realm in a position
like that of the Princess Mary during the life of her
brother. She would be free to receive her friends, to
correspond with whom she would, to enjoy whatever
pleasure an English country life would offer, and a tacit
understanding would gradually establish itself that she
was to succeed on the Queen's death. It was true that
the Queen had a deeply rooted fear of the probable
effects of her liberty; she believed that when Mary
Stuart was at large, her own reign would be at an end.
It was therefore likely, that the present overtures were
merely artifices to gain time for the settlement of Scotland. In that case, the Queen of Scots had merely to
wait on Providence, and to hold herself ready for the
deliverance, which in all human and divine reason could
not be distant; his Holiness and the King of Spain
being determined not to neglect her, and God, as the
cause was his own, being likely to provide opportunities.[1]

[1] Mendoza to the Queen of Scots, May, 1583.—*MSS. Simancas.*

Mendoza took credit to himself for the cleverness of his answer. His object was to prevent her from leaving England for fear lest she should fall back upon France; and he had argued on the grounds of her own interest instead of betraying his anxiety for Spain.[1] She, perhaps, saw that he was not entirely frank with her; she could hardly have failed to observe that he said nothing about the Duke of Guise. She thanked him for his advice, and agreed that England was the best place for her; but she wished evidently to make him feel that she had resources besides Spain, and that if Spain wished for her friendship, it must exert itself. Elizabeth, she told him, so far as she could herself see, was dealing honestly and kindly with her.[2] Her cousin of Guise, she added (careless of the reflection which she was passing on her own good faith in the matter), had written to her to say that he was as determined as ever on the invasion of England, and as soon as ever his arrangements were completed, was coming over in person.[3]

By this time, Col. Stewart and Sir John Colville

---

[1] 'He usado del mayor artificio que he podido en el significalle no estar la cosa mejor por todo buen respecto que el no aumentar su persona de la Isla, desamparando esta causa, y esto proponiendole todas las partes donde puede tener libertad y inconvenientes que hay en ellas, para que vistos, juzgue ser mi parecer mas conforme á razon que dirigido solo á la mira del servicio de V. Mag⁴, no necesitandola á vivir perpetualmente á prision ni tampoco aqui por salir della arriesgo lo que tan de veras ha de procurar conseguir, teniendo tan ciertas esperanzas en él.'—*Mendoza al Rey*, 6 Mayo, 1583. *MSS. Simancas.*

[2] 'La Reyne m'a escripte une fort honneste et gracieuse lettre, et jusques ici los dicts commissionaires ne m'ont demonstré que toute apparence de bien. Dieu veuille tout conduire à son honneur et gloire plus que à mon estat et contentment.'—*Mary Stuart to Don Bernardino*, June 5. Cifer. *MSS. Simancas.*

[3] 'Par les derniers paquets que j'ay reçue de France, mon cousin M. de Guise m'a escript qu'il persistoit en sa premiere determination de descendre luimesmes en Angleterre, et que si tôt que les choses y seroient disposées il ne faudroict de marcher en personne.'—*Ibid.*

had arrived in London. Sir Robert Bowes had made known to the King the offers which had been made by Lennox, and the King, startled at his friend's real or apparent treachery, had consented to proposals which, if honest, were as simple as they were moderate, and if accepted would have closed Scotland to Jesuit intrigues. Colville was a tried Protestant; Stewart was selected as having long lived in England with Lady Lennox, and having been personally acquainted with Elizabeth. Both had been chosen as professedly favourable to the English alliance, and of the party of Angus and Gowrie. Mary Stuart flattered herself that her son was on his guard against Elizabeth, and knowing her to be treacherous, was repaying her in her own coin. Stewart, she said, had been an old instrument of communication between Lady Lennox and herself, and had been bribed to conduct his negotiation in Mary Stuart's interest.[1] She was deceived in both of them. If they could have obtained what they wanted, the confederate lords, and the King also, intended to adhere to their own part of the bargain.

The commissioners were directed to lay before Elizabeth the condition of the Scotch finances. The King asked for his grandmother's estate, or an equivalent of 5,000l. a year. If she would give him either the one or the other he promised to be guided by her advice in his marriage and in the administration of the kingdom. He would abandon France and rely only on England. As 'a testification of his amity,' and 'a terror to disloyal

---

[1] 'Mon fils est suffisamment averti de la dissimulation et artifices de la Royne avec luy. Quant au Capitan Stuart, il asseure mon fils de sa fidelité et a reçeu un presente qui luy a este presenté pour le ramener du tout à ma devotion, comme aultrefois il y estoit beaucoup, ayant traicté fort avant entre la Comtesse de Lennox ma belle mère et moy.'— Mary Stuart to Mendoza, May 15. MSS. Simancas.

'subjects,' he declared himself willing to ratify the treaty of Leith, and to make a further defensive league for mutual protection, should religion in either realm be made a plea for invasion or rebellion.[1] Nothing was said about his mother. Her name was not so much as mentioned. It was, however, intimated that if the request for so small a sum of money was refused, the King would be compelled by poverty to seek help elsewhere. Shortened down to the mere rents of the Lennox lands, his demands, if nothing lay behind, were singularly modest. Rumours of course were flying that the commissioners were confederate with the Queen of Scots—that the King would take the English money and go over to the other side.[2] La Mothe Fénelon had been heard to say that the English politicians were looking for 'a white crow;'[3] 'that their doings in Scotland were but as if they were thrashing the water.' 'We do what we can,' wrote Walsingham to Sir Robert Bowes, 'to remove these unprofitable jealousies, that 'Colonel Stewart may receive such answers at her 'Majesty's hands as may be to the King's liking and 'satisfaction, and the common benefit of the realm.'[4]

Mendoza was of opinion that the Scots were essentially honest; they were really ready, that is to say, to run Elizabeth's fortune if she would make it worth their while. The 5,000*l.*, however, would not be all which she would be required to pay. An additional sum was asked for a guard about the King's person. In this demand, too, Walsingham desired the Queen to

---

[1] Instructions to Col. Stewart going to England, April 24, 1583.—*MSS. Scotland.*

[2] Secret information given to Walsingham, May 1583.—*MSS.*
Scotland.

[3] 'Ung corbeau blanc.'

[4] Walsingham to Bowes, April 25.—*MSS. Scotland.*

acquiesce, but she persisted against his advice on mixing the treaties with the mother with the treaty with the son. She had feared nothing so much as the association between them in the crown of Scotland; but having ascertained that the Scots were disinclined to consent, she made it a condition of Mary Stuart's release.[1] Before she would receive the commissioners she sent a copy of Mary Stuart's offers to James, and she asked if he would agree to the association provided it was managed by England. James, acute as he already considered himself, fell into the snare which she had laid for him. He told Bowes 'that his mother being 'defeated, and desperate in her intended plots and purposes, and seeing how matters were likely to proceed 'between her Majesty and him,' was now affecting to desire an amicable arrangement; but in reality she desired nothing less. She was only 'casting a bone to stick 'between their teeth.' 'He wished,' he said, 'that his 'mother would give over her plots, and would turn 'truly to the religion received in the two realms;' in a draft of the association which she had sent him to look at she had claimed precedence; 'she was a determined 'Papist,' and French to the heart; he must look to his future as well as his present interests; and the English, he said significantly, 'justly dreaded another Queen Mary;' 'when his mother first proposed the association to 'him, she spoke of it only as a means to recover her 'liberty;' and she promised, as soon as she was released,

---

Esta Reyna ha dicho sobre la instancia que la de Escocia hace en su libertad, que aunque sea negocio tan peligroso y mal seguro por ella, cuando esta concluyda de todo punto la asociacion del Rey de Escocia y su madre por los nobles de aquel Reyno, holgara tratar de su libertad —cosa que la Reyna impidiera cuando los de Escocia lo deseáren, siendo solo el decirlo cumplimiento y palabras.' &c.—*Don Bernardino al Rey*, 20 Maio, 1583. *MSS. Simancas.*

to repeat her abdication; she had afterwards altered her note; she had shown that she intended to reclaim the whole or a part of the government, and to this he was determined never to consent: he declined to be a party to any agreement in which he was himself to be compromised till he saw deeper 'into his mother's 'meaning.'

James had thus revealed his own inward disposition. Lennox had failed to make a Catholic of him, and by his real or seeming treachery had for a time frightened him out of conspiracies. He had made up his mind to stick to Elizabeth if Elizabeth would allow him, to leave his mother in an enforced retirement which removed her from the political stage, and to look forward, with Elizabeth's consent and in the Protestant interest, to succeeding eventually to her throne.

'The King,' wrote Bowes, 'attends how her Majesty 'will deal. The French and Papists look that he shall 'receive a dilatory answer, persuading him to provide 'otherwise for his standing and welfare. The well 'affected must be comforted and sustained by her 'Majesty's kind dealing with the King, otherwise they 'shall be utterly cast down. The King and the realm 'can now be won or lost. I need not persuade the 'necessity of her Majesty's timely resolution, for the 'King's own necessity and the conditions of the time 'and personal causes will constrain the King and the 'realm to resolve speedily to provide for themselves 'without further trust to us.'

But Elizabeth had now, as she supposed, the control of the situation. Mary Stuart and James were separated, and as long as they could be kept at issue, she conceived

---

[1] Bowes to Walsingham, May 3, 1583.—*MSS. Scotland.* [2] Bowes to Walsingham, May 8. —*MSS. Scotland.*

that she had them both in her power—that she could hold James in check by threatening to release his mother, force Mary Stuart into submission by proving to her that she was neglected by her son, and remain supreme arbiter of both their fortunes without risk, and still better without cost.

She was the less disposed to favour James, as he had just given her special cause of offence. The Jesuit, Gaspar Holt, after lying concealed for some weeks at Seton, had been surprised and taken. On his first examination he had confessed that 'there was a purpose in 'hand between the Pope and the Princes Catholic, for a 'war against England; that the pretext was to be re-'ligion and the liberty of the Queen of Scots, and that 'they held the enterprise easy, considering their own 'preparation and the factions at home.' This was not enough. Elizabeth required further particulars as to these factions, and desired that either ' Holt should be ' substantially examined and forced by torture to deliver what he knew,'[2] or else be handed over to herself as an English subject. The second alternative meant Little Ease, the Tower rack, and the Tyburn quartering knife; and Mendoza, in some alarm, could but pray ' that ' God would give Holt constancy that he might earn his 'martyr's crown, and confess nothing that would do ' harm.'[3] But the poor wretch was spared the trial. James, with some pity for him, ordered his prison door to be left unlocked. He escaped and went again into a safe hiding place. Elizabeth had been very angry, and her resentment had not passed off when the commissioners arrived in London.

[1] Davison to Walsingham, March 4, 1583.—*MSS. Scotland.*
[2] Walsingham to Bowes, April
[3] Don Bernardino to Philip, April 4.—*MSS. Simancas.*

The first difficulty, as Mendoza anticipated, was about the King's guard. The King would have been seized and carried off had he been left unprotected. It had been necessary—and the necessity continued—to keep 300 men-at-arms at the Court. 'The life of the cause 'depended on the guard,' yet the King had not a penny to pay their wages;[1] and unless something was done immediately, they would disband in mutiny. Present temporary assistance was all that had been so far hinted at. The Queen stopped them at once with an absolute refusal. Declining to give a sixpence, she consented, only with extreme difficulty, that Sir Robert Bowes might, if he liked, lend the King 300*l*.

'I pray you,' said Walsingham, in informing him of her liberality, 'stretch what you may for the perfor- 'mance hereof, weighing the necessity of the cause, and 'how much it concerns her Majesty's service, that the 'guard should not as yet be discharged. If her 'Majesty should happen to leave the burden upon you, 'I will not fail to see you myself discharged of the 'same.'[2]

A fortnight then passed while the Queen was considering the reply which she should make to their main demands. The answer, when it came, would have been unfavourable without fresh provocation; but some one had whispered to her that Leicester, who had been planning a marriage for his son with Lady Arabella, had been feeling his way also towards finding a wife for James in one of his step-daughters. If there was a person in the world whom Elizabeth loathed it was the woman who had dared to become the wife of the only man that she had thought of seriously for herself. She

---

[1] Colville to Walsingham, May 7.—*MSS. Scotland.*

[2] Walsingham to Bowes, May 9.—*MSS. Scotland.*

was in such a fury when she heard of it that she said
she would rather see James stripped of his crown than
wedded to that she-wolf's cub. If there was no other way
to check the pride of her and her traitor Leicester, she
threatened to publish her wickednesses and her husband's horns to all the world.[1] Her exasperation
vented itself on the Scots. She told them at first she
could make no treaty unless their Queen was a party to
it, and that as for money she would give them none.
She had supposed, she said, that the gratitude for past
kindness and conformity of creed would of itself have
secured the King's good will towards her. She was
sorry to see that sordid considerations had such weight
with him. If he was in absolute want she would lend
him a small sum, if the large towns and 'chosen per-
' sons of the nobility of both factions would be sureties
' for the repayment.' The Lennox succession was
under examination by lawyers, and the rents must
remain sequestered till the right of aliens to inherit
was decided. To the lords who had risked life and
fortune in the raid of Ruthven she refused to give
anything at all.

Col. Stewart reminded her, with some resentment,
' of the promises of help in men and money, which
' were made at the beginning of that action.' The
guard, he said, had been maintained at Court by the
confederate lords solely to keep the English party in
power. At least, he expected that she would allow
them two months' wages.[2]

[1] 'La Reyna se encendió en la materia, de suerte que dixó que antes consentiria que el Rey le quitase su corona que verlo casado con hija de una loba, y cuando se hallase otro medio para reprimir su ambicion y del traydor Leicester, ella la publicaria por tal mala muger por toda la X^{ad} y los cuernos de su marido.'— *Don Bernardino al Rey*, 11 de Junio, 1583. *MSS. Simancas*.

[2] Stewart and Colville to Walsingham, May 18.—*MSS. Scotland*.

Then was then, and now was now. She complained to Burghley of the Scotch beggars, who were using religion as a pretext to rob her treasury.

Walsingham, with some warmth, tried to bring her to be more reasonable; but at times she had the very insanity of avarice. 'Her servants and favourites,' she said, 'professed to love her for her high qualities, 'Alençon for her beauty, and the Scots for her crown; 'but they all meant the same in the end. They wanted 'nothing but her money, and they should not have it.'[1]

Walsingham carried her refusal to Stewart. He said she would live to repent it, at a time, perhaps, when there would be no remedy.

Again and most solemnly he remonstrated. At last he brought the Queen to say that she would allow James half the pension which he had asked for—two thousand five hundred pounds—but not a farthing more could be extorted from her; and even this Walsingham doubted if she would really pay.[2]

The commissioners did not waste time in endeavouring to move her further, and in fierce resentment returned to Scotland. James, accepting this second refusal either of the lands or their equivalent as a declaration against his succession, turned once more to the party from whom he had been for a time divided; and besides other tragical consequences soon to be related, Elizabeth had

---

[1] 'Le respondió que sus criados domesticos y favoridos profesaban amalla por sus buenas partes, Alençon por su porsona, y los Escoceses por su corona, y si bien eran estas tres causas diferentes, venian todas á parar á un fin, que era pedille dinero, que ella defenderia.'—*Don Bernardino al Rey,* 4 Junio. *MSS.*

Simancas.

[2] 'Thus you see, notwithstanding it importeth us greatly to yield all contentment to that nation, how we stick at trifles. I pray God we perform the rest of things promised.—*Walsingham to Bowes,* May 29. *MSS. Scotland.*

to spend thousands of pounds for every hundred which she had saved by her thrift.

She on her part, having shaken off her troublesome petitioners, turned to her treaty with the Queen of Scots, which was to save her from the effects of their displeasure. On the departure of Stewart and Colville, Secretary Beale, accompanied by Sir Walter Mildmay, went again to Sheffield to tell the Queen of Scots that the offers which she had made deserved consideration. They were directed to read them over to her that she might not afterwards pretend her meaning to have been mistaken. If she made no exception, they were to turn particularly to the treaty of Edinburgh, and to ask by what authority she now undertook to ratify it for her son as well as for herself. Had she obtained her son's consent, or had the act of association gone secretly further than either she or he had as yet acknowledged?

The Queen of Scots, made acquainted perhaps with James's words to Sir Robert Bowes—at any rate, weary to death of her long captivity, and eager at any cost to be free, answered with extreme submissiveness. She acknowledged and expressed regret for her early faults, but she said she had been young and ill-advised. To the ratification of the treaty, she thought that her son had consented. She had imagined that she might safely undertake for him; but if the Queen wished, she would send to Scotland for the necessary powers. She accepted Beale's version of her promises as accurate, and repeated them as exactly and concisely as language would allow. She bound herself never to trouble Elizabeth more with pretensions to the crown; never to communicate with Jesuits or conspirators, and to leave the succession after the Queen's death to be decided by the

English Parliament. She undertook never to meddle with the established religion. She declared herself willing to remain in England as an evidence of her good faith, and to take an oath in the House of Lords, if the Queen wished it, to observe the treaty. The Kings of France and Spain, the Duke of Lorraine, the Duke of Guise, would together be securities for her good behaviour. She would live in any castle or park which Elizabeth might be pleased to assign to her, and some nobleman or gentleman in the neighbourhood might be appointed to keep an eye over her actions; while for herself she would promise never to go more than ten miles from the place of her abode.[1]

These conditions were very much what Mendoza had sketched out for her. She was not to be credited with having abandoned any one of her purposes; but liberty was sweet, and relief by revolution was long in coming. The Catholic powers would gladly welcome a release from their responsibilities in an arrangement with which she could profess herself satisfied, and if they became securities for her at her own instance, they would be unlikely to move actively again in her favour; but she and they would exchange a precarious hope for a moderate certainty, and the treaty would amount to an acquiescence in her future claim on the succession.

Elizabeth admitted that these proposals were now all that she could wish. She suggested some additions, as, for instance, that the Queen of Scots should pay her own expenses out of her French dowry; but she did not insist on it, and she held out hopes that something now would be really done. But it seemed as if her main object was satisfied, when she had induced both

[1] Proceedings with the Queen of Scots, May 24 and June 2, 1583.—*MSS. Mary Queen of Scots.*

James and Mary Stuart to shew their hands. When a decision became necessary, as usual, she was incapable of the act of will which would incline the wavering balance. She found that in a treaty she must recognise Mary Stuart as a Queen—a Queen in some sense or other—and to recognise her in any sense would threaten the internal peace of Scotland. The very intimation that she was likely to be set at liberty set every Scottish household in vibration. Walsingham bade Bowes feel the tempers of the leading politicians. 'If,' he said, 'the Queen of Scots' offers were accompanied with 'good meaning, with the cautions and restrictions pro-'posed, he saw no inconvenience, but rather profit, 'likely to ensue from her liberty.' The doubt was of her sincerity. It was hard to obtain 'an impartial 'opinion' about her, 'the love and hatred that was 'borne her being either in the extremest degree.' 'It 'had been debated,' Walsingham said, 'whether she 'was to be sent to Scotland, or kept in England. The 'conclusion for the present had been to keep her; 'but if she could be placed in Scotland without any 'dangerous alteration, England would gladly be rid of 'her.'[1]

The longer Elizabeth considered, the more excuses she found for refusing to proceed. The King of Scots must be a party to any treaty which would hold, as well as the other princes, and James, and the leading nobles, whatever their political sympathies, refused to allow Mary Stuart, in any shape or form, the title of Sovereign.[2] The difficulty might of course have been overcome, had Elizabeth seriously wished it; but the

---

[1] Walsingham to Bowes, June 12.—*MSS. Scotland.*   [2] Bowes to Walsingham, June 29.—*MSS. Scotland.*

negotiation from her point of view had already answered its purpose. She had balanced one party against the other, and she meant to keep them there without gratifying either. 'I marvel,' said Sir Walter Mildmay, 'that finding the manners in Scotland so 'tickle, and this woman offering so much, there is no 'more regard of it. I doubt the death of Lennox has 'brought too great a security.'[1] But Elizabeth would not part with her money, and the release of the Queen of Scots was a measure which she preferred to hold in terror over James. When the lady at Sheffield was expecting to be established as a princess in England, free to correspond where she pleased, and to hold a second court of her Catholic admirers, she found after all that she had gained nothing, and was to remain where she was. She was informed that her offers were satisfactory, but that her son raised difficulties, which made her liberation for the present impossible, and that all her concessions had been in vain. After a few months' pause, the question was again brought up for consideration, but only again to be dismissed, and dismissed on grounds which, if valid at all, would be fatal against any treaty whatever. It was remembered that the Queen of Scots might disclaim the engagements into which she might enter, as she had disclaimed her abdication at Lochleven, on the plea that they had been forced from her in prison. She could escape with greater ease out of England, and her greater freedom if she was to continue there, would give life and hope to the disloyal Catholics. It would be an admission, moreover, that she had been detained hitherto unjustly. It would seem like an acquittal of the charge which had so

---

[1] Mildmay to Walsingham, June 17.—*MSS. Mary Queen of Scots.*

far clouded her fame, and would otherwise be a confession of weakness. 'Her Majesty,' by releasing her, 'would give the world to understand that the Queen of 'Scots was not in her opinion culpable of the murder of 'her husband—otherwise she would not shew her that 'favour.'

To require a ratification of the treaty of Leith was a quasi acknowledgment that the Queen doubted her own title. If the treaty proceeded a clause would have to be inserted 'that her Majesty did not clear her of the 'murder, but left her to God and her conscience, and 'the trial of Scotland, being a matter committed where 'her Majesty had no jurisdiction;' and with this qualification the Queen of Scots would refuse her signature, and her friends abroad their sanction.[1] The Council repeated their old opinion that 'the best and most sure 'way was for her Majesty to conclude with the young 'King;' 'so the treaty with the Queen would not be 'necessary, and she might remain as she was.'[2]

Elizabeth preferred to conclude with neither. She had money in abundance. She had half a million in bullion locked away as a reserve. But it was to be touched only in an extremity she could never believe to have arrived.[3] She had to choose, as Walsingham said, between her treasure and her safety, and she deliberately preferred the first.

The Reformed Calendar of Pope Gregory XIII. was published in the year 1582. Ten days were struck out of the computation, and the 5th of October was decreed to be the 15th. The Gregorian, or New Style, which was not accepted in England till 1752, was adopted at short in-

---

[1] Whether it be fit to treat and conclude with the Queen of Scots, Oct. 2.—*MSS. MARY QUEEN OF SCOTS.*

[2] *Ibid.*

[3] Mendoza and Mauvissière both mention this.

tervals by countries in communion with the Holy See. In Spain the same 5th of October, 1582, became the 15th of October. In France, the 10th of December, 1582, became the 20th. In the Catholic States of Germany, and the Catholic Netherlands, the 22nd of December, 1582, became the 1st of January, 1583. The English and foreign dates therefore no longer corresponding, the English first of January being in France and Spain the eleventh, all important letters and documents hereafter quoted will carry a double date.

CHAPTER XXXI.

THE visit of the Duke of Alençon to England proved an expensive one. The Queen had hoped to escape her suitor and to save her money. She had flung him off to croak as she said in the Dutch canals, but she had been compelled to gild his departure. She had prevented his return upon her hands by subsidies, which were almost as much wasted as if they had been buried in the sand-banks of the Scheldt; and those subsidies were so large that if expended on the objects which the most eminent of her Council had so often pressed upon her, they would have given order and good government to Ireland, and secured Scotland ten times over to the friends of England and the Reformation. The kiss bestowed at Greenwich with so much precipitancy cost at once sixty thousand pounds. Before six months was over the sixty thousand had grown into three hundred thousand, and in the year 1582–3 three hundred and fifty thousand in addition were wrenched out of her unwilling hands.[1] At no less price was she allowed to redeem the slight which she had passed upon the brother of the King of France. The war which she so much dreaded would not have been a heavier burden, and she

---

[1] A brief of the Duke of Anjou's receipts from May 1, 1581, to Oct. 31, 1583. — *MSS. France. Rolls House.*

failed after all in the object at which her manœuvres had been aimed, of embroiling France and Spain in an open conflict.

It was impossible indeed for the Duke of Alençon to undertake the protectorate of the King of Spain's insurgent subjects without in some degree compromising his brother. Philip was patient of affronts, and preferred to punish the house of Valois rather by intrigues than arms; but the Catholic powers remained divided, and Elizabeth bought off her lover's indignation and kept her alliance with France unbroken. So far her artifices had not been ineffective, nor her treasure wholly thrown away. Had she taken her place as the leader of Protestant Europe, had she held out her hand and her purse to the struggling defenders of the Reformation in France, and Scotland and the Netherlands, the result might have been as much grander as her course in itself would have been more honourable and straightforward. In the opinion of Burghley the path which she preferred was at once the most dangerous and the least effective, and those among her Council who most encouraged her were those who secretly desired her ruin.

Yet on the other side it is to be remembered that both Burghley and Walsingham held their places only through their mistress's pleasure. It was Elizabeth alone who enabled them to accomplish any fraction of their policy; and a government by majorities, an omnipotent House of Commons, elected by household suffrage, would at any moment have condemned them to obscurity or the scaffold. That she might have done more is not absolutely certain, and were it certain, does not deprive her of credit for the much which she did. The right cause is not always the strongest, and had France and Spain once combined, the Reformation, which had been made possible by their quarrel, might have been ended by their premature reconciliation.

So at least it seemed to Elizabeth. She saw no reason to risk her throne for a cause for which at best she had but a cold concern. She preferred to lie and twist, and perjure herself and betray her friends, with a purpose at the bottom moderately upright; and nature in fitting her for her work had left her without that nice sense of honour which would have made her part too difficult.

Alençon was thus installed in the Netherlands with a French army, paid jointly by Elizabeth and France. The States accepted him for the advantages which his presence promised. He was an unprincipled fool, but he was placed under the guidance of the Prince of Orange; and the Prince, who understood that he was saddled upon them to save the Queen from a husband, prepared to please her by making the best of him.

Orange was well understood to be the soul of the revolt. Could Orange be removed, Philip feared little either Alençon or any other person, and as all efforts to gain him over had been tried in vain, his life had been sought for some years past by the indirect means which are either murder or legitimate execution according to the character of the victim.[1] Bothwellhaugh, who killed Murray, had been employed to assassinate him in 1573, and party after party of English Catholic officers had tried it afterwards. In 1579 a youth introduced himself to Don Bernardino, in London, with a letter of credit from a merchant of Bruges. He said that he was in possession of a poison which if rubbed on the lining of a man's hat would dry up his brain and would kill him in ten days, and if the ambassador approved, he was ready

---

[1] The English Government had bought the head of Desmond. In our own time a reward has been offered for Nana Sahib, dead or alive.

to try its effects upon the Prince of Orange. Don Bernardino, not expecting much result, yet gave him his blessing, and bade him do his best.[1] Other experiments more promising were tried afterwards, but none had hitherto succeeded. Finally Philip declared the Prince outlawed, and promised a public reward to any one who would put him out of the way in the service of God and his country. The King's pleasure being made known, Don Pedro Arroyo, father of one of the royal secretaries, announced that he knew a man who would make the venture. Philip offered eighty thousand dollars, with the Order of St. Iago; and the reward being held sufficient, Don Pedro gave in the name of Gaspar de Anastro, a Spanish merchant at Antwerp. A formal contract was drawn out and signed,[2] and Anastro watched an opportunity to strike the blow.

Finding, however, that he could get the job done cheaper, and clear a sum of money without peril to himself, the merchant pretended that 'his courage was weak,' and asked if he might employ a substitute. Philip had no objection; provided the Prince was killed the means were of no consequence, and he left Anastro to manage as he pleased. In his house was a lad eighteen years old, the son of a sword cutler at Bilbao, named Juan Jaureguy. Ignorant, superstitious, undersized and paltry-looking, he was known to the cashier, Don Antonio Venero, to be a boy of singular audacity; and a present of three thousand dollars, and the persuasion of the chaplain, a Dominican priest, worked him into a proper state of mind. An Agnus Dei was hung about his neck; a

---

[1] Don Bernardino de Mendoza to Philip, Feb. 16–March 8, 1579.—*MSS. Simancas.*

[2] Confession of Don Antonio, a Spaniard, cashier to Don Anastro, March 21–31, 1582.—*MSS. Holland Rolls House.* Cf. Motley's *History of the Dutch Republic,* vol. iii.

wax taper and a dried toad were stuffed in his pocket, and he was told that they would render him invisible. A Jesuit catechism was given him for his spiritual comfort, and Parma promised that if the charms failed, and he was taken, he would compel his release by the threat of hanging every prisoner in his hands. Thus equipped and encouraged, and commending himself and his enterprise to the Virgin and the angel Gabriel, he prepared for the deed. The qualifications for successful political assassins are singularly rare. Jaureguy, however, possessed them all. Sunday the 18th-28th of March, was Alençon's birthday. Antwerp was to be illuminated in the evening, and the streets and squares were expected to be crowded. Some little jars had been felt already between the States and the French. Alençon was known to be impatient of the Prince's control, and the Spaniards calculated that if the murder could be accomplished when the people were collected and excited there would be an instant suspicion of treachery, and that an attack upon the French and a universal massacre of the citizens in retaliation by their allies would be a not improbable consequence.

The plot was ingeniously laid, and had all but succeeded. The Prince had dined in his own house. He had risen from the table, and had passed with his son, Count Maurice, and a few friends into another room, where he was seated on a low chair. Jaureguy had introduced himself among the servants, pretending that he wanted to present a petition. He approached Orange so close as to be able to touch him, and then snatching a pistol from under his cloak fired it full in the Prince's face. At the moment of the shot the Prince was rising from his seat, and happened to be turning his head. The ball entered under the right ear, passed through the

roof of his mouth, and went out below the left eye. He
staggered and fell. The assassin tried to draw a dagger,
and finish his work, but he had overloaded his pistol,
which had broken his thumb in the recoil. An instant
later, and before he could speak, half a dozen swords were
through his body. All was immediately confusion. A
cry of horror rung through the city. Suspicion fell, but
too naturally, where the Spaniards expected. Shouts
were heard of ' Kill the French, kill the French,' and had
Jaureguy waited till night when the fête had commenced,
Alençon and his suit would have probably been slaughtered on the spot.[1] Orange himself had swooned, and
was at first supposed to be dead. He recovered consciousness, however, in time to allay the worst alarm.
Believing that he had but a few minutes to live, and anticipating the direction which popular fury might assume,
he sent for the burgomaster, and assured him that to his
certain knowledge it was the work not of France but of
Spain. The assassin was identified by papers found
about his person. Anastro, when the police went for
him, had fled, but Antonio Venero was taken, and at
once confessed, and before darkness fell the truth was
known throughout the city.

The Prince lay in extreme danger, and but for his
extraordinary calmness, the wound would have been
certainly mortal. One of the large arteries of the
throat had been divided, which the surgeons were
unable to tie. Again and again the bleeding burst out,
and his death was every moment expected. Daily
bulletins were sent to England, and the delighted

---

[1] ' Si bien afirman todos que si el moço aguardaria dar el pistoletazo á la noche en un gran banquete que hacia al Alençon, le mataran á él y á cuantos Franceses habia.'—*Don Bernardino al Rey*, 1-11 Avril, 1581. *MSS. Simancas.*

Catholics watched eagerly for the news which was to make their satisfaction complete.

'The Prince was gasping when the post left,' wrote Mendoza on the 4th–14th of April. 'The physicians gave 'no hope, and the Queen hears that all is over. We may 'assume his death as certain, and we can but give 'infinite thanks to God that he has thus chastised so 'abominable a heretic and rebel.'[1] 'We have news 'from Antwerp of the 9th–19th,' he wrote a week after. 'The Prince was still alive, two surgeons holding 'the wound closed with their fingers, and relieving one 'another every hour. On the 7th–17th, conceiving 'that in human reason it was not possible for him to live, 'they laid open his right cheek in the hope of reaching 'the injured vein. We may suppose it to be the good 'providence of God to increase his agonies by prolong-'ing his life. The pain which he suffered, they say, is 'terrible. In the opinion of those here, a few hours 'must now bring an end.'[2]

Mary Stuart's gratification was no less than that of the Spanish Ambassador. 'I have heard,' she said, 'that an artery is cut, and that the Prince is in danger. 'I praise God for this his mercy to the Church, and to 'the King my brother, the Church's chief protector.'[3]

Equally great was the consternation in Protestant England, and beyond all in the Queen. Ill as it had pleased her to use him, none knew better than she the value of William of Nassau. Her own life had been

---

[1] Mendoza to Philip, April 4–14.—*MSS. Simancas.*

[2] Mendoza to Philip, April 11–21.—*MSS. Simancas.*

[3] 'J'ai eu advis du danger auquel estoit dernierement le Prince d'Orange par le grand flux de sang que luy estoit survenu d'un artere, dont je loue Dieu en consideration du bien qu'en reviendroit à son Eglise et au Roy mon bon frère, aujourd'huy principal protecteur d'elle.'—*Marie Stuart à Don Bernardino*, Avril 22–Mai 2. *MSS. Simancas.*

threatened as often as his, and his fate, when he was thought to be dying, appeared but a foretaste of her own. The first news entirely overwhelmed her.[1] The realm had its own fears. The very thought of a sudden vacancy of the throne was simply appalling; and in the midst of her terrors, Burghley had to remind her of the duty which she had so long refused to perform of naming a successor.[2] In her first excitement, her thoughts turned into the stereotyped track. She swore she would send for Alençon and marry him;' and Walsingham, who knew what would follow, and feared that a fresh affront to France might be fatal, prevented her with difficulty from sending a gentleman of her household to recall the Duke into the realm.[3]

Both hopes and fears were this time disappointed. The Prince's fine constitution and admirable courage gave him a chance of recovery when a weaker person must have died. Once more Philip had failed, but he nursed his purpose; and the Catholic faith, which has influenced human character in so many curious ways, was singularly productive of men who would risk their lives to deliver the Church from an enemy.

On the 2nd–12th of May, Orange returned thanks for his recovery in the Cathedral at Antwerp. The commonwealth, unfortunately, was sick of diseases which were less easy to cure. In all countries the noble part of the people is but a minority, and the trials of a protracted

---

[1] 'Se anichiló aquel dia tanto como le hubieran quitado la corona.' —*Mendoza al Rey*, 1-11 April. *MSS. Simancas.*

[2] 'Entiendo que el Thesorero le ha persuadido muy de veras estos dias hiciese cierta prevencion para declarar el successor deste Reyno, si las vidas, hijos y bienes de sus vasallos no queria que se perdieren.'— *Ibid.*

[3] 'El Walsingham, por estar cierto que no piensa casarse, teme que será parte semejante demostracion tras las pasadas para iritar al de Francia, perdiendole de todo punto.'—*Ibid.*

war bring the baser elements into prominence. The
Catholics of Brabant and Flanders, weary of a freedom which brought with it religious toleration, were
sighing for reabsorption into Spain. The presence of
Alençon and the French was an excuse to the States to
relax their own energies. They conceived that they
had fought long enough and spent money enough, and
that their allies might now relieve them of the burden.
Peculation and corruption, the besetting sins of commercial communities, were rife among them. Sixteen
thousand officials intercepted and consumed the revenues, while the English volunteer army, under John
Norris, was left unpaid. Elizabeth found money for
them, but with more right than usual resented the
States' neglect. Alone, Norris could do but little service, yet Alençon neither helped him nor appeared to
be conscious that he was in the country for any object
except to sit still. Everywhere and in everything
there was confusion of purpose, heartburning and
jealousy. Parma, meanwhile, was pushing forward
slowly but irresistibly. Town was falling after town;
and though his success was checked once in a brilliant
action before Ghent, in which, after the States troops
had fled, Norris and his English sustained and repulsed
an attack of the whole Spanish army, a single defeat did not affect the advance of the Spanish conquest,
and by the end of the summer the States frontier had
been pushed back, till all that they held of Flanders was
the coast from Dunkirk to Ostend, and the great towns
of Bruges, Ghent, Alost, and Brussels, which formed a
line covering Antwerp. Alençon laid the blame on the
States, and the States upon Alençon. The towns,
fearing that Alençon was betraying them, began privately to treat with Parma, while Alençon, suspect-

ing treachery on their side, was meditating a grand surprise as an employment for his hitherto idle army. He was plotting to seize simultaneously upon Ghent, Bruges, and Antwerp; and thus holding Flanders in his hand and master of the situation, either to hand it over to his brother to be incorporated with France, or to fall back upon his mother's second policy—buy Philip's pardon by the restoration of his Flemish provinces, and offer his precious hand to the Infanta.

Either he kept in his hands the money which he received from Elizabeth, or it was insufficient for the maintenance of his forces. At any rate, he exasperated them against the States by leaving them unpaid and pretending that they were robbed. He sent for reinforcements from France, and when Orange remonstrated with him for increasing his army when he could not maintain what he had already, he pretended that he was acting for the Queen of England; that he had her sanction as well as his brother's for what he was doing; that she was his wife in the sight of God, and could not abandon him. By representations of the same kind, he borrowed large sums of private persons,[1] and being thus supplied with men and finances, he came to a private understanding with the Catholic factions in the cities

---

[1] 'El de Orange tratando con Alençon la sospecha que tenian los Estados de que hiciese venir tanta gente tras no tener con que pagar la que se hallaba en ellas, le habia respondido que en tanto que él fuese ministro de la Reyna de Inglaterra su lugarteniente capⁿ general en aquella empresa, no le faltarian dineros, asistiendole juntamente el Rey de Francia su hermano para la paga de tantos soldados los quales no venian sin su licencia y particular consentimiento; asegurandole que esta reyna era delante de Dios y del mundo su muger, y que no podia abandonarle en aquella guerra sin mayor peligro de su persona y reyno. Que asimismo el duque de Alençon se habia servido del nombre de la Reyna para sacar dineros de algunas personas aficionadas á sus cosas.'—*Mendoza al Rey*, 16-26 de Enero, 1583. *MSS. Simancas.*

which he was preparing to surprise. The French garrisons were quietly increased: his principal camp was brought close to the walls of Antwerp, and the soldiers were told that as their wages were withheld they should have an opportunity of paying themselves. Their plan was to rise at nine or ten places on the same day, overpower the burgher guards, and make themselves masters of Flanders. Secrecy was admirably observed, and in the smaller towns they were completely successful. On the 5th–15th of January, they took possession of Dunkirk, Ostend, Dixmuyde, Dendermonde, Alost, and Vilvoorde, without striking a blow. At Ghent, Bruges, and Antwerp, fortune was less propitious. Ghent proved too Spanish to be attempted; at Bruges the citizens had received information, and were on their guard; at Antwerp, where the Duke commanded in person, his own imbecility made his defeat more absolutely fatal. He had waited to hear of his success elsewhere. The delay brought notice to the Prince from Bruges, and he had leisure to prepare. The French camp contained four thousand men, trained soldiers all of them. The Provost of Antwerp was in Alençon's confidence, and had promised, so far as lay in him, to betray his trust. The Prince, saying nothing, made an excuse for calling the city guard under arms, and bidding them hold themselves in readiness to form at a moment's notice, went frankly to the Duke for explanations. The Duke swore, with seemingly equal openness, that he was absolutely innocent of any bad intentions whatever. He disclaimed all knowledge of what had happened at Bruges, and professed himself a faithful and loyal servant of the States. The Prince was not satisfied. The city remained all night on the alert. In the morning he went again with a deputation of the magistrates to request that the camp should be withdrawn to a greater distance from the gates. The Duke agreed, still swearing that no harm was intended. He occupied a palace inside the walls, and the Prince asked him to prove his sincerity by remaining within the gates for a day. He gave his word only to break it: he remained quiet till the afternoon, that the French might do their work under cover of the early darkness, and then galloping out to them, where they were drawn up waiting for his coming, he pointed to the city and bade them go in and take it. The gate from which he had issued remained open. A party of horse plunged forward, killed the sentinels, and held the end of the street, while their comrades swarmed after them with shouts of 'Vive la messe! Vive le Duc d'Anjou! ' Vive la messe! tuez! tuez! tuez!' The affair did not last half-an-hour. As they dashed into the narrow streets, barricades rose as if by magic behind them. Maddened by the terrible recollections of the Spanish fury, and exasperated at the treachery, the citizens flew out on their false allies from alley and cross-way, while tiles, stones, and boiling water were rained upon their heads from the parapets. Before the night fell in which they had promised themselves a surfeit of lust and plunder, two hundred and fifty officers and fifteen hundred men lay dead on the pavement. Two rows of corpses, piled ten feet high, were at the gate where they had entered, and which they were trying in vain to recover. Of the whole number, about half escaped at last by springing from the walls, plunging into the ditches, and so miserably groping their way back into the camp. Alençon, craven as well as traitor, had not trusted his own precious person into danger. Not daring to abide till the morning, he started at once for Dendermonde, under cover of the darkness, followed by all of his men that were able to march. The alarm outran him: the citizens of Mechlin cut the dykes, and another thousand of the miserable wretches were drowned. Never had treachery encountered a more immediate or more absolutely disastrous retribution.

Whatever else might follow, the catastrophe was utterly fatal to Elizabeth's diplomacy. Alençon had only been borne with for her sake; and one universal cry rose over the whole province that they would submit to Spain rather than allow him to remain any longer among them. With her card castle all in ruins about her, she first fell on the wretched Duke himself. Orange made haste to tell her that the Duke had many times threatened to be revenged upon her for jilting him;[1] and that be his other objects what they might, it was quite certain that he meant no good to England. She spoke 'abominations' of him. She said 'he was a 'false villain like his mother;' that 'he kept faith 'neither with God nor man,' and she flew out at every one who had advised her to marry him.[2] The first impression was that Alençon must have been in secret alliance with Parma. Mendoza hinted that it might be part of a plan between Alençon and Orange for a partition of the Low Countries. Walsingham, not professing to understand Alençon's motive, and offering no conjecture 'what might have happened if so desperate an 'enterprise had succeeded,' yet conceived that he saw

---

[1] 'Siempre habia entendido de Alençon en platicas que con él habia tenido el de Orange el tener gran rencor contra la Reyna, y desseo de satisfacer la injuria que le habia hecho, rebusandole por marido.'— *Mendoza al Rey*, 16-26, 1583. *MSS. Simancas.*

[2] 'Entiendo que está desbridissima con la nueva, y que dice abominaciones de Alençon, y de cuantos le persuadian su casamiento por ser un tirano y sin ninguna fee como su madre por no guardarla á Dios ny á las gentes.'—*Ibid.*

but too clearly what was likely now to follow. 'He 'feared, with too much reason, that France and Spain 'would unite for the subversion of the Low Countries, 'and the overthrow of religion. Monsieur would 'marry the King of Spain's daughter, and then would 'come nothing else but what he had long looked for.'[1]

But the thing which Elizabeth considered policy very soon resumed its place with her, and her anger turned from Alençon to the States. Antwerp and Bruges, in anticipation of her changed humour, had thrown themselves at once prostrate before her, deprecating her displeasure. She refused to hear them, and insisted that the Duke should be recalled. She blamed Norris, who had been in Antwerp at the attack, for the miseries of Alençon's retreat. She said that he ought to have protected her dearest friend, and she ordered him either to place himself at Alençon's disposition, or instantly to leave the States. Norris pleaded that he had taken no part against Monsieur. When he heard the French cry, 'Vive la messe,' and 'Kill the heretics,' he had simply looked to the safety of his own people, as he conceived himself to have been bound to do. He would obey her Majesty's pleasure if she persisted; but he said plainly, that in obeying, 'he would cause that to follow 'which her Majesty would not like of; the people 'were in that humour they would undoubtedly treat 'with the Spaniards.'[2] The Prince wrote to ask whether, if France made war on the States in revenge for the slaughter, Elizabeth would stand by them? She replied by a demand that Alençon should be replaced in the Protectorate; and the Prince, not wishing to add France to the list of his enemies, with Elizabeth in her

---

[1] Walsingham to Cobham, Jan. 17-27.—*MSS. France.*
[2] Norris to Walsingham, Feb. 3-13, Feb. 8-18.—*MSS. Holland.*

present humour, did his best to please her. Negotiations were opened, in which Monsieur was alternately insolent and cringing, and Elizabeth, at a loss what to do, was tossed to and fro in uncertainties. Alençon said truly that he had involved himself in the quarrel of the Low Countries only for her sake, and that she was bound to adhere to him. He wished to be rid of Norris, and he boasted that if the English were sent away, he could soon settle with the States.[1] The Queen dispatched Sir Arthur Darcy to apologise for Norris's behaviour. Darcy, with half-a-dozen of Alençon's suite, went to Norris to tell him that it was his mistress's pleasure that the English contingent should immediately withdraw. It seems, however, that she had sent a private message along with her order that he need not comply. Norris, with an affectation of bluntness, replied that he was a second son with not a yard of land in England; that he had taken an oath to the States, and would not desert them without an order under the Queen's hand.[2] She abused him in public: she said in private that he had answered well.[3] Messenger was dispatched after messenger to bring about a reconciliation. The Prince of Orange exerted himself so earnestly as to throw suspicion on his patriotism. The English commander received fresh orders to remain at his post, but to be exclusively under Alençon's authority. But nothing could heal a wound so envenomed with treachery. Norris, knowing well that if mischief happened through the English contingent

---

[1] 'Alençon embió á pedir á la Reyna que pues desea tanto su acrescentamiento y tener su partido contra todo el mundo, mande luego salir los Ingleses que estan en los Estados, que como él quede solo con Françeses se avendra muy bien con los Estados.' —*Mendoza al Rey*, 7-17 Marcio, 1583. *MSS. Simancas.*

[2] *Ibid.*

[3] 'Diciendo malas palabras del dicho Norris en publico y en secreto bien.' — *Mendoza al Rey*, 18-28 Marcio, 1583. *MSS. Simancas.*

the blame would be laid on himself, declared that if he was to continue his command he would take his orders only from the States.[1] He had doubtful gentlemen in the service who would be ready for any villany on which Alençon might choose to employ them. Even as it was, the town of Alost, a few months later, was sold by an English officer to the Spaniards.[2]

Thus baffled, and false as he was cowardly, the Duke addressed himself to Parma, and attempted to bargain for the towns which he had succeeded in securing. But this paltry practice failed also. His garrisons were obliged to withdraw, and on the 28th of June, deserted, disgraced, and broken with disease and disappointment, the petted instrument of Elizabeth's political genius went back to France, not yet utterly cast aside—she could not wholly part with him—but disabled for further action, and with his miserable part in the world's drama played out.

Meanwhile, the cause of the Low Countries appeared to be totally ruined. The friendship of France was gone. The spirit of the people, thus scandalously abandoned after their splendid struggle, was broken. The Prince of Parma, who alone, of all the parties interested, saw his way clearly, and had his work definitely cut out, pushed forward slowly but irresistibly. The towns which Alençon would have sold he recovered easily by force. On the sea-board he took Dunkirk, Gravelines, and Nieuporte, places which were of vital moment to him when England's turn came to be attacked. On the other side, Ipres, Zutfen, and afterwards Bruges surrendered. Almost everything which had been gained by the great revolt of 1576, was again

---

[1] Norris to Walsingham, April 28.—MSS. Holland. [2] Norris to Walsingham, Nov. 27.—MSS. Holland.

lost, and once more a languid despondency palsied the
policy of England. The effects of the raid of Ruthven
had been undone by the rejection of Col. Stewart's overtures. Scotland had again fallen under anti-English
influences, and was reopened to the designs of the Duke
of Guise. On all sides the cause of freedom, which so
many times had been all but won, seemed finally collapsing; and some general compromise—something
equivalent to a universal submission, by which the revolted Provinces would be restored to their master, and
the Queen of Scots released and recognised in Parliament as heir presumptive in England, appeared now
inevitably approaching.

Under these circumstances, Elizabeth reverted to the
purpose which she had begun to execute in 1576. In
the expected crash, she wished to be able to say that she
had been no friend to the revolted Provinces. If she
assisted in their overthrow she might claim a voice in
the disposal of them; at all events, she might recover
part of the treasure which she had lavished on the
wretched Alençon. It will be remembered that six
years before, the States had borrowed twenty thousand
pounds from her, and she had made herself afterwards
security for forty thousand pounds in addition. The
debt had never been paid. As she held the jewels of
the house of Burgundy in pawn, the States had thought
no more about the matter. But she may have possibly
reflected that these jewels would have to be given up to
Philip after the reconquest, and either for this or some
other reason she determined, while the States had still
a corporate existence, to repay herself both principal
and interest. Notwithstanding the war, an extensive
trade continued between the United Provinces and
Spain. Their merchant fleet was expected in the

Channel on its return from Cadiz. She proposed quietly to take possession of it.

'The causes of the loans' were first formally 'set 'down,' as Elizabeth pleased to describe them.

She had justified herself, from the first, for assisting the States, on the ground that she could not allow them to be annexed to France. She still maintained the same position, distinctly denying that she had been influenced by hostility to Spain.[1] 'Hard it is,' said the secretary who was employed upon the duty, 'to deal in these 'causes that are so perplexed, especially to such as are 'not accustomed to swim between two waters. The 'care that is to be taken is that her honour may be 'preserved, and yet her turn served in this her 'pleasure.'[2]

She had her own notions of honour and of the means to preserve it. Once more—and this time in serious earnest—she sent orders for Norris and the volunteers to leave the Provinces,[3] while she directed Captain Bingham, an officer of her own navy, to go out into the Channel and there seize the best of the ships of the States as a punishment for their want of gratitude, 'considering 'the extraordinary favours which she had shewn them.'

---

[1] 'I have set down,' said Walsingham's secretary, 'the causes of those loans. Her Majesty doubted that one or the other would follow, if they were not holpen. My master directed me to name those causes, though in truth I do not see how it will stand with honour et fœderum fide. I could wish they were spared, and some other colour set upon the matter. The States in all intendment of her Majesty are taken as the King of Spain's subjects. She never otherwise liked of any of their proceedings, and from time to time in her own writings, taketh and nameth them so.'—*Lawrence Tomson to Mr. Hammond*, Aug. 13. *MSS. Holland.*

[2] *Ibid.*

[3] She offered Norris the marshalship of Berwick, as a reward for his past service, but thrifty in her liberality, she required five or six hundred pounds for it, and the bargain was too hard for him.—*Norris to Burghley*, Sept. 13. *MSS. Holland.*

'You will apprehend,' she said, 'any ships which you
'may discover to be richly laden, either passing west-
'wards or returning homewards; you will encounter
'with them and assail them, yet without force if it con-
'veniently may be. Assure yourself beforehand what
'substance is in any ship or ships, so as the prize may
'countervail the debt, and also all such other charges as
'may in justice be demanded. The interest now
'amounts to thirty-five or thirty-six thousand pounds.
'If you are not certain of the value, you shall, on first
'boarding, search, pretending that you are to look for
'certain notorious traitors escaped out of England. Be
'sure to capture the entire fleet: let not one escape
'you.'[1]

Ingenuity may invent excuses for Elizabeth. There may have been secret circumstances or secret intentions which might make her conduct not wholly indefensible; yet the reverting a second time to the same resolution on the recurrence of the same circumstances, indicates a principle and a policy. She would have protected the United Provinces at all times, had she seen her way to it without open war; but war, with its certain costs and uncertain issues, she did not choose to encounter; and if the States were to be conquered, she hoped, by assisting Philip, to obtain a moderating voice in the terms of their submission, and a share at any rate in the spoils.

The good genius of England stood between its Sovereign and discredit, and the bad purpose was left unexecuted. Three months later the Prince of Orange was again Elizabeth's dearest friend. Hopes of compromise had vanished, and the war which she had waded through so many manœuvres to avoid, stared her in the face. She was convinced, perhaps for the first time, that

---

[1] Instructions to Captain Bingham, Aug. 18, 1585.—*MSS. Holland.*

if Philip conquered, her own deposition was to be a condition of the pacification of Europe; and again without a blush she sought the friendship of the only allies on whom she could rely.

The raid of Ruthven and the expulsion of Lennox had disconcerted the plot which had been first formed for the invasion. In the original programme the Duke of Guise was to enter Scotland as the ally of the King, and with the consent of the party in power there. Savage as James had shown himself on his capture, he had been persuaded to make another trial of Elizabeth's good-will. De Mainville, La Mothe Fénelon's companion in the French embassy, was Guise's friend and confederate, and had laboured to persuade the King that his English prospects depended on the Catholics. But so long as he had hopes of an English pension, and of being recognised as successor in preference to his mother, he had held aloof, giving hesitating answers. He had declared his intention of remaining a Protestant, and evidently, if Elizabeth had been willing to meet his wishes, was prepared to take his chance at her side. De Mainville, therefore, while Colonel Stewart was still unanswered, had returned to Paris with an opinion that Scotland was not to be relied upon; that the Kirk was too strong, and that Protestantism had too firm a hold upon the country. The Duke of Guise in consequence, not abandoning his enterprise, but changing the direction of it, turned his eyes upon England itself. The Jesuits assured him that the people were ripe for insurrection. He had about him a knot of young English gentlemen, cadets of Catholic families, who were in regular correspondence with their friends. Mendoza's six noblemen, though refusing to move alone, were waiting only for help from abroad; and the Queen of Scots, while she was affecting to treat with Elizabeth, had agents in Paris, between whom and herself there was a constant interchange of ciphered letters. The most active of these were Charles Paget, son of Henry VIII.'s minister, and younger brother of Lord Paget, who was perhaps one of the six; William Parry, who, pretending to be a spy of Burghley's, was in fact betraying him; Charles Arundel, brother of Sir Matthew Arundel of Wardour; and a person who was afterwards the unwilling cause of the Queen of Scots' execution, named Thomas Morgan.[1]

---

[1] In the natural exasperation of the Catholic conspirators, when their plots were defeated and exploded, Morgan was suspected of treachery. He was seized, carried to Brussels, and examined by Parma, to whom he related his history. As he became a person of so much consequence it is worth recording. He was the son of a Welsh gentleman, and was born in 1543. When he was eighteen he was put into the household of the Bishop of Exeter, and became afterwards secretary to Young, the Archbishop of York, with whom he remained till the Archbishop's death in 1570. These two prelates, he said, were violent Calvinists. He was himself a Catholic, but had concealed his creed, and had received church preferment from them, though a layman, worth four thousand crowns a year. When Young died, excited by the rising of the north, he resolved to devote himself to the service of the Queen of Scots. Lord Northumberland and the Earl of Pembroke recommended him to Lord Shrewsbury, and in the loose custody in which the Queen of Scots was held, he was soon able to be useful to her. He managed her correspondence, and as Shrewsbury's secretary he was able to read and communicate to her whatever passed between his master and the Court. When her rooms and boxes were to be searched he had notice beforehand, and concealed her papers. After three years of this employment, he was discovered, and sent to the Tower under a charge of having been acquainted with the Ridolfi conspiracy. There he continued ten months, and the most suspicious circumstance about him was that at the end of that time he was dismissed unpunished. The Tower gates, he admitted, were rarely opened to Catholic prisoners, except on condition that they turned traitors. Many Catholics, he confessed, had escaped in that way, and had afterwards become servants of the Government. He denied, however, entirely that he had himself purchased his release by treachery. Lord Burghley, he said, had interceded for him, he knew not why. And he retained and deserved the confidence of the Queen of Scots, whose most trusted instrument he ever after remained. She recommended him to Guise and the Archbishop of Glasgow. He lived at Paris, where she allowed him 30 crowns a month out of her dowry. He managed her ciphers, and corresponded for her with the Pope, the

These gentlemen agreed in representing the enterprise against England as offering no serious difficulties, and the noble families as eager to rid the country of the disgrace of heresy. On the 24th of April (May 4) Baptista de Tassis spoke of Guise as almost ready, and as endeavouring, meanwhile, to find some one who would do what Alva always recommended as a preliminary step, that is, shoot or stab Elizabeth.[1]

Beyond the general resolution, however, there was still great uncertainty, and wide divergence of opinion. At a consultation at the Nuncio's house at Paris in June, the Duke of Guise announced that Duke Albert of Bavaria would take a part in the invasion, and supposing the King of Spain to approve, but to be unwilling to appear in the matter personally, he said that he was ready himself to cross immediately to the coast of Northumberland with four thousand of his own people. His brother the Duke of Mayenne would land with as many more in Sussex, and if Parma would allow the use of Dunkirk, Duke Albert would pass from thence to Norfolk with five thousand Germans. This plan appeared to him to be on the whole the most desirable. It could be

---

Nuncio in France, the English Catholics at home and abroad, with Allen, Sanders, and every other person concerned in the conspiracies against Elizabeth. The Queen of Scots entrusted him with her deepest and darkest secrets, and though her connexion with him proved fatal to her, there is no doubt of his genuine fidelity. — *Cargas contra Tomas Morgan, fecho en Bruselas en doze de Hebrero*, 1590. *MSS. Simancas.*

[1] 'La traça en que andaba Hercules (Guise), y que apunté á V. M. á 4 de Mayo, era un hecho violento contra essa señora.'— *Juan Baptista de Tassis al Rey*, 14-24 de Mayo. TEULET, vol. v. Three sets of conspirators besides the Jesuits were meditating the Queen's murder at that very moment: Somerville and Arden in Warwickshire, Thomas Morgan and his friends at Paris, and a third party, whose names were unknown.—See the trial of the Earl of Arundel *State Trials*, vol. i. It is uncertain to whom de Tassis referred. Opposite de Tassis's words Philip wrote, 'Así creo que lo entendimos acá, y con que lo hicieran ellos no fuera malo, aunque habian de prevenir algunas cosas.'

executed at once; the danger of discovery from delay would be avoided; while France itself could provide arms and men.

From this proposal, prompt and decisive as it was, the English Jesuits dissented. Their leanings were entirely Spanish, and although they were ready to accept Guise as their leader, they wished him to act only under Philip's directions. They made objections to a triple combination. They said that unless the King of Spain was supreme, they would quarrel among themselves— one party would think only of re-establishing religion, another of placing Mary Stuart on the throne, while a third would be for letting Elizabeth remain, and for giving the Queen of Scots only the succession. Again, supposing Mary Stuart Queen, the Scots, they said, would look to have precedence at Court, to which the English would never yield. Catholic England was ready to take her as its Sovereign, but only as the representative of Philip. The people were strongly attached to their old alliance, and could only be relied on to rise if Spain was distinctly in the field. Father Allen, who was present, recommended strongly that the force employed should be Spanish and Italian, and not French. The Pope might gratify France by appointing the Duke of Guise to the command. The King of Spain need not appear, but must keep the control of everything in his hand. Four thousand men, Allen thought, would be sufficient, with arms for those who would join them, and money to pay their way, that they might not have to prey upon the country. Volunteers would crowd to the standard. Allen himself offered to go first and take possession of the see of Durham, to which the Pope had appointed him. God, he thought, could be relied upon for the rest.

As Allen drew the picture, de Tassis admitted that it was a tempting one. Guise was ready to sacrifice his own scheme, if the other was preferred. The invasion it was thought ought not to be postponed beyond the coming September at latest, but 4,000 men might be sent off with no great difficulty. In the interests of England, of France, of Flanders, of all Europe, de Tassis recommended Philip to consent, at all events he pressed for an immediate answer. All were agreed on the danger of delay. If Allen's plans were disliked, Guise and Maienne were ready to fall back upon their own.[1]

Promptitude was an element of human success which Philip II. neither commanded nor understood. The fitness of the Duke of Guise to conduct the English invasion had been canvassed for years; yet now, when the enterprise was on the eve of execution, he preferred to reconsider the whole question. When de Tassis's letter of the 4th of May reached him, he sent Guise word that he was glad he was so well employed, that he wished him success, and would give him money; but he desired first to learn particularly what he meant to do—while, as it was contrary to Spanish political tradition to allow a Frenchman to gain a footing in England, and as de Tassis was under Guise's influence, he wrote to Mendoza to send him a confidential opinion.[2]

Mendoza's answer throws admirable light on the complications which embarrassed the Catholic cause.

'Your Majesty asks me,' he wrote, 'what I think of the
'Duke of Guise: whether his coming to England is open
'to the objection which we entertain generally against
'the introduction of the French into the island; and

---

[1] Tassis to Philip II. April 24
—May 4, June 14-24.—TECLET,
vol. v.

[2] Philip to de Tassis, June 6.
Philip to Mendoza, June 6.—TEC-
LET, vol. v.

'whether it will be sufficient to help him with money,
' or if your Majesty should do more. I have many times
' insisted to your Highness that if the French invade
' Scotland or England in the interests of the Queen of
' Scots, and if they gain entire control of the situation,
' this much is certain, that the island will not be re-
' covered to the Catholic faith. The French care little
' enough for it at home. Religion with them is but an
' accessory of politics, as they have shown in their trans-
' actions with the Low Countries. You can consider,
' therefore, the inconveniences which will arise. The
' English will be in a frenzy, the French being their
' natural enemies, and when so just an object is pre-
' tended as the conversion of the people, and the rights
' of the Scottish Queen, your Majesty will be unable to
' interfere on the Queen of England's behalf.

'Well then, to obviate this, and to neutralise the
' jealousy which cannot but arise between France and
' Spain, if either of them attempt alone the conquest of
' England, God has been pleased to introduce the
' Queen of Scots as a neutral person between us.
' Other causes besides religion make it desirable both to
' us and to France that the Queen of Scots should have
' this Crown. She will put a stop to the mischief which
' the English have done, and are doing, in Flanders and
' France also; only there must be a clear understanding
' that whoever comes hither at the head of an army,
' comes with no other object but to set her at liberty,
' and replant religion. I do not know what is passing
' between the Catholics here and the Duke of Guise.
' They say nothing of it to me; but the Duke knows
' them of course—being what they are—to wish well to
' himself and his house; and they know him to be the de-
' fender, with your Majesty's help, of French orthodoxy.

'I cannot think, therefore, that inconvenience can arise
'from his coming, either to this country or to Scotland.
'Rather, I think, we should invite him to undertake the
'enterprise, there being no other person in whom so
'many advantages concur. He is the Queen of Scots'
'near kinsman, and possesses her fullest confidence. He
'will be himself interested in preventing France from
'gaining too strong a hold here. His concern will be
'for the imprisoned Queen, from whom we have so much
'to expect in the way of service to God and your
'Majesty. The Duke will take charge of her interests.
'He will see that the son does not supplant the mother
'in England as he has done in Scotland. From the
'son, until he be reconciled to the Church, there is
'nothing more to be looked for than from any other
'Scot or heretic. The Catholics will not admit him
'here while he is unconverted. They will not even ac-
'cept his mother except in concert with and under the
'authority of your Majesty, and it is on your Majesty
'assuredly that the Queen of Scots will lean. She
'knows the hatred borne to her by the Queen-mother,
'and the animosity between her kinsmen the Guises
'and the houses of Bourbon and Montmorency. As to
'the form and quality of your Majesty's assistance, I can
'advise nothing till I know more of your Highness's
'intentions. It must depend on whether your Majesty
'means to declare yourself openly—whether the King
'of France is to take a part, or whether it is to be left
'to his Holiness and the Duke of Guise, your Majesty
'reserving a power to interpose if the French go too far.
'As to the amount of force, you remember what the
'Duke of Lennox asked for when the invasion was in-
'tended through Scotland. Baptista de Tassis and the
'Nuncio have talked over matters since that time with

'the other parties concerned, but I know not what they
'have resolved. If England is to be invaded imme-
'diately, I should like to know in what strength the
'Duke calculates the Catholics here will join him. He
'may either come over with three or four thousand tho-
'roughly trusty men, or he may come with a large army
'regularly appointed. If the first, your Majesty will
'do well to provide him with a number of experienced
'officers. Some of those in Flanders may seem to quar-
'rel with the Prince of Parma, and be turned adrift to
'seek service elsewhere. If the second, and if your Ma-
'jesty will not commit yourself by sending Spaniards,
'the army ought to consist of Italians and German
'Catholics, wholly devoted to your Majesty. The Duke
'of Guise will make no objection, for he will be assured
'that your Majesty will ensure him a safe return to
'France, and will guarantee him against his rivals
'during his absence. The realm is ripe for revolution.
'It is full of sects and faction. The people will not
'bear control, and the doings of the Council and clergy
'are scandalous. There is every reason, therefore, to
'expect success. The French Ambassador tells them
'that the Queen of Scots may count on the help of
'Alençon. For the honour of God, let your Majesty
'beware of this false and ambitious Prince. If you
'mean to do anything here do it promptly, and trust
'only to Guise. Do not let Alençon fancy that you will
'allow him to conduct the enterprise, or give him time
'to hinder it if he is refused. Guise alone can be safely
'trusted. It is not for your Majesty's interests that any
'other Frenchman should come hither, unless indeed
'for every hundred of his countrymen he bring as many
'Spaniards also. If they are coming to restore religion,
'your Majesty's soldiers are as zealous as they. If they

'have ulterior objects, it will be well to have our own
'people on the spot to share the game.'[1]

Scotland, it will be seen, was now dropped out of the scheme of invasion. Scotland, and with it the interests of Scotland's young King, who had been intriguing with the other side, and as long as he was unconverted, was to be excluded from further advancement. But James and the politicians with whom he was surrounded had no intention of being thus thrust into the shade. The English succession was the loadstar on which James's eyes were permanently fixed. He had hoped to secure it for himself over his mother's head; he had offended her and the Catholics, and he had as yet obtained nothing. He might still wait humbly, and so at last hope to propitiate Elizabeth. On the other hand Guise might come over, and the Catholics might rise and make a revolution, and his chances would be forfeited for ever. Could he but have commanded the second sight of his countrymen, how easy would have been his course! If he turned Catholic prematurely, and after all the Protestants won the victory, he was lost equally that way. It was a tremendous position, but the scoundrels who surrounded him were equal to it. The first step was to beg his mother's pardon for having coquetted with Elizabeth. Colonel Stewart had brought his orders with him to London, and instantly that he and Colville were dismissed, with their requests refused, he found means of communicating with Sheffield, and telling the lady that her son had acted under constraint. In Scotland preparations were made swiftly and secretly to undo the effects of the raid of Ruthven, shake off the English lords, and place the country once more at the disposition of the conspirators at Paris, if they cared to use

---

[1] Mendoza to Philip, July 6–16. Abridged.—*MSS. Simancas.*

it. Gowrie himself, blinded by the phantom of the
succession, and exasperated at the broken promises of
Elizabeth, imagined that he had no more interest in
holding James prisoner. John Maitland lent abilities
to the new intrigues, which were second only to his
brother's. Colonel Stewart came back from London
with as keen a hatred of the English alliance, as he
had carried thither a desire to make it perpetual.[1]
The Catholic noblemen were burning to recover their
ascendancy. The King was at Falkland in charge of
Angus and Mar, and a plot was rapidly formed, with
James's privity, to rescue him. Young Seton stole off
to France to tell de Tassis that a revolution was coming,
and that Scotland would soon be Spanish again.[2] Warnings were sent to Huntley, Montrose, Crawford, and
others of the Catholic faction, to hold themselves in
readiness, and on the 7th of July[3] the King and Colonel
Stewart slipped away to St. Andrew's, and shut themselves up in the castle there. The two Earls followed in
haste, but Huntley had the start of them. St. Andrew's
was swarming with Gordons, the King was in the midst
of his mother's friends, and they were obliged to retire
as they came. A second messenger went off to Paris
with the news, and with a promise that the work so
well begun would soon be finished, that Gowrie, who
had been made a tool of, would be shaken off, and that
the Catholics would have Scotland at their feet. It was
the rebound of the stone of Sisyphus. After years of

---

[1] 'Col. Stewart est retourné d'Angleterre, où les choses luy sont si mal succedées qu'il n'a peu choisir meilleur party que de se ranger du côté du Roy et abandonner l'aultre faction du tout, de sorte que le Roy mesme est beaucoup refroydy.'— Letter from a nobleman at St. Andrew's to M. de Mayneville, July 3-13. TEULET, vol. iii.

[2] Tassis to Philip, June 29–July 9.—TEULET, vol. v.

[3] New Style.

anxiety and miracles of diplomatic adroitness, the neglect which had destroyed Morton had been repaired. The cards had been once more in Elizabeth's hands, she had flung them in the face of her friends, and they, as usual, were left to perish, and her ministers to begin their ever recurring and ever hopeless toil.

Utterly discomfited, Mar, Angus, and Lindsay could but sit still. They knew not what to do, or in which direction to turn. Only the ministers saw their way clearly. A deputation from the Presbytery at Edinburgh came over to St. Andrew's, demanded an interview with the King, and warned him against 'new 'courses.' James, whatever his shifts of politics, had never wavered in his hatred of the Kirk. He turned fiercely on them. 'Never king in Europe,' he said, ' would have borne at their hands what he had borne.' David Fergusson, one of the party, coolly answered that he had been well brought up, and they did not wish him to be like other kings. If they saw occasion to speak to him they intended to speak, whether he liked it or not. ' There was not the face on flesh that they would ' spare, if they found rebellion to God, whose message ' they carried.' He might despise them, but his contempt would not alter facts. ' There was never one in ' that realm that prospered in authority after the ' ministers began to threaten him.'[1] It was disrespectful language from a subject to a Sovereign—disrespectful and, as some might think, vain and absurd—yet no more, after all, than the literal truth. Nothing in the history of these times is more remarkable than the correctness of the political judgment of John Knox and his successors. They believed that the world was governed

---

[1] Calderwood.

by justice and truth, and not by intrigue and chicanery, and the event proved that they were right.

Meanwhile it was the enemies' day. Every officer, either of state or household, known to be attached to England was removed, and those who had been in exile for fidelity to the Queen of Scots were recalled and promoted. When Sir Robert Bowes remonstrated, he was taunted with his mistress's parsimony. When he asked if they would accept the pension which she had offered the King, he was told that sooner than the King should disgrace himself by accepting so vile a sum the lords would subscribe double the amount for him themselves.[1] An agent of Walsingham's sent word that if the Queen interfered with force, France would take it 'as if she had declared war;' the King had distinctly told him so;[2] and perplexed and penitent too late Elizabeth flew from counsel to counsel, cursing the changeableness of the Scots, as if she had given them cause for constancy. Secretary Beale went again to Sheffield, carrying proposals, ignominious now because extorted by fear, to go on with the treaty. Elizabeth might have spared herself the humiliation. In the exulting confidence of expected triumph the Queen of Scots refused now to be bound by her past promises. If she was to ratify the treaty of Leith, she must have her right of succession recognised by Act of Parliament, or at least by private deed under Elizabeth's hand and seal. She declined to pledge herself against alterations of the established religion. She would consent to remain in England—it was part of the scheme which she had arranged with Guise and Mendoza—but she required the free use of the Catholic ritual for herself

---

[1] Bowes to Walsingham, July 13-23.—MSS. Scotland. [2] ——— (sic) to Walsingham, July 1583.—MSS. Ibid.

and her household, free access to her person from all parts of the world, and the title of an English duchy.[1] Walsingham cynically advised that his mistress should go even further and replace Mary Stuart in Scotland, and when reminded of his past objections, answered that times were changed and that wise men must change with them.[2] 'You are not so resolute there,' he wrote to Bowes, 'as we are irresolute here.'[3] Sir Walter Mildmay, who had been with Beale at Sheffield, was ordered to prepare to accompany Lord Hunsdon to the Scotch Court,[4] while Bowes, on the same day, was bidden renew for the twentieth time the as often broken promises, look out the noblemen affected to the English crown, and promise them help in arms and money if they would again combine.[5]

Frightened off this course by fear of France, she directed the ambassador to remonstrate sharply with the King. In a second letter she bade him 'not re-proach, but rather expostulate.' Next she resolved to do nothing, expecting 'that the King would do what was right of his own mind.'[6] Finally after a violent scene with Walsingham, she insisted that he should go to Scotland himself, and either by persuasion or by any means that he could find, undo the effects of her

---

[1] Mauvissière to the King of France, July 21-31.—TEULET, vol. iii.

[2] 'Le Sieur de Walsingham a dict que il luy sembloit que l'on debvroit contenter ladicte Royne d'Escosse, et qu'elle demeureroit par-delà, avec asseurance de la Royne d'Angleterre pour demeurer sourement en son Royaulme sans que luy feust faict ny mal ny desplaisir. Aulcuns luy ont respondu qu'il n'avoit pas toujours tenu ce langage ny esté de ce conseil. Il a respondu que aussy voyoit-il qu'il se falloit accommoder et changer selon les temps.'—M. de Castelnau à la Royne mère, 31 Juillet-10 Aoust, 1583. TEULET, vol. iii.

[3] Walsingham to Bowes, July 22-Aug. 1.—MSS. Scotland.

[4] Walsingham to Bowes, July 10-20.—MSS. Ibid.

[5] Ibid.

[6] Walsingham to Bowes, July 27-Aug. 6.—MSS. Scotland.

own neglect of his advice. Walsingham said 'that he would most willingly have used his travail therein if the Queen did embrace and go through with things as effectively as she should do.'[1] As it was he received his order 'with as ill a will as ever he undertook any service in his life.' He 'feared he could do little good.' He 'would most willingly have avoided the journey if he could have done it without her Majesty's extreme displeasure,' and not choosing to be the means of tempting Scotch noblemen to rely upon promises which he knew would not be observed, he sent word to the Earl of Mar, who had applied for advice to Sir Robert Bowes, 'to follow the way of counsel that might be best for his own safety, without further regard to England.'[2]

He was curious to see James, however, and form his own impressions about him, while Elizabeth prepared the way by a letter of condescending and contemptuous superiority, which, however truly it might represent the essential relations between herself and the young prince, was not calculated to make the latter unwilling to quarrel with her.[3] She said she intended to deal as an affectionate sister with him. With how much truth may be inferred from Walsingham's unwillingness to go. She intended in fact to tempt him to forsake his

---

[1] Walsingham to Bowes, July 27–Aug. 6.—*MSS. Ibid.*

[2] Walsingham to Bowes, Aug. 6–16.—*MSS. Ibid.*

[3] 'My dear brother and cousin,—It moveth me much to moan you when I behold how diversely sundry wicked spirits distract your mind, and bend your course to crooked paths, and like all evil illusions, wrapped under the cloke of your best safety, endanger your estate. You deal with one whose experience will not take dross for good payment, and with one who will not easily be beguiled. No, no, I mean to set to school your craftiest councillors. I beseech you proceed no further in this course till you receive an express messenger, a trusty servant of mine, by whom I intend to deal as an affectionate sister with you.'—*Elizabeth to James*, Aug. 7–17. *MSS. Scotland.*

new friends, with vague assurances which might or might not be realised after her death, but for which he would certainly receive no value till the grave had closed over her. She said she would enlarge his pension if the sum which she had offered appeared too small, but be must replace in office the lords of the English party, and send their opponents away. For Lady Lennox's estate, which was the symbol of the succession, and the point therefore of especial soreness, she bade Walsingham say that she had suspended her answer for his own sake. She could not consent till the opposing claims had been heard of the Lady Arabella, and as the issue might be such as would offend him she preferred to leave it undecided.[1]

How far evasions of this kind were likely to influence James in his present mood, or how far Elizabeth's admonition was likely to work favourably on him, may be gathered from a letter which he now wrote to the Duke of Guise. He was infinitely delighted with himself for having recovered his liberty. He assumed that Guise was ready as ever to use Scotland as his stepping-stone to England, but was anxious to let him know that he claimed for himself a right to a share in the enterprise.

'Your proposal to send troops here is most agreeable
' to me,' he said. 'I will accept or not accept it as cir-
' cumstances shall require. I hold myself happy in
' having so brilliant and distinguished a kinsman, the
' first captain of his age, ready to take arms in my
' behalf. M. de Mainville, you tell me, has been pleased
' to speak *of the virtues and rare qualities which God has
' bestowed upon me.*[2] I am the more bound to imitate

---

[1] Instructions to Walsingham, Aug. 13-15.—*MSS. Scotland.*

[2] This letter is preserved in a Spanish translation, sent by de Tassis to the King of Spain. The words in italics were underlined by Philip, who remarked upon them 'a modest young gentleman' ('bien las confiesa de sí').

'the ever memorable deeds of my ancestors of the noble
'house of Lorraine. If there be anything in me de-
'serving praise it is to that house from which through
'my mother I derive my origin, that I attribute all.
'Had I, at the receipt of your letter, been in the con-
'dition in which M. de Mainville left me, you would
'have excited in my breast an ardent desire of liberty;
'but God be praised I had already extricated myself by
'my own prudence and patience. I am now free, and
'eager for an opportunity to revenge myself. My
'mother, in a letter which I have just received from
'her, refers me to you for directions. You propose, I
'understand, to set her free and establish our united
'right to the English crown. I admire your object. I
'approve of the means which you intend to use, and
'which have only to be handled with dexterity. I will
'send you my opinion in a few days. I have much of
'great consequence to say to you, which I dare not
'commit to paper except in cipher.'[1]

The writer of such a letter as this was not likely to take patiently a lecture upon his pliancy to evil. While it justifies Elizabeth's extreme distrust of his character, it shews also the imprudence of trifling away the control over him which the raid of Ruthven had placed in her hands. Having a more slender estimate of James's abilities than he had formed for himself, Guise was not anxious to take him into partnership. The escape of the young King was so recent, and the changes had been so many and so sudden, that the scheme which he had formed originally with Lennox no longer seemed advisable. The Scotch Protestants were evidently very strong; it was enough if for the present they could be neutralised. England was the point to strike at, and to

---

[1] James VI. to the Duke of Guise, Aug. 9-19, 1583.—TEULET, vol. v.

strike at with speed. Guise's position at home was critical. The King feared him. Catherine de Medici hated him. His personal safety, as he told Mendoza, required the support of an army. Action somewhere was a necessity to him, either in France or England, and he preferred to transfer the miseries of war to a foreign country.[1] Philip, after due consideration, had decided against an over trust in the French, and on himself supplying at least part of the force which was to be employed. Parma could easily spare four or five thousand men, and it had been settled that a Spanish fleet was to hold the Channel to protect the crossing. For the fleet, and for the fleet only, Guise was now waiting. All else was ready. Notice had gone round to the principal houses in the northern counties in England to be on the alert. The Queen of Scots was prepared either to fly or to defend herself. The 'principal noblemen,' Northumberland, that is, and the Earl of Arundel, had sent word that her friends were prepared.[2] The Earl of Westmoreland was in Flanders, waiting for the moment to return to his tenants. Durham was reported ready to welcome Allen as Bishop. A brother of Leonard Dacres, who now claimed the title, undertook for Gilsland and the English border. Lord Wharton, the Earl of Cumberland, and the Percies had promised six thousand horse between them; Fernihurst and Maxwell three thousand Scots from Teviotdale and Dumfries. It was calculated

[1] 'Dióme el clerigo particular cuenta en nombre de Hercules de la resolucion hecha, y juntamente de que á él le habia de ser fuerça y á su hermano, por el termino con que procedia con ellos el Rey de Francia tomar las armas en aquel Reyno ó en Inglaterra.'—*Don Bernardino al Rey*, 9-19 Agosto. *MSS. Simancas.*

[2] 'Habiendo escrito la Reyna de Escocia y dado aviso los principales señores de aquel reyno que las cosas estan muy bien dispuestas, principalmente hacia los confines de Escocia, donde debe descender la armada de España, tandem se ha hecho resolucion que bastará que el Rey Catolico embie una armada de cuatro mil buenos soldados,' &c.—*Instruccion por los negocios de Inglaterra*, 12-22 de Agosto. TECLET, vol. v.

that twenty thousand men at least would take arms on the instant that Guise was known to have landed. The Earls of Rutland, Arundel, and Worcester, Lord Montague, and several others had promised to declare themselves when the insurrection was once in motion. The plan had been minutely arranged. Mendoza was to remain quietly in London till the last moment, and then to slip away to Dunkirk. Guise and Allen were to join him there. Parma was to supply the troops. They were to run down the French coast, double the Land's End, and land in Morecambe Bay, where they would be least expected. The Pope had prepared a Bull, declaring that the King of Spain and the Duke of Guise had undertaken the execution of the Church's censures against Elizabeth. Allen, as Nuncio, was to issue it immediately that they were on shore, while the Duc de Mayenne, with a second army, was to throw himself on the coast of Sussex, where Lord Paget and Arundel of Wardour had engaged to receive him.

The arrangements being thus forward, Guise was naturally restless. The ships from Spain were long in coming, and to employ the time he sent Charles Paget privately across the Channel to arrange with his friends the exact spot where Mayenne should land, and to remove at the same time any lingering alarm which they might feel of danger to English liberty by assuring them that he and his brother were coming over merely and simply to re-establish the faith of Christ, and make Mary Stuart Queen;[1] that when these objects were ob-

---

[1] 'Y para poner la Reyna de Escocia pacifica de la corona de Inglaterra, la cual de derecho le pertenece.'—*Instructions of the Duke of Guise to Charles Paget*, Aug. 18-28. TEULET, vol. v. These instructions were not intended for Philip's eye. De Tassis, however, copied, translated and sent them to him. He underlined the words referring to the Queen of Scots, writing on the margin an 'Ojo,' to draw special

tained both French and Spaniards were to withdraw from the country, and that if the Spaniards hesitated he was prepared to compel them.

The murder scheme had failed. The unknown person whom Guise had employed had gone to England for the purpose, but had made no progress, and at last gave up the business, returned ineffectually to the Continent, and with a rare conscience for an assassin returned his reward.[1] Mendoza concluded with a sigh that it was not God's pleasure that this easy method should prosper. Paget's errand answered better. He went over to the coast of Sussex in disguise, accompanied by one of the Throgmortons. He saw the Earl of Arundel, and he saw also the Earl of Northumberland, gave Guise's message, and obtained all the assurances and all the information which Guise desired. He took soundings in Rye harbour. He fixed apparently on Rye as the most appropriate landing place, and returned safely to France, having been seen and suspected, but having escaped arrest or identification. No more could be done till the coming of the fleet. Guise wrote to Mendoza asking him candidly for his opinion as a soldier how far the English Catholics were to be depended on.[2] He apparently was satisfied with the answer,

---

attention to them. He was not at all sure after all that he wished Mary Stuart to be Queen. He was quite certain that he did not mean James to be King. He knew that Guise aspired — on the failure of the house of Valois — to the French crown. Guise, if a Catholic, was a Frenchman, and it was of as much importance to Philip to divide England from France as it was to Elizabeth to keep France apart from Spain.

[1] 'Á la persona que escriví á V. S. en mis antecedentes se le ha ordenado por un caso accidental no vaya adonde esta la otra, por lo cual él ha vuelto á dar lo que se le habia entregado, diciendo que no quiere engañar á nadie, pues falta ocasion, que se muestra de que procedia con llaneza y que Dios no quiere que se haga el negocio en aquella manera.' —*Autograph of Don Bernardino to Secretary Idiaquez*, Aug. 19-29. *MSS. Simancas.*

[2] 'Me pedia le advirtiese precisamente como soldado lo que se podria esperar de los Catolicos de Inglaterra y parciales de la de Escocia, con lo cual él se satisfaria, y no con relacion

and waited only till Philip sent the means to carry him over.

While the mine was thus dug under her feet, and on the point of explosion, Elizabeth was totally unconscious that she was in unusual danger. Rumours had reached her of intended mischief, but such only as she had been accustomed to hear every day for twenty years. She was uneasy about Scotland, but rather for the ultimate consequences of the revolution there than for any mischief to be immediately apprehended. Notwithstanding Alençon she was on good terms with the French Government. Catherine de Medici had written affectionately to her after Alençon's return from the Low Countries, regretting that the marriage had come to nothing, but expressing a hope that the friendship between the two crowns might remain unbroken,[1] and that then and always they might act together in the interests of Christendom.[2] Even Walsingham was satisfied that nothing was to be feared from the King and the Queen-mother,[3] and as to Guise and his brother, a small subsidy to the Huguenots would find them occupation at home.[4] In Scotland Elizabeth recognised that mischief was working, but she had played into Guise's hands by the way in which she had dealt with it. Her letter to James 'mightily 'stirred the coals.'[5] The more angry she shewed herself the less he regarded her admonitions. The Queen of England, he said, ruled her subjects, and he intended

---

de otra ninguna persona.'—*Don Bernardino al Rey*, 19 de Agosto, 1583. *MSS. Simancas.*

[1] Catherine de Medici to Elizabeth, July 16-26.—*MSS. France.*

[2] Walsingham to Cobham, Aug. 6-16.—*MSS. Ibid.*

[3] Walsingham to Bowes, Aug. 20-30.—*MSS. Scotland.*

[4] 'La Reyna con la libertad del Rey de Escocia ha juzgado ser lo que mas le importa, as remover guerra en Francia, en la cual de por fuerça se han de ocupar los de la casa de Guisa.'—*Don Bernardino al Rey*, 19 Agosto. *MSS. Simancas.*

[5] Bowes to Walsingham, Aug. 20-30.—*MSS. Scotland.*

to rule the Scots. Confident in Guise and in the expected invasion, he no longer thought it necessary to carry a fair face to Gowry. He proceeded to call to account both him and all the others who had been concerned in the raid, and insisted that if they were not to be punished they should apply for their pardons. Gowry, whose eyes were soon opened to his mistake in letting the King escape, at first refused. 'He was brought into 'such a passion,' wrote Sir Robert Bowes, 'that he 'cursed the time that he obeyed the King's letters to 'come to him—seeing promises had been doubly broken 'with him—and also accused himself of great beastli- 'ness,[1] by the which those mischiefs were suffered to 'spring, wishing himself rather banished than accept 'pardon for the act which his conscience testifies to be 'good.'[2] Afterwards seeing that he was in real danger he made a sullen acknowledgment of his fault, and withdrew from the Court. The ministers, as usual, stood their ground. They were required 'to condemn 'the act of Ruthven.' They said that the King himself had admitted it to have been good, and to have delivered religion from great perils; the Kirk had approved it in general assembly, and the judgment of the Kirk was law. They were threatened, but they stood to their word. 'Sundry barons and chief burroughs' were seen to approve of their answer, and the King, not wishing to provoke a further quarrel till Guise had arrived, controlled himself, and let them go.[3]

It was at this moment, when Guise was watching for the Spanish sails, and Paget had stolen over upon his secret errand, that Walsingham was started at last upon

---

[1] *Bétise*, folly.
[2] Bowes to Walsingham, Aug. 17-27.—*MSS. Scotland.*
[3] Bowes to Walsingham, Aug. 22-Sept. 1, Aug. 25-Sept. 4.—*MSS. Ibid.*

his journey to the Scotch Court. His dislike of his mission made him ill; and he lingered long upon the road. Believing France to be secure, and that Guise could not move without his master's consent, he would have preferred to see James 'go his own way and taste 'the fruits of his folly.'[1] 'The Court was ruled by 'those who were devoted to the King's mother, directed 'by her counsel, and hated by the people,'[2] 'and was 'wholly bent upon a violent course;' but the ministers of the Kirk could be relied upon; 'the burroughs, who 'lived by traffic, and were grown wealthy by long-'continued peace with England, would not willingly 'hear of a breach;' 'the existing state could not long 'continue,'[2] and if neither France nor England interposed, Walsingham thought the Scots might be safely left to settle their own differences.

He found James at Perth. The Earl of Arran was now his first favourite as Lennox had formerly been, and by Arran and Colonel Stewart he was ruled. When Walsingham was introduced, the King began with complaints. The Queen, he said, found fault with his councillors; what had she to do with his councillors? he made no objection to hers. Walsingham, out of humour already, told him that 'if he made so 'little account of her Majesty she would leave him 'to his own direction;' England had no need of his friendship, nor had he come to seek it; he was sent 'to charge him with unkind dealing, and to require 'satisfaction, excuse, or reparation.'

Excuse was not considered necessary, and reparation was not intended. Arran and Stewart affected innocent

---

[1] Walsingham to Bowes, Aug. 20-30.—*MSS. Scotland.*
[2] Walsingham to Burghley, Aug. 30-Sept. 9.—*MSS. Ibid.*
[2] Same to the same, Sept. 6-16.—*MSS. Ibid.*

surprise. Walsingham would not listen to them, and on the whole formed a worse opinion than he had even expected, both of them and their master. 'I have no 'hopes of the recovery of this young Prince,' he wrote to Burghley. 'If his power may agree with his will he 'will become a dangerous enemy.' He described James as 'full of contempt for her Majesty, into which he 'had grown altogether by the advice of his mother, 'who put him in hope of a great party in England.' His mother had told him 'that the more alienated he 'shewed himself from her Majesty, and the more in-'clined to change the religion,' the more his party would increase. He was evidently 'depending on Spain 'and the Pope,' and 'shewing himself bent by degrees 'to follow that course.' At times, perhaps, he hesitated; 'but if he proceeded not as was meant he should, his 'mother, who was the layer of the plot, would work his 'confusion; and, though she could not live many years, 'yet before their end would see his overthrow.'[1]

Walsingham remained a week, and was then going; when James, not wishing to be utterly defiant while there was still a chance of the non-appearance of Guise, made a faint attempt at conciliation. He assured the English minister that he was really anxious to please the Queen, and that if she desired it he would say no more of 'the raid of Ruthven;' he was ready to pass an act of oblivion, and to replace the English lords in the Council. Walsingham, not trusting him, said coldly, that he had been ill-advised in surrounding himself with so many passionate ambitious young men; he was treading in the steps of the English Edward II., and might come to the same end; the execution of Morton had

---

[1] Walsingham to Burghley, Sept. 11-21. To Elizabeth, Sept. 11-21, 12-22.—*MSS. Scotland.*

been a bad beginning; princes fancied themselves absolute, but princes were as much bound to rule justly as subjects were bound to obey, and if they broke the law they were no longer kings but tyrants.[1]

But James had spoken fairly, and to try his sincerity, Walsingham sent him a note of his offers in writing, and asked if he had understood his meaning. 'A 'dark and ambiguous answer' was returned. It was obviously idle to depend upon him; and Walsingham being on the spot consulted with the old friends of England on the feasibility of some new raid and of 'forcing' James, whether he would or no, to depend on her Majesty's favour. Gowry, Angus, Mar, Lindsay, were all willing, provided that this time the Queen would give them a definite sum of money to work with. Walsingham neither would nor could make promises, but he said that he would write to his mistress, wait at Durham for her answer, and send them word.[2] He was afraid that she would prove impracticable,[3] and the event proved to be as he expected.

Money Elizabeth would give none. She was incredulous of the danger with which she was threatened. She probably believed that the Scotch Protestants would move on their own account without her interposition. Walsingham's letters were ineffectual; and his personal arguments, when he returned to London, were equally powerless. He could prevail neither with his ministers nor with Burghley, and he sent word to the lords that

---

[1] Heads of a conversation between Secretary Walsingham and the King of Scots, Sept. 12-21.—*MSS. Scotland.*

[2] Walsingham to Elizabeth, Sept. 15-25.—*MSS. Ibid.*

[3] 'If the answer I receive from our Court be not such as was to be wished, and the necessity of the present times require—whereof I stand in some doubt, for security did never more possess us than at this present—I would have you retire from thence with as convenient speed as you may.'—*Walsingham to Bowes, Sept. 25-Oct. 5. MSS. Ibid.*

they must provide for their safety and not depend on England, in the hope that the message would reach them in time to prevent them from committing themselves. They had been over sanguine and had gone far; not only Gowry, Angus, and Mar, but Glamys and the Earl of Rothes, had been in consultation. Angus had laid a plot to carry off James when hunting. Rothes, though unwilling 'to be an executor in the action,' had consented to join afterwards. The rest were more seriously compromised. Glamys and Mar fled to Ireland, and lay concealed at Knockfergus. Gowry and Angus imagining, as it proved untruly, that they had not been discovered, remained at home, waiting till circumstances again compelled Elizabeth to espouse their cause.[1]

Meanwhile another overture of no less consequence had been made to Elizabeth from France. Mendoza had said that she meditated rekindling the civil war there as a counterpoise to the change in Scotland. It was at all times an easy process, but if the war would kindle without her assistance, she naturally preferred to be a spectator. The French King, lying between the two factions of Catholics and Huguenots, was neither able nor particularly anxious to keep the peace between them; and the King of Navarre and the Duke of Guise raised armies, occupied towns, and enforced or suppressed the edicts of toleration where each happened to be strongest. As Alençon's health failed, and the accession of the house of Bourbon to the Crown became more probable, the bitterness between them became naturally aggravated. The Duke of Guise, to spare France from being the battle-field of the rival creeds, became more impatient every day to be moving, knowing that to overthrow Protestantism in England and Scotland

---
[1] Bowes to Walsingham, Dec. 19—Jan. 1.—MSS. Scotland.

was to overthrow it everywhere. The King of Navarre was equally aware that the liberator of Mary Stuart and the conqueror of England would be a rival, whose power and popularity it would be idle for him to attempt to resist.

In September, therefore, while Walsingham was in Scotland, Navarre sent his secretary, M. Ségur, to London, to lay before the Queen once more the scheme for a Protestant alliance which waited only for her consent to organise itself. M. Ségur pointed out to her, what her own ministers were weary of repeating, that the Protestants in France and the Low Countries had so far saved England from a joint invasion by the Catholic powers. The Prince of Orange and the King of Navarre had been fighting her battle as well as their own, and the assistance which they had received from her had so far been almost nothing. She imagined that she had done wonders for them. In the last thirteen years, her solitary contribution to the Huguenot cause had been a loan of sixty thousand crowns, for which the King had given her jewels of five times the value as a security. He hoped that now, with the Low Countries almost at the last gasp and the Catholics everywhere recovering the ascendancy, she would see her way to a more liberal co-operation with those who were her best if not her only friends. Nothing, he was convinced, but inability would hold her back at such a time. If it could not be, M. Ségur was instructed to request the restoration of the jewels on payment of the sum for which they were pledged.[1]

Some intention of encouraging Navarre may have passed over her mind among her shifts of purpose; but, as the reader has seen, she had fallen off like a

[1] Memorial of M. Ségur, 1583.—MSS. France.

vessel unable to contend against the wind. Her thoughts were once more of compromise, and Captain Bingham was waiting for his final orders to make an end of the commerce of the Hollanders. 'Such,' wrote Walsingham on his return from Scotland, 'as are at 'Court for the King of Navarre, to solicit an association 'for the common defence of religion, will be dismissed 'I doubt with no very good satisfaction, and yet was 'there never more cause to embrace such a motion than 'now.'[1] Dismissed they were. Slight as was the goodwill with which struggling Protestantism was regarded by Elizabeth, the Huguenots had earned her special disfavour by turning upon her at the occupation of Havre. She had assisted Alençon when Alençon was their leader, but rather for his sake than for theirs. The King of Navarre, as Ségur said, had been one of the supports on which her throne had rested, but she recognised her obligations but lightly. She was not contented with rejecting his suit. She declined to restore his securities. Acquisitiveness of precious stones was a kind of madness with her. She had already collected (and there is no sign that she had parted with them) the Crown jewels of three countries—of Scotland, which had been sold by Murray; of Burgundy, which had been pledged by the States; of the house of Braganza, which she had manœuvred out of Don Antonio. The Navarre diamonds were a brilliant addition. The rights of the case cannot be decided, since there is but Ségur's statement on one side and the Queen's contradiction on the other. It is only certain that Burghley was in favour of the King of Navarre and against his mistress.[2] Either she credited the King

---

[1] Walsingham to Bowes, Sept. 25-Oct. 5.—*MSS. Scotland.*

[2] 'J'ai esté bien adverti qu'il n'a tenue à vous que la Rayne n'ait rendue au Roi de Navarre ses bagues.'—*Ségur to Burghley*, Oct. 9-19. *MSS. France.*

with part of the money which she had advanced to Alençon or she calculated interest against him by tables of her own, as she had done against the States. Ségur at any rate insisted that she had lent his master but sixty thousand crowns. Elizabeth said that he owed her three hundred thousand. Ségur demanded either that the diamonds should be given up to him or that they should be valued and that she should let his master have the surplus. Elizabeth contended that there was no surplus, that the diamonds were hers, and that she would keep them.[1] The friendship of the King of Navarre, as M. Ségur well said to Burghley, was of more importance to her than a thousand diamonds; at least, he said, she ought to be contented with her lawful debt without extorting five times the amount of it. He left England in supreme indignation, and before long the Queen found reason to reconsider the wisdom of what she was doing. A letter of extravagant flattery from the King of Navarre to her in the following December, shows that, as far as he was concerned, she had repented of her sharp practice.[2]

Guise meanwhile, himself chafing with eagerness, was reproached day by day for his inaction by letters from the Queen of Scots, and vexed with the fretful pleadings of the Jesuits and refugees. 'Hours,' wrote de Tassis, 'appear like years to those poor afflicted crea-

---

[1] 'Au lieu de cela sa Ma^{té} se laisse persuader qu'elles sont engagées pour deux cent cinquante ou trois cent mille escus, et le Roy de Navarre croit qu'elles ne sont tenues que pour cinquante ou soixante mille. Voila pourquoy j'escri à sa Ma^{té} à ce qu'il luy plaise faire averer pour combien elles sont engagées, à fin que le sachant j'en donne avis au Roy de Navarre, qui trouvera moyens de les desengager; ou si la Reyne les veut retenir, je la supplie les vouloir faire priser et m'en vouloir faire delivrer le surplus de la juste valeur desdictes bagues que le Roy de Navarre entend estre employé comme le reste qu'il a entre ses mains pour la conservation de l'Eglise de Dieu.'— *Ségur to Burghley*, Oct. 9-19. *MSS. France.*

[2] The King of Navarre to Elizabeth, Dec. 1583.—*MSS. Ibid.*

'tures, pining as they are for deliverance.'[1] Nothing could be done without the Spanish ships, and no Spanish ships appeared. Instead of them came letters preaching patience, and insisting on elaborate preparation as a condition of success. The days wore away. October passed, and with the broken weather the season for action passed also. Philip promised everything in the spring, but the Pope had now grown suspicious. He was still ready to issue Bulls, make Allen Nuncio, and give his blessing to assassins. He was less liberal about money, and contracted miserably the extent of his contributions. The Duke of Guise, weary of his dilatory allies, turned his thoughts once more to Scotland, and had resolved to use the fishing boats of Normandy, and make a sudden descent on the coast of Fife. But his English friends again interposed. They represented to him that a French army invading from Scotland would irritate the national sensibilities, and that the patriotism of the Catholics would prove stronger than their creed. Unwillingly the Duke consented to wait till the spring. Too many persons had been taken into confidence under the impression that the invasion would be immediate, and the English, as experience had proved, were ill keepers of dangerous secrets.

Walsingham had apostate priests in his service, who had saved themselves from the Tower rack by selling their souls. Some of them were in the seminary at Rheims, some were still prisoners in English dungeons, sharing the confidence of their comrades by seemingly partaking of their sufferings. Others were flitting in the usual disguises about country houses saying mass, hearing confessions, and all on the watch for information; and a number of curious notes from unknown hands,

---
[1] De Tassis to Philip, Nov. 5-15.—TEULET, vol. v.

written or signed in cipher, survive as evidence of the
hundred eyes with which Elizabeth's secretary was peering into the secrets of the enemy. It was not for nothing that de Tassis and Guise had recommended haste.
So furnished, and with such instruments, it was scarcely
possible that a secret of so much magnitude could for
many months escape Walsingham's knowledge.

Among the Catholics themselves, too, there were differences of opinion, which were indicated rather than
openly expressed in the conference of the conspirators at
Paris. Some were for James, some for Mary; some had
looked to Henry III. and Alençon; some considered the
Valois King to have inherited a poison from the English
King after whom he was named, and 'to have been appointed of God to be a scourge to religion in other
'countries as King Henry VIII. had been in England.'
Allen, Parsons, and the Jesuits were intensely Spanish,
while still more curiously the English layman's contempt
of the clergy survived in the Catholic camp. Charles
Paget and Thomas Throgmorton had set themselves to
thwart and contradict Parsons, 'liking not that gentlemen
'should be directed by priests.'[1] The longer the invasion was postponed the more these divisions widened, and
with them grew also the peril of discovery. Towards the
end of 1583 an account of the plot was sent in to Walsingham, so accurate that it must have been furnished
by some one who knew every part of it. The King of
Scots, some informant said, was secretly practising with
the Duke of Guise and the Jesuits for the invasion of
England; whether the descent would be first in England or in Scotland was uncertain, but he gave in
a catalogue of the English confederates, and the names

---

[1] Miscellaneous notes in 1582-1583, scattered through the Domestic MSS. of those years, and through the collection referring to the Queen of Scots.

of the Earls of Cumberland, Rutland, Northumberland, Arundel, and the Pagets, agree accurately with the lists of de Tassis. He mentioned Charles Paget's coming to England, as well as his interview with the Earl of Northumberland.[1]

A little after a warning came that Lord Morley was about to leave England, to be out of harm's way in some expected convulsion.[2] Lord Morley went without permission asked or given, and so far confirmed the story; and one more, Sir Edward Stafford, who had succeeded Cobham as Ambassador at Paris, heard a rumour there that England was to be invaded through Scotland, and that the dockyard and ships at Chatham would be set on fire at the same time.[3]

Reports of this kind, however, were so frequent that on Elizabeth they had ceased to produce much effect. She was personally fearless even to callousness. Disaffected English gentlemen had been leaving the realm for many years past, and the Queen had encouraged them by refusing to let the Act of Parliament be put in force, and by allowing them to draw the rents of their estates. Even Sir Francis Englefield, the most restlessly mischievous of all the refugees, had lived in luxury at Brussels or Madrid for twenty-five years on the income of his English property. Those who went abroad merely in search of priests and masses were in no danger of molestation, and all were considered innocent of further ill intentions till they were proved to be guilty. Lord Morley wrote to say that he had gone to join his mother, and his excuse was accepted. Not much else of a positive kind had transpired which could be definitely noticed. Orders were given indeed for a

---

[1] MS. endorsed 'Extracts from B.'s letters,' Aug. and Sept. 1583.—*MSS. Mary Queen of Scots.*
[2] *Ibid.*
[3] Stafford to Walsingham, Oct. 27-Nov. 6.—*MSS. France.*

more extensive and frequent training of the militia, but the militia was a double-edged weapon, on which the conspirators were calculating. Many a magistrate who would call out men for the defence of the realm was expected by the Jesuits to carry them over to the camp of the invader.

At the beginning of October one of the half-dozen plots exploded, which have been already alluded to, for the murder of the Queen. The attempt of Jaureguy, which had so nearly succeeded, had quickened the imagination and spurred the ardour of the would-be regicides. While Guise lingered, one blow boldly struck for Holy Church would place Mary Stuart on the throne; and the carcase of the Jezebel cast, as she had deserved, to the dogs, the faith of Christ would be reinstated in its old supremacy. So for ever sang the Jesuits, and many a youth was found to listen wistfully, and dream of writing his name among the chivalry of heaven by one brave shot or dagger stroke.

The Ardens of Park Hall, in Warwickshire, were among those who were waiting for the good time which was so long in coming. They kept a priest, of course —his name was Hall—who lived with them disguised as a gardener, and was an eloquent preacher of this kind of wickedness. Among his most attentive hearers was the son-in-law of the house, a certain John Somerville, who had married an Arden, and resided in his father-in-law's family. This young gentleman had a friend at Coventry, who had seen the Queen of Scots when she was brought thither by Lord Huntingdon in 1569, had done her a service there, and had been rewarded by a couple of gold buttons, which he wore ostentatiously in his doublet. The buttons excited Somerville's emulation.[1] The priest

---

[1] Examination of Somerville in the Tower, Oct. 6-16, 1583.—*MSS. Domestic.*

fed him with the pamphlets of Allen and Parsons and Sanders, till he had come to look on Elizabeth as the spawn of a devil and a witch.¹ He began to talk of killing her at old Arden's table, and Arden said nothing to forbid him. Then he took his friends into confidence; he told them he was going to London 'to shoot the 'Queen with his dagg, and he hoped to see her head set 'upon a pole, for she was a serpent and a viper.'²

Though Guise's emissary had failed, there was no real difficulty. The only requisite was courage. Never was Princess more easy of access than Elizabeth, or more entirely regardless of the dangers to which she knew that she was exposed. Nor was escape, though unlikely, at all impossible. There was a danger, of course, of being killed upon the spot, but the Royal Household was full of friends of the Queen of Scots, who might try to please her by saving her champion. Half the Babington conspirators were connected with the Palace. Even Hatton—the spoilt and petted Hatton—though not false to his mistress, had a second loyalty for the lady who was likely to succeed her, and had sent Mary Stuart word that on the instant of Elizabeth's death he would go down to Sheffield with the guard and take charge of her person.³ Somerville had studied Jaureguy's exploit, and notwithstanding his fate, imitated him in his preparations. He too assumed an Agnus Dei for an amulet,

---

¹ 'He admits that he was moved to that wicked resolution touching her Majesty, being moved to hatred of her by certain speeches of one Hall, a priest, which touched her Majesty, and also by certain English books, containing exhortations to that wicked enterprise.'—*Somerville's Confession*, Oct. 31–Nov. 10. *MSS. Domestic.*

² Examination of R. Cross, Thomas Sanders and others, before John Doyley of Merton, Oct. 1583.—*MSS. Ibid.*

³ 'Hatton luy a faict divers bons offices, luy offrant par la Contesse de Shrewsbury que la Reyne d'Angleterre venant à deceder, il seroit prest de venir trouver la Reyne d'Escosse avec la garde.'—*MS. Endorsed 'Nau's private notes of reminiscences,'* Nov. 1584. *MSS.* MARY QUEEN OF SCOTS.

and confessed and received the sacrament from Father
Hall before setting out on his journey;[1] but he was a
loose-tongued blockhead, and betrayed himself on the
road by idle speeches. Some one by whom he was over-
heard sent notice to the Council. He was intercepted
and carried up to the Tower, where the rack, or the
threat of it, made short work with him. He was craven,
and made a full confession. He denounced his father-
in-law as his accomplice, and the priest as the instigator
of his crime. They were all three tried, found guilty, and
sentenced to be executed. Somerville strangled himself
in his cell; Arden was hanged at Tyburn, and his head
and Somerville's were set on London Bridge beside the
skull of the Earl of Desmond. The priest was spared,
having paid, it is easy to see, the only price by which he
could have saved himself, and undertaken to be a spy.

The affair had been of spontaneous growth, uncon-
nected with the main conspiracy. Nothing had come
out which connected it with ulterior designs, and de
Tassis, when he heard of the story, flattered himself
that the Queen was on the wrong scent, and that the
principal secret was still safe. He was congratulating
himself too soon. Accident, immediately after Somerville's death, revealed the whole mystery.

The Cheshire Throgmortons were among the stoutest
partisans of Mary Stuart in England. Sir Nicholas, a
politician chiefly, had saved her life at Lochleven, and
as long as he lived had defended her and her title. His
brother, Sir John, being required to take an oath after
the coming in of the Jesuits, and being unable to comply,
had forfeited an office which he held in Cheshire, and
had thereupon become malcontent with the rest of his

---

[1] MS. endorsed, 'Mr. Wilkes touching the cause of Somerville,' Nov. 7-17.—*MSS. Domestic.*

family. Sir John's second son, Thomas, was with Charles Paget at Paris, and, as has been seen, had come over with him into Sussex in September. Francis, the eldest, had also spent a year or two on the Continent, and had been, among other places, at Madrid, where he had discussed the invasion of England with Englefield. His father, to whom he wrote, 'seeing no probability of 'success, had dissuaded him from further meddling.' On his way home he had met Morgan in Paris, who, seeing that he was of the right metal, had admitted him to share the honours and the dangers of the great conspiracy. He had a house in London at Paul's Wharf, to which he returned, and became the medium through which Morgan communicated with the Queen of Scots, and the Queen of Scots with Mendoza. The secret police observed him frequently leaving the Spanish Ambassador's house. He was watched. Other suspicious circumstances were noted, and an order was issued to seize his person and search his rooms. When the constables entered he was in the act of ciphering a letter to Mary Stuart. He darted up a staircase, destroying the paper on his way. He had time to entrust a casket of compromising letters to a maid-servant, who carried them to Mendoza. But a list was found of the Catholic English confederates, plans of harbours sketched by Charles Paget, and described as suitable for the landing of a foreign force, treatises in defence of the Queen of Scots' title, and 'six or seven infamous libels against 'her Majesty, printed beyond seas.' With these he was taken to the Tower, and the Council prepared to examine him.

This time they had struck the true trail, and the party in Paris were in dismay.[1] Throgmorton found

---

[1] De Tassis to Philip, Dec. 12-22.—TEULET, vol. v.

time before he was carried off to cipher a few hasty words on the back of a playing card and to send them with the casket to Mendoza. He said that he had denied all knowledge of the papers, and had explained that they must have been left in his house by some one who desired to injure him. He bade the ambassador have no fear for his constancy; he promised to die a thousand deaths before a word should be wrung from his lips.[1] But the rack, as Mendoza well knew, was a terrible persuader. He thought it not unlikely that Guise, on the news of the arrest, would hesitate no longer, and either go at once to Scotland or fling himself desperately into Sussex. He sent to entreat him to pause, but he doubted whether Guise would listen to him, and he wrote to the Queen of Scots, bidding her keep up her courage, and above all not to let distress make her ill, as if her friends moved her life would be in danger, and she would need all her energies.[2]

There was still a hope that Throgmorton might remain firm. But his fortitude was not equal to the trial. Interrogated in the gloomy cell which had rung with the screams of the Jesuits, the horrid instrument at his side, with the mute executioners standing ready to strain his limbs out of their sockets, his imagination was appalled, his senses refused to do their work. He equivocated, varied in his story, contradicted himself in every succeeding sentence. Pardon was promised him if he would make a free confession. He still held out, but he could not conceal that he had much to tell, and the times did not permit humanity to traitors to

---

[1] Mendoza to Philip, Nov. 16-26.—*MSS. Simancas.*

[2] 'Yo he escrito á la señora presa el suceso, animandola no le de pena que cause daño en su salud, negocio que es de temer por el peligro que correra su vida si se vienen aclarar de todo punto los que platican en Francia.'—*Mendoza al Rey,* 16-26 de Noviembre. *MSS. Simancas.*

imperil the safety of the realm. The Queen gave the necessary authority to proceed with 'the pains.' 'Her 'Majesty thought it agreeable with good policy and 'the safety of her person and seat, to commit him to 'the hands of her learned Council, to assay by torture 'to draw the truth from him.' Again he was offered pardon: again he refused, and he was handed over 'to 'such as were usually appointed in the Tower to handle 'the rack.'[1]

His honour struggled with his agony. 'On the first 'racking he confessed nothing;' but he could not encounter a second trial. When he was laid again upon the frame, 'before he was strained to any purpose, he 'yielded to confess everything that he knew.'[2] Sitting in wretchedness beside the horrid engine, the November light faintly streaming down the tunnelled windows into the dungeon beneath the armoury, he broke his pledged word, and broke his heart along with it. The accuracy of his narrative can be tested by the letters of de Tassis and Mendoza, and a comparison between them proves, if not the lawfulness, yet the tremendous efficiency of the method by which Elizabeth's statesmen baffled the conspiracies of the Catholics. All was revealed: the spot where Guise or the Duc de Mayenne was to land; the force that was coming over; the names of the noblemen and others whose assistance had been promised. Then came the past history of the plot, the correspondence between the Jesuits, the Pope, the King of Spain, the Queen of Scots and the two Spanish Ambassadors; then Charles Paget's visit, the particulars of which he knew from his brother, who had come up secretly to London at the time, and had brought with

---

[1] Throgmorton's treason. Official narrative, June 1584.—MSS. Do- [2] Ibid.

him the plans of the harbours. He acknowledged the
sending the casket to Mendoza. It was past recovery,
but the general contents of it were admitted to be
traitorous. He confessed that Mary Stuart had been
consulted upon every detail: he described the plans
which had been formed in England for her rescue as
soon as the invaders should have landed: he told how
Mendoza was to communicate ' with sundry recusants,
' being in the commission of the peace, to raise the Catho-
' lics when the Duke of Guise should arrive, under pre-
' text of her Majesty's levy, afterwards to use them
' against her Majesty.'[1] Then at last, when all was
out, and there was nothing more to reveal, he drew
himself up upon his seat and sobbed in misery, ' Now
' I have disclosed the secrets of her who was the dearest
' Queen to me in the world, whom I thought no tor-
' ment could have drawn me so much to have preju-
' diced. I have broken faith to her, and I care not if
' I were hanged. Che a perso la fede a perso l' honore.'[2]

Hanged the poor wretch naturally was: a free confession would have secured him a life of shame. A confession on the rack did but sentence him to the death
which he desired, and left him so much of the honour
which he thought that he had lost, as was equivalent to
the torture which he had borne. He was detained a
few months till his evidence could be of no more service. He was then tried, and executed, as usual, at
Tyburn.

Meanwhile he was known to have sunk under the
test, and as an instant effect, there was a flight of
Catholics over the Channel, thick as autumn swallows.
It was a race between the fugitives and the officers of

---

[1] Throgmorton's treason, June, 1584.—*MSS. Domestic.*
[2] *Ibid.*

justice. Suspected persons everywhere were either sent to prison or ordered to keep their houses under surveillance. Mendoza calculated that by the middle of the winter, eleven thousand were under arrest in one form or other. Lord Paget escaped to France, writing, on his way, to Burghley, that he found life unendurable without free enjoyment of the sacraments. The Earls of Arundel and Northumberland, who had arranged the landing place for Guise with Lord Paget's brother, were taken and sent to the Tower. They swore they were innocent; and historians whose business has been to make the Government of Elizabeth odious, insist still that there was no shadow of proof against them. If proof was wanting, it was not from the falsehood of the charges. Two servants of Northumberland were arrested; one of them his secretary. 'If these men 'confess,' Mendoza scornfully said, 'as easily as English 'prisoners generally do, it will go hard with their 'master.'[1]

The revelations of Throgmorton startled Elizabeth at last out of her dream of security. The visions of compromise faded away, and with them her intentions of assisting in the collapse of the miserable Netherlands. She recognised, for a time, that her wrestle with Spain was a mortal one, and that she must win or perish. She had suspended her extravagant orders to seize the ships of the States; if they knew what she had meditated they had remained prudently silent. But they had seen themselves abandoned—had taken counsel with despair, and were preparing to surrender to the

---

[1] 'Tan bien han prendido dos criados del Conde de Northumberland, y el uno su secretario, que si confiesan con la facilidad que lo hacen los demas Ingleses, harán harto á su amo.'—*Don Bernardino al Rey*, 8-18 Enero, 1584. *MSS. Simancas.*

Spaniards. 'They do not even care for religion,' wrote
M. Busenval to Walsingham from Middleburgh, ' so
' they may have their lives in peace. If the Spaniards
' come they will send their ships to receive them.'¹
Three months earlier, the Queen had persisted in
calling them Spanish subjects. Now, excusing her
neglect on the score of their past unthankfulness, she
allowed Walsingham to tell St. Aldegonde that 'Spain
was revengeful;' that no safety was ' to be looked for
' that way,' and that sooner than 'they should come to
an accord with Spain,' she would reconsider the possibility of assisting them.²

Her own danger was still most imminent: any
morning might find Guise upon the coast, and swarms
of French pouring into Kent or Sussex. Stafford
reported from Paris that there had been another consultation at the house of the Nuncio; that Guise was
present, and that the conspirators had separated in high
spirits and full of hope and enthusiasm. The King of
Scots, they were satisfied, was for them: the Earl of
Shrewsbury, they believed, was Catholic at heart, and
would protect Mary Stuart; and very soon they looked
to have ' beau jeu ' in England.³

The English Council was divided in opinion: Walsingham, as usual, was for the straight course—an open
alliance with Orange and the Scotch Protestants. Others
were for making terms with James only. Conditions
were sketched out which James ' would have liked well,
' by reason they were a direct answer and good' to all
his demands. Archibald Douglas, who was in London
in James's interests, was bidden to prepare to go down

---

¹ Nov. 4-14, 1583.—*MSS. Hol-*
land.
² Instructions for Ed. Burnam,
Nov. 19-29.—*MSS. Holland.*
³ Stafford to Walsingham, Jan.
8-18, 1584.—*MSS. France.*

CHAP. XXXI.
1584 January.

to Scotland and tell his master that the Queen was willing to recognise him.[1] 'This resolution continued hot for a 'certain space.' But there came news from Scotland that the Protestant lords were conspiring again, that the country was in confusion; that 'the proudest 'there was ready to make friends with the Queen of 'England; so that she was persuaded that she held the 'balance in her hands, and could smooth over matters 'with fair words,'[2] 'and as usual nothing was done.'

The navy, however, was sent to sea—not now on the unworthy errand intended for it in the autumn, but to lie in three squadrons—in the Downs, in the Isle of Wight, and at Scilly, to guard the coast. 'The strength of 'the realm' was called under arms, and Catholic or malcontent officers were weeded out of the service. The forts and bulwarks were repaired, the arms were looked to, and drilling and training went forward in town and village. A visitation was instituted of the Inns of Court, the legal profession being still constant to precedent and the old faith, and in consequence, a most dangerous stronghold of disloyalty. Conformity in religion was made henceforth a condition of admission to the bar. Commissions were issued in every county to examine suspected magistrates on their allegiance; and if they gave uncertain answers, to remove or imprison them. There were, or were believed to be, still five hundred Jesuits and seminary priests in England. A great many had been seized, and batches had from time to time been executed. The Council ordered that every priest now under arrest in any house or gaol, should be examined on the authority of the Pope;

---

[1] MS. endorsed by Burghley. Scotland.
[2] 'Copy of Archibald Douglas's letter to Scotland,' Jan. 23-Feb. 2.—MSS. Ibid.

and that those who would not swear without reserve to be loyal to the Queen, should be condemned as traitors. 'As many as should be thought requisite 'should suffer death;' others should be banished 'with 'judgment to be hanged if they returned;' others 'should be straitly imprisoned' where they could infest no one with their doctrines; 'while the charge of their 'diet' was to be furnished out of the forfeitures of the recusants.[1]

Under these instructions, seven priests—Oxford converts most of them—of the same race as Campian, were immediately executed; five at Tyburn and two at York. Each martyr's death was counted a victory of the faith; and these triumphs, of which the Jesuits could not be deprived, were the more welcome as their secular prospects were again clouded. In the training of these happy or unhappy youths, Allen had been thoroughly successful. He had desired to compel Elizabeth into persecution, and he had provided willing victims who had forced her to sacrifice them. They perished as he hoped and intended, and their heroic deaths were now trumpeted over Europe with all the hideous details to stir rage and hatred against the Antichrist of England. The reproach was felt, felt the more keenly as Elizabeth had tried so hard to avoid giving occasion for it. So loud was the clamour, and so sensitive the Queen, that Burghley took pen to reply to it, and the publication of the libels was the occasion of an elaborate and noble defence of Elizabeth's Government, containing the entire history of her relations with the Catholics, her steady forbearance to retaliate for the Marian persecution, her resolution that at no time and under no

---

[1] Memoranda of resolutions of Council, Dec. 2, 1583. Burghley's hand.— *MSS. Domestic.*

circumstances should any one of her subjects suffer for persevering in the faith of his ancestors. In this spirit she had begun her reign, and in this spirit Lord Burghley said she would have continued, had not the Pope forced a change of policy upon her by making treason a part of his creed. The principle of the administration remained unchanged. He repeated what he had declared many times already, that no Catholic had been or would be punished for his opinions on the Christian mysteries; but, with a just disdain, he refused to recognise the pretence that the Pope could make rebellion a religious duty, or could elevate men into martyrs who had suffered deaths for conspiring against their Sovereign.

Equally decided was the course taken with Don Bernardino de Mendoza. Four times the experiment of a resident Spanish Ambassador in Protestant England, had evidenced the reluctance of the old allies to drift into hostility. Four times the separative tendencies of the creeds had proved too strong for the efforts of statesmanship. The chief obligation which devolved upon the representatives of Spain was to encourage the Catholics to persevere in recusancy, to sustain their spirits, to hold out indefinite prospects to them of better days that were to come; and it was a duty which lay so near conspiracy that the step from one to the other was almost inevitable. The Bishop of Aquila had escaped expulsion only by death. De Silva, a layman and a gentleman, had managed better, but he too had found his position become intolerable. He had seen the Catholic nobility made restless by the presence in the realm of the Queen of Scots. The emissaries of the Pope had been too strong for him. The ferment had gathered under his eyes towards the first insurrection, and de Silva made an excuse to demand his recall to escape a quarrel in which he foresaw that he would be involved. Up to this time, Philip had laboured loyally to prevent the Catholics from embarrassing Elizabeth with insurrection. Don Guerau de Espes represented a different policy. Pope Pius having excommunicated her, though against Philip's wishes, the King was drawn reluctantly into acquiescing in her deposition. Under the advice of the Duke of Feria and the Archbishop of Toledo, he allowed Vitelli to undertake to assassinate her, and directed Alva to invade England. The intention was discovered, the Duke of Norfolk was executed, and Don Guerau, who had been the soul of the conspiracy, was driven out with infamy. Philip, shrinking from war, again acquiesced in the insult, and relapsed into his attitude of expectation. The embassy was suspended, and Spain was represented in England only by a commercial factor, Don Antonio de Guaras. But the same necessity made de Guaras the focus of insurrection. Elizabeth, who always reserved alternatives on which she could fall back in extremity, took de Guaras more than once into her confidence; more than once talked to him about her relations with Philip, and her desire to be on more cordial terms with so old a friend. But the Queen of Scots and the priests drew de Guaras, like his predecessors, into the charmed circle. He too, after a severe and protracted imprisonment, was desired to leave the country and never to return.

War would then have followed but for the great revolt of the Low Countries, which tempted the ambition of France and united the circle of the Provinces against the Spanish Sovereign. The breach with England was indefinitely postponed: a fifth representative, a soldier, a statesman, and a Mendoza, was dispatched to renew the efforts at conciliation. An English Minister was allowed with impunity to insult the Grand Inquisitor at Madrid. The services of the volunteers in Flanders, and the piracies of Drake, were condoned or passed over with a faint complaint. The honour of Spain was trailed in the dirt to prevent Elizabeth from allying herself with the Prince of Orange. It was all in vain. The Jesuits had stirred the fire till the flame could no longer be kept under. Once more a grand combination had grown up for invasion, rebellion, and regicide: once more a Spanish Ambassador was at its heart. Mendoza foresaw what must follow when he heard that Throgmorton had confessed. On the 9th-19th of January, the Queen sent to tell him that the Council were in session at the house of Lord Chancellor Bromley, and had a message of importance to deliver to him. Mendoza replied that when Ministers of State desired to speak with Ambassadors, their usual practice was to repair themselves to the Ambassador's residence. Since the collected Cabinet wished to speak to him, however, he would wait on them and hear what they had to say.

The party which he found assembled consisted of the Chancellor, the Earl of Leicester, Lord Charles Howard, Lord Hunsdon, and Walsingham. Burghley for some cause was absent. They rose as Don Bernardino entered, raised their hats gravely, and withdrew with him into an inner apartment, where they sat down and motioned him also to a chair. Don Bernardino spoke English imperfectly, and Walsingham, as the spokesman for the rest, addressed him in Italian. 'The Queen,' he said, 'regretted that he had given her serious cause to
'be dissatisfied with his conduct. From the time that he
'had come to England to reside, he had troubled the
'quiet of the realm. He had connected himself with
'the Queen of Scots, had written to her, encouraged her

'to rely for support on Spain, and contrived plans for her
'escape. He had fomented the discontent of the
'Catholics. He had corresponded with Charles Paget,
'with the traitor Throgmorton, and with the Earl of
'Northumberland, and had concerted plans with them
'for bringing in the Duke of Guise. His house had
'been the rendezvous of conspirators, Jesuits, seminary
'priests, and other disaffected subjects. It was now
'her Majesty's pleasure that he should leave the country,
'and leave it within fifteen days.'

Mendoza had been careful in his communications. He knew that Francis Throgmorton was the only witness that could be produced against him, and that Throgmorton's confession had been extorted by the rack. He answered boldly that the Council were dreaming. The Queen of Scots was heir presumptive to the Crown. What, he asked, had she to gain by conspiring? or he by conspiring with her? She would but ruin her prospects, forfeit her French dowry, and throw the cost of her maintenance on the King of Spain. Experienced men did not hatch treason with boys like Throgmorton; and with the Earl of Northumberland he swore that he had never exchanged a word.[1] He challenged Walsingham to prove his charges. What had he said, and when, and to whom? How had he planned the Queen of Scots' escape? Her Majesty found fault with him. She should look rather to what she had done herself. She had lent money to the revolted States, and three thousand English under English officers were serving at that moment

---

[1] Telling the truth in this, as he explained to Philip, all his communications with the Earl having passed through Mary Stuart. 'Como es verdad, no he hablado jamas al Conde de Northumberland, por haber procedido siempre en estas materias con gran recato y de manera que no me pudiesen clarificar nada dellas, no habiendo platicado con persona fuera de la de Escocia de particular ninguno, sino fuese escribiendo ella que confidentes suyos me adviriesen dellos.' — *Mendoza al Rey*, 16-16 Enero, 1584. *MSS. Simancas.*

in the Low Countries. She had assisted Don Antonio. She had supported the Duke of Alençon. Again and again and again she had taken possession of treasure belonging to Spain, and had always refused redress. If she wished him to depart he declared that he was ready to go; he had no desire to remain where he was unwelcome; but uncertain whether the Council were in earnest, he said that he must first inform his master, and receive an answer from him.

The Council swiftly convinced him that they were serious. They again rose from their seats while Walsingham said for them that delay could not be allowed. The Ambassador must leave the country at once. He had done ill service to the King of Spain, and he had cause to congratulate himself that her Majesty had not ordered him to be chastised.

The blood of the Mendozas flamed up at the word chastisement. Starting on his feet also, and, as he admitted, bursting with passion, he replied that he would answer for his conduct to his master alone. None else should touch him unless sword in hand. Chastisement was a fool's word. Let the Queen send him his passport, and he would begone. She was quarrelling with her best friend, but being a woman she was acting after her kind. As he had not pleased her as a minister of peace, he would endeavour for the future to satisfy her better in war.[1]

Not feeling quite certain whether Philip would approve of his violence, he said in his report that he had been so angry that he could not control himself. To be sent away thus suddenly was supremely incon-

---

[1] 'Pues no le habia dada satisfaccion siendo ministro de paz, me enforçaria de aqui adelante para que la tuviese de mi en la guerra.' The Ambassador was proud of the vigour of his expression: 'palabra,' he adds, 'que han ramiado ellos entre si despues aca, baptizandola por muy sacudida y preñada.'—*Mendoza al Rey*, 16-26 Enero, 1584. *MSS. Simancas.*

venient. He had swarms of foreigners on his hands,[1] whom he would have to carry away with him. 'He 'could not leave them on the horns of the bull.' The Channel pirates would probably catch him if he attempted to sail for Spain. He must go to France, and he distrusted his reception there. His exchequer was embarrassed, and the expense would ruin him; while so great, he said, was the fury of the people in London, that he was like to be torn in pieces. He was charged publicly in the churches, and even by a Court preacher in the presence of the Council, with having conspired against the Queen's life.[2]

'The insolence of these people,' he wrote to Secretary Idriaquez, 'so exasperates me, that I desire to live only 'to be revenged upon them. I hope in God the time 'will soon come, and that He will give me grace to be 'an instrument in their punishment. I will walk bare'foot over Europe to compass it. His Majesty, I am 'certain, will send them the answer which they have 'deserved.'[3] 'God,' he wrote to Philip himself, 'has 'made your Majesty so great a Prince, that you cannot 'overlook such insolence, though they offer you all the 'world to forgive them.'

He was obliged to go, leaving Northumberland in the Tower, where Arundel, who had been released after his first arrest, speedily rejoined him, the conspiracy dislocated, and the chance of overthrowing Elizabeth by surprise finally gone. He applied for a Queen's ship to carry him across the Channel. He was told

---

[1] Come over probably to take part in the expected rising.

[2] 'Teniendome todos tanta indignacion, que se ha acrecentado mucho mas con la fama que han echado de que me mandan salir por haber tratado de matar á la Reyna, lo cual dixó un ministro en sus predicas en la misma corte adelante de todos estos consejeros.'—*Mendoza al Rey*, 16-26 Enero, 1584. *MSS. Simancas.*

[3] Mendoza á Don Juan de Idriaquez, 16-26 Enero. *MSS. Simancas.*

that such courtesies were for friends, and not for those who had concerted revolutions. He sued no more, but took his leave with Castilian haughtiness. 'Don 'Bernardino de Mendoza,' he said to the officer who brought him the message, 'was not born to revolu-'tionise kingdoms, but to conquer them.'[1]

Unwilling to give the dismissal of the Ambassador a character of abrupt defiance, Elizabeth sent Sir William Wade to Madrid to explain the causes of it. Philip refused to admit Wade to his presence, or to listen to any justification. A second and more pressing application for an audience was equally unsuccessful. The English Ambassador, like Mendoza, was directed to depart, and was told also, 'in dark and doubtful terms,' 'that he was favourably dealt with, and might have 'looked for worse entertainment.' He returned as he went, and the diplomatic relations between Spain and England were at an end.[2]

War sooner or later was now inevitable; but, between the 'leaden foot' of Philip and the Pope's unwillingness to part with money, it was likely to be rather later than sooner. The assassination of Elizabeth alone would certainly precipitate the convulsion. On this, therefore, the eyes of the crew at Paris were fastened with deadly earnestness. As one plot failed another grew in its place, and in their first rage of disappointment they sent over a chosen instrument of villany carefully disciplined for the work, whose history is peculiarly illustrative of the character of the time.

Among the correspondents whose letters from abroad to Burghley and Walsingham are preserved in the

---

[1] 'No podia dexar de decille que Don Bernardino de Mendoza no habia nacido para revolver Reynos, sino por conquistarlos.'—*Mendoza al Rey*, 20-30 Enero. *MSS. Simancas.*
[2] Mission of Sir William Wade, 1583-4.—*MSS. Spain.*

Record Office, one of the most regular was William Parry. He had been educated in the palace, and for many years had held an office about the Queen's person; he had attracted her notice, and was on terms of easy intimacy with her. Being a ruffling scoundrel, he had some discreditable quarrel with a gentleman of the Temple, whom he attempted to run through the body. He was tried, found guilty, and left for execution, but was saved by his mistress's interference. He went abroad in July 1582, with permission to remain till his crime was forgotten; and to recover favour, he proposed to Walsingham to make himself useful, by collecting information, and sending it home to the Council. He had no particular principles. The Court was the most lax of all places in England in its religious observances. The Queen chose that half the household should be Catholics. Every one was left, in consequence, to his own conscience, and Parry had not 'communicated' for twenty years. In this condition he fell an easy victim to the Jesuits. He was secretly 'reconciled' in Paris. From thence he went to Milan, where he 'justified himself' before the Grand Inquisitor. In the warmth of conversion he desired to do something great for the cause which he had espoused. Meditating much on the afflictions of the English Catholics, and pondering how he could deliver them from 'captivity,' he thought for himself of the obvious means, which his knowledge of the Queen and Court would give him special opportunities to execute, and he consulted a Jesuit acquaintance at Venice. The Jesuit commended his devotion, introduced him to the Nuncio as a chosen vessel, and sent word of him to Pope Gregory. He returned in the autumn (1583) to Paris, where, being a Welshman, he fell in with his countryman Thomas

Morgan. The two worthies were not long in understanding each other. The assassination was a constant subject of conversation between them; but Parry, professing conscientious scruples, desired the opinion of certain learned divines. If his doubts could be resolved, he promised to undertake the business. He was aware already of the opinion of the Jesuits, but accident brought him across a priest of the old school; and there were clergy still with antiquated notions, to whom murder was still a crime, and regicide was sacrilege. This man strongly condemned what Allen as warmly commended, and, distracted between his counsellors, he agreed at last to refer the question to the Vatican. If the Pope would sanction his purpose, and give him absolution for it beforehand, he promised to be satisfied. Morgan took him to the Nuncio at Paris. The Nuncio undertook to lay the case before his Holiness, and meanwhile to remember him in his prayers.

Other influences, however, were brought to bear upon him—persuasion, possibly—if he was the person alluded to by de Tassis—from the Duke of Guise. Before an answer came from Rome, he had started for England, resolute, as he professed, for the deed, and due preparation was made on the Scotch border and elsewhere to take advantage of the confusion when the Queen should be known to be dead. He landed at Rye. He assured himself of access to Elizabeth's person by writing word to her that he had brought information of consequence to communicate. It was at the moment of the discovery of the plot. He knew that she would send for him to London, and he had made up his mind that she should not escape his hands alive.

The age was a theological one, and crimes were curiously balanced. There was a peculiar baseness in taking advantage of the Queen's unsuspicious nature, and of her regard for and kindness to himself. But dishonour was not among the offences which were graduated by the canon law, and the special facilities which he possessed appeared rather indications of Providence that he was elected to do service to the Church. But murder in itself was one of the seven mortal sins. He was never weary of talking to priests about it. Their opinions differed, and to mistake might be damnation. An English confessor once more shook his resolution. He saw Elizabeth alone. He came to her with a purpose half overthrown. He left her, if not penitent, yet unwilling, till his scruples could be removed, to proceed further, and he wrote to Morgan to tell him so.[1]

---

[1] The letter was found among Morgan's papers at Paris, and is beyond doubt in Parry's hand.

'London, Feb. 24, 1583-4.
'Good Mr. Morgan,

'I do most heartily thank you for your friendly letter of the 6th, and am glad that by your and my dear friend Mr. Charles Paget's example I may so safely send to you. I have not been careless of the debt undertaken, but being meanly satisfied before my departure from Paris, I laboured by conference with a singular man* on this side to be fully informed what might be done with conscience in that case for the common good. I was very learnedly and substantially in reason, policy, and divinity overruled, and assured it ought not to fall into the thought of a good Christian. The difficulties besides are many, and in this vigilant time full of despair. The service you know did never pass your hand and mine, and may therefore with more ease and less offence be concealed and suppressed. I am out of doubt that the divine with whom I had conference in Paris by your appointment is secret and honest. If you will travail to satisfy the greatest and to retain my better sort of friends in good opinion of me, I shall hold it for a singular pleasure, and if you can use me in any other possible service on this side for you and yours, be bold and assured for me. I have not been careless of the Lord Paget and his brother. Neither do I yet, notwithstanding the proclamation, see any great cause why they should be hasty or overforward in seeking or embracing foreign entertainment. I find the Queen very calm, and heard that she termed some cormorants for their greediness in seeking men's livings. Mr. Charles Arundel is condemned to have dealt unthankfully with the Queen, unkindly with his friends, and unadvisedly with himself. I write thus much of them to you to the intent you may make them privy to it, for I know you do honour and love them all.

'Read and burn.   W. PARRY.'

* This was probably William Crichton.   See Holinshed, vol. iv. p. 571.

To gain her confidence, and to explain his coming over, he had the audacity to tell her that overtures had been made to him to kill her, concealing, indeed, nothing of the story but his own assent. According to his own story, he wished to frighten her into a change of policy.[1]

'The Queen,' he says, 'took it doubtfully.' She told him that no Catholic who would live as a loyal subject 'should be troubled either for religion or for the 'supremacy;' but her manner was cold and stern, and 'he departed with fear.' Soon after this the answer came from the Vatican. The Cardinal of Como wrote in the name of the Pope to bid him at once and for ever lay aside his needless scruples. The father of Christendom sent his benediction, with indulgences and remission of sins for the faithful son who would do the Church so great a service, and promised not only favour in heaven, but substantial acknowledgments upon earth.[2] Thus encouraged, Parry resumed his half-abandoned purpose. He was allowed to remain at the Court. He saw the Queen continually, and again and

---

The 'greatest' who was to be satisfied was either Guise or, more likely, the Queen of Scots. Philip evidently knew what was intended, and so did other Spanish statesmen. Writing to Count Olivarez of the discovery of the general conspiracy, he adds, 'Siento mucho lo que padescen, y quiera Dios no se acabe de descubrir lo principal.'—*El Rey al Conde de Olivares*, 10 Hebrero. *MSS. Simancas.*

[1] All these circumstances, and Parry's whole history, were related by himself on his trial.—*State Trials,* vol. i.

[2] 'La Santità di N. S. ha veduto le lettere di V. S. con la fede inclusa, e non può se non laudare la buona disposizione e risolutione che scrive di tenere verso il servitio e beneficio publico, nel che la Santità sua l'esorta di perseverare con fama riuscire li effetti che V. S. promette; et acciochè tanto maggiormente V. S. sia ajutata da quel buon spirito che l' ha mosso, le concede sua Benedittione, plenaria Indulgenza e Remissione di tutti li peccati secondo che V. S. ha chiesto, assicurandosi che oltre il merito che n' haverà in cielo, vuole anco sua Santità constituirsi debitore a riconoscere li meriti di V. S in ogni miglior modo che potrà, &c.—Di Roma, a 30 di Gennaro, 1584.'—*Trial of William Parry, State Trials,* vol. i.

again endeavoured to screw his courage to the striking point; but he was made of the wrong material, and he found or made excuses for delay. Once, when he was about to stab her, he was appalled by her likeness to Henry VIII. At last he decided that he would not do it till other means of working upon her had been tried and failed; he would obtain a seat in the next Parliament, and appeal in behalf of the Catholics to the representatives of his country.[1]

While 'the principal matter' was thus halting, the conspirators abroad were in no good humour with each other. Every post from England brought news of arrests and imprisonments of their friends in England. The leaders, on whose assistance they had calculated, were disarmed and confined. Guise and the Pope blamed Philip. Philip defended his caution by appealing to the evident fact that the English Catholics were weaker than they had pretended. He had himself collected ships and troops. He had even thought of accompanying the expedition in person, to secure the benefit of the expected conquest.[2] He described himself as being as much mortified as Guise, and as anxious to find means of repairing his disappointment. He felt but too sure that after the expulsion of Mendoza, Elizabeth would ally herself in earnest with the Netherlands. But if he had sent the handful of men which Guise had asked for, the Catholics, he said, who were now in prison, would all have been in their graves.[3]

His fears about the Netherlands seemed likely to be realised. St. Aldegonde, in reply to the message sent by Walsingham in November, had answered that the

---

[1] Parry's Confession.—*State Trials*, vol. i.
[2] Roger Bodenham to Burghley from Seville, May 8-18.—*MSS. Spain.*
[3] Philip to Olivares, Jan. 31-Feb. 10, 1584.—*MSS. Simancas.*

States were at the last extremity. They could not hold out beyond the following summer without help, and if England continued to hold aloof, there were but two alternatives before them. If the whole of the States, including Holland and Zealand, would consent to be annexed to France, the French, notwithstanding the accident at Antwerp, were still ready to risk a war for the acquisition; otherwise necessity was a law of iron, and they must submit to Spain.[1]

It was hard to say which of these two results would be most unwelcome in England. It was a received political axiom that the acquisition of the Provinces by France would be fatal to English independence, while for Spain to recover the seaboard of Zealand, with a war impending, was equally formidable. The States, St. Aldegonde said, were ready to contribute 60,000 crowns a month if England would add 30,000. Fifteen thousand men could then be kept in the field, or maintained in garrison, and would suffice to hold Parma at bay for ever.[2] The sum was not large in itself, but the expenses of war were usually undercalculated, and thousands often grew to tens of thousands. Not wholly trusting St. Aldegonde, Elizabeth sent over a favourite of her own, Sir Edward Dyer, to learn the real condition to which the States were reduced. Dyer reported that 'the cause was panting, and all but dead.' It was not yet utterly desperate, but the moments were running away. Sir William Wade returned from Spain while the Queen was hesitating, with news that Philip would not see him, and she allowed Dyer to tell the Prince of Orange that her fleet should unite at once with that of Holland to hold the seas against Spain, and that she

[1] St. Aldegonde to Walsingham, December 1583.—*MSS. Holland.*
[2] Roger Williams to Walsingham, Jan. 26-Feb. 5.—*MSS. Holland.*

would listen to proposals for the joint defence of the two countries.[1]

Many a shift of purpose lay yet between resolution and performance; but Orange, sanguine always, believed that his long-cherished hopes were at last about to be realised. A hearty alliance with England, a bold defiance of Pope, Spain, and devil, had been his dream for fifteen years. France might then be sent to the winds. He 'blessed God that He had opened the eyes of 'the Queen.' He undertook to keep twenty good ships in the Channel, besides defending his own waters. Holland, Zealand, and Utrecht, he said, now that their spirits were revived, would alone maintain 12,000 men,[2] and if her Majesty would accept them for her subjects, were still eager to become part of the English Empire. The Queen, perhaps, fancied that she was in earnest. Perhaps she had other thoughts, which she did not like to acknowledge. She retained her coolness, at any rate, and chose to stand prepared for all contingencies. She dispatched Secretary Davison to say that she compassionated the Prince's condition, and was anxious to help him; but she had 'not forgotten the Protestants in France, who, 'after embroiling her in war, made their own peace, 'and then turned against her.' 'Her Majesty had been 'cooled towards them'—towards the Huguenots, and towards all others in the same position 'from that time 'forth.' If she went to war for their sakes—and it pleased her to pretend that her motive was purely disinterested —she said 'she must have assurance.' She could not

---

[1] 'Sa Mᵗᵉ trouve necessaire pour obvier aux forces de mer du Roy d'Espagne, joindre forces avec celles de ces pays semblablement par mer.

'Sa Maᵗᵉ desire avoir l'advis de Son Excellence à ce qui est le plus expedient de faire proceder en mutuelle defense.'—*Articles presented to the Prince of Orange by Mr. Dyer*, March 3-13. *MSS. Holland*.

[2] Answer of the Prince of Orange. *Ibid.*

accept the States as subjects, but she was willing to be their protectress on condition that Flushing, Brill, and Enchusen were made over to her to be occupied by English garrisons.[1]

A few months before, the Queen of England was on the edge of becoming an open enemy. These three towns were the keys of the States' independence, and it was possible, though blasphemy to dream of it, that she might be nursing some secret purpose of making terms with Philip for herself by betraying them. The negotiation not unnaturally 'cooled a little.'

It was a peculiarity of Elizabeth that no matter how great her danger, or how obvious her interest in a straightforward and open course of action, she exhibited always the same obliquities. She could not write an English sentence without the most intricate involutions. Like animals which move only sideways, she advanced, when she advanced at all, in zigzag lines, with her eyes everywhere except directly in her front. She never adopted a policy, she never ventured on an action, where her retreat was not secured, or where she had not some unexpected and crooked reason to allege in its defence. To become an ally of the revolted States on the ground of a common religion, was to furnish her own Catholic subjects with a justification of a revolt against herself; and to call on Parliament to grant subsidies for a war in a cause which half England abhorred, might provoke the Catholics' patience beyond anything which she had hitherto ventured. She intended, if she again moved for the States, to maintain her old position. The safety of England required that they should not become French. She required the towns as a guarantee for the repayment

---

[1] Davison to Walsingham, April 3-13. Burnam to Davison, April 21-May 1.—*MSS. Holland.*

of her expenses, and to use them also for such further purposes as the turn of events might make necessary.

It was a dangerous manœuvre, for meanwhile 'the 'grass was growing.' The circle of Brabant which held out against Parma was narrowing day by day. Ghent had submitted, Brussels had submitted. Of all the Belgian provinces the narrow strip of coast from Ostend to the Scheldt alone remained besides Antwerp. Antwerp was now threatened. There was a large peace party in Holland, which, if Antwerp fell and Parma gained a footing among the Islands, would immediately make itself felt. 'A general revolt' was not impossible while Elizabeth was haggling; and as 'a long 'and severe war,' in the opinion of all intelligent people, was hanging inevitably over England, the narrowest prudence recommended her to strike in before the States were further weakened and disheartened.[1]

Nor was this her only or her most pressing peril. The irony of fate had flung on Elizabeth, who disdained the name of Protestant, the task of defending the Reformation in the countries where Protestantism was most pronounced. The prim, self-satisfied Anglo-Catholic prided himself on the gulf of separation which divided him from the Calvinist. The Anglo-Catholic had his Apostolic succession, his episcopate, and his sacraments. He fasted twice in the week, he gave tithes of all that he possessed. He was not as Knox or Beza, and was clamorous in his demand to be distinguished from them. He was a thing

---

[1] 'Si les malcontents ou les Espagnols, par subtilité, ou par gaigner aulcuns Seigneurs ou Capitaine, prennent deux ou trois villes, soit en Holland ou Zealand, il est à craindre ainsy que l'on cognoit bien ceux de Holland, non pas les Seigneurs mais le comun peuple, qu'ils feront sortir le Prince d'Orange hors du Pays, et accorderont avec le Roy d'Espaigne, car ils ne vouldront point combattre comme ils ont faict cy-devant.'—*MS. endorsed by Burghley,* 'Advice to make an army in Brabant, May 1584.' *MSS. Holland.*

of vapour, but he depended for his existence on the Protestantism which he despised. Elizabeth had been taught already, and the lesson was to be repeated till it was learnt, that the cause of the Reformation in Scotland was identical with her own cause. If she was to escape herself from being dethroned, it was necessary for her to uphold the Assembly against King, Bishop, or Jesuit, as the Assembly had upheld her.

Notwithstanding the completeness of his success, and the defiant tone which he had assumed, the young King was not altogether satisfied. The fixed idea of his life was the English crown. With his mother or without his mother, before, or if not before, then after her, he had fastened his hopes on this one prize, and he meant to have it; and it was with no easy feelings that he had learnt the modification of the first plan of the Duke of Guise, and the substitution of England for Scotland as the point where the invasion was to be made. Under the original arrangement he was to have come forward as the champion of his mother, to have demanded her release, and to have invited the co-operation of his cousin. Carried out thus, he could not have been cheated of the profits of the enterprise. The direct invasion of England was a different matter. His first act on his escape from Gowrie had been to invite Guise over, and no notice had been taken of him. Were Guise and the Spaniards to throw themselves into Sussex or into Northumberland, were a Catholic insurrection to follow, and were Elizabeth to be dethroned, his mother would become Queen; but after the double play in which he had been engaged, he began to fear that his own subsequent succession need not necessarily follow. It was of no great moment that his conversion would be insisted on—James was not a youth who would lose a crown for a confession of faith —but Philip would have the controlling voice; he knew

that Philip did not like him; and a conversion after
the event might not be accepted. In Scotland, also,
it was no less clear that on his mother's elevation he
would have to descend to the position of a subject. He
had broken with Elizabeth; he had refused her pension,
and turned his back upon her minister; yet he did not
wish absolutely to quarrel with her. He wished so to
act that whatever happened, and whichever party was
uppermost, he should himself still be the winner. He
dared not at once declare himself a Catholic, for the
Catholics might fail after all, and then he would be
ruined. He wished to avoid committing himself, and
yet to secure the Catholic support. He was now not
perfectly sure that he wished Guise to come over at
all; but if he came it was all important that he should
come first to Scotland. His position was a very difficult
one. The cunning which he displayed was altogether
beyond his age, and must be attributed to the counsels
of the Earl of Arran.

The arrest and confession of Throgmorton having
disarranged for the moment the plan for invading England, he sent off Seton to Paris to see Guise, and tell him
that Scotland was still at his service; and by Seton's
hands he sent two letters, one to his cousin, and the
other through his cousin to the Pope. To Guise he
wrote that, following his advice, he had now thoroughly
espoused his mother's cause, and had separated himself
from the English connexion. The Queen of England,
he said, desired to revolutionise Scotland, to imprison
him, perhaps to take his life from him, or his honour,
which he valued more. He besought Guise, therefore, to
intercede in his behalf with the Holy Father, and to bring
the Catholic Powers to his aid. Support from them and
from his good friends in England would enable him to
conquer his difficulties. Guise, he promised, should be

his guide in everything, and he would take his place definitively at his side, in religion as well as in policy.¹

The letter to the Pope is even more curious, and deserves particular attention. Whether it was the composition of James himself, or of the subtle heads with whom he was surrounded, there is no evidence to shew.

'The affection and goodwill,' so the letter runs, 'which your Holiness and your predecessors have always borne towards this Crown and my ancestors, together with the fatherly care which the Holy See has exercised over the Queen, my most dear mother, have emboldened me to address your Holiness at this present. I desire as well to thank your Holiness for your exertions in my mother's behalf, as to explain the difficulties in which my having placed myself in the position towards her which my duty requires, has involved me. The prejudices of my education, the temptations of ambition, the advice or pressure of those who are more masters of my dominions than I am myself, combined to lead me into another course; but I have preferred rather to be guided by the laws of God and nature, and the advice of my near and loving kinsmen of the house of Guise, whom I understand to be devoted to your Holiness. Thus it has come to pass that the faction who expelled my said lady and mother, who made use of my young years as the veil and shield of their own tyrannous appetites, seeing that I was beginning to comprehend their evil deport-

---

¹ 'Si par votre moyen je puis obtenir quelque bon secours, j'espere, aidant Dieu, qu'avec l'assistance du bon nombre de serviteurs que j'ay, tant en ce mien Royaulme qu'en Angleterre, je sortiray bien tôt de ces difficultes, et lors j'en serois en plein liberté de pouvoir embrasser votre bon conseil et advis en toutes choses, tant de religion que d'estat, comme je desire toujours de me ranger en tout ce que sera raisonable.'—*James of Scotland to the Duke of Guise*, Feb. 9-19, 1584. MSS. Simancas.

ment towards their natural Princes, have now banded themselves together against me, and with the help of my neighbour, the Queen of England, who has encouraged every bad enterprise attempted in this country throughout her reign, they intend if they can to destroy me altogether. I confide, however, both in your Holiness's prudence, and in your love for my mother. I have myself as yet deserved nothing at your hands, but it shall not be always thus.[1] Those under whose advice I am now acting have told me always to look to your Holiness rather than to any other Prince. My extremity, however, is such that if I receive no help from abroad, I see that I soon may be forced to play into the hands of your Holiness's worst enemies and mine. Traitors, abusing my youth and my authority, have taken possession of my government, of the revenues of my estates, of the chief fortresses in the realm. They have deprived me of every means of defending myself, or of delivering my mother, or recovering the rights which she possesses, along with myself, in the realm of England.[2] How best to remedy these things I shall be advised by my dear cousin of Guise, by whose counsel I am at present acting, in undertaking the defence of my dear and honoured lady and mother. I look also to satisfying your Holiness in all other things, especially if in this my great necessity your Holiness stands my friend.[3] I must beseech your Holiness to let no one know that I have written to you. Should it get abroad, it will embarrass my position, and may prove my utter destruction, so weak am I, and so powerless to defend myself if I am assailed

---

[1] 'Sans que jusque à present j'ai encore rien merité, que je ne permettray pas qu'il en soit ainsi.'

[2] 'Pour delivrer madame ma mere et recouvrer le droit qu'elle et moy avons au Royaulme d'Angleterre.'

[3] 'J'espere aussi de pouvoir satisfaire à Vostre Santité en toutes aultres choses, principalment si je suis secouru en une si grande necessité par vostre Santité.'

at once by my rebels, and by my neighbour of England. God grant your Holiness health and a long and happy life, with all spiritual graces. From my palace at Holyrood, Feb. 19, 1584.

'Your Holiness's most humble and affectionate

'JAMES R.'[1]

In forwarding this letter to the Vatican, the Duke of Guise, through whom it was sent, added his own entreaties that Gregory would espouse the cause of 'the poor young man.'[2] But 'the poor young man's' cause was complicated by cross politics and purposes extremely difficult to reconcile. Spain and France, while jealous of each other, were neither of them anxious to facilitate the union of Scotland and England. The English Catholics were Spanish in their sympathies. The Scotch Catholics were French. The Duke of Guise, whose views had been already turning again towards Scotland, responded to James's invitation. He insisted to Allen and de Tassis on the military advantages of landing in a friendly country. If he invaded England out of Scotland, he would be able to take James along with him,[3] present him to the English people as heir to the crown, and introduce him as having come thither to redress the wrongs under which the Catholics were suffering.[4]

---

[1] *MSS. Simancas.*

[2] Guise to the Pope, April 5-15.—*MSS. Simancas.*

[3] 'Sospecho que tienen intencion de que lleve el Rey de Escocia el ejercito en persona y entre con el en Inglaterra.'—*Tassis to Philip,* April 8-18. TEULET, vol. v.

[4] 'The title of the crown was of great efficacy with the English nation. Whenever any prince did govern evil, if the successor did take upon him to remedy the same, never any to whom the succession did belong did at any time take arms to reform the government but he had good success.'—*Discourse on the Invasion of England, found on Crichton, the Jesuit,* May 1584. *MSS. Domestic.*

On the other hand, there were many Catholics in England, whom even the prospect of the restitution of the faith could not reconcile to a conquest by a Scoto-French army. They were ready to accept a Scotch princess as their sovereign, but their own arms, or the arms of Spain, must place her on the throne. England, if the crowns were united, expected to remain the superior. In the dread of being overborne by Scotland and France, the party represented by Allen and the Jesuits intended, after Mary Stuart became Queen, that she should remain inseparably connected with Spain. Guise had undertaken through Charles Paget that if Spaniards accompanied the invasion, they should be compelled to retire when it had succeeded. Allen insisted through de Tassis that there should be no invasion unless the Spaniards bore a part in it, and that a Spanish force should remain in the country after the conquest had been completed, and the Queen of Scots was on the throne.[1]

A subtle divergence of opinion divided the whole party. The choice of Guise to lead the enterprise had diminished, but had failed to remove, the national rivalries and suspicions. De Tassis said that if James was to accompany the Duke into England he must first declare himself a Catholic.[2] It was answered that many English Protestants favoured the Scotch title, and that to alienate them prematurely would be unwise. The objection being still maintained, Lord Seton applied to Catherine de' Medici, and held out 'the direction and

---

[1] 'No quieren Ingleses otro patron que V. M. No solamente tienen ojo á que V. M. les remedie á la primera entrada, pero que aunque se les constituya Reyna la de Escocia, no les desampara tan presto hasta tener todo aquello bien asegurado.'—*Tassis to Philip*, May 17-27. TEULET, vol. v.

[2] Tassis to Philip, April 9-19.—*Ibid.*

'disposition of the cause' as a temptation to the French crown independent of Spain altogether.[1]

Mauvissière, who had been the minister of the Anglo-French alliance, and had hitherto clung to Elizabeth, had begun to doubt her stability, and to hint that James's star was perhaps the rising one. 'The Queen 'of Scots,' he wrote to Catherine, 'is a thorn in this 'Queen's foot. Every moment she suffers from it, but 'she cannot pluck it out. She lost Scotland when she 'lost Morton. None but he could have mastered the 'young King; and the young King means to be monarch 'of this island, as one day he will and must be.'[2]

Rumours reached de Tassis that the conspirators, weary of his master's delay, were turning their thoughts in a direction mischievous to Spanish interests, and he made haste[3] to send word to Philip. Mauvissière's prophecy was right, but the day of its fulfilment was still far distant, and the jealousies which had so long protected Elizabeth continued to paralyse her enemies. Both Spain and France, it was thought, could have agreed to trust the Duke of Guise, but opposite policies and opposite principles ravelled out the coalition as fast as it was woven. The King of Spain, like de Tassis, insisted on the immediate conversion of James, and perhaps was not anxious at heart that James should comply. He feared James's connexion with France, as he had feared his mother's; and though, like the Jesuits, he was willing that Mary Stuart should reign if she would lean on Spain to uphold her, he coveted,

---

[1] Words of Lord Seton to the Queen-mother, April 9-19, 1584.—TEULET, vol. iii.

[2] Mauvissière to the Queen-mother, March 30-April 9.—TEULET, vol. iii.

[3] 'Melino ha me dicho en confiança que andan entre los Escoceses enfadados de la dilacion platicas, de ver si seria posible guiar este negocio por otras manos que las de Vuestra Majestad.'—J. B. de Tassis al Rey, 17-27 de Maio. TEULET, vol. v.

as became afterwards clear, the reversion of the title for himself.

Meanwhile in Scotland itself James was going merrily forward. In his letter to the Pope he had been more desponding than the occasion called for.

Disconcerted by Elizabeth's backwardness, Gowry and his friends had attempted to make their peace with the King and Arran. They had been met coldly and ambiguously. Angus's plan of seizing James when hunting had been betrayed. The King had held his tongue, in fear of provoking England prematurely, but none the less it was clear that he knew something, if not all. The confession of Throgmorton may perhaps have made Elizabeth more encouraging. Sir Robert Bowes, at any rate, reported in January, as a thing which she would be pleased to hear, that a conspiracy was again on foot which would soon be executed. 'The chief 'instruments,' Gowry himself among them, were said to be 'hanging back,' and 'shewing much faintness;' but they were provided with unlooked-for allies in the two Hamilton brothers, Lord Claude and Lord John, the natural chiefs of the Catholic faction, who had been deprived of their estates by Morton, and had been kept out of them to feed the avarice of the Earl of Arran. In lending support to men who had suffered for their fidelity to Mary Stuart, who had fought for her at Langside, who had murdered Murray and Lennox to please her, Elizabeth could not be accused of partisanship. The brothers undertook, if she would restore them, to break up the present faction which ruled the King. She sent them down to the border, and made a shew of collecting a force at Berwick. Mar and Glamys stole back from Knockfergus, and an unnatural alliance was secretly formed between the chiefs of the

Protestant faction and the sons of the Duke of Chatelherault. Gowry, Rothes, Angus, and several others undertook to surprise the King, and deal with him as might afterwards be found convenient. If they failed, or if they could find no convenient opportunity, their plan was to fall back upon the border. The Hamiltons were then to join them, and their united parties were to march on Edinburgh, drawing supplies from Berwick, and perhaps attended by an English fleet.[1]

Elizabeth's promises, however, were still ambiguous. She gave good words in plenty, but neither from her nor from Sir Robert Bowes could the lords obtain a definite engagement in writing; and experience of her conduct on other occasions was less encouraging than Bowes would have had them believe. He perceived the thing ' to lie coldly on their stomachs,'[2] and either he or some one else in the secret intimated that the Queen was waiting for them to do something decisive for themselves. England, he sent them word, could not interpose till there was an open ground for interference, and an open party to be helped. The Queen had sent an army to Berwick to save Morton, but none of the Scots took arms for him, and she was obliged to withdraw with shame. They ought to be up and doing. If they

---

[1] Mauvissière, writing on the 23rd of April, says distinctly that they looked for help from England, but they were purposely misled by Sir Robert Bowes, whose instructions were to tempt them to commit themselves while evading a distinct engagement on the part of his own Government.

[2] 'By such discreet messengers as I employed,' he wrote, ' I satisfied the chief solicitor in this cause and the rest of the party, of his late letters sent to me. In this I have advised to behold the goodwill shewed in like matters in time past, whereby they may have good experience that neither the good cause nor the well-affected have been abandoned in time of necessity. I have not nor dare not write any particular promise or comfort to them otherwise than by words and effects rehearsed with like generalities, to continue them in good hopes, without any bond or promise from me.'—*Bowes to Walsingham*, April 4-14. *MSS. Scotland.*

[3] *Ibid.*

had written to England for advice 'before Davie was
'slaughtered, or the Queen taken prisoner, neither of
'those things could have been done,' but the lords
knew 'how well they were taken afterwards.' It was
time 'to draw sword,' and not 'to be hanging on uncertainty.'[1]

Translated into plain language, these words meant that
the lords were to venture something decided, at their
own risk, and that if they succeeded Elizabeth would
accept the benefit of their enterprise. The allusion to
the capture of the Queen of Scots was an unhappy one,
for relieved from danger by the Queen of Scots' deposition, Elizabeth had sought credit with other established
governments by threatening to chastise the instruments
of it. Morton's skull over the Tolbooth gate was a
grinning evidence of the value of these misleading
promptings; but Gowry's fate was coming upon him, and
he allowed himself to be persuaded. Angus and Mar
undertook the capture of the King. Gowry pretended
that he was going over into France, and went down to
Dundee, intending to cross by water to Tantallon, where
Lord Lindsay, the two Hamiltons, and, as he hoped,
the English had agreed to join him.[2] As it was with
Guise and the invasion of England, however, so it was
with the plots against James. There were too many
confederates. There had been too much talk beforehand, and the secret had been betrayed to the Earl of
Arran. Stewart, who had been in England with Colville, followed Gowry with a party of horse to Dundee,
captured him, and carried him off to Holyrood. Angus
and Mar were more successful. They missed James,
but, accompanied by Glamys, they surprised and cap-

---

[1] Letter endorsed by Burghley, 'Mr. Colville;' and in another hand, 'Copy of my last letter to Scotland, April 16-26.'—*MSS. Scotland.*

[2] Bowes to Walsingham, April 14.—*MSS. Scotland.*

tured Stirling Castle, and sent out a proclamation inviting the country to rise and join them. 'The King,' they said, 'was abused by persons of low estate.' He was surrounded 'by a young and insolent company of 'papists, atheists, and furtherers of the bloody Council 'of Trent.' 'The fearers of God'[1] were in danger of massacre, and had taken arms in the King's interests, and their own. Couriers flew to Lindsay at Tantallon, to the Hamiltons at Berwick, and on to London to the Court, to entreat for help. The conditions were fulfilled which the Queen had required; a distinct party was in arms with a public cause. If she would but order her ships to the Forth, to intimate by their presence that she favoured their enterprise, if she would check Maxwell and Fernyhurst on the border, and give or lend a little money, the three Earls, notwithstanding Gowry's capture, were confident of success.

Half Scotland was waiting to see what England would do. Had Gowry escaped, the Queen's interference would perhaps not have been needed. His capture had so far inclined the scale, that many who had promised their assistance hung back till they saw for certain that they might depend upon Elizabeth.

There was of course the usual difficulty, the treaty of non-intervention, which had been tacitly formed with France. Mauvissière objected in the name of his Court, and the established battery of traitorous or timid counsels was brought into play. That the movement had been undertaken at Elizabeth's instigation, or at least with her knowledge, consent, and approval, passed for nothing. Her first impulse was to send the couriers back with the answer that she could not comply with

---

[1] 'Effect of the petition delivered by the credit of Mr. Colvillo, in the names of the Earls of Angus, Mar, and Glamys, entered into the action of Stirling, April 1584.'—*MSS. Scotland.*

the Earls' requests. A few days later, Secretary Davison was dispatched with directions to give fresh encouragement and to threaten the King into moderation; and she sent a thousand pounds to the border to be used in the service of the confederates. But it was too late. The first refusal had decided the fate of the rising. The Earl of Arran, promptly collecting a few thousand ruffians, marched at their head to Stirling, and the Earls, believing themselves deserted, escaped before his arrival to Berwick. The Edinburgh ministers followed, conscious of the vengeance that they had provoked, and knowing that it would not now be delayed. Fernyhurst, seeing the English motionless, rose with the Kers and the Humes; and Tantallon, which was to have been the rallying-point of the confederates, was changed into Lindsay's prison. Stirling Castle surrendered, the captain and his chief followers were hanged, and the only effect of the conspiracy had been to raise James at last into an absolute sovereign.

There was a moan of indignation, heard alas! too often in Scotland, at Elizabeth's broken faith. Sir Robert Bowes, the instrument of their deception, did not seek to conceal his own shame and humiliation. He covered his mistress in public by taking the blame upon himself; but to Walsingham he did not scruple to describe the Earls 'as foully abused and betrayed.'[1] The friends of the Queen of Scots, on the other hand, sent her exulting word of her son's victory, bidding her remind him that now was the time for vengeance, and tell Guise to be quick in coming.[2]

The Queen of Scots needed no urging. Morton,

---

[1] Bowes to Walsingham, April 27-May 7.—*MSS. Ibid.*

[2] 'Madame, escrives au Roy d'avoir souvenance du temps passé. Oultre, Madame, advertissez M. de Guise d'accelerer toutes choses pour mettre fin à ces énormités.'—— *to the Queen of Scots*, April 26-May 6. Decipher. *MSS.* MARY QUEEN OF SCOTS.

Gowry, and Lindsay, were the three noblemen who had extorted the abdication at Lochleven. Morton was gone, and Gowry's turn had come. There was no question that he had conspired a second time against the person of his Sovereign. When he saw that all was over he made a free confession, and in a natural resentment at his desertion, he said, perhaps untruly, perhaps half truly, that if he had succeeded this time, and if he had listened to English overtures, both the King and his mother would have been put to death.[1] If he hoped to save himself by the revelation, he was mistaken. He was carried to Stirling immediately on the surrender, and a court was extemporised for his trial, of which Colonel Stewart, who had taken him prisoner, was President. Argyle, who had been his friend, declined to sit; even Huntley, though he was present, did not vote; but of his literal guilt, if guilt could be said to attach to any kind of political action in the anarchy of Scotland, there could be no question. The forms were

---

[1] 'Le feu Conte de Gowry estant l'an passé sur le poinct d'avoir la tête tranchée pour la mesme conspiration que ces seigneurs Escossoys, desdits complices du dict Gowry, ont à present executée, déposa et conferra voluntairement au maistre de Gray, qui m'en advertist par lettres encores extantes, qu'en Angleterre (je ne veulx nommer par qui) il avoit esté faict projecté et arresté de nous faire mourir moy et mon fils en ung mesme jour.'—*Marie Stuart à M. de Chateauneuf*, 8 décembre 1585. LABANOFF, vol. vi. When it is considered how extremely convenient James's death would have been, how many misgivings he had caused and was still causing to English statesmen, how bitterly both countries had suffered from Elizabeth's interference to save Mary Stuart, how universal had been the expectation that James would not emerge alive out of the confusions of Scotland, it is not unlikely that this way out of their difficulties had presented itself to more than one eminent politician, and that small enquiry would have followed had it been reported that the young King had died of some sudden disorder. Beyond doubt this would have been his fate and the Queen of Scots' fate also, everywhere in Europe in any previous century. Times were changing, but the traditions of the old ways survived, and many a wistful eye might be cast back at them.

hurried over, and execution instantly followed. Angus and Mar were proclaimed traitors, and their estates confiscated. The forfeiture of lands followed the sentences; Lady Gowry and her children were turned adrift to starve; and the vast inheritances of the Douglases, the Erskines, and the Ruthvens were divided between Arran, who was already gorged with plunder, and the young Duke of Lennox, whom James had sent for from France.[1]

Lindsay only now remained of the three. On that wild evening, when Mary Stuart was brought in a prisoner from the field at Carberry, she swore to Lindsay that she would one day have his head, and oaths of this kind she was not apt to leave unfulfilled. Now that he was in James's power, she required peremptorily that his treatment of her should not be forgotten; and James, eager to atone for his refusal of the association by the sacrifice of an enemy of his own, promised that not Lindsay only but every one of the confederates that he could catch should receive exemplary chastisement.[2] So good an intention was not to be allowed to cool. She sent her son a present of a sword. She bade him go forward boldly, and above all not spare Lindsay.[3] He laughed as he girded on her gift, telling the bearer that he would be his mother's true knight, and that before many

---

[1] Davison to Walsingham, May 11.—*MSS. Scotland.*

[2] 'Sans aultre recommandation de vostre part, la sympathie et conformité de nos complexions avec le sentiment que j'ay des injures et trahisons commises à l'endroit de vous par My Lord Lindsay, m'avoit ya tout resolu d'en faire punition exemplaire; comme j'espere de ses semblables, sans qu'il m'en eschappe un seul de ceulx que je pourray attraper.'—*The King of Scots to Mary Stuart*, July 23. Decipher. *MSS. Scotland.*

[3] 'Pour Lindsay le Roy obeira à ce que la Royne luy en mande à la premiere occasion, n'attendant que preuve et proces contre luy.'—*Instructions secretes de M. Fontenay*, Aug. 1583. *MSS. MARY QUEEN OF SCOTS.* Incorrectly dated in the State Papers Jan. 1583.

days the heads of Lindsay and others besides him should prove how religiously he would observe his oath.[1] The confederate lords had risked their lives in a wild belief that Elizabeth would be true to them. As they had failed, she was not content with leaving them in Scotland to James's vengeance; but, with a repetition accurate as an automaton's of her behaviour to Murray, she endeavoured to prove that she had never been in any way connected with them, by hard treatment of Angus and Mar and the other fugitives who had taken refuge in Northumberland. Outward displeasure, had it gone no further, might have been politic affectation, but the Court had veered round with the altered prospect, carrying Elizabeth with it, and the opposite policy was in the ascendant altogether.

'The poor gentlemen that are retired into this realm,' wrote Walsingham, 'are like to receive but cold comfort, 'having fewer favourers than I looked for, and such be-'come their enemies as neither the authority of their 'place nor the care they ought to have of her Majesty's 'safety doth make allowable in them. But it agrees with 'the course we now hold here in displacing and depriv-'ing the best affected ministers.[2] I look for no better 'fruits from them that use religion for policy, and many 'here do abuse it for faction.'[3] And again, a few days later: 'The noblemen receive no great comfort, and as 'for the poor ministers retired into the realm, who have 'shewn themselves good instruments for entertaining 'the amity between the Crowns, they are but hardly 'thought of here, and therefore not likely to be used

---

[1] Fontenay to the Queen of Scots, Aug. 15.—*MSS. Mary Queen of Scots.* Decipher.

[2] Several Puritan clergy had been just prosecuted under the Act of Uniformity, and deprived of their benefices.

[3] Walsingham to Davison, June 3-13, 1584.—*MSS. Scotland.*

'with the kindness that either Christianity or policy re-
'quireth. I write this with extreme grief, for that I
'hold it a presage of God's judgment towards us.'[1]

For the few weeks which followed the arrest and confession of Throgmorton, Elizabeth had almost resolved to take a decided part at last. She had dismissed Mendoza, imprisoned the Catholic noblemen, held out her hand to the Low Countries, and had invited her party in Scotland to take arms and make a revolution. But a purpose of this kind never long resisted influences which combined to undermine it. There was no longer a French marriage for the Queen to fall back upon, but there was still a French alliance. The Court at Paris feared the ascendancy of the Duke of Guise almost as much as England feared it; and Mauvissière, in London, represented the principles of compromise so dear to Elizabeth, by which moderation and good sense were to control the passions of the opposing creeds. It was possible that Catherine de' Medici might be tempted by the offers of Lord Seton, but her preference was still for the alliance with Elizabeth, if that alliance could be maintained. Her own and her son's influence in Europe, and even their authority in France, depended on the continuance of the balance which had hitherto been hardly preserved. If once the Protestants combined, and the war of religion broke out, the chieftainship of the two great parties must devolve on Elizabeth and Philip, and the temporising uncertain House of Valois would be inevitably shipwrecked. Philip had still to settle with Henry for Alençon's proceedings in the Low Countries, and the day of reckoning would assuredly come with the completion of Parma's reconquest. The object from the French point of view, therefore, was a triple

[1] Walsingham to Davison, June 17-27.—*MSS. Ibid.*

union between France, England, and Scotland, to which Mary Stuart and James should be parties in opposition to Spain and to Spanish influences. Mauvissière, from the first moment of the troubles of Scotland, had never ceased to urge this solution of the situation. He undertook himself to reconcile all quarrels there if the Queen would allow him to go to Edinburgh. Alençon, though not yet dead, was notoriously dying; and if the completion of the treaty with the Queen of Scots and her consequent release was to be one condition, the recognition of the King of Navarre as heir presumptive in France was to be another.

There was much to be said in favour of such a policy, especially when the alternative was a gigantic convulsion of which no one could foresee the end. Could Mary Stuart and James be depended on, no prudent Sovereign would prefer the chances of the sword. The French Court itself undertook to become responsible for the Queen of Scots, and the state of Scotland was less unfavourable than it might have seemed. The Earl of Arran, by whom the King was now controlled, was a hard, clear-headed, and entirely unscrupulous villain, to whom creeds appeared fools' playthings, and power and wealth the only concern of a reasonable man. His title and his estates depended on the exclusion of the Hamiltons, and the Hamiltons had deserved too well of the Catholic cause to be left dispossessed of their patrimony in the event of a religious revolution. On the capture of Gowry and the flight of the lords to England, Arran had made advances, therefore, to Lord Hunsdon at Berwick, in the spirit of Mauvissière's proposals to Elizabeth. It was hinted that if there was to be a general reconciliation, the Earls of Angus and Mar might be allowed to return, supposing the Queen

of Scots would intercede for them. The settlement of
Scotland, on the English episcopal pattern, was held out
as a further temptation, and it was through these considerations that Gowry had been sacrificed, and the resolution had been ultimately arrived at to abstain from
interference by arms.

Spain was hopelessly slow—Throgmorton had confessed—discovery and disappointment had clung like a
shadow to every plot in which Philip had borne a part.
Mary Stuart, afraid of what might follow to herself,
were Elizabeth to be forced finally into open war, had
written to Mauvissière, expressing sympathy with the
policy which he advocated. She consented eagerly to his
proposed mission; she empowered him to assure Elizabeth, on her word of honour as a princess, that if the
treaty were renewed and completed, she would compel
her son into compliance.[1] She called God to witness, in
a letter to the Queen, that if the English succession
were secured to James, she would herself remain for the
rest of her life in retirement. To accept these advances would gratify France, rivet afresh the Anglo-
French alliance, and, without war or expenditure of
money, throw a diplomatic shelter over the Low Countries, and secure England from all danger of invasion
on the northern border. Mauvissière assured Elizabeth that his master's wish 'was to compound matters
'in Scotland in a reasonable course,' to persuade the
Queen of Scots 'to give counsel to her son to her
'Majesty's best liking,' 'to unite the crowns of England,
'Scotland, and France, in good perfect friendship and
'amity.'[2]

---

[1] The Queen of Scots to Mauvissière, March 11-21, 1584.—LABAN-
OFF, vol. v.

[2] Points contained in the French
Ambassador's letter of May 13-23.—
MSS. Scotland.

Elizabeth trusted these fair words only so far as she knew them to represent her brother of France's interests. Mauvissière, on the other hand, trusted Elizabeth not a jot further: an experience of twenty-five years had taught him, he distinctly said, that the English Queen would promise anything, and was utterly indifferent to the performance of what she promised. Could she be assured otherwise of Scotland, she would care for no Power in Christendom.[1]

But Elizabeth could not afford to quarrel with France, and Catherine and Henry were equally concerned in preventing a revolution which would make over England and Scotland to Guise and Philip. Permission, therefore, was given to Mauvissière to go down and do his best in Scotland; the treaty, which had become almost a jest, was reopened with Mary Stuart, and the Queen of England appeared once more in the position of a suitor to her prisoner.

So abrupt a change of attitude could hardly be executed without ungracefulness. The Paris conspirators had avowedly calculated on the support of Lord Shrewsbury: he was expected if not to join the insurrection, which was to break out on Guise's landing, at least to secure the safety of his charge; and in the short interval, when a bold course was half resolved on, the removal of the Queen of Scots into the custody of some firmer person, had been part of the general scheme. Elizabeth herself had informed Shrewsbury of Throgmorton's confessions, and of the double part which she had ascertained that the Queen of Scots had been playing.[2] She had sent the Queen of Scots a threatening message, that she must abandon conspiracies

---

[1] Mauvissière to the King, April 26-May 6.—TEULET, vol. iii.

[2] Elizabeth to the Earl of Shrewsbury, March 8-18.—*MSS. MARY QUEEN OF SCOTS.*

if she ever hoped for favour. Sir Ralph Sadler had been selected as her future keeper, and on the 26th of March a commission had been issued to Sadler and Sir Henry Neville to take charge of her person, to carry her to Melbourne Castle in Derbyshire, to allow no excuses, and to use force if she refused to move.[1]

The order had been suspended till the intended 'practice' in Scotland should be executed, and on the confederates' failure, had been abandoned with the policy to which it belonged. A M. Mason came over from France in April to see the Queen of Scots on business connected with her dowry. The news of Angus's and Mar's flight had just reached London, but was perhaps still unknown at Sheffield. The occasion was used to send down Wade as Mason's escort, with orders to reopen negotiations for the treaty with as much dignity as circumstances would allow.

It was no very easy task. They arrived at Sheffield on the 23rd of April,[2] and the next day were introduced to the lady. As was hoped, she had heard nothing recently from Scotland. She began to talk to Mason in French. She knew that Shrewsbury was ignorant of it, and, trusting that the rest were in the same condition, said something imprudent. Wade struck into the conversation in a way that shewed his easy familiarity with the language. He irritated her by doing so, and she exploded into one of her passions. She asked after her son, observing, satirically, that she had no other means of hearing whether he was alive or dead. She was eloquently pathetic about France. Then turning upon Wade, she said that she had humbled herself before Elizabeth into the very dirt, and had been cheated after all of her reward.

---

[1] Commission to Sadler and Neville, March 26–April 5.—*MSS.*
[2] May 3.

'I told her,' said Wade, 'her son's conduct was the cause, and it appeared that she had sought to amuse her Majesty with the treaty to give her son time to work that alteration: it was time for her Majesty to break off when the foundation failed.'

Quoting the words once written with a diamond by Elizabeth on a window, when imprisoned by her sister,

> 'Much suspected by me,
> But nothing proved can be,'

she ran fiercely over the story of her wrongs, 'using bitter speeches of her misery.'

Wade replied that her treatment was regarded abroad 'as one of the rarest examples of singular mercy and good inclination that was ever heard of, considering the provocation her Majesty had received.'

She flamed out at the word mercy. She said she was an absolute Prince as much as her Majesty. She was no inferior of hers. She had been a Queen from her cradle, and had been afterwards 'Queen of France, the greatest realm in Christendom.' Mercy was for subjects; for her there had been nothing but extremity.

'All this was said with extreme choler.' She cooled afterwards and became quieter, but there were three things she said which she would die a thousand deaths rather than allow to be sacrificed—her honour, her interest in the English succession, and her child.

Her Majesty, Wade answered, had taken care of the first and the last; the second she must deserve. England would never accept her as Queen without her Majesty's consent. She was deceiving herself if she expected support from France. He had himself heard Mauvissière say that 'France would spend forty million crowns before she or her son should reign in England.' After her double dealing with Spain, it was but too

likely that this might be true. She began again 'to moan
'her grief and her woful estate.' She complained of her
friends' neglect of her, of her imprisonment and misery.
She was younger in years, she said, than the Queen
of England, but suffering had made her older to look
at. 'God would avenge her enemies and those that
'were the authors of her overthrow, whom she stuck
'not to curse.'

When the torrent of eloquence began to slacken,
Wade reminded her of certain things which she had
forgotten—intrigues, practices, and conspiracies.

She said that the Queen had never trusted her, and
could not justly blame her. She did not deny that she
had begged her friends to exert themselves for her, but
she had meant innocently, and if they had done wrong,
the fault was theirs.

Wade spoke of proofs. She said, angrily, that 'he
'was not of calling to reason with her.' He answered
that he was not of calling either to hear his own mistress
found fault with. There were few princes in Christendom
who would not have made shorter work with her;
and if she would seriously consider what she had done,
she would rather wonder that the Queen had consented
to treat with her at all.

So the argument ran on, Wade being intentionally
harsh, to prepare for concessions afterwards. At
length her anger died away into pleading and tenderness.
She sang the song which she had sung before to
Mauvissière. If the Queen would but trust her, she said,
she should never find her confidence misplaced. Anything
which her sister wished she was ready to do;
the first and last desire of her heart was to please her.[1]

---

[1] Mr. Wade's narrative of what passed at Sheffield, April 25-May 5.—
MSS. MARY QUEEN OF SCOTS.

Could the Queen of Scots, when she learnt what could not long be concealed from her, have bridled her temper, and been prudent and moderate, she might possibly at this particular crisis have really recovered her freedom. At no time were so many circumstances in her favour. It was true that the continuance of the pressure which France was exerting in her behalf was contingent on her separating herself from Spain; and to break with Spain was to break with the whole party of revolt and revolution. Yet it would have been her best chance. Spain clearly would not risk a war in her interest with France and England combined, and could hardly be tempted into a quarrel with England single-handed. Guise's enterprise hung fire through the jealousies which split up the party; and could she have parted with her passionate desire for revenge, she might have either taken the benefit of a treaty in which England, France, and Scotland would have been held together on terms of compromise; or else, which would have equally served her purpose, she would have broken up the Anglo-French alliance.

But Mary Stuart, notwithstanding her affected plaintiveness, was proud and fierce as when she stood with Bothwell on the hills of Musselburgh. The one absorbing hope of her life was to see those who had humbled her rolling, all of them, in the dust at her feet. The least gleam of success she construed into a turn of the tide; and the news of the defeat and flight of the confederates, and the execution of Gowry, scattered her despondency and filled her with dreams of coming triumph. Walsingham was distinctly of opinion that if she would adhere to what she had said to Wade, her offer ought to be tried. 'The impediment,' he said, ' grew principally through a jealous conceit that either of

'the two Princesses had of the other, which could hardly
be removed.'¹ But alarm had so far superseded the
'jealous conceit,' that Elizabeth had yielded to necessity.
When Wade returned with an account of his conversation, she brought herself to write a courteous letter to the
Queen of Scots, and Secretary Beale was once more sent
down to Sheffield to take up again the dropped threads of
the treaty of the past year. He was empowered to tell
her that if her son, at her intercession, would recall
Angus and Mar, would pardon Lindsay, and proclaim
a general amnesty, if she would herself relinquish
her intrigues and forbid the Archbishop of Glasgow to
prosecute further the conspiracy at Paris, Sir Walter
Mildmay would resume his place on the commission,
and an arrangement should be concluded with her without further delay. If the Queen of Scots said that the
lords, by their late rebellion, had placed themselves
beyond the pale of forgiveness, Beale was instructed to
tell her that the lords had many friends in England,
that they had meant no ill, and that if she refused,
'inconvenience would grow,' and such an offer would
never be made to her again. Her transactions with the
Duke of Guise for the invasion of England had been
discovered, and a harder course would be taken with
her.²

Wade had left her tender and compliant. When
Beale arrived, the mood had changed. Her son was now
absolute; her enemies were dispersed, the Queen of
England dismayed. She understood now the cause of
the late advances to her and was proportionately resentful. Guise, she fondly thought, would soon be

¹ Walsingham to Sadler, Oct. 17–7, 1584.—*MSS. Mary Queen of Scots.*
² Elizabeth to Secretary Beale, May 4–14.—*MSS. Ibid.*

over, and there was no occasion for her to humiliate herself. She stood upon 'very proud terms;' she refused to promise to control the diplomacy of her representatives abroad. If she was to interfere for the pardon of the lords, she said it should be when she was free, and not otherwise. She required ampler conditions than those which she had accepted in the past; above all, she required to be allowed, if she wished it, to leave England. She said that Sir Walter Mildmay, if he came to Sheffield, must bring powers to conclude the treaty, or she would not discuss it with him; and unless it was concluded immediately, she would regard her concessions as withdrawn.[1]

'With all the cunning that we have,' wrote Beale privately, 'we cannot bring this lady to make any abso-
'lute promise for the performance of her offers, unless
'she may be assured of the accomplishment of the
'treaty. Since the last break off she is more circum-
'spect how she entangle herself. She seems marvellous
'glad of the late success in Scotland, and especially
'that her son had a heart to go into the field himself.
'She will deal for Angus and Mar, but she seems to
'retain another mind towards Gowry and Lindsay upon
'the ancient quarrel of Lochleven.'[2]

Elizabeth might as well have abdicated as have yielded to such terms so demanded. She sent a cold intimation to Lord Shrewsbury that the treaty was at an end, and that Beale might leave Sheffield.[3] But she was extremely troubled—troubled especially about the noblemen who had taken refuge in England, and whose restoration she had hoped to effect through the Queen of

---

[1] Beale to Walsingham, May 16–26.—*MSS.* MARY QUEEN OF SCOTS.
[2] Same to the same, May 17–27.
[3] Elizabeth to Shrewsbury, May 24–June 3.—*MSS. Ibid.*

Scots' mediation. Mauvissière was to have been the bearer of her intercession, and since it could not be obtained, his mission was abandoned. Lord Livingston came up from Scotland to demand their surrender as traitors. Elizabeth was unable to give them up, but she was afraid to assist or countenance them. She treated them as she had treated Murray nineteen years before, whom she equally employed and deserted; and Walsingham naturally feared that the lords, being left to starve, would make terms with James, purchase their pardon at the price of deserting for ever the ungrateful English cause, and leave Elizabeth without a friend in the only country where friends were absolutely indispensable to her.[1]

The prudence or imprudence of Elizabeth, and the chances of success to the Queen of Scots in the attitude which she had dared to resume, turned more and more on the character of her boy, who sate on the throne of Scotland, and who, young as he was, already exerted a personal influence on the politics of his country, which, as parties were balanced, was likely to turn the scale. In the hands of the different factions who had successively been his masters, he had shewn a pliancy inevitable from his circumstances. Yet he had evidently a purpose of his own, which was visible through all his changes, and while the ministers of the Kirk had found

---

[1] 'The intended journey of the French Ambassador into Scotland is now broken off, for that the Queen of Scots stands upon very proud terms, refusing to mediate the restitution of the distressed noblemen unless her Majesty will grant her liberty and ratify the treaty between the Earl of Shrewsbury, Sir Walter Mildmay, Mr. Beale, and her. So that now I do not see what means her Majesty can use to procure their relief, but fear greatly they will be left to seek their own peace, which cannot but breed to us a war. This, I pray you, reserve to yourself, for we may alter our purpose.'—*Walsingham to Davison*, May 20-30. *MSS. Scotland.*

him always as hostile to them as his mother had been, yet neither his mother nor the Jesuits had found him as docile as they had hoped and looked for. He had written to the Pope, but he had not been converted. He had shewn himself entirely willing to please Mary Stuart by the execution of the lords who had been the instruments of her overthrow; but he had shewn no great desire to see her again in Scotland, or to share his power with her, or even to acknowledge that he held his crown by her will and pleasure. He had been, no doubt, influenced greatly by Lennox and Arran; but he had opinions which, as he grew older, became more decided, and it now becomes important to look more closely at him, and to examine in detail the figure of the youth who was to play so large a part in the history of Great Britain. The materials are fortunately provided in a singular and minute account of him, which was furnished to his mother by an acute and observing Frenchman.

On the death of the Cardinal of Lorraine, the Cardinal's secretary, M. Nau, passed into the service of Mary Stuart, and while M. Nau resided with her at Sheffield, and thenceforward managed her correspondence, his brother, M. Fontenay, became one of her many agents abroad, and passed his time carrying her messages, and advocating her cause in Rome, Paris, and Madrid. He, too, occasionally visited her at Sheffield, and when the last defeat of the lords gave her back her spirits and her energy, she sent M. Fontenay through France to Scotland to see her son, to urge the execution of Lindsay and the Abbot of Dunfermline, to arrange a common course of action, and bring him above all to consent to the long-talked-of association.

M. Fontenay's letters from the Scotch Court are long and complicated, but they bring the scene and the

actors in it upon the stage with a completeness which leaves nothing to be desired.¹ 'The King,' wrote M. Fontenay to his brother—and James himself stands before us as we read—'is for his age one of the most remarkable princes that ever lived. He has the three
' parts of the mind in perfection.² He apprehends readily,
' he judges maturely, he concludes with reason. His
' memory is full and retentive. His questions are quick
' and piercing, and his answers solid. Whatever be the
' subject of conversation, be it religion or anything else,
' he maintains the view which appears to him to be true
' and just. In religious argument I have known him
' establish a point against adversaries who in the main
' agree with him, and I venture to say that in languages,
' sciences, and affairs of State, he has more learning than
' any man in Scotland. In short, he is wonderfully
' clever, and for the rest, he is full of honourable am-
' bition, and has an excellent opinion of himself. Owing
' to the terrorism under which he has been brought up,
' he is timid with the great lords, and seldom ventures
' to contradict them. Yet his especial anxiety is to be
' thought hardy, and a man of courage. He has so good
' a will that nothing is too laborious for him. Hearing
' lately that the Laird of Dun³ had passed two days
' and two nights without sleep, he passed three; but if
' he once finds himself beaten in such exercises, he ab-
' hors them ever after. He dislikes dances and music,
' and amorous talk, and curiosity of dress, and courtly
' trivialities.⁴ He has an especial detestation for ear-

---

¹ These letters fell into the hands of Elizabeth on the seizure of the Queen of Scots' papers at Chartley, and were deciphered by Walsingham's secretary.

² The *simplex apprehensio, judicium*, and *discursus*, of the logicians.

³ Sir John Erskine.

⁴ 'Mignardises du cour.'

'rings.'¹ From want of instruction, his manners are
'rough and uncouth. He speaks, eats, dresses, and
'plays like a boor, and he is no better in the company
'of women. He is never still for a moment, but
'walks perpetually up and down the room, and his
'gait is sprawling and awkward. His voice is loud,
'and his words sententious. He prefers hunting to
'all other amusements, and will be six hours together
'on horseback, galloping over hill and dale. . . . His
'body is feeble, yet he is not delicate; in a word, he is
'an old young man.² Three unfavourable points only
'I observe in him. He does not understand his own
'insignificance. He is prodigiously conceited, and
'he underrates other princes. He irritates his sub-
'jects by indiscreet and violent attachments. He is
'idle and careless, too easy, and too much given to
'pleasure, particularly to the chase, leaving his affairs to
'be managed by Arran, Montrose, and his secretary.
'Excuses, I know, must be made for so young a man;
'but it is to be feared that the habit may grow upon
'him. I once hinted something of this kind to him.
'He told me that whatever he seemed, he was aware of
'everything of consequence that was going on. He
'could afford to spend time in hunting, for that when
'he attended to business he could do more in an hour
'than others could do in a day. He could listen to one
'man, talk to another, and observe a third. Sometimes
'he could do five things at once. The lords could
'attempt nothing without his knowledge. He had his
'spies at their chamber-doors evening and morning, who
'brought him word of all that they were about. He

---

¹ Then coming into fashion with French courtiers. Henry III. wore large pendants of pearls, and they may be seen in the early pictures of Charles I.

² 'C'est ung vieulx jeune homme.'

'said he was his mother's son in many ways. His body
'was weak, and he could not work long consecutively,
'but when he did work he was worth any other six
'men put together. He had sometimes tried to force
'himself, and had continued at his desk without inter-
'ruption for a week, but he was always ill after it. In
'fact he said he was like a Spanish gennet, which
'could run one course well, but could not hold out.
'This was the very expression which he used.'[1]

The personal portrait was drawn for Nau. The
political and spiritual account was given to Mary
Stuart, and was far less favourable. It was unnecessary,
Fontenay told her, to urge her son to severity against
the ministers of the Kirk, for he was himself sufficiently
bent on their destruction;[2] 'indeed, he had promised to
'hang one or two of them as an example to the rest.'

'But I fear,' Fontenay continued, 'that your son may
'constitute himself head of the Church. He is neither
'Lutheran nor Calvinist, but in many points much
'nearer to us. He thinks, for instance, that faith is dead
'without works, that there is no predestination, and so
'forth. But he holds a false opinion, though it can be
'turned to the advantage of Catholics—that faith in
'God alone is sufficient to save a man, let him belong to
'what religion he may.[3] As to the Pope, he abhors
'him,[4] and will not hear his name mentioned. His
'mind is filled with a thousand villanies about Popes,
'and monks, and priests.'[5] This last sentence throws a

[1] Fontenay to Nau, Aug. 5-15, 1584.—*MSS. Mary Queen of Scots*.

[2] 'Car il est de soymesmes assez preparé à leur ruine.'

[3] 'Il tient une faulse opinion, qui toutefois est profitable aux Catholiques. C'est que la seule foy en Dieu suffist pour sauver l'homme en qualque religion que ce soyt.'

[4] 'Quant au Pape, il l'abhorre extrêmement.'

[5] Fontenay to the Queen of Scots, Aug. 5-15.—*MSS. Mary Queen of Scots*.

curious light on James's letter to the 'abhorred' Pontiff. With the Duke of Guise also he had not been entirely sincere. So far as concerned Lindsay and the Abbot of Dunfermline, his replies were entirely satisfactory.[1] But Fontenay had been instructed also to make arrangements for the coming over of the Duke; and he found, to his surprise, that while James was most unwilling that the Duke should go to England without his participation, he was not particularly anxious to see his cousin in Scotland. He was afraid of Spain. He was afraid of the Pope. He objected to foreign troops; preferring, if the invasion were to take place, that only Scots should be employed upon it. If Guise conquered England he feared he might be inclined to keep it, or else Philip might be inclined to keep it. It could not be for his sake, he said, that his mother had been conspiring with these people, for she had been busy at it for fifteen years. It was that she herself might recover her liberty, and possibly the Scotch crown. Moreover, the secret was out—the King of France objected. The Queen of England had received notice, and was on her guard. All that Fontenay could gather from him was that he would not renounce the scheme entirely. He would keep it as a second string to his bow, in case the Queen of England would not come to terms with him. He professed to wish well to his mother, but his tone was cold. Fontenay observed that he asked few questions about her, shewed no curiosity about her health, her treatment, or her occupations.

On the third point of importance that was spoken of,

---

[1] 'Quant aux instructions secretes, le Roy me promit ce que ensuit, pour le premier article la mort de Mylord Lindsay et de l'Abbé de Dunfermline.'—*Fontenay to the Queen of Scots*, Aug. 5-15. MSS. MARY QUEEN OF SCOTS.

the association in the throne, he was equally unsatisfactory. Mary Stuart had not been easy about him. She knew that at one time he had been ready to sacrifice her if he could obtain his own recognition. She had hoped better things since the late revolution, but she was not certain, and she had charged Fontenay, if he trifled, to threaten him with her curse. He tried to evade the question when Fontenay brought it before him. He went off upon the detestation which he had felt always for those who had ill-used her, especially for Knox and Buchanan. When Fontenay indicated what might be in store for him, he trembled and was evidently frightened. He promised to pass the Association Act; but Fontenay's impression was that, so long as Arran and his infamous wife were in favour, it could never be. Both the Earl and Countess were clever, subtle, avaricious, ambitious persons, extremely adroit, untroubled with scruples, and utterly opposed to Mary Stuart's restoration in any form or shape.

A fourth point was marriage. James had promised to let his mother choose his bride for him, and he gave fresh assurances to the same purpose. Yet Fontenay learnt that he was actually speculating on a marriage with Elizabeth, as his surest road to the English crown.[1] She was old and would soon die, and he would then be his own master. Or, again, there was another plan, that he should marry Elizabeth's cousin, Lord Hunsdon's daughter, with a condition of being declared next heir

---

[1] 'Madame, non obstant ceste honneste response, Sir R. Melville et aultres conseillers d'Estat m'ont asseuré qu'il faict traicter par Gray son marriage avec la Royne d'Angleterre. Le Comte d'Arran luy ayant persuadé de lo faire s'il se veult asseurer la couronne d'Angleterre.'— *Fontenay to the Queen of Scots*, Aug. 5-15. *MSS. MARY QUEEN OF SCOTS*.

in England; Lady Arran pointedly telling Fontenay that the King need not wait for his mother's death, and had but to separate his cause from hers to obtain a declaration in his favour immediately.

Once more Mary Stuart had desired that James would present a formal demand to Elizabeth for her release. Thus much, at least, she had a right to expect from him, and again his professions were most warm. But the same subtle influence was at work to persuade him that so long as her life was in no danger—'for that 'would touch his honour'—it would be more convenient 'that she should remain in captivity some years longer.' If she was free, she would disturb Scotland, and perhaps take the crown from him; perhaps, also, 'she 'might marry again, being still of an age to bear 'children.'

Coming to him as this information did from Sir Robert Melville and other of the Queen of Scots' best friends, Fontenay had not been able to discredit it; he had, therefore, asked James, frankly, how much of it was true; whether it was possible that he meant, after all, to forsake his mother and sell himself to the false Englishwoman. James had given him a sharp answer, saying he would take good care of his mother, but bidding Fontenay be less curious in matters which did not concern him. It was equivalent to a confession. Fontenay discovered that an intrigue of some kind with England was undoubtedly going forward. The King, it was likely, really would marry Elizabeth if she would have him, and, at any rate, had a most dangerous inclination towards an alliance with her. He pretended that he was deceiving her. But he had recently entertained Davison, the English Ambassador, at a banquet in Edinburgh Castle; and Fontenay, who was present, told Mary Stuart he had seen noblemen, pretending to be her friends, contending for the honour of kissing the Englishman's hands. He said he looked at James, and James had blushed and turned pale.[1]

Nor was Arran the King's only dangerous adviser. The young, treacherous, and accomplished Master of Gray had been for some time stealing his way into Scotch diplomacy. He had been in Paris with Guise, and had shared the secrets of the great conspiracy. Like Arran, he had professed to be devoted to the Queen of Scots. He had once proposed to lead a party of horse to Sheffield, cut her out, and carry her off; but, like Arran, he hated her at heart, wished her to remain for ever a prisoner, and was in favour of a reconciliation with Elizabeth. Gray was a politician of the school of Maitland of Lethington, to whom 'God' was 'a 'bogle of the nursery;' and his theory was a bad copy of the tyrannous type of Anglicanism, the destruction of the Kirk and the establishment of episcopacy, with the King for head of the Church—Protestantism overthrown and a decent State system erected on its ruins with a contemptuous infidelity at the root.

'Money and preferment,' wrote Fontenay, 'are the 'only Sirens which charm the lords of Scotland. To 'preach to them of duty to their Prince, of honour, 'justice, virtue, noble actions, the memory of an illus- 'trious life which they should bequeath to their pos-

---

[1] 'Je voyois tous les Seigneurs, tant l'inconstance de ce monde est grande, courir à l'envie l'un de l'autre pour baiser les mains de ce venerable Angloys et à le caresser en presence du Roy, qui rougissoit et pâlissoit, me voyant, ma face luy presentant continuelment l'idée de vostre Majesté.'—*Fontenay à la Reyne d'Escosse*, 5-15 Août. *MSS. Mary Queen of Scots.*

'terity, they count the merest folly. They can dis-
'course of these things like the best of the philosophers,
'but in their deeds they are like the Athenians, who
'know what is good but will not do it. To our sorrow,
'they will not look beyond the point of their shoes.
'They care nothing for the future and less for the
'past.'

There was but one way, M. Fontenay sadly concluded, in which his mistress could recover the devotion of the Scottish nation. She must buy it. Every one was poor, every one was extravagant, and every one was corrupt. The King himself was so impoverished, that though he had but a handful of servants, he could neither pay nor feed them. He was deep in debt, and lived by borrowing, yet he was so thoughtless, that if his French cousins sent him money he gave it or flung it away.[1]

For the first time in these letters Mary Stuart was presented with an authentic picture of her son. She had dreamt of him, through the weary years of her imprisonment, as her coming champion and avenger. She had slaved, she had intrigued, she had brought her kinsmen in France to espouse his cause. His image had been the one bright spot in the gloomy circle of her thoughts, and this was the end. Here he stood before her drawn by no enemy's pen, but by the hand of her own devoted servant, coarse, ugly, vulgar, uncouth, inflated with vanity and selfishness, and careless whether she lived or died. It must have been a terrible moment, perhaps the worst that she had ever known in all her miserable life. He had gratified her revenge, for in doing so he gratified himself. In all else he

---

[1] Fontenay à la Reyne d'Escosse, 5–15 Août. *MSS. Mary Queen of Scots.*

threatened to be the most dangerous obstacle which had yet risen in her path. The only hold that she possessed upon him was through his fears. He was craven at heart, he dreaded her malediction,[1] and he knew that she would not spare him.

---

[1] 'Il est fort craintive de la malediction de Dieu et de vostre Majesté.'—*M. Fontenay à la Reyne d'Escosse*, 5-15 Août. *MSS. Mary Queen of Scots.*

END OF VOL. XI.

www.ingramcontent.com/pod-product-compliance
Lightning Source LLC
Chambersburg PA
CBHW021218300426
44111CB00007B/349